CRUCIBLE OF COMBAT

Germany's Defensive Battles in the Ukraine, 1943–44

Rolf Hinze

Translated and edited by Frederick P. Steinhardt, MS, PhD.

Helion & Company Ltd

Dedicated to those who were not granted the opportunity to report the incredible achievements of the troops.

Helion & Company Limited
26 Willow Road
Solihull
West Midlands B91 1UE
England
Tel. 0121 705 3393
Fax 0121 711 4075
Email: info@helion.co.uk
Website: www.helion.co.uk

Derbyshire County Council	
DRO	
2681962	
Askews	11-Jan-2010
940.542177	£35.00

Published by Helion & Company 2009

Designed and typeset by Farr out Publications, Wokingham, Berkshire
Cover designed by Farr out Publications, Wokingham, Berkshire
Printed by The Cromwell Press Group, Trowbridge, Wiltshire

This English edition © Helion & Company Limited 2009. Translated and edited by Frederick P. Steinhardt, MS, PhD.

Originally published as: *Rückzugskämpfe in der Ukraine 1943/44*. German edition © Verlag Dr Rolf Hinze 1991. All rights reserved.

Checking by: Fritz Brandenburg, Alexander Scheele, Dr Wilhelm Schiffers, Dr Hella Hinze.
Maps by Alexander Scheele, Michael Riess.
Photographs © Bundesarchiv.

ISBN 978 1 906033 39 2

British Library Cataloguing-in-Publication Data.
A catalogue record for this book is available from the British Library.
All rights reserved. No part of this publication may be reproduced, stored in a retrieval system,or transmitted, in any form, or by any means, electronic, mechanical, photocopying, recording or otherwise, without the express written consent of Helion & Company Limited.

For details of other military history titles published by Helion & Company Limited contact the above address, or visit our website: http://www.helion.co.uk.

We always welcome receiving book proposals from prospective authors.

Contents

List of maps	x
Key to map symbols, map glossary	xvi
Translator's notes	19
Publishers' note	22
Foreword	23
Introduction	24

1   Fighting Retreat of the Southern Wing of the German Eastern Front, 1943/44 — 26
  From the Dnjepr [Dnieper] to the Dnjestr [Dniester] — 26
  Race for the Dnjepr — 32
  Retreat of the Right Wing of *Heeresgruppe* A — 34
  Overcoming the Dnjepr-Barrier — 36
  Fighting on the Left Wing of the *Heeresgruppe* (4th *Panzer Armee*) — 38
  Fighting in the 1st *Panzer Armee* Sector — 40
  First Battle of Kirowograd/Kriwoi Rog — 42
  The Frontal Salient Northwest of Dnjepropetrowsk — 48
  Soviet Intentions — 48
  Building Additional Bridgeheads — 49
  Fighting in the Dnjepr Knee — 51
  New *Schwerpunkt* in the Krementschug Area (northwestward) — 54

2   Defending the Dnjepr — 57
  The Situation — 57
  Fighting in the Dnjepr Knee — 60
  The Tscherkassy Bridgehead — 68
  The Situation South of Krementschug — 72
  Fighting West of Krementschug — 75
  Breakthrough between the 47th *Panzer Korps* and 11th *Armee Korps* — 77
  The Big Picture — 88
  Evaluation of the Overall Situation — 90
  Fighting East of Kirowograd — 91
  The Fedwar *Kessel* — 95

3   Fighting in the *Heeresgruppe* A Sector — 97
  Fighting in and around the Dnjepropetrowsk Frontal Salient — 97
  Loss of the 'Franken – Line' — 100
  Soviet Attack on the German 'Fist' near Saporoshje — 103
  Fate of the Nikopol Bridgehead — 105
  Critique of the Fighting in the Nikopol Bridgehead — 112
  The Chersson Bridgehead — 115

4	**Second Battle of Kirowograd**	**120**
	Situation South of Kirowograd	122
	Further Development of the Situation	122
5	***Heeresgruppe Süd* at the Dawn of the New Year**	**124**
	Reorganization	125
	Consequences of Command Decisions	126
6	**Fighting on the Left Wing of *Heeresgruppe Süd***	**128**
	Heeresgruppe Mitte [Center] Attempts to Regain Contact on the Right	128
	Hitler's Unconcern with the Left Wing of *Heeresgruppe Süd*	129
	Combat Sector Kiew	130
	Loss of the Kiew Bridgehead	130
	Soviet Advance into the Area North of Kiew	132
	Situation at the Left Wing of the 4th *Panzer Armee*	135
	The Start of the Soviet Offensive	135
	Thrust toward Korosten	138
	Fighting around Korosten	138
	Recapture of Korosten	139
	New Thrust to the East and Retreat	140
7	**New Push to the West**	**142**
	Soviet Advance Directly North of Kiew	142
	Events North of Kiew	142
	Soviet Thrust to the West	143
	The Shitomir Situation	144
	Advance to the South	144
8	**German Counterattack**	**147**
	Recapture of Shitomir	147
	Preparations for a German Counterattack	147
	Battle of the Brussilow *Kessel*	149
	Battle of Radomyschl	151
	Fighting East of Meleni	152
	The Situation East of Shitomir	154
	Defense in the Shitomir Area	156
9	**Renewed Soviet Offensive**	**157**
	Soviet Christmas Offensive	157
	Establishing a New Line of Defense	160
10	**Defensive Battles at the Start of 1944**	**162**
	Situation South of Kiew	162
	Fighting in the Berditschew – Kasatin Area	162
	Defensive Fighting near Winniza	166
	The Gaissin *Kessel*	167
	The Situation	170
	Operation '*Watutin*'	172
	Soviet Advance from East and West	174
	Closing the Ring around the 'Dnjepr-*Balkon*'	177

11	**Battle of Tscherkassy**	**180**
	Difficulties in Bringing Up the German Relief Forces	180
	Delays in Bringing the Forces Up	182
	Preparations for a Relieving Attack	183
	First Relief Attempt	183
	Further Relief Attempt	184
	Hitler Becomes Involved	186
	The Development of the *Kessel*	187
	The 'Wandering *Kessel*'	188
	'*Gruppe Stemmermann*' Breaks Out	188
	Formations Involved	191
12	**Situation after the Breakout from the Tscherkassy Pocket**	**193**
	Situation of the 6th *Armee* in the Dnjepr Bend	193
	Situation of the Left Wing of the *Heeresgruppe*	194
	Gap Between the *Heeresgruppe Süd* and *Heeresgruppe Mitte* Fronts	194
	The Front Line of the 4th *Panzer Armee*	195
	The Balance of Forces	195
	Precautionary Measures Taken by *Heeresgruppe Süd*	197
13	**Retreat of *Heeresgruppe* A**	**199**
	Evacuation of the Dnjepr Frontal Salient (6th *Armee*)	199
	Attack on the Dnjepr Salient	199
	Defense in the Line East of the Basawluk (Busuluk)	202
	Northern Front of the *Kessel*	205
	Fighting Clear the Retreat Route	206
	Recapture of Bolschaja – Kostromka	207
	Fighting after Securing the Breakout Route	207
	New Defensive Front Facing East	209
	Soviet Breakthrough at Kriwoi Rog	209
	Clearing the Way Again to the Ingul	211
	Employment of the 24th *Panzer Division*	214
	The Right Wing of the 6th *Armee*	216
	Loss of the Line of Defense at the Lower Dnjepr	216
	Crossing the Ingul	221
	Evacuation of the Bug Line	221
	Step by Step Retreat	222
	Fighting Through to the Dnjestr	225
	Additional Formations Retreat from the Bug to the Dnjestr	226
	'*Gruppe Wittmann*' Breaks Out	228
	The 302nd *Infanterie Division* On Its Own	230
	The Dnjestr Position	233

14	**Soviet Advance to and past Kriwoi Rog**	**235**
	The Situation of *Heeresgruppe* A	235
	Enemy Attack in the Kriwoi Rog Area	236
	Advance to the Bug	236
	Fighting in Bessarabia	237
	The End of the Movements	237
15	**Retreat in the Central Sector of *Heeresgruppe Süd***	**239**
	Estimate of Soviet Intentions	239
	German Troop Redispositions	241
16	**Soviet Attack against the Left Wing of the 8th *Armee***	**242**
	The German Lines are Broken	242
	The German Retreat	247
	Loss of Additional Ground – Loss of the Bug	247
	Retreat to the Upper Dnjestr	249
	Further Retreat to the Pruth	250
	Fates of Individual Divisions	251
	Fighting Retreat of the 4th *Gebirgs Division*	251
	Actions of the 14th *Panzer Division*	253
	Train Elements Sent to the Rear	254
	Further Movements of the 14th *Panzer Division*	255
	Transfer of the 14th *Panzer Division* to its New Area of Operations	256
	Initial Fighting in the New Area of Operations	258
	The 13th *Panzer Division*	259
	Elimination of Two Soviet Bridgeheads	260
17	**Soviet Attack against the Right Wing of the 8th *Armee***	**261**
	Evacuation of the Area East of the Bug	261
	The Situation	261
	Withdrawal of First Elements from the Kirowograd Area	263
	Withdrawal of *Panzergrenadier Division 'Großdeutschland'*	264
	Retreat to the Bug	266
	Concentration of the Withdrawn Elements West of the Bug	268
	Evaluation of the Situation	269
	Further Evacuation East of the Bug	270
18	**Soviet Advance into the Vacant Area Between the 8th *Armee Korps* and 1st *Panzer Korps***	**272**
	The Situation Between the Bug and Ssawranka	274
	Defense Facing North between the Bug and Dnjestr	274
	The Situation	276
	Penetration near Perelety	277
19	**Defense toward the Northeast and East**	**280**
	Fighting in the Area Between the Dnjestr and Pruth	280
	Change of Command	284
	Rearguard Combat of Individual Formations	284
	Renewed Commitment of the 24th *Panzer Division*	285

20	**Battle of Targul-Frumos**	**289**
	The Situation	289
	Preparations for the Battle of Targul-Frumos	291
	The Offensive Opens	292
	The Second Day of Battle	295
	The Third Day of Battle	295
	Conclusion of the Battle	296
21	**Situation at the Beginning of May**	**297**
	The Big Picture	298
22	**The Battle of Tarnopol**	**299**
	The Situation in the Sector of the 1st and 4th *Panzer Armee* (Kirowograd – Winniza – Uman)	299
	Gap in the Front Southwest of Schepetowka	300
	Commitment of the First German Formations	301
23	**Operations in the Tarnopol Area**	**305**
	First Battle of Tarnopol	306
	'Fortress' Tarnopol	306
	Soviet Advance to the West and Southwest	307
	Offensive of the 1st Ukrainian Front	308
24	**Fighting in the Tarnopol Area**	**311**
	Reinforcement of the 'Fortress' Troops	311
	Envelopment of 'Fortress' Tarnopol	313
	Final Encirclement of Tarnopol	314
	The Battle for 'Fortress' Tarnopol	315
	First Relief Attempt	316
	Situation of the 'Fortress'	317
	Further Relief Attempts	326
	Final Battle in the 'Fortress'	327
	Withdrawal of the Relief Forces	328
25	**The Situation on the Left Wing of *Heeresgruppe Süd***	**330**
	Advance on Rowno	331
	Battle of Rowno	332
	Fallback to the Dubno Area	333
26	**The Soviet 'Second Blow' Against the German Lines**	**335**
	Brody Surrounded	339
	The Brody *Kessel*	341
	The Situation Around Brody at the Beginning of April	341
27	**Review of the Situation**	**343**
28	**Advance Against the 1st *Panzer Armee***	**346**
	The Soviet Attack	347

29	**The 'Second Blow' from the Area Southwest of Schepetowka**	349
	1. Time of Preparation	349
	2. Preparatory Attacks Southwest of Schepetowka	352
	3. Preliminary Attack against the line of the 19th *Panzer Division*	355
	4. Additional Formations Brought Up	355
30	**The Offensive**	359
	Defensive Fighting on the Wings of the 59th *Armee Korps*	359
	First Day of Major Fighting (3 March)	359
	Situation in the Central Sector (19th *Panzer Division*)	362
	The Second Day of the Offensive	364
	Fighting to Prevent the Encirclement of the 59th *Armee Korps*	365
	The Situation of the 59th *Armee Korps*	366
31	**Fighting Retreat of the 59th *Armee Korps***	367
	Staro Konstantinow Bridgehead	367
	Evacuation of Staro Konstantinow	369
	Further Retreat of the 59th *Armee Korps*	372
	The Bushok Line	373
	Attempts to Close the Gap in the Front to the 48th *Panzer Korps*	374
32	**Development of the Situation of the 1st *Panzer Armee***	376
	Organization of Formations	379
	'Fester Platz' Proskurow	380
	Situation of the 1st *Panzer Armee* to the Time of its Encirclement	383
	Defensive Battles of the 24th and 46th *Panzer Korps*	384
	New Defensive Front in the Pruth Valley	384
	The Wandering 'Hube *Kessel*'	385
	Crossing the Zbrucz	389
	Change in the Direction of the Breakout	390
	Further Advance to the Seret	393
	Advance to the Strypa	394
33	**The Breakout of the *'Hube Kessel'***	396
	Preparation for the Breakthrough	396
	Breakout to the West	399
	The March Out	400
	The Situation after the Breakout	400
	Final Conclusion	402
34	**Situation of the 17th *Armee*, Evacuation of Crimea**	403
	Defense of the Kertsch Peninsula	406
	Enemy Landing at Eltingen	408
	Additional Landings	409
	Defensive Fighting North of Kertsch	410
35	**Attack against the Isthmus near Perekop**	412
	New Front at the Siwasch	414
	Fighting at the Tartar Wall	415

36	**Fighting at the Kertsch Front, Eltingen and Mitridat**	**418**
37	**The Situation of the 17th *Armee***	**420**
	Fighting Continues in the 'Nose' North of Kertsch	420
	Preparations for an Attack on the Crimea	423
	Attack on the Northern Flank (Perekop and Siwasch Front)	424
	Further Soviet Advance	425
	Holding the Northern Line	428
	The 5th *Armee Korps* Withdraws	429
	The Formations of the 5th *Armee Korps* Retreat	431
	Retreat of the 49th *Gebirgs Armee Korps*	432
38	**The Battle of Sewastopol**	**434**
	The Situation before the Battle of Sewastopol	434
	The Battle of Sewastopol	435
	The Soviet 51st Army Offensive	436
	The Final Soviet Offensive	437
	Evacuation of the German Positions	439
	Embarkation of the Last Formations	441
	Conclusions	443

Epilogue	445
Photographic Essay	448
Appendix: Orders of Battle	472
Glossary	491
Bibliography	496

List of maps

1. Operation *Zitadelle*, 5 to 17 July, 1943. — 28
2. Combat Area, *Heeresgruppe Süd*, later divided into *Heeresgruppen Süd* and A. — 29
3. Railway map of the *Ostbahn* in the combat area of *Heeresgruppe Süd*, later *Süd* and A. — 30
4. *Heeresgrupe* A, 17th *Armee*. Evacuation of the Kuban Bridgehead; Situation on the Kertsch Peninsula as of 8/9 October, 1943. — 35
5. Railroad net East between Kiew and Charkow with the most important junctions. — 50
6. *Heeresgruppe* A and 6th *Armee* situation as of 9 October, 1943 after the evacuation of the Kuban bridgehead; intense defensive fighting at Melitopol and Saporoschje. See also maps 97-104 inclusive. — 59
7. Situation of the 24th *Panzer Korps*. Commitment of Soviet paratroops on 24 September, 1943. Hasty counterattack of the 19th *Panzer Division* on 29 September in the Dnjepr-knee. — 62
8. The Battle of the Dnjepr-knee. Development of the situation from 11/12 October to 25 October, 1943. — 63
9. Area of the Dnjepr-knee. — 66
10. (upper right corner) – 4th *Panzer Armee* and 8th *Armee* end of September, 1943: Crossing of the Dnjepr in the Krementschug – Kiew sector, Situation in the bridgeheads as of the evening of 23 September, 1943 and organization of the Dnjepr position 3 October, 1943. (lower left) – Dnjepr knee south of Perejasslaw 22-24 September, 1943: Aerial attacks day and night on artillery firing positions, bridges and train areas. 24/25 September, 1943: Commitment of Soviet paratroops in the rear of the front. Massive concentration of Soviet artillery. — 67
11. Left wing of the 8th *Armee* Sector of the 3rd *Panzer Korps* and 24th *Panzer Korps*. Situation from 3 to 16 November, 1943 in Dnjepr-knee. — 69
12. Situation in the Krementschug Bridgehead 23 September, evening, to 30 September, 1943, night. Position and Organization at the bank of the Dnjepr 3 October, 1943, evening. — 71
13. The Soviet 2nd Ukrainian Front extended their Dnjepr bridgeheads between Koleberda and Litwinowka and linked them up. Situation on the left wing of the 1st *Panzer Armee* in the night of 13/14 October, 1943. — 74
14. (top right) On 25 October, 1943 the Soviet army group '2nd Ukrainian Front' also attacked to the southwest in the Werchnednjeprowsk – Woiskowoje sector. (bottom center) The left wing of the 1st *Panzer Armee* tore open in the Mischurin – Annowka sector under the mighty Soviet attacks from the Dnjepr bridgeheads between Litwinowka and Koleberda on 13/14 October, 1943. — 76
15. Situation on the left wing of the 1st *Panzer Armee* from 22 October to 2 November, 1943. — 78
16. Situation on 3 November, 1943 between Kriwoi Rog and Alexandrija after the counterattack of the 30th *Panzer Korps*; The gap in the front was closed. Soviet bridgehead in and around Petrowo cannot be eliminated. — 81

17.	Defensive fighting in the sector of the 11th *Armee Korps* and 47th *Panzer Korps* on the right wing of the 8th *Armee*. Development of the situation from 14 October to 10 December, 1943.	82
18.	Situation of *Heeresgruppe Süd* on 10 December, 1943, evening, between Korosten and Saporoshje.	83
19.	Development of the situation between Kirowograd and Tscherkassy from 10 to 26 December, 1943.	86
20.	Soviet offensive between Krementschug and Alexandrija. Development of the situation from 24 November to 1/2 December, 1943.	87
21.	Development of the situation between Kirowograd and Tscherkassy from 10 to 26 December, 1943	89
22.	Situation on both sides of Kirowograd on 26 December, 1943, evening.	93
23.	Situation in the Sector of the 1st *Panzer Armee* as of 23 September, 1943. Crossing the river by the 57th *Panzer Korps*, the 52nd *Armee Korps*, the 30th *Armee Korps* and the 40th *Panzer Korps* – from 21/22 to 30 September, 1943, Soviet Dnjepr bridgehead at the start of October. Situation and organization in the Dnjepr Position as of 9 October, 1943, evening.	98
24.	*Heeresgruppe* A, 6th *Armee*. Situation between Saproshje/ Dnjepr, Melitopol and Sea of Asov (*Asowsches Meer*) 9 to 14 October, 1943, evening.	99
25.	Saporoshje Bridgehead, The Fist. Action until 14 October, 1943.	101
26.	Nikopol Bridgehead. Action until the end of November, 1943.	104
27.	Excerpt from *Heeres* Map sheet X49/Y47.	108
28.	Nikopol Bridgehead. Situation of the 6th *Armee* in January, 1944.	111
29.	4th *Gebirgs Division* in the Dnjepr Bridgehead at Aleschki east of Chersson until 20/21 December, 1943.	113
30.	*Heeresgruppe* A. Situation on the lower course of the Dnjepr between the Nikopol Bridgehead and the mouths of the Dnjepr and the Bug, 20/21 January, 1944.	114
78.	Bridgehead at Chersson. Chersson before completion of the bridge and the connection to the Chersson – Nikolajew *Rollbahn*.	115
31.	*Heeresgruppe Mitte* and *Süd*. Situation at the end of September, 1943 on both sides of the *Heeresgruppe*n boundary in the Kiew – Gomel sector.	131
32.	*Heeresgruppe Süd*, left wing. Situation of the 59th *Armee Korps* at the beginning of October, 1943.	133
33.	Soviet offensive against the left wing of *Heeresgruppe Süd* 3 November, 1943. Fighting Retreat of the 13th, 59th and 7th *Armee Korps*. Loss of the Kiew, Fastow, Shitomir and Korosten transportation hubs.	136
34.	Situation of the 59th *Armee Korps* on 23 November, 1943, 2400 hours. Intended conduct of attack on 24 November, 1943, 0600 hours.	137
35.	Attack and breakthrough of the 48th *Panzer Korps* to the Shitomir – Kiew *Rollbahn*, 12 to 24 November, 1943, leading to building a new eastern front, to the Brussilow *Kessel* and to the recapture of Shitomir.	148
36.	Attack of the 48th *Panzer Korps* on 6 December, 1943. Continuation of frontal straightening between Fastow – Radomyschl and Malin.	150
37.	48th *Panzer Korps* Attack on 19 December, 1943. Situation at 1800 hours. [Lage 10 00 = situation 1000 hours; zweigleisig = twin-tracked railroad].	153

38. Continuation of the Attack. Situation on 20 December, 1943, 2000 hours. Situation on 22 December, 1943, morning. Situation on 22 December, 1943, evening.   155
39. *Heeresgruppe Süd* / 4th *Panzer Armee*. Soviet Offensive on 24 December 1943 against the Fastow – Korosten sector.   158
40. Situation of the 59th *Armee Korps* from 28 December, 1943, 0700 hours until 31 December, 1943, 0800 hours.   159
41. 4th *Panzer Armee*. Defensive fighting in the Kasatin – Berditschew – Schepetowka sector, 7 to 16 January, 1944. See Map 86 for 7 January to end of February 1944.   163
42. The Situation in the sector of the 1st *Panzer Armee*. *Unternehmen* [operations] '*Gaissin*' and '*Watutin*' 20 to 31 January, 1944. Map 43 covers larger area.   165
43. 4th *Panzer Armee*, *Unternehmen* [operations] '*Gaissin*' and '*Watutin*', relief attempts for the Tscherkassy *Kessel*.   168
44. Soviet breakthrough southeast of Fastow; Envelopment of the 42nd *Armee Korps* and 7th *Armee Korps* between Bogusslaw and Dnjepr. Development of the situation from 27 December, 1943 to 20 January, 1944.   169
45. The Dnjepr-Knee. Situation in the sector of the 24th *Panzer Korps* on 26 December, 1943, evening.   171
46. Armoured formations of the 2nd Ukrainian Front break through the positions of the 8th *Armee* south of Smela, widen the gap to 30 kilometers and link up with armoured spearheads of the 1st Ukrainian Front in the Swenigorodka area. Development of the situation from 10 to 31 January, 1944.   175
47. Soviet armoured wedges of the 1st and 2nd Ukrainian Fronts close up to the left wing of the 8th *Armee* in the Tscherkassy, Swenigorodka and Boguslaw area. Situation from 25 to 31 January, 1944.   178
48. The Tscherkassy *Kessel*. Relief attempt by the 3rd *Panzer Korps* and 47th *Panzer Korps*. Situation from 3 to 12 February, 1944. See Map 50 for rail lines and more detail between Schanderowka and Lebedin.   181
49. The attack of the German *Panzer* divisions, which had been in constant action for weeks, comes to a standstill. The relief attempt fails. In addition there have been command errors, shortages of replacements and weather-occasioned losses of time. Development of the situation from 12 to 16 February, 1944   185
50. Breakout of the 42nd *Armee Korps* and 11th *Armee Korps* from the *Kessel* at Komarowka 16/17 February, 1944.   189
51. Right wing of the 1st *Panzer Armee*. Situation on both sides of Saporoshje on 5 December, 1943, evening.   200
52. Situation of the 6th *Armee* from 2 to 25 February, 1944. Fighting retreat in the Nikopol – Apostolowo sector. 24th *Armee Korps*, 4th *Armee Korps* and 17th *Armee Korps* fight clear the route of retreat and force the breakthrough to the west at Bolschaja Kostromka.   203
53. Situation of the 6th *Armee* on 5 March, 1944, evening. Ingulez-sector south of Kriwoi Rog. The weight of the Soviet attack hits the German front before it solidifies, with *Schwerpunkt* in and around Schirokoje.   210

54.	Retreat of the 335th *Infanterie Division* to the Bug. The report of the 335th *Infanterie Division* can represent the experiences of all the formations of the 6th *Armee* in the fighting retreat from the Dnjepr to the Bug from 8 to 19 March, 1944, in snow, mud and cold. The direct 'as the crow flies' distance was 150 kilometers, the distance as fought, however, at least 200 kilometers.	217
55.	Situation of the 6th *Armee* during the period from 5 to 18 March, 1944. Fighting retreat between the Ingulez, Wissun, Ingul, Gromoklej and Ghiloi Jelanez.	219
56.	6th *Armee*, Situation on 20 March, 1944. Evacuation of the Bug bridgehead; positions at the Bug; 26/27 March, 1944, beginning withdrawal to the Dnjestr. (The situation map of the General Staff of the *Heeres Operations Abteilung* III shows almost all the divisions as *Kampfgruppen*).	223
57.	Retreat of the 6th *Armee* to the Dnjestr. Soviet Dnjestr bridgehead. 5 to 29 April, 1944.	229
58.	Situation of the 8th *Armee* during the period from 3 to 16 March, 1944. Soviet breakthrough between Swenigorodka and Shaschkow. Adjoined to the northwest by Map 69, to the west by Map 89, continues to the southwest on Map 60, adjoined to the south by Map 62.	243
59.	Crossings over the Bug. *KoPiFü Gruppe* von Knobelsdorf.	244
60.	The positions on the Bug between Sawran and Brazlaw had to be evacuated on 12/13 March, 1944.	246
61.	Situation between the 8th *Armee* and 1st *Panzer Armee* between the Bug and Dnjestr in the Mogilew-Podolsk and Shmerinka sector. 13 to 28 March, 1944. Map 90 of *Hube Kessel* overlaps this map and carries on to the west.	248
62.	Development of the situation in the Perwomaisk/Bug brigehead. Fighting retreat between Bug – Ssawranka and Dnjestr 15/16 to 27 March, 1944. See Map 63 for 18-28 March, and for more details of the north-west quadrant of this map. Map 64 covers 26 March-3 April 1944. Map 60 adjoins and overlaps to the north.	252
63.	Fighting Retreat of *Armee*-Gruppe Wöhler (8th) between the Bug – Ssewranka and Dnjestr from 18/19 to 28 March, 1944. Defensive battle on both sides of Balta.	257
64.	The situation of *Armee*-Gruppe Wöhler (8th) between the Dnjestr and Pruth from 26 March to 3 April, 1944.	282
65.	Gap in the front between the inner wings of the 8th *Armee* and the 1st *Panzer Armee*. Situation on 27 March 1944, evening. Map 90 overlaps northern portion as of 27 March 1944.	283
66.	*Armee – Gruppe General Wöhler* (8th). Defensive fighting between the Pruth and Sereth from 4 to 30 April, 1944.	287
67.	The Battle of Targul-Frumos 2 to 6 May, 1944.	293
68.	1st *Panzer Armee*, left wing: Soviet breakthrough attempt at the boundary between the 1st and 4th *Panzer Armeen*. Situation on 5 March, 1944, evening.	302

69. 4th *Panzer Armee*, left wing, *Heeresgruppe Süd*. Situation from 5 to 16 March, 1944. See Map 80 for 27 January-18 March 1944. Map 70 shows Tarnopol, 2-12 March 1944. Map 68 adjoins to the lower right. Map 79 shows Rowno, 26 January-1 February 1944. 303
70. Sector of the 48th *Panzer Korps*. Development of the situation on both sides of Tarnopol, 2 to 12 March, 1944, evening. Map 68 adjoins to the right. 309
71. '*Fester Platz*' Tarnopol with defensive sectors. 315
72. Development of the situation from 5 to 12 March, 1944 318
73. Development of the situation from 13 to 20 March, 1944. 320
74. Development of the situation from 21 to 24 March, 1944. 322
75. The Thrust toward Tarnopol on 25 March, 1944 by *Panzerverband Friebe*. 324
76. The Relief Attack toward Tarnopol from 15 to 17 April, 1944. 325
79. Fighting at Horyn. Beginning of the battle of Rowno, 26 January to 1 February, 1944. See Map 80 for larger picture. 333
80. 4th *Panzer Armee*. Development of the situation between Schepetowka and Luzk; Battle of Rowno, Dubno and Brody. 27 January to 16/18 March, 1944. See Map 69 for 5-16 March, Map 81 for 16-26 March, Map 82 for 7-16 April 1944. Map 85 adjoins to lower right. 336
81. 4th *Panzer Armee*. Retreat of the 13th *Armee Korps* from the front Kremianez – Dubno – Radomyschl 16 to 26 March, 1944. Brody *Kessel*. Map 82 adjoins lower left corner. 337
82. 4th *Panzer Armee* / 13th *Armee Korps*. Fighting on both sides of Brody; Opening of the Brody *Kessel* 7 to 14 April, 1944. Map 81 adjoins upper right corner. 338
83. 4th *Panzer Armee* – Extreme left wing sector on both sides of Kowel. Retreat and fighting until encirclement of the city, 1 February to 29 March, 1944. See also Map 84 which extends farther northward. 340
84. *Heeresgruppe Süd* / *Heeresgruppe Mitte*. Closure of the gap in the front between the *Heeresgruppen* by the 2nd *Armee* – 7th *Armee Korps* 56th *Panzer Korps*. *Heeresgruppen* boundary was initially shifted to the south (1 April, 1944). The 2nd *Armee* took over the Kowel sector and action. 3 to 12/18 April, 1944. 344
85. 4th *Panzer Armee*, left wing. Fighting retreat of the 59th *Armee Korps* and 13th *Armee Korps* in Schepetowka – Rowno sector 16 – 31 January, 1944. See Map 87 for 7 January-29 February 1944. See Map 89 for 4-12 March 1944, overlaps this map. See Map 68 which adjoins to the right. 350
86. Fighting and situation on the right wing of the 4th *Panzer Armee* in the Staro Konstantinow / Schepetowka sector from 7-12-16-29-31 January, 1944 plus 29 February, 1944. See Map 41 for 7-16 January, Map 85 for 16-31 January, Map 87 for 19 February 1944 near Ljubar and Tscherna. Map 88 adjoins to the right. Map 91 for 12 March 1944 adjoins bottom, and Map 90 for the Hube *Kessel* overlaps. 351
87. Situation on 19 February 1944, 20 00 hours. 353
88. 1st *Panzer Armee*, right wing. Situation on 5 March, 1944, evening. Map 89 shows the left wing. Maps 89, 41 and 43 adjoin to the left. Map 58 shows lower right and adjoins. 360

89.	1st *Panzer Armee*, left wing. Fighting around Staro Konstantinow. Retreat to Proskuros, 4 to 12 March, 1944. Map 88 shows right wing, adjoining to the right. Map 61 overlaps the lower right corner. Map 41 covers 7-16 January 1944, Map 86 7-29 January.	363
77.	Situation on 7 March, 1944, 1000 hours. Staro Konstantinow Bridgehead	370
90.	The Hube *Kessel*. Situation 20-27 March 1944. Map 65 overlaps bottom for 27 March. Map 61 overlaps to the right, 13-28 March.	378
91.	1st *Panzer Armee*, left wing. Situation on 12 March 1944, evening. Map 86 adjoins to the north for 7 January-29 February 1944.	381
92.	The important rivers in the combat area of *Heeresgruppe Süd*.	386
93.	(upper center) Situation of the 1st and 4th *Panzer Armee*n from 29 March to 3 April, 1944 (lower left) The divisions are neither more nor less than strong *Kampfgruppen* lacking armour, heavy weapons, guns and prime movers, which impacts their combat effectiveness and their mobility.	388
94.	Encirclement of the 1st *Panzer Armee* between Smotritsch, Seret and Dnjestr 2 to 5 April, 1944. Snow storms, drifts, air-dropped supplies to a limited degree.	392
95.	1st *Panzer Armee*, Development of the Situation between the Zbrucz and Strypa,5 to 7 April, 1944. Air-dropped supplies, 292 tons.	395
96.	Situation of the 1st *Panzer Armee* in 'Hube *Kessel*' 8 to 12 April, 1944; Soviet attack on Stanislau; 2nd SS-*Panzer Korps* and 100th *Jäger Division* close gap north of Buczacz.	397
97.	Situation on the *Krim* [Crimean Peninsula] 11 March to 12 May, 1944. [*Schwarzes Meer* = Black Sea; *Asowsches Meer* = Sea of Asov; *Strasse f. Kertsch* = Straits of Kertsch.]	404
98.	Fighting on the Kertsch Peninsula 30 October 1943 to 2 June 1944.	407
99.	Situation at the Tartar Wall [*Tatarenwall*] and at the northwestern Ssiwasch from 30 October to the start of November, 1943. See also Map 6.	413
100.	Fighting on the Kertsch Peninsula, 30 October , 1943 to 6 February, 1944.	416
101.	Northern Front of the 17th *Armee*. Defensive fighting at the entrances to the Crimea; Soviet offensive on 7 April, 1944.	421
102.	Withdrawal of the 17th *Armee* in the Crimea from 12 to 14 April, 1944. [*Sowj. Schwarzmeer-Flotte* = Soviet Black Sea Fleet].	426
103.	17th *Armee*, 5th *Armee Korps*. Fighting retreat on the Kertsch peninsula to the Parpatsch position (12 April, 1944).	430
104.	17th *Armee*, Final Battle in the Crimea, 12 April to 13 May, 1944. [*Letzter Geleitzug* = last convoy; *Kap u. Leichturm* = cape and lighthouse; *Tal* = valley].	438
105.	Eastern Front. Situation before the Soviet 1944 summer offensive. Length of front of *Heeresgruppe Mitte*: about 1,100 kilometers. Number of formations: 40 Divisions.	442

Key to map symbols, map glossary

German Formation Symbols

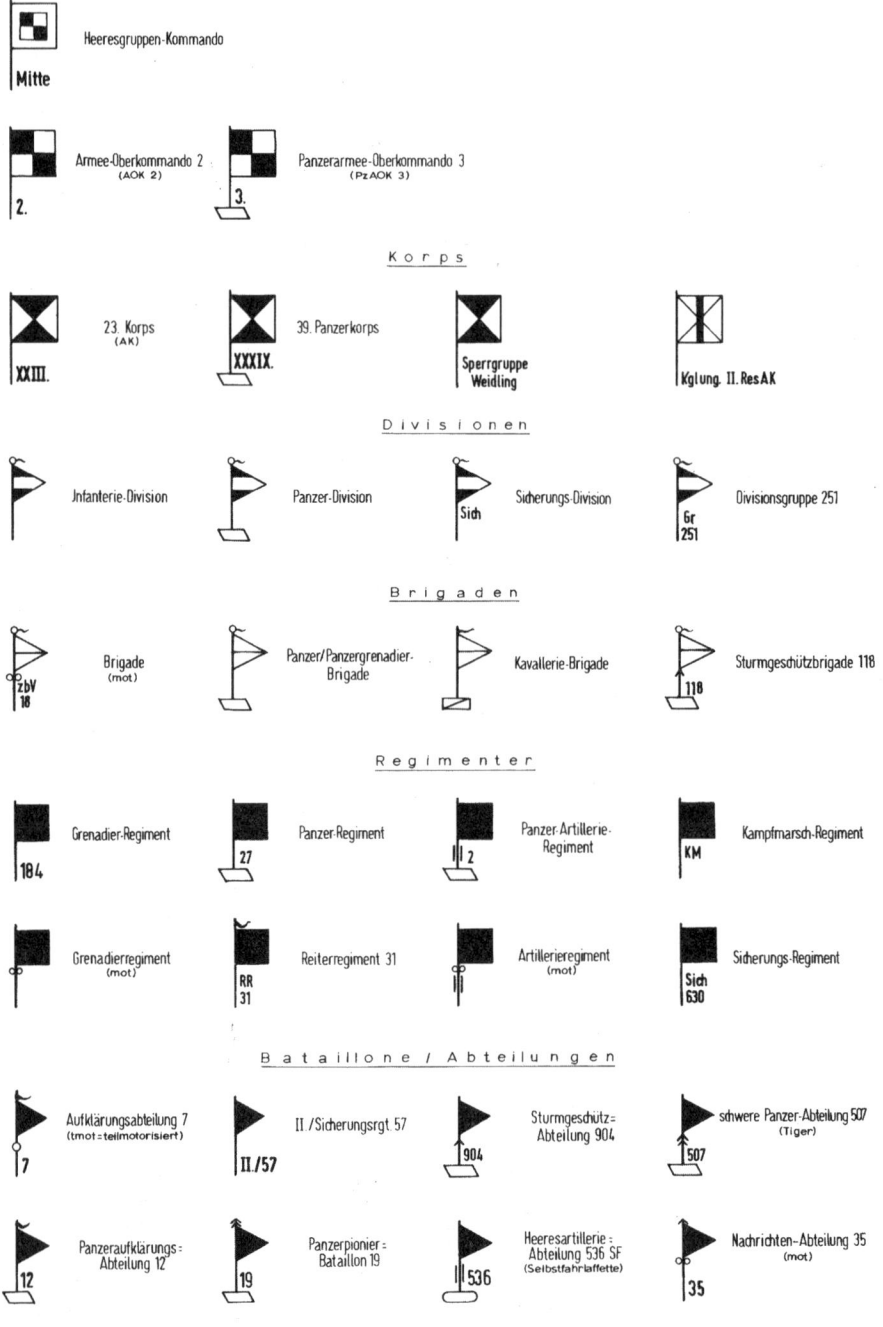

KEY TO MAP SYMBOLS, MAP GLOSSARY xvii

Soviet Formation Symbols

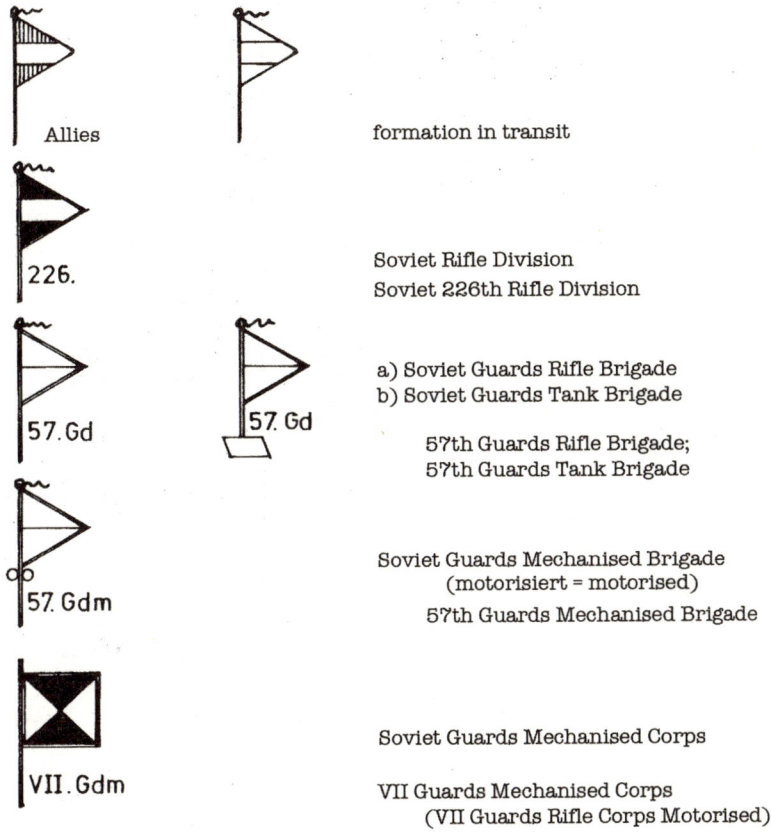

Allies

formation in transit

226.
Soviet Rifle Division
Soviet 226th Rifle Division

57. Gd
57. Gd
a) Soviet Guards Rifle Brigade
b) Soviet Guards Tank Brigade

57th Guards Rifle Brigade;
57th Guards Tank Brigade

57. Gdm
Soviet Guards Mechanised Brigade
(motorisiert = motorised)
57th Guards Mechanised Brigade

VII. Gdm
Soviet Guards Mechanised Corps
VII Guards Mechanised Corps
(VII Guards Rifle Corps Motorised)

Other Symbols

German troops

Soviet troops

Tactical Boundaries

Army group boundary

Army boundary

Corps boundary

Divisional boundary

Regimental boundary

Battalion boundary

Map glossary

The following is a glossary compiled by the translator to help the reader with German legends and notes in the bodies of the maps which are not translated.

abends	evening	*Kriegsbrücke*	military bridge, – bridges
alt, alte	old	*Lage am...*	situation at...
am	on	*Leichtturm*	lighthouse
anfang	beginning, start of	*letzt(er)*	last
Behelfsfähre(n)	makeshift ferry(ies)	*Liman*	lagoon
bereits	already	*Ma, Masse*	main body
Bewegung(en)	movement(s)	*Marine-Fährprahme*	navy landing craft
Bf., Bahnhof	railroad station	*Meer*	sea
B-Gerät	type of military bridge	*nach*	to, toward
bis	until	*Ponton*	pontoon
Brückenkopf	bridgehead	*Raum*	area
Bucht	bay, bight	*Schiff(e)*	ship(s)
einschl.	inclusive	*Stab(es)*	staff(s)
Eisenbahn	railroad	*Stellung(en)*	position(s)
Fähre (n)	ferry(s)	*Strasse*	strait(s), sea-route; road
Fährstelle	ferry site	*Sumpf*	swamp
Floßsack	inflatable rubber raft	*Tal*	valley
Gr. G. G.	*Gruppe General-Gouvernement*	*Tle, Teile*	elements
Geleitzug	convoy	*über*	via (as used on these maps), over
Halbinsel	peninsula	*Verband(e)*	formation(s)
hinter	behind	*Verlegt*	transferred
Holzbrücke	wooden bridge	*Zeichenerklärung*	explanation of map symbols
Kap	cape	*zweigleisig*	twin-tracked
Kgr	*Kampfgruppe*		

Translator's notes

The reader should be aware of the translator's choices in dealing with the following.

When German words are retained, I have used the nominative case, singular or plural, regardless of the grammatical situation. The reader should be aware of some German words where the singular and plural are identical, such as *Tiger*, *Panther* and *Panzer*. I nave retained the German *ß* for the double 's' as in *Großdeutschland*. Foreign (non-English) words are italicized.

The author generally refers to the German side as *'eigene'*, 'own' which would generally be translated as 'friendly', in accord with English and American usage. However, when reading a German account of the war with Russia, the English speaking reader may not so automatically identify with the German side as 'his own', so I chose to replace 'friendly' or 'own' with German.

I have retained the German *Kampfgruppe* for German combat groups, since the German term is generally used, both, as in English usage, for a balanced team of combat elements created for a particular task, and also in referring to battered remnants of divisions that no longer have sufficient strength to justify being considered divisions.

Another German term which has found its way into worldwide usage is *Schwerpunkt*, literally 'center of gravity', as a physicist or engineer would use it, but, in military usage, referring to the point of main effort.

The only unit designation that calls for explanation is that of battalions, or *Abteilungen*, as the case may be, of regiments. To avoid tedious and lengthy expansion into words, I have retained the usual German designation, such as 'I./PGR 26', which I have expanded to I./ *Panzergrenadier Regiment* 26, means First Battalion, *Panzergrenadier Regiment* 26, or II./ *AR* 291 becomes II. / *Artillerie Regiment* 291, which means 2nd *Abteilung, Artillerie Regiment* 291. The author used a variety of informal designations for *Waffen-SS* divisions. To avoid confusion, all such references have been standardized to the official designations applicable at that time, as per Bender and Taylor, *Uniforms, Organization and History of the Waffen-SS*. To reduce the sometimes ponderous nomenclature, *'Leibstandarte SS Adolf Hitler'* has, in regimental references, been abbreviated to *'LSSAH'*.

To maintain consistency with German records, maps and other sources that the reader may refer to, all Russian place names are given as rendered in the German original. The reader will note that, in most cases, English versions of Russian place names employ the letter 'v' where the German version employs the letter 'w', as, for example, Kiev vs Kiew, Brussilow vs Brussilov.

I have made no attempt to create consistency between the maps and text. There are numerous minor differences in spelling that the reader should be prepared to recognize, as, for example, Showtnewoje in the text and Showtenoje, which appears to be in the right location for that reference on the map. The translator had no way of knowing which, if either, might be 'correct', since both are German renditions of Cyrillic names. Furthermore, the translator could only assume that he had correctly identified the equivalency but could not see that as justification for altering the original.

Despite such minor frustrations, these maps are by far the best, if not the only ones, available for most of the actions and areas referred to in the text. In extensive studies over many years of German memoirs, histories and unit histories describing events on the Eastern Front, the translator has repeatedly turned to Hinze's books to supply geographic and military information that is so seldom provided by maps in other accounts. Hinze's series on the collapse of *Heeresgruppe Mitte* and on the retreat and defeat of the German forces in the Ukraine are the invaluable background for gaining perspective needed to comprehend the local settings of memoirs and unit histories.

The German original lacked any reference in the body of the text to the relevant maps, leaving that entirely up to the reader to discover. The translator has employed this history for years and, in the process, made his own marginal references to relative maps. These fall into two classes, references to a map or maps illustrating the action described and references to a map or maps which, while illustrating action at a different point in time, at least show the relevant geography. These references have been displayed in the margins of the page for ready reference. For the most part, all of the maps relevant to a paragraph are referred to in a single note in the margin at the start of the paragraph. In a few cases, references have been inserted at the relevant point within or at the end of a paragraph.

Because it proved economically unfeasible to redraw and re-letter the many maps, English captions have been provided but the body of the maps remains in the original German. A brief glossary for special application to the maps has been provided to assist with German terms such as *Lage* and *HKL*. To assist the reader in identifying features on the map, German geographic and geomorphic terms such as *'Bucht', 'See', 'Meer', 'Insel'* and the like have in most cases been retained in the text, since those are the terms that appear on the map. When such terms appear in the text, an English equivalent immediately follows in brackets, and is also included in the main glossary at the end of the text. Similarly, to make it easier to identify locations on the maps, German geographic names have generally been retained in the text, sometimes with a bracketed English equivalent. There are a few exceptions, where I did use the English name, such as Black Sea, rather than *Schwarzes Meer*, Crimea rather than *Krim*, and Carpathian Mountains rather than *Karpaten*.

The translator apologizes for the use of the term 'AFVs' respecting Russian armoured vehicles when the German term is *'Panzer'*. However, only a few references indicate whether the Russian vehicles referred to were tanks or assault guns and, in general, the Russians employed both types, so I chose to use the later English language term, 'AFV' to indicate that both tanks and assault guns were probably involved. I also apologize for using the awkward term, 'Localities' on occasion where the reference was to a Russian population center and I was unable to determine its size and, therefore, use a more informative term such as village, town or city.

In many cases, where numbered regiments were referred to in the text and it was not clear from their numbers or the context what divisions they belonged to, I was able to check their affiliation in Tessin, *Verbände und Truppen der deutschen Wehrmacht und Waffen-SS, 1939–1945*. Where I was able to determine their parent division I added a bracketed note. In some cases Tessin did not provide such a solution, but I was able to find the necessary information in a unit history or other source, and was able to add a translator's note with the correction. All such outside references are included in my own, 'translator's bibliography'. Most of the units lacking such bracketed references or obvious parent division were *Korps, Armee* or *Heeresgruppe* troops or independent units.

Fred Steinhardt

Publishers' note

Producing an English language edition of this book has been extremely challenging from a technical point of view. Maps had to be scanned by hand from a clean copy as none were available from the original German publishers; we have decided to retain the German legends within the maps, with the necessary translation appearing as caption below each map. The reader will note several maps (maps 78 and 79) are out-of-sequence. This is a deliberate effort to keep the original map numbering between German and English editions. However, these particular maps were out of sequence in the German edition, and have now been restored to their appropriate place. The schematic orders of battle have been retained from the German edition – resetting these in new type would have been both extremely time-consuming and expensive, and rather pointless since the terminology used is that present in most cases throughout the remainder of the text.

We would like to extend our thanks to this book's editor and translator, Frederick P. Steinhardt, who has kindly gone beyond the call of duty in providing extensive notes and annotations (surrounded by square brackets within the text) that clarify and assist the reader in picking their way through this complex military campaign.

Foreword

The mission of writing history is to research the history, thus what has happened, and to set it down for posterity. The first task is to determine the events that took place. Its mission does not stop there, since many facts – documented to some extent – do not necessarily agree in all points. In addition, gaps remain in the overall picture that must be filled by depending on circumstantial evidence. Such evidence, and other facts, must be considered and evaluated. Only in rare cases do records exist revealing the intentions of an army commander or of lower military commanders.

In addition we are exclusively dependant on German sources for presentation of the events on the Eastern Front. It is to be hoped that, with continued softening of the Communist dictatorship, Soviet records may become available to compare with the German documents. The extant official German military records reveal extensive gaps that might be filled with information from Soviet sources. That is the only way that can provide a complete representation of the course of events.

There seems no further justification, so long after the end of the war, to wait in hopes of the opening of Soviet archives in which it is highly probable that there will be found a large number of German division and *Korps* histories that were captured by the Red Army. This opinion is based on the belief that it will be extremely difficult for a later author, who did not, himself, experience the events, to comprehend the achievements and endeavors of the troops and to be able to evaluate the significance and meaning of the decisions at the various military command levels.

Just the evaluation of the available records, some of radio traffic between various levels of command and also the reports, demands knowledge of the realities of the extant combat situation, the plight of the troops facing overwhelmingly superior forces, often with inadequate supplies, in hostile climate in terrain severely impacted by unfavorable weather. The content and tone of many reports and orders are only comprehensible in light of combat conditions existing at that time. Without a sympathetic understanding of those conditions, there is no way that one could write a history that would in any way do justice to the soldiers living and fighting at that time.

In light of the existing gaps in available records, this work that follows must be seen as an attempt at a historical presentation that, in the opinion of the author, is the best and most complete possible in the given circumstances.

It would, certainly, be fortunate if future historians will be able to expand and complete what this work presents when the Soviet archives are opened to the public.

Introduction

The present work does not describe a successful (*Blitz-*) campaign, like those of the German *Wehrmacht* at the start of the war to the east, north south and west – and, indeed, initially into the Soviet Union. Rather it depicts the bitter defensive battles of a force involved in a two – later multiple – front war. The German command had to distribute its forces among all the fronts and anticipated combat zones. Thus it was unable to provide those elements that were engaged in heavy combat with the forces deemed necessary as is usual in offensive warfare where one holds the initiative. On the other hand, even though the German army lost its aura of invincibility as a result of the Battle of Stalingrad, it still managed to hold the fronts in the East and was able to conduct further successful battles. Above all, the troops had avoided the evacuation of hard-fought-for terrain and costly retreat – so long as it was possible to provide the fighting forces with personnel and materiel. The combat morale of the fighting troops, particularly the experienced frontline 'old hands' of the Eastern Front, had not yet, in 1943 and 1944, suffered. To the very end the soldiers met the demands put upon them for self-sacrificing devotion – as the end approached, in hopes that by such sacrificial effort they might spare the German homeland from being overrun by the Red Army and thereby protect it from Communism, whose consequences the soldiers had learned in occupied Soviet Russia.

Soviet superiority steadily mounted, in part as a result of materiel from the USA. Uniforms, made of good material, arrived, ready made complete with the re-instituted Czarist shoulder-straps. A significant portion of the troops' rations came from the USA. Of decisive combat significance was the provision of about 500,000 all-terrain Studebaker lorries, with all-wheel drive and ten-speed transmissions. In addition came American Sherman and English Mark V tanks. Neither matched the performance of the Soviet T – 34. The same held true for the construction of artillery. Armour and artillery were Stalin's 'hobbyhorses' with which he hoped to make up for the declining quality of Soviet infantry. The Soviets were able to offset the immense losses in infantry, so far as quantity went, by inducting White Russian and Ukrainian citizens who had attained military age in territory formerly behind German lines. They also drafted older men, including those who had been released from German captivity as prisoners of war in the Ukraine in 1941. Although the situation did not allow for adequate military training of these men, they were immediately thrown into action. According to statements by prisoners of war, these men were greeted with a certain mistrust in the Red Army because they had learned to view the German occupation forces from a different perspective. Harnessed in the Soviet system of supervision and control by commissars, with the support of armour and vast masses of infantry and artillery, the Soviets enjoyed immense superiority of forces confronting the overextended sectors held by combat-fatigued German grenadiers in strongpoints.

The superior mobility the Soviets derived from the American vehicles that had been provided proved decisive to their successes in combat. The Soviets knew no shortages of fuel. Again and again they could overtake and outmaneuver the German grenadiers, who were, in most cases, marching on foot. The German troops were forced to accomplish wonders in marching and, after slipping out of impending encirclement, always committed to yet new costly defensive operations.

A glance at the situation map as 1943 turned to 1944 gives the initial impression that *Heeresgruppe* A and *Heeresgruppe Süd* wielded a massive concentration of German troops. However, the number of *Korps* and divisions committed reveals nothing of the actual available manpower and combat strength. In many cases the actual units involved consisted merely of remnants of a division that had been reduced to *Kampfgruppen*. The shrinkage of troops continued to worsen on the retreat to the Bug, Dnjestr [Dniester] and, finally, to the Pruth.

Initially the question was raised with the command, and also with the troops, how they were to stand against the overwhelming superiority of the Soviet forces with such scant manpower and equipment? Finally, however, it became clear that it must be accepted as irresponsible to attempt to build another line of defense with what was left of the troops, thereby exposing them to an attack by superior Soviet forces, in expectation or hopes that they would be able to stand fast yet one more time against the Soviet pressure.

After the Soviet southern offensive ran its course the German remnant formations merely profited from the fact that every offensive eventually 'runs down'. The attacking troops were simply worn out. Above all else, they found it difficult to bring up supplies. The impassability of the softened roads of the black-earth region of the Ukraine in periods of alternating frost and thaw, which was such a burden to the Germans with their horse-drawn vehicles, also hampered the Red Army supply service with its largely motorized or (horse) mounted combat groups, serving warning on the Soviet command to exercise caution regarding further advances.

I

Fighting Retreat of the Southern Wing of the German Eastern Front, 1943/44

From the Dnjepr [Dnieper] to the Dnjestr [Dniester]
In light of the combat situation at the end of 1943 it is difficult to find a clear-cut, well-defined starting point for this account of the actions of the German formations in the Ukraine between the Pripjet Marshes and the Black Sea.

The Battle of Stalingrad had exhausted – at least a portion of – the Red Army while, at the same time, building the self-confidence of the Red soldiers. These no longer looked on German soldiers as the experts to whose mercy they were hopelessly delivered. Instead, they had, certainly with gratification, seen either directly or on the weekly newsreels the winding column of destitute, starving, freezing German soldiers from the Stalingrad pocket. Henceforth, and also in other combat zones of the Red Army, the glorious aura of 'invincibility' that had been such an advantage for the German troops became a thing of the past.

This impression of invincibility had been based on the overwhelming successes of the German forces in their advance deep into the Soviet Union. This came, in part, as the result of skilled tactical command, of incredible marching accomplishments and of the great endurance of the German soldier, sometimes in far-reaching, independently operating groups. In part this respect arose from recognition of the tactical superiority of the German grenadiers and armour in action right at the front.

Driven by necessity, the Red Army had been forced to learn, and had done so. The German tactic of breakthrough, overhauling pursuit and rapid formation of pockets that earlier brought such success for the Germans in varied campaigns had impressed the Soviet command. Repeated Soviet imitation produced varied results. Already the Battle of Stalingrad and the subsequent westward advance to Charkow [Kharkov] – granted, with changing objectives and, thus, at the start, lacking clear and consistent direction – reflected the concern of the Soviet command to employ the former German tactic to Soviet advantage. These initial Soviet attempts demonstrated inadequacies and errors. The advance on Charkow at the start of 1943 did, indeed, bring initial ground gains but then ended with significant losses of troops and armour. In most instances the failure could be traced back to inadequate freedom of initiative at the mid and lower levels of command, as well as to difficulties in command by radio and, not least, to inadequate supply and insufficient training of the Red soldiers.

As a result the Germans lost territory, but, considering the weakness of the fought-out German formations, inferior in both numbers and armament, these losses were held in check. Consider that the Germans had lost an entire army of experienced East-Front formations with the fall of Stalingrad, an army now missing and which could not be replaced. As if that weren't enough, the German command had to reckon on invasion of both the channel-coast and southern Europe even as it was already in combat with the Western Powers in Sicily, then in southern Italy. All combat theaters required additional forces, with the result that the Eastern Front had to accept significant extension of individual units frontal commitments, thus a practical 'thinning' of the manpower and weapons density at the front.

Every participant of combat operations at that period remembers still the resultant decline in tactical superiority *vis à vis* Soviet units even as Soviet superiority in infantry, armour, artillery and other weapons and aircraft steadily increased – in part thanks to the materiel provided by the Western Powers to the USSR. Increasing levels of Soviet motorization became evident, particularly as a result of American Studebaker lorries arriving via Persia or Murmansk. These largely equaled and then reversed the earlier German superiority in mobility. Above all, in addition to the lorries, came armour, ammunition, rations and uniforms. Nor was there any shortage of fuel in the USSR.

For the German troops on the Eastern Front 1943 had developed into a terrible tragedy. The final desperate German effort had been the 5 July 1943 offensive to eliminate the Kursk salient, 'Operation *Zitadelle* [Citadel]'. For that operation new tanks were introduced into combat, the *Panzer* VI *'Tiger'*, already proven on other fronts, and, direct from the factory, the *Panzer* V *'Panther'*, without which Hitler would not allow the operation to begin. Manufacturing delays held up delivery for two months, so that the start of the attack was repeatedly postponed from its original 15 May, finally being set for 5 July 1943.

In addition, through their *'Rote Kapelle* [Red Orchestra]' espionage organization, which extended into the German ministries, the Soviets received exact information complete to the smallest detail about the strong German formations, their equipment and German plans. The delay in the start of the operation cost it any chance of surprise and granted the Soviets time to construct a massive defensive system organized in the entire depth of the defensive area. They brought in four thousand armoured fighting vehicles, some of which were dug in.

The northern pincer of the German attack gained no significant ground south from Orel but the southern pincer did better toward the northeast. News of the American landings of troops crossing from Sicily into southern Italy burst in the midst of the attack operation. Hitler reacted to this news with a 'panic' decision. He immediately pulled combat-worthy formations out of the successful attack of the southern pincer. The greatest armoured battle of World War II near Prochorowka, in which the Red Army had already lost more than twice as much armour as the German formations – this in particular as a result of the superior gunnery performance of the *'Tiger'* tank with its main gun developed from the 8.8 cm *Flak* gun of the same caliber had to be broken off in the midst of a promising German advance. Over the objections of the

See Map 1

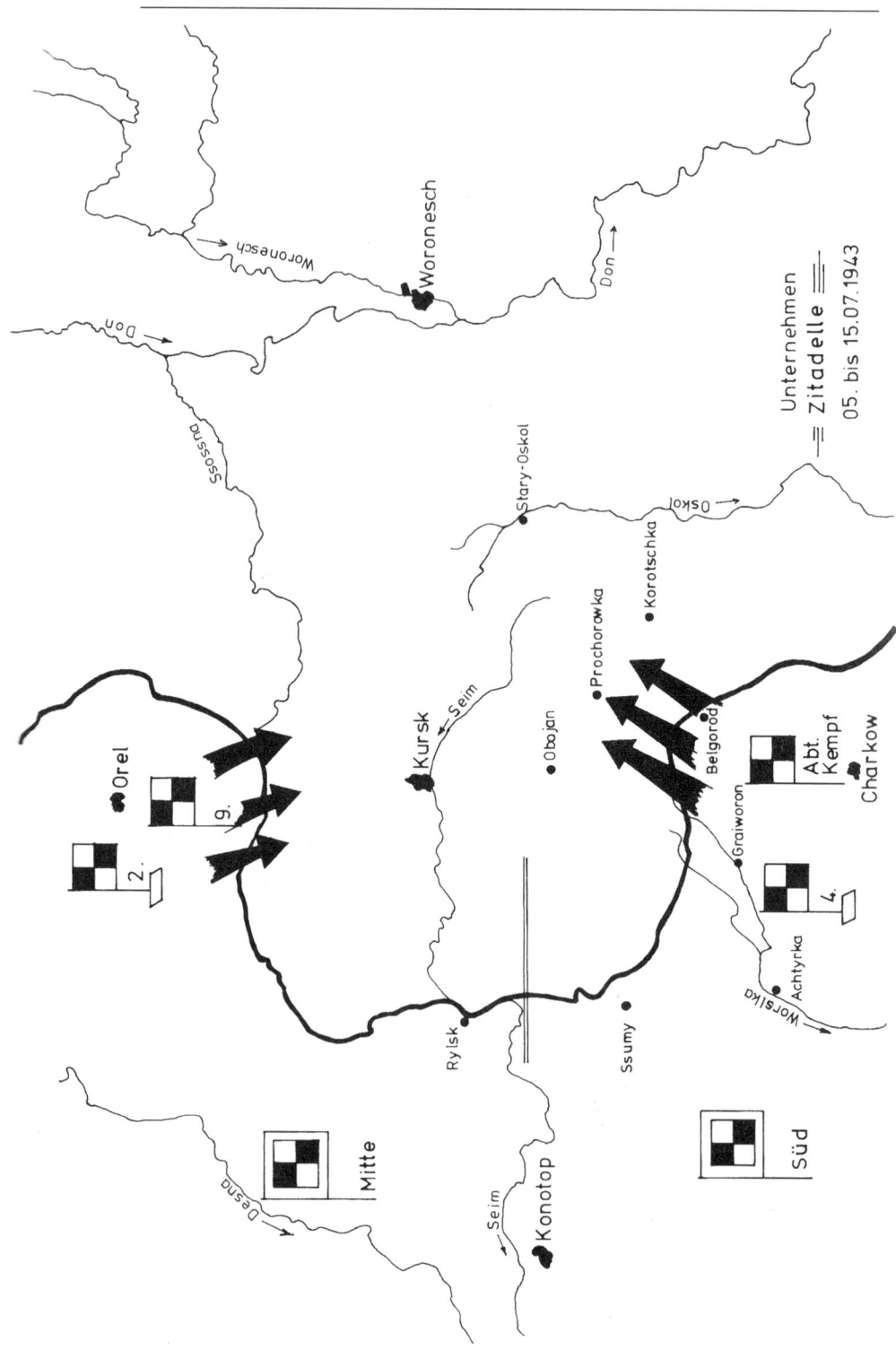

1. Operation *Zitadelle*, 5 to 17 July, 1943.

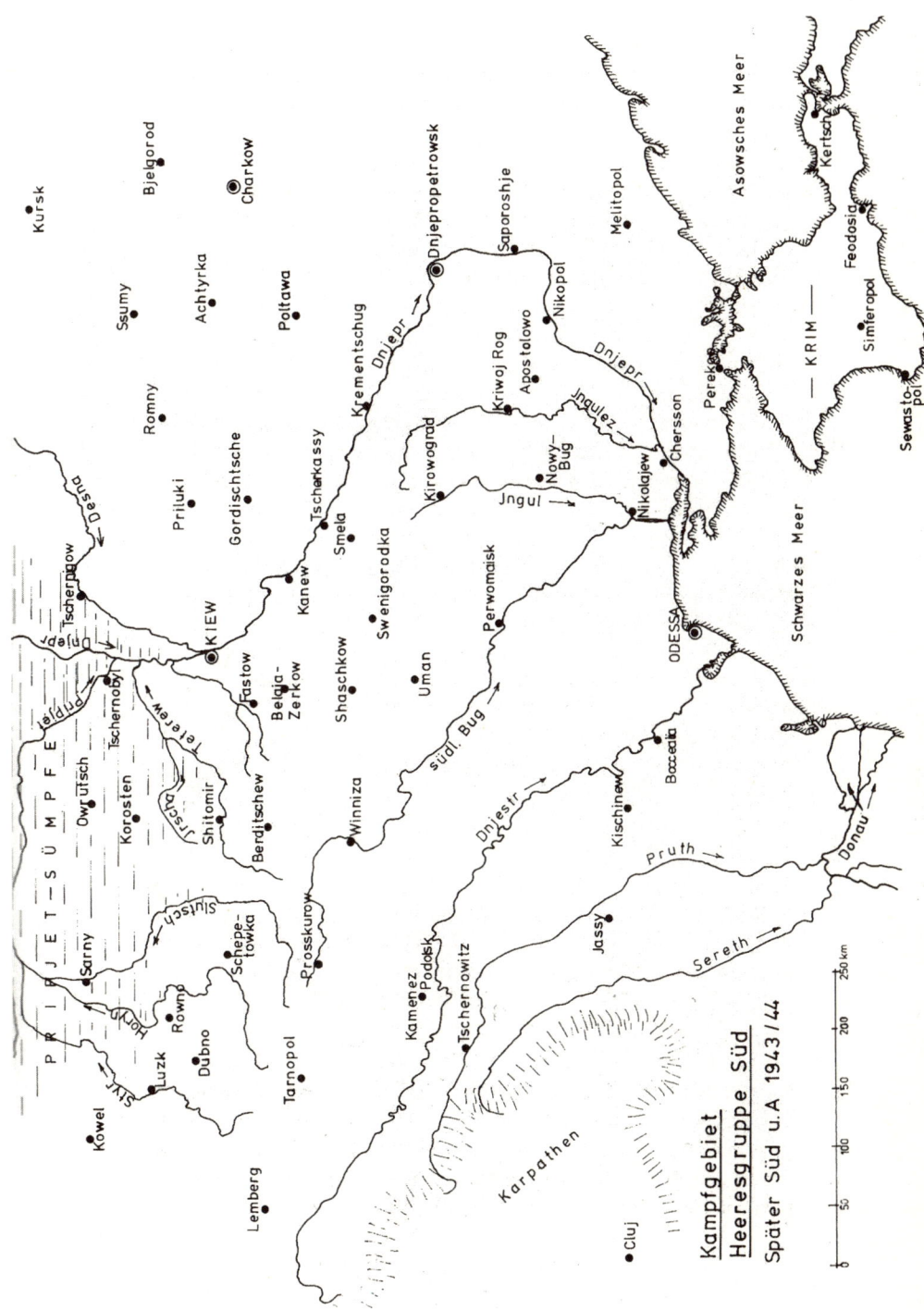

2. Combat Area, *Heeresgruppe Süd*, later divided into *Heeresgruppen Süd* and A.

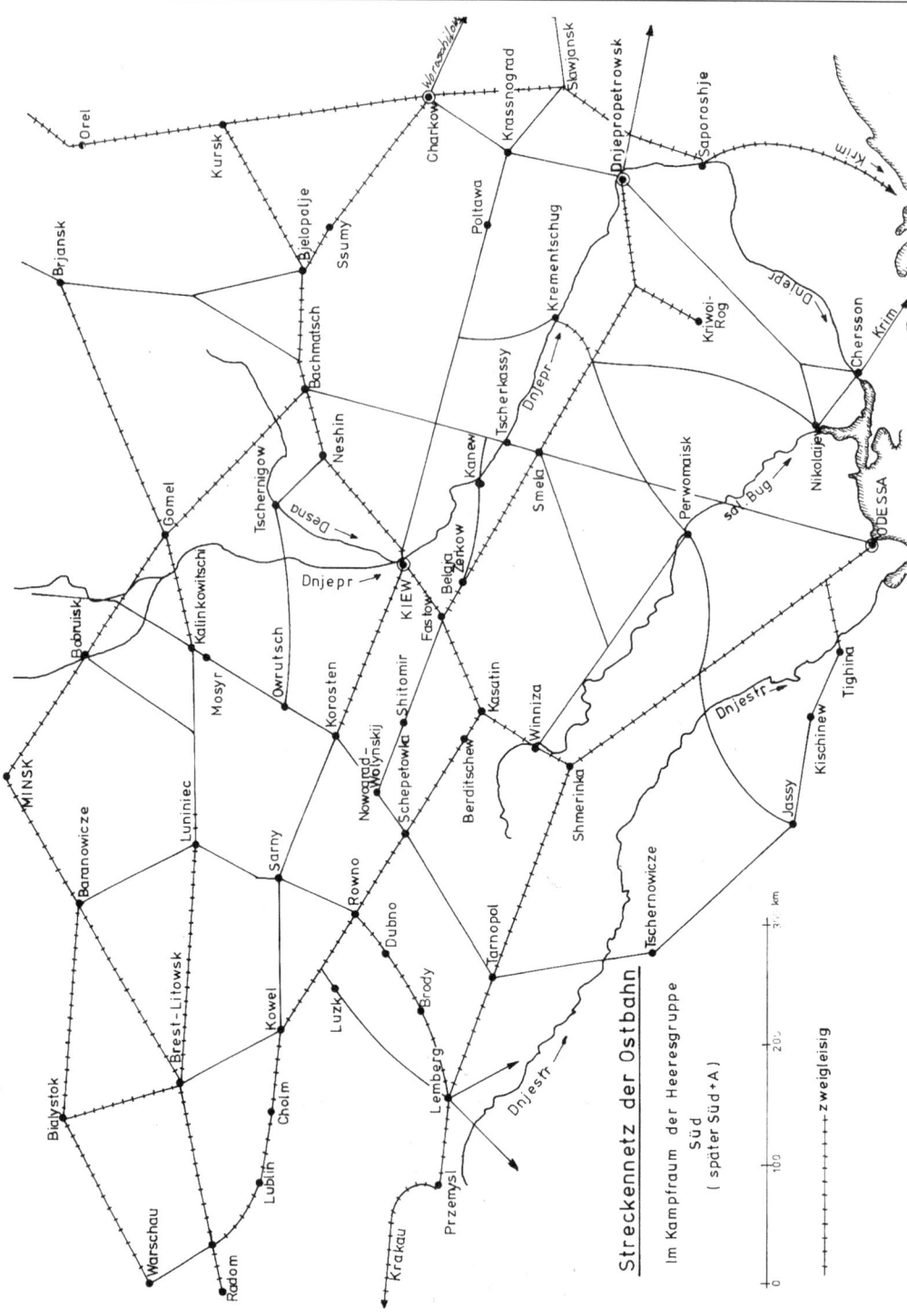

3. Railway map of the *Ostbahn* in the combat area of *Heeresgruppe Süd*, later *Süd* and A.

Wehrmachtsbefehlshaber [Commander of the Armed Forces] the 2nd *SS-Panzer Korps* was pulled out of the midst of the attack to load for transport to Italy – leaving a substantial gap in the front. The Red Army took advantage of this undreamed of opportunity, truly a miraculous seeming chance, to advance into the gap and, by then turning to the sides, to set the German front in motion.

The retrograde movement continued and, for want of adequate reserves, proved unstoppable. *Generalfeldmarschall* von Manstein attempted to get permission to evacuate the entire area east of the Dnjepr.

On 4 August, after the capture of Bjelgorod, troops of the Soviet 'Steppe' Front advanced to the southwest and forced the German MLR (main line of resistance) back against the Charkow – Ssumy railroad line. On 13/14 August a Soviet tank corps and an infantry division broke through the 8th *Armee* line of defense. *Panzergrenadier Dvision 'Großdeutschland'*, which had, in January 1943, long before the start of Operation *'Zitadelle'*, been transferred from *Heeresgruppe Mitte's* sector to that of *Heeresgruppe Don'*, restored the situation in a rash advance. The *'Tiger'* tanks immediately smashed any opposition, especially that arising from Soviet antitank guns or assault guns.

Nevertheless, the Soviet 'Steppe' Front carried on their attack on 22 August and took Charkow. The further thrust toward Poltawa was parried. The Soviet troops then regrouped, granting the troops of the German 8th *Armee* and 4th *Panzer Armee* a short breather.

Farther to the south, the Soviet armies of Generals Malinowsky and Tolbuchin broke through the German defenses at the Donez and Mius Rivers, the defense lines of the German 29th *Armee Korps* and cut off elements of the German formations near Taganrog. The Soviet forces captured Stalino and broke into the 'Donetz Basin' industrial area. General Konjew's forces thereupon resumed their attack against the 4th *Panzer Armee* front (von Knobelsdorff's 48th *Panzer Korps*).

Generalfeldmarschall von Manstein presented *Heeresgruppe Süd's* critical situation to *Führer* Headquarters, but was unable to gain approval for his resultant demands until the danger loomed of *Heeresgruppe Süd* being split into several isolated groups. Hitler then granted permission to fall back behind the Dnjepr.

The troops hoped, with this prospect, that they would go into what would be described as a well constructed and prepared position and, finally, get some rest there. This wishful thinking soon turned out to be an illusion, for Hitler followed a fundamental principle of never permitting construction of positions to the rear, because he believed that a soldier who had his gaze fixed on a position to the rear that promised a few days freedom from combat and danger would fight with less determination. Hitler had the same feelings toward his generals. Accordingly, there were no prepared fallback positions on the west bank of the Dnjepr.

In September began the evacuation of the former rear area of the *Heeresgruppen* in the Ukraine. Over 200,000 wounded had to be brought back over the Dnjepr from the front and rear-area hospitals. A large portion of the grain harvest that had already been harvested and stored in large amounts at the railroad stations was left behind. The same fate awaited agricultural machinery that had been brought from the *Reich* and stockpiled for distribution to the peasants. Ration and ammunition dumps established in a variety of locales were also abandoned. The rations dumps freed the Soviets from concerns about such supplies, but the ammunition dumps were of little use to them. The German command was additionally concerned with transporting youths who had reached military age to the west, since they would otherwise be immediately drafted into the ranks and directly into service against German forces. However, there was neither time nor rail transport available for that purpose. All movement to the rear had to move via the five functional Dnjepr crossings: Kiew [Kiev], Tscherkassy, Krementschug, Dnjepropetrowsk and Saporoschje. That included, not only evacuation of troops and materiel, but also columns of refugees with a host of Panjewagons [the standard sturdy two-wheeled Russian peasant cart]. They, too, required a clear passage, crossing over the Dnjepr and provision for quartering in villages west of the Dnjepr.

Evacuation of troops and depots took place by both rail and road. Because the carrying capacity was limited, supplies for the withdrawing formations suffered. Again and again reports reached the higher command of shortages of fuel or ammunition, and also of the greatly reduced personnel levels of the individual units – concerns which could not be fully addressed in the context of this hasty and comprehensive withdrawal. The *'Feldgraue'* railroad ['Field gray' railroad, meaning the military railroad] east of the Dnjepr worked closely with the 'Blue' railroad west of the Dnjepr. [The nicknames *'Feldgraue Bahn'* and *Blaue Bahn'* referred to the color of the uniforms of the men running the respective roads, army *Feldrau* and German civilian railroad *Blau* uniforms.] As a result of the major combat operations in the Kuban bridgehead the [civilian] *'Blaue'* railroad was already burdened with massive supply operations and had difficulty picking up massive transport demands to the east. In addition, the railroad's carrying capacity suffered from repeated demolition of tracks in the partisan areas, especially between Owrutsch, Shitomir, and Fastow to Kasatin, as well as in the single-track stretches between the double-track Lemberg – Odessa and Fastow – Dnjepropetrowsk lines (along the Dnjepr), where the direction of railroad traffic alternated from one day to the next.

Race for the Dnjepr

The withdrawal of the 2nd *SS-Panzer Korps* certainly took the Red Army by surprise, since the *ad hoc* decisions of the German command could not have been discovered by the *'Rote Kapelle'* spy organization. There was no way that the Soviet command could have planned for such an opportunity since the withdrawal of an entire army corps in the midst of a successful attack contradicted all the basic principles of military command.

The Soviet command utilized the resulting opportunity to advance the formations of their 'Steppe Front', which had, initially, been in their second line. The way to Kiew seemed virtually wide open. This city was desirable as an important transportation hub with both railroad and highway crossings over the several-hundred meter wide Dnjepr River. The road and rail crossings at Tscherkassy and Dnjepropetrowsk and the rail-crossing at Krementschug offered additional objectives. Melitopol or an advance north of the Sea of Asow to cut off the Crimean Peninsula, thereby endangering *Heeresgruppe* A, provided more distant objectives. This latter objective was less tempting to the Soviet command, because, if they gained a bridgehead over the course of the Dnjepr between Kiew and Dnjepropetrowsk, they would be able to sever the usable supply railroad for *Heeresgruppe* A, including the 17th *Armee* in the Kuban Bridgehead. The only other supply route for supplying Crimea was a single-track line from Odessa via Chersson to Dshankoj/Crimea. It is possible that the favorable military situation for the Soviet command that was produced by the withdrawal of the 2nd *SS-Panzer Korps* came too suddenly for it to be incorporated into large-scale planning. In any case, it seemed to the Germans that the Soviets initially lacked clear objectives for further tactical advances and merely strove to gain ground to the west and thereby reach the Dnjepr. Thus, on a broad front they pursued the retreating German troops, reaching the Dnjepr [River] in a variety of locations. In general, wherever possible, they attempted to build bridgeheads on the west bank of the Dnjepr before German troops retreating over the Dnjepr bridges could occupy them. In addition they hindered or prevented formation of a coherent German defense, particularly by deception regarding the strengths of the isolated Soviet elements that had crossed to the west bank.

See map of *Ostbahn* rail network, Map 3.

In evaluating possible Soviet intentions the German command had to deal with the repeatedly demonstrated Soviet tactic of having two *Schwerpunkte* [The German term, *Schwerpunkt*, meaning point of main effort, has become such a common and useful term in English military writing that it will be used, henceforth, without further explanation.]. Thus there were two *Schwerpunkte*, north and south of Kiew, as, also, north of Dnjepropetrowsk and south of that locale or south of Saporoshje. The German command was unable to recognize a predetermined ranking of priorities for the *Schwerpunkte* so far as right versus left was concerned. They had to reckon with an attempt to cross the river, at least in the Kiew area and, again, at Dnjepropetrowsk, as well as at Krementschug. In any case, the swamp, brush and wooded area west of the Dnjepr offered crossing opportunities at a variety of locations.

See Map 2 for geography.

The river offered numerous favorable opportunities for crossings, as at bends in the river that were not open to observation – perhaps at night – where assault troops could be put across and, under the cover provided by high sand dunes on the west bank, establish ferry and bridgeheads and take advantage of usable fords. The Dnjepr did not always flow with a breadth of 300 meters. Sometimes it was far wider, with shallows and islands. The Dnjepr - knee about 80 kilometers south of Kiew appeared especially favorable. Accordingly, the first concern of the German command had to be to secure such dangerpoints near Kiew, Dnjepropetrowsk – Saporoshje and Krementschug, along with the Dnjepr-knee. On the other hand, the German estimate of Soviet intentions was affected by the need to restrict the Soviet advance by holding the major Dnjepr crossings and building bridgeheads around these. Thus the Soviets would be denied the paved roads and railroad crossings over the Dnjepr, which were their obvious objectives. Regardless, Hitler always strove to hold such bridgeheads on the east bank for possible use in later renewed advances to the east. The Kuban Front had, in the meantime, lost any such significance, wherefore the German command finally completed its evacuation between the end of September and 9 October.

Retreat of the Right Wing of *Heeresgruppe* A

See Map 4, *Heeresgruppe* A, 17th *Armee*, Evacuation of the Kuban Bridgehead, situation on the Kertsch Peninsula, 8/9 October 1943.

In the Kuban Bridgehead the month of September was marked by repeated Soviet attempts to squeeze the area defended by the 17th *Armee*. On 4 September they attempted to land southeast of Ssakataj, shelled the embarkation harbour of Noworossisk, landed southwest of Noworossisk and at Myshako-*Berg* [hill], as well as in the Noworossisk harbour in order to prevent withdrawal of German forces therefrom. It was no longer possible to prevent Soviet reconnaissance from detecting preparations for evacuation of the bridgehead – under the code-name *'Krimhild'*. The objective of this initial operation was to withdraw from Crimea *Heeres* artillery, especially the heavy *Flak* which had been committed without its own prime-movers, as well as field-replacement battalions. Operation *'Brunhild'* ensued to evacuate the bridgehead.[1]

German forces repeatedly beat the Soviets back at individual points in bitter, eventful fighting. Despite unavoidable losses of ground, and inevitable delays, they secured the systematic evacuation of German forces over the Sea of Asow. The 17th *Armee* built one line of defense after another, as at Noworossisk and at the Starotitarowskaja lagoon front. During this time the crossing-operations mounted daily under air-cover provided by the *Luftwaffe*. Between 8 and 17 September the daily average was 8,223 men, 721 motor-vehicles, 2,040 horses and cattle, 780 horse-drawn vehicles and 3,797 tons of supplies. To disrupt German movements the Soviets launched attacks supported by armour, always with rapid forward-displacement of artillery as well as local attacks against the *'kleine Gotenstellung'* ['small Goth position'] along the Dschiginskoje – Wosroshdenadija road and, in addition, by landing operations aimed at cutting in behind the line of defense.

A Soviet landing-fleet stood by off the Asow coast between the Kuban Bridgehead and Golubizkaja – the Black Sea Fleet in the background – threatening landings on Crimea as well.

As of 29 September the daily averages for the evacuation operation increased significantly to 10,549 men, 745 motor-vehicles, 3,209 horses and cattle, 1,068 horse-drawn vehicles and 4,423 tons of supplies. These totals did not include materiel evacuated to Kertsch via the aerial cable-railway.[2]

In an attempt to disrupt this withdrawal on 1 October the Soviets occupied the Talman Peninsula in the Straits of Kertsch. Nevertheless, during this the formations of the 17th *Armee*, *i.e.* the 98th *Infanterie Division* and the 97th *Jäger*

1 Translator's note - On all the maps Crimea is referred to as Krim.
2 Beginning on 14 July 1943 an aerial cable-railway ran from Jenikale on the Kertsch Peninsula to the tip of the Kossa – Tschuschka tongue of land with a daily carrying capacity of 1,000 tons. It was constructed by railway pioneers and the Organisation Todt. More than ten bridge-piles from the planned highway-bridge across the Kertsch Straits were no longer serviceable. A narrow-gauge railway ran from the terminus of the cable-railway to Temrjuk. Swampy terrain prevented transport of supplies beyond that point. Therefore the connecting railroad from the aerial cable-railway was constructed via Stennaja with a link to the narrow-gauge supply rail-spur from Taman to Warenikowskaja, connecting there to the regular-gauge railway to Krymskaja, provided with 109 locomotives and 1,450 wagons. It was possible to withdraw all of the locomotives.

FIGHTING RETREAT OF THE SOUTHERN WING

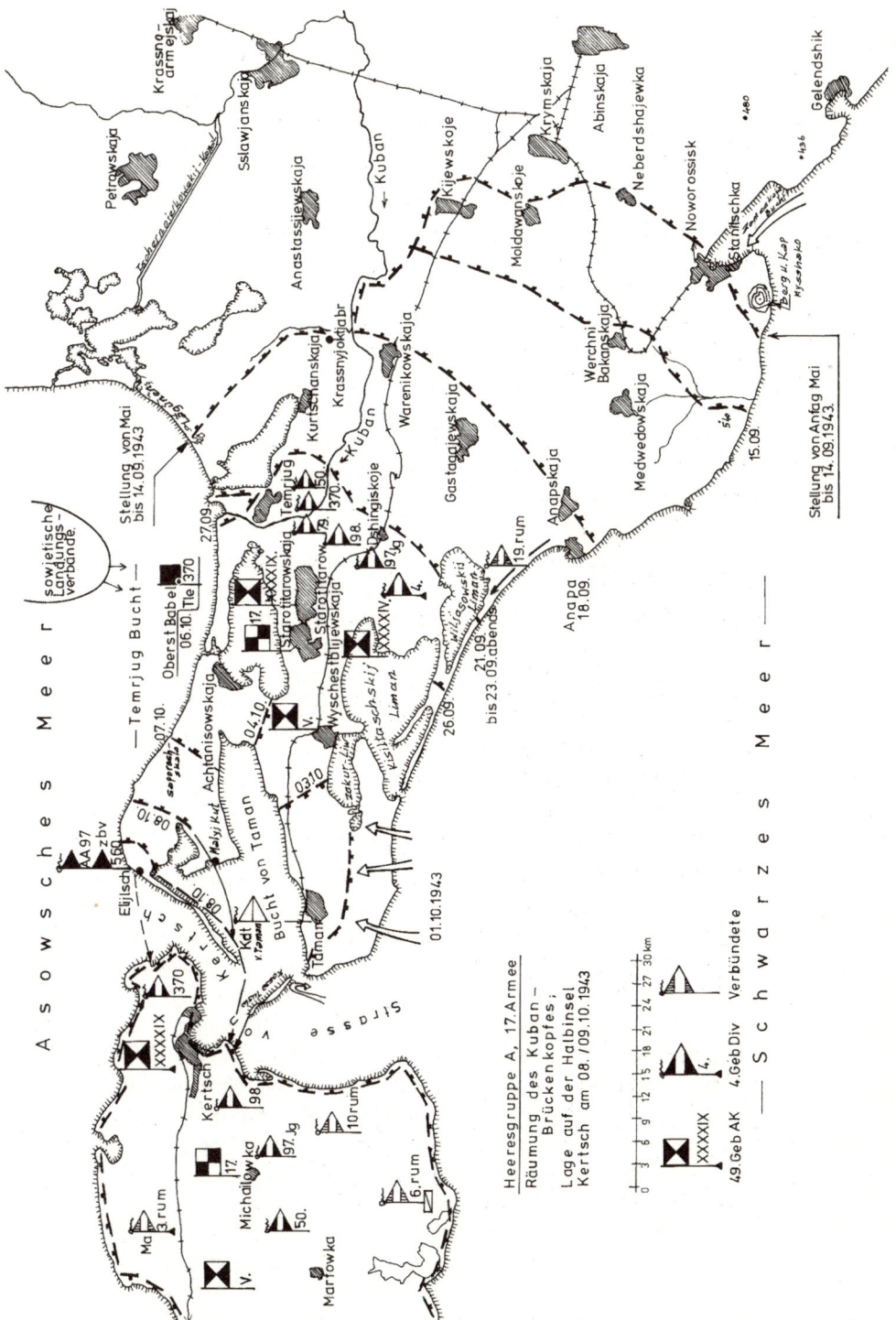

4. *Heeresgrupe* A, 17th *Armee*. Evacuation of the Kuban Bridgehead; Situation on the Kertsch Peninsula as of 8/9 October, 1943.

Division, fell back undeterred from one prepared position to another (Wien-, Bukarest-, Berlin positions) and knocked out attacking armour. As a result of the initial withdrawal of the heavy weapons and the movement from more-or-less fortified positions into improvised lines of defense these movements inevitably tempted the Soviets to harassing operations. They committed five or six divisions against the German formations.

On 6 October they landed on the southern point of the Kossa Tusla island in the Strait of Kertsch. German units succeeded that same day in forcing the forces that had landed back onto the southern point of the island. Under cover of a smokescreen the Soviets made another landing attempt on the island the following day, with the apparent intention of disrupting German embarkation of the Kuban forces.

The final withdrawal was to take place on 8 October at 0100 hours in the night from the Münchener [Munich] and Breslauer [Breslau] positions. All available ferries assembled for this operation off of Elijtsch, Kossa Tusla and Maly Kut to complete the operation in a single move. The withdrawal went as planned, covered by the concentrated, heavy fire of the heavy *Flak* positioned northeast of Kertsch. The Soviets did, indeed, lay down heavy artillery fire on the evacuated Münchener position with additional sudden concentrations of fire from heavy rocket-launchers on the embarkation points, without, however, disrupting the embarkation. As planned, the embarkation took 1 hour 20 minutes. At 2230 hours of that day the main body of the 97th *Jäger Division* was afloat, the withdrawal covered by two battalions (*Bataillon zur besondere Verwendung* 560 [a penal battalion, which would normally be employed for extremely hazardous operations]) and *Aufklärungs Abteilung* 97 in the 'Ulmer [Ulm] Position'.

At 2245 hours this rearguard, under similarly heavy fire from artillery and Stalin-Organs [multiple rocket launchers], commenced its withdrawal and, without losses, made it to the assault-boats that were standing ready on a broad front. At 2235 the garrison of Kossa Tusla Island also received orders to pull out. All of the landing craft from the Kuban Bridgehead reached Crimea by 0200 hours on 9 October. The garrison of Kossa Tusla Island arrived at Cape AK-Burnu at about 0400 hours.

That marked a notable defensive success for the 17th *Armee*. However, it did free up the Soviet formations that had hitherto been committed there either to be landed on Crimea or employed against the left wing of *Heeresgruppe* A in the Ukraine on the line between Saporoshje and the Sea of Asow. The right wing of *Heeresgruppe* A, the 3rd Rumanian *Armee* stationed in Crimea, directly organized for defense of the long southern front of the Crimean Peninsula from Kertsch via Feodosia to Sewastopol.

Overcoming the Dnjepr-Barrier

During the successful evacuation of the Kuban Bridgehead developments on the Dnjepr Front were far more confusing. Obviously the German command had expected to employ the broad Dnjepr River as a naturally strong line of defense. However, it had overlooked the fact that the Soviets had the initiative and that there were numerous stretches where the Soviets could cross, shielded from observation from the west bank

Each of the multitude of such crossings along the stretch of river between Kiew and Dnjepropetrowsk could be accomplished with a minimum of manpower, confusing and unsettling the German command, especially disrupting the orderly construction of an effective line of defense. The Soviets counted on support for these operations from partisan bands operating west of the Dnjepr. These partisan bands were frequently reinforced by paratroops dropped behind the arriving German elements.

See Maps 10, 13 and 14.

The Red Army pursued the German troops so closely that they often attained the east bank of the Dnjepr before German troops reached the corresponding west bank. Thus the German divisions and other formations committed west of Bjelgorod fell back toward Kiew and, briefly, manned the defensive position east of Kiew. As reports arrived of Soviet crossings south of Kiew, several formations immediately withdrew, as ordered, from this position, crossed the highway bridges in Kiew and proceeded to the Dnjepr-knee 80 kilometers southeast of Kiew.

This projecting knee offered good opportunities for cover for the Soviet operations. The dune-terrain on the west bank was particularly favorable, blocking observation of the east bank of the river. On 22 September the Soviets established a footing there on the west bank and immediately initiated movement to the south. Hastily brought up *Kampfgruppen* of the 7th *Panzer Division* and 23rd *Panzer Division* disrupted the marching columns and drove the remnants back into the Dnjepr-knee.

See Maps 7 and 8.

The leading elements of the 19th *Panzer Division*, ordered in forced march from the suburbs of Kiew, arrived during the night of 21/22 September via Rschtschitschew, Balyka in the area southwest of Perejasslaw in the line drawn across the Dnjepr-knee [cordon position]. During the night of 25/26 September the Soviet paratroopers disrupted the construction of an orderly line of defense, suitably adjusted to conform to the curved course of the river, with landings in Monastyrek and Sarubenzy, as well as behind the German lines. Accordingly the German formations could only take up their defensive positions in the cordon-position on the heights rising east of Maly Bukrin and Welikije Bukrin, utilizing Hill 199. Before long aerial reconnaissance reported that the Soviets were building three underwater bridges in a stretch of the river in the Dnjepr-knee that was shielded from observation.³ Upon completion heavy weapons, especially armour were brought forward over these bridges. *Stuka* airplanes repeatedly knocked these bridges out during the day. The Soviets repaired them during the night.

See Map 7.

The Soviets followed the same course of action in other sections of the river's course – separate from the river crossings initially denied to them by the German bridgehead-forces remaining east of the Dnjepr.

---

3   Translator's note - The Soviets regularly built bridges whose decks were concealed from observation by being just below the surface of the water.

Fighting on the Left Wing of the *Heeresgruppe* (4th *Panzer Armee*)

Until the end of September 1943 German formations brought back from the area east of the Dnjepr crossed the Dnjepr bridges that were still accessible to take up their assigned positions along the west bank of the Dnjepr River. The troops hoped that they would find here the presumably prepared positions they had been promised. However, they found no such arrangements, not even preparations for them. In addition, there was a shortage of formations that, in such a situation where the enemy had the initiative, could have adequately defended every conceivable crossing-site against enemy attempts.

Already the bridgehead position around Kiew proved undermanned and untenable against the pursuing Soviets. Accordingly the 4th *Panzer Armee* (291st *Infanterie Division*) evacuated the bridgehead on 28 September, blowing up the Dnjepr bridges. In the meantime, however, the Soviets had already gained ground north of Kiew.

See Maps 31, 32 and 33.

Directly north of the city the Desna River joins the Dnjepr, giving the Soviets two rivers to cross. Both rivers, however, had a very gentle gradient, flowing slowly with great breadth. Islands and shallows provided opportunities to ford the rivers. Just north of Kiew the Soviets ran into opposition on the west bank of the Dnjepr east of Ljutesh and Demidowo [Demitowo on Map 33], which initially halted them. The Koselez crossing site via Oster (Desna), then over the Dnjepr north of Gornostaipol and, in addition, the crossing with highway bridges at Tschernigow over the Desna and the Dnepr to Pritjet near Tschernobyl seemed more important to them.

Repeatedly the Soviets had chosen the *Schwerpunkte* of their advances with an eye to supplying their troops with appropriate roads or rail connections to the rear. Thus in this sector the Soviets initially tried their luck in the boundary area between *Heeresgruppe Süd* and *Heeresgruppe Mitte*, accordingly toward Gornostaipol and Tschernobyl. Bitter fighting developed directly north of the Gornostaipol – Oster road. Contributing to the concerns of the German command, there was also fighting in the area immediately north of Kiew both from the bridgehead the Soviets had built near Jassnogorodka and also further north near Rotitschi and Starosselje.

South of Kiew the Soviets had also gained a small crossing which, however, they failed to develop. Initially they played on the alternation between Ljutesh and Demidowo on the one hand and north of Tschernobyl – Starosselje, as well as south of Tschernobyl (Opatschizy), and also near Rotitschi, with the attack directed toward Gornostaipol.

See Maps 31 and 32.

By constantly shifting the *Schwerpunkte* the Soviets repeatedly broke through the overextended German line of defense. Each time a shortage of defending forces forced the line to be pulled back. Elements of the 7th *Panzer Division* and 8th *Panzer Division* forced the Soviets from their crossings at Janowka and south of Tschernobyl and recaptured Tschernobyl, which had, in the meanwhile, fallen into enemy hands. They battled enemy forces near Staro-Petrowzy, launched a counterattack from Ljutesh and Demidowo against enemy forces in the woods northeast of Rasiljudesh and Lepimedowo. On 8 October the Soviets broke through between Ljutesh and Demidowo with

FIGHTING RETREAT OF THE SOUTHERN WING

three rifle divisions, enabling them to attack the 183rd *Infanterie Division* from the rear.

In the ensuing days the fighting was extraordinarily eventful. On 11 October the Soviets broke through the forest position west of Ljuteshy, crossed the Irpen Stream and advanced to the Sinjak – Demidowo road. On both sides of Jassnogorodka thay broke through as far as the artillery positions of the 291st *Infanterie Division*. The last, however, was subject to a successful counterattack by hastily thrown-together German forces.

Eventful fighting developed reaching the bend in the railroad 15 kilometers northwest of Kiew. [Map 33 shows the geography, though illustrating action at a later date.] In this action a Soviet combat group was cut off. This, however, broke out again at the north wing of the 291st *Infanterie Division* and established contact with an enemy group that had been cut off west of Opatschitzy and then, immediately turned to attack Wiankowka from the south. The 7th *Armee Korps*, accordingly, was ordered to have its left wing smash through along the Wischgorod – Moschtschun line. Counterattacks ensued by the 7th *Panzer Division* with elements of the 340th and 183rd *Infanterie Divisionen*. See Maps 31 and 33.

On 18 October the *Schwerpunkt* of the Soviet attack was near Wyschgorod and Muschtschun. An enemy group that had been cut off at the northern wing of the 13th *Armee Korps* broke out of its encirclement. An attempt by the 7th *Panzer Division* to reestablish the encirclement with an armoured group failed.

On 20 October the Soviets renewed their attack on a broad front against the northern front of the 7th *Armee Korps*, without, however, achieving success. The 291st *Infanterie Division* was able to improve its positions at its extreme northern wing by advancing over the Gornaipol – Tschernobyl road. On 23 October the 7th *Panzer Division* and 217th *Infanterie Division* surrounded an apparently stronger enemy group east of Rowy.

It appeared that the German command treated the area north of Kiew as a sideshow. *Generalfeldmarschall* von Manstein informed Hitler repeatedly that the 4th *Panzer Armee* needed reinforcement because, without adequately strong German defense, the Soviets would be able to advance rapidly to the west, farther than in the sector of the right wing of *Heeresgruppe Süd*. In the event, *Generalfeldmarschall* Model's promises regarding providing troops remained empty. *Heeresgruppe Mitte* was supposed to take over the area around Tschernigow, but that fell through because the formations intended for that purpose had to be employed elsewhere. It is possible that the high command had let itself be deceived by conclusions based on Maps regarding terrain conditions, for further movement of combat action between the two *Heeresgruppen* to the west would get into the difficult terrain of the Pripjet Marshes, crossed by few roads or railroads. What this overlooked was that around Tschernobyl and farther north were thickly settled areas and, above all – what seems most significant, the rivers that had to be crossed, the Desna, Dnjepr and Pripjet offered numerous shallow places where the Red soldiers could wade through the water holding their weapons above their heads, followed by their guns and ammunition carts drawn by *panje* horses. [The Russian peasant horses, called *panje-* horses or ponies, were tough, shaggy, extremely sturdy small horses capable of amazing endurance and performance.] Thus, in a variety of sectors these three rivers were scant hindrance, and the Red soldiers knew well how to take advantage of the opportunities.

The weak German manning of the entire area north of Kiew would, necessarily, stimulate the Russians to employ this area for their further advance. Despite *Generalfeldmarschall* von Manstein's repeated warnings, OKH [*Oberkommando des Heeres*] only began to pay attention when the Soviets turned south from Demidowo and Ljutesh – two roads led from there to Kiew – thereby threatening Kiew from the rear. Shortly the German formations operating there, comprising three fought-out infantry divisions (183rd, 339th and 217th *Infanterie Divisionen*), were put together to make *Korps Abteilung* C.[4] As for other divisions, all that was left in action of them were *Kampfgruppen,* as the 323rd, 327th, 340th *Infanterie Divisionen,* 8th and 7th *Panzer Divisionen,* along with the 454th *Sicherungs Division.* [*Sicherungs Divisionen* were mobile *Landesschützen* divisions, normally employed for rear-area guard duties, lacking the transport and heavy weapons of normal infantry divisions.] The only combat-capable divisions were the 68th, 88th and 291st *Infanterie Divisionen* and *Korps Abteilung* C. The neglect of this frontal sector would later cost heavily. After the Soviets' intentions foundered with their other various bridgeheads over the Dnjepr, especially at the Dnjepr - knee, they turned to this sector for which, in addition, it appeared important to block use of Kiew as a railroad hub to prevent rapid shifting of German formations behind *Heeresguppe Süd's* front from south to north.

Fighting in the 1st *Panzer Armee* Sector

In their advance to the west, the Soviets initially attempted to gain a foothold at as many places as possible on the west bank of the Dnjepr River before the Germans could build a line of defense there. Which sector would then become the *Schwerpunkt* of the Red Army attack and where in the several hundred kilometer course of the Dnjepr they would then attempt to build a western bridgehead clearly hung on the success of these endeavours. An obvious candidate appeared to be the section of the Dnjepr where a great bend stretched far to the east, thus likely to be the first stretch reached by Soviet troops. Above all else, in several places (Dnjepropetrowsk, Saporoshje) there were good roads and bridges and, in addition, suitable highways and railroads in the hinterland for bringing up troops and supplies. Thus it was that the Soviets initially turned in strength to the sector of the 1st *Panzer Armee*.

As usual, they formed two *Schwerpunkte,* one north of Dnjepropetrowsk, the other south of Saporoshje, as well as other attempts, possibly to excite the German command or distract attention from the functioning bridgeheads.

See Maps 13, 14 and 23.

They crossed the Dnjepr-arm to the island southwest of Koleberda (29/30 September) and built a bridgehead near Uspenskoje with the only usable ferry location in this section of the river. They established additional crossing

See Map 13.

---

4   Translator's note: The term 'Abteilung', sometimes used as meaning a detachment, was here used in the simple sense as 'unit', which was, in fact, a way of indicating that the three battered infantry divisions lacked sufficient strength to operate as divisions, but were put together to come up with a single combat-worthy unit, more or less equal to a division in strength and designated as a Korps Abteilung. Korps Abteilung C proved extremely effective, a 'division' that anyone could be proud to belong to, with its own excellent unit history. (Wolfgang Lange, *Korpsabteilung C*).

points, apparently in hopes of linking them together, thereby gaining a wider continuous section of the west bank of the Dnjepr in which to build a greater bridgehead. Whether the Soviet plans, at this time, were more far-reaching cannot be ascertained, but seems unlikely, since any further tactical planning awaited the successes of the initial endeavors, namely, gaining bridgeheads sufficient for future enlarging.

North of Werchnedjeprowsk the Soviets gained a bridgehead, attacked from north and northwest near Mischurin Rog and forced the 23rd *Panzer Division* back to the north edge of Nesamoshnik. German reconnaissance identified preparation of materiel for crossing seven kilometers north of Saporoshje and also west of Dnjepropetrowsk. The Soviets put up extraordinarily tough opposition to a German counterattack against the enemy bridgehead northwest of Werchnedjeprowsk. Nevertheless, the 9th *Panzer Division* with elements of the 355th *Infanterie Division* gained ground in counterattack. The main body of the 6th *Panzer Division* forced the Soviets out of Annowka and back to the Kalushino high ground so that the main line of resistance could again be continuous, though now already south of the Dnjepr. *(See Maps 23, 14 and 17.)* *(See Map 14.)*

The 9th *Panzer Division* and *Panzergrenadier Division 'Großdeutschland'* narrowed the enemy bridgehead northwest of Werchnedjeprowsk, the 9th *Panzer Division* with 306th *Infanterie Division* doing the same to the Soviet bridgehead south of Orlik. The Soviets, however, gained a *Schwerpunkt* west-northwest of Dnjepropetrowsk near Romankowo, where the Dnjepr is extremely broad with shallows and even sandy islands in its course. They had also, in the meantime, gained a landing south of Orlik. *(See Map 14.)*

On 13 October the Soviets also attacked the east and south fronts of the Saporoshje bridgehead, with strong support from artillery, armour and ground-attack aircraft. This support showed that they were seeking the same success here as north-northwest of Dnjepropetrowsk in order to encircle the German bridgehead that yet remained east of the Dnjepr. The Soviets achieved numerous penetrations and also breakthroughs. Lack of available forces made it impossible to seal these off. The Soviets attained a deeper penetration on the east bank of the Dnjepr near Podoporoshnyi against the German bridgehead there. They then shifted their *Schwerpunkt* to the Nowo-Alexandrowka area and on both sides of the Krassnoarmeiskoje – Saporoshje railroad line (at the Charkow – Saporoshje – Dnjepropetrowsk railroad line) with their objective aimed at the German bridgehead, itself. South of the railroad line the Soviets penetrated to the Nowo-Alexandrowo – Balabino ridge. *(See Maps 23, 24 and 25.)*

The Soviets put extreme effort into utilizing local ground-gains on the west bank. The intensity of the defensive battle is shown by the 61 AFVs knocked out by the 30th *Armee Korps* near Schtuschinka. The Soviets attacked the German bridgehead east of Saporoshje with support from 116 AFVs, thereby compressing the German bridgehead into a small area. On 14 October the main line of resistance ran through the center of the city, still denying the Soviets their desired advance to the dam and the Dnjepr bridges. That day, however, the dam and the railroad bridges were blown up. The new main line of resistance then ran along the west bank of the river, including the Chortiza island.

The Soviets attempted to widen and deepen the bridgeheads they had built north-northwest of Dnjepropetrowsk in order to then establish contact between the individual bridgeheads. Where they had sufficient depth in a bridgehead they moved heavy weapons to the west bank of the Dnjepr and prepared for their attacks with heavy artillery fire, as from the bridgeheads south of Shulgowka, south of Orlik and also Annowka.

See Map 14.

In light of the results of aerial reconnaissance it now seemed difficult to the German command to determine where the Soviets were actually planning to advance westward from a bridgehead, or, if such plans had not yet been made, to identify where the Soviets could and would build *Schwerpunkte* for further westward advances.

One such *Schwerpunkt* soon became evident in the Shulgowka – Ssoloschino sector, where the Soviets committed 180 – 200 batteries of artillery, as well as ground-attack aircraft and armour. The count of enemy equipment knocked out gave even better evidence of the bitterness of the fighting. A breakthrough to the south and southwest was prevented in mid October with the destruction of about 100 enemy AFVs. Nevertheless, the Soviets were able to establish continuous contact on the west bank of the Dnjepr from Litwinowka as far as the 8th *Armee* – 1st *Panzer Armee* boundary and to extend the bridgehead in the Mischurin Rog area to a depth of 15 to 16 kilometers.

See Map 13.

Dissatisfied with these successes, the Soviets extended additional bridgeheads, as in the sector northwest of Werchnedjeprowsk as far as the area of Lichowka – Popelnastoje, Matrenowka, Pjatichatki and Nikolajewka (25 kilometers northwest of Popelnastoje). The Soviets were able to do this because of a gap in the German defenses that was over 70 kilometers wide. In the early-dawn of 19 October the Soviets reached Pjatichatki and, at numerous places, broke through the lines of the 355th *Infanterie Division* and 306th *Infanterie Division*, which were only held as a series of strong-points. They achieved an additional breakthrough toward Petrowo. 700 to 800 enemy AFVs were, in the meantime, identified, feeling their way forward to the south, southwest and west in the area of the breakthrough, employed in groups of 10 to 20 AFVs with motorized infantry. In the evening of 20 October these reached Ziwok, advanced southwest of Pjatichatki over the railroad line to Nowo-Iwanowka, forcing their way via Selenojo into Petrowo, advancing east of Nowo-Starodub and reconnoitering to the Tscherwona – Kamenka front and Prijutowka and Kukolowka.

See Map 14.

In the evening of 21 October the enemy spearheads were already near Raj Pole in the Ssaxagan sector, as well as directly southeast of Annowka. A group of 15 enemy AFVs was advancing west of the Ingulez river near Kupani. Another enemy armoured group that had broken through was wiped out in the rear area. With that the Soviets achieved a deep penetration west of Dnjepropetrowsk toward Kirowograd. The Germans simply did not have the troops required to hold the margins of this penetration.

First Battle of Kirowograd/Kriwoi Rog

The Soviets were not satisfied with the successes they had striven for, but attempted to further extend the area of their penetration by gaining additional

FIGHTING RETREAT OF THE SOUTHERN WING

crossings west of Dnjepropetrowsk. On 22 October they failed against the 387th *Infanterie Division*. Further fighting developed in the depth of the Soviet frontal salient, as in the salient between the Saxogen and Ingulez rivers between Wesselyje Terny and also near Losowatka (12 kilometers north of Kriwoij Rog). The available *Kampfgruppen* [combat groups] of the 40th *Panzer Korps*, the 24th *Panzer Division*, 3rd *SS-Panzer Division 'Totenkopf'* and the 11th *Panzer Division* launched counterattacks, flank attacks in particular, to seal off penetrations, as did the available elements of the 14th *Panzer Division* that were arriving in transport from France.

See Maps 14, 15 and 16.

Six Soviet rifle divisions and one armoured brigade attacked to broaden this Soviet penetration area on 24 October in the Woiskowoje area and achieved significant penetrations into the thinly held German front that was sealing off the breakthrough. The Soviets opened a great, yawning gap between Kalkowka and Woiskowoje, north of the Dnjepr knee between Dnjepropetrowsk and Saporoshje. In light of the immense superiority of the Soviet forces and the lack of German reserves, the *Armee* had to pull its line of defense back farther to the south.

See Map 14.

On 25 October persistent fog favored further Soviet efforts to broaden their penetration, whereby they attacked the 46th *Infanterie Division*, which adjoined the 387th *Infanterie Division* to the right, near Stary Kojdaki, forcing back its left wing so that the Soviets could also gain a foothold on the west bank of the Dnjepr at that location. The attackers also took advantage of the fog to build a bridgehead at the left wing of the 387th *Infanterie Division* north of Ssuchatschewka. German formations launched counter attacks, which the Soviets again countered with new advances supported by armour, as from Tschernyj Wyssoki, where ten enemy AFVs were knocked out. The Soviets utilized the withdrawal movements of *30th Armee Korps*, attacking into them and again attaining a new, deep penetration near Blagoweschtschenko – Rogowski. The necessity of closing the gaps in the front, at least with a series of strongpoints brought about the withdrawal of the *Korps* left wing to the general line Krinitschki – Showtenewoje. German attacks at the apex of the German frontal salient in the Saporoshje area on 26 October brought only local success, but did force enemy forces that had crossed the Dnjepr back to the east bank and also cleansed the Chortiza Island.

See Maps 14, 25.

See Map 26.

The situation became increasingly critical due to the lack of mobile, combat-worthy German formations with which to seal off the lengthening frontal salient of this Soviet advance west-southwest of Dnjepropetrowsk. The Soviets enveloped the southern wing of the 57th *Panzer Korps* with a total of 30 AFVs and reached the area Spassowo – Dubowyj – both sides of Nowo-Starodub, as well as near Ismailowka with a confirmed 75 AFVs, primarily to broaden the area for the Soviet approaches. The Soviets had also, however, targeted successes to the south, as in the attainment of Kriwoi-Rog. Hastily brought up elements of the 11th *Panzer Division* counterattacked, driving the Soviets from the city. The *Heeresgruppe* command urgently awaited the arrival of additional formations, since there was no other way of halting the strong Soviet forces that were advancing. The divisions that were then in action proved to be fought out and decimated, unable to take over additional sectors of the

See Maps 15, 16, 17, 18.

front. Formations arriving from western and southern Europe initially had to become acclimated to autumn in the Ukraine. Nevertheless, elements of the 24th *Panzer Division* began arriving in rapid-transport, initially from Vienna via Krakau – Przemysl – Winniza to Uman, the leading elements arriving on 17 October 1943. *Panzeraufklärungsabteilung* 24 was immediately committed in the Alexandrija area with the 40th *Panzer Korps*. The *Abteilung* organized in a blocking position defending Nowo Starodub with a completely open right flank and with a great gap on the left to the 376th *Infanterie Division*, which was arriving from Holland – without heavy weapons and, initially, with inadequate logistical support.

In the morning of 23 October the Soviets surprised the *Abteilung* combat outposts with over 20 AFVs and forced their way into Nowo Starodub. The two *Abteilung Schwadronen*, however, blocked the crossing over the Ingulez river. The Soviets then crossed the river during the night and the following morning with armour and infantry over makeshift bridges north and south of the city. Several T 34 tanks rolled over an *Abteilung* command post from the rear and were only knocked out when they penetrated the city. The situation was relieved as an armoured *Schwadron* [troop] of the *Aufklärungsabteilung* approached to within ten kilometers of the city and knocked out numerous enemy AFVs. Nevertheless, the Soviets drew their ring ever tighter in the terrain, which was closed to observation. A strong attack against the left wing and advance to the *Abteilung* command post of *Panzeraufklärungsabteilung* 24 on 25 October put the *Abteilung* in a nearly hopeless situation. The last counter-assault of the 3rd *Schwadron* brought relief. On 27 October additional elements of the division arrived in the Nowo Starodub area, including an armoured flamethrower *Schwadron* and a *Werfer-Abteilung* [rocket-launcher battalion], which freed the *Panzeraufklärungsabteilung* from its perilous situation. The *Abteilung* took a commanding hill west of the city, thereby opening access to it. Nevertheless, it was unable to establish contact with the 376th *Infanterie Division* in the face of tough enemy resistance. On 28 October the *Aufklärungsabteilung* of the 3rd *SS Panzer Division 'Totenkopf'* relieved *Panzeraufklärungsabteilung* 24. In order to secure the withdrawal route a pioneer platoon had to repulse enemy infantry near Woloschino – Orlowka. The amounts of ammunition expended bear witness to the type and ferocity of this fighting, with 134,000 rifle and machine gun rounds, 710 mortar shells and 12,000 hand grenades.

Enemy pressure then was not only directed against Kriwoi Rog, but especially against Kirowograd, so that, once it was assembled, the 24th *Panzer Division* initially had to stop the enemy pressure over the Ingulez river to the west. There the Soviet 5th and 1st Guards Mechanized Corps advanced from the Sselenoje area westward with the intention of advancing to Snamenka via Nowo Starodub and Nowaja Praga, where they then ran into *Panzeraufklärungsabteilung* 24 at Nowo Starodub.

On 27 October the Soviets attacked, enveloping additional elements of the 24th *Panzer Division* with greatly superior forces. These Soviet forces were smashed in eventful fighting that resulted in 500 dead left on the field and 32 AFVs knocked out. One armoured brigade of the Soviet 1st Guards Mechanized Corps, which advanced toward Kirowograd,, broke through the

FIGHTING RETREAT OF THE SOUTHERN WING

security lines of the II./ *Panzerartillerie Regiment* 89 [2nd *Abteilung, PAR* 89, 24th *Panzer Division*] and caused losses.

That day, however, the 14th *Panzer Division* and 24th *Panzer Division* were fully committed under the 40th *Panzer Korps* in an assault on the flank of the enemy advancing on Kriwoi Rog, with the initial objective of forcing the enemy armour that had broken through to Snamenka – Kirowograd back over the Ingulez river. For this purpose the *Heeresgruppe* attached *Panzergrenadier Division 'Groß Deutschland'*, along with the 376th *Infanterie Division* to the 24th *Panzer Division* . Only the 24th *Panzer Division*, however, was to be committed to the attack, while the two attached divisions were assigned to cover the flanks of the attack. However, the division did not come out of a single concentrated assembly position but had to start out from widely separated villages against an enemy that was assembled, ready to attack with strong forces and who had already carried out strong local advances. The first order of business was to destroy strong enemy forces that were south and southwest of Nowaja Praga, wherefor several *Panzer* of the group set off from the northwest, *Panzerregiment* 26 from the west and *Panzergrenadierregiment* 21 [24th *Panzer Division*] from the north toward the Scharowka railroad station. Because of the enemy situation at Nowo Starodub *Panzeraufklärungsabteilung* 24 and II./ *Panzergrenadierregiment* 21 did not start on time. The thrust led from Dubrowyj after turning to the south-southwest to Spassowo, Wodjana and Krassno-Konstantinowka, building a bridgehead over the Ingulez river at Losowatka and Ternowatka. 40 enemy AFVs were knocked out on the first day of the attack. During the night of 28/29 October the *Kampfgruppe* on the left, which was in the lead, advanced via Dobrowyj and Spassowo, reaching Wodjana by dark. The *Kampfgruppe* advancing on the right reached Werbljushka.

On 30 October the armoured spearhead renewed its attack in the dark. Against strong resistance, that included anti-tank guns, it advanced north of Losowatka via Krassno-Konstantinowka. Near Werschino – Wlassijewka it dispersed a Soviet artillery division and, near Bairak, the 1317th Soviet Artillery Regiment with the loss of all its guns. The elements of the 24th *Panzer Division* then turned eastward to fight for a bridgehead over the Ingulez river at Ternowatka, with a new direction of attack toward Annowka and Pjatichatki. The bridgehead was successfully built in the face of well organized, stubbornly defending enemy forces and despite an enemy counterattack in the dark.

The Red Army soldiers fleeing from the area of the German breakthrough assembled on the east bank. Newly brought-up formations attacked the *Panzer* Division. The Soviets put up such strong resistance along the Srja-Ssanowka line, particularly with anti-tank guns and artillery, that ground-gain was extremely slow. Nevertheless, on 10 October the attack continued with concentrated forces. Despite heavy enemy losses, there was no decisive breakthrough. When the German armour came up against a strong *Pak-Front* [a carefully organized, mutually supporting array of anti-tank guns and infantry], *Panzergrenadierregiment* 21 launched an infantry attack through the halted armour and gained ground until the *Korps* halted the attack with the order to hold at the foremost line of ground gained.

See Map 15.

This courageous thrust into the flank of the Soviet attacking forces halted the Soviet advance, thereby relieving the 1st *Panzer Armee*.

The 24th *Panzer Division*, however, was not the only German formation attacking the Soviets in a tactically favorable commitment. The 14th *Panzer Division* also did so. It, too, had come a long 2,400 kilometers from the warmth of France to autumn in the Ukraine via Lemberg, Stanislau – Kischinew – Tiraspol – Odessa and detrained in the Kamenka – Snamenka area. By 27 October it took security positions facing southeast, east and north around Nowgorodka. During its march from Snamenka to Moschorino to the south, *Panzeraufklärungsabteilung* 14 ran into the first enemy forces near the Mederowa railroad station. It destroyed these forces, knocking out several T-34 tanks.

The German command took into account the Soviet tactic of forming its armoured spearheads exclusively out of armoured formations, in that it attached grenadiers, artillery and pioneers to the German armoured commands. The first formed armoured group of the 14th *Panzer Division* assembled at Jelisawetgratowka. The command initially faced the difficult question of deciding at which of the two danger points it would commit this force, whether frontally against the Soviet thrust into the intricately dissected terrain about 30 kilometers east of Kirowograd, which was not open to observation, or at the left wing of the 1st *Panzer Armee* north of Kriwoi Rog, the more so since the Soviet thrust to the south had been blocked, but not, however, the Soviet attacks that were simultaneously being conducted to the west and northwest. Accordingly the division initially had to secure the terrain between the two areas of penetration that was still in German hands and to cut off the Red armoured formations that had advanced farthest to the west from their rear connections. Finally they were to attack in the framework of the 40th *Panzer Korps* together with the 24th *Panzer Division* and 3rd *SS-Panzer Division 'Totenkopf'* to the east and southeast and regain the Ingulez sector as a basis for defense.

Directly west of Wladimirowka the *Kampfgruppe* assembled and advanced along the railroad line to the north as far as the Tschabanowka train-stop. There it met with the first weak enemy resistance, turned to the west and attacked the garrison of the Pawloka settlement, which it wiped out in hard fighting. Shortly thereafter the Schorowka collective was captured. The *Kampfgruppe* then reached the highway intersection west of Werschina Kamenka, knocking out 33 enemy AFVs, six anti-tank guns, 12 lorries and capturing numerous prisoners while so doing.

Another *Kampfgruppe* of the 14th *Panzer Division* attacked out of the security position at Woronzowka and forced the Soviets back far to the northeast, knocking our four tanks. *Panzergrenadierregiment* 108 [14th *Panzer Division*] advanced from Tschetschelewka via the railroad line to the east and, by the time darkness fell, reached the west edge of Werbljushka. Disregarding a confirmed enemy threat from the line Dobljanka – Nowo Tschewtschenkowo – Bukowa – Warwarowka, the 40th *Panzer Korps* stood firmly by its order to advance against the identified assembly position at the Ingulez, near Petrowo.

FIGHTING RETREAT OF THE SOUTHERN WING   47

To cover the right flank *Panzeraufklärungsabteilung* 14 received a howitzer battery as reinforcement in order to advance into the area north of Gurowka. This advance would relieve the pressure on the *Korps* that was fighting hard around Kriwoi Rog. *Panzergrenadierregiment* 108 of the 14th *Panzer Division* thereby supported the advance of elements of the 24th *Panzer Division* by capturing Wodjana, with the support of dive-bombers and a *Gruppe* [section] of tanks.

Together with the 24th *Panzer Division* the 14th *Panzer Division* delivered several powerful attacks against the still-forming enemy front with the capture of Losowatka described above and the building of a bridgehead on the east bank of the Ingulez river.

Another *Kampfgruppe* launched attacks against the Ssaxagan river sector and, in the face of notably stiffening opposition, attained the line Nowo-Iwanowka – Krassny. Yet another group advanced east of Alexejewka.

On 1 November the Soviet resistance stiffened, particularly as a result of newly formed *Pak*- and armour- fronts and intense employment of Soviet air force formations which caused disruptions and losses. Nevertheless, despite enemy employment of reinforced artillery, it was possible to take the Soviet positions in frontal attacks, so that the I./ *Panzergrenadierregiment* 108, swinging far to the right, was able to advance, with the help of several *Sturmgeschütze*,[5] past the Lenin mine to Hill 109, about two kilometers west of Nowo Pawlowka. Premature darkness, however, prevented full completion of the combat mission. The 23rd *Panzer Division* relieved the 14th *Panzer Division* in the achieved security position.

With that, the Soviet advance appeared initially to be stopped.[6]

Judging by previous experience, the German command now had to expect that the Soviets would attack anew from the south near Apostolowo or Nikopol, simultaneously exerting pressure in the area of the Dnjepr knee.

Again, on 6 November, the formations attempted to break through the Soviet lines. However, the tempo of the advance dropped increasingly after breaking through the first weakly-secured field positions under fire from extraordinarily strong anti-tank and artillery from the east, north and west. Several further attempts, with support from *Stukas*, failed to achieve success, the more so since the ravines provided good concealment for artillery and anti-

---

5   Translator's note – assault guns. The German *Sturmgeschütz*, essentially a tank hull with no rotating turret, the main gun firing forward, thus with a lower profile than a tank, was the first 'assault gun'. The *Sturmgeschütz* defined the new type of AFV. Therefore I am retaining the German term.
6   LVII *Panzer Korps*:
     Left group, *Generalleutnant* Buschenhagen
     Panzergrenadier Division 'Großdeutschland', elements 15th *Panzer Division*, *Kampfgruppe* 9th *Panzer Division*, elements *Waffen-SS Kavallerie Division*, staff, elements 62nd *Infanterie Division*, Elements 15th *Panzer Division* [sic.], *Kampfgruppe* 23rd *Panzer Division*, occasionally 11th *Panzer Division*, 14th *Panzer Division* from 2 to 6 November.
     Right group, *Generalleutnant* Schwerin
     Marine Bataillon 62, *Kampfgruppe* 38th *Infanterie Division*, *Marsch Bataillon* 16th *Panzergrenadier Division*, *Kampfgruppe* 306th *Infanterie Division*, *Kampfgruppe* 328th *Infanterie Division*, remnants 355th *Infanterie Division*, *Kampfgruppe* 161st *Infanterie Division*, *Kampfgruppe* 293rd *Infanterie Division*.
     These are a mass of unit designations that give the impression of a substantial combat force.

tank guns. In addition, the Soviets were strongly supported by fighter-planes. Therefore the German command terminated this operation. *Panzergrenadier Division 'Großdeutschland'* then relieved the 14th *Panzer Division*. Further combat operations bogged down in the mud of the softened terrain.

The Frontal Salient Northwest of Dnjepropetrowsk

See Map 14.

As a result of the enemy penetration between Alexandrija and Kriwoi Rog, as well as the Soviet efforts to widen the frontal salient they had achieved west of the Dnjepr — roughly north of the dam across the Dnjepr and in the sector of the 30th *Armee Korps* (257th *Infanterie Division*, 46th *Infanterie Division*, 387th *Infanterie Division* and 15th *Panzer Division*)– the 1st *Panzer Armee* pulled its entire front in this area back to the general line Shirokoje – Alexandrowka-East – Alexandrowka-west – Tscherkereskaja – Adamowka. Regardless of that the Soviet *Schwerpunkt* remained in the sector of the Soviet penetration near Kriwoi Rog, with an estimated hundred enemy AFVs. An enemy armoured group of 35 AFVS that was behind German lines was completely destroyed.

See Maps 23 and 25 for geography.

The fighting in the area of the penetration and in the German frontal salient near Saporoshje continued to ebb and flow. Thus there was heavy fighting in the enemy bridgehead on the Chortiza Island, as well as north of the Saporoshje dam, where the Soviets extended their bridgehead to a width of 1,200 meters and a depth of 800 meters. The Soviets gained several deep penetrations, with infantry and armoured escort, against the 62nd *Infanterie Division* and 306th *Infanterie Division*, which made it necessary to pull back the German lines there, too.

See Map 15.

While all this was happening the 11th *Panzer Division* was engaged in heavy fighting with fiercely attacking enemy forces and knocked out 30 enemy AFVs on 29 October. A concentric advance of the 23rd *Panzer Division*, 14th *Panzer Division* and 24th *Panzer Division* in the area north of Kriwoi Rog set off an intense battle with strong enemy groups. The formations involved achieved limited gains of terrain to the Kriwoi Rog – Moissejewka-Geikowka highway and to Petrowo.

The simultaneous effort of the Soviets to drive their advance forward, not only to the west, but to widen the entire area of their penetration may well have been based on the fear of flank attacks out of the Dnjepropetrowsk, with the additional enticement that the German units positioned on that flank were fought-out, but still experienced in combat on the Eastern Front. Flank attacks proved particularly effective against motorized formations, whose march-columns were especially vulnerable to attacks from the side.

Soviet Intentions

In addition to the above the fact was that the Soviets usually advanced with two *Schwerpunkte* with the intention of then having the formations of the two arms of the pincers come together in the German rear area. With both the 4th *Panzer Armee* and also with the 1st *Panzer Armee* a peculiarity had developed, whether by intention or by chance, that the right-hand arm of the advance developed more strongly than the one on the left. That had occurred

FIGHTING RETREAT OF THE SOUTHERN WING

at the German Dnjepropetrowsk – Saporoshje salient, at Tscherkassy and at the Dnjepr knee, as also at Kiew.

Not only had the Soviets in the area of the 4th *Panzer Armee* recognized that the German command treated the area north of Kiew extraordinarily like an unwelcome stepchild, ignoring the advantages that the terrain offered the Soviets to there press forward to the west, but they also had the advantage offered by the German *Armee* boundary there. The Soviets preferred such situations because of the difficulties they presented to the Germans of command with tactical boundaries and overlapping responsibilities. In addition there was the fact that the land behind the Pripjet front offered few through-passages and possibilities for supply, consequently complicating shifting German forces parallel to the line of defense. Here, too, however, the Soviets followed the principle of making the right-hand arm of the attack stronger than the left, whereby they made no significant efforts to broaden their bridgehead south of Kiew. *See Maps 31, 32 and 33.*

In the area of the 1st *Panzer Armee* the emphasis on the right arm of the advance probably was based on the same considerations as with the 4th *Panzer Armee*. Here there was not a *Heeresgruppe* boundary, at most an *Armee* boundary, though there was a *Heeresgruppe* boundary at the right wing of the German front south of Saporoshje – after the removal of the 6th *Armee* from the command of *Heeresgruppe Süd*. *See Maps 23, 24 and 25.*

The direct advance against the Saporoshje bridgehead and on both sides of it had not led to the desired success. The advance in the area of *Heeresgruppe* A via Melitopol to the west could hardly replace such an arm of the advance, since combat operations with the support of heavy weapons and the necessity for constant supply of fuel and, especially, ammunition, were difficult there because of the difficult transportation situation. There was no direct railroad line west beyond Melitopol, only a roundabout route to Chersson.

At this point, however, the Soviet command did not plan to that depth, nor was it really required, considering the success in the area northwest of Dnjepropetrowsk. That did not stop them from repeatedly committing forces in the Saporoshje bend and also, later, against the German bridgehead southeast of Nikopol. It is possible that they intended to cut off the German frontal salient, or to force the German command to withdraw from it, or, merely, to induce the German command to shift troops into the salient, thereby exposing the Kriwoj Rog and Kirowograd areas in the direction of the Soviet advance by removing those troops. *See Maps 2 and 3 for general geography and railroad net in combat sector of Heeresgruppe Süd, later Süd + A, and Map 5 for rail net between Kiew and Charkow.*

The German command could only suspect the existence of such Soviet intentions. It is probably, however, that the Soviet command did not, at that time, have any clear conception of the future course of their advance, since the area that they had captured north of Dnjepropetrowsk to the Kriwoj Rog area did not yet suffice for the concentration of an attack-army or the bridges over the Dnjepr had not yet been prepared for the requisite logistical support.

Building Additional Bridgeheads

Other locations along the river offered similar possibilities, with the help of paratroops dropped west of the Dnjepr at the time. Accordingly, the elements *See Maps 7, 10 and 11.*

5. Railroad net East between Kiew and Charkow with the most important junctions.

FIGHTING RETREAT OF THE SOUTHERN WING

of the 106th *Infanterie Division*, 282nd *Infanterie Division*, SS-*Panzergrenadier Division 'Das Reich'*, but especially the 3rd *Panzer Division* and elements of the 11th *Panzer Division,* which held the narrow bridgehead in the line Ssomonizy – Dublinka – Krassnoje, had to repulse the paratroops that had dropped, wherein the 5th *SS-Panzer Division 'Wiking'* helped. Several groups, some of which had radio equipment, were thereby destroyed. The German command, however, was unable to determine the strength of the paratroopers that had landed, the more so since the survivors of such groups of paratroops probably linked up with the partisan bands.

The Soviets also attempted river crossings in the sector of the 24th *Panzer Korps* at Kanew and Chodoroff, as well as by attacking the Grigorowka -South – Welikijm defense line, putting troops over the river at Grigorowka and Sarubenzy.

See Map 10.

See Maps 7 and 8.

Reconnaissance revealed that strong forces were being brought into the Perejasslaw area, which suggested that a *Schwerpunkt* was being built in the Dnjepr knee – together with paratroops being dropped in the Dudary area.

Fighting in the Dnjepr Knee

In order to mislead the German command the Soviets started new landing operations, such as landing at least a regiment south of Ssoloschino (in the Krementschug area). In their advance to the northwest they ran into the counter-thrust of elements of the 282nd *Infanterie Division.* The Soviets also reinforced their troops that had crossed to the west bank at Rschitschtschew, north of the Dnjepr knee. In the meantime, German reconnaissance identified at least three tank corps – one of them fully reconstituted – and one mechanized corps in this area. In the bridgehead of the Dnjepr knee, itself, three rifle divisions and elements of two tank and one mechanized corps were identified, which rendered unlikely the complete cleansing of the bend, given the existing force ratio. Nevertheless, the German *Armee* command believed that the capture of the commanding high ground (244.5 meters), north of Grigorowka, by local *Schwerpunkt*-attack, made possible cleansing of the bridgehead at Schtshutschinka and northwest of Rshischtschew.

See Maps 12 and 13.

In the event, however, disregarding the operations in other sectors of the river – possibly in planned coordination with the advance east of Kriwoi Rog – the Soviets concentrated their support in their bridgehead at the Dnjepr knee.

Even as the first elements of the 19th *Panzer Division* arrived the Soviets secured a foothold on the west bank of the river, even to the extent that they could bring armour forward to their forces in areas that were protected from observation on underwater bridges and launch attacks to gain more ground – also to bring over heavy artillery. Finally, the Soviets brought up an entire artillery division, so that they had an estimated 1,200 tubes of all calibers. They committed strong aerial forces to this selected *Schwerpunkt*, which kept the German heavy weapons and, especially, the access routes, under constant strafing and bombing attacks.

The paratroops that had been dropped further west failed to accomplish their assigned missions, most of them being wiped out by the rear-area troops of the units committed there.⁷ Furthermore, the partisan bands also failed to penetrate the area occupied by troops behind the main line of resistance, thereby failing to significantly interfere with the German defense. However, they increased their railroad demolitions on the vital Berditscheff – Fastoff supply route and on the single-tracked one-way traffic railroad lines through the western Ukraine. These disruptions led to delays in bringing up forces and, above all, to interruptions in ammunition supply. The effect on the troops was that they could not combat identified river crossing points and other identified targets with the requisite volume of fire.

The forces of the 48th *Panzer Korps* that were committed in the cordon-position across the Dnjepr knee, especially the 19th *Panzer Division* and 72nd *Infanterie Division*, renewed their attacks against the Soviet forces in the river-knee of the Dnjepr and, by the evening of 29 September, attained the line at the high ground directly southwest of Lukowiza – south slope 206.4 – north bank of the stream, thus the commanding high ground north of Grigorowka and north of Welikij. In accord with *Armee* orders, the troops went over to the defense in the line attained, thereby leaving the enemy capable of further reinforcement from the east bank.

See Map 8.

As the Soviets attacked in the Dnjepr knee in subsequent days enemy pressure also increased from the bridgehead southwest of Ssoloschino in the Krementschug area with the objective of breaking through before Kuzewolowka to the west. In addition, reconnaissance revealed the attempt to bring up two artillery divisions and mortar units to support the crossing attempts northwest of Krementschug – apparently as part of a relief operation for the attack in the Dnjepr knee, primarily to build a larger bridgehead in the Derejewka – Nowo - Georgjewsk sector. The 11th *Armee Korps* reported fighting on the peninsula north of Uspenskoje that included destruction of several AFVs and three ferries, south of Ssoloschine – one carrying armour. A new *Schwerpunkt* made itself evident by the appearance of strong enemy groups in the area northeast and north of Nowo-Georgjewsk with 15 to 18 batteries of all calibers. Northwest of the Ros position the Soviets extended their bridgehead to about 13 kilometers width.

See Maps 12 and 13.

The attacks against the line of defense of the 11th *Armee Korps* as well as the 47th and 3rd *Panzer Korps* alternated with each other, without the Soviets giving up their intentions in the Dnjepr knee. Moreover, on 15 October they launched a widespread offensive with the objective of breaking through the German cordon position and uniting that bridgehead with the bridgeheads at Studenez and Schtschutschinka – this with a heretofore unseen intensity of artillery preparation by an entire artillery division. Supported by armour and air, several waves of Soviets infantry charged the German positions. 34 AFVs were left knocked out in dune terrain that was unfavorable for armour, four of them destroyed at close-quarters by infantry weapons. However, German losses in personnel and matériel resulting from the massed enemy artillery fire were significant.

See Maps 7, 8 and 10.

---

7   See Map 7.

FIGHTING RETREAT OF THE SOUTHERN WING   53

The Soviets shifted the *Schwerpunkt* of their attack to the sector of the 19th *Panzer Division*. The enemy attack, a concentrated group of 12 AFVs against the left division sector resulted in the destruction of all the attacking armour. Day after day the Soviets worked over the German positions twice a day, each time with nearly two hours of artillery bombardment of all calibers. On 21 October the Soviets resumed their attack with the 3rd Guards Tank Army in order to unite the three bridgeheads in the Dnjepr Knee so as to break through the cordon position of the 48th *Panzer Korps*. Initially they launched the attack against the entire width of the Studenez bridgehead and the Dnjepr bend, as well as against the eastern portion of the Schtschutschinka bridgehead, with the *Schwerpunkt* against the inner wing of the 48th *Panzer Korps* and 24th *Panzer Korps*.

See Map 7.

The Soviets achieved several breakthroughs at these positions with 3 – 5 kilometers ground gain to the south, southwest and west, with *Schwerpunkt* at Chodoroff . The breakthrough to the southwest foundered on a German counterattack. The attempt to establish contact on the south bank of the river with Schtschutschinka also failed. However, the Soviets brought up additional forces over the, at times, smoke-screened crossing points. The force ratio between the opposing forces continued, in the meantime, to develop ever more strongly in favor of the Soviet forces. The German airforce attacked. *Stukas* repeatedly destroyed Soviet underwater bridges over which they brought up heavy weapons, especially armour. In the event, however, that had limited effects, because the Soviets always immediately set about repairing the bridges.

In the sector of the 72nd *Infanterie Division* the Soviets launched an attack with support of 150 AFVs and rolling ground-attack and fighter attacks, with strong infantry forces and heavy artillery fire-support. The Soviets reached Romaschki and Chodoroff, but were forced back as far as the center of the place. In the fighting on 21 and 22 October with the 19th *Panzer Division* and 72nd *Infanterie Division* 74 enemy tanks and one Soviet assault gun were knocked out and left on the battlefield. The Soviets then brought in larger caliber, longer range artillery. That evidenced continued the Soviet intention of breaking through at the Dnjepr knee. Again and again, with shifting *Schwerpunkt* and employment of strong infantry formations the Soviets tried to break through the 19th *Panzer Division* and the left wing of the 72nd *Infanterie Division*. Before opening the attack they leveled the German trenches each time with several hours of heavy artillery and mortar fire of all calibers. They then laid smoke screens over the German front lines so the artillery observers and grenadiers would not see the approaching Soviets until the last moment. Nevertheless, all the Soviet attacks failed.

See Map 8.

The 48th *Panzer Korps* halted the counterattacks of the 19th *Panzer Division* and 72nd *Infanterie Division* as well as those of the *SS-Panzergrenadier Division 'Das Reich'* after initial local successes due to the strong defense. On 30 October the 11th *Armee Korps* was able again to clean up the penetration at Losowatka and north of Mlinok, as well as west and northwest of Datscha. The 47th *Panzer Korps* constricted the enemy penetration southeast of Starolipowo.

See Maps 14 and 15.

New *Schwerpunkt* in the Krementschug Area (northwestward)

> See Maps 10 and 12. Map 11 shows geography.

The German bridgehead west of Krementschug and the Tscherkassy bridgehead, which barred Soviet access to the bridges there, initially held. In the Krementschug area the Soviets launched an attack from Maximowka with 25 AFVs carrying infantry, which came to a halt in Kriwuschi, so that the Soviets were still denied the Dnjepr bridges. On 29 September the German forces transferred the main body of their artillery across the river and finally evacuated the bridgehead.

> See Map 8.

Farther northwest on the Dnjepr the 3rd *Panzer Division* was pulled out of the fighting and assigned to eliminate the enemy bridgeheads southeast and north of Kanew.

> See Maps 7 and 12.

In the other bridgeheads, as at Schtschutschinka (24th *Panzer Korps*) with the capture of the high ground southeast of Schtschutschinka the Soviets brought in more forces. With the capture of the island southwest of Koleberda, the Uspenskoje bridgehead – here with one of the usable ferry locations in this sector of the river –, the Sselischtsche and Rschischtschew bridgeheads, the Soviets had, in the meantime, built so many bridgeheads that they only had to assemble formations to cross the river. Especially at Krementschug German reconnaissance confirmed strengthening of the enemy forces. Apparently the Soviets intended to build there a bridgehead in the Derejewka – Nowogeorgjewsk sector.

> See Maps 10, 12, 15, 17 and 18.

The 11th *Armee Korps*, too, reported heavy fighting with the destruction of several AFVs, with fighting on the peninsula north of Uspenskoje. The German command judged that crossing attempts and local attacks from the existing bridgeheads at Krementschug were diversionary attacks for the fighting in the Dnjepr knee. In addition, however, these were considered to indicate the intention of a further advance of Soviet forces to Kriwoi Rog and Kirowograd, now extending further to the north as they had to the south. The 198th *Infanterie Division* significantly reduced the bridgehead north of Tschernomorowka (11th *Armee Korps*) by attacks. The island northeast of Nowogeorgjewsk in the area of the 47th *Panzer Korps* was cleansed of enemy forces in heavy fighting. On the adjoining island the Soviets were compressed into a narrow area. Local bridgeheads north of Smytnizar were sealed off and the island north of Woronowka was cleansed of enemy forces.

All of these did not, however, prevent the Soviets from crossing to the west bank of the Dnjepr at other locations, nor from reinforcing their forces in peaceful crossing traffic at the bridgeheads they had previously built. On the German side, at that point, a not-inconsiderable shortage of ammunition became evident, resulting from railroad demolitions by partisan bands in the army's rear area, and also from overloading the railroads with bringing up troops. This shortage prevented the artillery from interfering with the Soviet crossing activity through appropriate fire.

> See Map 12.

Near Krementschug additional reinforcement of Soviet forces became evident, especially east of the Pssel in the area around Maximowka – Gradishek and in the bridgehead north of Uspenskoje, including the penetration location southeast of Tschikolowka (elements of six divisions) and in front of the sector north of Taburischtsche to Smytnizar (four divisions positively identified, with two more probable). German formations complained about the lack of local reserves, as well as inadequate ammunition supply and dwindling combat strengths.[8]

The active ferry traffic in the area east of Chutor, Chmelna and the bridgehead north of Sselischtsche (here anew with armour) made it seem probable that the Soviets intended to strengthen their attack out of the Dnjepr knee against the cordon position of the 48th *Panzer Korps* with simultaneous operations out of the Sselischtsche bridgehead. Good weather favored the action of the Red Air Force, whose attacks – also in the Dnjepr knee – with machine gun, rockets and bombs often made it impossible to bring up ammunition or reserves to the positions. The fact that 104 of the over 250 attacking AFVs were knocked out indicates the ferocity of the fighting. *See Maps 7 and 8.*

Captured enemy documents revealed that the mission of the eastern combat group was to advance concentrically out of the Sselischtsche bridgehead, as also from the Grigorowka area initially to the high ground around Tschermischa and to prepare an adequate operational basis to link up with the Duschinka bridgehead. 100 enemy AFVs were knocked out on 12 October, alone. Aerial reconnaissance reported additional heavy logistical railroad traffic with transport of armour on the Charkow – Poltawa railroad. *See Map 8.*

The Soviets also initiated relief- and diversionary- attacks on the *Korps* boundary with the 11th *Korps*, where they achieved a penetration at the junction of the 6th *Panzer Division* and 106th *Infanterie Division* with a group of 12 AFVs, possibly for an advance on Uskenskoje. Diversionary attacks took place in the penetration area southeast of Tschikalowka, probably to gain possession of the crossing at Krementschug. There were additional attacks in the adjoining sector of the Dnjepr bend with the apparent objective of uniting the Studenez and Schtschutschinka bridgeheads through the penetration in the Dnjepr bend. To the rear, partisan bands were inactive, a danger that would be successfully eliminated in the Tschigrin area. On all of the other sectors of the front the Soviets were active, quite possibly with the intention of forcing the withdrawal of the German forces from the cordon position west of the Dnjepr knee. *See Maps 7, 10, 12 and 17.*

Then ensued, again with the 11th *Armee Korps*, a Soviet advance with 40 AFVs against Datscha, whereby 12 AFVs broke through to Uspenskoje, but were knocked out by evening. The penetration was eliminated in a counterattack. On 30 October the 11th *Armee Korps* also succeeded in eliminating the penetrations at Losowatka and north of Mlinok, as well as west and northwest

---

8 In illustration of the logistical difficulties of the retreating formations of *Heersgruppe Süd* and *Heersgruppe* A it should be pointed out that the military field railroad had to meet substantial commitments in bringing up new formations, and at a pace that, in a few days in the Snamenka – Kamenka – Kirowograd area, required unloading of 350 to 400 or more transport trains, with 60 – 74 trains required for each division. That resulted from the transport of the 376th *Infanterie Division* from the Netherlands to the Eastern Front, the 384th *Infanterie Division* from northwest France, the 24th *Panzer Division* from northern Italy, the 14th *Panzer Division* from northwest France and the 76th *Infanterie Division* from northern Italy. All of this took place in the course of the month of October in the area of *Heeresgruppe Süd*, In addition to the above, the 1st *SS-Panzer Division 'Leibstandarte SS Adolf Hitler'* and the 1st *Panzer Division* were also transported from the west.

of Datscha. Southeast of Starolipowo, the 47th *Panzer Korps* compressed the site of the enemy penetration.

2

Defending the Dnjepr

The Situation

Lacking the opportunity to examine Soviet sources it appears difficult to present the actual intentions of the Soviets at this point in time. It is only from the detailed reports of our own troops and from aerial reconnaissance that conclusions can be drawn about Soviet planned transfers of forces, losses, difficulties with supplies and the like.

As October gave way to November the course of the line of defense already showed a total change. In the sector of *Heeresgruppe* A the Soviets had continued to gain ground to the west, cutting Crimea off from its connections to the rear. The defense of *'Festung Krim'* ['Fortress Crimea'] seemed, at first glance, to be simple, since the isthmus along the *Tatarenwall* [Tartar Wall], directly south of Perekop, was only ten kilometers across and, from there, the *'Faule Meer'* ['Putrid Sea'], which was proof against armoured movement, stretched almost to the Utljuskij *Bucht* [Bay], 80 kilometers to the east. There it met the narrow Arabat – a tongue – of – land which paralleled the east coast of Crimea, similar to a *Nehrung* [the long, very narrow spits of land along the German Baltic coast that enclose extensive lagoons between them and the mainland].

See Map 6.

See Maps 101 and 102.

From Perekop to Genitschesk at the entrance to the Utljukskij Bay it was 90 kilometers as the crow flies, a line of defense along the coast of the *'Faule Meer'* at least longer by half. The tongue of land – in the north locally up to four kilometers wide, in the South only 300 meters at the most – stretched from Genitschesk via Tschokrak-Ssredni Dshankoi to Ak Monai with a length of about 120 kilometers. The 17th *Armee* had two *Korps* to defend Crimea with three German and seven Rumanian divisions available. In addition there were formations and stragglers that had been forced southward to Crimea in the fighting between Melitopol and the Sea of Asov [Asowsches Meer].

The formations of *Heeresgruppe* A on the mainland fell back on the Dnjepr river in the Nikopol sector in the face of the danger of being broken through, overtaken and cut off, there to maintain a bridgehead, so far as the extent of the line of defense seemed possible. Initially there were no formations southwest to the Dnjeprowski bay.

As October gave way to November the front line of the 1st *Panzer Armee* extended from its sector boundary to the right, near Belenkoje south of Saporoshje along the west bank of the Dnjepr north via the Chortiza island to the Dnjepr meander and there turned via Kanzeropol – Shirokoje to the west. It then continued in a more northerly advanced bend via Alexandrowka – Tschekereskaja (localities inclusive) to the Saxagan River, downstream to Wesselyje Terny and west thereof from Ternowatka up the Ingulez river to the left sector boundary at Nowo Starobud.

See Maps 14, 16, 23 (for geography), and 26.

See Maps 14 and 16.

See Maps 31 and 32.

The front line of the adjoining 8th *Armee* again met the Dnjepr at Uspenskoje and ran along the west bank past Krementschug – Tscherkassy along the cordon position in the Dnjepr knee to the sector boundary with the 4th *Panzer Armee* south of Kiew. In the sector of the 4th *Panzer Armee* between Kiew and Tschernobyl/Pripjet the Soviets already held numerous bridgeheads on the west bank that could not be eliminated. The front line ran from there, in places, far west of the Dnjepr and first met the Pripjet River at Tschernobyl.

The Soviet command now enjoyed not only the possibility to advance to the west and south, based on the serviceable roads and numerous Dnjepr crossings and the large concentration area between the Dnjepr and Ingulez rivers but also the opportunity to launch an attack to the west from the bridgeheads they had built facing the 4th *Panzer Armee*.

After their breakthrough at Melitopol the Soviet assault armies faced the Nogaische Steppe, terrain favorable to armour, with an adequate and serviceable network of unpaved roads. These not only linked the east with the Genitschesk harbour on the Sea of Asow and with the entries to Crimea at Tschongar and Perekop, but also led to the Dnjepr crossings at Nikopol, Bolschaja Lepaticha, Kachowka / Berisslaw and Chersson. On the basis of such favorable pre-existing conditions the Soviets had already, in 1941, when the German troops attacked, constructed a 60 kilometer long anti-tank ditch between Balki and Nowo Nikolajewka / Melitopol, which they were still working on when the 49th *Gebirgs Korps* [Mountain Corps] crossed the Dnjepr at Berisslaw / Kachowka.

On the other hand, there were no railroad lines in the Nogaische Steppe in the direction of the single crossing of the troublesomely broad mouth of the Dnjepr that were usable for transport of supplies. From the Stalino transportation hub in the east all railroad connections ended at the Dnjepropetrowsk – Saporoshje – Melitopol – Dshankoi/Crimea north-south railroad line until the one stretch in the south departing at the Nowo Bogdanowka railroad station, 27 kilometers north of Melitopol, which was given up on 25/26 October 1943. (Airline distance 200 kilometers, Melitopol – Chersson.)

The initially, at times apparently deficient operational planning of the Soviets made it seem that they attacked indiscriminately in nearly all frontal sectors. In their chosen tactic they alternated, here with an infantry attack following artillery preparation, there without support from heavy weapons, with or without mounted infantry riding on AFVs. Or, in the expectation of strong German defenses, they prepared the terrain, as at the Dnjepr knee, according to the 'hammer' system with bombardment, in hopes of smashing the defense in this line to help the following infantry, supported by armour.

The areas of attack shifted, presumably with the intent of testing the strength of the German defense, to reconnoiter the blocking fire and locations of artillery, to scout out the terrain or, simply, to irritate the German command. Frequently this involved operations without any large-scale preparations visible to reconnaissance, so that the German command could not adequately anticipate them. In the course of such attacks the Soviets repeatedly achieved local penetrations which made it necessary to bring up German troops. Such

DEFENDING THE DNJEPR 59

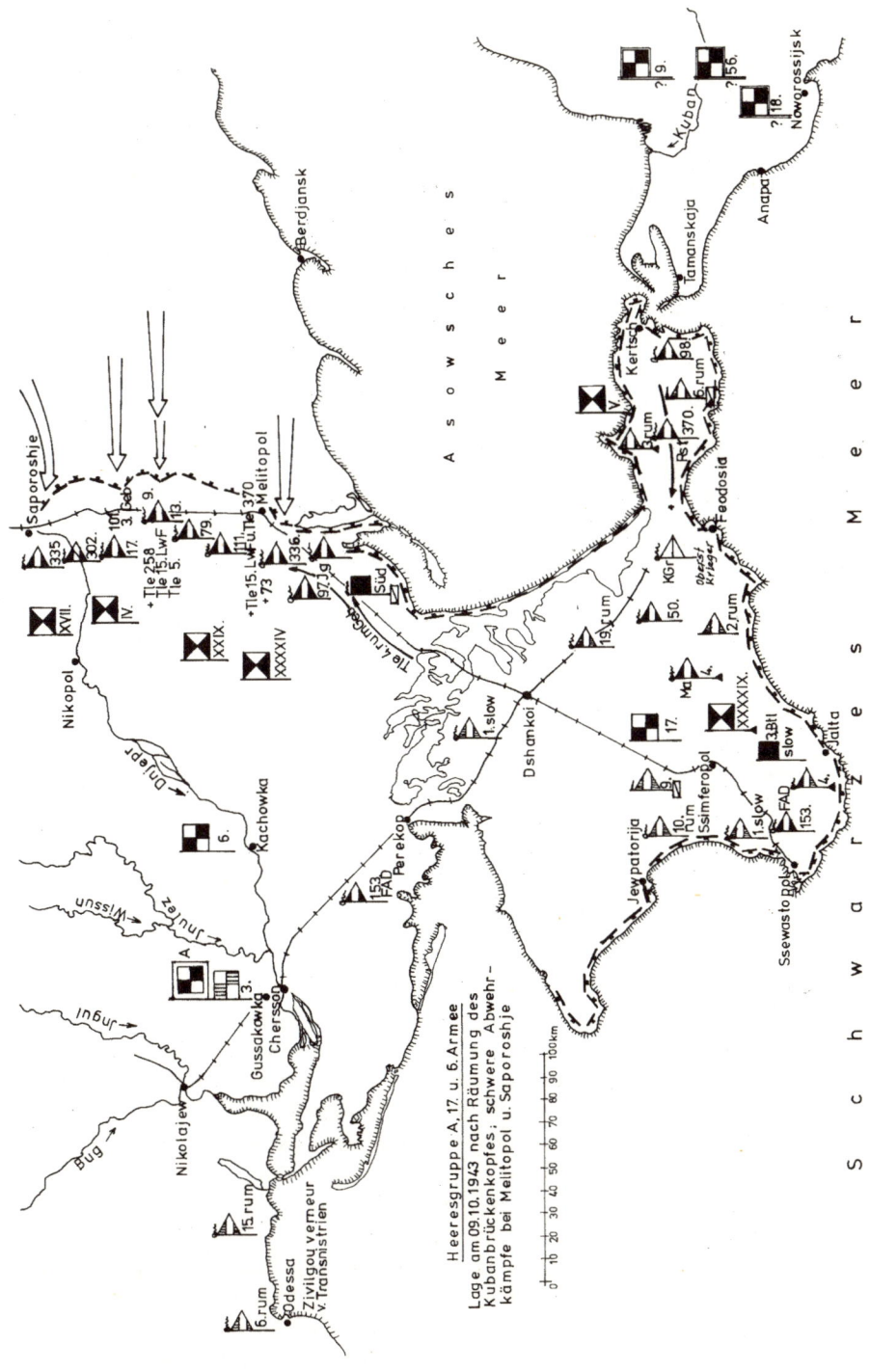

6. *Heeresgruppe* A and 6th *Armee* situation as of 9 October, 1943 after the evacuation of the Kuban bridgehead; intense defensive fighting at Melitopol and Saporoschje. See also maps 97-104 inclusive.

new countermeasures, however, frequently resulted in immediate Soviet attacks on the locations thus stripped of troops, requiring, in turn, the most rapid transfer of troops back to those locations. Such reports arrived daily from the divisions. Some of these were satisfying reports of success that indicated constant heavy fighting, as, on 28 October, the report that after an eventful back-and-forth struggle, 24 enemy AFVs had been knocked out in the area of the 8th *Armee*.

Since an operational coordination between the advance in the sector of *Heeresgruppe* A, north of the Black Sea [*Schwarzes Meer*] and the advance west of Dnjepropetrowsk was rendered impossible by terrain conditions, the Soviets considered other possibilities. The situation prevented linkage between the advance north of Kiew toward Korosten and the advance against the 1st *Panzer Armee*. Recognition of this probably resulted in the fact that the Soviets attempted forcefully to widen their bridgeheads at other locations, namely in the Dnjepr knee. Granted, there were no bridges there, only the three underwater military bridges that the Red Army constructed. The Perejasslaw area, however, had two promising sites for railroad access. Reconnaissance reported that troops were being brought up by rail, and also by lorry, from the direction of Kiew, definitely not consisting of formations being withdrawn from Kiew, but from formations brought in from the east via Kiew.

Fighting in the Dnjepr Knee

Reconnaissance of the enemy thus identified a stream of enemy forces converging on Perejasslaw from several sides and proceeding from there to the Dnjepr knee. On 22 September, after crossing the river, infantry forces infiltrated into the Dnjepr knee, which jutted far out to the east. The *Kampfgruppen* of the 7th *Panzer Division* and 20th *Panzergrenadier Division* that were hastily brought in completely disrupted the Soviet march-columns that were, shortly, marching to the south and forced the remnants back into the bend of the river, until the 19th *Panzer Division*, which had been pulled out of the defensive position in the bridgehead east of Kiew, occupied the river bank, so far as possible. However, it was impossible to force the Soviet infantry formations completely back over the river, the more so since only elements of the 19th *Panzer Division* were available. On 22 September the Soviets gained ground from the bridgehead as far as north of Grigorowka against weak security forces. They were, however, immediately forced back by the slowly strengthening elements of the 19th *Panzer Division*. That did not prevent the Soviets from extending their bridgehead in ensuing days to the Grigorowka – Lukowiza – Sarubenzy line and from occupying an island farther north in the western bend of the river.

See Map 8.

The Soviets crossed the river with ferries at several locations. A crossing attempt west of Rschichtschew was repulsed. Both ground and aerial reconnaissance identified concentrations of forces on the north bank of the Dnjepr from Gorodischtsche to the area west of Staroje, as well as the arrival of armour on the north bank of the river-knee in terrain favorable for an attack across the river and then from north to south. That made it apparent that the Soviets were preparing a large scale operation against that sector. On 24

September they extended their bridgehead to the line along the northern edge of Grigorowka / northeast edge Welikij Bukrin and built a wider bridgehead at Balyka and Monasstyrjok. Elements of the 112th *Infanterie Division* and the main body of a *Kampfgruppe* of the 19th *Panzer Division* and 10th *Panzergrenadier Division* attacked Balyka. The 57th *Infanterie Division*, which had been brought up, took position in the Kanew area. The 34th *Infanterie Division* arrived by lorry in the Rshischtschew sector, reaching to the left *Armee* boundary. The Soviets dropped paratroops at the level of Trosse and to its rear in support of their operations.

The Soviets selected these crossing points at the Dnjepr knee, even though they were not established bridge-crossings, because of the logistical possibilities they offered by rail and highway. In addition, the west bank of the Dnjepr knee, which the Soviets held, with its dune-topography, provided cover for vehicle movements. Furthermore, the Soviets expected, or, at least, hoped, for support by partisan bands in the area west of the Dnjepr. The repeated dropping of paratroops and supply gliders helped to involve them. The intention was for disruption of the rear communications of the German forces, and, thus, of their supply, but there were also to be attacks from the rear. These enemy combat groups behind the front defended themselves, but the German rear area troops, field-cooks, drivers, *Hauptfeldwebel* and the like hunted, surrounded and destroyed the Soviet parachute brigades. Numerous enemy dead were found in the terrain and it was saturated with white parachutes. It is possible that individual paratroopers escaped westward to the partisan bands. Additional German formations were *en route* to the front, other than the 72nd *Infanterie Division*, and cleaned up a wooded area south of Kanew that was still held by Soviet paratroopers. On 28 September at about 1600 hours the 48th *Panzer Korps* assumed command over the 112th *Infanterie Division* and 20th *Panzergrenadier Division* and, before their departure to the north, remaining elements of the 7th *Panzer Division*, 19th *Panzer Division* and 72nd *Infanterie-Division* in order to establish unified command over the entire cordon position in the Dnjepr knee.

On 29 September the 112th *Infanterie Division, Kampfgruppe* 55th *Infanterie Division,* 20th *Panzergrenadier Division,* a *Kampfgruppe* of the 7th *Panzergrenadier Division* and a *Kampfgruppe* of the 19th *Panzer Division,* as well as elements of the 72nd *Infanterie Division* launched an attack against the enemy forces in the river knee and attained a new line farther to the east. Enemy counter attacks, especially against the west wing of the 72nd *Infanterie Division* foundered with the loss of ten enemy AFVs. In this fighting on 29 and 30 September the Soviets lost 2,393 counted dead, 438 captured, 23 AFVs, three 7.2 cm antitank guns, two anti-tank/anti-aircraft guns, 78 antitank rifles, 53 heavy machine guns, 101 light machine guns, 334 machine pistols and 722 rifles. The *Armee* did not foresee further German attacks in the Dnjepr bend. Rather, the troops were ordered to organize for defense in the cordon position.

Thereupon the Soviets reinforced their forces. German reconnaissance identified 17 rifle divisions and elements of three tank corps as well as one mechanized corps in this combat sector. The forces of the 8th *Fliegerkorps* attacked and effectively destroyed the underwater bridges for bringing up heavy

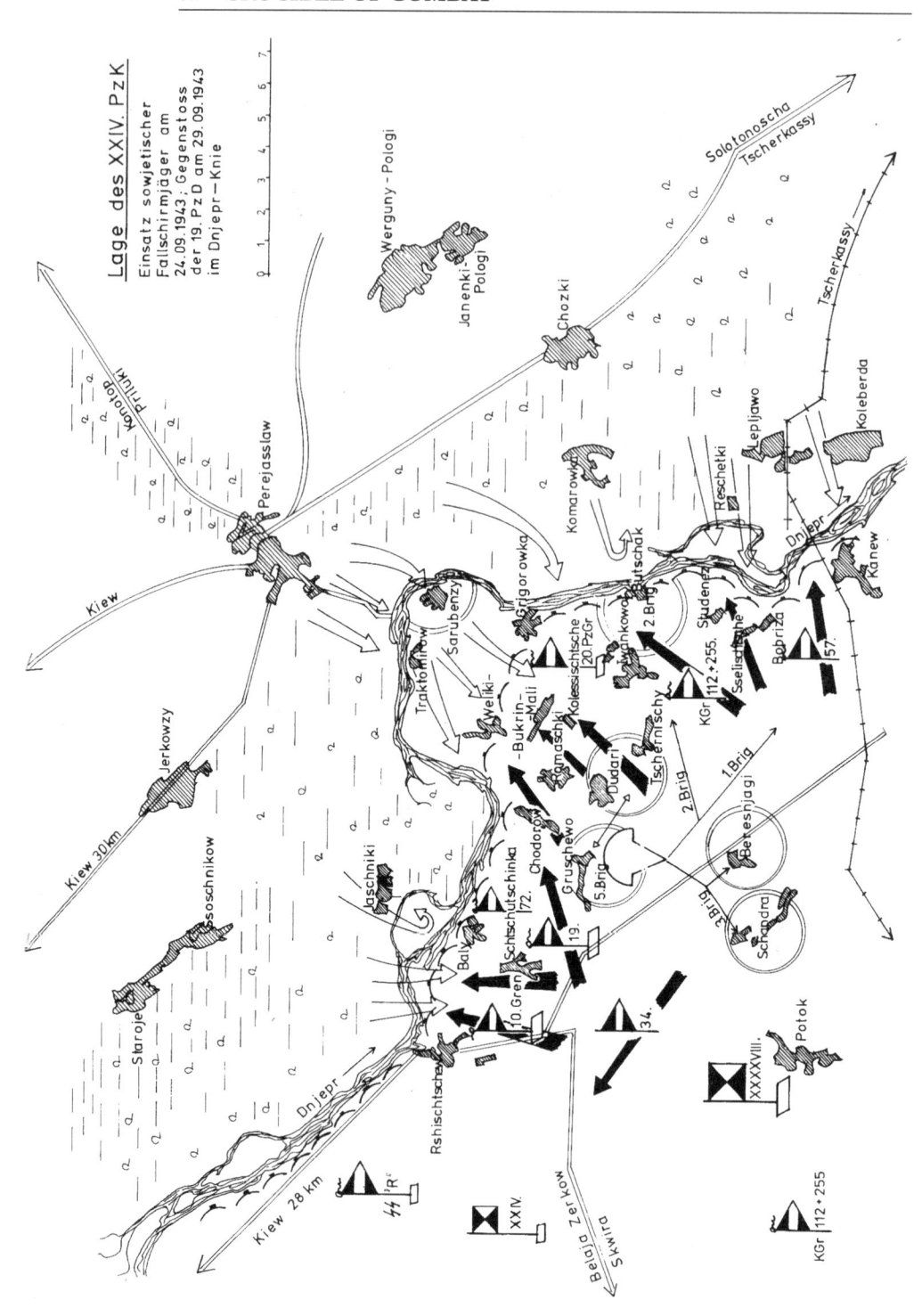

7. Situation of the 24th *Panzer Korps*. Commitment of Soviet paratroops on 24 September, 1943. Hasty counterattack of the 19th *Panzer Division* on 29 September in the Dnjepr-knee.

DEFENDING THE DNJEPR 63

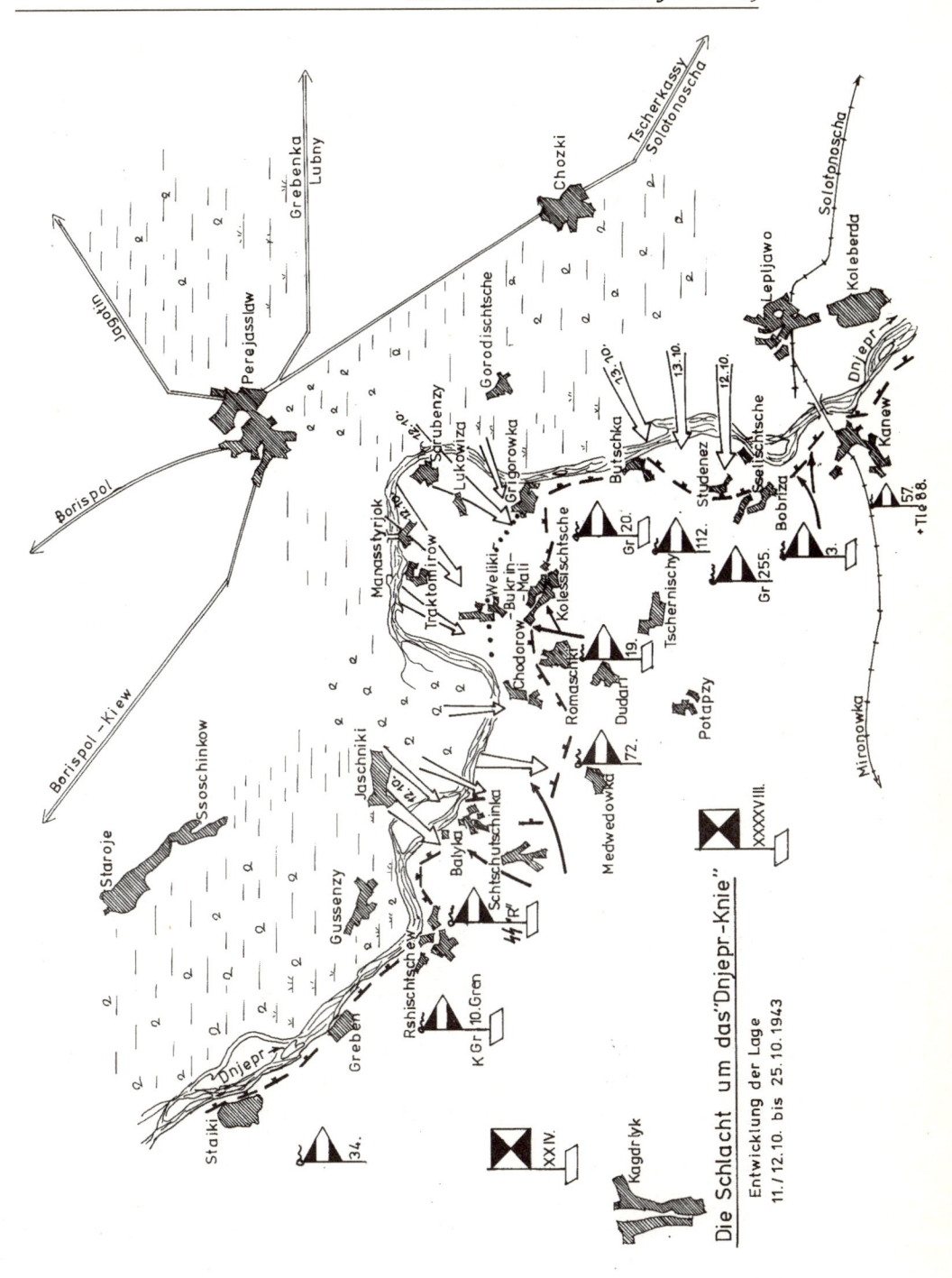

8. The Battle of the Dnjepr-knee. Development of the situation from 11/12 October to 25 October, 1943.

weapons that aerial reconnaissance had identified in the Dnjepr knee, which, however, did not prevent the Soviets from rebuilding them in the course of the next day. To the extent that observation was possible in the combat area the artillery of the 19th *Panzer Division* took worthwhile targets under fire. Not all of the riverbank area was open to observation and subject to observed fire. Thus, the Soviets constantly brought over new forces at Sarubenzy without observation or disruption by German artillery. North of Grigorowka, too, traffic crossing the river kept up in the ensuing days. The Red Army conducted continued reconnaissance probes on all portions of the cordon front. After the attack against the cordon position that was essentially held by the 19th *Panzer Division* and 72nd *Infanterie Division* failed to bring the Soviets the desired success, they attempted to attack the flanks of this defensive front, thus crossing troops over at Chodorow, north of the knee, and at Butschak, south of the knee.

After intense preparation and bringing up an immense superiority of forces, especially in artillery and armour – 70 AFVs in the sector of the 19th *Panzer Division* – on 12 October the expected offensive opened in the Dnjepr knee. After an hour and a half of artillery bombardment preparations, supported by strong formations of ground-attack aircraft, the Soviets began, with the initial *Schwerpunkt* on the Sselischtsche bridgehead south of the knee and on Sarubenzy, at the point of the knee. At about 1000 hours local forces joined the attack from the area west of Schtschutschinka, as well as two to three rifle divisions and one mechanized corps in the Sselischtsche area. In the Dnjepr bend, itself, were two tank corps, one mechanized corps and about six to eight rifle divisions.

As a result of matériel and numerical superiority the Soviets broke through the front at numerous locations. German countermeasures generally suffered from the shortage of ammunition. Accordingly, tempting enemy targets, particularly in the Sselischtsche area, could not be engaged. The intensive commitment of enemy ground-attack aircraft locally made movements of reserves and supply of ammunition impossible. As the afternoon progressed the attack came to a halt in a line west of Sselischtsche and west of Studenez, Kolessischtsche and Chodorow. Of the 250 attacking AFVs, 140 were left, knocked out, on the battlefield – and without having achieved any significant combat success.

Presumably, further enemy intentions were to attack from the Sselischtsche bridgehead in order to establish contact with the Schtschutschinka bridgehead over the Tschernischy high ground. For this purpose the Soviets attacked the next day from the Studenez bridgehead at the Dnjepr bend, and also from the bridgehead at Schtschutschinka, in part with groups of AFVs with infantry riding on them that had, in the meantime, been brought over. Lively support by formations of the 8th *Fliegerkorps* again brought some relief, bombing identified assembly positions, thereby preventing a combined attack. That day 61 enemy AFVs remained on the battlefield. Regardless of the losses, reconnaissance of the enemy reported additional forces being brought up, with concentrations in the area south of Butschak, concentrations of armour north of Iwankow and at Kolessischtsche, and armour and infantry assembly positions east of Chodorow. Aerial reconnaissance reported additional rail-transports of armour on the Charkow – Poltawa line, thus *en route* to the Dnjepr.

See Map 18 for this stretch of railroad.

In order to soften up the German positions the Soviets brought in an entire artillery division, which went into position around the 'knee'. There were also light batteries on the west bank, some of them in open positions. Twice a day, starting early, about 20 minutes after the 'Barbara' balloons[1] went up at 0300 hours, which reported weather conditions to the Soviet artillery, and again in the afternoon, came two hours of bombardment from all calibers, with extravagant expenditure of ammunition. At the same time the Soviets put smoke screens over the crossing sites over the river, so that the German *Luftwaffe* would be unable to disrupt bringing up armour. Starting with the shift of artillery fire to the rear of the German trenches onto the artillery positions, Soviet artillery laid down smoke on the foremost German trenches to enable Soviet infantry to approach the German trenches unseen. The Soviets expended matériel on a scale hitherto unknown in the Second World War.

For the combat troops of the 72nd *Infanterie Division* and the 19th *Panzer Division* these days of action were extremely nerve-racking. The damp sandy ground was good for digging in, but the systematic leveling of the German trenches by enemy artillery fire motivated the German soldiers to dig themselves individually into the sides of the trenches. Holding out during the artillery barrages, during which, again and again, in rapid succession, the eastern horizon would be a flare of light, presumably from 1,200 guns of all calibers, then, shortly following, the detonations of shells of various calibers in the area of one's own trenches, put a terrible strain on the nervous systems and self-control of the soldiers. One had to compare it with the artillery barrages of World War I at Verdun. Nevertheless, the Soviets did not achieve success. When they occasionally made it into the trenches, they were thrown back out of them in short order.

One of the Soviet *'Nebelkrähe'* [hooded-crow, nickname for a Soviet night-bomber] achieved serious results with one of its hand-dropped light bombs that hit the crest of a sand-dune. The bomb set the sand of the entire dune in motion, burying 21 men of the 7th company, *Panzergrenadier Regiment 73* [19th *Panzer Division*] beneath it.

After the Soviets had received a bloody nose here, despite extreme expenditure in armour, artillery, bombers and ground-attack aircraft and had been unable to break through the experienced east-front troops, they eased off. Against such a defense the Soviets were unable to utilize immense masses of men that they knew how to infiltrate in less defended terrain. Thereupon the Soviets gave up their intentions of attacking. This became evident on 29 October when a German attack that overcame the Soviet defenses in the Chodorow area ran into an enemy with a deeply organized, prepared defense (mines, built-in flamethrowers, massed anti-tank – and mortar blocking fire). In justification of the change of *Schwerpunkt* Soviet authors stated that the

---

1   Translator's note – weather balloons named after Saint Barbara, patron saint of artillerymen.

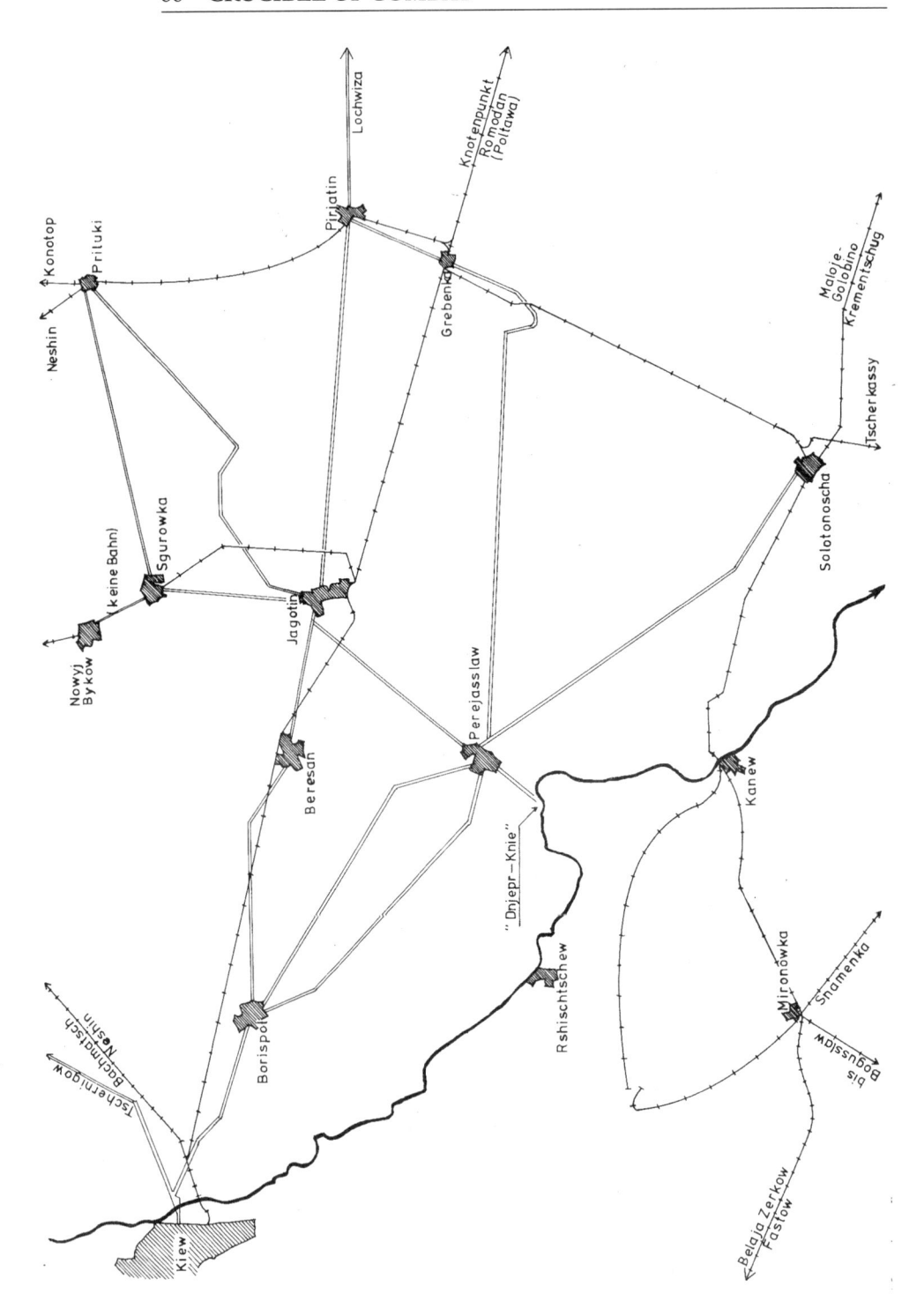

9. Area of the Dnjepr-knee.

DEFENDING THE DNJEPR 67

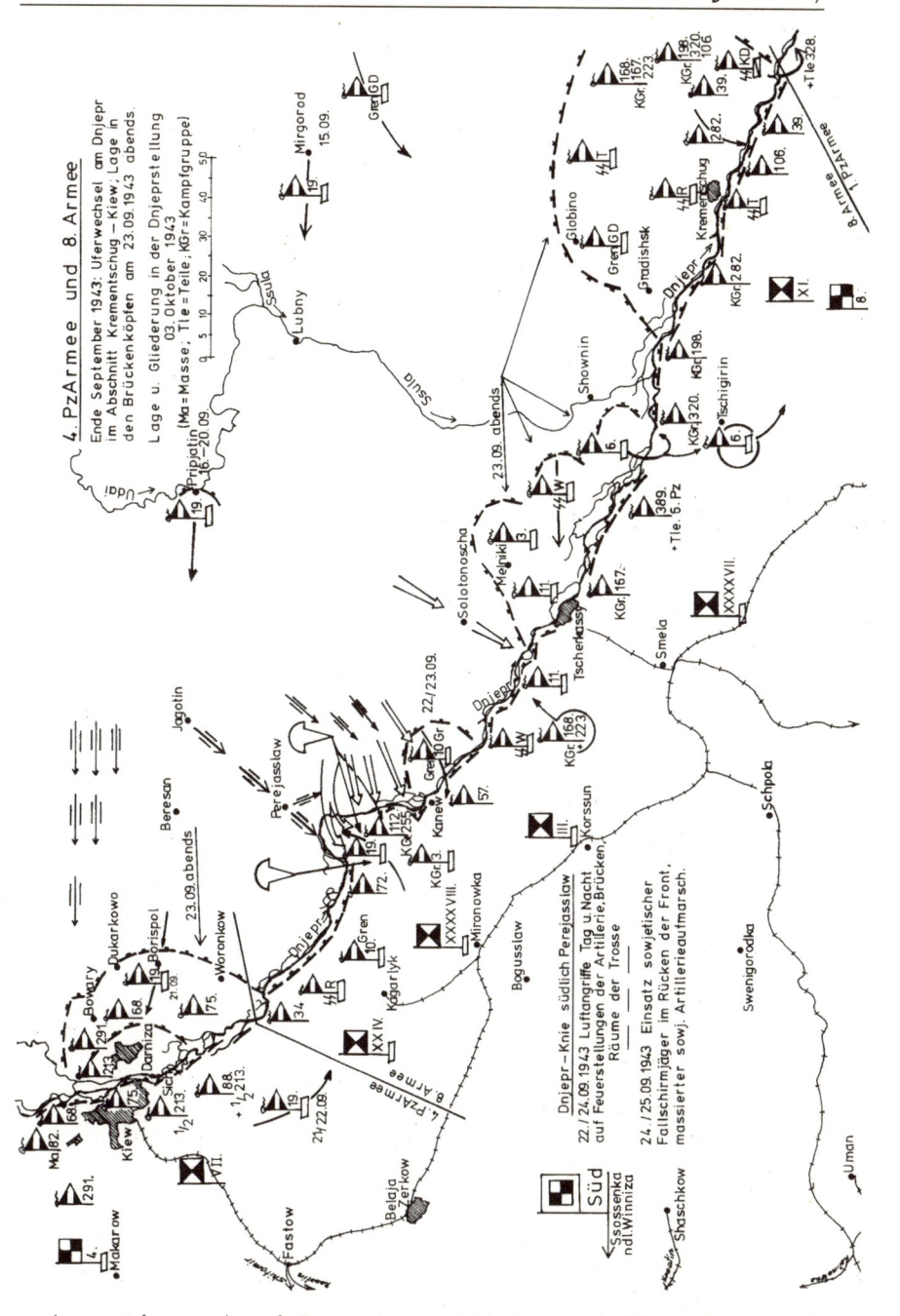

10. (upper right corner) – 4th *Panzer Armee* and 8th *Armee* end of September, 1943: Crossing of the Dnjepr in the Krementschug – Kiew sector, Situation in the bridgeheads as of the evening of 23 September, 1943 and organization of the Dnjepr position 3 October, 1943. (lower left) – Dnjepr knee south of Perejasslaw 22-24 September, 1943: Aerial attacks day and night on artillery firing positions, bridges and train areas. 24/25 September, 1943: Commitment of Soviet paratroops in the rear of the front. Massive concentration of Soviet artillery.

terrain in the bridgehead of the Dnjepr knee did not allow sufficient apace for armoured forces to fully deploy. That is unarguable.

The Tscherkassy Bridgehead

See Maps 10, 11 and, for rail connections, Map 18.

The nearest area in the Soviet consideration proved to be Tscherkassy, particularly since there were rail and highway bridges there, and, especially, good railway connections from the northeast for bringing up and supplying troops. There, too, the Soviets could count on help from partisan bands in the German rear areas, that, again, supported by dropping brigades of paratroops (12 – 25 October).

The advance on 28 November opened with the occupation of several islands in the Dnjepr, including one island north of Taldyki (15 kilometers southeast of Tscherkassy). The Soviets tried with assault troops to gain a foothold on two more islands, but were forced back. They then landed, with simultaneous dropping of paratroops, on the west bank of the Dnjepr, west of Sswidowok, parallel to the above in the frontal area of the 5th *SS-Panzer Division 'Wiking'* with a landing northeast of Ssekirna (29 November). There were additional similar operations near Dachnowka. The partisan bands, however, fell back under the influence of the presence of German troops into the Tscherkassy forest.

On 30 November elements of the 3rd *Panzer Korps* smashed the bridgeheads southeast of Tscherkassy and north of Dachnowka and cleaned up the riverbank the next day. On the other hand, bringing up reinforcements, the Soviets extended their bridgehead north of Sswidowok – again, with a simultaneous attack by two strong partisan bands – and by groups of paratroops from the west. These, in part irregular, troops had the mission of advancing toward the north in order to link up with the regular Soviet troops attacking from the bridgehead at the Dnjepr knee. Conspicuous in the evening, starting at 1900 hours, was the arrival of enemy aircraft over the area of the penetration, dropping supplies, followed shortly by an attack by partisan bands and groups of paratroops (about 500 men) from the woods south of Sswidowok (14 October). These troops took the east edge of the town, which, initially, was lost in costly, hard fighting. The next day, however, the attack was brought to a standstill.

On 16 November the Soviets undertook a new attempt from the bridgehead northwest of Tscherkassy. In two groups they broke through the weak security lines between the bank and the edge of the woods northwest of Dachnowka and forced their way into the northwest part of Dachnowka. Statements by prisoners made it clear that the Soviets intended to build a new bridgehead at the site of the former Tscherkassy bridgehead to gain a bridge-crossing with good bridge-approaches and exits through the city. Aerial reconnaissance identified heavy troop concentrations in the area around and south of Solotonscha, the Soviet de-training station.

The German situation made it necessary to pull forces out of the front southeast of Tscherkassy, only keeping an eye on the sector with combat-capable patrols. The wooded terrain on both sides of the Irdyn-swamp, which

DEFENDING THE DNJEPR 69

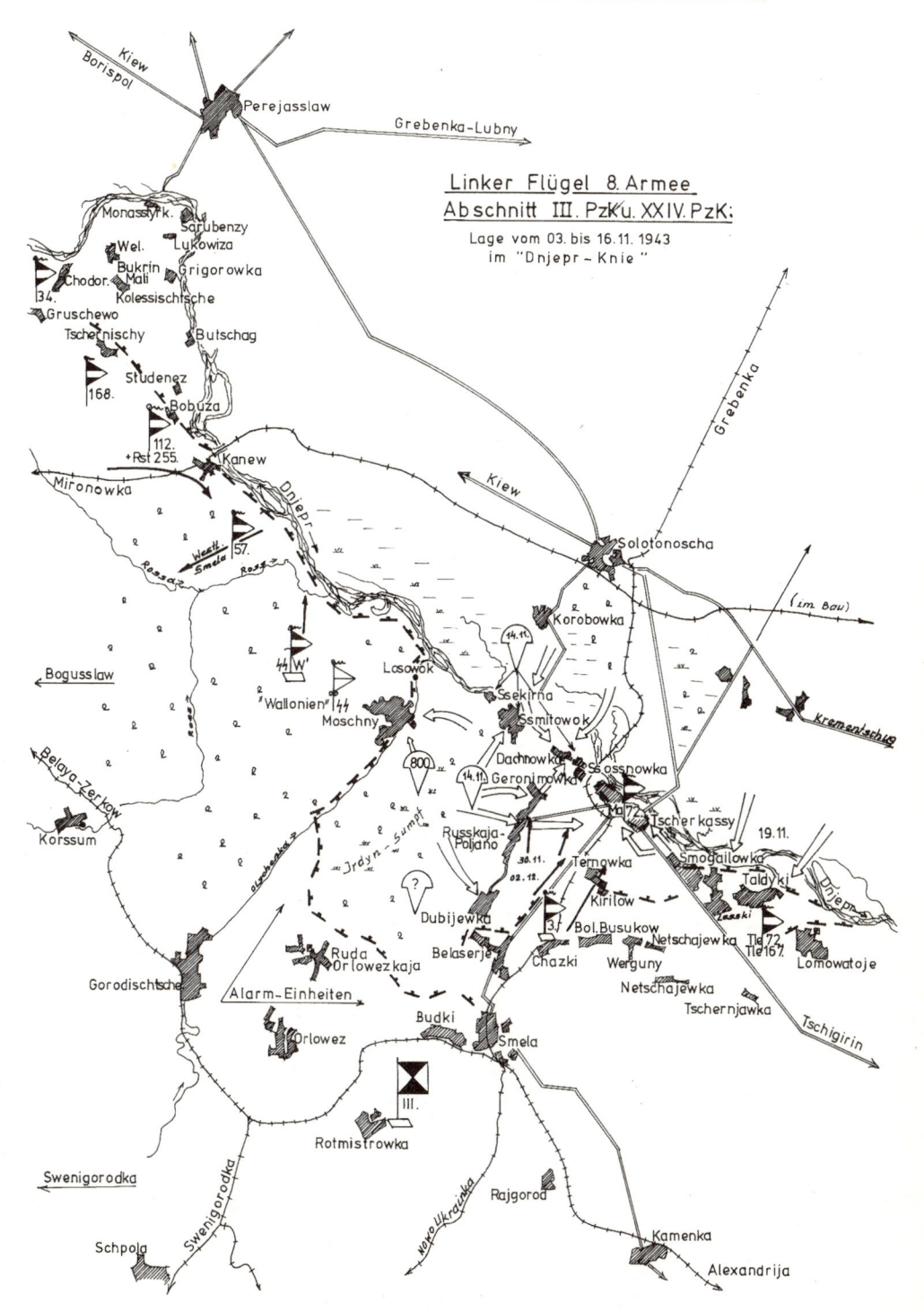

11. Left wing of the 8th *Armee* Sector of the 3rd *Panzer Korps* and 24th *Panzer Korps*. Situation from 3 to 16 November, 1943 in Dnjepr-knee.

was occupied by partisan bands and paratroops, continued to be outside of German control.

Thanks to superior infantry forces, the Soviets extended their bridgehead northwest of Tscherkassy. With 500 – 600 men they pushed into the woods south of Sserkima, as well as Geronimowka and the north part of Russkaja – Poljana. Reliable sources reported additional paratroop and partisan groups of about 800 men assembling in the woods southeast of Moschny, with the mission of attacking from Moschny. In light of this situation and considering broad gaps existing elsewhere along the Dnjepr front, the 8th *Armee* had to withdraw forces that had been committed there. There were no forces available to seal off the wooded terrain between Russkaja-Poljana and Moschny. The Soviets attacked from Geronimowka toward Dachnowka. As a result of the flanking effect of an enemy group of 500 men from the woods southwest of Sswisdowok, the German lines had to be pulled back to the departure positions.

In this state of combat operations the 8th *Armee* complained about the lack of replacement personnel, especially officers and trained soldiers, because the combat strengths of the divisions that were in action sank as a result of daily losses. In addition there was a critical shortage of weapons, equipment and ammunition. The shortage of ammunition even prevented training on the new weapons, such as the *'Offenrohren'* [literally, 'Stovepipe', the German version of the American bazooka, a portable, reusable infantry anti-tank weapon launching shaped-charge rockets.] – the new infantry anti-tank weapon. The troops had to be miserly even with machine gun ammunition, living, so to speak, 'from hand to mouth'.

See Maps 8, 15, 17.

On 19 November the Soviets occupied the island east of Tscherkassy, attempting to get into the city from there. Reconnaissance further revealed that enemy troops were concentrating in that combat area. Their lack of success in that sector again caused the Soviets to shift their *Schwerpunkt*. While the operations in the southern edge of the Dnjepr knee [Studenez – Sselischtsche] with an advance to the south served to relieve pressure on the Soviet troops in the Tscherkassy area, the Soviets also advanced westward in the Krementschug area, to the south. There they had already achieved success at the end of October on the right wing of the 8th *Armee* in the 11th *Armee Korps* sector as far as the left wing of the 1st *Panzer Armee* by forcing back elements of the 57th *Panzer Korps* and breaching the front of the 167th *Infanterie Division* between Woroschilowka and Tscherwony. With subsequent forces the Soviets turned against the weakly secured, stationary wing. They apparently included this fighting in their plans for the Tscherkassy sector without, however, initial success.

The wing of the attack that had been driven forward north of Tscherkassy strove for Smela, southwest of Tscherkassy, with the probably intention of severing the twin-tracked Gorodischtsche – Kamenka rail line. Elements of the 5th *SS-Panzer Division 'Wiking'* recaptured Dubijewka in a hasty counter attack. The enemy, however, took the place back in a renewed attack.

On 22 November, between the two arms of the assault discussed above, two enemy regiments broke through in the Tscherkassy combat area, frontally attacking the positions on the west and south edge of Tscherkassy, enveloping

DEFENDING THE DNJEPR 71

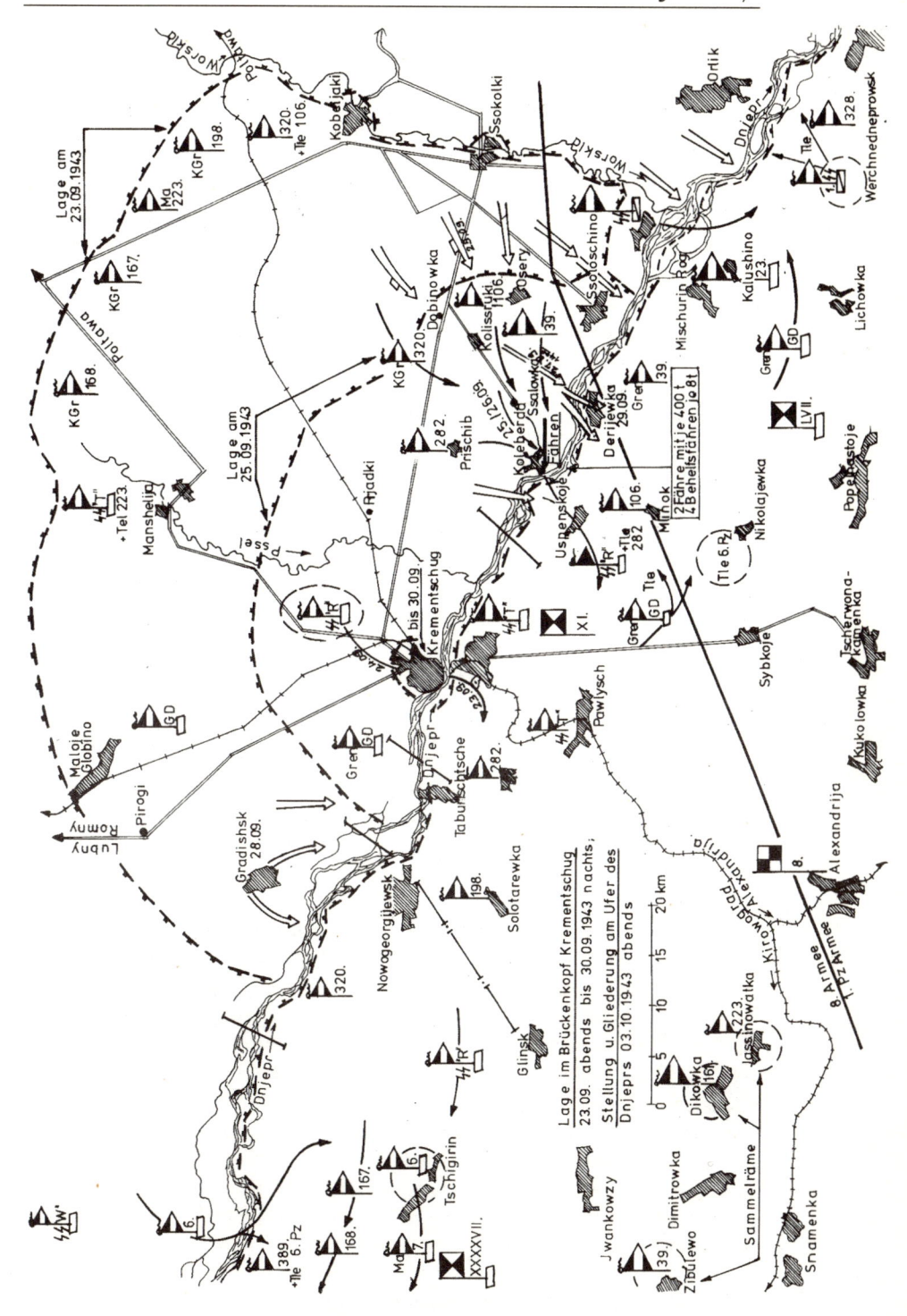

12. Situation in the Krementschug Bridgehead 23 September, evening, to 30 September, 1943, night. Position and Organization at the bank of the Dnjepr 3 October, 1943, evening.

the latter to the south. They advanced toward Smogailowka, thereby cutting off Tscherkassy. The 3rd *Panzer Division* was able to break the ring by attacking out of Tscherkassy and from the southwest.

See Map 11.

Reconnaissance of the enemy identified billeting of strong forces in the area of the northern Soviet advance, especially south of Moschny, and armoured traffic over the military bridge north of Sswidowok and through the woods west of Russkaja Pojana. Such movement of forces in the Tscherkassy area raised concern in consideration of the steadily decreasing combat strengths of the German forces. Construction of the bridge north of Tscherkassy and a further advance in that area enabled the Soviets to relieve pressure on their front facing Krementschug. Despite weather-determined unfavorable terrain conditions the 3rd *Panzer Division* captured Russkaja Poljana and cleansed the area west of Tscherkassy. North of Buda Orlowitskaja German assault troops ran into two fortified and occupied partisan camps, which they destroyed.

Fog set in during the days following, which favored the Soviet attack in the line Tscherkassy – west edge of Dubijewka and their penetration into the positions along the western edge of the city. In the face of weak German security the Soviets crossed the Smela – Tscherkassy road at several places. Enemy forces cut off near Russkaja Poljana broke out to the east. Finally enemy forces with about 25 AFVs followed by 600 infantry broke through the security line at the Smela – Tscherkassy road and to Kirilow (southwest of Tscherkassy). Therefore on 29 and 30 November the *Armee* had to arrange for aerial delivery of supplies to the German Tscherkassy forces, along with a relief attack.

The 3rd *Panzer Division*, reinforced with attached elements of the 72nd *Infanterie Division* and 5th *SS-Panzer Division 'Wiking'*, then advanced toward Tscherkassy. The garrison of the city fought its way toward that force. The two forces linked up between Smogailowka and the southwest edge of the city (from the south, along the railroad). In so doing the German forces cut off substantial enemy forces in the Kirilow area, knocking out several AFVs, antitank guns and guns.

As November gave way to December the Soviets had to recognize that they could no longer hope for the desired success at Tscherkassy, just as, in October, the same had happened in the Dnjepr bend. They had been unable to capture the needed bridges at Tscherkassy. The Soviets had, apparently, overestimated the help of the partisan bands and paratroops, but especially the load-carrying capacity of the terrain in the crossing and penetration area north of Tscherkassy, namely, from Sswidowok to the west. After these failures the Soviets turned to the bridgeheads lying farther south, to those north of Krementschug (Gradishsk) – along with further attempts to attack from the Dnjepr bend between Krementschug and Dnjepropetrowsk. By advancing from the penetration area at the right wing of the 8th *Armee* toward Pawlysch they hoped to attack the German line of defense at Krementschug, the cornerpost of the German defenses, from the rear.

See Maps 12 and 13.

The Situation South of Krementschug

After an exhausting retreat over mud-bound roads, soaked to the skin, the formations selected for the crossing at Krementschug over the 'Rundstedt'

DEFENDING THE DNJEPR

Bridge, that had been built by the *Organization Todt,* and the double-decker railroad and highway bridge ran into the massive jam of march columns before the bridges. In places there were six lines in parallel. There seemed no way out without strict controls. To make matters worse, the *Waffen-SS* units claimed priority.

See Map 12.

At the end of September the 282nd *Infanterie Division* found another route, getting the bulk of their own elements and also those of other formations across over a self-operated ferry at Koleberda. That offered the advantage of being able to occupy the new positions on the west bank of the Dnjepr immediately after crossing. Other divisions, which made the detour via Krementschug, first had to march southward on the west bank of the Dnjepr, only to find the areas designated for them already in part held by the enemy.

Southeast of Krementschug the Dnjepr goes through a bend where it is divided into several arms. Between the separate channels of the river are large islands with firm ground that made it possible on the enemy side to cross without being observed by the Germans. In many cases all that was left for the enemy to cross to the west bank was a narrow arm of the river. In several places the Soviets had undertaken such attempts as at Gradishsk, north of Krementschug, and at several locations south of Krementschug, including at Krjukoff, Kamenno-Potozkoje, Tschikanowka and Muschurin Rod, but especially at Uspenskoje and Derijewka.

See Map 12.

See Map 13.

Of the German formations intended for this sector of the front, the 106th *Infanterie Division* reached the river bank in good time. Elements of the *SS-Kavalerie Division* followed in support of the 106th *Infanterie Division*. The main bodies of the 384th *Infanterie Division* and 376th *Infanterie Divison,* coming by rapid transport from the west, from the latter of which a few elements arrived before the Soviet attack on 14 October, only arrived after the counterattack of the 40th *Panzer Korps* in the new eastern front of the 52nd *Armee Korps* at the Ingulez river. As the elements arrived they had to be committed widely separated from each other in building a thin security line. In some places the divisions had to take over sectors that were more than 20 kilometers wide, and that with a strength of about 1,000 men each in the trenches. The remnants of the 39th and 327th *Infanterie Divisionen* were assigned to other divisions as *Kampfgruppen* after the division staffs were sent off to France.

The Soviets reinforced their bridgeheads facing the security lines and advanced on Uspenskoje toward Mlinok, taking Mlinok against the opposition of the 106th *Infanterie Division*, but also pushing farther south to Popelnastoje and on to Tscherwona – Kamenka, without the German forces being able to do anything to stop them. Reconnaissance daily produced the same reports: arrival of infantry, some on trucks, batteries registering their fire and assembly of about 140 AFVs.

See Map 17.

Near Sybkoje the Soviets broke through the lines of the 3rd *SS-Panzer Division 'Totenkopf'* on a broad front. Cleaning up the site of the penetration had to be halted as darkness fell. Accordingly, Soviet forces infiltrated through as far as Solotarewka. Other enemy groups advanced southeast from the bridgehead from Tschikanowka.

See Maps 15 and 17.

Shown as Tschikalowka on the Map on 17.

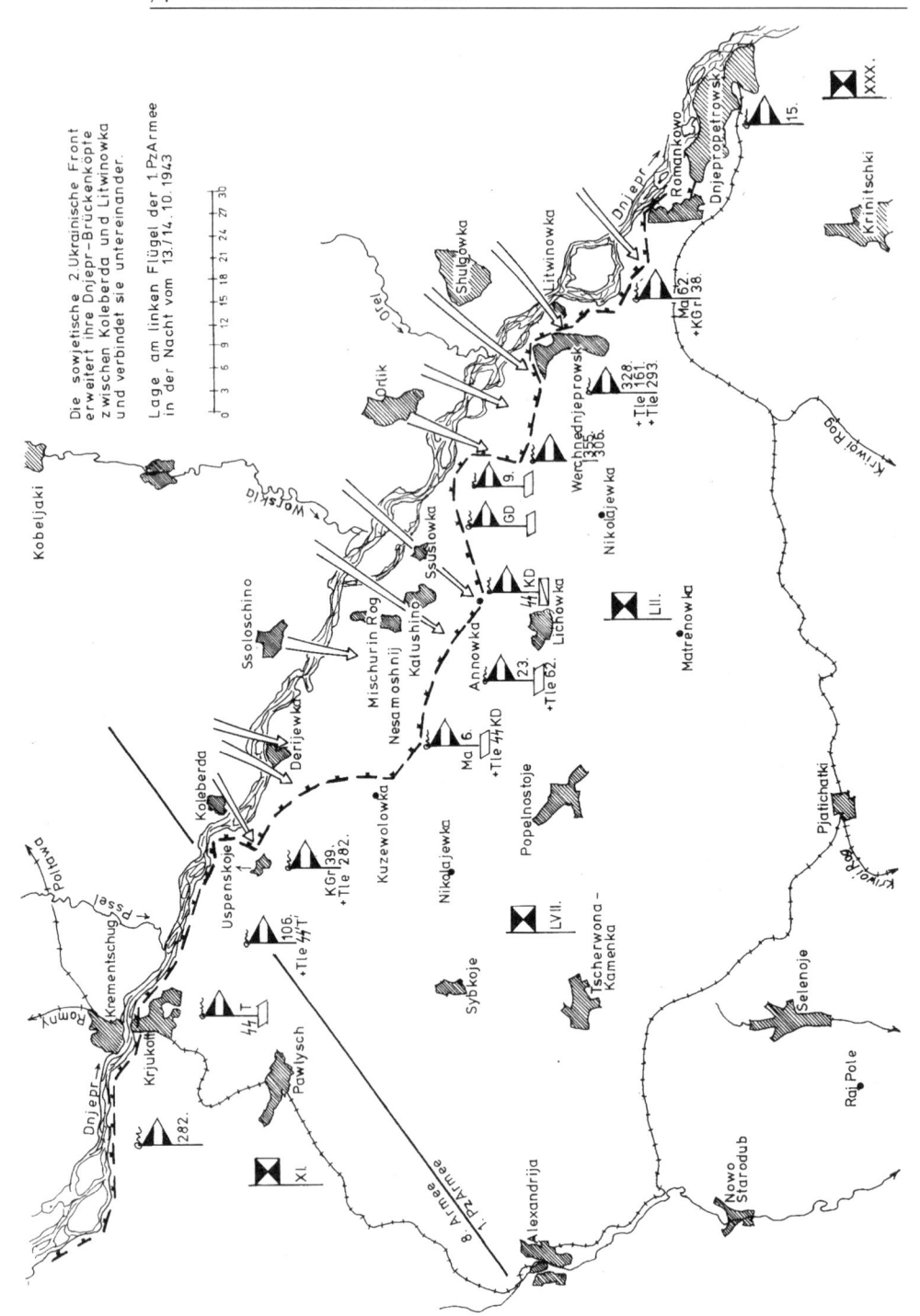

13. The Soviet 2nd Ukrainian Front extended their Dnjepr bridgeheads between Koleberda and Litwinowka and linked them up. Situation on the left wing of the 1st *Panzer Armee* in the night of 13/14 October, 1943.

25 October was particularly marked by lively enemy air and artillery activity. Bombers dropped fire-bombs, particularly in the Uspenskoje area. With the capture of Kukalowka, just in front of Alexandrija, the security line ran south from there to Nowo Starodub.

With that the Soviets had already reached the intended line of defense along the Dnjepr at the end of October/start of November 1943. The formations of the 40th *Panzer Korps* that had been intended to hold the Dnjepr bend by the command of the *Heeresgruppe* had not arrived in time in their intended combat area as a result of their initially being held in the bridgehead east of Dnjepropetrowsk, later in the old city section of Dnjepropetrowsk on the south bank. The last formations were only freed up in the Dnjepropetrowsk sector on 27/28 October. In any case, it seemed questionable whether, after the recent heavy fighting, these formations would be able to develop their full defensive strength. Regardless of that, and above all else, they were absent from the areas planned for them in the Dnjepr bend.

For geography see Map 23.

It was evident that the intentions of the Soviets in this sector were not, initially, aimed at simply gaining ground to the west. It appeared that the objective was aimed, by turning this advance toward to south, to cut off the entire German Dnjepropetrowsk – Saporoschje frontal salient. Therefore the Soviets substantially broadened their breakthrough between Dnjepropetrowsk and Krementschug. Mechanized corps and the main body of the enemy armour broke through as far as Unitrofanowka. In reaching that place they had nearly reached their objective – within thirty kilometers. Hurriedly committed elements of the 1st *Panzer Armee* and 6th *Armee*, however, prevented the Soviets from closing a *Kessel*.[2]

Fighting West of Krementschug

Reconnaissance reported accumulation of construction materials north of Krementschug and near Gradishsk. The Soviets quickly made good use of small bridgeheads in Staro Lipowo, west-northwest of Krementschug, from which they advanced toward Nowogeorgijewsk, with local penetrations at the 389th *Infanterie Division* as well as farther northwest from Bushin and Borowiza (half-way between Krementschug and Tscherkassy). This was a matter of small, weakly held bridgeheads whose establishment resulted in a scattering of forces. Therefore the Soviets set the capture of Krementschug, as a corner-post, as a further objective, attacking it from the southeast, particularly against the sector of the 167th *Infanterie Division*.

Up to this point aerial reconnaissance identified each Soviet move in good time from the reported troop movements, as on the Rschetilowka – Krementschug road. While this was happening the Soviets started

See Maps 15, 16 and 17.

---

2   Translator's note - The German term, *Kessel*, literally kettle, is usually translated as 'pocket'. However, The significance and dimensions of the *Kesselschlachten* (pocket battles) that the Germans fought in World War II, whether the Uman and Smolensk *Kesseln* where the Germans encircled and captured or destroyed hundreds of thousands of Russian troops and vast amounts of equipment in the early days of their invasion of Russia, or those, later in the war, where the roles were reversed, as in the Falaise *Kessel* and the great *Kesselschlachten* on the Eastern Front: Stalingrad, Tscherkassy and the wandering *Hube Kessel* exceed the usual associations of the English term, 'pocket'. Therefore I have chosen to retain the German *Kessel*.

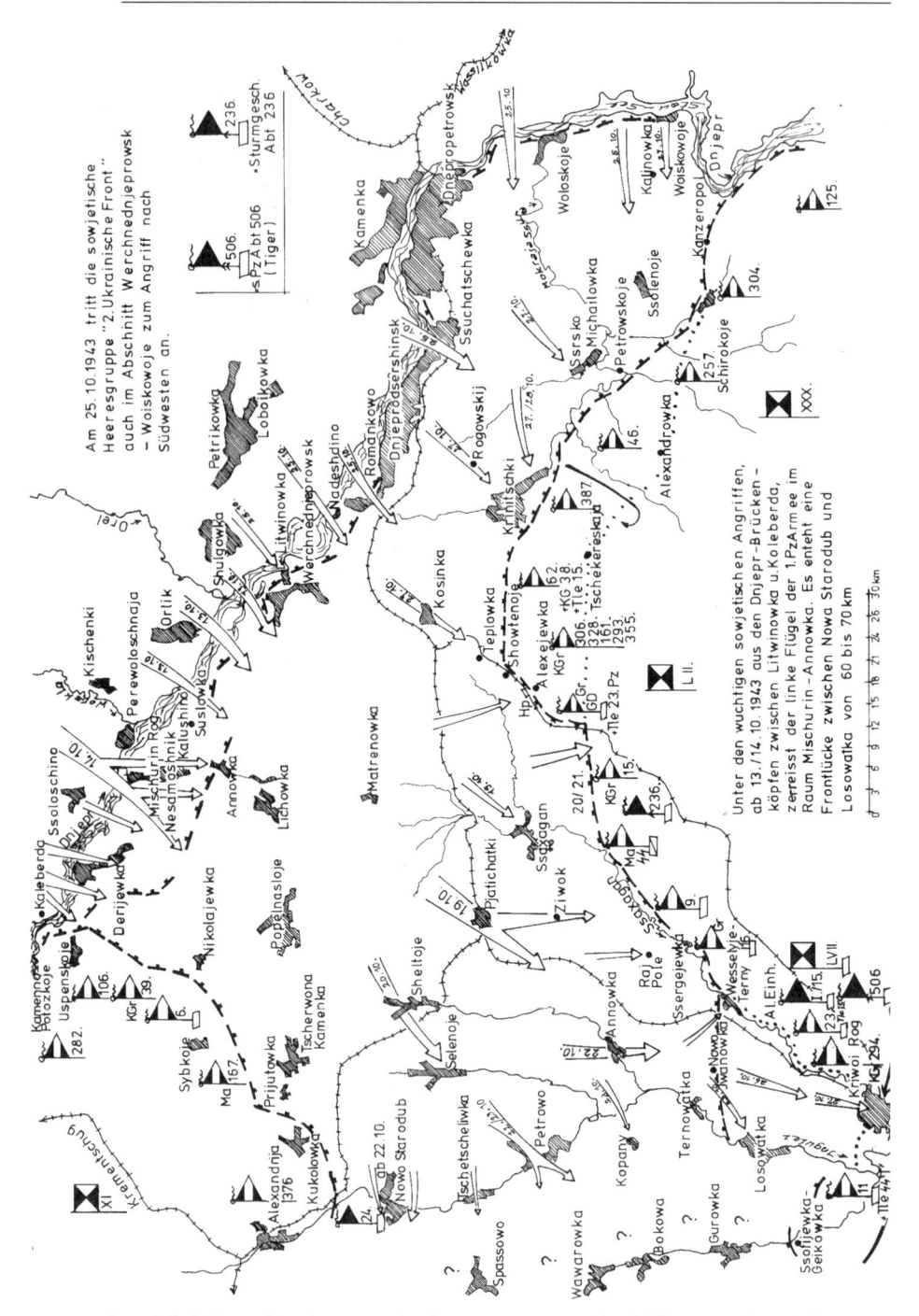

14. (top right) On 25 October, 1943 the Soviet army group '2nd Ukrainian Front' also attacked to the southwest in the Werchnednjeprowsk –Woiskowoje sector.
(bottom center) The left wing of the 1st *Panzer Armee* tore open in the Mischurin – Annowka sector under the mighty Soviet attacks from the Dnjepr bridgeheads between Litwinowka and Koleberda on 13/14 October, 1943.

reconnaissance thrusts as a distraction, not only in the 47th *Panzer Korps* sector but also in the adjoining sector of the 11th *Armee Korps*. An attack against the southern wing of the 47th *Panzer Korps* seemed obvious, to strike from the rear the bend in the 8th *Armee* front where the front had already been bent back toward the west. The Soviets well knew that an attack against this sector of the front line, which was held by formations with plenty of experience on the Eastern Front, but which were weak in personnel, was likely to achieve further success. Accordingly, they strengthened their efforts, not only against the front of the 11th *Armee Korps* of the 8th *Armee*, but also against the positions of the left wing of the 1st *Panzer Armee*.

Their tactics constantly changed. If a bluff proved successful, the Soviets concentrated a mass of armour to simulate formation of a *Schwerpunkt* for a breakthrough – which, if it actually proved successful, would then be carried forward. That, in various places, resulted in pure armoured battles. However, with that arm of the service operating alone, territory could not be occupied nor, accordingly, held. For that the Soviets required their infantry, which they seemed to have in inexhaustible amounts which they constantly brought forward. These did not always consist of battle-proven soldiers. In this sector they were frequently young recruits who had reached military age during the time of the German occupation of the Ukraine. After a mere four weeks of training they emerged in the formations of the Red Army as infantry. Such vast masses of infantry, which the Germans could only behold in amazement and envy, required some inner reinforcement, which was provided by individual AFVs assigned to the infantry.

Breakthrough between the 47th *Panzer Korps* and 11th *Armee Korps*

The repeated attacks against the south front of the 47th *Panzer Korps* foundered, each time with heavy Soviet losses in armour and infantry, so that the Red Army shifted the *Schwerpunkt* of its attacks at the end of November to the area between Alexandrija and Protopowka. They opened with an attack by about 100 AFVs. Elements of the 11th *Panzer Division* intercepted these in the high ground east of the Ingulez – with assistance by the 4th *Fliegerkorps* – and knocked out about 66 enemy AFVs on that day, 82 on the next day. However, the Soviets did, thereby, attain an initially narrow penetration in the German line of defense.

See Map 17.

The wing of the 11th *Armee Korps* that was initially near Alexandrija and east of the Pawlysch – Krjukoff (south of Krementschug) line was, obviously, to be forced back by the assault to Kirowograd – Snamenka. Nevertheless, at that point the line of defense between Pawlysch and Krjukoff held. On 24 November the Soviets were able to envelop this frontal salient and attain penetrations at several places. In light of the massive Soviet superiority in numbers and the lack of German reserves, the *Armee* was unable to restore the situation and found itself forced to pull the east wing of the 47th *Panzer Korps* back to a cordon position. It thereby hoped to enable the badly battered divisions to mount an effective defense.

See Maps 15 and, especially, 17.

78   CRUCIBLE OF COMBAT

15. Situation on the left wing of the 1st *Panzer Armee* from 22 October to 2 November, 1943.

DEFENDING THE DNJEPR

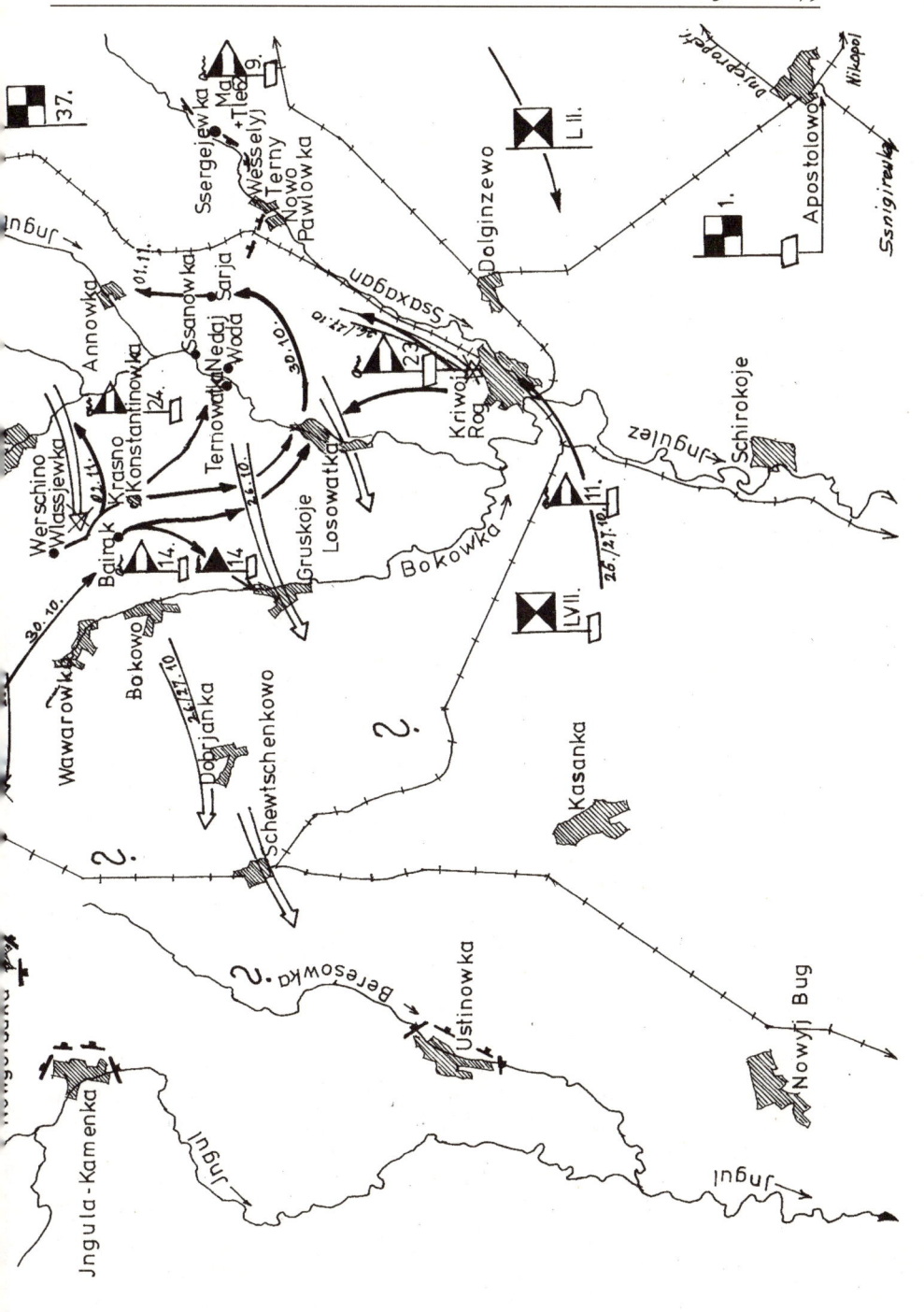

Between the left wing of the 11th *Armee Korps* and the right wing of the 47th *Panzer Korps*, however, there was still a gap in the line of defense into which the Soviets poured armour, infantry and cavalry. That did not, in fact, give them a breakthrough in the desired location, but in another, where, however, it was feared that again the German forces would seal it off in a short time. The Germans repulsed attacks against the then – forming flank security of the 47th *Panzer Korps* along the Auditorowka – Mironowka line, taking Mironowka in a hasty counter attack. On 25 November the 11th *Panzer Division* was to attempt to at least partially close the gap between Protopowka and Mironowka with a *Kampfgruppe*, thereby relieving pressure on the south wing of the 47th *Panzer Korps*. Success in that venture, however, required that weather-sensitive terrain be in passable condition and, above all, timely arrival of elements of the 14th *Panzer Division*. The 6th *Panzer Division* repulsed enemy attacks north of Ssacharjewka and Mironowka on another margin of the breakthrough at the 47th *Panzer Korps*, recapturing Mironowka after its earlier loss.

[See Map 17.]

On 26 November, west of Kossowka, the forces of the 11th *Panzer Division* finally cut the rear connections of the enemy forces that had broken through to the west and established loose contact with the southern wing of the 47th *Panzer Korps*. Enemy forces that had advanced westward via the Kossowka sector were thereby taken in the flank, partially destroyed and partially thrown back to the east.

At that point in the fighting the Soviets made use of the 'interior line' and daily shifted their jump-off points and the direction of their attacks. An attack astride the Pawlysch – Alexandrija road resulted in a penetration at the road to the northeast edge of Alexandrija . The Soviets then attacked the security line of the 11th *Panzer Division* between Alexandrija north and Beresowka south, as well as Nowo Alexandrowka, on a broad front. They also attacked the lines of the 14th *Panzer Division* on the heights northwest of Protopopowka. There was also the successful penetration in which, according to German estimates, the Soviets, sent in 100 to 150 AFVs. Throughout the entire day these formations received reinforcement from the Alexandrija sector and from the area of penetration west of Kossowka, as well as by rail on the Pjatichatki – Alexandrija railroad line, detraining east of Nowo Sswetlopol and on foot and by motorized march. On 27 November strong enemy fighter-defense prevented adequate aerial reconnaissance in that combat sector.

[See Map 17.]

By attacks from east, north and northwest the Soviets attempted to eliminate the frontal salient around Nowo – Georgijewsk. The 389th *Infanterie Division*, however, held firm. The 282nd *Infanterie Division* lost high ground southwest of Swinarka, the 389th *Infanterie Division* lost Taburischtsche. Above all else, the fighting again resulted in heavy losses in personnel and matériel. The 282nd *Infanterie Division* lost one regimental and four battalion commanders in an attack on a decisive hill. In many places such losses prevented orderly tactical command which, in turn, caused the troops, which had become apathetic after months of action under excessive strain, in many places to be deficient in steadfastness. The state of exhaustion increased, the more so as the combat situation locally prevented regular logistical support.

[Margin note: See Map 17.]

DEFENDING THE DNJEPR

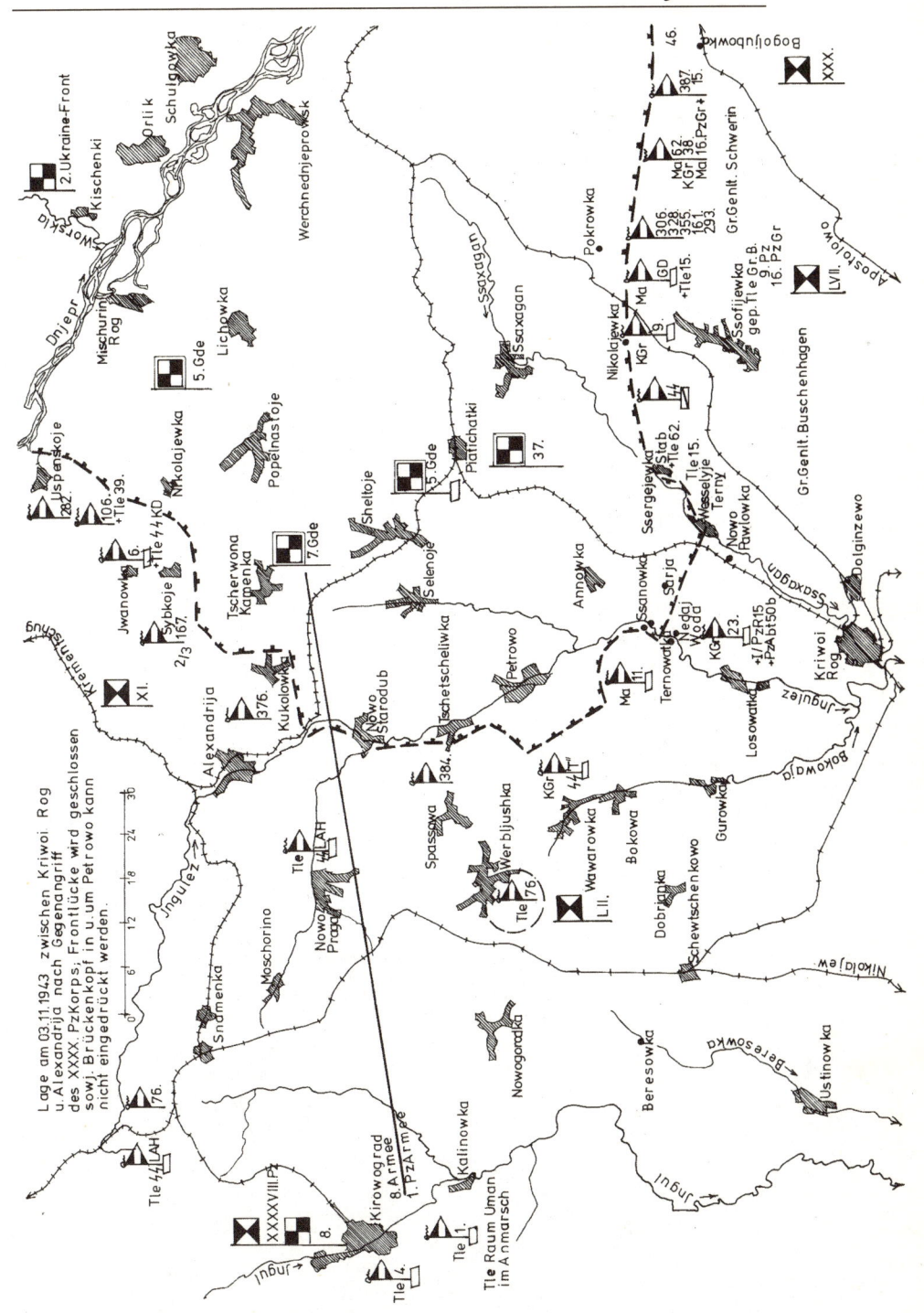

16. Situation on 3 November, 1943 between Kriwoi Rog and Alexandrija after the counterattack of the 30th *Panzer Korps*; The gap in the front was closed. Soviet bridgehead in and around Petrowo cannot be eliminated.

17. Defensive fighting in the sector of the 11th *Armee Korps* and 47th *Panzer Korps* on the right wing of the 8th *Armee*. Development of the situation from 14 October to 10 December, 1943.

DEFENDING THE DNJEPR

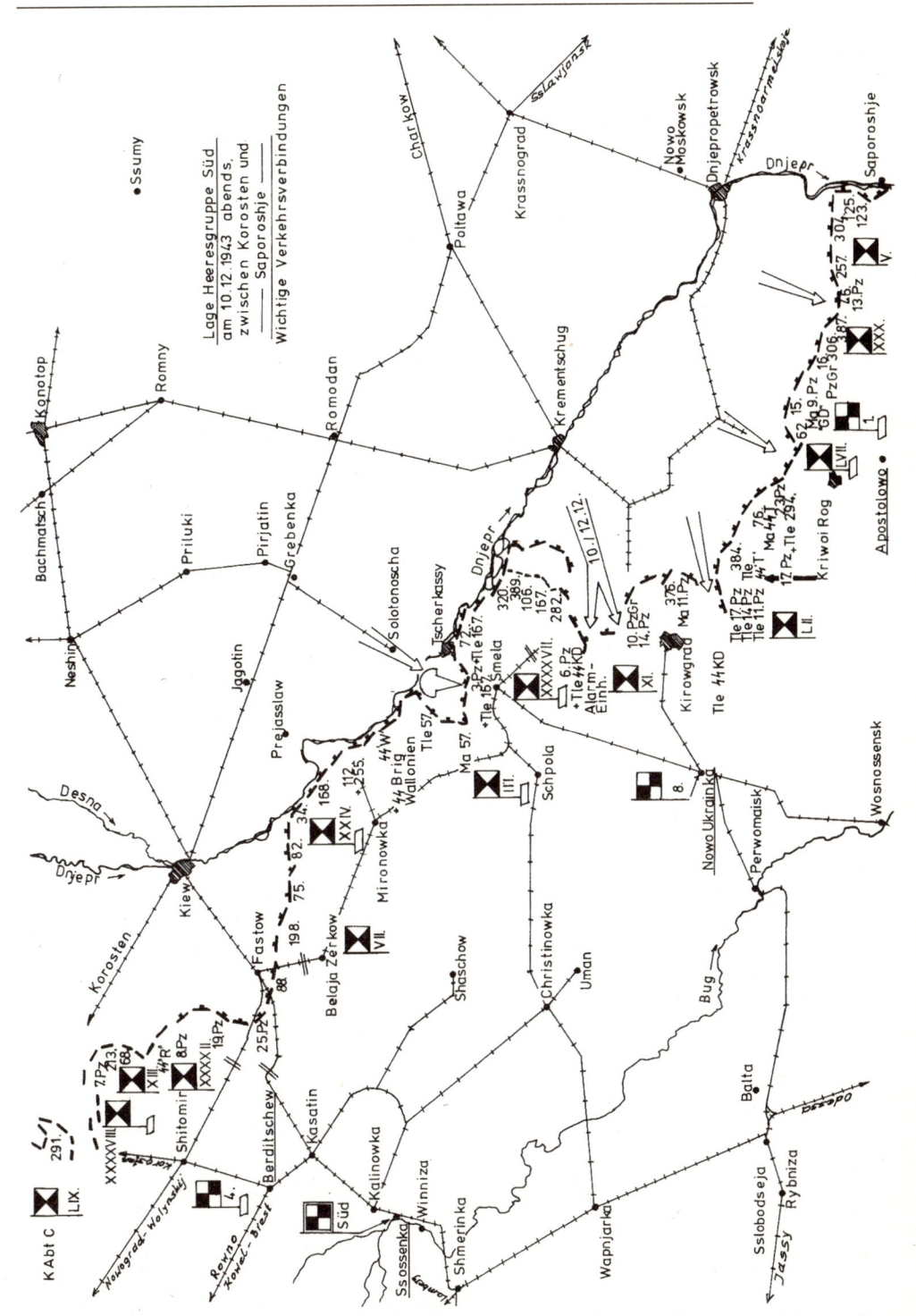

18. Situation of *Heeresgruppe Süd* on 10 December, 1943, evening, between Korosten and Saporoshje.

In order to prevent movement of forces of the 47th *Armee Korps* to the site of the breakthrough, the Soviets attacked in the east from the Gradishsk bridgehead and advanced northwest of Nowo Lipowo. The Germans, however, lacked reserves to restore the situation in this area. On 28 November the Soviets also captured the other cornerstone of the German defense by attacks near Alexandrija on an 11 kilometer front. Thanks to fierce resistance by the 376th *Infanterie Division* and elements of the 11th *Panzer Division* the attack ground to a halt with heavy Soviet losses. A complete defensive success! Local forces of the southern enemy attack group, presumably committed to envelop Alexandrija, were repulsed with loss of six AFVs on the hills northwest of Protopopowka.

In ongoing fighting against strong infantry and armour, elements of the 14th *Panzer Division*, reinforced with elements of the 11th *Panzer Division*, advanced in the afternoon of 28 November to the area southwest of Kossowka, thereby cutting the Soviet east-west march route. The left wing of the German attack advanced to the center of Dikowka and east to Bolschaja Makarischa, thereby constricting the area of the Soviet penetration from south and west, while knocking out 27 enemy AFVs and numerous personnel carriers, antitank guns and heavy weapons, and scattering enemy infantry march-columns with heavy losses to them. Forces were lacking, however, to close the gap between Bolschaja Marakrischa and Sacharjewka. The Soviets thrust into that gap with armoured reconnaissance and infantry that had been brought up.

See Maps 17 and 20.

While fixing the front at Alexandrija with local forces, predominately armour and motorized forces, on 29 November the Soviets swung their main body to the south and attacked the Ingulez line Bandurowka – Dikowka. with strong infantry and armoured forces (a total of 80 – 100 AFVs). At the same time armoured reconnaissance forces advanced to Bolschaja Makarischa.

The strong ground-attack and fighter plane commitment in support of the ground fighting against the 11th *Armee Korps* and 47th *Panzer Korps* typified the Soviet *Schwerpunkt* formation. The aircraft bombed and strafed transport routes and billets, heavily bombing the Snamenka railroad station. Elements of the 4th *Fliegerkorps* flew numerous sorties supporting the *Korps*. Partisan bands again made themselves evident and occupied locales north of Snamenka that were not garrisoned by German troops. They fortified these places making it necessary for German antitank guns and tanks to block the Glinsk – Snamenka road at Krassno Uralsk.

See Map 20.

The next day the Soviets appeared initially to desire to defend themselves against the threat to their flank from the Protopopowka area by eliminating this cornerstone even before they aimed at capturing the Snamenka crossroads. The attacks failed. The 14th *Panzer Division* attacked in the flank and essentially thwarted a Soviet advance supported by about 30 AFVs against the Bandurowka bridgehead. German interference prevented the assembly of armour and a concentration of partisan bands estimated at about 2,000 men in Dikowka for an attack. The fighting on 29 and 30 November cost the Soviets 31 AFVs, three rocket-launchers and 16 antitank guns. One tank and one assault gun were captured in towable condition. The Soviet attacks against

See Maps 17 and 20.

the southern corner-post of the southern wing of the 47th *Panzer Korps* also foundered.

In ensuing days advances of the 11th *Panzer Division* as well as the 14th *Panzer Division* alternated with Soviet attacks – the actions were locally complicated by weather-related terrain problems. The final result was that the Soviets achieved limited ground gains. Thus they advanced via Dikowka to Dmitrowka. The anti-aircraft and alarm units committed to secure the Ingulez river crossings in the southern part of Dmitrowka prevented a further Soviet advance in heavy defensive fighting. That day partisan bands, some in German uniforms, attacked from the west toward Soviet troops. *See Map 17.*

The retrograde movements of the 8th *Armee* and, indeed, of the 11th *Armee Korps* and 47th *Panzer Korps* took place, despite problems with the roads, without enemy pressure. The Soviets only followed the 11th *Armee Korps* with weak infantry forces. With the 47th *Panzer Korps*, however, the Soviet forces locally pushed into the newly occupied main line of resistance in battalion strength. An attack with armour and infantry against the Dmitrowka bridgehead foundered with the loss of 11 AFVs. On 1 and 2 December the Soviets lost 26 AFVs in this sector of the front. The attacks against the southern wing of the 47th *Panzer Korps* now appeared directed at Tschigrin. *See Maps 17, 18 and 20.*

The Soviets supported utilization of the penetrations they had achieved with simultaneously delivered attacks against the front of the 1st *Panzer Armee*, where the isolation of the 376th *Infanterie Division* remained a feared possibility. With strong armoured forces the attackers reached Trojanka, nine kilometers southeast of Snamenka. They lost three AFVs in the fighting for the Dmitrowka bridgehead, around Wassowka and also at the north and west edges of Snamenka. The Soviets again gained ground across the Chirowka, Zibulewko – Krassnosselja line with armour and infantry, partisan bands and small groups of cavalry, as far as the Chirowka – Alexandrowka line, thereby disrupting detraining of the 10th *Panzergrenadier Division* in the Zibulewo railroad station, even temporarily blocking the railroad line. *See Maps 18, 19 and 20.*

To take advantage of the penetration, the Soviet 5th Guards Army advanced with strong infantry forces and elements of the 1st Mechanized Corps through the gap made by the penetration and over the Beschka sector into the flank and rear of the southern wing of the 8th *Armee*. That resulted in the premature withdrawal of the 376th *Infanterie Division* to the Grigorjewka – Pantajewka line, which succeeded despite flank attacks by enemy infantry and armour and aggressive followup in the direction of the attack. The 11th *Panzer Division*, however, severed the rear communications of the enemy force-group that had broken through with a bold and resolute advance to Pantajewka, thereby stopping the enemy force. *See Maps 17 and 20.*

In the meantime, however, the Soviets brought up forces to utilize, broaden and deepen the breakthrough. Facing the 8th *Armee* on 8 December reconnaissance of the enemy identified 25 rifle divisions, 14 of which were guards rifle divisions, two tank corps, three mechanized corps, one to two tank brigades, of which about 13 rifle divisions, two tank corps, and two mechanized corps were concentrated to form a *Scherpunkt* before the southern wing of the *Armee*. The German forces opposing these consisted of eight

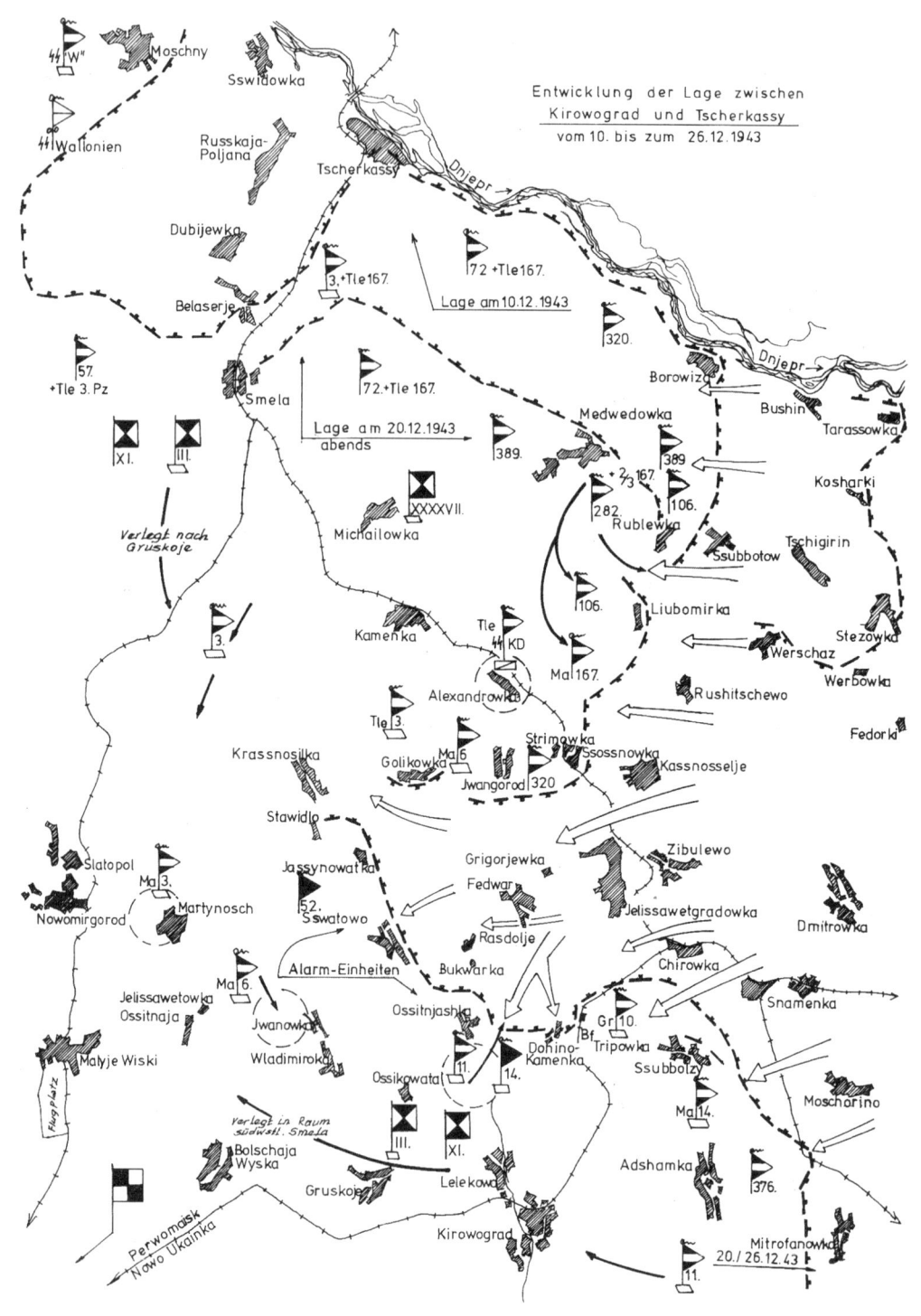

19. Development of the situation between Kirowograd and Tscherkassy from 10 to 26 December, 1943.

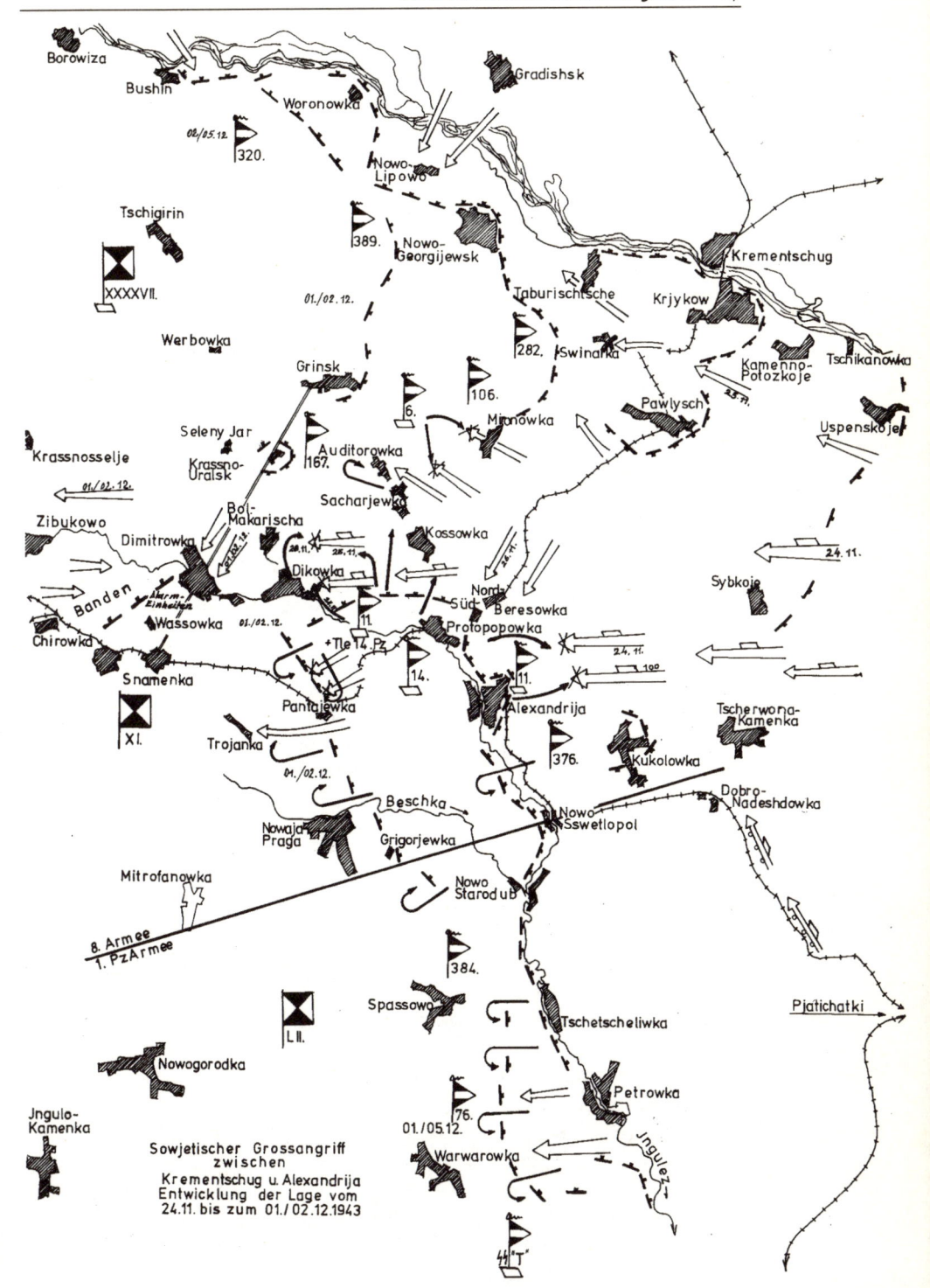

DEFENDING THE DNJEPR 87

20. Soviet offensive between Krementschug and Alexandrija. Development of the situation from 24 November to 1/2 December, 1943.

infantry divisions, four of which were badly battered (167th, 376th, 282nd and 72nd *Infanterie Divisionen*), the 6th *Panzer Division* or, as the case may be, 10th *Panzergrenadier Division*, none of which, as the result of high losses of personnel and equipment, were at their full combat effectiveness. Every day brought new losses that were not replaced. One *Panzergrenadier Regiment* of the 11th *Panzer Division* lost 95 wounded, not counting killed and missing!) out of its combat strength of 350 men on the single day of 7 December in the heavy fighting at the Dikowka railroad stop. Conditions were similar for the 376th *Infanterie Division*, which also suffered heavy losses in its heroic battle against vastly superior enemy forces on 7 December.

The 6th *Panzer Division* and 106th *Infanterie Division* of the 47th *Panzer Korps* then attacked the 6th Guards Mechanized Corps and captured the hills northwest of Selnyj Jar and South of Werbowka, thereby providing the prerequisites for an orderly evacuation of the angle of the front of the 47th *Panzer Korps* west of Krementschug.

The Soviets, however, were not satisfied with their penetration between the 47th *Panzer Korps* and the 11th *Armee Korps*, but also attacked the *Armee* boundary between the 11th *Armee Korps* (8th *Armee*) and 1st *Panzer Armee* at Mitrofanowka [see bottom right corner of Map 19] in greater strength in order to further complicate the defense with steadily changing jump-off positions and varying objective directions, as well as multiple attacks daily.

The Big Picture

See Maps 10, 12 and 23.

Withdrawal of the German forces that were east of the Dnjepr had to take place over the existing Dnjepr crossings. There were not, however, sufficient such crossings, so traffic jams developed before several of the crossings by 20 September. There was still a German bridgehead on the east bank of the Dnjepr at Dnjepropetrowsk, so that retreating elements of troops could flow into that bridgehead. A great mass of troops built up in a jam before the bridges at Krementschug, one road bridge and a two-level road and railroad bridge, so that it was only by good fortune that weather conditions prevented greater involvement of the Russian airforce, which would otherwise have caused substantial losses in the march columns that had built up in several parallel lines. The crossing, however, was complicated by the fact that the armoured divisions were assigned priority in crossing, so that other formations had to wait. The rearguard was formed from elements of *Panzergrenadier Division 'Großdeutschland'*.

See Map 12.

The 282nd *Infanterie Division* found another solution. It took a barge that it found and a small steamer that had stopped on its journey to the Black Sea and set up its own ferry. With the help of these two vessels the division set up an effective crossing point near Koloberda (see above).

Except for the bridgehead east of Dnjepropetrowsk that was farther to the south or southeast, there were no bridges, so the units that crossed the river at Krementschug and were assigned to defend that sector first had to march to that southern area of the riverbank. Partisan bands, however, sometimes got there before them and, in cooperation with the Red Army, occupied various sectors of the river bank, thus preparing bridgeheads there for the Red Army.

DEFENDING THE DNJEPR 89

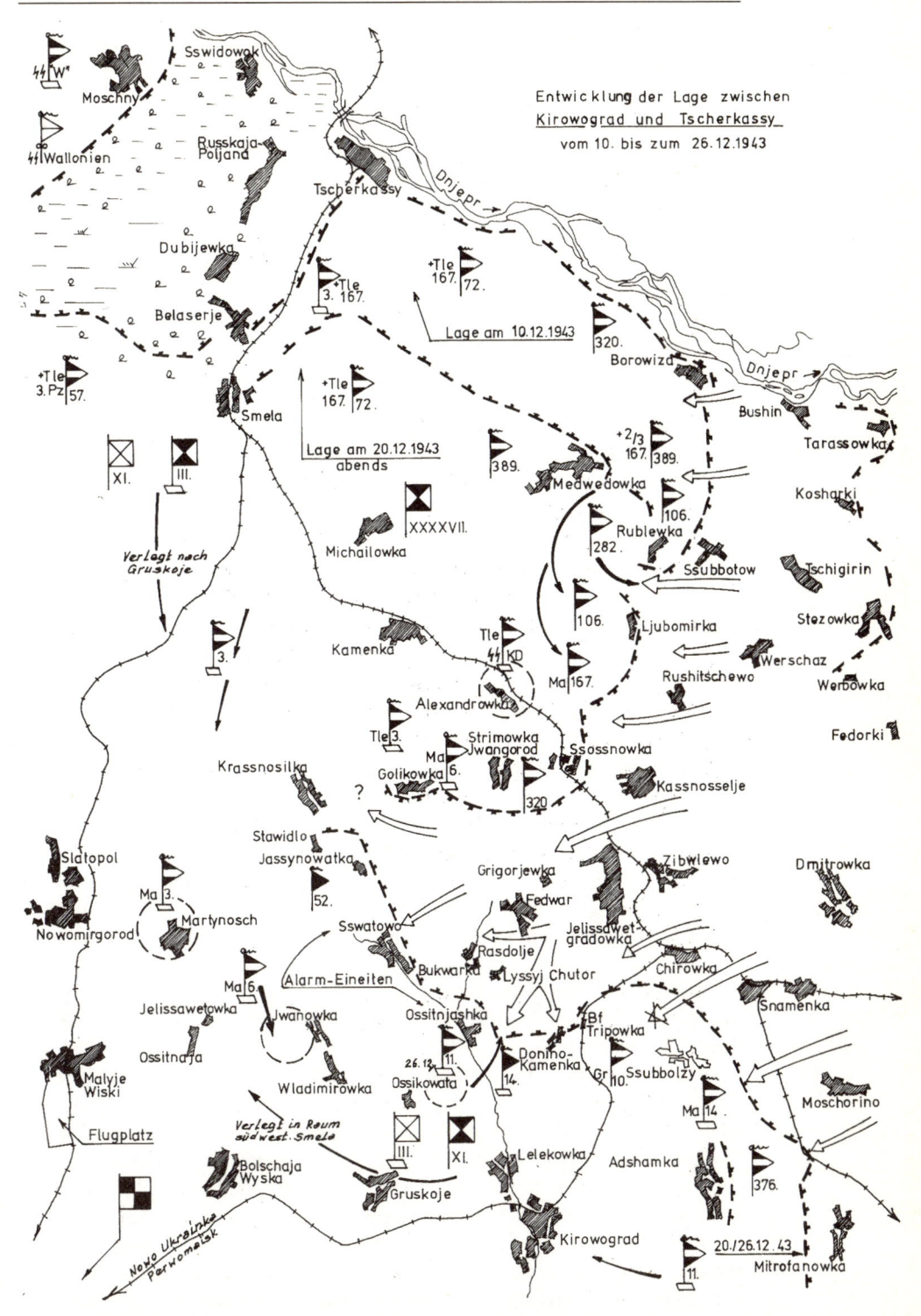

21. Development of the situation between Kirowograd and Tscherkassy from 10 to 26 December, 1943

At various places the German units that were marching on foot simply arrived too late and in totally inadequate strength, so that a further retreat to the west seemed unavoidable.

Thus the Soviets established a broad and, finally, a deep basis for an attack for the concentration of heavy weapons, especially armour, for the continued advance to the west. The Germans lacked the forces requisite to put a halt to such operations. Accordingly the Soviets gained a great frontal salient reaching nearly to Kirowograd in which the 11th *Panzer Division* and the newly brought up 24th *Panzer Division* and 14th *Panzer Division* had to go into action as *Kampfgruppen* to halt the Soviet advance.

See Map 18.

Evaluation of the Overall Situation

It was not always possible to determine from their advance how far ahead the Soviets at that time had clear operational plans. The Red Army more often attempted, by choice of varying *Schwerpunkte*, to find weak points in the German defense and then take advantage of them for an advance to the west. Since, however, it was impossible to foresee where such a success might take place, the prerequisites for far-reaching operational tactical planning were lacking.

The Soviet attack operations against the southern wing of the 57th *Panzer Korps* and the north wing of the 11th *Armee Korps* were not restricted only to the area between the 11th *Armee Korps* and the 1st *Panzer Armee*, but also extended to the other lines of defense of the 57th *Armee Korps* of the 1st *Panzer Armee*. The varying support of the ground troops by the Red Airforce made it possible to identify which part of the front was the *Schwerpunkt* of the day. In the face of this immense Soviet superiority in armour, artillery and, above all, in infantry forces, it was impossible for the German command to bring up combat-worthy formations with experience on the Eastern Front. When reports speak of 'divisions', one must keep in mind that, many times, the unit in question was no more than an assemblage of *Kampfgruppen* that was fighting with significantly reduced personnel, most particularly with soldiers who had already been in unbroken action for several months, while the Soviets constantly brought up fresh troops in rotation. At times shortages of ammunition were evident, as, also, of fuel. The German supply over one single-tracked railroad line from Odessa that was subject to disruption by partisan bands proved seriously strained and, after the loss of supply via Fastow, downright overloaded.

The same railway line had also brought the 14th *Panzer Division*, newly reconstituted after its destruction at Stalingrad, from France over a stretch of about 2,500 kilometers, via small secondary rail lines: Lemberg – Stanislau – Kischinew – Tiraspol – Odessa (70 – 80 goods trains). The troops came from the warmth of France to the Ukraine winter and, generally, lacked any combat experience. The different branches of the service had not yet learned to work together. Nevertheless, this division was immediately sent into action, and not even as a coherent unit. Rather, its elements were thrown into action in the order of their arrival, then assigned to *Kampfgruppen* to enter the battle at the individual hot spots of the defense. Despite all that they repeatedly succeeded in breaking into the as-yet unfortified Soviet defensive positions. Most important, their mobile commitment prevented a further Soviet advance to the west.

The Soviets now had several possible courses of action after the breakthrough between the right wing of the 47th *Panzer Korps* toward Andronowka and at the left wing of the 11th *Armee Korps*. One was to carry out the initially intended advance against the southern front of the 47th *Panzer Korps*, now shifted farther to the west, with some modification, with the direction of the thrust toward the enemy formations advancing in the reciprocal direction from Tscherkassy, with assistance from Soviet forces working toward [the main thrust] from other – smaller – Dnjepr bridgeheads north of Tscherkassy. That possibility must have become less tempting when the 47th *Panzer Korps* pulled back the angle in the front west of Krementschug. Nevertheless, there were still German forces remaining along the Dnjepr from Krementschug to the northwest that the Soviets could attack from the rear.

Fighting East of Kirowograd

After the Soviets failed to achieve the desired success with their operations further northward, they turned anew to the new sector between Krementschug and Dnjepropetrowsk, in which they had previously succeeded in establishing crossings over the Dnjepr at several locations, where the bridgeheads had communications with the rear and where the bridgeheads had been deepened enough to proved adequate area for the assembly of strong formations and heavy weapons. Aside from the advances from Tscherkassy, from the area of the penetration to the north, to eliminate the angle in the German front near Krementschug, the Soviets turned farther to the west, especially against the lines of the 47th *Panzer Korps* of the 1st *Panzer Armee*. It was apparent that, at that time, the Soviets did not yet have a clear objective. Probably they initially wanted to provide flank support for the advance into the gap between the 47th *Panzer Korps* and the 11th *Armee Korps*, and, in addition, to tie down German forces by advancing to the west, thereby preventing those units from being shifted to the southern wing of the 8th *Armee* or to other bridgehead fronts along the course of the Dnjepr.

See Maps 14 and 18.

Nevertheless, the 8th *Armee*, at that time, still had available local stretches of the functional twin-tracked rail line south from Fastow, namely, between Belaja – Zerkow and Smela. The severing of that rail line farther north, however, caused logistical difficulties since, for the entire frontal sector, there were only two single-tracked approaches, via the Shmerinka transportation hub, Wapnjarka – Christinowka to Smela and via Tschernowitz – Jassy – Permowaisk – Nowo Ukrainka to Smela. Therefore the entire logistical support now had to function via the twin-tracked Lemberg – Odessa rail link and via the Brest – Kowel – Berditschew – Shmerinka approach. The branch-lines ending farther to the rear leading to Shaskow and Uman were of little significance.

See Map 18.

The penetration that had been achieved also offered the possibility of advancing to the south, into the rear of the front of the 57th *Panzer Korps* of the 1st *Panzer Armee*, with supporting attacks from the other side or diversionary attacks against the German bridgehead south of the Dnjepr at Nikopol. Such an advance could serve the purpose of forcing the evacuation of the frontal salient as far as Saporoschje, or, – a bold conception – of cutting the salient off.

However, the elements of the 14th *Panzer Division* that were committed scuttled that southward-directed opportunity so the only remaining possibility was to advance westward toward Kriwoi Rog and Kirowograd. The concentration of strong attack forces made that seem to be a justified fear. That made it apparent that the Soviets planned an advance into the Kirowograd area with one arm in the area north of Kirowograd and another, after breaking through the lines of the 57th *Panzer Korps,* into the area south of Kirowograd. Such an advance proffered the prospect, should the occasion arise, of cutting off Kirowograd.

See Maps 19 and 21. Close examination reveals a few small differences between these two maps, even though the caption is the same.

To achieve the above objective, the Soviets committed an assault group before the inner wing of the 1st *Panzer Armee* and of the 11th *Armee Korps* of the 8th *Armee* – north wing near Mitrofanowka – southwest of Alexandrija. Another group, consisting of strong armoured formations (1st Mechanized-, 8th Mechanized – and 18th Tank-Corps) stood between the Adshamka – Nowoja Praga road and Snamenka (the 3rd Division north and northwest of Snamenka). In the gap north of Snamenka the Soviets primarily sent in infantry formations. They started with massed armoured and infantry attacks against the Beschka line, but were intercepted in heavy fighting by elements of the 376th *Infanterie Division* and 14th *Panzer Division*, as well as elements of the 10th *Panzergrenadier Division* on the heights southwest of Moscherino and at the railroad line south of Snamenka. As a result of the intense snow-squalls the fighting was extraordinarily difficult and demanded extreme commitment from the troops.

The Soviets did not, at this time, launch their various assaults simultaneously, but varied the starting time, location and style of their attacks in changing tactics. The western attack group jumped off at noon on 9 December with two assault elements in a frontal attack against the northern front of the 11th *Panzer Division*, with one group enveloping from the west, and broke through the widely stretched security line at several places. 25 AFVs remained, knocked out, before the lines of the 11th *Armee Korps*, five before the 47th *Panzer Korps* and seven before the 3rd *Panzer Korps*.

In this situation the 11th *Panzer Division* established contact with the northern wing of the 1st *Panzer Armee* in Werschine Kamenka with an armoured group advancing to the south. The 11th *Panzer Division* repulsed, with heavy losses to the Soviets, an enemy attack in battalion and regimental strength turning in to the east from the Mitrofanowka area and south of Mitrofanowka and, above all, Soviet advances astride the Nowaja Praga road <aside>See Maps 21 and 22.</aside> with infantry and individual AFVs. On the next day the luck of the battle again favoured the Soviets in that they forced back the inner wing of the 376th *Infanterie Division* and 14th *Panzer Division* about three kilometers to the west and captured the high ground east of Ssubotzy, losing, therein, 13 AFVs south-southwest of Snamenka. The Soviets attained a deep penetration on the Snamenka – Ssubotzy road.

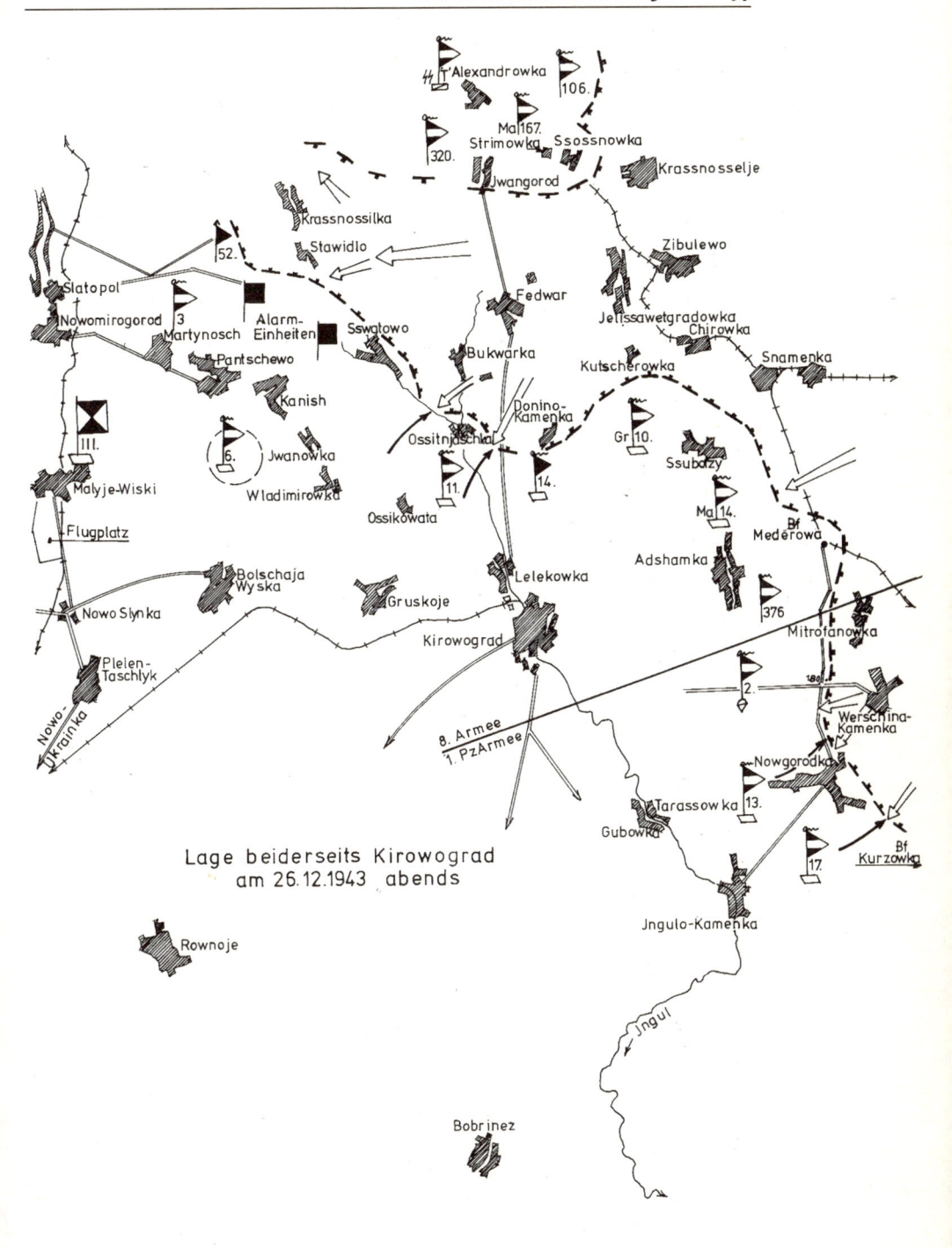

22. Situation on both sides of Kirowograd on 26 December, 1943, evening.

During all this the Soviets secured the flanks of their advance between the right wing of the 47th *Panzer Korps* and the left wing of the 11th *Armee Korps* with armoured forces brought up from the Ssossnowka area and pressure against the lines of the 6th *Panzer Division*, without, however, altering the direction of march. That was aimed from the area south of Wershaz and Tschigirin, probably to disrupt the eastern front of the 47th *Panzer Korps*, if the opportunity permitted, in cooperation with the landing attempt in the Bushin – Borowiza sector southeast of Tscherkassy. At the same time the Soviets launched relief attacks in the Tscherkassy area, regaining the railroad station land in Tscherkassy, losing, in the attempt, 18 AFVs – 24 AFVs during the entire day (10 December). The activity in this area was clearly linked to the advance through the gap in the front between the 47th *Panzer Korps* and 11th *Armee Korps*.

See Map 21.

Farther south the 11th *Panzer Division* attempted with a *Kampfgruppe* to prevent the clearly intended Soviet breakthrough attempt from Adshanka (elements of the Soviet 18th Tank Corps, 29th Tank Corps and strong artillery forces). Involving the 376th *Infanterie Division* and elements of the 14th *Panzer Division*, the fighting resulted in the destruction of 54 enemy AFVs. That makes clear the fierceness of the combat operations in that area. The next day the Soviets advanced with a combat group to the Ingul river at Tarassowka with the possible intention of turning in from there to the north and relieving the combat group that had been employed to open the line leading through Adshanka.

See Map 22.

The Soviets fiercely pursued the withdrawal of the 47th *Panzer Korps*, so that on 10 and 11 December the 6th *Panzer Division* and 282nd *Infanterie Division* were able to knock out no less than 134 enemy AFVs.

The breakthrough through the open flank of the 47th *Panzer Division* again offered the Soviets the possibility of advancing with armoured reconnaissance to the area southeast of Kamenka and launching attacks against the Iwangorod – Strimowka line in a direction south of Kamenka. These operations, too, could be related to the reinvigorated combat activity of the Soviets in the Tscherkassy bridgehead. Their apparent intention was to block the Alesandrowka [Alexandrowka] – Smela railroad line and road. That intention against the 47th *Panzer Korps* did not, however, prevent the Soviets from also sending spearheads farther west out of the penetration between the 47th *Panzer Korps* and 11th *Armee Korps* and reaching the Ingul river at Sswjatowo. In hard fighting, by capturing Kamenka, the 6th *Panzer Division* eliminated the dangerous situation near Kamenka where the Soviet 5th Guards Mechanized Corps was concentrating with three mechanized and one tank brigade south and southwest of Kamenka. It was further intended to cut the Soviet forces that had advanced into this area off from their connections to the rear. Instead of that, the Soviets concentrated in the unoccupied area of the breakthrough. The Germans lacked blocking forces. All that could be accomplished was to remove the threat to Kamenka by the attack by elements of the 3rd *Panzer Division* and 6th *Panzer Division* and to narrow the gap in the front north of Krassnosselje by an advance of the 320th *Infanterie Division* and 106th *Infanterie Division*. On the other hand, while widening the penetration

See Map 21.

southwest of Ssubbotow, the Soviet 138th Rifle Division broke through the blocking positions of the 389th *Infanterie Division* and, utilizing terrain that was not open to observation, advanced to the area near Rublewka.

The Fedwar *Kessel*

The 47th *Panzer Korps* continued to concern itself with narrowing the gap near Zibulewo up to the point when the first Soviet shells fell on the northern edge of Kirowograd (16 December). The Soviets assembled forces in the northern part of the gap between the 11th *Armee Korps* and 47th *Panzer Korps* southeast of Fedwar. Apparently these forces were to attack toward the Tscherkassy bridgenead, to at least capture the area around Smela and to establish contact with the 4th Guards Army. The 6th *Panzer Division* and 320th *Infanterie Division*, along with the 106th *Infanterie Division* drove their attack against heavy resistance to the northern edge of Michalowka. It was possible to seal off in makeshift fashion the Soviet's further penetrations that they had achieved against the isolated German outposts thanks to their masses of manpower.

See Map 21.

In the meantime, strong Soviet artillery formations marched into the Beloserje bridgehead west of Tscherkassy, which suggested that the Soviets intended coordinated attacks from the Tscherkassy bridgehead working toward their forces advancing through the breakthrough from the south. A German counterattack conducted on 21 December to restore the situation at Nowo Nikolajewka ran into concentrated heavy artillery and mortar fire, which prevented it from achieving striking success. The only success was the destruction of the exit from a mine south of Kirowograd in which, according to reports, a partisan band of over 800 men had assembled. Troop movements starting on 25 December for *Unternehmen 'Stephan'* [Operation 'Stephan'] suffered from weather-related road problems (ice glare). Aside from the occupation of Jassnyawatkos in the Ingul river sector, action in the next few days was limited to patrols and assault troops and there was no aerial reconnaissance.

That, however, did not prevent the battered German formations from launching attacks with limited objectives, as that of the 3rd *Panzer Korps*, which achieved a notable success against the surprised enemy forces. A concentric attack against enemy forces in the Donino – Kamenka area made rapid forward progress, resulting in capture of the commanding terrain west of Iwanowka and the sector near Bogdanoka. The northern wing of the attack group blocked communications between Fedwar and Jelissawedgradowka. The *Schwerpunkt* of the Soviet resistance was in the Fedwar area, where the Soviets fiercely and stubbornly defended strongly held, well-fortified strongpoints.

It is true that the Soviets regrouped their forces in the area north of Fedwar in light of the looming danger facing them. After suppressing numerous opposing forces the 11th *Panzer Division* attacked into this movement over the Kirowograd – Fedwar road to Hill 101. Elements captured Iwanowka and the main body took the Bogdanowka sector. In difficult street fighting the 6th *Panzer Division* took the strongly-held localities of Lyssyi Chutor, Rasdolje and Bugwarka, the southern wing of the attack reaching the Kirowograd – Fedwar road, the northern wing attaining the high ground north of Rasdolje.

The 3rd *Panzer Division* forced its way into the northern and southern parts of Fedwar and remained in house-to-house combat with isolated enemy groups. An armoured group of the division bypassed Fedwar and blocked the Fedwar – Jelissawetgradowka road.

On 28 December the 3rd *Panzer Division* smashed enemy assembly positions in the woods directly north of Fedwar and took Grigorjewka in heavy fighting. As darkness fell the 3rd *Panzer Division* advanced to the hollow three kilometers northeast of Grigorjewka, there blocking the east-west road to the Soviets.

The initiative appeared to have reverted to the Germans. Weather-related problems with the terrain had a decisive effect on Soviet action but it is probable, however, that the necessary regrouping and troop reinforcements were prevented by enormous losses in armour and infantry. On 30 December this Soviet behaviour worked in favour of the concentric attack by the inner wings of the 3rd *Panzer Korps* and 47th *Panzer Korps*, where this established contact between the German attack groups at the eastern edge of the Fedwar woods. That closed the remaining gap in the front between the two *Korps*. The four-day offensive in the Fedwar area thereby achieved complete success. Soviet losses in this combat area between 27 and 29 December – to the extent that could be determined – amounted to 1,172 prisoners, 15 tanks and assault guns, eight self-propelled antitank guns, 36 guns of various calibers, 149 antitank and antiaircraft guns, 66 mortars of all calibers, 297 machine guns, 115 antitank rifles, numerous machine pistols, hand weapons, lorries, field kitchens and other equipment, two well-stocked ammunition dumps and over 100 horses. The fact that 10,000 mines were lifted or detonated emphasizes the difficulty of the combat conditions.

On 31 December a favorable main line of resistance was established southwest and west of Jelissawetgradowka and cleansing of the northeast portion of the Fedwar woods, whereby numerous additional prisoners were taken and 13 assault guns and 49 antitank guns were left, destroyed, on the battle field.

3

Fighting in the *Heeresgruppe* A Sector

Fighting in and around the Dnjepropetrowsk Frontal Salient
The Dnjepropetrowsk – Saporoshje frontal salient was bounded by the portion of the course of the Dnjepr river that swept in a great bend that reached to the east. That played a role in determining the German line of defense. The fighting in this sector of the front began in the *'Panther Stellung'* ['Panther Position'] that ran along the Dnjepr river from Dnjepropetrowsk to north of Saporoshje, with small bridgeheads on the east bank, then passing over to the *'Wotan Stellung'* to Melitopol and, finally, in a nearly straight line to the Sea of Asov [*Asowsches Meer*]. Initially the troops retreating from the Donez – and Mius fronts, evacuating Burlowka, Stalino, Taganrog, Wolnowacha and Mariupol, occupied this line. The retreat took place in stages, with improvised intermediate positions in which the retreating formations held off pursuing Soviet forces. The divisions arrived in the new positions with greatly reduced complements of personnel, each of them short by several thousand men from their authorized strengths.

See Maps 23 and 24. Map 6 may be useful for geography.

On 20/21 September the formations occupied their new position. The first Soviet reconnaissance thrusts in up to battalion strength immediately ensued. The 9th *Infanterie Division* arrived from the Kuban and occupied a sector in the *'Wotan Stellung'*, later followed by the 370th *Infanterie Division*, which took up position farther south in the Melitopol area.

Already in the forenoon of 26 September the Soviets launched an offensive against the 6th *Armee*, striking the left wing of the 29th *Armee Korps* and right wing of the 4th *Armee Korps*. They attained several penetrations, which were sealed off and later narrowed, in the sector of the 17th *Infanterie Division* and 3rd *Gebirgs Division*, losing ten AFVs. On 28 September the Soviets achieved a deep penetration south of the former German settlement of Heidelberg – later called 'Gendelberg'.[1] The requisite countermeasures resulted in unavoidable intermingling of various division elements. German reconnaissance identified participation on the Soviet side by three armies and four rifle divisions, one tank corps and one motorized mechanized corps, with a total of 14 rifle divisions and six tank-brigades, as well as motorized mechanized brigades with about 300 AFVs. During the five days of heavy fighting at the *'Wotan Stellung'*, despite limited loss of terrain, 181 enemy AFVs were left lying on the battlefield.

---

1 Translator's note – Starting in the time of Peter the Great, colonies of German settlers were encouraged by the Russian Czar (or Czarina) to emigrate to various areas in Russia and found agricultural colonies there. These settlements retained their German language and customs, in many cases, up to the time of the Nazi invasion of Russia, at which point many of the ethnically German residents were removed by the Russians.

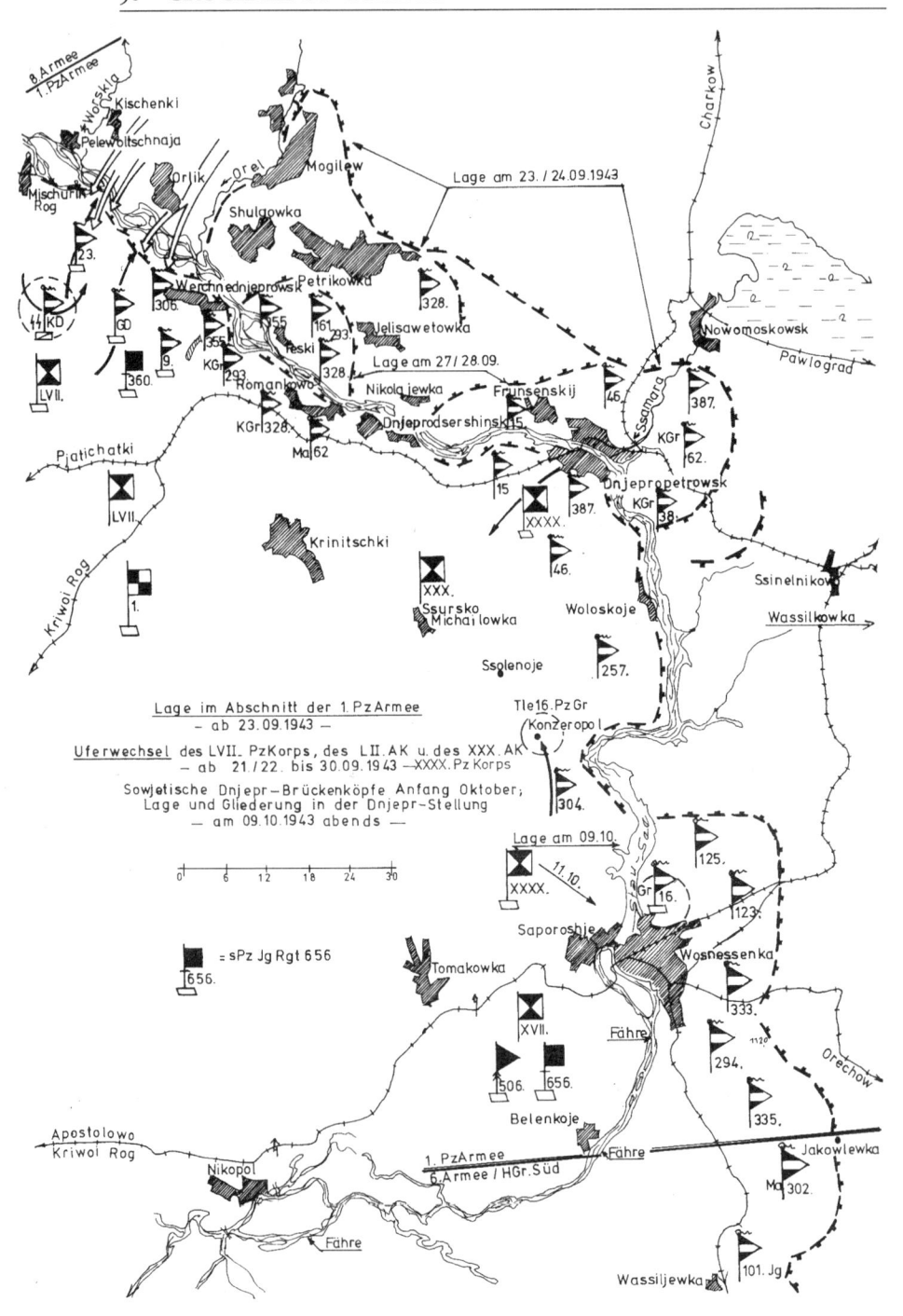

23. Situation in the Sector of the 1st *Panzer Armee* as of 23 September, 1943. Crossing the river by the 57th *Panzer Korps*, the 52nd *Armee Korps*, the 30th *Armee Korps* and the 40th *Panzer Korps* – from 21/22 to 30 September, 1943, Soviet Dnjepr bridgehead at the start of October. Situation and organization in the Dnjepr Position as of 9 October, 1943, evening.

FIGHTING IN THE *HEERESGRUPPE* A SECTOR 99

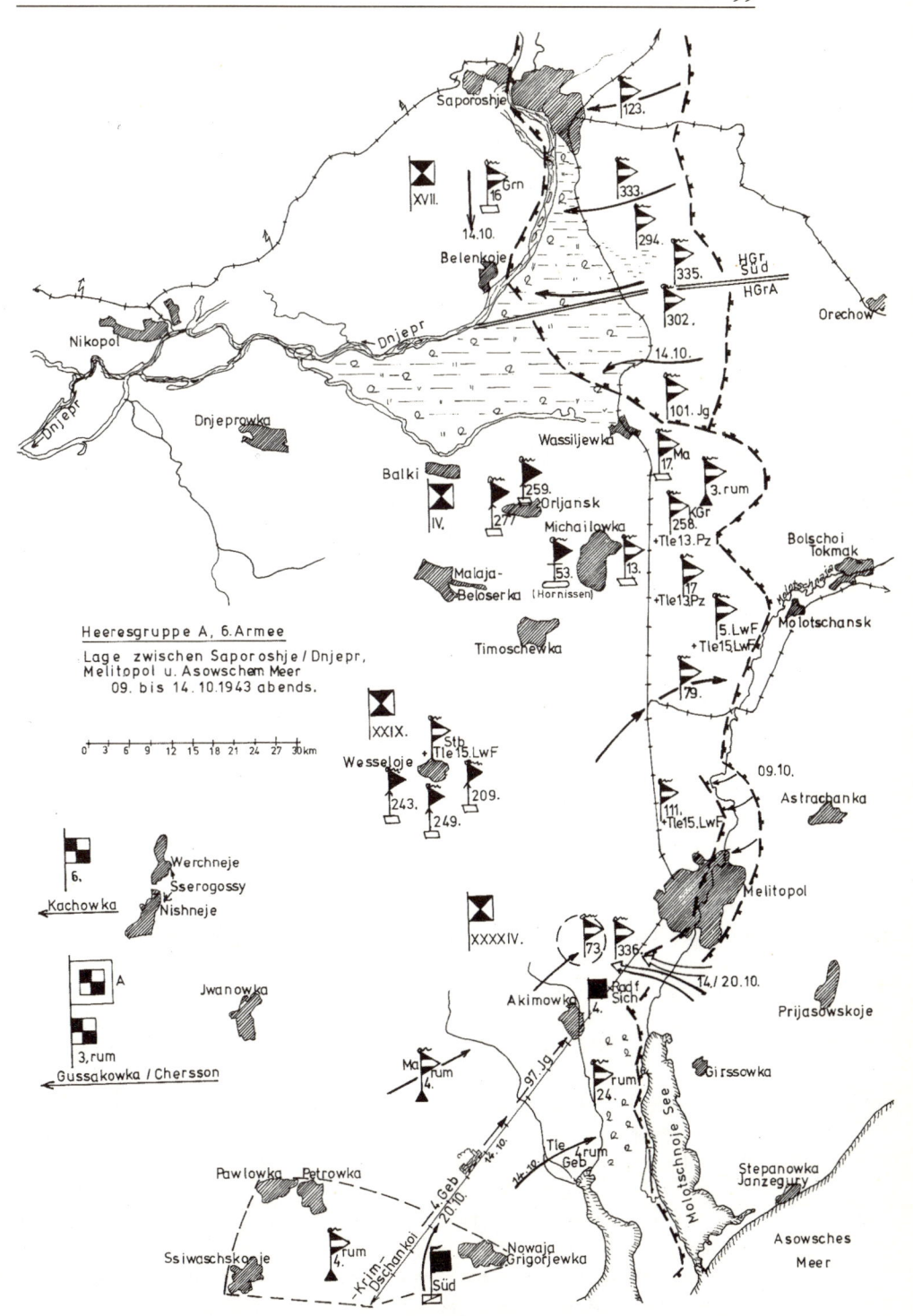

24. *Heeresgruppe* A, 6th *Armee*. Situation between Saproshje/ Dnjepr, Melitopol and Sea of Asov (*Asowsches Meer*) 9 to 14 October, 1943, evening.

The Soviet attempt to break through the new *'Wotan Stellung'*, which was still under construction, failed.

The German command initially counted on bringing in additional German formations as they were freed from the Kuban bridgehead. However, the Soviets, too, gained troops that were freed up there, which could then be employed against the 6th *Armee*. The German command placed great value on holding the *'Wotan Linie'* ['*Wotan*-Line'], since the supply railroad for the 17th *Armee* on the Crimean Peninsula still ran through Melitopol. Hitler desired, regardless, to keep open the possibility of later advancing again from this position into the Donez basin.

See Maps 24 and 25.   Constantly shifting locations of attack, the Soviets attacked in different sectors, one time attacking the 17th *Armee Korps*, the 40th *Panzer Korps*, then the 30th *Armee Korps* or the 4th *Armee Korps* of the 6th *Armee*. On 9 October reconnaissance identified the first Soviet formations that had been brought in from the Kuban, which were attacking the front of the 4th *Armee Korps* and 29th *Armee Korps* of the 6th *Armee*, especially the 258th *Infanterie Division*, 9th *Infanterie Division* and also elements of the 17th *Panzer Division* and 3rd *Gebirgs Division*. At the same time, however, the Soviets also attacked the bridgehead front east of Saporoshje, forcing its forward line back to the center of the city and, finally, all the way to the Dnjepr river. This development finally forced the left wing of the 4th *Armee Korps* of the 6th *Armee* (302nd *Infanterie Division*, 101st *Jäger Division*) to be pulled back in order to conform to the withdrawal of the lines of the right wing of the 17th *Armee Korps* of the 1st *Panzer Armee* (335th *Infanterie Division*). The attack against the adjoining divisions of the 4th *Armee Korps* (19th *Infanterie Division*, 258th *Infanterie Division*, 3rd *Gebirgs Division* and 17th *Panzer Division*) resulted in such significant losses that the combat effectiveness of these formations suffered thereby. These divisions accordingly reconnoitered a new line farther to the rear, the *'Franken' Stellung*, and occupied this on 22 October.

Loss of the *'Franken – Line'*

See Maps 18 and 26.   On 24 October the Soviets broke through south of Melitopol with armour and motorized infantry, thereby putting retention of the *'Franken*-Line' in doubt. There were no rested German formations available with full personnel complements. Eventually the 24th *Panzer Division* arrived from Italy, but *Heeresgruppe Süd* immediately claimed it for other employment, namely, together with the 14th *Panzer Division* under command of the 40th *Panzer Korps*, to fend off the Soviet advance on Kriwoi Rog. Thereupon the 4th *Armee Korps* prepared to evacuate the *'Franken'* position, pulling the line back to a bridgehead position designated *'Brückenkopf* [Bridgehead] *Nikopol'*, to the southeast, in front of the Dnjepr crossings at Nikopol and Bolschaja Lepaticha, effective 28 October. As of 3 December the formations employed there were placed under the command of *General* Schörner, under the designation *'Gruppe General Schörner'* (40th *Panzer Korps*). At the same time as this development the Soviets advanced over the Dnjepr river northwest of Dnjepropetrowsk. There the Soviets had already advanced to Kirowograd, as described above, and forced their way south from the northern front of the Dnjepropetrowsk frontal salient,

FIGHTING IN THE *HEERESGRUPPE* A SECTOR 101

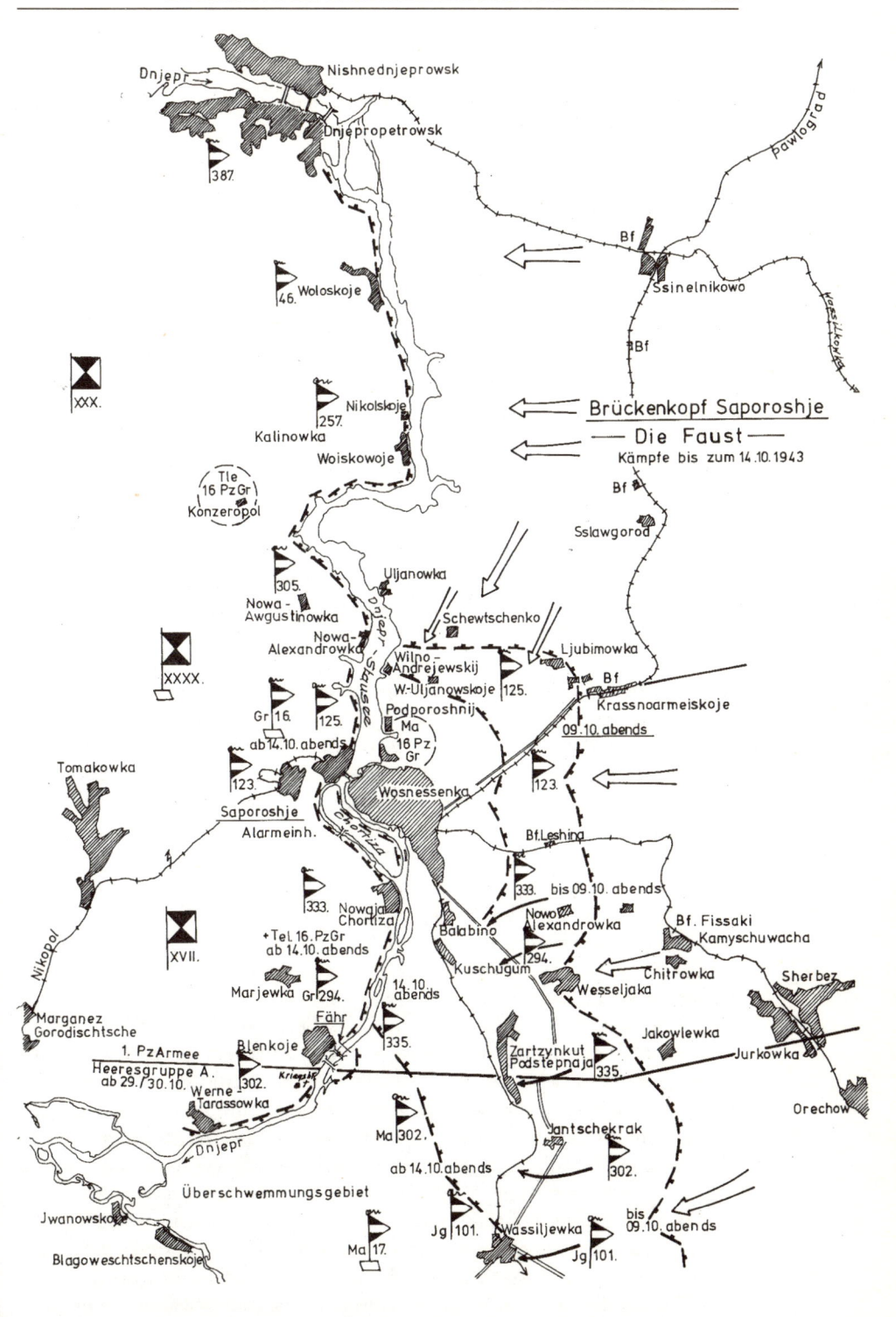

25. Saporoshje Bridgehead, The Fist. Action until 14 October, 1943.

doing this in coordination with the advance against the Nikopol bridgehead – this without negatively influencing the Soviet operations toward the west against Kirowograd and Kriwoi Rog. There, too, came the accustomed shifts in attack *Schwerpunkte*, shifting from the right wing of the 8th *Armee* to the left wing of the 1st *Panzer Armee*, in addition against the lines of the 1st *Panzer Armee*, and these attacks again linked with the advance against the Nikopol bridgehead (17th *Armee Korps*). Each time the Soviets alternated, attacking first in one sector, then in another, and so far as they attacked the northern front of the frontal salient (30th *Armee Korps*), again linked with attacks from the south against the Nikopol bridgehead, they attacked simultaneously the point of the German frontal salient at Saporoshje.

Timely reconnaissance of such operations led immediately to the movements of German forces that the Soviets obviously intended. The German command sent motorized mobile 'fire brigades', to the extent that these were available, into sectors that were exposed to an imminent Soviet attack. In light of the lack of rail lines that were usable for German troop movements, all movements had to be made by road. Softened or mud-bound routes required multiples of the normal fuel consumption and valuable time. In light of the German logistical difficulties over single-track partisan-endangered railroad lines it seems amazing that supplies actually arrived, even though only a trickle, but, in the end, barely sufficient. The Soviets, on the other hand, suffered from no concerns about fuel, and also were favored by good mobility thanks to the substantial number of American Studebaker lorries with multiple low-range gears and all-wheel drive. In precisely that mud-bound or apparently bottomless terrain the Soviets could shift their formations from one sector to another faster than the Germans, even though they had greater distances to cover than the German formations, which had the advantage of 'interior lines' in the Saporoshje frontal salient. In addition it was evident that the Soviets did not make frontal attacks on the defensive fronts their reconnaissance identified as a matter of course. Rather, they counted on binding German forces, as at the point of the German frontal salient at Saporoshje. They preferred to keep their advance on two axes, as in the attacks against the Nikopol bridgehead, with alternating or simultaneous attacks in the area of the 30th *Armee Korps*, and that, again, in alternation with advances of the spearhead of the Soviet 'wedge' toward Kriwoi Rog.

Shortening of the Saporoshje frontal salient would certainly have freed up a series of divisions, with whose help the other sectors could have been strengthened. Hitler, however, insisted that this salient had to be held. *Generalfeldmarschall* von Manstein flirted with this plan, based on the considerations that by holding a frontal salient both south of the Dnjepr, before Nikopol, as well as north of the Dnjepr, aggressive blows could be struck against the Soviets. Hitler, however, based his insistence primarily on continued utilization of the manganese ore mines, upon which the German armaments industry greatly depended, and planned a later advance to Perekop to reestablish contact with the 17th *Armee* on the Crimean peninsula.

The limited provision of fighting personnel caused *General* Schörner to ruthlessly comb out soldiers in the rear areas of his sector. He noticed that the staffs were still fully manned, which did not correspond to the diminution of strength in the trenches. He sent the 'combed out' personnel to the front. He carried out the same 'combing out' among the train troops, even though, as a rule, the train personnel consisted of older fathers of families without prior military service (members of so-called 'white age-groups') who were barely usable for service at the front. Schörner, however, grasped extremely harshly in the rear areas and did everything possible to provide logistical support for the troops in the foremost trenches.

Soviet Attack on the German 'Fist' near Saporoshje

In the meantime the Soviets had created a substantial frontal salient reaching to the west toward Krowograd, so that the German frontal salient to Saporoshje resembled a forward-reaching clenched fist. This course of the front stimulated the Soviets to attack it at the waist in order to cut off the salient. That attack would be linked with attacks at Saporoshje against the point of the salient to fix the German defensive forces there.

See Map 25 and, for geography, Map 18.

The only reserve in this 'fist' was the 16th *Panzergrenadier Division*. Elements of the 24th *Panzer Division* were, likewise, in addition to its commitment in the Nikopol bridgehead, assigned for commitment in the 'fist'. The mission of the formations consisted of immediately attacking penetrating enemy forces and restoring the old main line of resistance in hasty counterattack, whereupon the troops that had been holding that portion of the line would resume holding it.

It is true that the Soviet troops had also suffered during the aggressive combat of the previous months, but they were continually increased with newly arrived formations and reinforcements. The state of training of the Soviet infantry, however, proved to be inadequate. Repeatedly the Red Army had thrown untrained replacements right in amongst the fighting troops. Soviet combat methods were still characterized by ruthless commitment of masses of men. In addition to that it was evident that the lower and middle levels of command proved energetic and had gained in skill, even though, in German estimation, they were inferior to the German command in rapid grasp of new situations and flexible decision making.

A notably strengthened level of artillery served to make up for this deficiency in the state of training of the Soviet infantry. Entire divisions of artillery with guns of all current calibers were employed at *Schwerpunkte*. Soviet armoured forces, fully manned and well equipped, also supported nearly every Soviet attack, generally driving in line formation in order to avoid attack on the sensitive sides of the AFVs and present only the well armoured fronts to the German defense. The well armoured T 34, extremely adept at maneuvering on the terrain, also proved superior in firepower and mobility to the German tanks. The command of the Soviet armoured formations, however, suffered from a deficiency in radio equipment. Equipping with voice radio apparatus only extended down to the company commanders. Employment of armour, thus, followed a schematic plan laid down before the attack that extended right down to the individual AFV, without any possibility of requisite rapid decisions at the lower levels.

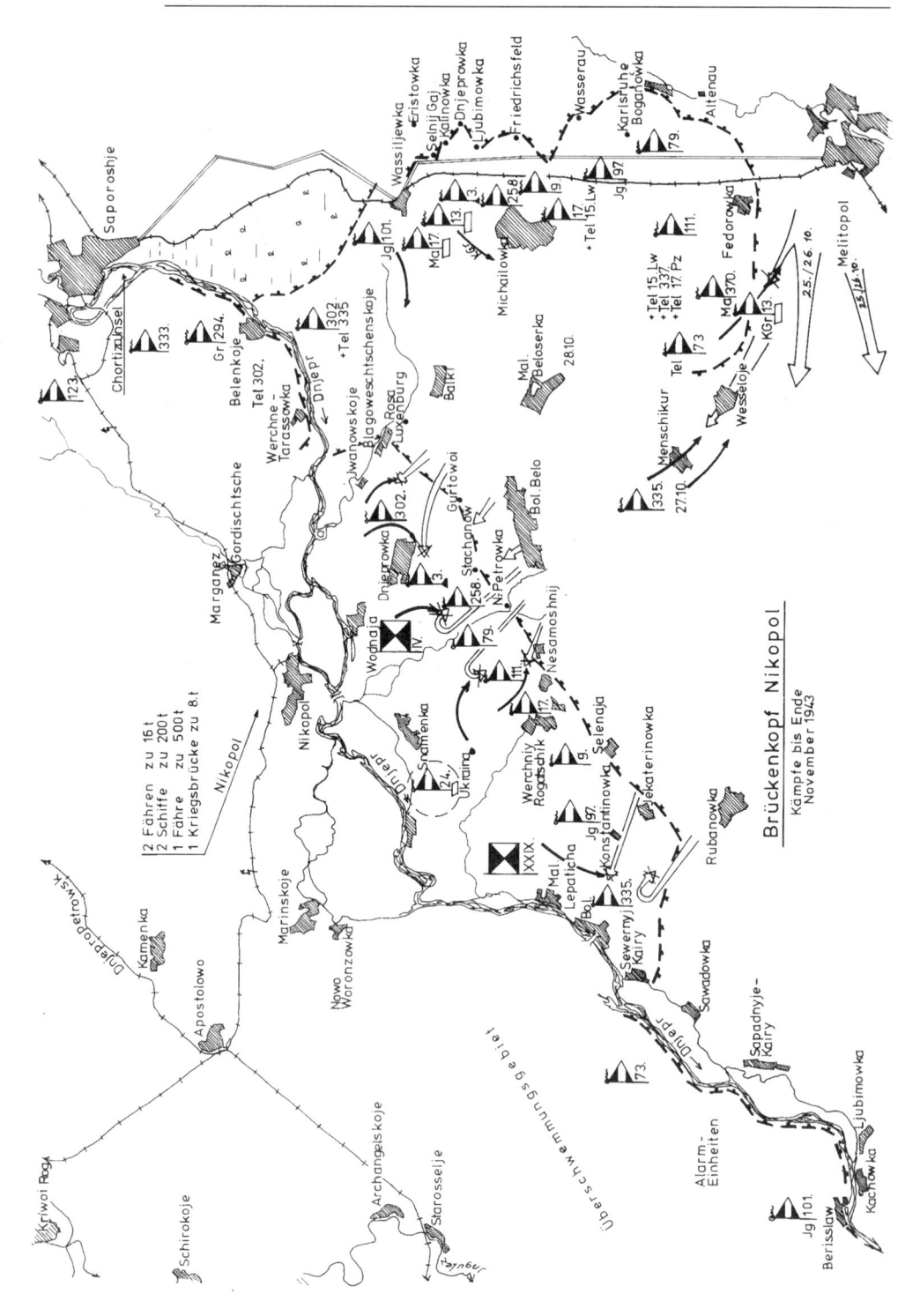

26. Nikopol Bridgehead. Action until the end of November, 1943.

FIGHTING IN THE *HEERESGRUPPE* A SECTOR

In support of the attacks delivered from the Dnjepr bridgehead between Koleberda and Litwinowka, on 8/9 October the Soviets attacked the German bridgehead in front of Saporoshje – the 'fist'. The 40th *Panzer Korps* commanded the northern sector, the 17th *Armee Korps* the southern.

The Soviets succeeded in cutting off the Bridgehead from the north and in splitting it in the center with powerful attacks against the 123rd *Infanterie Division*. Therefore both *Korps* evacuated the Saporoshje bridgehead by 14 October while retaining, however, possession of the Chortiza island. As of 14 October the front ran south from Belenkoje via Wassiljewka to Melitopol. After the later breakthrough at Melitopol on 25/26 October 1943 the left wing of the 6th *Armee* also had to fall back whereupon, on 28/29 October, the Nikopol bridgehead, with the ensuing fighting, existed for about 100 days. *See Map 26.*

On 25/26 October the Soviet attack started from the bridgehead between Litwinowka and Dnjepropetrowsk. As the Soviet formations succeeded in attacking over the Dnjepr south of Dnjepropetrowsk, the 30th *Armee Korps* also had to fall back to the south, eventually establishing contact with the 17th *Armee Korps* in the area northwest of Tschumaki. *See Map 14.*

See Map 28 for geography.

From this time forth the Soviets attempted to advance simultaneously toward Nikopol from the north and from the south, also advancing in the area south of Saporoshje, between Nowaja Chortiza and Belenkoje. There they built by surprise a ten kilometer wide bridgehead and broke through to the northwest in the sector of the 333rd *Infanterie Division* to Pawlowka, which was 15 kilometers distant. The Germans lacked forces to eliminate this bridgehead. During the period from 5 December to 26 December all that could be accomplished was to thwart Soviet attempts to widen the bridgehead or to break through. The situation came to a head for the 123rd *Infanterie Division* before Saporoshje and the 257th *Infanterie Division* in the Tschumaki sector. The counterattack by a *Kampfgruppe* of the 24th *Panzer Division* made no progress in the much-dissected terrain, secured with mines and flanking antiaircraft guns, that favoured the Soviet defense. Granted, the *Panzergrenadiere* reached their assigned objective, but, lacking support by German armour, they again had to give up their positions. *For geography see Maps on 25 and 26.*

Fate of the Nikopol Bridgehead

Against the Nikopol bridgehead the Soviets employed the 4th Ukrainian Front with the 44th, 5th Assault and 3rd Guards Armies, each army with two to four corps, each corps with two to five infantry divisions. In addition there were the 4th Guards Motorized Mechanized Corps and the 19th Tank Corps, with over 600 AFVs.

The Soviets now changed their tactics. The Soviets abandoned penetrations in the main line of resistance with advances by fast-driving armour-supported infantry, as well as the tactic of a slow breakthrough-advance with armour supported infantry. These tactics had not proven successful and offered opportunities for German formations to attack the flanks of such advancing wedges. Instead, the Soviets launched their attacks on a broader front with shorter-range objectives, thus striving for no more than a shift of the main line of resistance toward the Germans. They continued to support their attacks with numerous AFVs, against which the German divisions holding the positions lacked adequate defenses in the form of antitank guns or armour. The German artillery could only attempt to separate the enemy infantry from the armour with blocking barrages because the Soviet tank crews felt vulnerable without infantry. They saw themselves exposed to individual attack by German infantrymen who had allowed the tanks to run over their positions.

As soon as the Soviets had forced the German main line of resistance back in a sector of the front they organized the line they had achieved, securing it immediately with a *Pak-Front* [organized, mutually supporting array of antitank guns with infantry support] to meet the counter-attacking forces of the 24th *Panzer Division* that they had learned, by experience, to expect in short order.

See Maps 26 and 27.

It was advantageous to the Soviets that the terrain of the bridgehead was marked with two large eroded ravines running from the southeast to the northwest, the *'Rogatschik – Schlucht'* [*Schlucht* = ravine] and the *'Belosserka – Schlucht'*. These complicated lateral shifts of German reserves, especially in wet weather, for the rain in this black-earth terrain rapidly transformed the ground into bottomless mud that greatly interfered with the mobility of motorized forces. The two military bridges to the bridgehead, over which the entire logistical support traffic of both *Korps* ran, were at Bolschaja Lepaticha and Nikopol. As they still strove for breakthroughs, the Soviets locally succeeded

See Map 26.

in achieving deep penetrations, as, on 20 November, west of the Belosserka ravine with armoured forces consisting of about 100 T 34 tanks. While these advanced to the firing positions of the divisions holding the position, the Soviets also attacked in the Wesselyj – Nesmoshnik area, supported by ground-attack aircraft and fighters, which interfered with German movements by strafing and dropping a thick carpet of small high-explosive bombs – without interference by the German *Luftwaffe*, whose airfields west of the Dnjepr were often covered by ground fog.

Several *Panzerjäger* of the *'Ferdinand'* type, equipped with 8.8 cm antitank guns, made their debut in the Soviet offensive on 12 November. The resulting heavy losses in men and equipment may well have caused the Soviets initially to halt their attack. After they had abandoned their old tactic of attempting breakthroughs in depth, the Soviets made good use of the extensive fields of maize and millet. The latter, with their spaced rows of crops, offered good concealment for deeply organized field fortifications. An offensive advance against the occupants of such positions proved difficult, the more so since the terrain did not permit observation by German observers directing heavy weapons, without preventing the Soviets from employing their heavy weapons. Employment of large numbers of antitank guns in these maize fields occasioned heavy losses of German armour. The 24th *Panzer Division*, therefore, shifted over to attacking after darkness fell, the more so since the darkness denied the Soviets their superiority in weapons and forced them to rely upon their infantry. The German infantry continued to prove technically superior to the Soviet infantry.

The capture of such a maize field by the I./ *Panzergrenadier Regiment* 26 caused heavy Soviet losses. After several days wait, the Soviets attacked with a

FIGHTING IN THE *HEERESGRUPPE* A SECTOR

great mass of factory-new armour, achieving an initial penetration, in which they lost 60 AFVs and, finally, had to fall back to their jump-off positions. On 19 December the Soviets finally attacked the German bridgehead south of Nikopol, with a simultaneous attack against the 30th *Armee Korps* of the 1st *Panzer Armee*. In both sectors the Soviet command set Nikopol as the objective for their troops. In any case, after brief refitting of their troops, the Soviets attacked with local artillery preparations. Elements of the 24th *Panzer Division*, immediately thrown into the battle, blocked the assault, especially in the sector of the 258th *Infanterie Division* – knocking out 81 enemy AFVs, a total of destruction that bears witness to the intensity of the fighting.

The main body of the 24th *Panzer Division* then shifted to Krassnogrigorjewka (northeast of Nikopol) because the high command expected a breakthrough southwest of Saporoshje. From there the 24th *Panzer Division* had the opportunity of attacking such a breakthrough near Marjewka directly in the left flank. The commitment, however proved unnecessary, since the 123rd *Infanterie Division* initially continued to hold its positions. Only at the year's end did the 123rd *Infanterie Division* and the 257th *Infanterie Division* fall back to the west in the face of overwhelming enemy pressure. For geography see Map 25.

In the Nikopol bridgehead the Soviets first tried to capture the Dnjepr bridge at Bolschaja – Lepaticha in the sector of the 29th *Armee Korps*. At the same time they attacked anew on the opposite side, namely the northern front of the 30th *Armee Korps*, with strong forces in the Tschumaki and Medelejewka area, with three rifle divisions, one independent tank brigade and two brigades. *Kampfgruppen* hastily thrown together from rear-area troops and men returning from leave launched a counterattack in the darkness and surprised the Soviets, thereby delaying the Soviet advance. See Map 28 and, for geography, Map 26.

On the southern front, in the Ljubimowka area, the Soviets achieved a penetration that offered them the opportunity to deploy in the ravine-terrain north of Tschapojewo and west of the Bol. Belosserka – Dnjeproska highway. Both *Kampfgruppen* of the 24th *Panzer Division* attacked despite bad weather conditions along with remnant elements of the 258th *Infanterie Division*, intercepting the thrust and sealing it off with strongpoints. See Map 28 and, for geography, Map 26.

On the next day the Soviets continued in their plan to breakthrough toward Nikopol from the north and south with attacks in battalion and regimental strength against the lines of the 17th *Armee Korps* and the right wing of the 111th *Infanterie Division* of the 29th *Armee Korps*, which, after a reorganization of command, was now attached to the 1st *Panzer Armee*. A ground-attack plane and artillery *Schwerpunkt* became evident against the 258th *Infanterie Division* of the 29th *Armee Korps*. A *Kampfgruppe* of the 24th *Panzer Division* that came to the assistance of the 258th *Infanterie Division*, despite knocking out 20 Soviet AFVs, was unable in the steppe-like open terrain to gain any ground in a frontal attack. On 21 December other elements of the 24th *Panzer Division* brought enemy attacking formations to a standstill. On that day, however, a 700 meter wide gap in the front remained, guarded by artillery and heavy weapons. An attack into the enemy flank from the 3rd *Gebirgs Division* sector was enticing, but had to remain undelivered due to shortage of forces.

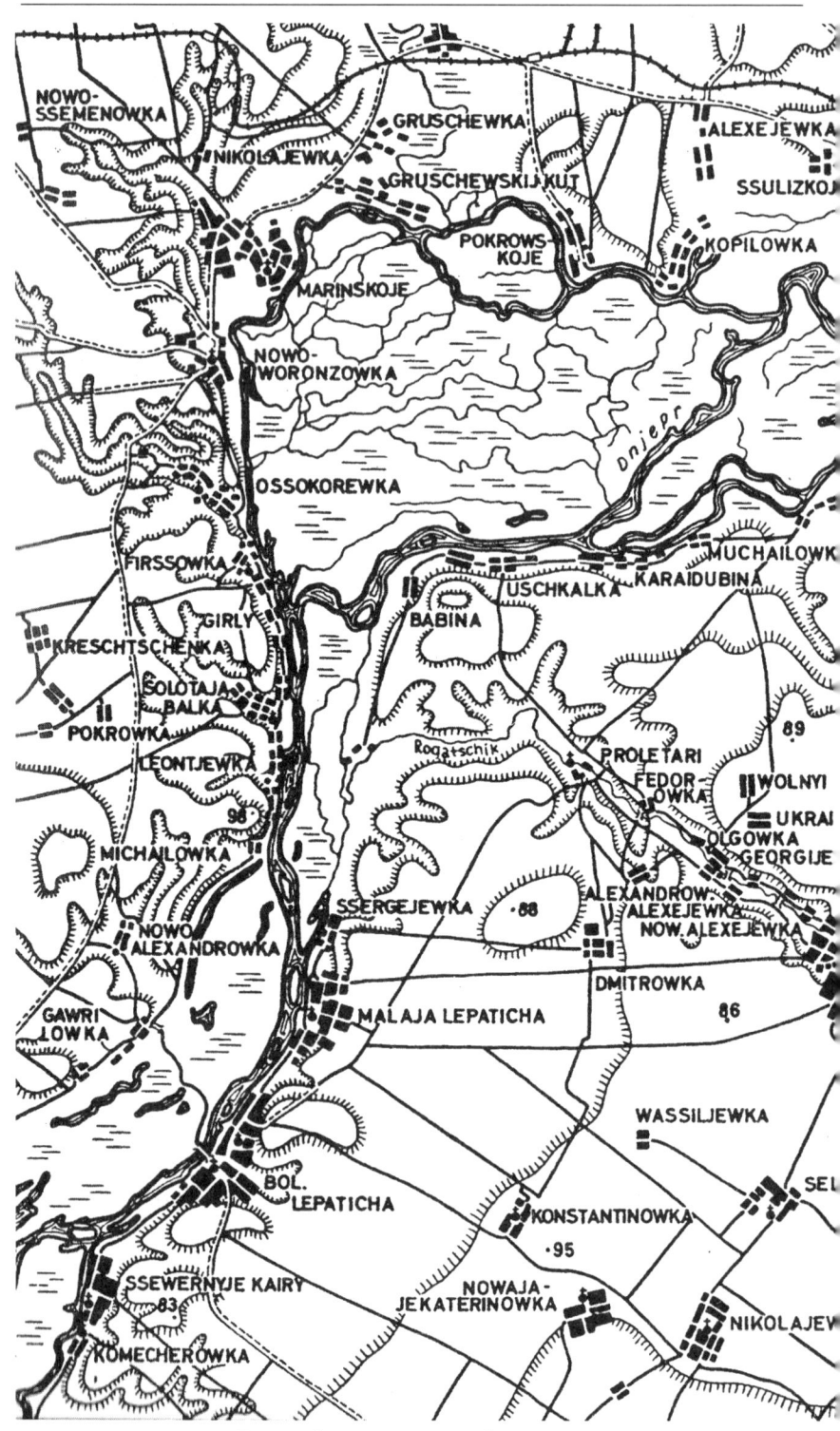

27. Excerpt from *Heeres* Map sheet X49/Y47.

FIGHTING IN THE *HEERESGRUPPE* A SECTOR

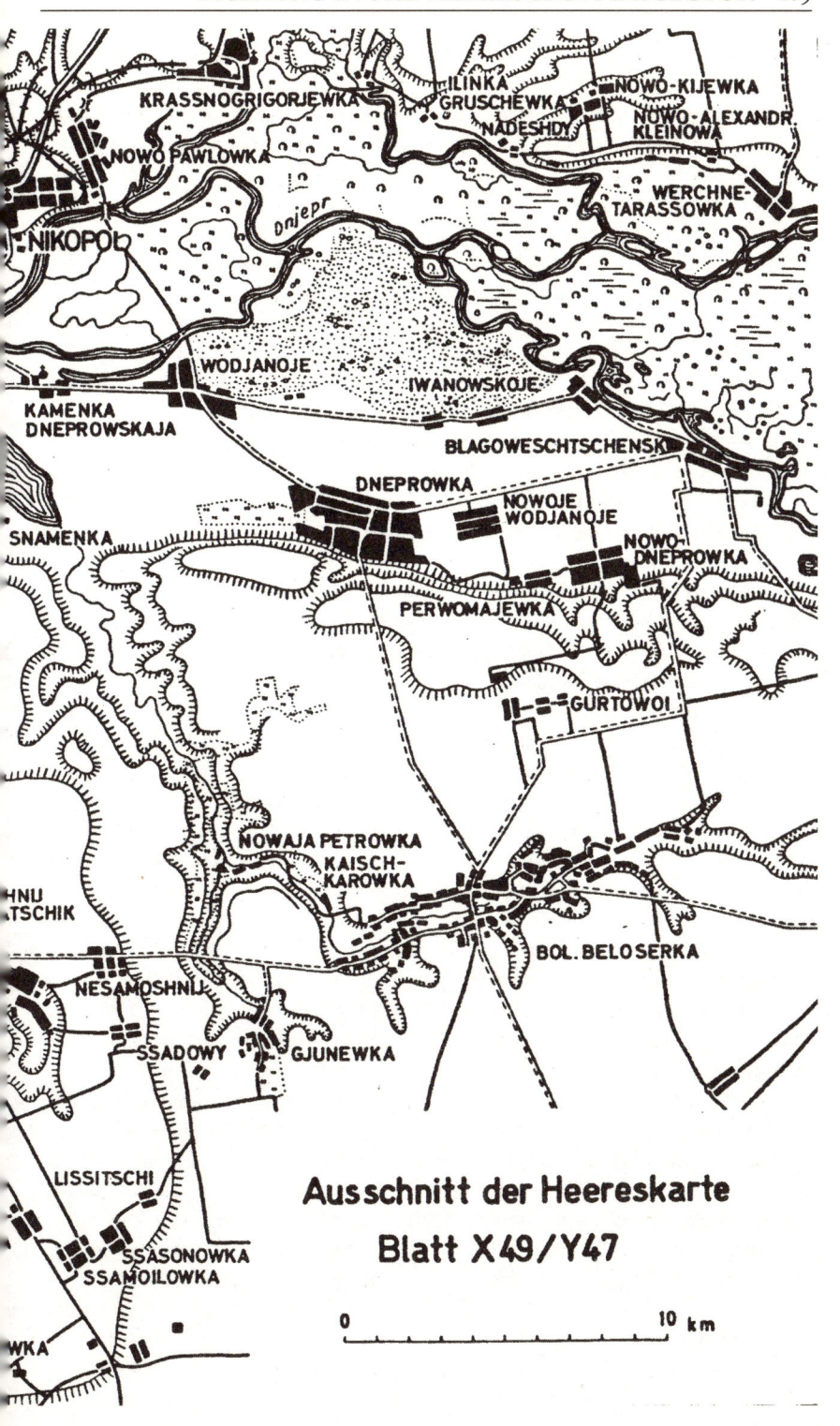

Ausschnitt der Heereskarte
Blatt X49/Y47

0   10 km

Heeresgruppe Süd issued guidelines for further combat: 'Spare the infantry! Make up for weakness with heavy infantry weapons, artillery and air!'

See Map 26.

In the ensuing days enemy armour broke through at the boundary between the 258th *Infanterie Division* and the 3rd *Gebirgs Division*, which led to a temporary crisis in that sector. A hasty counterattack by elements of the 24th *Panzer Division* eliminated that danger, knocking out 27 enemy AFVs. Simultaneously the artillery of the 111th *Infanterie Division* took the attackers under flanking fire. An afternoon Soviet attack also foundered with the loss of 64 AFVs and 11 aircraft. The Soviets started the final assault with strong infantry forces and about 40 AFVs against the front of the 258th *Infanterie Division* and 3rd *Gebirgs Division*. It turned into eventful hand-to-hand combat. This penetration came to an end in the depth of the main defensive area. The defending units then regained their old main line of resistance. Thereupon the Soviets let things rest. To that point they had failed to attain their objective, elimination of the Nikopol bridgehead.

The Soviets started the new year quietly, first attacking on 12 January between the Belosserka ravine and the highway to Dnjeprowka anew on a broad front with infantry. The penetration that they achieved was eliminated in a night-attack and the old main line of resistance regained. Another attack met the same fate on 14 January in the *'Hufeisen'* [horseshoe] ravine south of Dnjeprowka. Night attack German with armour had, as explained above, proven advantageous, but failed in the night of 16/17 January, where three German *Sturmgeschütze* that were knocked out and set ablaze cast so much light on the battlefield that the enemy antitank guns could spot the German armour.

Despite all the above, the Soviets succeeded with their later 'salami tactic', which was a surprise attack with overwhelming forces, in repeatedly forcing short sectors of the German main line of resistance back, securing this line against armoured counterattacks with antitank forces that were brought up and thus, a bit at a time, dangerously gnawing their way into the bridgehead.

The 24th *Panzer Division* eventually had to be withdrawn from the Nikopol bridgehead to start the march north to open the Tscherkassy *Kessel*. The Soviets utilized the opportunity for a new attack on 1 February, coming from the north along the Busuluk with the 4th Guards Motorized Mechanized Corps and the 4th and 29th Guards Rifle Corps, north of Woronzowka in order to cut off *Gruppe Schörner* in the bridgehead and elements of the 6th *Armee* north of Nikopol from their rear connections. Strong Soviet forces captured Apolstolowo and forced their way as far as Bolschaja-Kostromka. Encirclement of the German forces which had not been evacuated from the bridgehead in timely fashion thereby appeared inevitable. In that situation, the 24th *Panzer Division*, which was, at that time, on its way northward, received orders to turn around and head south. However, it did not arrive until the Soviets and already substantially 'cleared out' the formations of the 6th *Armee* in its rear area. Thus the 24th *Panzer Division* lost almost all its logistical elements and

FIGHTING IN THE *HEERESGRUPPE* A SECTOR

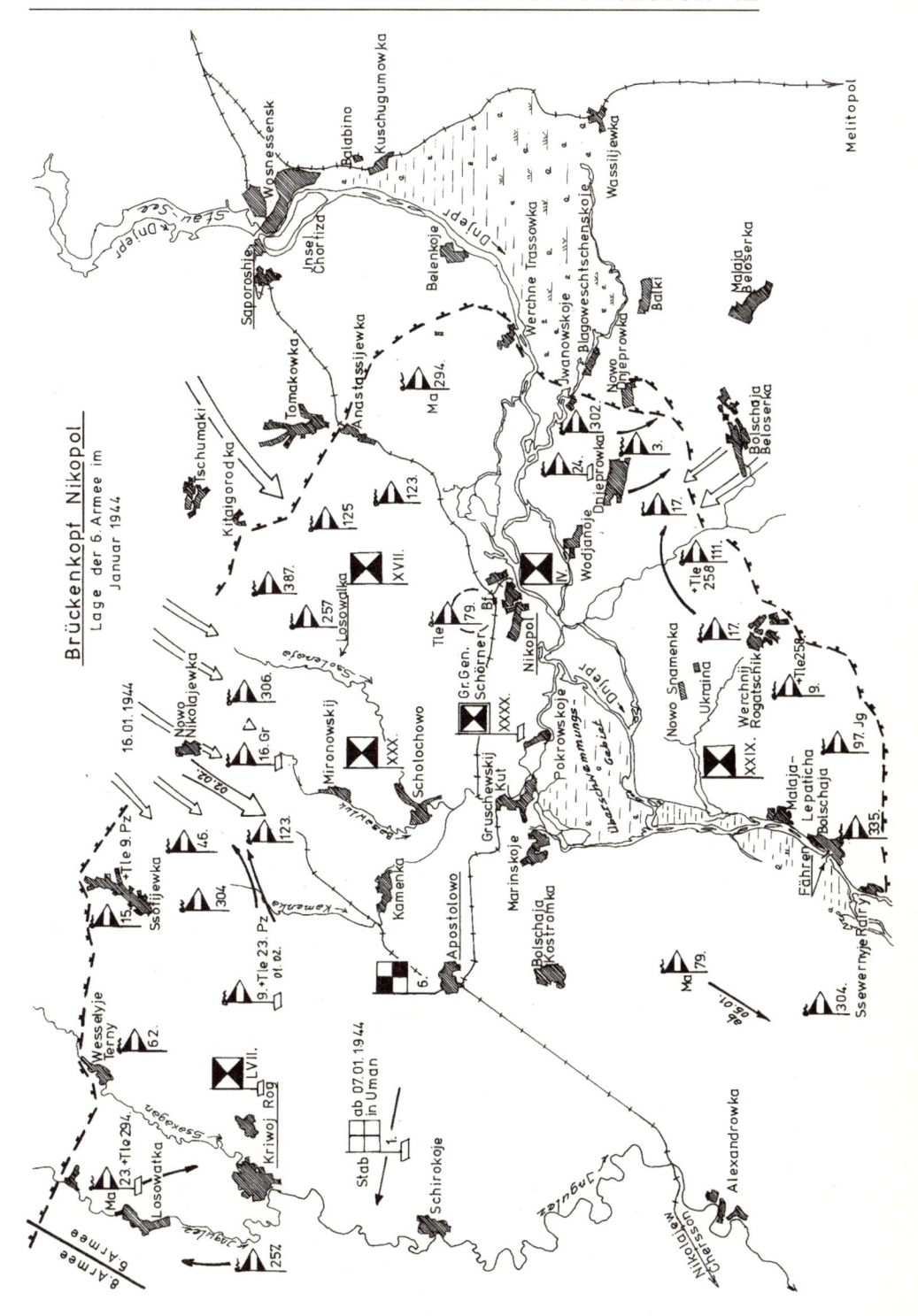

28. Nikopol Bridgehead. Situation of the 6th *Armee* in January, 1944.

had to receive logistical assistance that had been converted to horse-drawn columns through the adjoining division.²

Critique of the Fighting in the Nikopol Bridgehead

In light of the weakened condition of the infantry divisions, the defensive successes that had been achieved must be regarded as astonishing. In the fighting retreats of the summer of 1943 the divisions had lost an essential part of their fighting strength and heavy weapons. The battalions averaged 200 men. The divisions were committed in the front line without reserves. With fronts of up to 12 kilometers per division, the front line could only be thinly held in a series of strong points.

With consideration of the greatly increased mobility of the Soviets as a result of lorries provided by the Americans the German infantry divisions, as a rule, no longer received active missions. As a result of their personnel strength and limited mobility they were no longer capable of such. As it had been in the Kriwoi Rog area, so, in the Nikopol bridgehead, only *Panzer Divisionen* could be employed for offensive operations. They, alone, had armoured forces and the requisite mobility to react immediately and effectively to Soviet operations. One cannot forget the great number of AFVs that supported the Soviets in every attack, against which the German infantry divisions, without armour of their own, were defenseless, limited to infantry type anti-tank methods.

All of these defensive successes, especially in the Nikopol bridgehead, but also in the Saporoshje 'Fist', as earlier in the fighting around Kirowograd, were only possible because of extraordinarily sensible reconnaissance and a sensitive, flexible conduct of the combat. The Soviets would have been able to break through rigid fronts without difficulty, without significant German reserves to stop them in the hinterland. The *Kampfgruppen* of the individual *Panzer Divisionen* –here the 24th *Panzer Division* –took on the mission of these reserves, operating with extreme flexibility to attack the flanks of the enemy thrusts or to cut them off from their connections with the rear. Such defensive successes could only be achieved as long as Hitler did not interfere in the mobile conduct of the fighting by the *Heeresgruppe* and *Armeen* with orders to hold in place. The refusal to allow the evacuation of salients so often requested by *Heeresgruppe Süd* repeatedly bound the hands of the *Heeresgruppe* command and negatively impacted the mobility that was the only successful tactic remaining, given the existing force ratios, often leading to heavy losses, as

---

2 Formations employed in the Nikopol Bridgehead:
    29th *Armee Korps*   335th *Infanterie Division*
                            9th *Infanterie Division*
                            97th *Jäger Division*
    4th *Armee Korps*   17th *Infanterie Division*
                            111th *Infanterie Divsion*
                            79th *Infanterie Division*
                            24th *Panzer Division*
                            258th *Infanterie Division*
                            302nd *Infanterie Division*
                            3rd *Gebirgs Division*
In order to insure unified command in this area, both *Korps* were attached to the *Generalkommando* [command structure] of the 40th *Panzer Korps* and formed '*Gruppe Schörner*'.

FIGHTING IN THE *HEERESGRUPPE* A SECTOR 113

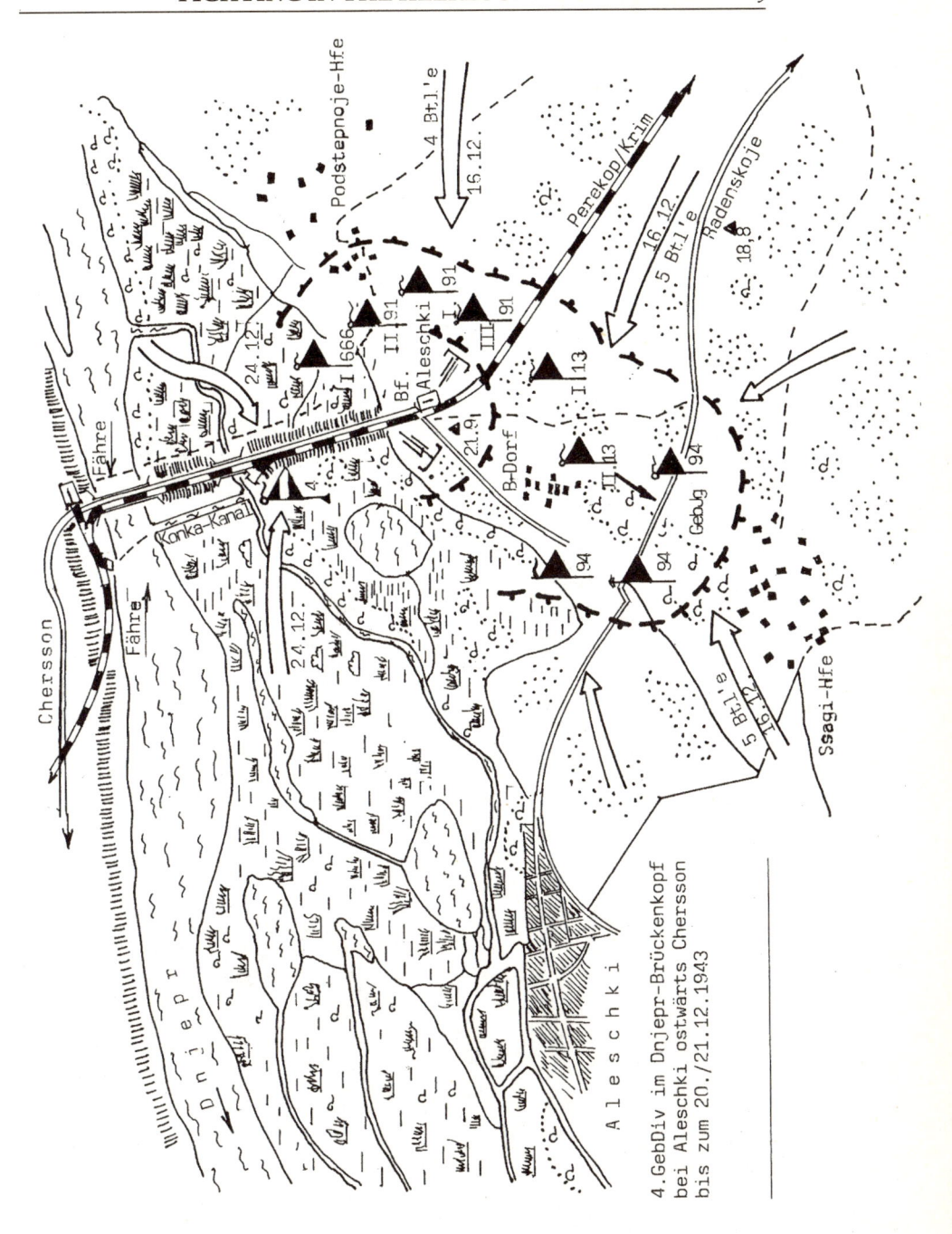

29. 4th *Gebirgs Division* in the Dnjepr Bridgehead at Aleschki
east of Chersson until 20/21 December, 1943.

114 **CRUCIBLE OF COMBAT**

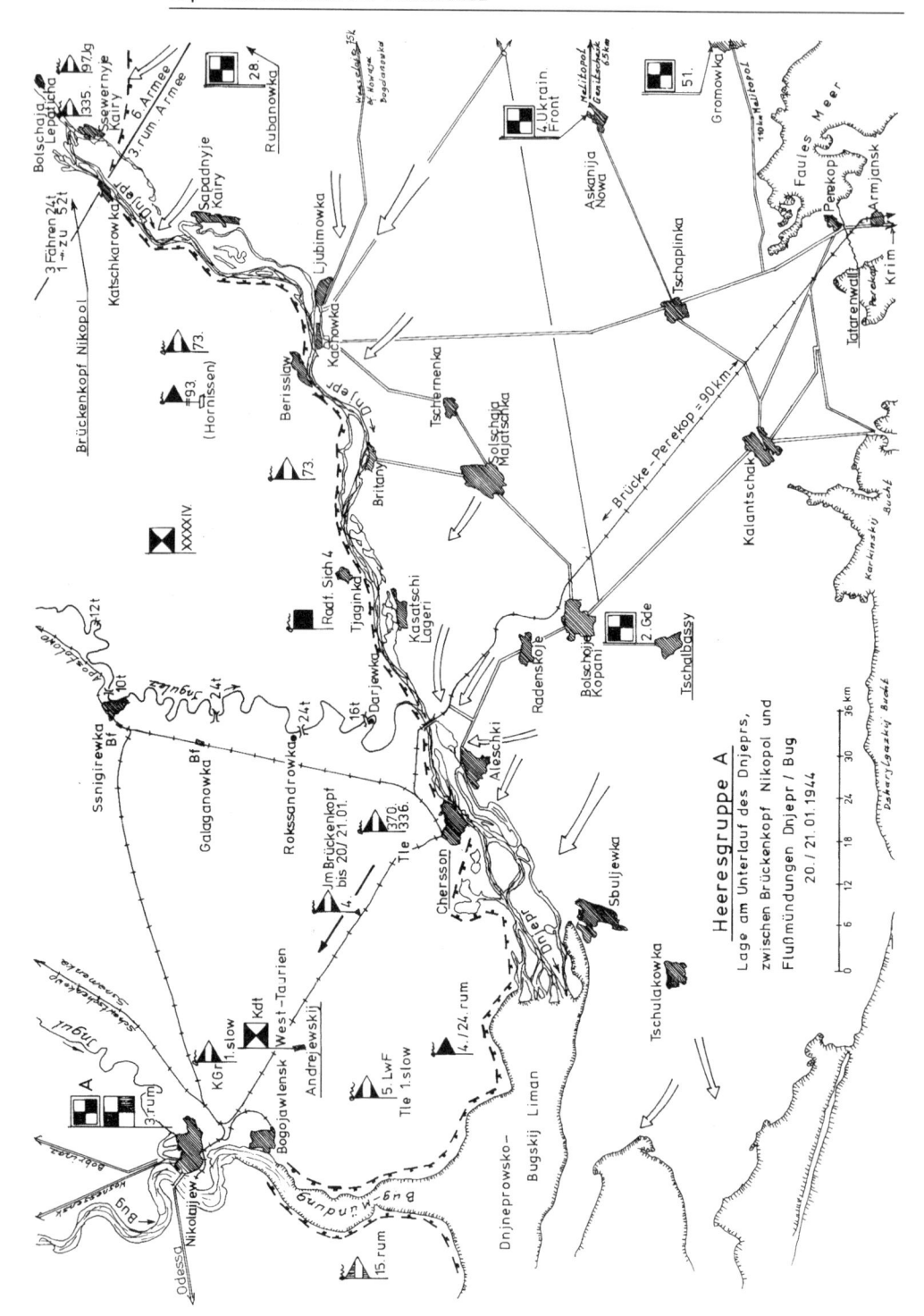

30. *Heeresgruppe* A. Situation on the lower course of the Dnjepr between the Nikopol Bridgehead and the mouths of the Dnjepr and the Bug, 20/21 January, 1944.

FIGHTING IN THE *HEERESGRUPPE* A SECTOR

at the Tscherkassy *Kessel* and, later, at *'Fester Platz'* Tarnopol, but also where retreat was forbidden at the Saporoshje 'Fist' or the Nikopol bridgehead.

The Chersson Bridgehead

For an overview of the situation developing at the start of the new year it is necessary to look in the adjoining sector of the 6th *Armee* of *Heeresgruppe* A, in the Chersson bridgehead. The Soviets had advanced through the Nogaische Steppe west of Melitopol to the west, not only to exert pressure on and capture the Nikopol bridgehead, but also, farther to the west, to capture the bridgehead held, essentially, by the 4th *Gebirgs Division* across from the city of Chersson.

See Maps 29, 30 and 78.

The significance of this bridgehead lay in the fact that, during the time of occupation, a sturdy bridge had been build over the mighty river to replace the

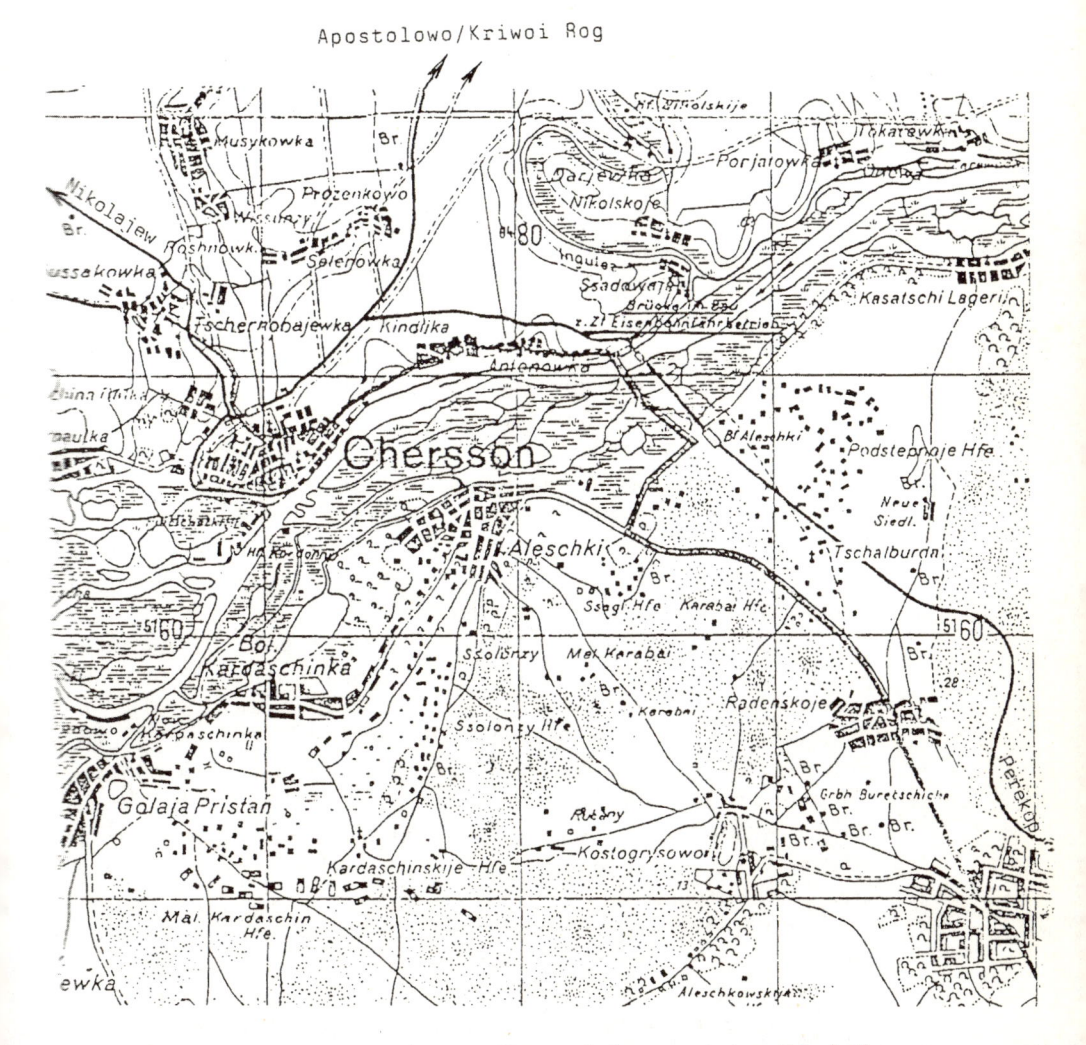

78. Bridgehead at Chersson. Chersson before completion of the bridge and the connection to the Chersson – Nikolajew *Rollbahn*.

previous railroad-ferry traffic, extending the railroad line to the southeast via Radenskoje to Perekop to the Crimean Peninsula. This bridge would provide the Soviets with good transportation, especially logistical support, for their advance on Odessa. That was something the German command wanted to prevent at any cost. Initially, however, it was a matter of threading the German formations that were arriving out of the Nogaische Steppe through the 'eye of the needle' of that railroad bridge. Those forces included *Heeres* formations, two Rumanian divisions and a great number of *Armee* and *Korps* units with a total of 15,000 motor vehicles and 15,000 horse-drawn vehicles. The 4th *Gebirgs Division* secured the retreat of those forces and also the evacuation of a great mass of railroad matériel and valuable supplies by holding the bridgehead.

See Map 29.

This bridgehead took in a semicircle approximately 20 kilometers in diameter around the railroad bridge and the Aleschki railroad station. After the retreating columns that had formed such a traffic jam had cleared the area, the 4th *Gebirgs Division* held the bridgehead position with inadequate personnel, about 30 to 50 men per company, with strongpoints or in a security fashion. That was to hold open the possibility of later advancing anew from the bridgehead to the Crimean peninsula. The division was supported by the I./*Grenadier Regiment* 666 [370th *ID*], 370th *Infanterie Division, schwere Feld Haubitze Abteilung* [heavy field-howitzer battalion] 607, I./*Flak – Abteilung* 32, *Panzer Jäger Abteilung* 150 [50th *ID*], five *Sturmgeschütze* and '*Hornissen*' ['Hornets', self-propelled 8.8 cm *PaK* 43/1 mounted on the same *Pz Kpfw* chassis as the *Hummel*, providing a highly effective mobile tank destroyer.] After the reduction in size of the bridgehead it had a maximum depth of three kilometers, and a maximum width of seven kilometers.

Behind the forces holding the bridgehead in their nearly oval sand-dune position ran the, in places, one kilometer wide Dnjepr river and a roughly 3.5 kilometer wide belt of lagoons and swamps with drainage canals and abandoned arms of the neighbouring Konka river. Yellow-brown reeds, taller than a man waved over this swampy area, from which, here and again, rose low ridges of land with dark, boggy woods. Farther to the east it was bordered by gently rolling dunes of loose, light-colored sand.

The railroad bridge that was being protected, with its massive concrete and steel construction, had been constructed with great expenditure of materials in the fall of 1943 (at a cost of 42 million *Reichsmark*). It stretched a total of 2,000 meters and had been built by the I./ *Eisenbahn-Pionier-Regiment* 3, together with the *Organisation Todt*. This bridge near the mouth of the Dnjepr at Chersson was then continued over the Konka river in a similarly long wooden bridge. The two bridges and the sand-embankment extending to the Aleschki railroad station covered several kilometers. This railroad station later was the center of the bridgehead.

The dune-sand was good for constructing positions, so the troops stationed there constructed a system of man-deep positions with fighting trenches, communications trenches and high-ceilinged covered bunkers for quarters.

The first Soviet attack – supported by 45 batteries of artillery– was easily repulsed. The 4th *Gebirgs Division* conducted the defense regardless of its numerical weakness. They kept the Soviets on edge with constant patrol and assault-troop activity, causing the Soviets losses in men and matériel. Thereupon the Soviets reinforced their forces, especially in heavy weapons, but also with sharpshooters, which made it necessary for the Germans to bring in reinforcements.

Throughout the day it was difficult to make it over the bridge or by the available ferries because the Soviet artillery kept the crossing under constant fire. During the night wagon loads of supplies crossed the bridge to Aleschki under harassment by *'Nebelkrähen'* ['hooded crows', Russian night-bombers] that dropped parachute-flares.

The peculiarity of this bridgehead was that it was nearly oval as it stretched around the Aleschki railroad station to the north and south, but left the swampy area to its rear untouched. That provided the Soviets with the opportunity on 24 November initially to make a frontal attack in the sectors of *Aufklärungs Abteilung* [reconnaissance battalion] 94 [4th *Gebirgs Division*], [Gebirgs-]Pionier *Bataillon* 94 [4th *Gebirgs Division*] and the I./ *Gebirgs [-jäger] Regiment* 13 [4th *Gebirgs Division*] – probably as a diversion – then, however, to suddenly break out of the uncovered flank facing the swamp. Under the cover of nighttime darkness the Soviets had landed troops in the rear of the I./[Grenadier Regiment] 666 [370th *Infanterie Division*], working their way forward from the west during the day under cover of the fog and reeds east of the Konka river through the unobservable lagoon terrain that had been considered practically impassable. Wading through ice-cold water and hiding in the thickets, the Soviets actually made it to the Rail – and highway embankment, the most sensitive part of the bridgehead, thereby creating a dangerous situation.

The 'swamp-Russians' stubbornly held out, skillfully concealing themselves, not letting themselves be driven out in repeated cleansing operations. Finally, on 30 November elements of *Gebirgs Jäger Regiment* 91 [4th *Gebirgs Division*] (III./13 and *Aufklärungs Abteilung* 94) brought up by the division, conducted a counterattack in which the *Grenadiere*, in hard hand-to-hand fighting, combed through the swamp and dune terrain, rooting out enemy nests and repulsing desperate hasty counterattacks. Supported by artillery, *Sturmgeschütze* and *Flak*, ignoring the ground-attack planes supporting the Soviets, they were finally able to wipe out the enemy forces that had advanced through the swamp.

After filling out the troops with a strong march-battalion on 5 December the division decided on 12 December to evacuate the bridgehead and to immediately pull out the heavy weapons. They revoked this evacuation order, however, the following day. The Soviets must have learned of the order. Therefore on 14 December they exerted pressure on the main line of resistance, first with an assault troop, then with a further reconnaissance assault, which merely led the Germans to bring up the I./[Grenadier Regiment] 667 [370th ID].

After numerous reconnaissance and scouting operations on 16 December the Soviets opened the offensive with strong artillery support. In a space of 45 minutes the group counted 3,000 shells of calibers ranging from 7.65 to 15.2 cm, 2,500 mortar rounds from 8 to 12 cm and about 500 *Wurfkörper* [special projectiles for signal pistols]. That amounted to over 139 rounds per minute.

See Map 28.

Armour initially attacked through the cratered dune land, locally breaking through into the hinterland in order to reach the great Dnjepr bridge in a frontal breakthrough. Soviet infantry followed them, but did not make it through the German lines. Five of the approximately 20 AFVs that had broken through the I./ *[Gebirgs Regiment]* 13 were destroyed in close-combat. Six rolled through the III./ *[Gebirgs Regiment]* 13 and four to five AFVs rolled through *Gebirgs Jäger Bataillon* 94. Six enemy AFVs forced their way into *B-Dorf* At about 1115 hours several T 34 tanks even broke into the artillery positions. One AFV after another was knocked out by infantry using close-combat means such as satchel charges, clustered hand grenades, *Panzerschrec*, *Panzerfaust* and the like. The last of the AFVs that had broken through fell victim to the *Panzervernichtungstrupps* [infantry tank-busting squads]. Not one made it back.

See Map 29.

That day the 13th Guards Rifle Corps and the 33rd Tank Brigade attacked. In accord with new orders, on 20 December the 4th *Gebirgs Division* evacuated the bridgehead. Contrary to initial expectations, that proved extraordinarily difficult. The demolition of the 500 meter long Dnjepr bridge played a significant role. To avoid giving the enemy a signal for a renewed assault on the remaining troops by demolishing the bridge during the day, the command put off the demolition until 2200 hours. A railroad train to bring back the artillery, antitank guns and *Sturmgeschütze* over the bridge was derailed and arrived too late on the north bank.

Various ferries, which were to bring over the remaining troops, were disabled by enemy action or engine problems. Others were frozen in where they were berthed on the Ingulez river. For security reasons the sluggish ferry traffic that had got under way had to be stopped one hour before the bridge demolition. At 2225 hours, with a great roar, the bridge flew in the air. The construction, which had only been completed a short time and barely put into service collapsed. After the demolition the train elements that were waiting in two columns on the road could count on being transported in ferries. At 2310 hours – similarly delayed – the wooden bridge went up with an even greater roar and glare. Some of the wooden members of this bridge caught fire and thereby endangered the last Konka bridge, which had already been prepared for demolition, and the columns waiting before it to move out. Steel beams that had been hurled onto the road blocked traffic.

The ice on the river was broken up by the demolition of the two bridges. Great ice-flows drifted downstream, endangering the ferry traffic. Therefore *Gebirgs Jäger Regiment* 13 and *Gebirgs Jäger Regiment* 91 had to hold the *Alex-Stellung* at the Aleschki railroad station an additional night. In the meantime they had sent elements that could be spared over the river and positioned the remaining artillery batteries on the sand island east of the bridge position, near the ferry crossing.

Traffic over the second Konka bridge initially continued, but the heat of the still-burning great bridge thawed out the ground. Pack-animals, vehicles and two *'Hornissen'* sank into the swamp.

With heavy supporting fire from the German artillery, especially from the north bank, the withdrawal from the *Alex-Stellung* to the fortified *Kamin-*

Stellung around the Konka bridge succeeded. The Soviet artillery remained relatively quiet during this change of position. The withdrawal, however, brought about new difficulties, for there was no 52 ton ferry that was suitable to bring over the *Sturmgeschütze* and *'Hornissen'*. These precious weapons had to be brought over with 24 ton ferries. The increasing amount of ice-flows nearly completely prevented employment of assault boats and inflatable rubber boats. As the ice on the river increased it threatened to bring the ferry traffic to a complete standstill. At 0430 hours the Konka bridge was blown up and the *'Kamin-Stellung'* evacuated. In boldly conducted hasty counterattacks *Gebirgs Jäger Regiment* 13 yet again repulsed Soviet flank attacks. The ferries plied their course until 0615 hours, at which point flow-ice put a halt to their activity, so that the rest of the matériel that had not been crossed over had to be blown up and a number of horses shot. The reinforcements that the Red Army had brought in, one Guards rifle corps, one tank brigade and two rifle brigades, had not managed to break through the front of the 4th *Gebirgs Division*.

4
Second Battle of Kirowograd

<small>See Map 46 and, for geography, Maps 22, 28 and 33.</small>

Independent of developments in the area of the Nikopol bridgehead and the northern 'Fist' front to its rear, the Soviets strove by attacking in other sectors to force the German command to withdraw troops from the German 'Fist'. Therefore they launched new westward advances from the apex of the Soviet frontal salient toward Kirowograd and Kriwoi Rog to gain ground there. It is not, however, possible in retrospect to determine to what extent, at that time, the Soviet command had formed concrete plans for a further operational advance. The shift of *Schwerpunkt* was in accord with a familiar Soviet tactic to utilize the advantage of an attacker, who could, himself, determine the *Schwerpunkt* and objective of his operations, in contrast with the defender, who must react to the operations of the attacker.

At that point in time the attacks at Kirowograd were markedly inopportune for the German command, since the emergency at the left wing of *Heeresgruppe Süd* urgently demanded that mobile formations be shifted to the left wing to the 4th *Armee*. Nevertheless, the German troops had to react to this renewed advance. Granted, the Soviets had suffered a reverse as the result of the German advance from the boundary area between the 8th *Armee* and the 1st *Panzer Armee* and the *Kessel* battle of Fedwar. Furthermore, the advance from the area of the penetration east of Kirowograd to the south had been initially shattered under flank attacks by the 11th *Panzer Division*

<small>For geography see Map 19.</small>

and 14th *Panzer Division*. Nevertheless, in the Kirowograd area the Soviets attempted anew to achieve their old objective, to advance simultaneously both north and south of the city.

The second battle of Kirowograd opened east of the city with an extraordinarily heavy artillery preparation on 5 January, at 0600 hours in the morning, with an estimated expenditure of 188,000 rounds, an amount corresponding to the carrying capacity of ten goods trains. Three enemy armies attacked the lines of the 57th *Panzer Korps* and 52nd *Armee Korps*, tearing open the German lines on both sides of Adshanka for further advance on Kirowograd. The 10th *Panzer Grenadier Division*, fighting north of Adshanka, fell back on Kirowograd, wherefore the 3rd *Panzer Division* initially advanced from its assembly area at Kirowograd to the north into the Lepikowka area to stop the retrograde movement of the 10th *Panzergrenadier Division* and close the resulting gap. According to reports, the Soviets that day advanced into the depth with over 600 AFVs on both sides of Kirowograd, thereby enveloping the 3rd *Panzer Division* before it could bring its forces into action.

On the following day the 3rd *Panzer Division* fought its way through the Soviet advance to the north behind its spearhead to link up with the forces of the 11th *Panzer Division* that were attacking towards it. In so doing they blocked the enemy's east-west supply route. Fifteen Soviet 7.6 cm antitank guns and several T 34 tanks were left, destroyed, on the battlefield. Furthermore, the 3rd *Panzer Division* captured Lelekowka, situated on a hill north of Kirowograd, and, shortly before dusk fell, the high ground near Roshnatowka. The 3rd *Panzer Division* had to halt its attack due to failing ammunition supply for the artillery, even though the distance to the spearhead of the 11th *Panzer Division* was only five kilometers. While the 3rd *Panzer Division* blocked the supply route for the advanced Soviet forces, the Soviets blocked the German *'Rollbahn'* [major highway designated for military transport purposes] west of Kirowograd, thereby cutting off supplies for the 3rd *Panzer Division*. In the meantime, house-to-house fighting raged in Kirowograd and there were problems rescuing the wounded and rear-area administrative and service personnel. The next day the Soviets completely encircled the city.

The 3rd *Panzer Division* launched a breakout, starting in a broad wedge formation to the north against the Soviet defensive positions. One of the spearhead-tanks was set ablaze by anti-tank fire and thereby illuminated the snow-covered battlefield. Without stopping, the other tanks continued a night attack against the Soviet positions. Some of these were taken without a fight. At about midnight the armoured spearhead ran into strong enemy resistance at the *Rollbahn*, which the tanks immediately crushed. As morning arrived the spearhead reached Wladinowka and Iwanowka where they linked up with the leading elements of the 11th *Panzer Division*.

The formations then changed direction to fight free the remaining forces in Kirowograd, elements of the 14th *Panzer Division,* 10th *Panzergrenadier Division* and 376th *Infanterie Division*. The elements of the 3rd *Panzer Division* so employed initially advanced to the east, where they ran into stiff resistance at Ossikowatka. The armour captured Ossikowatka and took about 500 prisoners. *Stukas* and *Luftwaffe* formations of *Oberst* Rudel joined in this conflict from the nearby Mal.Wiski airfield and destroyed numerous enemy AFVs.

For geography see Map 21.

As this indicated that, in the early dawn, the Soviets were starting to withdraw from the ground they had gained in their advance to the west, the forces of the 3rd *Panzer Division* launched a surprise attack into the flank of the Soviet troops. They knocked out all the enemy armour (14 – 16 T 34 tanks), captured much equipment and many prisoners. After penetrating into Mal. Wiski they established communication with the strongpoint of the *Luftwaffe* on the airfield south of Mal. Wiski, there securing a portion of the records of the *Korps* staff that had been surprised there two days earlier.

This advance brought the 3rd *Panzer Division* on 10 January far ahead of the intended line of defense, because, regardless of the penetration, to the north and farther to the south Soviet armoured spearheads reached to the west. Therefore, on 11 January the division evacuated its position at Ossikowata and fell back to the Petrowka – Alexandrowka line.

For geography see Maps 20, 21 and 22.

While the Soviets were finding success on the Dnjepr front against the 320th *Infanterie Division* (47th *Panzer Korps*), *Heeresgruppe Süd* had the 282nd *Infanterie Division* transported by lorry to the area of the 3rd *Panzer Division*. There, after a heavy artillery preparation, the Soviets launched yet another attack north of Gruskoje and forced the German lines slightly back. The 3rd

Panzer Division, reinforced with two regiments of the 282nd *Infanterie Division*, launched a counterattack on the following day.

The Soviets promptly attacked and achieved success in the sector from which the 282nd *Infanterie Division* had been withdrawn with lengthening the lines of the adjoining 106th *Infanterie Division* and 389th *Infanterie Division*. On 15 January, to support a company of *'Panther'* tanks of *Panzer Regiment* 15 and the 11th *Panzer Division* the 3rd *Panzer Division* initially advanced southeast from Ossitnjashka (north of Kirowograd) and caught the Soviets by surprise, who fled their positions, abandoning weapons and matériel and fell back. On the next day the elements of the 3rd *Panzer Division* that had been committed continued to advance via Reimentarowka. The Soviets, however, reacted with an attack on Jamki. Nevertheless, the advance of the 3rd *Panzer Division* cut the Soviet leading elements off from their rear connections. 3,871 prisoners marked the success of the twelve days of hard fighting of the second battle of Kirowograd, along with 490 AFVs destroyed, 100 captured guns, 564 antitank guns and 15 antiaircraft guns. On 17 January the Soviets gave up any further breakthrough attempts in this sector of the front, for the time being.

For geography see Map 22.

Situation South of Kirowograd

It seemed that the battle of Kirowograd was not yet over. As usual, the Soviets were not content with a single advance, such as that north of Kirowograd. Rather, they simultaneously launched another advance south of the city, at the border to the adjoining *Korps*. Before *Panzergrenadier Division 'Großdeutschland'* arrived to plug the gap the Soviets advanced strong forces to the west. At the moment, however, that *Panzergrenadier Division 'Großdeutschland'* drew near, the Soviet forces received orders to retreat. In long columns they marched from the west and southwest on foot and by horse, with lorries and individual horse-drawn vehicles, partly in halfway organized units, partly in motley bands, some with, some without weapons, in forced march to the existing gap in the front in a desperate attempt to get through the bottleneck to salvation in the last minute before it slammed shut. Nevertheless, two rifle divisions and elements of several tank brigades failed to escape. *Panzergrenadier Division 'Großdeutschland'* destroyed them. Elements of the surrounded Soviet forces managed to hide in concealed valleys and ravines and attempted in the ensuing days to get through the German positions to the east. Some pretended to be Ukrainian peasants, others, however, joined the local partisan organizations.

In spite of that the formations of the *Korps* succeeded in closing the front throughout its entire extent. Regardless of difficult situations, thin manning and inadequate logistical support they had 'done it one more time'. Amazing situations had to be overcome here: encircled Soviet forces, encircled German forces. Logistical support initially came with the support of an armoured railroad train that had been brought in from Nowo Ukrainka and that resulted in orderly supply of the troops.

Further Development of the Situation

The Germans were astounded that the Soviets failed to take advantage of their breakthroughs north and south of Kirowograd for a further advance to the west. Nevertheless the opportunity existed to advance from the south into the area west of the Dnjepr *'Balkon'*.[1]

Later the Soviets attempted that further north. Thus the fighting flared up in the Gruskoje – Krassnossilka area against the 376th *Infanterie Division* and against the 282nd *Infanterie Division*, which had been brought in from the north, as also against elements of the 10th *Panzergrenadier Division*. The Soviets buckled the German line in several places, but it held up against the pressure. That gave the German command an opportunity the assemble the 3rd *Panzer Division* and the 3rd *SS-Panzer Division 'Totenkopf'* behind the endangered sectors, ready to counterattack. Heavy German artillery fire and attacks both in the front and also in the flanks forced the Soviets back to their jump-off positions.

Reconnaissance then revealed that the Soviets again shifted their *Schwerpunkt* to the north. In the woods and localities west of the Fedwar – Alexandrowka road reconnaissance identified dense concentrations of forces of the 5th Guards Tank Army, the 18th, 20th and 29th Tank Corps. In addition came remnants of various independent tank brigades and the 5th Guards Cavalry Corps. The Soviets shifted the headquarters of the 2nd Ukrainian Front from Alexandrija to Zwetna, 40 kilometers east of Krassnossilka.

For geography see Maps 16, 17 and 22.

These changes, in combination with the Soviet advance to the south via Kiew, pointed to a new operation, cutting off the 'Dnjepr *Balkon*'.

---

1 Translator's note – The German *'Balkon'* can also refer to what the dictionary politely terms ' *vulg. Busen*, a heavy bust', which is a far better description of the 'frontal salient' in question and, probably, the sense intended by the soldiers who so-named it. The translator felt unable to select a 'mildly vulgar' term that would be equally meaningful to the readers on both sides of the pond, and thus decided on a footnote, so each could pick their own.

5

Heeresgruppe Süd at the Dawn of the New Year

In the Nikopol sector the Red Army was initially quiet, just as in the Kriwoi Rog sector, so that we can turn from the presentation of events in the southern and central sectors of *Heeresgruppe Süd* to developments in the area of the northern wing of the *Heeresgruppe*. These already caused considerable concern for the *Heeresgruppe* command before the end of the year, as to whether the thinly held lines of *Heeresgruppe Süd* – if the situation should arise – could still be held.

On the one hand, the troops could take pride in the fact that they had prevented operational Soviet breakthroughs in indefatigable combat against extraordinarily superior forces and held a nearly continuous line, even if locally only held as a series of strongpoints, here and there secured by no more than artillery firing positions.

The German *Ostheer* [Eastern Army] proved, in all operations at this time, entirely dependant on the arrival of of an adequate supply of fuel. Therefore the command had to protect the fuel sources, especially the crude-oil sources in Ploesti, Zisterdorf and also Celle, as well as the synthetic-fuel plants in Magdeburg, Leuna and the like. The mobility of the forces depended on preservation of the fuel sources. The constant shifting of the *Rollbahn* 'Fire Brigades', the *Panzer Divisions*, especially on unpaved roads and, even worse, during the mud-seasons, required considerably more fuel than normal movements. The troops often wondered where this quantity of fuel still came from and were amazed that logistical support, even though sluggish and scarce, still arrived at all.

The only good thing seemed to be that the Soviets did not take advantage of the opportunities presented to them. The reasons behind this tactical peculiarity can only be guessed at. The middle level of command, at the division and corps level, clearly lacked the requisite freedom of action. The higher command, however, appeared dependent on directives from Stavka [the Soviet high command, closely centered on Stalin]. Communications to and from Stavka obviously did not take place by the most rapid route, by radio, but by telephone or messenger – definitely time-consuming. Hitler's hindrance of the German command by his rigid hold-in-place orders and his interference in ongoing decision making, which eliminated the possibility for the weak German forces to gain success by greater mobility in utilizing space, must be seen as similar to these hindrances to command on the Soviet side.

Thus Manstein continued to endeavour to pull additional forces out of the southern area by shortening the Dnjepr bend in order to transfer them to the left wing of *Heeresgruppe Süd*. The Soviet offensive in the second battle of Kirowograd intruded into these considerations.

Reorganization

In response to *Generalfeldmarschall* von Manstein's proposals, on 29 November Hitler merely ordered the headquarters [*Oberkommando*] of the 1st *Panzer Armee* to the area of *Armeeoberkommando* 8 [the 8th *Armee* headquarters], turning over its former area of command to *Armeeoberkommando* 6. In addition, von Manstein received a lot of promises about strengthening the 4th *Panzer Armee*, such as the promised arrival of the 16th *Panzer Division*, 1st *Infanterie Division*, and 4th *Gebirgs Division*. *Armeeoberkommando* 6 assumed command of the line of defense along the lower course of the Dnjepr as far as the boundary with *Heeresgruppe* A. Two proven *Panzer* divisions, *Panzergrenadier Division 'Großdeutschland'* and the 3rd *SS-Panzer Division 'Totenkopf'*, previously employed at the most sensitive points of the front of the 1st *Panzer Armee*, received orders to shift to the northern wing of *Heeresgruppe Süd*. They were to be replaced by infantry divisions. In addition, from the 6th *Armee*, four infantry divisions, along with the 24th *Panzer Division* – hitherto supporting the defense of the Nikopol bridgehead – were to set out on their march to the north. The proposal that *Armeeoberkommando* 6, still responsible for the bridgehead, should evacuate the bridgehead ran into opposition from Hitler, as did the proposal to evacuate the already shortened Saporoshje salient, even though that would have shortened the defensive front by 200 kilometers.

The picture shown on the map, with its notations for divisions, was extremely deceptive, since none of the fighting formations could be rated as fully fit for action, hardly surprising in light of the great shortage of manpower amounting to a lack of over 1000 men per division. As if that was not enough, for several months the troops had been in incessant action. At some point they would have to be given a break for refitting and for incorporating and training the 'replacements' sent from the homeland, the recruits – the more so in light of their exceedingly short period of prior training before they were sent out. The vehicle and artillery parks required overhauling and restocking. Above all the formations needed, for once, to again be put back in order. Employment of *Kampfgruppen* formed out of separate individual elements resulted in a scrambling of the elements of the divisions. Often, however, there simply was no time for reorganization. Consequently, it was with great concern that the command had to consider the present front of *Heeresgruppe Süd*, always keeping in mind the question: How long can the soldiers still hold out against the immense Soviet superiority in artillery, armour and infantry? How long will it be possible, with sensitive reconnaissance and reaction to the reports arriving about the enemy, to continue to influence the developments with short, effective attacks, when possible in the vulnerable flanks of the Soviet advances? At some point the troops must finally reach the limits of their endurance. *Generalfeldmarschall* von Manstein therefore concerned himself, again and again, with freeing up troops, especially from the Saporoshje salient, because there was no other way of making good the steady decline in combat effectiveness of the fighting formations. *OKH*, itself, however, had no way to provide the personnel and matériel required to replenish the fighting formations. All the drastic representations to *OKH* and Hitler seemed to make no impression on the latter, which caused ever increasing concern for *Generalfeldmarschall* von Manstein regarding the inevitable moment when the situation would cross over the limits of what the troops could bear.

To counteract the efforts of *Generalfeldmarschall* von Manstein, Hitler again removed the 6th *Armee,* effective 2 February, from the command of *Heeresgruppe Süd* and attached it to *Heeresgruppe* A, apparently to limit the ability of *Heeresgruppe Süd* to call on the formations fighting at its southern wing. This action of Hitler's may have been based on his wishful thinking whereby he wanted to be ready to shift forces from the *Heeresgruppe* A sector to the Crimean Peninsula.

Consequences of Command Decisions

Into these deliberations and reorganizations came the additional realization that the events on the northern wing of *Heeresgruppe Süd* could no longer be considered in isolation. They affected the development of the situation in the center of *Heeresgruppe Süd's* sector and also on the right wing. In the meantime, a gap in the front between the Dnjepr front and Berditschew (24th *Panzer Korps* and 7th *Armee Korps*) had to be plugged with additional formations, for which the command foresaw the 6th *Panzer Division*, 17th *Panzer Division*, 16th *Panzergrenadier Division* and 101st *Jäger Division*. These, however, first had to be brought in from the Dnjepr bend or 6th *Armee* (24th *Panzer Division*), respectively. The enemy breakthrough east of Fastow to the south could be broadened toward Winniza. The 24th *Panzer Korps* and 7th *Armee Korps* had already been forced to substantially bend back their wing. That left a yawing gap of 75 kilometers in which the 3rd *Panzer Korps* was supposed to assemble. A new, thin German line (1st *Panzer Armee*) first made its appearance again southeast of Berditschew, essentially running just east of the Berditschew – Shitomir road, around Shitomir to the west, ending again to the north of that city. Between the 13th *Armee Korps*, which was fighting around Shitomir with its front facing east and north and the 59th *Armee Korps*, which had been forced back west of Korosten, stretched another gap of 75 kilometers, in which the 46th *Panzer Korps*, which was assembling in the rear, was to organize.

Up to this point the significance of the Soviet advance on the northern wing of *Heeresgruppe Süd* had not yet been seen as influencing the center of the *Heeresgruppe* sector. The Soviet advance to the south now forced recognition of the danger for the center and southern wing of the *Heeresgruppe*. A Soviet advance north of Gornostaipol and Tschernobyl to the west also raised the danger that the Soviets might reach the territory of the *Generalgouvernement*[1] and, thereby, more favorable terrain for attack and – if one disregarded the Weichsel [Vistula river] as an obstacle– even toward the territory of the *Reich*.

---

1 Translator's note – Area of German occupied Poland, and Ostrawa, Checkoslovakia, that Germany intended to make a province of Germany and which was governed entirely by and for Germans. The German intention was that, in the long run, there would be no ethnic Poles resident there, only people of German extraction.

HEERESGRUPPE SÜD AT THE DAWN OF THE NEW YEAR

At the moment this danger did not yet seem to be a burning issue, since, initially, disregarding the parallel advance from Shitomir, about 30 kilometer to the west, the assault to the south from Kiew via Fastow or past Fastow on the east toward Belaja Zerkow to Beresowka, seemed more dangerous, since that would bring the Soviets into the rear of the center of *Heeresgruppe Süd*. If, then, the Soviets achieved a breakthrough in the area east of Kirowograd, that would open up the opportunity for them there to get behind the German 8th *Armee* on the Dnjepr from the south. For *Generalfeldmarshall* von Manstein's *Heeresgrupps Süd* the provision of new troops became a vital necessity.

Help could not be expected from *Heeresgruppe Mitte*. The vast swamp and moor terrain of the Pripjet barred movements of troops between the two commands unless one were to accept loss of time that would be required for a round-about transport via Brest-Litowsk. This region surrounding the mouth of the Pripjet – stretching nearly 500 kilometers in its east-west dimension to the Dnjepr river and with a north-south breadth of about 180 kilometers – was, aside from the secured transport routes – almost entirely under the control of partisan bands.

In order to comprehend the difficulties of command it is first necessary to examine events in the sector of the northern wing of *Heeresgruppe Süd*. As the new year arrived, Soviet forces already were advancing into the gap between the 1st *Panzer Armee* and the right wing of the 4th *Panzer Armee* to about 30 kilometers north of Uman, the logistical base of the 1st *Panzer Armee*, and even close to Winniza, the headquarters of the *Heeresgruppe* command.

6

Fighting on the Left Wing of *Heeresgruppe Süd*

For geography see Map 31.

Since the end of *Unternehmen 'Zitadelle'* [Operation 'Citadel', the battle of Kursk] and the retreat to the west, the highest German command, (*OKH*) had attributed little significance to the northern wing of *Heeresgruppe Süd*. The *Heeresgruppe* repeatedly pointed out the weakness of the German formations in the area of the 4th *Panzer Armee*.

The neighbouring 2nd *Armee* of *Heeresgruppe Mitte*, adjoining on the left, fell back during the month of September to a line east of Gomel – Mogilew and, by the end of the month, behind the Dnjepr, though it still held one bridgehead at Gomel. *Heeresgruppe Mitte* failed to maintain contact with *Heeresgruppe Süd*, leaving a gap of about 90 kilometers.

Heeresgruppe Mitte [Center] Attempts to Regain Contact on the Right

See Map 31.

At the end of September the 2nd *Panzer Division* received orders from the 2nd *Armee* to establish contact with the 4th *Panzer Armee* of *Heeresgruppe Süd*. It reached Gomel by rail. From there on partisan bands prevented further progress by demolishing the railroad line. Several transport trains carrying the division ran onto mines, especially trains with armoured vehicles. The roads and byways, however, also turned out to be blocked by partisans blowing up or burning bridges.

Panzergrenadier Regiment 2, which had been sent ahead, succeeded in establishing contact to the south, and took part in the fighting around Kiew. However, the regiment soon lost contact with the 2nd *Panzer Division* because the elements following only reached the Tschernigow assembly area separately and delayed. Merely a portion of the division succeeded for a short time in coming under the command of the 4th *Panzer Armee* – *Generaloberst* Hoth. The main body of the 2nd *Panzer Division* remained attached to the 46th *Panzer Korps* (*General* Gollnik). Efforts to block the Soviet advance march areas, particularly from Tschernigow toward Tschernobyl came too late. Nevertheless, *Panzeraufklärungs Abteilung* 2 and *Panzerpionier* [*Bataillon*] 38 [belonging to 2nd *Panzer Division*] attempted to follow *Panzergrenadier Regiment* 2 toward Kiew. Hungarian troops and German police unites in Tschernigow had, however, already blown up all the bridges over the Dessna. The alternative routes along the Dessna proved in places to be extremely swampy, which interfered with forward progress. In Tschernigow were giant German supply and ration dumps. Therefore, the commander of the *Kampfgruppe* committed in this bridgehead by the 2nd *Panzer Division* – *Oberst* Schmidthuber, commander of *Panzergrenadier Regiment* 304 [2nd *Panzer Division*] sent *Panzergrenadier*

See Map 31.

FIGHTING ON THE LEFT WING OF *HEERESGRUPPE SÜD*

Regiment 2 after them to the south, in accord with his assignment, to cross the Dnjepr at Ljubetsch and thus to outflank the Soviets. The bulk of the enemy formations that had arrived, however, were partisan bands, not regular troops. This bears witness to the significance of the fact that, in the areas west of the Dnjepr that were only weakly held by German troops, partisan bands secured bridgeheads for the Red Army so that the Red Army troops could cross the river without having to fight for them. On 22 and 23 September there was heavy fighting at Guschtschin and Shukotki.

In the final days of September the *Panzergrenadier Regiment* crossed the Dnjepr, the self-propelled guns and armour going by ferry, wheeled vehicles crossing on a military bridge erected by the pioneers. Enemy aircraft interfered with this movement. Thus these elements of the 2nd *Panzer Division* (*Panzergrenadier Regiment* 304) again came under the command of the 2nd *Armee* of *Heeresgruppe Mitte* and were ordered, again, with attached elements of other formations, to attempt to establish contact with the northern wing of *Heeresgruppe Süd*. These efforts, however, bogged down in the sand dunes of the Pripjet triangle. There were night attacks, as, for example, south of Simowischtschje, Krassno and Kriwaja Gora. Since *Heeresgruppe Mitte*, however, was fully occupied with defending against enemy attacks from the east, it had to abandoned further efforts to establish contact to the south. Detachment of any forces for that mission dropped out of the picture in view of the critical situation.

Hitler's Unconcern with the Left Wing of *Heeresgruppe Süd*

Instead of concerning himself with the gap in the front between *Heeresgruppe Mitte* and *Heeresgruppe Süd* and the dangerous situation of the 4th *Armee*, Hitler turned his attention again to the right wing of *Heeresgruppe Süd*, initially the Donez and Mius front, later the Dnjepr front. That was a result, first, of the coal and manganese-ore deposits that had been developed there during the time of German occupation. Secondly, Hitler dreamed of new advances to the east from this advanced area. For these reasons he still hung onto the Kuban bridgehead. He feared that a pullback of the southern front would also negatively impact the attitudes of Rumania, Bulgaria and Turkey. The urgently needed reinforcements that had been promised *Generalfeldmarschall* von Manstein for the southern wing of the *Heeresgruppe*, however, did not arrive, even though the combat effectiveness of the formations committed in this area shrank daily due to the losses in men and armour.

The pull-back of the front of *Heeresgruppe Süd* to the Dnjepropetrowsk – Saproshje – Melitopol salient that Hitler later authorized did not result in a strengthening of the formations, because this new salient also had to be held and could only be inadequately manned due to its great extent. The divisions here took over 20 kilometer sectors of the front, even though they could each put only 1,000 men in the front line. The Soviets used this tying down of German formations at the southern wing of the *Heeresgruppe* to assist their attack against the left wing of the *Heeresgruppe*.

Combat Sector Kiew

The bridgehead front east of Kiew denied the Soviets an immediate entrance into Kiew, which was a vital transportation nodal-point for them. The Soviet penetration into the southern combat sectors of the Dnjepr, however, caused the German command to withdraw the 19th *Panzer Division* from the bridgehead east if Kiew – weakening the bridgehead – and hastily shift it 80 kilometers south into the Dnjepr knee. Nevertheless, the Soviets feared the German defense and undertook no direct advance against Kiew, instead attacking farther south and north of the city. To the south, they gained a foothold and built a bridgehead on the west bank of the river in the Dnjepr knee even before the 19th *Panzer Division* arrived. In an independent operation they attacked the German defensive strongpoints north of Kiew. Although terrain conditions there seemed particularly favorable for their operations, initially they only employed weak forces, achieving nothing.

The Dessna river enters the Dnjepr north of Kiew, so above that junction the Dnjepr has a smaller amount of water in its flow. Still farther north the Teterew river joins the Dnjepr, with the Pripjet joining still farther upstream. The Dnjepr has a very gentle gradient there, with a multitude of bends and islands. Below the junction of the Pripjet in the Dnjepr the Soviets could wade through the chest-deep water on foot, holding their weapons high, fording the shallow river with their *Panje* wagons and medium and heavy weapons. The river, here, provided no significant natural obstacle to aid the defense. In addition, west of the Dnjepr was a land of brush and woods, providing plenty of natural cover. Yet more, to the north stretched the nearly impassable Pripjet region, with its swamps and forests, crossed by few arterial roads, in which operations, even counter-operations of any great extent, were excluded. Even though the *Heeresgruppe* boundary ran there, a condition that the Soviets preferred for attack due to the resultant complications of command for the defenders, the German command still did not expect large-scale operations there because of the perceived terrain difficulties. But there were other reasons, too, as a result of the fact that the area north of Kiew had been treated like an unwelcome stepchild. The course of the fighting in other sectors of the Dnjepr, especially in the Dnjepr knee, but also the fighting around Dnjepropetrowsk and Saporoshje, gave the command sufficient cause to generally commit combat-worthy formations farther south at one of the *Schwerpunkte* of the Dnjepr front. There were entirely too many danger points, wherefore *OKH* paid too little attention to *Heeresgruppe Süd's* concern for the area north of Kiew, despite the favorable opportunities there for crossing to the west.

Loss of the Kiew Bridgehead

The withdrawal of the 19th *Panzer Division* from the eastern front of the Kiew bridgehead caused the command (7th *Armee Korps*) initially to entrust the 291st *Infanterie Division* as a combat worthy formation with responsibility for the bridgehead. Under massive, gradually increasing pressure from the pursuing Soviets this division evacuated the bridgehead during the night of 28/29 September 1943. The great Dnjepr bridge flew into the air with a mighty detonation in the gray light of dawn. The last *Grenadiere* and pioneers crossed

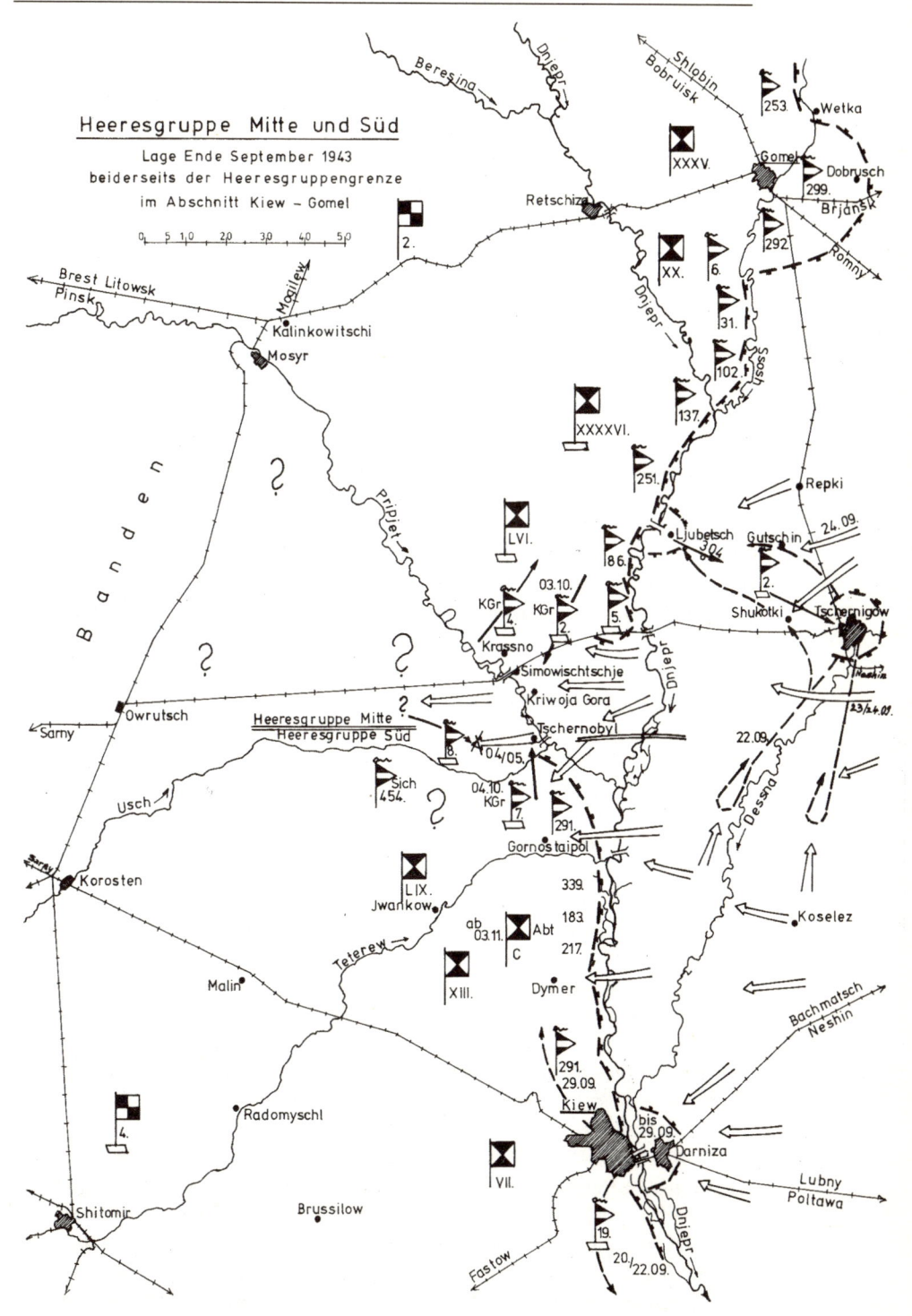

FIGHTING ON THE LEFT WING OF *HEERESGRUPPE SÜD* 131

31. *Heeresgruppe Mitte* and *Süd*. Situation at the end of September, 1943 on both sides of the *Heeresgruppe*n boundary in the Kiew – Gomel sector.

the river in inflatable rubber boats. From then on the line of defense ran through the city of Kiew.

To avoid the risks of house-to-house and street fighting, the Soviets infiltrated farther to the west through the Dnjepr river sector between the mouth of the Dessna and the mouth of the Pripjet, an inviting sector for them, thereby endangering the vital Korosten – Tschernobyl and Korosten – Kiew supply routes. For the Germans it thereby became a matter of blocking the east – west supply lines that were vital for the Soviet advance, especially for bringing up troops and supplying them. To accomplish this and to establish contact with *Heeresgruppe Mitte* on the left, the 8th *Panzer Division* was assigned to occupy the sector between the mouths of the Teterew and the Usch rivers and, for this purpose, to recapture Tschernobyl. The 291st *Infanterie Division* later was ordered to block the Koselez – Gornostaipol road to the west and Tschernigow – Tschernobyl.

Soviet Advance into the Area North of Kiew

The Soviets used weak forces to utilize the favorable crossing possibilities over the Dnjepr and Dessna rivers in order to secure precautionary bridgeheads on the west bank in the middle and lower course of the Dnjepr above Kiew for any situation that might develop. In this way they gained additional landing places and/or bridgeheads independent of the advance toward and past Tschernobyl. Some were, apparently, secured with the help of partisan bands operating in the rear of the German defense. Thus they secured:

See Maps 32 and 33.

1. At Ljutesch – Demidowo in the sector of the 13th *Armee Korps* a bridgehead facing the front of the 208th *Infanterie Division* with a *Kampfgruppe* of the 88th *Infanterie Division*.

2. At Jassnogorodka at the boundary between the 13th *Armee Korps* and 59th *Armee Korps* facing the front of the 340th *Infanterie Division* with a *Kampfgruppe* of the 327th *Infanterie Division*.

3. An almost 25 kilometer wide bridgehead between the mouth of the Teterew river in the Dnjepr and the mouth of the Usch river in the Pripjet river just south of Tschernobyl, facing the defensive sector of the 291st *Infanterie Division*.

In addition to these was the above mentioned advance at Tschernobyl at the boundary with the 2nd *Armee* of *Heeresgruppe Mitte* facing the *Kampfgruppe*n committed there, which were then in a state of flux, of the 7th *Panzer Division*, the 8th *Panzer Division*, the 2nd *Panzer Division*, elements of the 4th *Panzer Division*, at that time with elements of the 454th *Sicherungs* [security] *Division* and alarm units.

On 31 October the following formations were committed at the left wing of the 4th *Panzer Armee* between Kiew and Tschernobyl: The 7th *Armee Korps* defended in positions in and on both sides of Kiew with the 213th *Sicherungs Division* south of the city, 75th *Infanterie Division* and *Kampfgruppe* 323rd *Infanterie Division* as well as alarm units at the bank of the Dnjepr in the city, in the north with *Kampfgruppe* 82nd *Infanterie Division* and 68th *Infanterie Division* and remnants of other formations (the 68th *Infanterie Division* was attached to the 13th *Armee Korps* in the course of the following day). The

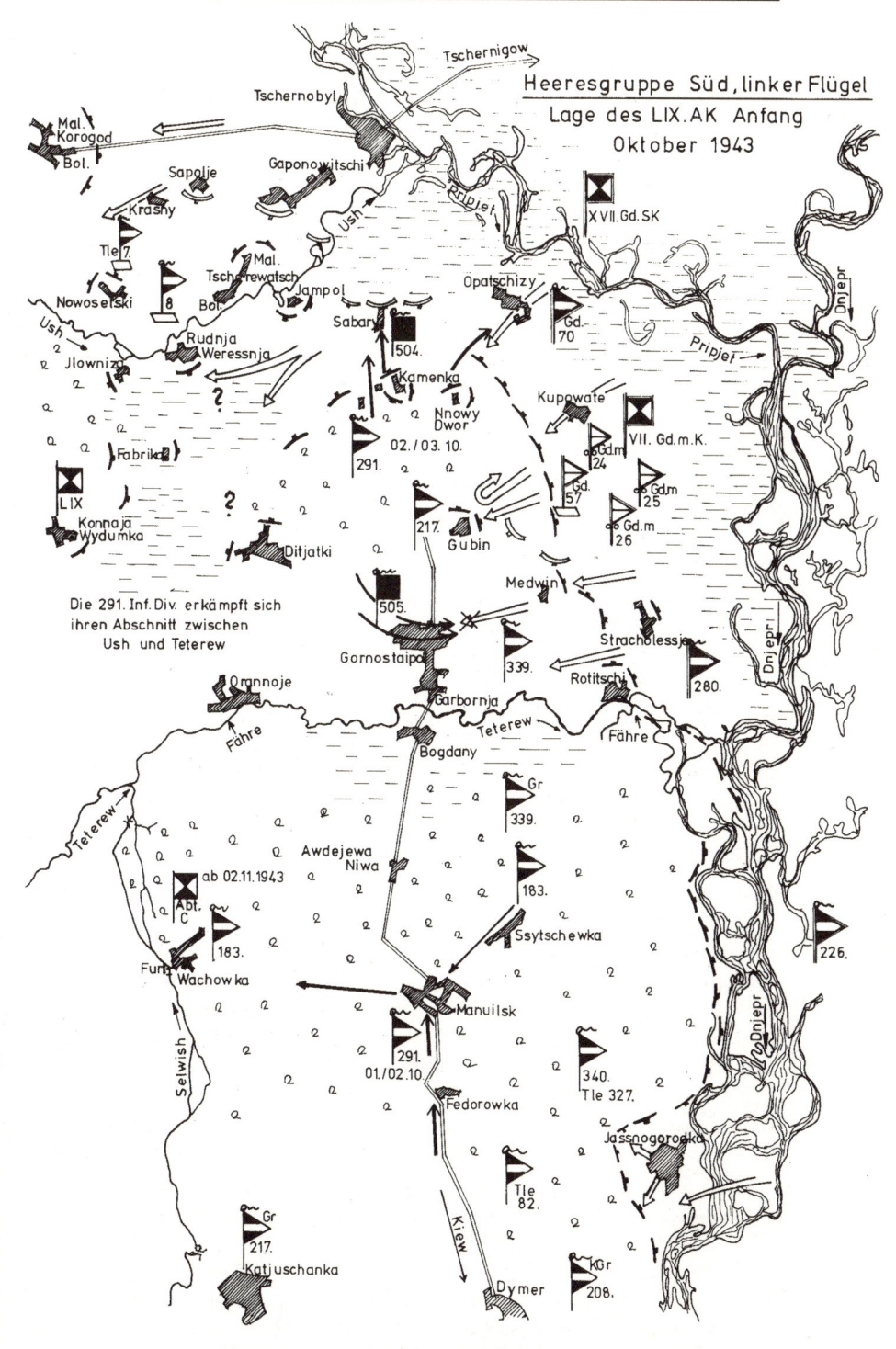

FIGHTING ON THE LEFT WING OF *HEERESGRUPPE SÜD* 133

32. *Heeresgruppe Süd*, left wing. Situation of the 59th *Armee Korps* at the beginning of October, 1943.

13th *Armee Korps* continued on the left later with the 68th *Infanterie Division*, *Kampfgruppe* 88th *Infanterie Division*, with, behind them, *Kampfgruppe* 9th *Panzer Division*, 208th *Infanterie Division* with *Kampfgruppe* 327th *Infanterie Division*, 340th *Infanterie Division*, then the left wing at Jassnogorodka inclusive with the 68th *Infanterie Division* – initially still attached to the 7th *Armee Korps*, later to the 13th *Armee Korps*.[1]

To regularize command relationships the command put together the remnants of the fought-out 217th *Infanterie Division*, 183rd *Infanterie Division* and 339th *Infanterie Division* on 3 November and called the formation *Korpsabteilung* C, comparable in organization and armament to one infantry division.

Next to the left was the 59th *Armee Korps* with *Korpsabteilung* C, organized as described above, with its left wing at the mouth of the Teterew, behind the right wing as of 1 / 2 November of I./ *Grenadier Regiment* 504 (291st *Infanterie Division*). The 291st *Infanterie Division* then stood between the mouths of the Teterew and Usch. At that time there existed loose contact – broken on 3 November – through a *Kampfgruppe* of the 2nd *Panzer Division*, later the 4th *Panzer Division* – with the southern wing of the 2nd *Armee* of *Heeresgruppe Mitte*.

The force ratio between the two sides was extremely unequal. The 340th *Infanterie Division* held its sector facing the Jassnogorodka bridgehead with no more than weak security. An infantry division that was dependant on footmarching and horse-drawn artillery and logistical columns had no possible way of securing the sector it was assigned against infiltration by mounted or motorized enemy forces in this brushy terrain that favoured the attacker. The line of defense – lacking any sort of terrain obstacles usable for the defense – was quite long.

The 291st *Infanterie Division*, which had been ordered there from the former Kiew bridgehead, received, after a long approach march, orders, advancing from the Gornostaipol area (at the Teterew) to the north, to establish contact with the southern wing of *Heeresgruppe Mitte* at the Usch river southwest of Tschernobyl. Considering the limited mobility of this unit and the terrain difficulties this was a difficult mission to accomplish. In addition, in the rear areas partisan bands did their sinister work. Here, for the first time, Ukrainian nationalist partisans were identified, who were ready and willing to cooperate with the Germans, their only desire being to prevent

---

1 Translator's note – Two points should be born in mind in reading the above list: First, units are usually listed, as here, from right to left as one faces the enemy. Secondly, The term *Kampfgruppe* is used in two different senses: A division, such as the 2nd *Panzer Division* might set up several independently operating balanced forces, assigning some of its armour and artillery to each of its *Panzergrenadier* regiments, with pioneer and medical support, designating each as a *Kampfgruppe*, usually named for the officer commanding it. Another common use of the term, as in most of the '*Kampfgruppen*' mentioned in the above list, is when a division has been reduced by constant fighting and attrition to the point where it would be too unrealistic to continue to refer to it as a division. For instance, the 327th *Infanterie Division* had, apparently, been reduced to the point where it was now designated '*Kampfgruppe* 327th *Infanterie Division*'. The next step in designating what was left of a further reduced division would be to mention it as 'remnants of the xxth *Infanterie Division*', which might be attached to another division. Finally might come what the subsequent paragraph describes.

FIGHTING ON THE LEFT WING OF *HEERESGRUPPE SÜD* 135

a renewed subjugation of the Ukraine to the USSR. Additionally, in the rear area, partly behind the left wing, the 454th *Sicherungs Division* along with Hungarian formations operated against partisan bands under the command of the *Wehrmachtbefehlshaber Ukraine* [military district commander in occupied territory, directly responsible to *OKH*]. These, however, were unable to prevent partisan bands from conducting disruption operations against the German troops in the Dnjepr line.

Situation at the Left Wing of the 4th *Panzer Armee*

After its long approach march, in order to fulfill its assigned mission, the 291st *Infanterie Division* initially had to cross a broad plain of bare fields and brushy terrain, then an extensive forested area, until it got to the villages of Kamenka and Sabary (3 October) in order, north of them, to reach the left-adjoining sector at the Usch. Unhindered by enemy groups to its right and left, despite difficult routes, the division made it through the terrain and captured Kamenka against stubborn enemy resistance. It then threw the Soviets off the hill north of Sabary in order, by so doing, to clear the way to Tschernobyl. The division, however, lacked sufficient forces to build a front to the east. Instead of that, during the night of 3/4 October, the division's reconnaissance identified Soviet battalions that had infiltrated into the rear of the division and had cut off the rear connections of the elements of *Grenadier Regimenter* 504 and 505 [both 291st *ID*] that were at Sabary. An alarm unit thrown together from artillerymen and supply column drivers fought free the rearward route via Kamenka. The Soviets suddenly appeared south of the forest terrain with armour and forced their way into Gornostaipol. The 217th *Infanterie Division* and elements of the 291st *Infanterie Division* threw them back out of Gornostaipol. That, however, did not prevent the Soviets from again infiltrating forward to the west north of Gornostaipol. With extreme effort, after firing off all the ammunition, the Soviet advance was stopped.

See Map 32.

In the next four weeks the front then held. During that time the Soviets reinforced their formations and brought armour and artillery, especially, into the area east of Demidowo and Gornostaipol.

See Maps 32 and 33.

The Start of the Soviet Offensive

Initially the Soviets, too, underestimated the significance that the favorable terrain conditions of the sector north of Kiew and the weakness of German forces there presented them. After they had to recognize that their action in the Dnjepr knee had proven fruitless, they suddenly turned with new emphasis to the sector north of Kiew. The advance at Tscherkassy had, until then, not attained the desired success, for which reason the 1st Ukrainian Front (formerly Woronesher Front [Voronetz Front] launched the attack to the west at several places north of Kiew (3 November).

Granted, this advance could not be brought into immediate tactical coordination with the operations of the Soviets at Tscherkassy or Krementschug or Dnjepropetrowsk, but it had the objective of affecting the withdrawal of German forces in this sector of the front. This advance into the depth of the

See Map 33.

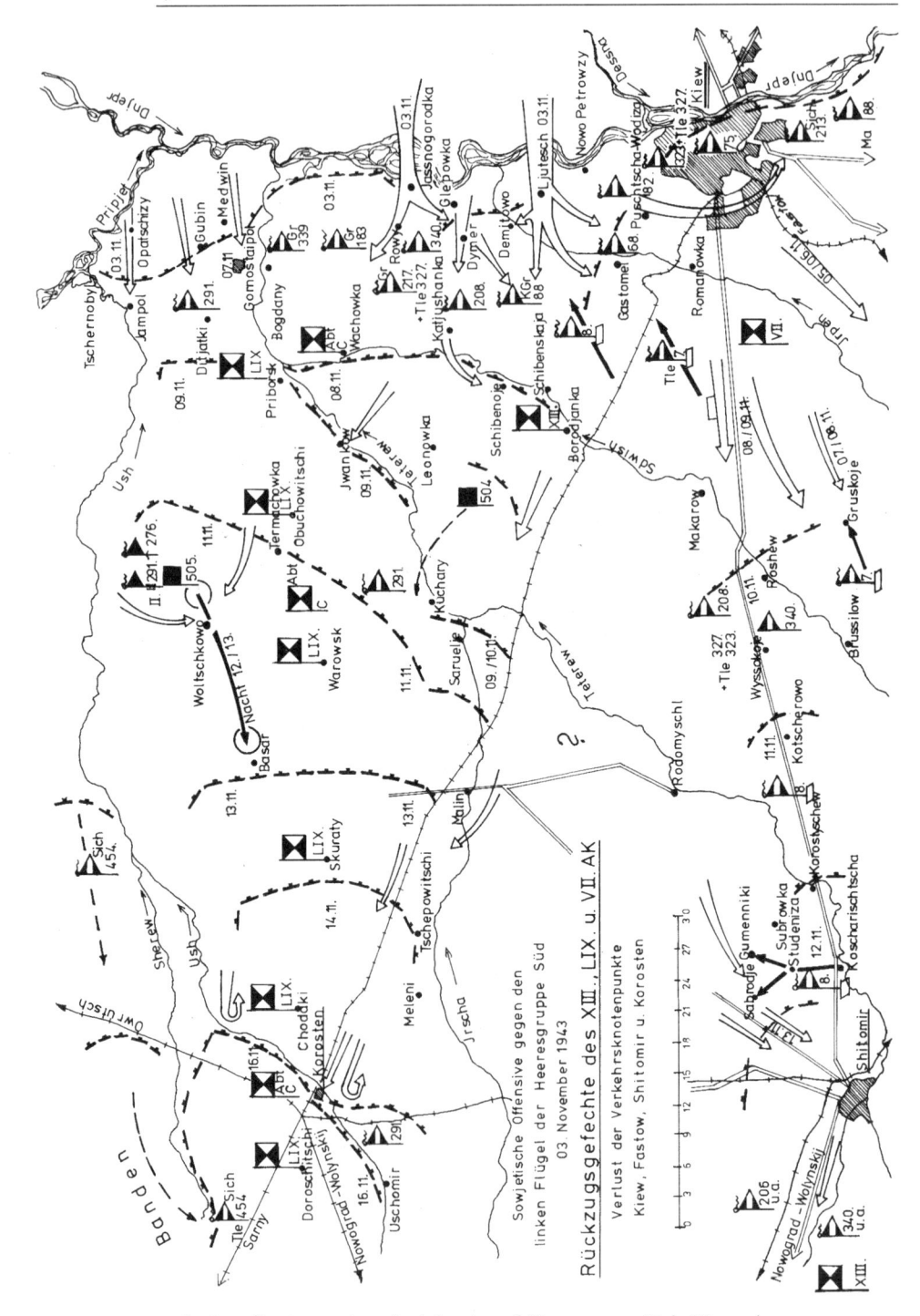

33. Soviet offensive against the left wing of *Heeresgruppe Süd* 3 November, 1943. Fighting Retreat of the 13th, 59th and 7th *Armee Korps*. Loss of the Kiew, Fastow, Shitomir and Korosten transportation hubs.

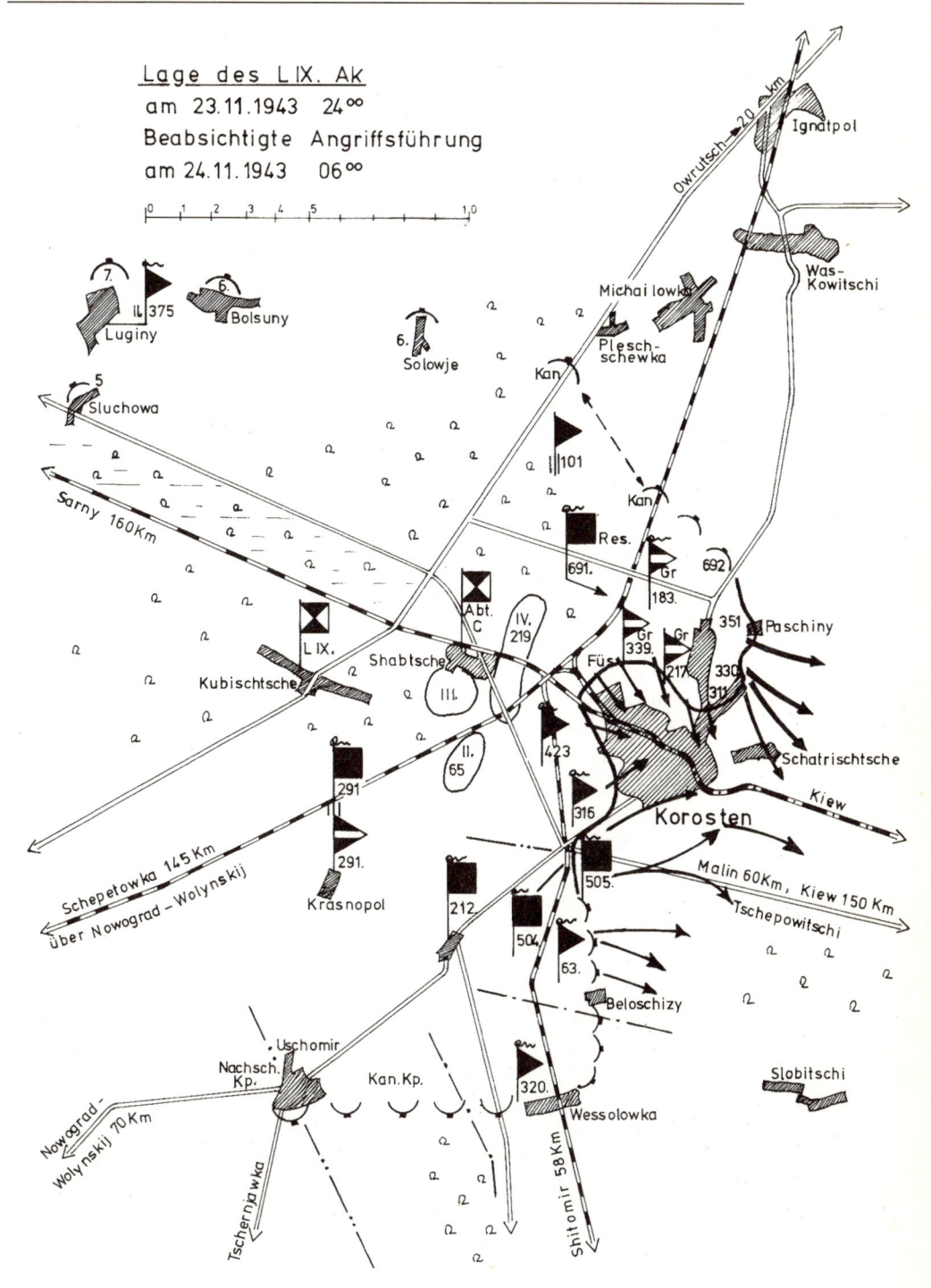

FIGHTING ON THE LEFT WING OF *HEERESGRUPPE SÜD* 137

34. Situation of the 59th *Armee Korps* on 23 November, 1943, 2400 hours. Intended conduct of attack on 24 November, 1943, 0600 hours.

Thrust toward Korosten

The Soviet advance could be divided into two sectors. Initially the Soviets attempted to free up the road connections toward the west by capturing Tschernobyl but also to gain ground to the west by following the road via Gornostaipol. *Korpsabteilung* C had to make a fighting retreat and, on 6/7 November, stood in the line northwest of Katjushanka, west of Manuilsk – Jampol at the Usch river. On 8/9 November the main body of the 291st *Infanterie Division* after shifting to the south was behind the Teterew river from the mouth of the Irscha to northwest of Iwankow (59th *Armee Korps*).

See Map 33.

The advance of strong Soviet infantry forces into the inviting gap disrupted contact right and left for all the German formations. They were, henceforth, alone, without logistical support, some of them without any adequate communications link. One bridgehead-like position at Iwankow could not be held. The 291st *Infanterie Division* was transferred in order to fill a 20 kilometer gap that was yawning between the 13th *Armee Korps* and 59th *Armee Korps*. On 10 November the Soviets crossed the Teterew river at several places with the *Schwerpunkt* of their attack at Iwankow, where they attained a 15 kilometer deep penetration.

The 59th *Armee Korps* now stood, with two divisions, in a 70 kilometer sector facing 11 – 12 Soviet rifle divisions, and that in terrain that was not open to observation, with two swampy river sectors and few bridges. The slender security line offered the Soviets opportunity enough to find additional weak points for further advances, so the regiments had to carry on the fighting, split up into isolated *Kampfgruppen*. The effort of the command to avoid leaving any gap on either side resulted in a brittle *Korps* front. Of the infantry formations committed there, the 291st *Infanterie Division* was the most combat-worthy, but it had to operate independently in empty space and had to attempt, while conducting a fighting retreat, to fall back on Korosten. To its west was a territory, infested with partisans and only held in strongpoints by Hungarian security troops.

See Map 33.

The 291st *Infanterie Division* was then assigned the mission of preventing the open left flank from being outflanked by a northward shift of *Grenadier Regiment* 505 with the attached II./ *Artillerie Regiment* 291 and *Sturmgeschütz Abteilung* 276, and, by artillery fire at the left wing to simulate a fighting retreat covering the retrograde movement of the 59th *Armee Korps*. Enemy forces thrusting toward Korosten separated the elements of the division that had been shifted to the north from the main body of the division. These elements broke through the encirclement during the night of 12/13 November and regained contact with the *Korps* in a 35 kilometer march.

Fighting around Korosten

See Map 33.

On 15 November there was an intense meeting engagement between the Germans and Soviets at Korosten. The train elements that were in the city abandoned it in panic. The 59th *Armee Korps* then built up a line of defense

FIGHTING ON THE LEFT WING OF *HEERESGRUPPE SÜD*

with *Korps Abteilung* C and the 291st *Infanterie Division*, with no contact to right or left, in a semi-circle around the city and secured the city of Zwiahel [Nowogrod-Wolynskij] as a logistical base, even though the road to it led through partisan territory. In the meantime, a roughly 150 kilometer gap had developed to *Heeresgruppe Mitte*. To the south the successful attack of German armoured formations on Shitomir brought immediate relief.

Moreover, the Soviets advanced to the west maintaining southern contact with the Pripjet swamp, apparently by so doing to screen the advance on Korosten from *Heeresgruppe Mitte*. The southern flank was west of Tschernobyl, initially still open, which gave little cause for concern given the natural protection provided by the Pripjet swamp. On 16 November Tschernobyl was lost, after several changes of hand, for the last time, which encouraged the Soviets to advance farther to Owrutsch. On 22 January the 2nd *Armee* of *Heeresgruppe Mitte* pulled its southern flank, which was hanging in thin air to the right and had been repeatedly broken through, back toward Mosyr.

The Soviet advance on Korosten gained particular significance, however, in light of the fact that the supply railroad from Kowel to Shitomir and Berditschew ran through Korosten – along with the twin-tracked Brest – Kowel – Rowno – Schepetowka – Kasatin – Fastow line. The Soviet advance could, however, lead farther into the rear of *Heeresgruppe Süd*. In the immediate area the 59th *Armee Korps*, 291st *Infanterie Divsion* and *Korps Abteilung* C found themselves in danger of envelopment as a result of this Soviet advance. Supplied only by air, on 15 November they evacuated the Tschepowitschi line and fell back, fighting, into a bridgehead position about 25 kilometers distant east of the Usch river, on both sides of Korostem, 12 kilometers southeast and 12 kilometers northeast of the city, respectively. When Korosten was evacuated it was not possible to remove all of the local men who had reached military age. Four weeks later these were facing the German formations in that very sector, incorporated into Russian rifle divisions, along with other Ukrainians who had been released from captivity as German prisoners of war in 1941.

See Maps 3 and 33.

Recapture of Korosten

The 59th *Armee Korps* in the Usch bridgehead position had to concern itself with fighting free the route to Zwiahel, 80 kilometers southwest of Korosten in order to thereby reopen its own supply route. In addition, the *Armee Korps* was ordered to concentrate forces on its wings and deliver powerful flank attacks against the advancing Soviet forces and to hold the positions to prevent the strong enemy from advancing toward Owrutsch or Shitomir. The gap between the 59th *Armee Korps* and 13th *Armee Korps* in the south extended about 40 kilometers, which allowed the Soviets to infiltrate through the gap and envelope the *Korps* on both sides. On 16 November, after heavy street fighting, the city was lost after an enemy penetration of the 291st *Infanterie Division* south of Korosten. The *Korps*' line of defense was, thereby, split. The *Armee* command had no unified concept regarding the tactics to be employed in this situation.

See Map 33.

On 24 November, following a heavy artillery preparation with support from *Sturmgeschütz Abteilung* 276 (4,000 rounds in 15 minutes) the 59th *Armee*

Korps launched an attack with *Korps Abteilung* C in the north and the 291st *Infanterie Division* in the south and encircled the city of Korosten. Relief attacks from outside and breakout attempts from the interior of the encircled city failed. Fighting house-to-house, the group cleaned out the heart of the city by 27 November. *Pionier Bataillon* 219 [183rd *ID*, then *Korps Abt.* C.] wiped out the last Soviets, hiding in cellars. Only a few Red soldiers escaped to the north. 1,500 dead and over 1,200 prisoners remained behind. The defenders repulsed Soviet attacks against the outer front of the ring around Korosten as well as attempts to encircle the Korosten front. The two enemy divisions that had been smashed in the German recapture of Korosten were shortly replaced by three newly introduced rifle divisions.

See Map 34.

New Thrust to the East and Retreat

See Map 34 and, for geography, Map 33.

Regardless of this situation the *Armee* ordered that the Korosten sector be held and an advance toward Tschepowitschi. The attack started on 7 December south of Korosten, departing from the railroad line at the Uschomir railroad station to the east. This attack was, again, the start of a pincers movement. At the same time German armoured formations attacked east of the Shitomir – Korosten railroad line from the south to the north to establish contact with the 59th *Armee Korps* at Korosten. The attack made good initial progress. Enemy resistance stiffened, however, in ensuing days. On 9 December the situation came to a head because Soviet units fell back before the German armoured thrust from south to north and broke into the rear area of *Korps Abteilung* C, at times breaking contact between the division staff and the combat troops. The advance to the south reestablished contact at the Kiew – Korosten railroad line between the 59th *Armee Korps* and the neighbour on the right, and, at the same time, destroyed the cut-off Soviet forces on the heights southeast of Korosten.

Thanks to the great supply dump in Korosten – the German command had set up supply dumps in nearly all the medium and large population centers of the occupied lands – there had been no interruptions in logistical support of the troops. There was, however, a lack of replacement personnel. The battalions of the 291st *Infanterie Division* were down to 50 men, so they were consolidated. The I./*Artillerie Regiment* 291 was disbanded, a *Kanonierkompanie* being formed from its personnel. The commander reported that his division was 'no longer combat-worthy'.

As a result of Soviet pressure farther to the south, the German command transferred armoured forces to the south, wherefore the divisions of the 59th *Armee Korps* (291st *Infanterie Division, Korpsabteilung* C) had to draw back their line of defense by stages in the face of increasing enemy pressure. Despite successful defense against the constantly repeated attacks on the positions west of Uschomir, the Soviets advanced with strong motorized and armoured forces into the gap in the front to its south toward Nowograd – Wolynskij (Zwiahel). Accordingly the German formations had to withdraw rapidly in order to gain contact with the German troops fighting to the south.

En route the march-columns crossed the partisan-infested forests and swamps, without paved roads, communication to *Korps* limited to radio, without normal logistical support, just emergency air-drops of ammunition for the *Sturmgeschütze* and antitank guns. Thus it was that the troops reached the Nowograd-Wolynski (Zwiahel) area via Bolschaja Zwiahel, there building a defensive front in contact with friendly forces. In light of the extreme attrition, there were extensive sectors of the front that were so stretched that they could not stand up to any real pressure.

7

New Push to the West

Soviet Advance Directly North of Kiew

The Soviet advance on the extreme left wing of *Heeresgruppe Süd* reached such a depth that combat operations and movements in this sector could not be further described without going into the additional advance of the Soviets farther south, the advance directly north of Kiew. Here the Soviets found favorable terrain for crossing the river at Ljutesh and Demidowo, though not as favorable as the Pripjet crossing at Tschernobyl of at Gornostaipol. At the end of the month of October/November aerial reconnaissance already reported Soviet assembly positions in the Ljutesh – Demidowo area. The German command was extremely sensitive to such reports, considering the two paved roads from Ljutesh to Kiew and from Demidowo to Kiew. The Soviet advance would, necessarily, have to gain these two roads in order, thereby, to take Kiew from the rear.

See Map 33.

Events North of Kiew

From the time before 3 November the only reports from the 68th *Infanterie Division* reported uncoordinated enemy attacks. Reports from the northern wing of the 7th *Armee Korps* spoke of advances in company and battalion strength against the inner wing of the 13th *Armee Korps* and 59th *Armee Korps*, until 3 November, when the expected attack – though not in the expected strength – opened against the 7th *Armee Korps*, with six Soviet rifle divisions with a sprinkling of armour.

West of the Ljutesh – Kiew road this attack broke through the positions of the 88th *Infanterie Division* and 68th *Infanterie Division*, reaching the Putschtscha-Wodiza summer-house settlement. The *Kampfgruppe* of the 7th *Panzer Division* that had arrived the previous day in the rear area was unable to restore the situation, whereupon the *Armee* had a new blocking position built from the northern edge of Kiew at Putschtscha, Wodiza to Gostomel by the 88th *Infanterie Division*. A *Kampfgruppe* of the 20th *Panzergrenadier Division* came to the aid of the 68th *Infanterie Division*.

See Map 33.

While the Soviets penetrated at the north wing of the 13th *Armee Korps* at Rowny and advanced from there south to Glebowka in order to envelop the center and northern wing of the 340th *Infanterie Division*, in the days that followed they particularly pressed against the lines of the 7th *Armee Korps*, there achieving local penetrations up to three kilometers deep west of the Kiew – Ljutesh road, with another small penetration just north of Demidowo. The German defensive forces could not be reinforced in such haste, the more so since Kiew was no longer able to serve as a railroad junction and unloading point for the passage of rail transports carrying the formations being brought in from the south. Moreover, there were no usable reserve formations at all to the rear.

The next day the Soviets attacked the thinly held line of the 7th *Armee Korps* with strong forces. The northern assault broke through the positions of the 68th *Infanterie Division* and deepened the penetration west of the Kiew – Ljutesh road to the west. The spearhead of the southern assault reached the west and southwest edge of Kiew (6 November) whereby elements of the 88th *Infanterie Division* that initially held on in their positions north of Kiew, were now outflanked in their deep flank. The 68th *Infanterie Division* was forced back to the Irpen river in heavy fighting.

The positions of the 88th *Infanterie Division* and also the city of Kiew had to be evacuated. The latter could no longer be held. After construction of bridges the Soviets now advanced through these farther to the west and south, practically unhindered. *See Map 33.*

The fact that there were two directions of Soviet advance raised hopes in the German command that the Soviets would be divided. The command did not consider the Soviet advance to the west to be as dangerous and threatening as the one aimed farther to the south, which threatened to overtake and envelope the 8th *Armee*.

Soviet Thrust to the West

The Soviets utilized the penetration in the Ljutesh – Demidowo area – constantly changing *Schwerpunkte* of attack and time of attack and making use of an additional small penetration directly north of Demidowo – to advance farther west. There were no reserves of any sort west of this area that could be thrown against them, so the Soviets advanced against a line of the northern wing of the 7th *Armee Korps* that was only held as a series of strongpoints. Enemy armoured formations advanced from the Romanowka and Irpen area over the Kiew – Shitomir road. An armoured *Kampfgruppe* of the 7th *Panzer Division* opposed them. The various Soviet attack *Schwerpunkte* had the effect that the fighting took place in a number of small engagements. That particularly complicated any unified conduct of the fighting by the *Korps* and division, due to the breakdown of telephone connections. *See Map 33.*

The 8th *Panzer Division* held its positions west of Kotschorowo at the Kiew – Shitomir road in heavy defensive fighting. On 11 November motorized enemy infantry pushed forward into the area just south of Chodorkoff and forced the *Korps* to pull its forward line back to this area. Alarm units formed from men returning from leave and rear area troops as well as security forces stood in the general line Kosharischtscha – 12 kilometers west of Korostyschew – Subrowka – and held off the next Soviet frontal attack on both sides of the Kiew – Shitomir *Rollbahn*. The 8th *Panzer Division* attacked to the northwest against advancing cavalry that was enveloping to the north, took Studeniza and Ssabrodja and advanced to Gumenniki. Nevertheless, the Soviets reached Shitomir on 13 November. Shitomir was a vital logistical and transport nodal point for the supply of *Heeresgruppe Süd*, with roads and, to a lesser extent, railroads fanning out from it to all points of the compass.

The Shitomir Situation

With that the Soviets attained a first operational breakthrough. Whether it could be considered successful depended, however, on the degree to which the Soviets knew how to make use of it and whether German countermeasures would be able to stop them from further progress. Certainly the Soviet command had not yet conceived of a great tactical pincers movement in conjunction with the advance on Kirowograd, first because this combat area was much farther west than the Kirowograd – Kriwoi Rog area and, second, because the two operational areas were so far apart. It is clear that, at that time of the war, neither Soviet planning nor boldness extended to include such far-reaching operations. Apparently the Soviet command merely concerned itself with gaining ground to the west and weakening the entire Dnjepr front by severing the Korosten – Shitomir – Fastow and Rowno – Berditschew – Fastow supply lines. Granted, on that day, alarm units were still fighting in the extreme southwest portion of the city of Shitomir, others in the stream sector south of the city. The 8th *Panzer Division* and elements of *Kavallerie-Regiment Süd* were west of the city in the general line Derman – Baryschewka (center). That did not prevent the Soviets from advancing farther from Shitomir toward Zwiahel with a group of 15 AFVs as far as the fork in the road south of Pulin, where remnants of the 208th *Infanterie Division* and 340th *Infanterie Division* stood with the mission of advancing on Shitomir. At that time, however there was no contact between the 59th *Armee Korps* and the left wing of the adjoining *Korps*, not even with *Korps-Abteilung* C in the Korosten area.

On 15 November the 7th *Panzer Division* reached the eastern edge of Stanischewka (four kilometers southeast of Shitomir) after a bold advance without significant enemy resistance and secured against the enemy in the woods north of the Iwniza – Shitomir railroad line. South of Shitomir alarm units supported by *Sturmgeschütze* launched an attack and ran into strong enemy resistance three kilometers south of Shitomir on the Berditschew – Shitomir road. West of Shitomir reconnaissance of the 8th *Panzer Division* and 208th *Infanterie Division* identified enemy forces in unchanged strength in their former positions.

In the ensuing days the German line of defense there grew stronger. Elements of the 1st *SS-Panzer Division 'Leibstandarte SS Adolf Hitler'*, 1st *Panzer Division*, 7th *Panzer Division* and 8th *Panzer Division* arrived to stop further Soviet advance in an arc around Shitomir. The Soviets paused there for several days, possibly to reorganize their troops, perhaps, also, in so far as their desire for victory went no further – to collect the immense amount of booty that they had found in the supply dumps in Shitomir, especially rations dumps.

Advance to the South

In addition to this thrust to the west the Soviets used the opportunity to advance past the west side of Kiew to the south. Elements of the 10th *Panzer Grenadier Division* of the 8th *Armee* that had, in the meantime, been brought in, initially brought the Soviets to a halt 50 kilometers south of Kiew, in order to prevent the Soviets from immediately rolling up the Dnjepr front by a continued advance past Kiew on the west to the south. The 7th *Panzer*

Division, with batteries of the 1st *Flak Korps*, alarm units and units made up of men returning from leave, received the mission of holding the important railroad center of Fastow. That, however, was not a success. This important railroad hub (60 kilometers southwest of Kiew), through which the entire logistical support for *Heeresgruppe Süd* passed from Brest – Kowel – Rowno via Tschepetowka – Berditschew – Kasatin on twin-tracked lines, was, thereby, lost. Soviet armoured forces even advanced on the Kiew – Biala Zerkwa road to the Pawlotsch – Poljnja area.

See Maps 3 and 35.

In the meantime the *Armee* concentrated all the forces that the *Heeresgruppe* believed it could free up from other sectors of the front, first, to recapture Fastow and, second, initially to secure the Shitomir supply base and, later, to recapture it. Accomplishing this mission proved extremely difficult, since all of the formations intended for this action first had to be brought in. To the extent that the twin-tracked railroad west of the Dnjepr was available for this function the movement was accomplished nearly to perfection. Considering the condition of the roads, local fog and also snow, bringing up units by wheeled vehicles was more difficult.

A division that had been activated in Norway and never been proven in battle, the 25th *Panzer Division*, was brought in from France by rail. Its wheeled elements made it to Berditschew, the tracked elements to Kirowograd as a result of some kind of incorrect instructions. An advance party of the 1st *SS-Panzer Division 'Leibstandarte Adolf Hitler'* received orders to assemble in the general direction of the Browki railroad station, the 7th *Panzer Division* behind the Ssywka stream between Tomaschewka and Gruskoje. Alarm units formed from rear area service troops stood on both sides of Roshew. Elements of the 8th *Panzer Division* recaptured the road crossing over the Sdwish river. The 340th *Infanterie Division* and 208th *Infanterie Division* continued to fall back.

See Map 35.

On 9 November the 25th *Panzer Division* captured Fastowez. However, a further advance by this division on Fastow failed. The division's vehicles bogged down hopelessly in the rain-soaked roads. The division lacked experience with such road conditions.

Among the prisoners were members of a Soviet formation that had earlier been in action at the Dnjepr bend south of Perejasslaw. The caused the German command, regardless of the now completely mud-bound roads, to also pull the 19th *Panzer Division* out of that area and set it in march with its motorized elements toward Fastow, the tracked elements going by rail. Further Soviet advance both via Shitomir to the west and also via Biala Zerkwa to the south had to be stopped at all costs to prevent the entire *Heeresgruppe Süd* front from teetering.

The German command, in an event, considered it necessary, despite severe mud conditions of the roads and resultant total traffic jams, to hastily bring in the 19th *Panzer Division*. The result was a dangerous state of confusion on the rear-area roads involving vehicles of the 1st *SS-Panzer Division 'Leibstandarte SS Adolf Hitler'* and, especially, those of the 25th *Panzer Division*, which had no experience at all with conditions of combat on the Eastern Front, and no driving experience on the muddy Russian roads. The 25th *Panzer Division* was, by no stretch of the imagination, fit to be rated 'combat-ready' for major commitment on the Eastern Front.

Against the advice and over the protests of the *Generalinspekteur der Panzertruppen, Generaloberst* Guderian, *OKH* had transferred this division, which had only been activated for a short period of time, in rapid-transport to the Eastern Front, and immediately thrown it into action. Since there were no other available formations, *Heeresgruppe Süd* had no other choice but to set the wheeled elements of the 25th *Panzer Division* in march toward Fastow as fast as they arrived, directly from their detraining station southwest of Berditschew. The elements that had assembled southwest of Fastow were ordered, on 6 November, to capture and hold Fastow in the fastest way possible – this in cooperation with a *Panzergrenadier Regiment* of the *SS-Panzergrenadier Division 'Das Reich'* that was *en route* – and then to defend Fastow against all enemy assaults.

On 7 November leading elements of *Panzergrenadier Regiment* 146 [of the 25th *Panzer Division*] ran into strong packs of Soviet T 34 tanks and panicked. The young, inexperienced elements fell back in great disorder. The division commander, who arrived shortly thereafter, reassembled them under his personal influence and then insured the stance of the regiment even under pressure from hotly pursuing Soviet armour. Nevertheless, these elements of the regiment thereby lost a portion of their vehicles on the approach march. With its remaining elements, which the division commander again led against Fastow, the regiment occupied a blocking position south and west of Fastow, thereby preventing a further enemy advance into the assembly area of the additional German units that were approaching.

Kampfgruppe von Wechmar (*Panzergrenadier Regiment* 146 of the 25th *Panzer Division*), together with the leading elements of *Panzer Regiment* 9 of the same division, which had arrived in Biala Zerkoff on 9 November, penetrated into the southern and southeastern outskirts of Fastow. However, limited enemy forces then held them in check there. At least this action provided a certain breathing-space during which the Germans could bring in the requisite armoured formations for a resolute attack.

In these actions the 25th *Panzer Division* lost so many men that it seemed it would be weeks before it could be used for major offensive operations. The bitter experience gained from the commitment of this division proved that the Soviets could out-maneuver such a unit lacking in experience on the East Front, and that inexperienced troops stood no chance against them. The 25th *Panzer Division* had lost heavily in both personnel, matériel also, since it had lost a large share of its vehicles. It was replenished with detachments of troops from both Greece and northern Italy, as well as from the west.

See Map 35.

8

German Counterattack

Recapture of Shitomir

During these Soviet advances to the south, the 48th *Panzer Korps* launched an advance of the 1st *SS-Panzer Division 'Leibstandarte SS Adolf Hitler'* from the south against the Soviet Kiew – Shitomir route of advance, the logistical support route and vital artery of the Soviets, thereby blocking this road. The 25th *Panzer Division* took over protecting the eastern flank of the *Leibstandarte* forces committed there. While this was happening the armoured *Kampfgruppe* of the 1st *Panzer Division* that was involved in the thrust to Kotscherowo advanced to the west and recaptured Shitomir in cooperation with the 7th *Panzer Division*, which had been brought up from the south. Elements of the 8th *Panzer Division* as well as the 20th *Panzer Division* were involved, as well as the 68th *Infanterie Division*, which adjoined behind the right wing of the southern group. Thus it was that the 1st *Panzer Division* attacking from the east and the 7th *Panzer Division* attacking from the south again took Shitomir during the night of 19/20 November. The significant logistical support base with its abundant supply dumps and depots was again in German hands.

Preparations for a German Counterattack

Attached to the 48th *Panzer Korps* for the counterattack west of Kiew that was so important to the forces fighting around Korosten were no less than six *Panzer* divisions and one infantry division (1st *Panzer Division*, 7th *Panzer Division*, 1st *SS – Panzer Division 'Leibstandarte SS Adolf Hitler'*, 19th *Panzer Division*, not available before 18 November, the 25th *Panzer Division*, weakened by losses, a weak *Kampfgruppe* of the *SS-Panzergrenadier Division 'Das Reich'* as well as the (horse-drawn) 68th *Infanterie Division*. The left-adjoining neighbour of the 48th *Panzer Korps* was supposed to be *'Armeeabteilung Mattenklott'* [*General der Infanterie* Franz Mattenklott], then the 13th *Armee Korps* and 59th *Armee Korps*, along with an assortment of alarm-units. The 68th *Infanterie Division* and 213th *Sicherungs Division* [security division] mopped up the forest region south of the Kiew – Shitomir road, across this to the north and relieved elements of the 1st *Panzer Division* and/or 7th *Panzer Division* respectively.

In addition, the 8th *Panzer Division*, 20th *Panzergrenadier Division*, 208th *Infanterie Division* and elements of the 2nd *Fallschirmjäger Division* supported the right wing. The right wing was to advance via Fastow and cut off the Soviet frontal salient west of Kiew in order to cripple any further enemy attempt to attack to the west, and to encircle and destroy whatever enemy forces might be there. The supreme command, however, considered that this plan was too ambitious and therefore limited it to the capture of Shitomir and the formation of a *Kessel* near Brussilow.

148 **CRUCIBLE OF COMBAT**

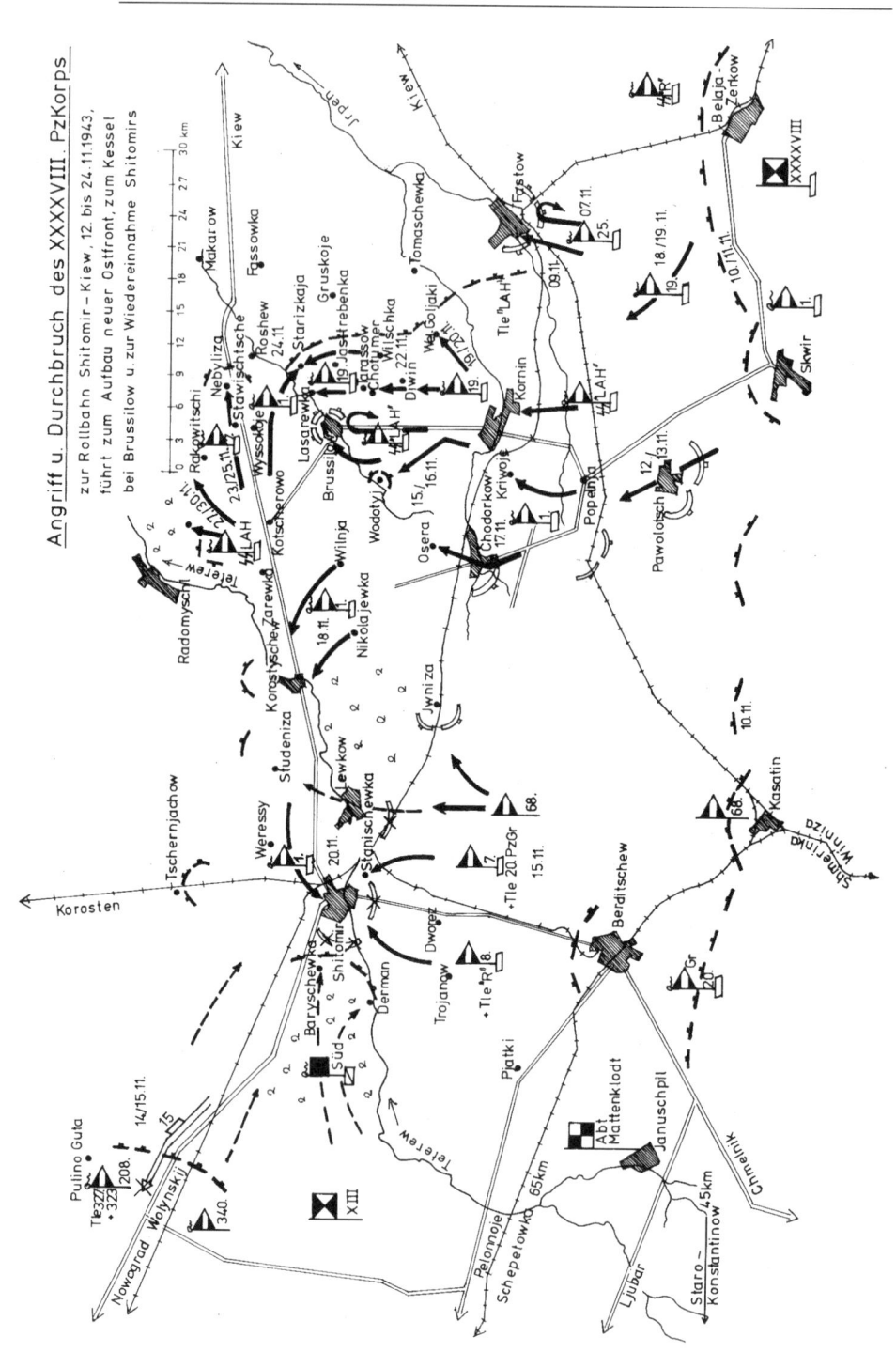

35. Attack and breakthrough of the 48th *Panzer Korps* to the Shitomir – Kiew *Rollbahn*, 12 to 24 November, 1943, leading to building a new eastern front, to the Brussilow *Kessel* and to the recapture of Shitomir.

Battle of the Brussilow *Kessel*

In the event, the command of the Soviet Southern Front recovered itself after the loss of Shitomir and, on 18/19 November, launched a new attack with its 1st Guards Cavalry Corps and the 5th and 8th Guards Tank Corps against the covering forces at Brussilow (1st *SS-Panzer Division 'Leibstandarte SS Adolf Hitler'*) and Korostyschew (1st *Panzer Division*) – without, however, achieving success. Soviet armoured formations appeared at Brussilow. Accordingly the 19th *Panzer Division* was ordered to move on Brussilow from the south, the *Leibstandarte* from the west, while the 1st *Panzer Division* moved along the Shitomir – Kiew road to the east, later turning to the southeast and south. The 7th *Panzer Division* was to advance past Radomyschl on the south in order to secure the defensive flank along the Teterew river along with 68th *Infanterie Division*, which was shifting along the left side of the 7th *Panzer Division*.

See Map 35.

The frontal attack of the 1st *SS-Panzer Division 'Leibstandarte SS Adolf Hitler'* on Brussilow failed, while the 7th *Panzer Division* accomplished its mission. After initial hard fighting the 1st *Panzer Division* thrust forward on both sides of the Shitomir – Kiew *Rollbahn* deep into the rear of the enemy forces that were east of Brussilow. Although still exhausted from the recent nerve-racking fighting in the Dnjepr knee and the forced march over mud-bound, traffic-jammed roads, the 19th *Panzer Division* broke through the enemy flank security on the right wing of the corps, advancing toward the 25th *Panzer Division* and *SS-Panzergrenadier Division 'Das Reich'*, thrust on to the northeast and, losing only four men, destroyed about 16 enemy AFVs and over 35 antitank guns. The 4th *Panzer Armee* ordered the 1st and 19th *Panzer Divisionen* (on 22 November) to carry on the attack. On 23 November the 1st *Panzer Division* took Wysokoje, about 12 – 15 kilometers northeast of Brussilow, on the main *Rollbahn* to Kiew and, after forming flank protection to the north and east, turned in to the south.

In a night attack *Oberst* Bradel led *Panzergrenadier Regiment* 113 [1st *Panzer Division*] and his armour and pioneers forward over the stubbornly-defended Sdwish sector, immediately pursued, when the enemy troops finally fell back, and there ran into the *Panzers* and *SPWs* of the fiercely fighting 19th *Panzer Division*, approaching from the south. Mopping up the resultant *Kessel* brought in a large number of prisoners, destroyed 153 AFVs as well as the capture of 70 guns and 250 antitank guns. The Soviets had over 3,000 dead to mourn. There were, however, several gaps in the ring of encirclement which gave the Soviet command the opportunity to bring all the staff officers and commissars, and several specialists, out of the encirclement. Not one higher officer was captured, nor were any staff-officers among the dead.

After this operation was concluded the temperature rose on 26 November, producing mud and morass. That led to cancellation of any further attacks against the Soviet front west of Kiew. At that time German reconnaissance of the front was excellent. The division radio interception units monitored radio traffic between Soviet troop elements and promptly deciphered all communications, passing them on to the *Korps*.

150 **CRUCIBLE OF COMBAT**

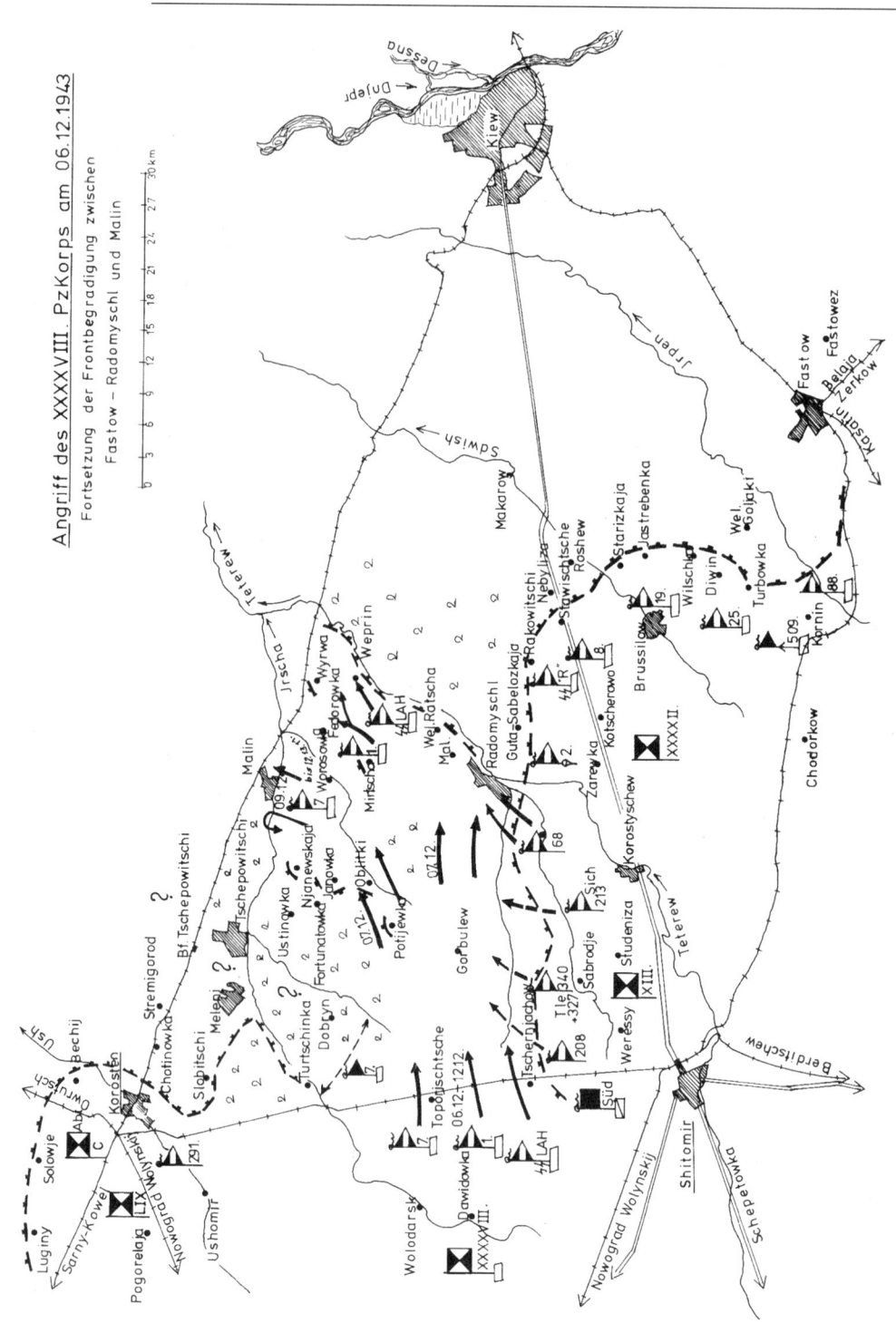

36. Attack of the 48th *Panzer Korps* on 6 December, 1943. Continuation of frontal straightening between Fastow – Radomyschl and Malin.

Battle of Radomyschl

In a night march in light frost and moonlight, the 7th *Panzer Division* attacked toward the east-northeast. Along the road to Korosten it ran into strongly fortified enemy field positions, though these were, generally, not fully manned. The defenders were totally surprised, in some places caught with front reversed, because they had not detected the enveloping movement of the German forces. That held true especially for the sectors of the 1st *Panzer Division* and 7th *Panzer Division*. After crossing the north – south road the attack moved forward smoothly, penetrating deep into the enemy's main defensive area. By noon the Soviet 60th *Armee* disappeared from radio traffic. Shortly thereafter the II./ *Panzer Regiment* 1 of the 1st *Panzer Division* rolled over elements of the Soviet army headquarters. In the evening of 6 December the formations had rolled up the Soviet front to a depth of 30 kilometers. Bombers of the 8th *Fliegerkorps* supported the attack.

See Map 36.

During the night of 7/8 December the 1st *SS-Panzer Division 'Leibstandarte SS Adolf Hitler'* thrust deeply through the enemy dispositions, but was then left without fuel. On the next day the fuel trucks had to search for the AFVs on the terrain before they could be refueled. The 1st *Panzer Division* again broke all enemy resistance and broke through in the area north and northeast of Radomyschl. The 1st *SS-Panzer Division 'Leibstandarte SS Adolf Hitler'* later closed up. The 1st *Panzer Division* continued to smash packs of enemy armour, advancing toward the northern suburbs of Radomyschl. It established contact northeast of Radomyschl with elements of *Panzergrenadier Regiment* 1 which had already gained the Teterew river. In fierce fighting the 7th *Panzer Division* wound its way through to the east, south of the Irscha, and smashed enemy forces on the west bank of the river at Malin. By 9 December it generally mopped up the area between the Irscha and Teterew rivers. Moreover it eliminated the Soviet bridgehead south of Malin and built its own bridgehead on the east bank of the Irscha. While this was happening the 68th *Infanterie Division*, as the leading division of the right wing of the *Korps*, closed up behind the armoured formations. The 1st *Panzer Division* , 1st *SS-Panzer Division 'Leibstandarte SS Adolf Hitler'* and the 68th *Infanterie Division* then smashed the remaining enemy forces in the Radomyschl area.

With that, the main body of the Soviet 60th Army was shattered. Judging by the massive ammunition dumps and the excellent available road network there could be little doubt that the Germans had forestalled a Soviet offensive with wide-ranging objectives.

Northeast of Radomyschl there was still a substantial Soviet bridgehead on the west bank of the Teterew. The 1st *Panzer Division* and 1st *SS – Panzer Division 'Leibstandarte SS Adolf Hitler'* smashed this, encircling 3½ enemy divisions in a closely coordinated attack. On the following day both *Panzer* divisions split this *Kessel*, wiping out the encircled enemy troops. Other forces that attempted to free their comrades in the *Kessel* north of Radomyschl suffered heavy bloody losses. The success of this battle included 36 enemy AFVs and 2-4 antitank guns.

See Map 36.

On 14 December the 1st *Panzer Division* and 1st *SS-Panzer Division 'Leibstandarte SS Adolf Hitler'* supported the 7th *Panzer Division*, which was fighting at Malin, with local limited attacks in the opposing direction, passing by Ferewoka [Federowka] on the northeast and, in bitter fighting, smashing another combat group between the Irscha and Teterew rivers. However, they were unable initially to link up with the 7th *Panzer Division*. The armour was withdrawn and assembled as a *Korps* reserve around and north of Gorbulew. At that time the Russians seemed extremely confused by this spectral German attack that seemed to come out of the night. Their radio traffic made clear the fragmented confusion and fear. This led, in any case, by 15 December to quieting down of the situation on both sides of Radomyschl.

Fighting East of Meleni

See Map 37 and, for geography, Map 36.

The 4th *Panzer Armee* suspected the presence of an unknown number of Soviet formations, including armoured formations, in the area east of Korosten and around Meleni. The 7th *Panzer Division* and 1st *Panzer Division* and the 1st *SS-Panzer Division 'Leibstandarte SS Adolf Hitler'* therefore were ordered to envelop these forces from both sides. By way of deception, elements of the 1st *Panzer Division* initially marched by day toward Berditschew, reversing their direction in the night. To conceal intentions, there was no German reconnaissance. The *Korps* set the start of the attack for 0900 hours on 18 December. The attack started with a heavy artillery preparation by 30 batteries and a *Nebelwerfer* brigade on the sector before the 1st *SS-Panzer Division 'Leibstandarte SS Adolf Hitler'* with 25 AFVs attached, initially to advance on Tschepowitschi, east of Meleni at the Irscha. After initial ground-gains the artillerists engaged other targets, namely the enemy positions to the northeast before the strongpoints of the right wing of the 291st *Infanterie Division*, (east of Dessjatin).

See Maps 36 and 38.

The 1st *Panzer Division* attacked Soviet security at and north of Meleni. Elements of the I./ *Panzer Regiment* 1 advanced against the flanks and rear of the enemy forces around Meleni. The 1st *SS-Panzer Division 'Leibstandarte SS Adolf Hitler'* forced its way to the area of Tschepowitschi. The 1st *Panzer Division*

Chatinowka on Map 37.

swung out to the north and then turned in to the southeast, advancing via Kasinowka into the area south of Stremigorod as far as six to eight kilometers north of the railroad station with the same name as Tschepowitschi. On the third day of the attack only 10–15 kilometers separated the spearheads of the 1st *Panzer Division* and the 1st *SS-Panzer Division 'Leibstandarte SS Adolf Hitler'*. The 7th *Panzer Division* likewise came from the southeast, so that the *Korps* command had justified hopes, on 20 December, that it would be able to conclude a successful *Kessel* battle in the area east of Meleni. Soviet relief attacks from the east foundered on the tough defense of the covering forces of the 7th *Panzer Division* and 1st *Panzer Division*.

Nevertheless, it proved impossible to close the 'sack'. Granted, the 1st *SS-Panzer Division 'Leibstandarte SS Adolf Hitler'* knocked out 65 AFVs south of the Irscha. While this was happening the 1st *Panzer Division* spent the entire day in fierce, incessant, eventful fighting south and east of the Tschepowitschi railroad station in the area east of Tremigorod – knocking out a large number of T 34 tanks. After, on the following day, the 7th and 1st *Panzer Divisionen* repulsed strong enemy relief attacks from the east and northeast in the rear of their armoured assault groups, on 22 December the Soviets also attacked

GERMAN COUNTERATTACK 153

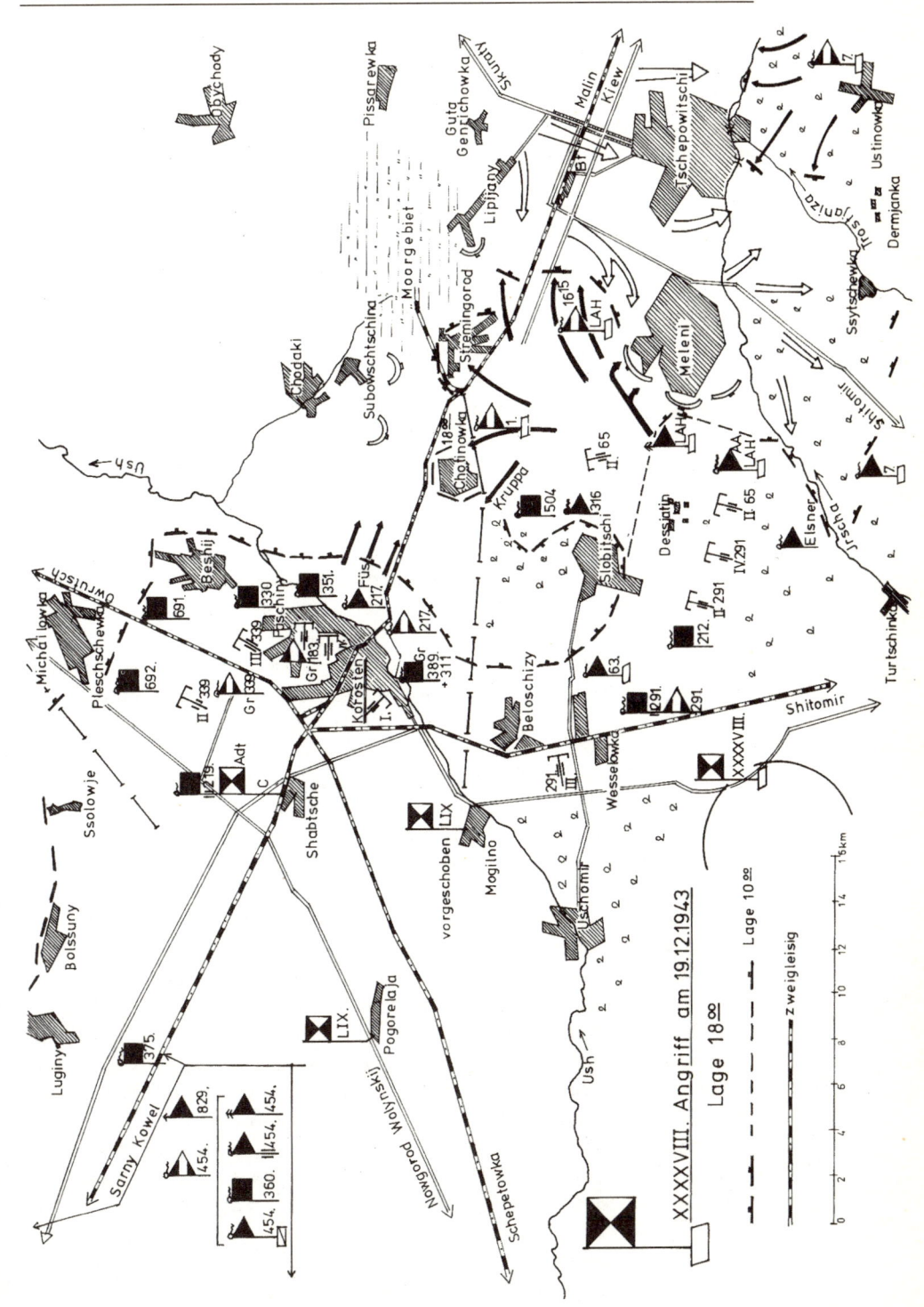

37. 48th *Panzer Korps* Attack on 19 December, 1943. Situation at 1800 hours.
[Lage 10 00 = situation 1000 hours; zweigleisig = twin-tracked railroad].

out of the 'sack' east of Meleni towards three sides in such strength that they knocked the breath out of the German formations. Nevertheless the German forces mastered every crisis. The *Panzer*-artillery shattered a series of strong counterattacks and numerous infantry attacks with armoured support at their very beginnings. The number of AFVs destroyed rose substantially. The enemy, however, proved to be far stronger than initially believed. Maps found on a fallen Soviet major revealed that one to two Soviet rifle divisions were west of Meleni and, in the 'sack' east of Meleni an additional three Soviet armoured corps and four Soviet rifle corps. In fact, the Soviet high command had assembled its forces for a massive offensive from the Meleni – Tschepowitschi area against Shitomir.

See Maps 38 and 39.

After this concentration of troops was recognized by the Germans, they had to reckon on a change of Soviet tactics. The intention to next attack the 48th *Panzer Korps* and eliminate it became apparent. The *Korps* command accordingly resolved to go over to the defensive. The 1st *SS-Panzer Division 'Leibstandarte SS Adolf Hitler'*, however, remained fixed in intense fighting south of Tschepowitschi. In the meanwhile, farther to the north, the 1st *Panzer Division* fended off repeated attacks by three tank corps and destroyed another 68 enemy AFVs, mostly T 34 tanks. On the next day (24 December) the *Panzer Korps* pulled its enveloping wings out of the area on both sides of Meleni, because the Soviets continued to attempt to envelop and cut off the forward-echeloned forces of the 7th *Panzer Division* and 1st *Panzer Division*. The 7th *Panzer Division* pulled back to Malin, the 1st *Panzer Division* to the area south of Stremigorod (southeast of Korosten). Both went over to the defensive.

With that the 48th *Panzer Korps* forestalled a painstakingly prepared and concealed enemy offensive against the Shitomir – Korosten area. If this offensive had been carried out it would have rapidly overwhelmed the northern wing of the 4th *Panzer Armee*, the weakened 13th *Armee Korps* and the 59th *Armee Korps*. Nevertheless, the formations of the 4th *Panzer Armee* could look back for this period on a total of 700 captured or destroyed enemy AFVs and 668 guns.

The Situation East of Shitomir

See Maps 33 and 36.

Of the three enemy troop concentrations that had crossed the Dnjepr north of Kiew in November, the first was, after being smashed and wiped out at Brussilow, no longer extant. The second had been smashed in the Radomyschl – Shitomir area and, at the very least, dispersed. The third group, southwest of Korosten, was badly battered. Such losses of armour and men would have to initially bring the Soviets to a halt and admonish them to be cautious. Nevertheless, they immediately made good their losses. The next day's prisoners, however, showed that the Soviet manpower consisted of 50 percent Asians, and, indeed, of men drawn from the most distant corners of the USSR, many of them old men. The remaining 50 percent consisted of young men who had reached military age during the German occupation of the Ukraine, some of them only 13 years old. The Soviets apparently employed the best age groups to fill out their Guards formations. Such evidence nourished the hope that the limits of Soviet manpower reserves could still be reached.

GERMAN COUNTERATTACK

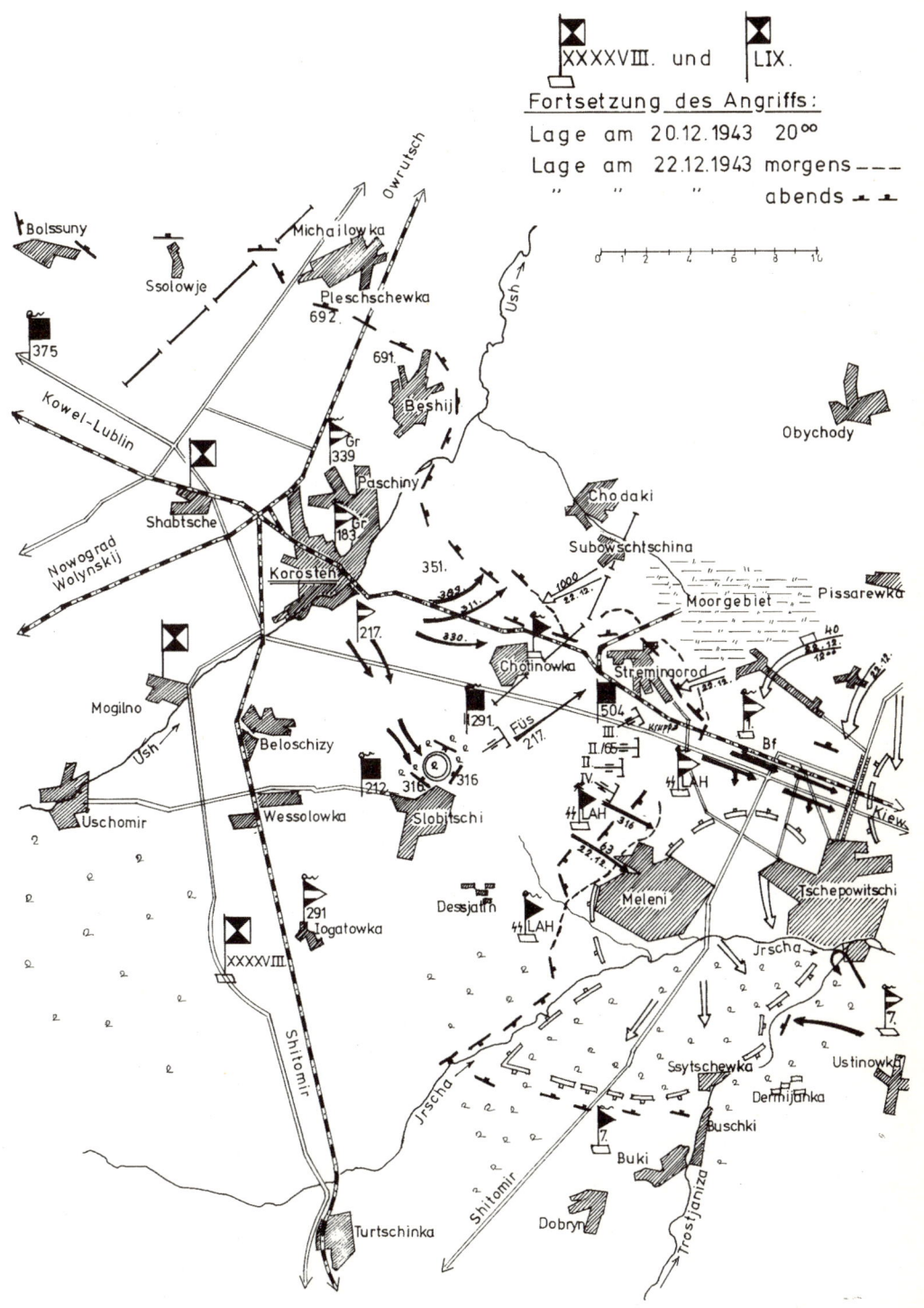

38. Continuation of the Attack. Situation on 20 December, 1943, 2000 hours. Situation on 22 December, 1943, morning. Situation on 22 December, 1943, evening.

Defense in the Shitomir Area

See Map 39.

Now the 48th *Panzer Korps* had to build a new defensive front in the line extending from Shitomir to east of Berditschew. The retreat through Shitomir caused chaos for traffic in the city. In addition to the logistical services of the fighting troops, the 4th *Panzer Armee* still had the 18th *Artillerie Division* in the city, with the result that more than 20,000 men and thousands of military vehicles were jammed into its streets. Despite energetic regulation of one-way traffic by the military police, Shitomir had turned into a regular 'mousetrap'. Because of the lack of good bypass roads the *Panzer* divisions arriving from the north, the 1st *Panzer Division*, 7th *Panzer Division* and 1st *SS-Panzer Division 'Leibstandarte SS Adolf Hitler'* had to pass through the city.

9

Renewed Soviet Offensive

Soviet Christmas Offensive

On 24 December the Soviets launched their offensive and continued it in the ensuing days, with *Schwerpunkt* on the southern wing in the Kornin area. Here they were again able to tear open the front and force the wing back to the west. The *Armee* made several attempts to construct lines of resistance. However, on 26 December the Soviet attack gained additional ground and forced the left wing of the 7th *Armee Korps* and the right wing of the 48th *Panzer Korps* back to the Kamenka – sector, Trylissy – Paripssy – Browki. Only isolated resistance groups of the 1st *Panzer Division* and 8th *Panzer Division* held on between the Shitomir – Popelnja road and Shitomir – Kiew in the Scaforostowka area and south of Korostyschew. The 1st *Panzer Division* was able to prop up the situation at the Shitomir – Kiew road in the Korostyschew area. North of the Teterew, however, the Soviets forced the front back up to five kilometers and took possession of Radomyschl.

See Map 39.

On 27 December the Red Army achieved the two-sided envelopment of Korostyschew by deep penetrations through elements of the 8th *Panzer Division* and *Kampfgruppe SS-Panzergrenadier Division 'Das Reich'* and forced both *Kampfgruppen* back to the Kmitoff – Studeniza line. The Soviets attacked the right wing of the 13th *Armee Korps* in division strength with support of 30 AFVs and forced it back to the Beresowka – Tschaikowka line.

See Map 39.

The weather (snow and fog) enabled the attackers to approach close to the German lines. At the very least, the Soviets regained the initiative, so that the 8th *Panzer Division* also had to pull its lines back, as did the 25th *Panzer Division*. The 19th *Panzer Division* gave up Brussilow, found its own route of retreat already blocked and 'hedgehogged' initially in Torbowka. *Panzer Regiment 27* [19th *Panzer Division*] knocked out 30 AFVs in repulsing the enemy attack. Radio contact broke down between the 19th *Panzer Division* and the 48th *Panzer Korps*, after the last report from the division that it was under attack by 30 enemy AFVs and had no more fuel. The 48th *Panzer Korps*, however, could not assist the 19th *Panzer Division* at that point because it, itself, first had to deal with the spearheads of the Soviet attack in the Shitomir area. The 19th *Panzer Division* had to fight free its own retreat route to Jelissawetiwka.

Siwawe, however, located on the route, was held by the enemy and was barred to through passage. With guidance from a Ukrainian peasant, the division was able to reach the Teterow crossing at Lewkoff via swampy woods roads in a torturous 40 kilometer detour that put great demands on fuel, matériel and men. With that the division could only hope for, but not expect, a quiet end of the year. On 28 December it took positions at the east edge of Shitomir.

158 **CRUCIBLE OF COMBAT**

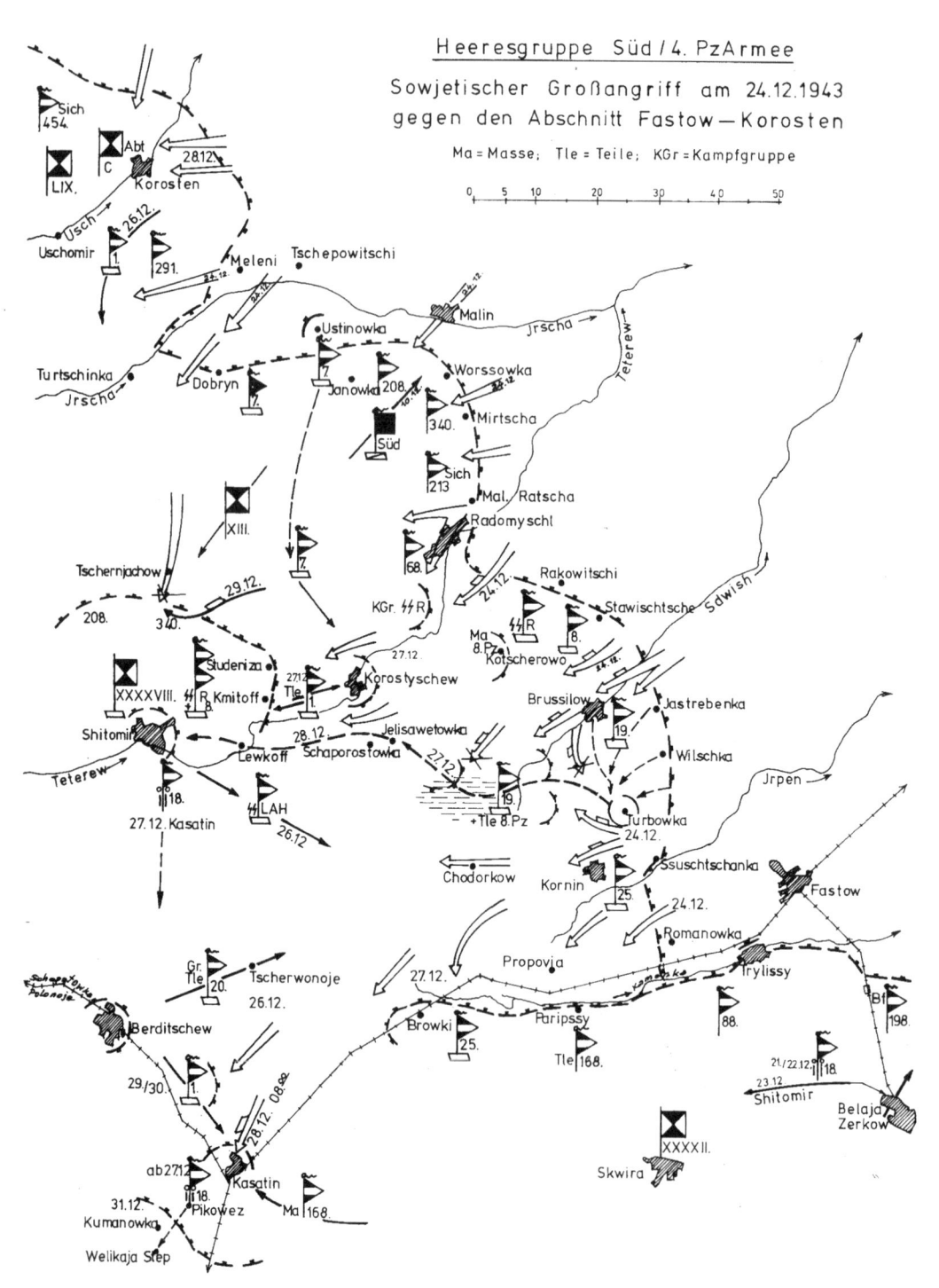

39. *Heeresgruppe Süd / 4th Panzer Armee.* Soviet Offensive on 24 December 1943 against the Fastow – Korosten sector.

RENEWED SOVIET OFFENSIVE 159

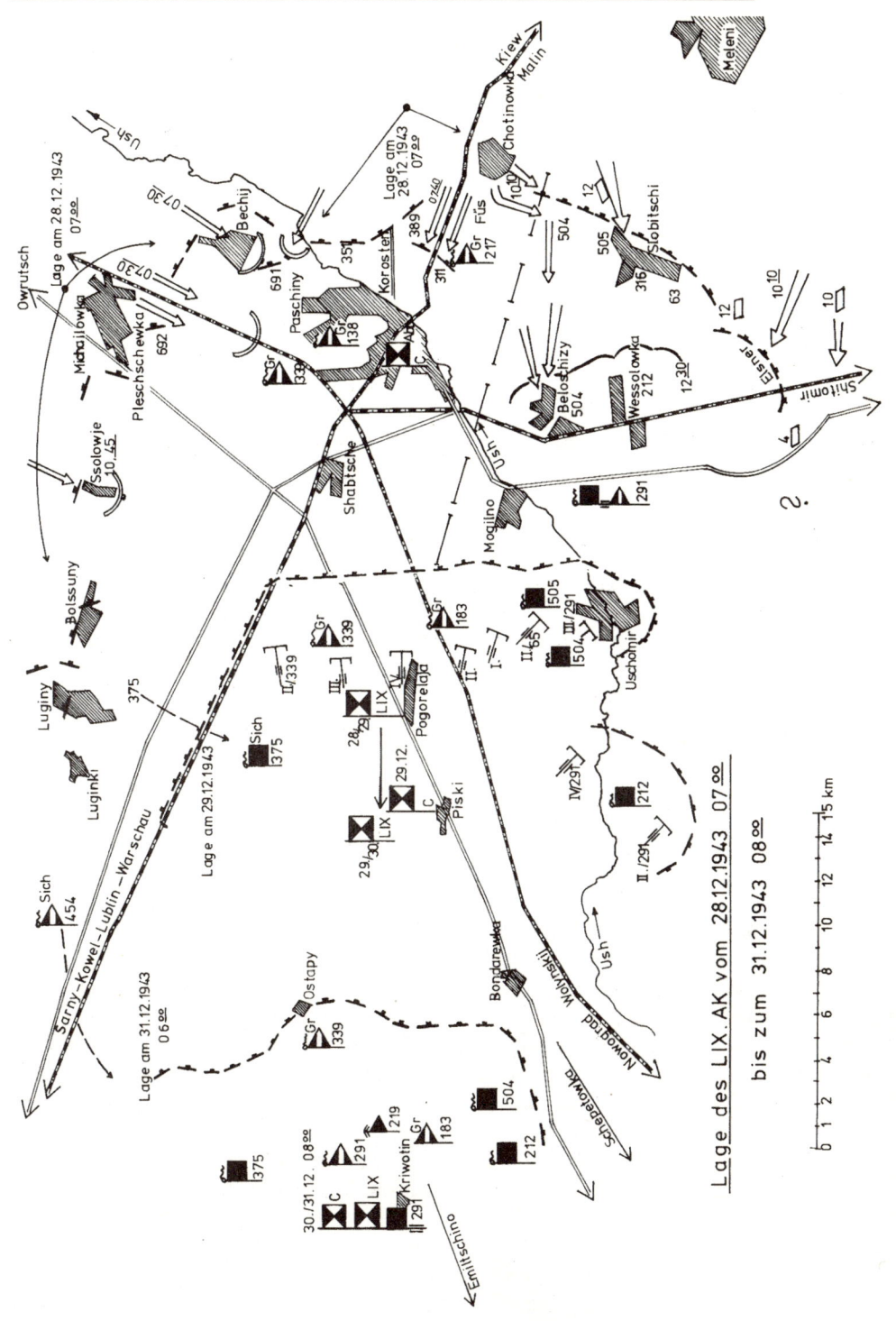

40. Situation of the 59th *Armee Korps* from 28 December, 1943, 0700 hours until 31 December, 1943, 0800 hours.

North of Shitomir the Soviets reached the western exit of the city. Their further advance to the south was blocked at Ssloboda Sslez with the help of *Panzergrenadier Regiment 74* [19th *Panzer Division*] and a *Panzergruppe* of *Panzer Regiment 27* [19th *Panzer Division*] . On 31 December, however, the Soviets broke through the line of defense of the infantry division north of Shitomir and thereby gained the road from Shitomir to Zwiahel [Nowograd – Wolinski], on which they immediately brought up additional forces.

The order to evacuate Shitomir arrived at noon of that day. Execution of that order proved difficult, for the exit roads from Shitomir to the west were filled with infantry trains-elements, horse-drawn artillery and long columns of vehicles, and were already under enemy fire from the north. Soviet AFVs caused extensive losses in the columns of German vehicles waiting to cross a bridge, causing combat elements of the 19th *Panzer Division* to choose a route over the swampy meadows and the stream. One heavy field howitzer of the 7./ *Panzerartillerie Regiment* 19 bogged down in the swamp and was lost.

At another point the Soviets fired on the retreat route with a row of AFVs. German armour joined the fray and anti-tank guns went into position. Thus the columns made their way to the Teterew and, finally, blew up the bridge over the river. At that point Soviet armour was already at the railroad and highway intersection 30 kilometers west of Shitomir.

The weather situation also caused a critical situation for the other formations with icy roads and byways. And that was during renewed fierce fighting with superior enemy forces at Shitomir! Among other things, the condition of the roads impacted the withdrawal of the 1st *Panzer Division*, which broke off its counterattack. The 1st *SS-Panzer Division 'Leibstandarte SS Adolf Hitler'* had to fight its way diagonally across the attacking Soviet columns in its retreat to the newly ordered line. The involvement of the 7th *Panzer Division* from the north suffered from both the road conditions and from the traffic jam in Shitomir. Nevertheless, on that day the *Panzer Korps* knocked out 32 enemy AFVs and 67 more the next day.

Establishing a New Line of Defense

The traffic chaos that resulted from various formations marching through Shitomir under the pressure of the Soviet formations from the north, to say nothing of the one-way traffic regulation, forced recognition of the fact that it was impracticable to station rear area services of every sort in such transportation nodal points. The transportation links provided by such a city along with its advantages for living and protection from partisan attacks repeatedly drew rear-area services to such collecting points with railroad unloading stations. In smaller population centers these services had more trouble with partisan bands, and, especially, had to provide more guards. The 48th *Panzer Korps* concluded from this observation that, in the future, it would distribute the rear-area services among individual villages in the hinterland, the more so because that had a pacifying effect on that area because it interfered with partisan activity.

After the capture of Shitomir on 31 December the Soviets were already moving forward again to the west on 3 January and reached the former Polish – Soviet border of 1939 (prior to the incorporation of eastern Poland into the Soviet Union). The German command, however, considered that the Soviet offensive power had been weakened, probably used up, which was advantageous to the Germans at that time, the more so since only weak, 'burnt-out' infantry formations could be committed against the Soviets. In addition, the *Heeresgruppe* considered that it was not in a position to adequately man the entire area from east of Tarnopol via Schepetowka to Berditschew. That evaluation, which applied to the Soviet advance to the west, was not applicable to the Soviet advance from Kiew via Fastow to the south (Berditschew). Here the Soviets had committed a series of offensive formations to the thrust to the south, which invoked the danger that the 8th *Armee's* line of defense that had hitherto been at the Dnjepr would be outflanked. The Soviets also concerned themselves with covering the flanks of their advance to the south, for, especially after their experiences at Kriwoi Rog, they had to expect that the German formations would disrupt this Soviet movement to the south with flank attacks.

The Soviet attack, initially southwest of Shitomir at Glubotschek, where two localities on the railroad line southwest of Tschudnoff (Stolpoff and Sserbinowka) were recaptured from Soviet hands, apparently served the objective of preventing the Germans from bringing up forces into this area. The *Heeresgruppe* also wanted to give this sector of the front stronger support. Accordingly, the 96th *Infanterie Division* was to be brought in from *Heeresgruppe Nord*. Deep snow, however, complicated movement for friend and foe, so that the left flank of the 19th *Panzer Division* at the upper course of the Teterew river remained open, for the time being. The 17th *Panzer Division* was to be committed to the right of this division.

The Soviets first attacked at the beginning of January, taking advantage of the winter weather, which was favorable for them, heavy snowfall and frost, which made it difficult for the *Grenadiere* to dig in. They attacked repeatedly in an effort to achieve at least one breakthrough. All they accomplished, however, were dents in the German line or that it was pulled back in isolated sectors, especially as a result of the alternation of snow and rain, frost and thaw, sometimes with frozen ground, but mostly with mushy or bottomless subsoil that put the foxholes under water or prevented digging in.

Despite all this, a certain abatement in the action set in about mid-January in the combat sector southwest and south of Shitomir, which gave the German command an opportunity to turn its attention again to the Soviet advance on Berditschew.

10

Defensive Battles at the Start of 1944

The situation of *Heeresgruppe Süd* as the new year opened seemed by no means rosy. Just the course of the front line gave rise to serious concern. In the area of the 4th *Panzer Armee* the Soviets had again taken Shitomir and were advancing to the northwest toward Nowograd – Wolynski (Zwiahel) as well as to the west (Schepetowka). The Soviets were also advancing to the southwest from Shitomir (Ljubar) where, initially, the 19th *Panzer Division* and 8th *Panzer Division* blocked them.

Situation South of Kiew

See Map 44, also Maps 39, 41 and 43.

While this was happening, however, the Soviets gained ground south from Kiew. On the second day of Christmas, 1943, after a heavy artillery preparation, they attacked in the area of the division boundary between the 88th and 198th *Infanterie Divisionen* northwest of Biala Zerkwa. A few days later they broke through the positions of the over-stretched 198th *Infanterie Division* at Dossjatin and there thrust on past the northwest side of Biala Zerkwa toward the south. Additional attacks against the lines of the 88th *Infanterie Division* northwest and north of the city were initially unsuccessful. However, the advance to the south soon reached the Biala Zerkwa – Taraschtscha road about four kilometers south of Biala Zerkwa. As a result of strong enemy attacks against its extreme left wing the 88th *Infanterie Division* pulled its lines back to Schkarowka. The fate of this division seems to have been sealed with the later encirclement in the *Kessel* of Tscherkassy, while the 198th *Infanterie Division* had to attempt to be forced aside to the west in order to counteract the further Soviet advance on Berditschew.

Fighting in the Berditschew – Kasatin Area

See Maps 39 and 41.

The *Heeresgruppe* had to try to shift some sort of formations into this area in order to halt the Soviet advance. Accordingly, the hastily brought-in 1st *Panzer Division* received the mission of securing the logistical support point of Kasatin, with its rich supply dumps of all sorts, from the grasp of the Soviets. However, it ran into stiff resistance from superior Soviet forces when it was still about ten kilometers from Kasatin. The division then took up a long, drawn-out front extending from Berditschew to about 15 – 20 kilometers southeast of the city and established contact with the 18th *Artillerie Division*, with the alarm units of the *Armee* and *Heeresgruppe* that were attached to it, for example, *Alarm-Kompanie Nachrichten* [communications] – *Regiment Süd* (558), *Feld Ersatz Bataillon* [field replacement battalion] 25th *Panzer Division*, *Panzer Aufklärungs Abteilung* 25, *Tiger-Abteilung* 503 [schwere *Panzer Abteilung*

DEFENSIVE BATTLES AT THE START OF 1944 163

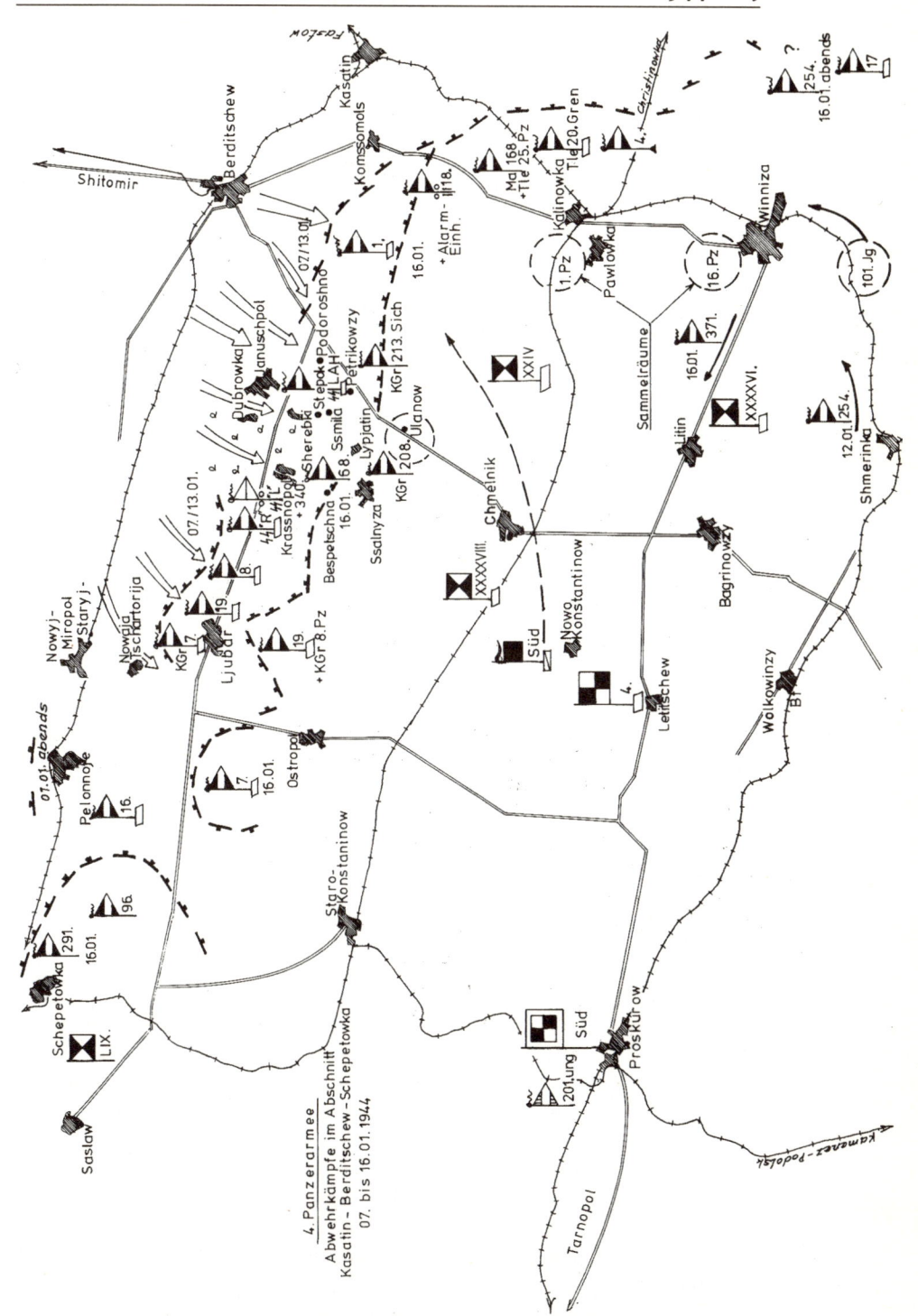

41. 4th *Panzer Armee*. Defensive fighting in the Kasatin – Berditschew – Schepetowka sector, 7 to 16 January, 1944. See Map 86 for 7 January to end of February 1944.

503, also known as *schwere Tiger Abteilung* 503]. With that, optimistically, the gap in the front between the 24th *Panzer Korps* and 48th *Panzer Korps* was closed for a short period.

North-northeast of Winniza stood the 4th *Gebirgs Division*, which had been brought out of the Chersson bridgehead by rail. The 7th *Panzer Division* with *Panzer Abteilung* 506 [*schwere Tiger Abteilung* 506] provided no more than weak security[1] in the area which had not yet, at this time, been stripped of German troops. It could not, in the long run, prevent further Soviet advance to the south toward Uman. Thereby arose the danger that the Soviets would be able to cut off the 'Dnjepr *Balkon*', the formations of the 7th *Armee Korps*, 42nd *Armee Korps* and 11th *Armee Korps*, that were farther east from Belaja Zerkwa to the Dnjepr, from their connections to the rear.

Heavy fighting developed in the Kasatin area, especially in and around Berditschew. Based on their experience in the fighting between Shitomir and Kiew and from the fighting around Kriwoi Rog, the Soviets may well have sensed danger for their concentration of troops to the south, danger of German flank attacks from the west into the march-columns moving south. They therefore repeatedly attempted to broaden the area of the advance in order to secure the advance to the west.

See Map 41.
In the first half of January the Soviets had not yet given up on their operations in the Berditschew area. In two days of heavy fighting they lost over 100 AFVs to the formations of the 1st *SS-Panzer Division 'Leibstandarte SS Adolf Hitler'* with attached elements of *Kampfgruppe* 2nd *SS-Panzer Division 'Das Reich'* and *Kampfgruppen* 208th *Infanterie Division* and 68th *Infanterie Division*. In the ensuing days the Soviets repeatedly attempted to find weak points. Early on 8 January about 40 enemy AFVs with mounted infantry rolled forward against the German lines and penetrated into the hollows northward against Sherebki and Stepok. *Panzeraufklärungs Abteilung* 1, *Panzer Regiment* 1 and *Panzer Zerstörer Bataillon* 473 [Tank Destroyer Battalion 473] knocked out 33 T 34 tanks and seven assault guns. At other locations one *'Panther' Gruppe* knocked out eight T 34s and two assault guns.

See Map 41.
On the next day the Soviets captured the woods west of Dubrowka in order to capture the place from the east and west with support from multiple-rocket launchers. Eight T 34 tanks broke out of the woods southeast of Januschpol against the positions of *Kampfgruppe* 208th *Infanterie Division*, penetrating into Podoroshno. The situation was cleaned up in a counterattack.

The next day the Soviets tried, again and again, to find some weak point in the German positions. Nevertheless, although occasionally a limited amount of land had to be given up, it was possible to restore the situation, destroying some enemy armour in the process. So, on 9 January, 12 T 34s and three assault guns were knocked out.

On 10 January The 1st *SS-Panzer Division 'Leibstandarte SS Adolf Hitler'* with attached *Kampfgruppen* 208th *Infanterie Division* and 68th *Infanterie Division* took up a new second position in the line north of Petrikowzy – Ssmela – Besbetschna. In the meantime the trains elements constructed a

---

1   To its left were security forces of the 16th *Panzer Division* with loose contact with the 59th *Armee Korps* –291st *Infanterie Division*.

DEFENSIVE BATTLES AT THE START OF 1944   165

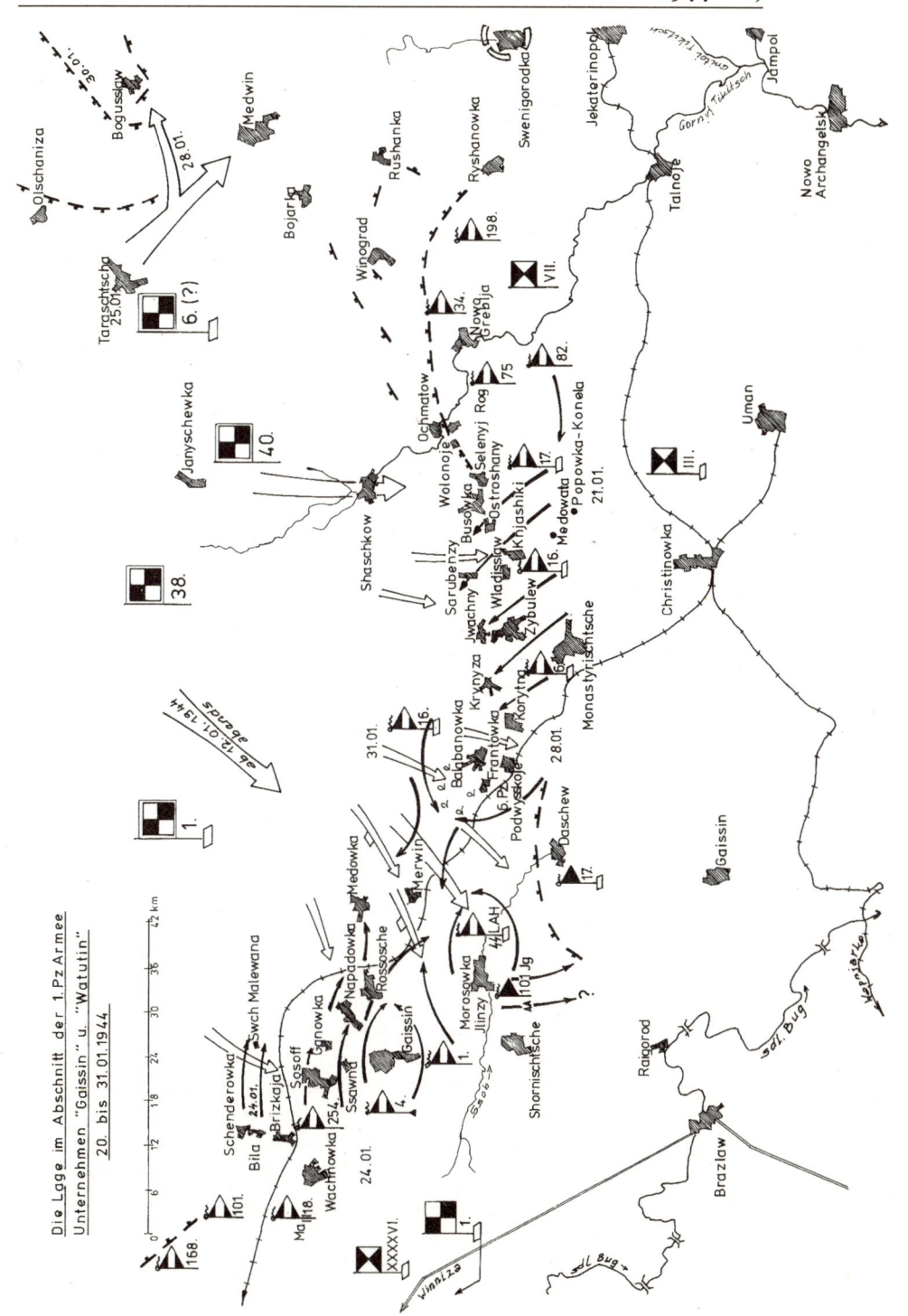

42. The Situation in the sector of the 1st *Panzer Armee*. *Unternehmen* [operations] '*Gaissin*' and '*Watutin*' 20 to 31 January, 1944. Map 43 covers larger area.

third position between Petrikowzy and Ssmila as well as the northern edge of Lisjatin and Ssalnyza.

During the night of 12 January ensued a renewed armoured assault against the left wing of *Kampfgruppe* 68th *Infanterie Division*. After breaking through and unloading the infantry that they had brought with them, the AFVs turned north behind the main line of defense. Another penetration of 12 AFVs followed at the same location, advancing past Lipjatin on the east to Ulanoff, blocking the supply route. After 12 T34s were knocked out, the second wave was forced to turn aside, and the enemy was pursued to the south edge of the Chutorysko farmstead. Several hours later the gap in the main line of resistance was sealed again. After turning to the east into Ulanoff, the remaining armour that had broken in was destroyed by two *Tiger* tanks and *Panzer-Zerstörer Bataillon* 473. The Soviets initially assigned special significance to this sector of the front because rail and highway links running from here to the west would be particularly advantageous for a further advance.

On 13 January came an armoured advance to Tschessnowka, which was totally wiped out with the destruction of 37 T 34 tanks and seven assault guns. The next day brought renewed attacks with penetrations into the German lines. These, too, were cleaned up, as at Bespetschna. A counterattack against an identified Soviet troop movement with the objective of gaining the Berditschew – Ljubar *Rollbahn* and capturing Krassnopol resulted in gaining the northern edge of Krassnopol and the capture of Molotschki. In conjunction with an armoured group of the 2nd *SS-Panzer Division 'Das Reich'* this counter attack knocked out a large number of vehicles, 20 antitank guns and two T34 tanks.

See Map 41.

Defensive Fighting near Winniza

See Maps 41, 42 and 43.

Given their basic intention of gaining ground to the west, the Soviets did not need to limit themselves to the Berditschew area, despite the favorable highway and railroad supply possibilities this area offered for continued logistical support of formations advancing westward from there. There were other possibilities farther south, as toward Winniza and Uman. Whether or not the Soviets at that point already held further plans for making such an advance to cut off the left wing of *Heeresgruppe Süd*, appears dubious. The direction of the thrust makes it appear far more likely that their intention was to support the successful attack against *Heeresgruppe* A with an advance from the central sector to the south, namely by way of a further swing to the west, thereby involving additional sectors of the front of *Heeresgruppe Süd* (8th *Armee*) in the retrograde movement of *Heeresgruppe* A.

While the left wing of *Heeresgruppe Süd* could still be supplied from the *Generalgouvernement Polen* over adequate highway and railroad lines, the central sector and southern sector of *Heeresgruppe Süd* and/or *Heeresgruppe* A, respectively, lacked such advantages. The latter, in particular, would be more vulnerable to Soviet attacks than the left wing of the *Heeresgruppe*, especially since, with the loss of the Fastow supply railroad along the Dnjepr, the twin-tracked Lemberg – Odessa line was left as the only functional supply route. After that, the only remaining route for logistical support was the extremely difficult route through Hungary, Siebenbürgen and Bessarabia, with mostly single-tracked lines that were rendered vulnerable by easily demolished structural components. With regard to the amount of logistical support required for large-scale combat, the Soviets had the opportunity of creating a critical shortage of supplies for the German formations fighting in the south by advancing in the center of the *Heeresgruppe* front, which, again, was favorable to the Soviets in their operations. The capture of Bessarabia additionally promised the prospect of undermining the steadfastness of the troops of other nationalities that were fighting alongside the Germans.

The Gaissin *Kessel*

Considering this danger the *Heeresgruppe* attempted to head off the spearhead of the Soviet formations reaching nearly to Winniza. The 1st *SS-Panzer Division 'Leibstandarte SS Adolf Hitler'* received this mission. Fixed in the fighting west of Berditschew, this division could not immediately carry out its assignment. Instead, the defensive mission went to the 4th *Gebirgs Division*, which was, at the end of the old year, approaching in high-speed transport via Odessa. The 4th *Gebirgs Division* initially took over a 49 kilometer sector around Kalinowka (20 kilometers north of Winniza) with elements reaching to Losowataja – Swerdlowka, a sector that could only be held in a security fashion, between Strutinka (seven kilometers southwest of Gaissin) and Nowo Greblija. At that time the *Schwerpunkt* of the Soviet southward advance via Wachnowka appeared to lie there.

See Maps 42 and 43.

The penetrating cold complicated the developing fierce defensive battle against the Soviet attack, which was supported by armour and ground-attack aircraft. There was contact on the right with the 1st *Infanterie Division*, on the left with the 254th *Infanterie Division*. Farther to the left was the 101st *Jäger Division*. The division was supported by elements of the 18th *Artillerie Division*, finally also by elements of the 1st *SS-Panzer Division 'Leibstandarte SS Adolf Hitler'*. The 4th *Gebirgs Division* was, however, in the *Schwerpunkt* of the fighting.

On 24 January the 4th *Gebirgs Division* was, in close coordination with the 254th *Infanterie Division* and 101st *Jäger Division*, attacking on the left, to gain the Jassenki – Rotmistriwka north-south road and capture Sosoff. The troops thus had to accomplish two missions, neither of them easy. The first was to attack an enemy who was in a deeply organized system of positions with the strongest possible forces. The second was, with elements not involved in that attack, to hold a roughly 18 kilometer stretch of front against the expected relief attacks.

Gebirgs Jäger Regiment 91 [4th *Gebirgs Division*] launched the attack with two battalions forward north of the road to Sosowka through thick mine fields and systems of positions, while the III./*Gebirgs Jäger Regiment* 91 mopped up the east part of Wachnowka, which was strongly held by the enemy. Under constant flanking fire from Britskoje it took the ridge halfway between Wachnowka and Sosowka. The troops remained there in totally open terrain under heavy Soviet defensive fire. After darkness fell, *Gebirgs Jäger Regiment* 91 made a fresh start and, after stubborn fighting – destroying six enemy AFVs – forced its way into the northwest part of Sosowka. The Soviets had secured

See Map 42.

43. 4th *Panzer Armee*, *Unternehmen* [operations] '*Gaissin*' and '*Watutin*', relief attempts for the Tscherkassy *Kessel*.

DEFENSIVE BATTLES AT THE START OF 1944 169

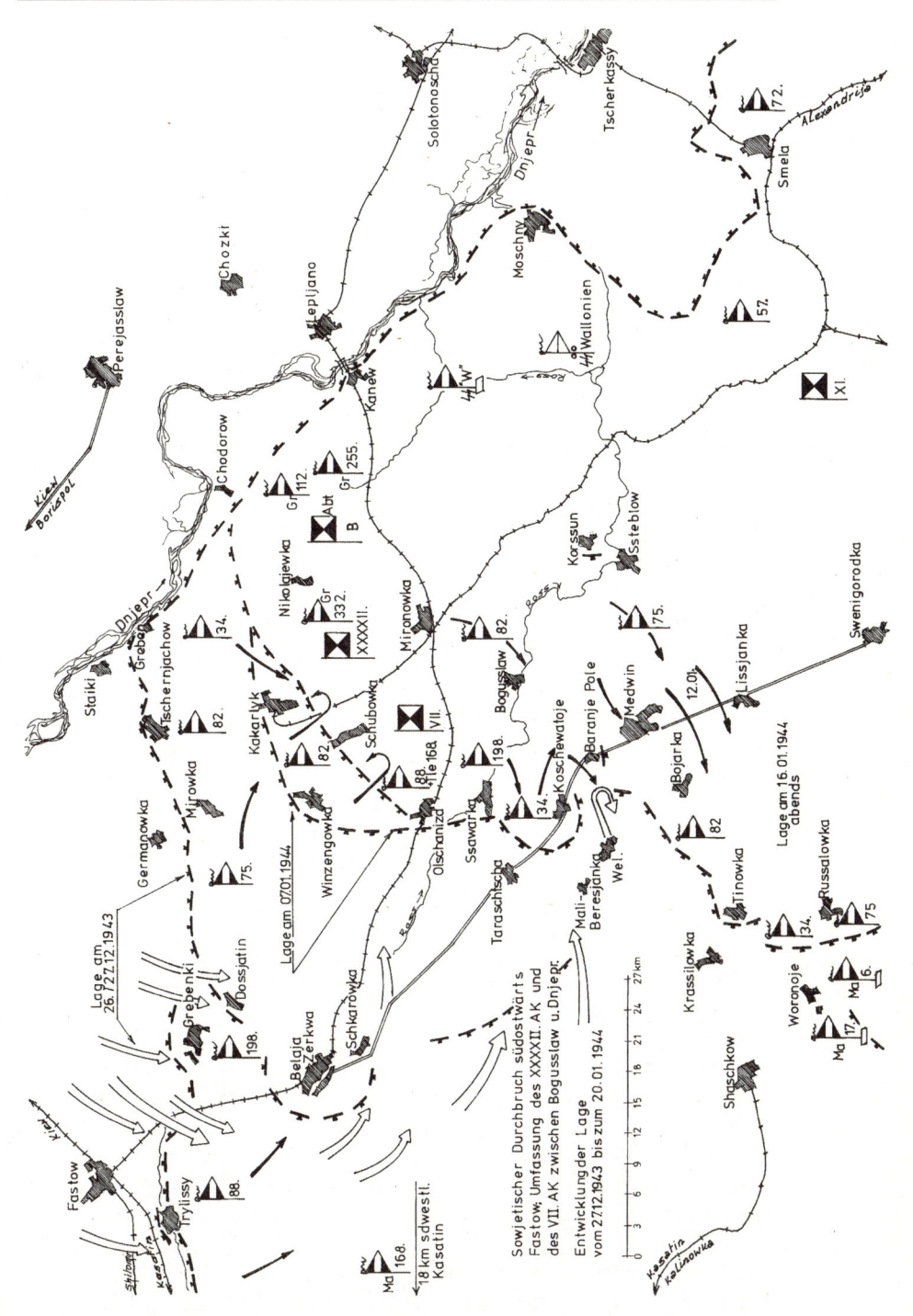

44. Soviet breakthrough southeast of Fastow; Envelopment of the 42nd *Armee Korps* and 7th *Armee Korps* between Bogusslaw and Dnjepr. Development of the situation from 27 December, 1943 to 20 January, 1944.

Sosoff, Sosowo and Sosowka with a mass of artillery and antitank positions as well as assembly positions for armour.

The forward pressure of the 254th *Infanterie Division* on the left assisted *Gebirgs Jäger Regiment* 91 in its advance, until the Soviets launched a counterattack from Sosoff in regimental strength with armoured support. This came to a halt in concentrated fire by all weapons, locally in bloody hand-to-hand combat. The 254th *Infanterie Division* then forced its way into the northern portion of Sosowka and Sosoff, while *Gebirgs Jäger Regiment* 91 fought its way through to the southern part of Sosoff, supported by the heavy firepower of the 18th *Artillerie Division*, and had to undergo fierce house-to-house fighting with bayonet and rifle-butt. *Gebirgs Jäger Bataillon* 94 finally reached a hill north of Wyssedki, thereby establishing contact with those elements of the 4th *Gebirgs Division* that were in Sosowo and Sosowka and, thereby, initiating the turning movement to encircle the Soviets in Gaissin.

The III./ *Gebirgs Jäger Regiment* 13 [4th *Gebirgs Division*] attempted to crush the front around Jassenki, but the attempt failed in the face of resolute resistance by an enemy who blew up all bridges and roads in his retreat. The enemy fell back in flight to Gaissin under the forceful attack by *Gebirgs Jäger Regiment* 13 and *Gebirgs Jäger Bataillon* 94 that followed their capture of Wyssedki and Narzisowka as well as that by *Gebirgs Jäger Regiment* 91 after its capture of Sslawna. In order to prevent the Soviets from retreating out of this *Kessel*, the regiments advanced past the north side of Gaissin in a strenuous night march in icy cold, and reached the defensive positions at Rossosche and Napadowka where the 4th *Gebirgs Division* relieved the elements of the 1st *SS-Panzer Division 'Leibstandarte SS Adolf Hitler'* that were securing there.

The Soviet forces that were cut off in the Gaissin *Kessel* repeatedly attempted to break out to the rear. They were opposed by elements of the 1st *SS-Panzer Division 'Leibstandarte SS Adolf Hitler'*. Individual elements escaped from the *Kessel*, abandoning their weapons and equipment.

The Situation

Concluding observations regarding the overall situation seem hardly possible, in light of the pressing events of the day. For the command there was only the constantly recurring question of where they could get forces with which to hold the long, inadequately manned line.

The capture of Kiew had granted the Soviets the opportunity to divert some elements of their forces advancing to the west (Shitomir) to advance with these to the south in order to get them into the border area between the 4th *Panzer Armee* (right wing) and the left wing of the 8th *Armee*. There were adequate possibilities for logistical support, on the one hand over the available bridges in Kiew as well as over the highways capable of carrying loads near the great city and the twin-tracked railroad via Fastow to Wassilow. The Red Army had availed itself of this opportunity to advance toward Belaja – Zerkwa by starting one part of the forces to the west via Berditschew and also Kasatin and, then, continuing with an advance to the south toward Winniza and Uman.

Granted, the Soviets had, in this area, suffered perceptible losses, especially in armour. The German troops had been forced to fall back a step at a time, each

DEFENSIVE BATTLES AT THE START OF 1944

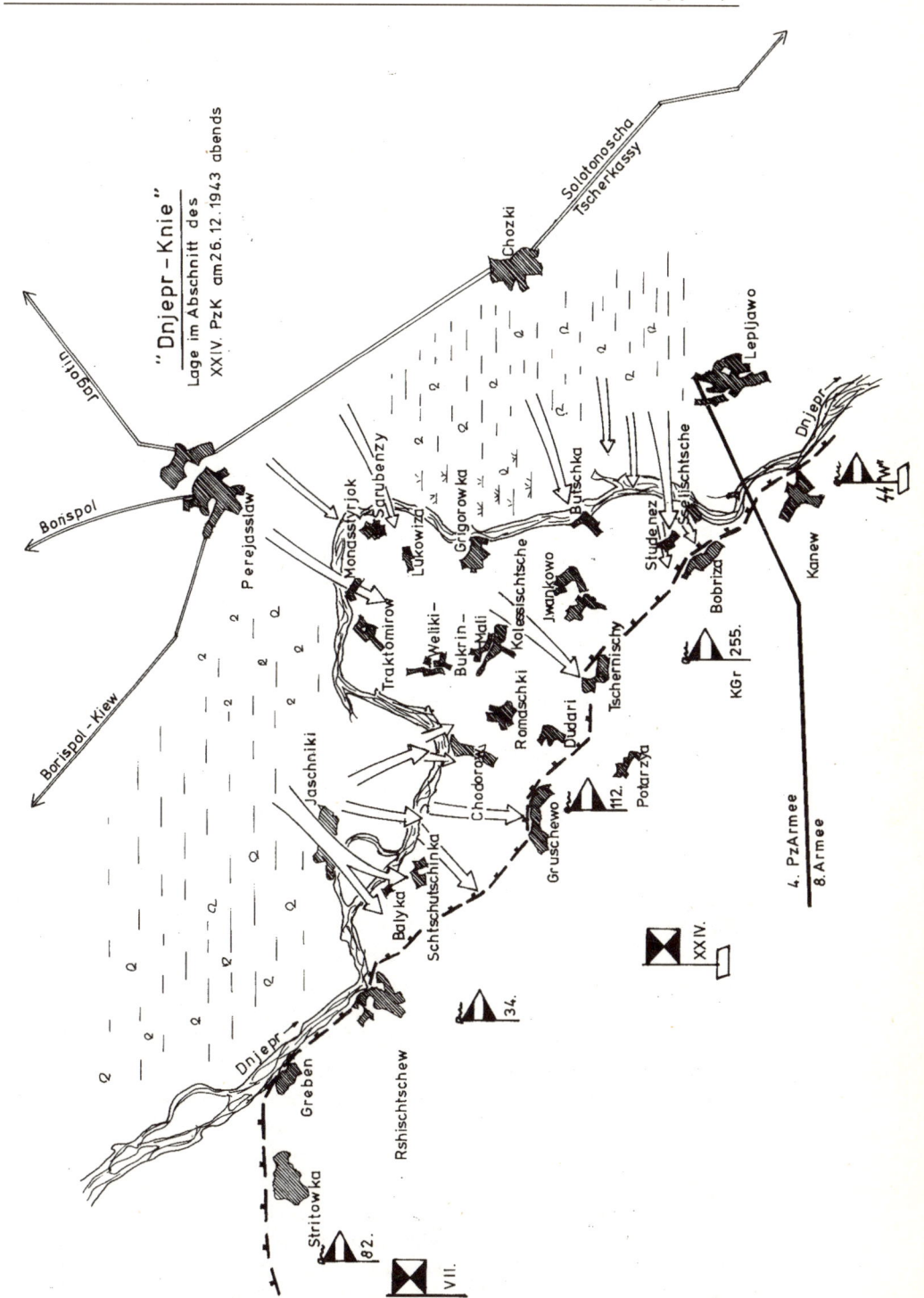

45. The Dnjepr-Knee. Situation in the sector of the 24th *Panzer Korps* on 26 December, 1943, evening.

time giving up some ground, before the heavy Soviet pressure. Nevertheless, the end result was that they still held a nearly continuous line, held thinly or by strongpoints, as the case might be.

Lacking the opportunity to examine Soviet records, it is only possible to guess at the intentions of the Soviet command at that time from the results of German reconnaissance. It is possible that the results of the *Kessel* battle of Gaissin played a role, even though some of the Soviet soldiers made their way back to the Red Army, without weapons or equipment. The spearhead that was stretched to the south had, however, had a damper put on it.

During this stage of the battle, the German command attempted to learn by reconnaissance what was the Soviet objective. The radio-intercept work of prisoner-of-war *Hiwis* employed by the 1st *SS-Panzer Division 'Leibstandarte SS Adolf Hitler'* produced valuable information.

See Maps 43, 44 and 46.

The 42nd *Panzer Korps* held, with its northern front, a sector extending 75 kilometers with a total of three battalions and five batteries of *Korps Abteilung* B. In light of such weakness on the German side it is not surprising that the Soviets succeeded in a deep penetration to Nikolajewka, Schubrowka and Olschaniza. With a *Schwerpunkt* group the Soviets attacked the Boguslaw – Ssteblow sector along the Ross river and attempted to envelop the wing of the 42nd *Panzer Korps* and 7th *Armee Korps* that was at Ssteblow. The advance of strong forces to the southeast toward Schpola apparently served the purpose, in conjunction with the eastern group advancing from Smela, to cut off the German forces in the 'Dnjepr knee' from their connections to the rear.

The Germans did not have forces available to eliminate the penetration that had been achieved. Weather conditions and organizational problems complicated bringing in forces to deal with the developing situation. As darkness fell the 11th *Panzer Division,* 13th *Panzer Division* and 376th *Infanterie Division* of the 47th *Panzer Korps* were withdrawn from the front line as a reserve in the Nowo Mirgorod and Pantschew area – this resulting in extension of the already far-too-wide sectors held by the infantry divisions. The 11th *Panzer Division* was at Krassnossilka, where the German command expected the first further Soviet breakthrough to the south. The main body of the *Korps'* artillery marched behind the 11th *Panzer Division,* which later proved useful. The evacuation of the 'Dnjepr *Balkon* ' (11th *Armee Korps* and 42nd *Armee Korps*) would, indeed, have given the opportunity to free up sufficient forces to reestablish a nearly defensible line of defense. This withdrawal, however, foundered on Hitler's refusal. The 11th *Armee Korps* completed a small withdrawal movement behind the Irdyn swamp (57th *Infanterie Division* and 72nd *Infanterie Division*).

Operation *'Watutin'*

See Map 43.

As soon as the extended spearhead of the Soviet forces advancing toward Winniza had been cut off at Gaissin, and before the Soviet forces advancing from north to south toward the Soviet forces advancing from east to west could close the ring around the 'Dnjepr knee', the German command planned to also cut off the Soviet armoured forces that were behind the spearhead that had been encircled at Gaissin from their rear connections, thereby preventing

DEFENSIVE BATTLES AT THE START OF 1944

any further advance to the south. The 3rd *Panzer Korps* essentially was assigned this mission. To accomplish this mission the *Korps* had the 1st *Panzer Division*, elements of the 1st *SS-Panzer Division 'Leibstandarte SS Adolf Hitler'* as – they – successively – arrived, as well as the 4th *Gebirgs Division*, 101st *Jäger Division* and the 254th *Infanterie Division*, coming out of the battle at Gaissin.

The 3rd *Panzer Korps* concentrated north of Uman with the 1st *Panzer Division*, 16th *Panzer Division,* 17th *Panzer Division* and the 1st *SS-Panzer Division 'Leibstandarte SS Adolf Hitler'*, all of them hastily brought in and arriving one after another. The 48th *Panzer Korps* advanced with five divisions at Iskrennoje – Swenigorodka into the rear of the Soviets that were facing the southern front of the 11th *Korps*. The 3rd *Panzer Korps* launched an advance with four divisions from the area north of Uman via Bojarka and Medwin into the rear of the Soviets facing the southern front of the 42nd *Korps* – this, however, with less than the entire force that had been intended, since the 16th *Panzer Division* and 17th *Panzer Division* had, as a result of bad road conditions, been unable to get to their intended jump-off point in time.

In any case, these plans did not consider the poor road conditions in this time of weather varying from rain and mud to snow and frost, nor the strength of the Soviet formations of the 4th Guards Army, the 27th and 53rd Soviet Armies, to say nothing of the 5th Guards Cavalry Corps, coming from the east, with three divisions and substantial elements of the 5th Guards Army from the Kirowograd area, as well as the 52nd Soviet Army from the Tscherkassy area. The force ratio between these enemy formations and the German *Kampfgruppen* seems extraordinarily unequal, so that it appears extremely improbably that the German formations could achieve their objectives against such overwhelmingly superior forces.

See Maps 44 and 45.

Against the slowly assembling 3rd *Panzer Korps* the Soviets stood with strong forces south of the Gornyj – Tikitsch river sector. Concentrating its forces closely, the *Korps* advanced into the combat sector knocking out several enemy AFVs and destroying or capturing 89 antitank guns, with the 17th *Panzer Division* at Sarubenzi, the 16th *Panzer Division* at Iwachny and the 6th *Panzer Division* at Krynyza. The 3rd *Panzer Korps* closed a gap in the front between Selenyj Rog and Ostroshany and mopped up the area west of Ssekolewk. On 21 January the 17th *Panzer Division* captured Medowata from the west. The *Korps* also launched a concentric attack from the north, west and south against Popowka – Koleka and captured Knjashiki and Wladisslawtschik.

For geography see Maps 42 and 43.

On 24 January the 46th *Panzer Korps* attacked, thrusting through the line of enemy combat outposts and, in heavy fighting, took the first Soviet main position in the general line Brizkohe – Bila – Schenderowka, knocking out ten enemy AFVs. The *Korps* continued to advance via Rodmistrowka to the fork in the road at Sonjoze Malewano, getting, however, into an intense armoured battle with strong enemy elements, in which 60 enemy AFVs were knocked out.

On 27 January, after crushing initial strong enemy resistance and the destruction of three enemy battalions, the 3rd *Panzer Korps* gained ground to the northwest in a fast-moving attack, with the 16th *Panzer Division* and 6th *Panzer Division*. The 46th *Panzer Korps* repulsed repeated attacks in the

Napadowka area with the 1st *SS-Panzer Division 'Leibstandarte SS Adolf Hitler'* and *Panzerregiment Bäke* and thrust farther to the southwest to link up with the 3rd *Panzer Korps*.

See Map 42.

The 4th *Gebirgs Division* and right wing of the 254th *Infanterie Division* captured Sslawna, as well as Ganowka and continued to the east. The main body of the 254th *Infanterie Division* repeatedly repulsed enemy attacks against the east and north fronts. On 28 January the 3rd *Panzer Korps* destroyed strong enemy forces, took Schabastowka, Krytna and Podwyssokoje with the 17th *Panzer Division,* compressed strong enemy forces in the area around Frantowka, and beat back breakout attempts.

The 46th *Panzer Korps* thrust deep into the *Kessel* with the 1st *SS-Panzer Division 'Leibstandarte SS Adolf Hitler'*, the 4th *Gebirgs Division* fending off enemy attempts to break out from Gaissin to the north, as well as relief attacks against the Lipowez railroad station and Napadowka. On 29 January the 3rd *Panzer Korps* compressed the encircled enemy forces into a constricted area in the woods west of Balabanowka, repulsing a regimental-strength relief attack from Juschkowzy against the 6th *Panzer Division*.

Against the 46th *Panzer Korps* enemy forces advancing against the ring of encirclement that had yet to be firmed up attempted to break out of the closed ring and to populate the *'Watutin' Kessel*. *Gruppe Bäke* and the 1st *SS-Panzer Division 'Leibstandarte SS Adolf Hitler'* exacted particularly heavy losses from the enemy. The 1st *SS-Panzer Division 'Leibstandarte SS Adolf Hitler'* attacked to the south and forced enemy forces at and east of Morowoka back via Szudow. The successes of this *Kessel* included 13,500 prisoners and enemy dead, as well as 700 AFVs and 680 guns that the Soviets abandoned on the battlefield. These losses were essentially the result of the advance of the 1st *SS-Panzer Division 'Leibstandarte SS Adolf Hitler'* attacking to the east and the 16th *Panzer Division,* attacking from east to west in a matching attack from the opposite direction.

On 30 January the enemy group encircled west of Balabanowka was reduced to remnants. The 1st *SS-Panzer Division 'Leibstandarte SS Adolf Hitler'* fought south of the Ssob. *Gruppe Bäke* knocked out 46 enemy AFVs on both sides of Merwin.

Soviet Advance from East and West

For geography see Maps 42 and 43.

Even before the start of the Gaissin *Kessel* battle and Operation *'Watutin'*, which halted the Soviet advance from north to south, other elements of the Red Army advanced as relief from east to west into the combat sector toward Schpola, indeed, from the Tscherkassy bridgehead via Smela and from the sector north of Kirowgrad to the west. On 10 January they were before Kamenka and reached the *'Sperber'* position at Balandino at the same time as the retreating German forces, achieving local penetrations. The German forces suffered difficulties in salvaging all of their heavy weapons and equipment and in conducting an orderly evacuation of the terrain as a result of the road conditions (sheet-ice) and over-stressed troops, as well as the lack of towing equipment. In the meanwhile the Soviets attacked toward Swenigorodka from the north, counterbalancing the advance from the east at the Krassnossilka – Smela front.

DEFENSIVE BATTLES AT THE START OF 1944

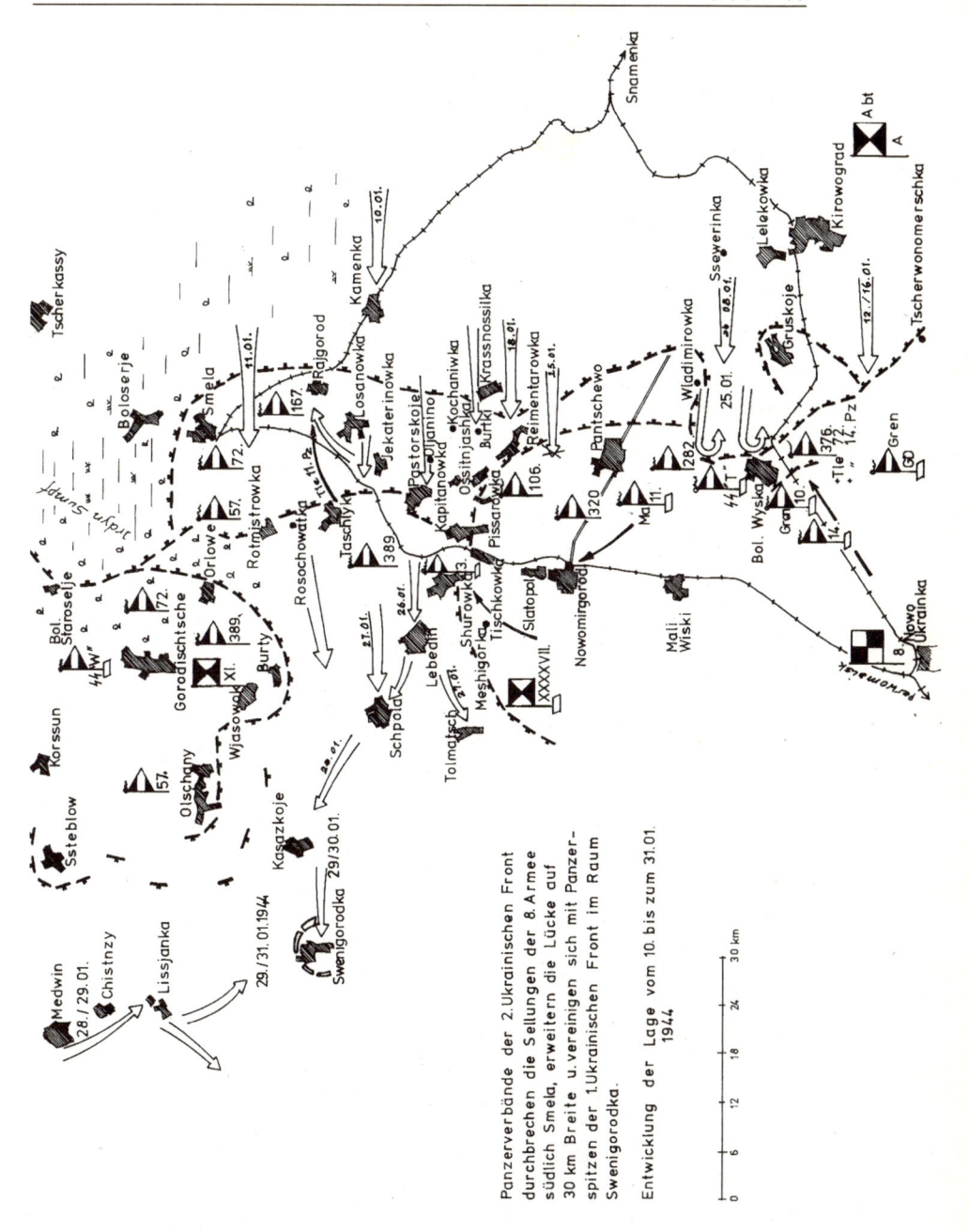

46. Armoured formations of the 2nd Ukrainian Front break through the positions of the 8th *Armee* south of Smela, widen the gap to 30 kilometers and link up with armoured spearheads of the 1st Ukrainian Front in the Swenigorodka area. Development of the situation from 10 to 31 January, 1944.

Again and again the Soviets achieved penetrations, as, on 11 January, south of Smela, at Boda-Orlowskaja. The ferocity of the fighting is evident from the total of 380 Soviet AFVs and 374 guns and antitank guns destroyed by the 8th *Armee* between 5 and 12 January.

On 15 January, after half an hour of artillery preparation, the Soviets attacked anew in the southern sector between the Nowo Ukrainka – Kirowograd railroad line and the Nowo-Mirgorod – Kirowgrad road with eleven rifle divisions and armoured escort. North of the Wladimirowka road, simultaneously with the attack in the northern sector, they tore open the German front in a breach that was 12 kilometers wide and up to five kilometers deep. At Krassnossilka a German counterattack in the Reimantarowka area was successful. Nevertheless, the Soviets broadened their area of penetration at Krassnossilka on 18 January. There was no respite in this, either, because they were finally forced to attempt to provide relief for the elements that were fighting from north to south. On 24 January they achieved penetrations at Burtki and Oljanino. The German forces had to restrict themselves to seal off such penetrations after the fact. Thus, they recaptured Burtki and sealed off the area of the penetration in the line Burtki – Kochaniwka – hills west of Radwanowka.

On the next day there were crossings at Reimentarowka and the capture of the Nowo – Mirgorod – Kapitanowka railroad line. At Reimantarowka the Soviets expended 27 AFVs on 25 January, alone. They then committed a new Guards division with an unknown number of AFVs at Pissariwka and felt their way forward against the Tischkowka – Kapitanowka line, as well as against Ossitnjashka, this with a loss of 15 Soviet AFVs.

The 14th *Panzer Division* launched an attack to close the gap between the inner wings of the two *Korps*. By the evening of 25 January the spearheads of the attack gained the high terrain east of Rosochowatka, while the 72nd *Infanterie Division* had to pull its southern wing back to the southern edge of Ragorod – Losanowka – Jekaterinowka.

The attack on the 26th clearly showed that the objective was to link up via Schpola with the Soviet forces advancing from north to south. The Soviets, accordingly, committed 12 – 14 rifle divisions and armoured formations of the 5th Guards Tank Army, with, presumably, also the 20th Tank Corps, against the eastward-facing German defensive front. All in all, on 26 January 120 to 130 Soviet AFVs attacked, of which the Soviets lost 31 knocked out (a total in this combat area of 90 AFVs between 24 and 26 January).

With offensive covering of the flank to the south with armoured groups and with the employment of numerous antitank guns in the Rosowatka – Tischkowka line, the Soviets carried on their advance westward from the Pissariwka area with an armoured group of 30 – 49 AFVs, including numerous KW 1 heavy tanks. They captured Kapitanowka and, diverting some forces toward Slatopol and Schurowka, continued their advance. In order to support the forces advancing from north to south they launched attacks in regimental strength in waves supported by armour in the northern portion of the area of penetration and forced the German line back to Pastorskoje – railroad line west of Jekaterinowka. In so doing they suffered heavy bloody losses and

DEFENSIVE BATTLES AT THE START OF 1944

lost 20 AFVs. East of Jekaterinowka an enemy group reinforced with armour advanced to the north and got into the rear of the 72nd *Infanterie Division* in the Rajgorod area.

That day the Soviets lost 31 AFVs in the fighting against the northern wing of the 47th *Panzer Korps*. In the Kapitanowka – Shurowka – Lebedin area. However, the enemy formations felt their way forward to the Schpola bridges, in fact, to the Tolmatsch area, 12 kilometers south of Schpola. Other forces broke through the inner wing of the 389th *Infanterie Division* and 72nd *Infanterie Division* between the railroad northwest of Jekaterinowka and west of Krassnyj Chutor and crossed the railroad line to the west. This Soviet success forced the *Armee* command to pull back the Smela salient in the front to a cordon position east of Taschlyk, east of Rotmistrowka – Balakleja in order to eliminate the threat to the rear of the 72nd *Infanterie Division* and 5th *SS-Panzer Division 'Wiking'*. That involved ruthless weakening of the front in the Kanew area with the transfer of the 320th *Infanterie Division*.

See Maps 46 and 47.

The 11th *Panzer Division* was to sever the rearward connections of the Kapitanowka enemy group in the Pissariwka rea. Regardless of the fact that the roads had turned to bottomless mud – alternating with glare from sheet ice – the division made it to the line of the hill west of Pissariwka – Tischkowka and there ran into an enemy column that was marching from east to west, from which they exacted substantial losses. The division blocked the ridge-line east of Tischkowka – Kapitanowka on 27 January, thereby preventing the advance of strong enemy forces west via Schpola.

Closing the Ring around the 'Dnjepr-*Balkon*'

On 28 January the Soviets thrust through the 11th *Panzer Division's* blocking line on the heights east of Tischkowka – Kapitanowka and thereby reopened the rear communications for their breakthrough group. On that same day the breakthrough forces coming from the east linked up with the forces coming southward from the north between Schpola and Swenigorodka, thereby closing the ring around the 'Dnjepr-*Balkon*'. Immediately the Soviets brought strong forces into this area around Ossitnjashka – Pissariwka, about 150 AFVs and 3,000 men, with over 100 lorries. A German armoured thrust aimed at closing the gap east of Kapitanowka ran into a solid enemy front of armour and antitank guns on the hills between Pissariwka and Tischkowka. After achieving considerable initial success it failed to break through. In heavy fighting with significant German losses (20 AFVs lost) 25 enemy AFVs were destroyed.

See Maps 46 and 47.

The Soviets concerned themselves with widening the breakthrough they had achieved with commitment of armour and strong infantry forces, thereby losing 10 – 12 AFVs that day. After capturing Swenigorodka, the Soviets advanced with armoured forces to the line of the railroad station south of Swenigorodka – Bogatschewka – Kasazkoje.

In fact, on 29 January, with 16 – 17 rifle divisions and three tank corps, the Soviets were able to hold the Kapitanowka gap open. Indeed, with 60 AFVs they thrust through the east front of the 11th *Armee Korps* between the Jekaterinowka railroad station and Taschlyk, making an eight to ten kilometer

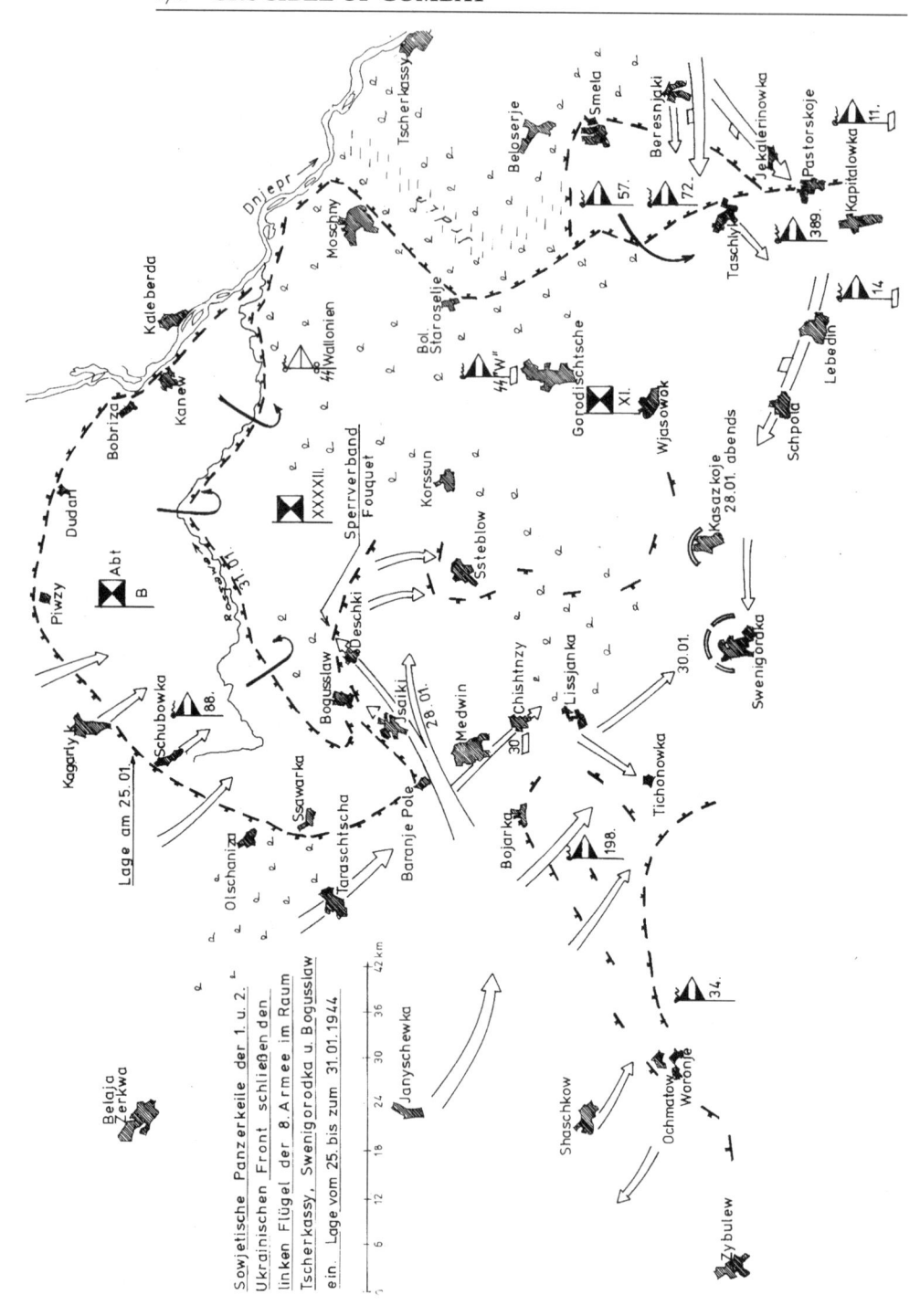

47. Soviet armoured wedges of the 1st and 2nd Ukrainian Fronts close up to the left wing of the 8th *Armee* in the Tscherkassy, Swenigorodka and Boguslaw area. Situation from 25 to 31 January, 1944.

DEFENSIVE BATTLES AT THE START OF 1944

breach, thereby splitting the front. Nevertheless, the Soviets lost another 19 AFVs on 29 January in their effort to widen their breakthrough. German forces mopped up Meshigorka in a counterattack.

With that, the Red Army cut off the Dnjepr *'Balkon'* with its *Schwerpunkt* apparently from the east from the Tscherkassy – Smela area toward Schpola, and with weaker attacks from the north toward Swenigorodka. These attacking forces closed up on 30 January in this area of the front against the Ross river line at Bogusslaw and Ssteblow and brought up forces into the Kwitki and Olschana area.

See Maps 47, 48 and 49.

11
Battle of Tscherkassy[1]

In the previous events it has not been possible to unequivocally determine from the surviving *Heeres* reports which formations served exclusively in 'Operation *Watutin*' amd which were already pursuing the objective of relieving the 'Dnjepr *Balkon*', thus, the Tscherkassy *Kessel*. The latter mission already appeared and became ever more urgent during the formation of the Gaissin *Kessel* and the further Operation *'Watutin'*, considering that 50,000 German soldiers were encircled there. Supply by air did not seem secure, in light of the Soviet anti-aircraft forces that had been brought in and also considering the miserable weather. 70 tons of supplies appeared to be necessary each day. However, because of the fog and the heavy Soviet anti-aircraft forces that could not always be landed in Korssun. A series of *Ju 52* took wounded back with them on their return and were shot down.

Difficulties in Bringing Up the German Relief Forces

The *Heeresgruppe* command was repeatedly faced with the necessity of stripping sectors of the front to supply troops to other endangered sectors. Again and again Von Manstein had stressed the need for timely evacuation of the Nikopol bridgehead, and, also, the Saporoshje frontal salient, in order to free up troops for the central front of *Heeresgruppe Süd*. Von Manstein had, likewise, pushed for permission to pull back the 'Dnjepr *Balkon*'. Hitler, however, insisted that this *Balkon*, which included Korssun, west of Tscherkassy, and still extended to the Dnjepr, had to be held. He still cherished hopes to regain Kiew by attacking north from this Dnjepr position, or, later, to again advance eastward over the Dnjepr crossings, this in complete refusal to recognize the condition of the fought-out troops and actual force-ratio between the two sides.

See Maps 42 and 48, and for geography, Map 50.

The time for the increasingly urgent provision of relief troops proved to be extraordinarily unfavorable. Almost daily weather changes from frost with snowstorms to thaws with spring mud and softened ground transformed the unpaved roads locally into viscous, apparently bottomless mud. Men on foot sometimes sank in calf deep. Wheeled vehicles remained hopelessly bogged down. The only means of locomotion were prime movers and AFVs, and that caused excessive wear and tear on the machines and extremely high fuel

---

1 Translator's note – The 'Tscherkassy *Kessel*' is sometimes called the 'Korssun – Schewtschenkoskij *Kessel*'. For more detailed maps of the Battle of Tscherkassy, see Vopersal, Wolfgang, *Band IVa, Soldaten, Kämpfer, Kameraden, Marsch und Kämpfe der SS-Totenkopf – Division*, Biblio Verlag, Osnabrück, 1988; *Der Kessel von Tscherkassy, 5. SS-Panzer-Division 'Wiking'*, Munin Verlag, Osnabrück, 1969 and the dustjacket of the German 1977 3rd edition of Strassner, Peter, *'Europäische Freiwillige, Die 5. SS Panzerdivision 'Wiking'*, Munin Verlag, Osnabrück, 1977. I found that the map on that particular dustjacket was so helpful that I laminated it and used it in my own studies of Tscherkassy more than any other single map. See also, an excellent study of the battle in English, Douglas E. Nash's, *Hell's Gate: The Battle of the Cherkassy Pocket January – February 1944*, RZM Imports, Inc., Stamford CT, USA, 2005.

BATTLE OF TSCHERKASSY 181

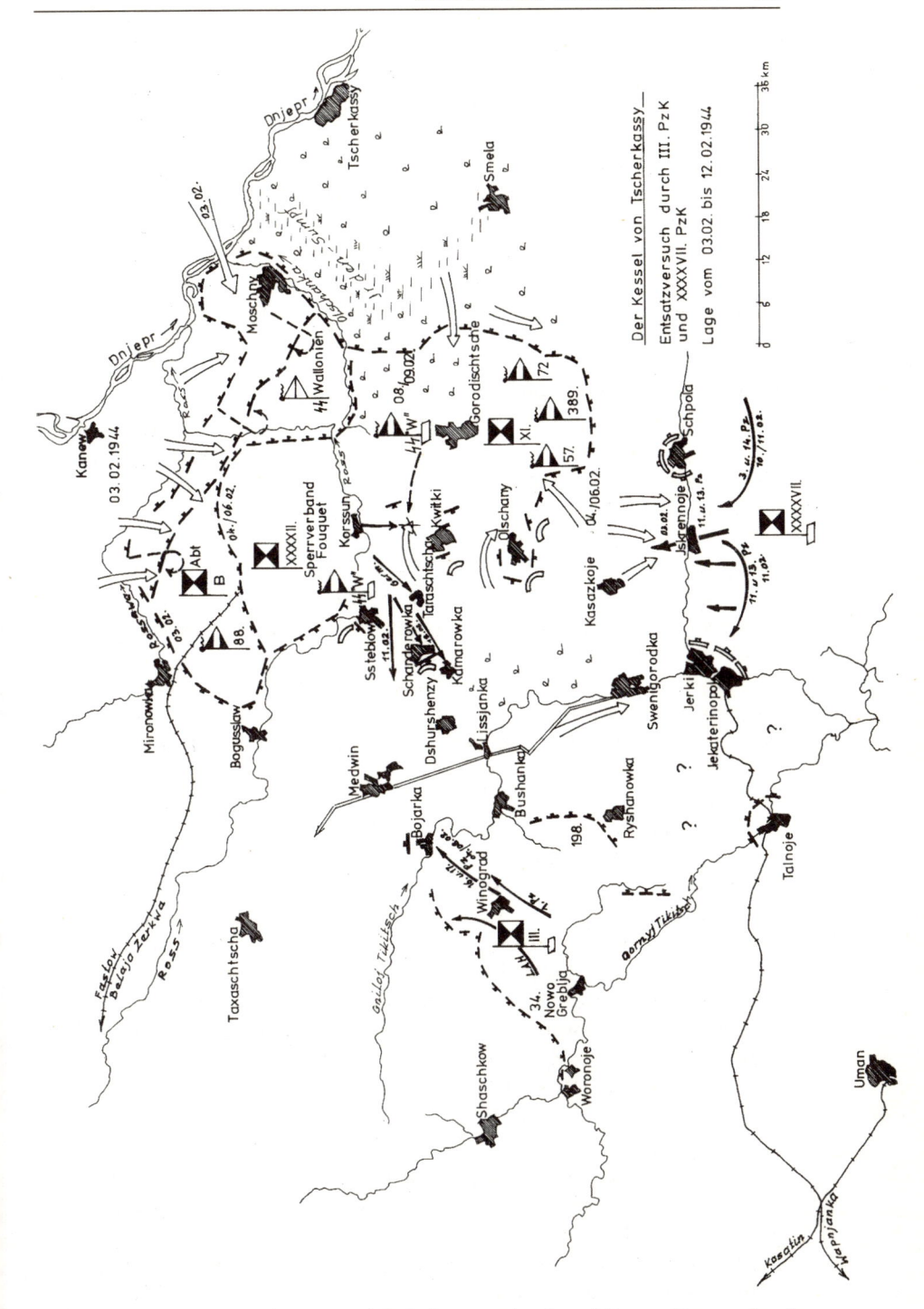

48. The Tscherkassy *Kessel*. Relief attempt by the 3rd *Panzer Korps* and 47th *Panzer Korps*. Situation from 3 to 12 February, 1944. See Map 50 for rail lines and more detail between Schanderowka and Lebedin.

consumption. At night the muddy roads re-froze. The changes in temperature proved extremely bad for the health of the troops, who were out in rain-soaked uniforms by day and exposed at night to temperatures dropping as low as – 20 degrees Celsius (-4 degrees Fahrenheit), all this under the open sky. Nevertheless, the divisions that had been assigned slowly laboured forward, using the AFVs as towing machines. The 24th *Panzer Division* had the longest approach route from the combat sector of the 6th *Armee*. It came to Jampol, some elements to Malij Jekaterinopol. Weak remnants of the 14th *Panzer Division*, and then the 3rd *Panzer Division* were to follow. The 11th *Panzer Division* and 13th *Panzer Division* came from the Iskrennoje bridgehead, to enter action later, adjoining to the right.

Delays in Bringing the Forces Up

The changes in direction of advance of the 3rd *Panzer Korps* to the Tscherkassy *Kessel* following abandonment of Operation *'Watutin'* resulted in delays, as could only be expected. The 16th *Panzer Division* and 17th *Panzer Division* finally arrived, so that, instead of the planned nine *Panzer* divisions, the *Korps* had three *Panzer* divisions or, at any rate, elements of them, at its disposal, thus, a far more limited force than had been intended and was necessary.

In general, the Soviets held back in other sectors. To be sure, on the right wing of the 6th *Armee* they overran the Nikopol bridgehead and attacked north of Apostolowo toward the southwest, probably to drive hard on the heels of the withdrawal of the 24th *Panzer Division* to the Korssun sector – the rear area services here fell, in part, victim to the Soviets. However, the attack in the area of the 6th *Armee* resulted – certainly in accord with Red Army plans – in the sudden and, from the viewpoint of the command, entirely unjustified, order from Hitler that the 24th *Panzer Division*, just before the start of the intended Tscherkassy attack, was to be pulled out of the Tscherkassy attack and set in march back whence it had come. That order came when the division was already in its jump-off positions for the next day's attack to relieve the Dnjepr *'Balkon'*. *Generalfeldmarschall* von Manstein's objections were ignored by Hitler. The 24th *Panzer Division*, which had already been on the march for several days, thereby was no longer available for the action. Its reverse march to its former combat sector also required time, so that it took several more days for the division to churn its way through this stretch of over 300 kilometers of mud-bound roads, with great wear and tear on strength and matériel and expenditure of fuel. During the critical days this division was available for action neither at Swenigorodka nor at Apostolowo because it arrived back there too late.

See Map 48.

Instead of the planned number of *Panzer* divisions the 8th *Armee* did not have a single *Panzer* division available for the 4 February attack south of Swenigorodka. The 11th *Panzer Division* and 13th *Panzer Division* were still fighting at Iskrennoje. The 14th *Panzer Division* was south of Lebedin and the 24th *Panzer Division* was churning through 300 kilometers of mud back to Apostolowo, the original starting point of its arduous march. With that, the fate of the 'Dnjepr *Balkon*', namely, of the 11th *Armee Korps* and 42nd *Armee Korps* seemed sealed. Hitler had, with his directive regarding the reversal of the

BATTLE OF TSCHERKASSY

movement of the 24th *Panzer Division*, repeated the same mistake that had, apparently, caused the loss of the battle of Kursk, whereby, in the middle of a successful action he pulled the 2nd *Waffen-SS Panzer Korps* out of the battle, regardless of the favorable state of this greatest armoured battle of World War II at Prochorowka.

Preparations for a Relieving Attack

In order to pull the 3rd *Panzer Division* and 14th *Panzer Division* out of an exposed 40 kilometers wide front and free them up for service elsewhere, particularly for commitment at Swenigorodka, additional infantry division had to work their way through the mud from the Kirowograd area to the north. Regardless of this, there was a 60 kilometer gap in the front at Swenigorodka – Ryshanowka to the 3rd *Panzer Korps*.

See Map 48.

Contrary to German expectations, the Soviets attacked with their 29th Tank Corps south from Lebedin into the gap between the 320th *Infanterije Division* and the Iskrennoje bridgehead to take advantage of the apparently identified withdrawal of German forces. The 3rd *Panzer Division* and 14th *Panzer Division*, which were supposed to set off in haste to the north, immediately hurled themselves against the attackers. With great sacrifice they managed to again close the front. Only on 11 February did the 106th *Infanterie Division* reach its new sector in order to free up the 14th *Panzer Division*. Accordingly, the advance of the Soviet 29th Tank Corps, shortly joined by the Soviet 18th Tank Corps, had far-reaching consequences, even though neither corps achieved successes of their own. Fortunately, the Red 20th Tank Corps initially remained inactive around Swenigorodka.

See Map 48, which shows the Soviet attack, but not the name of Lebedin, and, for geography, Maps 46, 47 and 50.

In order to fill the existing gaps with infantry forces, the 8th *Armee* gathered up men returning from leave in the homeland and assembled them at Jampol in about two regiment's strength, attaching them to the 48th *Panzer Korps*. The combat effectiveness of such motley outfits in which nobody knew one-another must seem extremely dubious. Such units lacked the normal cohesiveness of troops. Everyone concerned felt that he was involved in a lost cause.[2]

First Relief Attempt

With that, the intention of utilizing the Iskrennoje bridgehead as the jump-off position for an advance and thereby to cover the eastern flank of a breakthrough attack via Swenigorodka and, after linking up with the 3rd *Panzer Division* and 14th *Panzer Division* on 4 February south of Lebedin, to advance, appeared to have been rendered impossible. The 8th *Armee* could, in any case, still force the Soviets to withdraw forces from the southern edge of the *Kessel*. That called for the formation of a new front. The Iskrennoje bridgehead, however, had to be evacuated. This projecting wedge had to be abandoned. The 14th *Panzer Division* had to extend itself to the west and take over securing of the resultant cordon position with isolated outposts in addition to its former mission. This division could not put up any significant resistance in such a broad sector

See Maps 48 and 49.

---

2   Translator's note – Regardless of Hinze's remarks, from a Western Allied point of view, German makeshift units performed far more effectively than did similarly formed western units.

that was so scantily manned. At best, it could only hope to observe the enemy. It had lost heavily in the fighting east of Kirowograd without receiving any replacements to fill its ranks. In addition the division had lost command over an entire *Grenadier* regiment of the 282nd *Infanterie Division* [formerly attached], which, after a successful hasty counterattack at Kapitanowka, had been forced aside into the *Kessel*. In any case, the 11th *Panzer Division* and 13th *Panzer Division* regained freedom of movement.

Further Relief Attempt

See Map 49. The attack of the 3rd *Panzer Korps* with the 16th *Panzer Division* and 17th *Panzer Division* to the north to the Gniloi – Tikitsch river sector remained bogged down in the mud. The Soviets then stirred and thrust with their armour into the deep flank of the still 40 kilometer wide gap to the 8th *Armee* at Malij Jekaterinopol, threatening the vital Talnoje supply railroad station.

The various groups of the 1st *SS-Panzer Division 'Leibstandarte SS Adolf Hitler'* and the 1st *Panzer Division* came into action, one after another, covering the flanks and carrying the attack forward again. On 8 February the 16th *Panzer Division* and elements of the 1st *SS-Panzer Division 'Leibstandarte SS Adolf Hitler'* reached the Gniloi – Tikitsch sector west of Bojarka and forced a crossing over the river. With that, the 3rd *Panzer Korps* jutted like a pointed wedge 30 kilometers into the enemy forces. However, another 30 kilometers still separated the *Korps* from the *Kessel* of the 11th *Armee Korps*, which had, in the meantime, been forced eastward around Gorodischtsche and Korssun – Schewtschenkoskij. The 3rd *Panzer Korps* then received orders to give up its former combat objective and to cut off the spearhead of the Soviet north-south advance, and to swing to the east in order to advance via Bushanka – Lissjanka to Kwitki, toward the *Kessel* of the 'Dnjepr *Balkon*'.

See Map 49. Light frost on 11 February favoured the German movements. The new direction of advance of the 3rd *Panzer Korps* apparently surprised the Soviets. That assisted the 1st *Panzer Division*, pressing forward, to take Bushanka at the Gniloi-Tikitsch on its first attempt, covered on both sides by the 17th *Panzer Division* and 16th *Panzer Division*.

In the sector adjoining the 8th *Armee* on the right, the 11th *Panzer Division* and 13th *Panzer Division*, attacking to the west, initially took Malejo Katerinopol and then turned north at the Gniloi Tikitsch. On 11 February, together with the 13th *Panzer Division*, they forced a crossing over the Schpola river. This operation involved a risky concentration of forces that stripped the defensive front to the east and north.

See Maps 49 and 50. The winter weather hardly allowed support by the *Luftwaffe*. Therefore supply, especially of fuel, which only arrived by air-drop, halted. On 12 February the 16th *Panzer Division*, advancing to the east under constant threat to its northern flank, took Daschukowka. That same day, assisted in its movement by frost, the 11th *Panzer Division* reached the hills south of Swenigorodka. At this point, the 8th *Armee* wedge projecting into the enemy was still 25 kilometers from the 3rd *Panzer Korps* in Lissjanka, about 30 kilometers from the southern boundary of the dangerously diminished *Kessel* at Komarowka. The German forces, however, proved to be totally exhausted. Armour received

BATTLE OF TSCHERKASSY 185

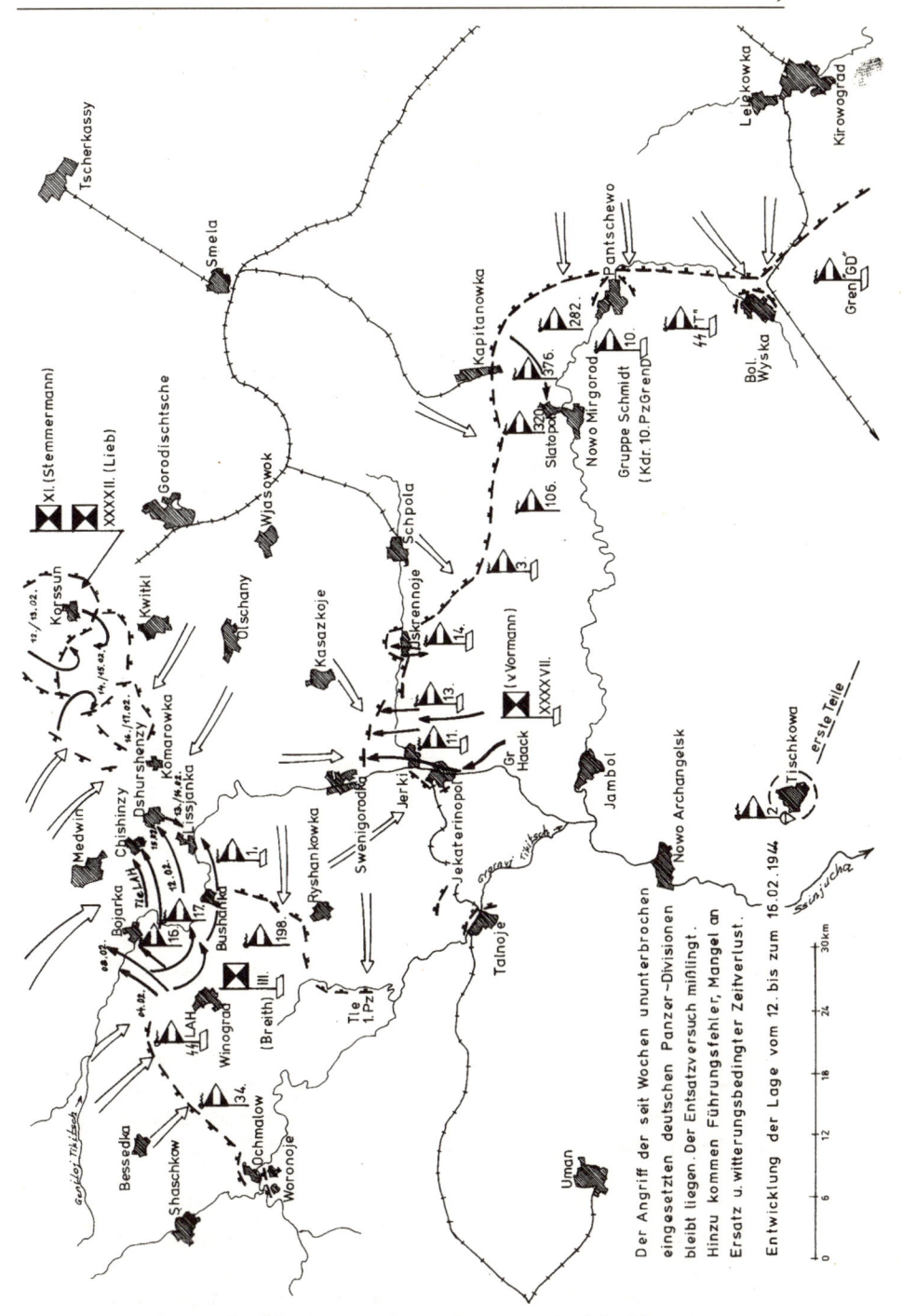

49. The attack of the German *Panzer* divisions, which had been in constant action for weeks, comes to a standstill. The relief attempt fails. In addition there have been command errors, shortages of replacements and weather-occasioned losses of time. Development of the situation from 12 to 16 February, 1944

no replacement engines or parts. Only a few *Panzer* were still serviceable, while the Soviet armoured and infantry forces steadily grew.

The German relief forces could not undertake any additional operations without more support and flank-cover to both right and left. Thus, the only remaining hope was for the encircled forces to fight their way through to them. Furthermore, the encircled forces had received no more orderly logistical support after 28 January, just a few morsels of necessities that the *Luftwaffe* landed or dropped at the Korssun airfield.

Later the Gniloi-Tikitsh river would acquire great significance. It could only be crossed by bridges. Thus, at this time of the year it constituted a major obstacle, 20 meters wide and deeper than the height of a man. Ice covered margins extended on both sides from soft, boggy banks that offered no footing out into the river where great ice flows swept past in the middle in the slow current.

13 and 14 February brought no significant changes. The 1st *Panzer Division* forced its way into Lissjanka, but then had to pull back out of it. The division was not able to cross the Gniloi-Tikitsch. After the 16th *Panzer Division* penetrated Chishinzy only ten kilometers remained to the *Kessel*. Concentric attacks by the Soviet 5th Guards Corps forced the 16th *Panzer Division* to fall back again to the west.

Hitler Becomes Involved

Hitler's orders entered the situation, that the 11th *Armee Korps* in the 'Dnjepr Balkon' should continue to hold the entire former salient-position as the basis for launching a great operation against Kiew, meaning that it would have to hold a front of at least 100 kilometers and repulse attacks, and, in addition, form a 100 kilometer southern front between Bojarka and Kapitanowka. As if that was not enough, it would have to assemble strong forces somewhere around Morenzy – Kwitki, which would serve as a breakthrough group to the two relief spearheads of the 3rd *Panzer Korps* and 47th *Panzer Korps* at the appropriate time. Apparently Hitler had given no thought to how such an order, which was totally irrelevant to the actual situation, was to be carried out. However, it complicated command at the *Armee, Korps* and division levels.

It remains to observe that the onset of the change in the weather, the 'Rasputitza', transformed the landscape into knee-deep mud, crusted at night with frost, moistened by day with drizzle that alternated with snow storms. In such terrain vehicles required three to four times their normal fuel allotments. Gasoline was scarce, ammunition even worse, rations and clothing completely inadequate.

On 15 and 16 February the 3rd *Panzer Korps*, screened on its rear and northern flank toward Bojarka and Medwin by the 16th *Panzer Division* again attempted to break through. In Lissjanka, however, the only bridge collapsed for unfathomable reasons, which prevented crossing. The armoured attack failed to develop and aborted.

The Development of the *Kessel*

Already, on 29 January the Soviets streamed via Medwin toward Korssun and Buguslaw at the Ross river, while, in the east, armour and cavalry turned north toward Olschana. There was no *Kessel* front, which was contrary to the usual Soviet practice of splitting such a *Kessel* into small parts. The first action was for the encircled *Korps* to evacuate the Dnjepr front on its own initiative – disregarding Hitler's orders – and immediately commit the formations thereby freed up to attack to the south toward and to capture Morenzy – Kwitki. Between Kwitki and Olschana at the southern edge of the *Kessel* the distance was a bare ten kilometers. At times in a race with the Red Army, the German forces were able, by the evening of 4 February, to establish by attack a continuous front in an arc around Wjasowok. In the meanwhile, instead of turning toward this breakout position of the *Korps* – as the result of a nearly incomprehensible order – the 3rd *Panzer Korps* continued initially to advance to the north, thereby bringing no relief to the encircled *Korps*. In addition, the help that the *Luftwaffe* provided to the 3rd *Panzer Korps* thereby reduced its support for the forces in the *Kessel*. At this point the 24th *Panzer Division* was lacking for commitment toward the *Kessel*, because Hitler had ordered it back over the 300 kilometers it had come to the 6th *Armee* at Apostolowo.

See Maps 47 and 48.

On 5 February the Cossacks stormed past Kwitki toward Korssun, and its airfield that was so vital for supplying the encircled forces. That heightened the danger of splitting up the forces in the *Kessel*.

See Map 48.

The outer ring of the *Kessel* still measured 250 kilometers, greater, therefore, than six weak divisions could hold in heavy fighting. The *Kessel* formations therefore further evacuated the northern area, pulling the front back to the Starusselje – Jannowka line and forming a large arc around Korssun to the north. It was more difficult to give up the southern salient around Wjasowok, because the lines of the *Kessel* there were closest to the approaching relief forces. Thus, giving up that salient increased the distance to the main body of the 8th *Armee*. The Korssun supply airfield was farther to the north. The 57th *Infanterie Division*, weak remnants of the 389th *Infanterie Division* and the 5th *SS-Panzer Division 'Wiking'* fell back on Gorodischtsche by 8 February. That freed up the 72nd *Infanterie Division* on 9 February and helped close the gap east of Kwitki in counterattack. The perimeter of the *Kessel* then amounted to about 130 kilometers.

See Maps 48 and 49.

Hopes for relief continued to diminish. The 47th *Panzer Korps* was bogged down in the Kapitanowka – Iskrennoje line, fixed by superior enemy forces. The 3rd *Panzer Korps*, 30 kilometers distant, west of Bojarka, had, indeed, finally received orders to attack to the east toward Komarowka, but first had to regroup.

The Soviets considered that the situation was suitable to demand that the forces in the *Kessel* surrender. A Soviet colonel-general brought the message across the lines east of Medwin as a proper parliamentary, complete with trumpeter and white flag. The expected reply was to be given the following day by a fully-empowered representative in Chirowka, a locality 15 kilometers west of Korssun. At the same time the Soviets dropped leaflets from the air. In addition members of the *'Nationalkomitees Freies Deutschland'* ['National

Committee of Free Germany'] encouraged the encircled soldiers to surrender. Especially active were *General* von Seydlitz-Kurzbach, *General* Korfe, *Major* Lewerenz, *Oberst* Steidle and *Major* Büchler, as well as *Leutnant Graf* von Einsiedel.

The 'Wandering *Kessel*'

General Stemmermann, who was also placed in command of the 42nd *Korps*, now guided the *Kessel* like a battleship, as the 'Wandering *Kessel*', toward the southwest, initially foregoing any sort of logistical support. He wanted to move toward the 3rd *Panzer Korps* and 47th *Panzer Korps*. He had Kwitki, Gorodischtsche and Starosselje, north of Jannowka, evacuated and pulled the extreme front line back to both sides of Korssun, so that the airfield was still barely usable, but lay now under observed enemy fire. That freed up *Korpsabteilung* B and the 5th *SS-Panzer Division 'Wiking'*. They, together with the 72nd *Infanterie Division*, were to launch an attack on 10 February on Schandarowka and, on 12 February, on Chilki and Komarowka. The movements were impacted by impassible roads and difficult weather conditions, at times as frost and temperatures as low as – 20 degrees Celsius or more [– four degrees Farenheit or more], with entire days of thaw, rain and snow. As if that wasn't enough there were shortages of ammunition, lack of rations and failure of communications equipment. Attributable to that last failure was probably the unrecognized Soviet thrust into the withdrawal movement at Gorodischtsche. Formations specified for the attack to the southwest again had to turn to the east to prevent a breakthrough. In the meantime, about 4,000 wounded, for whom there was no possibility of transport, were assembled in the *Kessel*. *General* Stemmermann did not let anything divert him from his resolution. He concentrated the divisions that were under his command closely around Schandarowka and, on 13 February, evacuated Korssun, and, on 15 February, Ssteblow, to its southwest. The *Kessel* now measured only seven by eight kilometers, with about 50,000 men, included 4,00 wounded who could not be transported. All of this awaited success of the last decisive advance of the 3rd *Panzer Korps*.

In the meantime the Soviets were even calling German radio stations with demands for surrender. The people from the *Nationalkomitee* had letters dropped to the German commander. However, nobody among the encircled troops replied to the repeated demands for surrender. All such efforts,, even those of the *Nationalkomitee*, seemed to have failed in light of the troops' own knowledge of the treatment of prisoners, such promises of good treatment in captivity were totally unconvincing.

'Gruppe Stemmermann' Breaks Out

The 3rd *Panzer Korps* did not move forward, remaining with its vehicles stuck in the mud, so that now the encircled formations – *Gruppe Stemmermann* – itself had to carry out the decisive breakthrough at Dshurshenzy – Hill 239.0 with its own forces to link up with the spearhead of the 3rd *Panzer Korps*. On 16 February the formations were supposed to set out, in three assault wedges, deeply echeloned, without preparatory fires, from the Chilki – Komarowka

BATTLE OF TSCHERKASSY 189

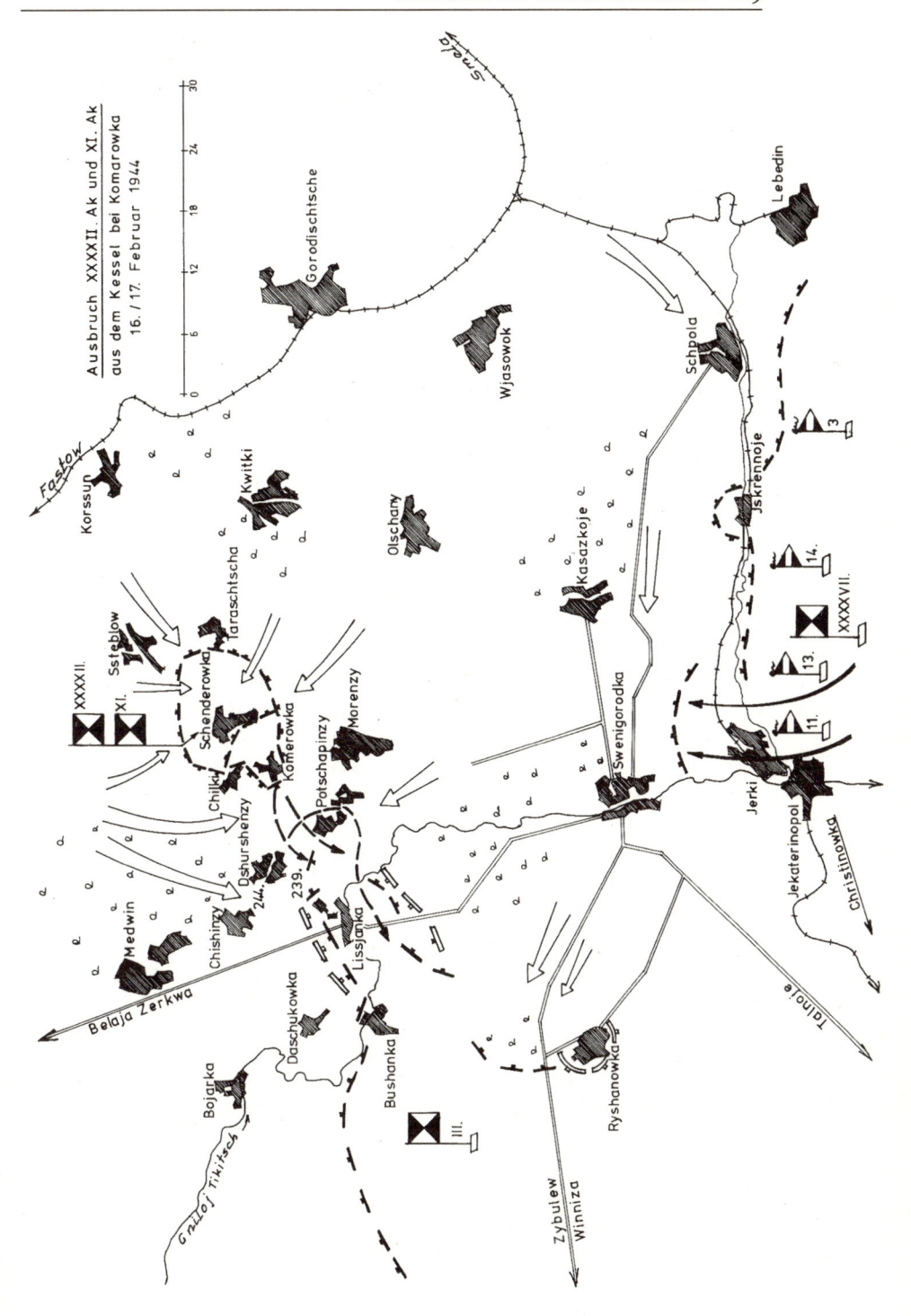

50. Breakout of the 42nd *Armee Korps* and 11th *Armee Korps* from the *Kessel* at Komarowka 16/17 February, 1944.

line. Working their way forward, without a sound, they were to fall on the enemy with cold steel and break through the Soviet lines in a single thrust. At daybreak the 8th *Fliegerkorps* was to screen the flanks. The 3rd *Panzer Korps* and 47th *Panzer Korps* were to resume their attacks in the former directions to draw as many enemy forces upon themselves as possible. The 57th *Infanterie Division* and 88th *Infanterie Division* formed the *Kessel's* rear guard. About 1,500 wounded were to remain in Schandarowka, accompanied by physicians and the necessary medical personnel.

See Map 50.

The difficulty for the break-out formations was that all three break-out groups had to use a single route, through Schandorowka, which was under observed enemy artillery fire. There was no bypass. In the northeast, south of Steblew, the Soviets attacked into the withdrawal movement of the rear guards of the 88th *Infanterie Division* and 57th *Infanterie Division*. The dangerous penetration, however, was successfully intercepted, though not until it was only three kilometers from Schandorowka.

Komarowka changed hands four times on 16 February. The Soviet lines, however, were only a scant three kilometers from Schandorowka here. Now 46,000 men and all their equipment were crowded into 50 square kilometers, barely able to move, no longer subject to command, waiting for the specified time for the breakout.

The first troops set out at 2300 hours without any preparatory fire, and ran over the Soviets. They thereby broke the ring. Thus would the breakout have to succeed, because it started based on the assumption that the 3rd *Panzer Korps* was in Dshurschenzy on Hill 239 and in Potschapinzy. As planned, the second and third waves moved out of the assembly position area under the impression that the first wave had successfully broken through. About 40,000 men now flowed in a swelling stream to the west. Now only a few kilometers separated them from the relief formations with whom they hoped to link up.

As daylight broke, however, the advancing formations ran into murderous fire from armour, antitank guns and artillery. The last of the material that had been brought along – guns and *Sturmgeschütze* – were abandoned after they had fired their last remaining rounds, Here the fate of the wounded that the troops had carried with them was consummated. The disorganized remnants of the troops now sought a way out of the chaos with all the courage of desperation. Individual groups composed of a motley collection of all arms and specialties led by the best officers on the spot forced their way on to the west. Soviet infantry barring their way were swept aside with cold steel. Nevertheless, the defenseless masses were exposed to the fire of Soviet artillery and armour and suffered heavy losses.

It was now discovered that the spearheads of the 3rd *Panzer Korps* were not where the formations that were breaking out had expected to meet them, at Llishinzy, Oktjabr and Lissjanka. Instead, Soviet troops, ready for defense, blocked the crossing over the Gniloi – Tikitsch.

Shielded by darkness and snow squalls individual groups of Germans made their way forward to the first German armour in Oktjabr, making it to salvation. The majority of the thoroughly intermingled troop-remnants, however, with nothing more than hand-held weapons, initially remained, lying hopelessly. Since, to them, the sound of fighting seemed weaker to the south, great masses turned in desperation to the south. Soviet infantry fled before their assault from the eastern part of Potschapinzy. They dispersed the Soviet forces defending the river at the banks of the Gniloi-Tikitsch. However, they found no bridge. The ice covering the river did not hold. In their desperation, throwing aside their weapons, the masses of the arriving soldiers finally threw themselves into the icy flood. Many drowned. Those that reached the other side were still under fire of the T 34s and artillery from the open ridge southeast of Lissjanka. Thos who made it to the spearhead of the 1st *Panzer Division* in the southern part of Lissjanka could consider themselves saved.

During the night of 17/18 February the last soldiers of the rear guard, who had initially held off the pursuing enemy in exemplary devotion to duty, slogged, dry-shod, over a bridge that the pioneers had hastily erected to the German lines, half-frozen, starving, some without weapons. About 25,000 men reached the objective of their break out from the *Kessel*. The veil of silence fell over the fate of the wounded left behind, as it did over those who entered the hopeless situation of captivity. Individuals from among these prisoners returned after many years, mostly starting in 1949, and reported what they had seen – that the Soviets had, as was their custom, immediately shot the wounded who were incapable of walking. Only the lightly wounded had the opportunity, after days of marching without any rations, after having their boots taken from them, their feet wrapped in rags, of reaching the collecting points and, later, of surviving what was, for most, five years of captivity that had nothing to do with what the Soviets had promised.

The 11th *Armee Korps* and 42nd *Armee Korps* ceased to exist. They were missing from the later defense. These formations with their Eastern Front experience could not easily be replaced, and even if it was possible to gather the requisite personnel for activating new formations, the equipment was lacking. The German economy could not equip two entire *Armee Korps* in a foreseeable time with new vehicles and guns. Above all, the loss of these two *Armee Korps* opened the way for a great Soviet breakthrough farther to the west.

Formations Involved

The formations involved in the fighting from 5 January to 17 February 1944 (Battle of Tscherkassy):

8th *Armee*
11th *Armee Korps*
42nd *Armee Korps*
52nd *Armee Korps*
47th *Armee Korps*
57th *Infanterie Division*
72nd *Infanterie Division*
88th *Infanterie Division*
106th *Infanterie Division*
282nd *Infanterie Division*
320th *Infanterie Division*
376th *Infanterie Division*

384th *Infanterie Division*
Korpsabteilung A
Korpsabteilung B
Gruppe Haack (made up of men returning from or going on leave)
10th *Panzergrenadier Division*
Panzergrenadier Division 'Großdeutschland'
3rd *Panzer Division*
11th *Panzer Division*
14th *Panzer Division*
24th *Panzer Division*
2nd *Fallschirmjäger Division*
3rd *SS-Panzerdivision 'Totenkopf'*
5th *SS-Panzer Division 'Wiking'*
SS-Brigade 'Walonien'

1st *Panzer Armee*
7th *Armee Korps*
3rd *Panzer Korps*
34th *Infanterie Division*
198th *Infanterie Division*
1st *Panzer Division*
16th *Panzer Division*
17th *Panzer Division*
1st *SS-Panzer Division 'Leibstandarte SS Adolf Hitler'* [schwere Panzer Abteilung 503 (sPzRgt Bäke)]
[4th *Gebirgs Division*]

8th *Flieger Korps*

12

Situation after the Breakout from the Tscherkassy Pocket

The evaluation of the situation had to raise grave concerns for *Heeresgruppe Süd*. Granted, the battle for the relief of the Tscherkassy *Kessel* had drawn forces together, with whose help it had been possible to close the gaps in the front line to the west. That seemed to have prevented the Soviets from utilizing the hitherto neglected opportunity to advance with all available forces toward Uman – Winniza and further to the west. On the other hand, if the German forces that had been assembled there were withdrawn, that opportunity could again be open for exploitation. It was scarcely possible to judge whether the attack on the left wing of *Heeresgruppe Süd*, southwest of Shitomir, in particular against the 11th *Armee Korps*, or the constantly repeated attacks against the Nikopol bridgehead, against the positions of the 30th *Armee Korps* or in the Kirowograd area served the objective of opening this possibility. Experience showed that the Soviets, with few exceptions, directed their attacks against sectors of the German front that were not strongly held, as against the cordon position in the Dnjepr bend, especially preferring to attack sectors that had been 'stripped' of troops, since that promised faster advances and lower losses. That was the case in the Dnjepr frontal salient between Krementschug and Dnjepropetrowsk, as also on the extreme left wing, particularly in the gap in the front to *Heeresgruppe Mitte*.

Situation of the 6th *Armee* in the Dnjepr Bend

Hitler finally decided to approve the order for *General* Schörner to evacuate the Nikopol bridgehead (see below), but only after the Soviets had taken Apostolowo and threatened to cut off the formations in the entire Dnjepr bend, including the Nikopol bridgehead. This approval, again, came too late, the retreat too sudden. A force that has constantly had to be in readiness to repulse attacks could not weaken itself by withdrawal of matériel and heavy weapons and of the slow-marching elements. So long as the defensive mission remained in effect, all of the formations so employed had to hold themselves in total readiness, particularly because of their weakened condition. In addition, at that time the 24th *Panzer Division* was not available as a reserve that could have thwarted the Soviet intentions.

There was only one single-tracked railroad line available in that area and no paved roads over which the withdrawal movement could have moved smoothly. The evacuation order for the German frontal salient came at a time when the roads had all been turned to mud as a result of the weather. The retreat – under constant enemy pressure – therefore was extremely exhausting for the infantry, marching on foot, as for the motorized elements. Losses of vehicles, armour under repair, rear-area services and – not an exception – also of ammunition and rations dumps was inevitable.

See Maps 46 and 58.

The fate of the 6th *Armee* and the Dnjepr frontal salient that it held was essentially dependant on the situation in the Kirowograd area. There, too, the withdrawal of *Panzer* divisions and various infantry division for service farther north, relieving the Tscherkassy *Kessel*, left only a thin security line. It was not difficult for the Soviets to break through this and gain ground to the west.

Situation of the Left Wing of the *Heeresgruppe*

See Maps 39 and 43.

Even greater danger threatened the left wing of the *Heeresgruppe*, where a broad gap between the 59th *Armee Korps* and the 13th *Armee Korps* still yawned north of Shitomir, and an even greater gap stretched from its left wing to the police forces around Kowel that were attached to *Heeresgruppe Mitte*. The formations in the lines of defense of the 59th *Armee Korps* and the 13th *Armee Korps* had, at the time, such wide sectors to defend that the necessarily thin manning left plenty of gaps through which the Soviets could infiltrate to the west, either undetected or, at the very least, without it being possible to prevent them.

The road from Kiew via Shitomir to Rowno was an invitation to a continued advance straight to the west. Accordingly the *Heeresgruppe* shifted the 13th *Armee Korps* to block this land-bridge on the extreme northern wing. Despite its weak forces the *Armee Korps* was able to delay the advance of vastly superior Soviet forces during the months of February and March, and that on both sides of this road, skillfully avoiding repeated Soviet attempts at envelopment.

Any further Soviet advance to the west in this area must, therefore, require that the Red Army get to Lublin or Lemberg in the central Polish area in order to sever the supply arteries for the entire *Heeresgruppe Süd* sector. If these attacking forces swung to the south that would result in cutting off the 1st *Panzer Armee* and 8th *Armee*, which were fixed by a westward counter-thrust from the area west of Tscherkassy or, respectively, Kirowograd with a later turn to the north.

There was a universal shortage of combat-worthy formations. The six divisions that had experience on the Eastern Front that had been smashed in the Tscherkassy *Kessel* were absolutely irreplaceable.[1] The remnants that had broken out of the *Kessel* were initially transferred into the *Generalgouvernement* for reactivation. After several months of unbroken action the formations committed in the line of defense could no longer be rated as sufficiently combat-worthy for major fighting, particularly in light of the wholly inadequate provision of replacement personnel for the losses they had suffered.

Gap Between the *Heeresgruppe Süd* and *Heeresgruppe Mitte* Fronts

East of Kowel a group of police units secured the railroad leading from Kiew to the *Generalgouvernement Polen*. The 13th *Armee Korps* could not assist these, since this *Korps* had to fall back to the west on Dubno after the fall of the city of Rowno at the start of February. In this area, too, the possibility existed and

---

1   These included the *Waffen-SS-Sturm Brigade 'Wallonien'* with four grenadier companies, one infantry-gun company, a *Panzer-Jäger* company and an antiaircraft battery.

had to be feared of an enveloping Soviet advance, initially to the west, later swinging in to the south. To counter this danger *Heeresgruppe Süd* repeatedly requested the positioning of an army in the Rowno area. This request, however, was left unfulfilled, even though, in Manstein's opinion, additional formations could have been made available by withdrawal from *Heeresgruppe Nord* as well as by evacuating Crimea.

The Front Line of the 4th *Panzer Armee*

The Soviets did not even have to swing out widely enough to get in the rear of the 1st *Panzer Armee* and 8th *Armee*. An attack against the lines of the 4th *Panzer Armee* with the direction of advance to the southwest or south — the small solution – would offer the Soviets the same possibility for an envelopment of the German forces that were farther to the east.

Merely twelve weak divisions that could be considered as combat-worthy only with reservations (eight infantry-, two *Panzer* – and two *Panzergrenadier* – divisions) under three *Generalkommandos* [*Korps* commands] were available for the entire 240 kilometer front line of the 4th *Panzer Armee*. Aside from the fierce defensive fighting west of Berditschew, the rest of the line of defense held, for the time being, because, except for local operations, the Soviets paused in their activity in February 1944. There was no doubt at that time that the German forces could hardly be considered capable of holding in the face of an attack by a far-superior enemy.

This superior enemy force would not, however, even have to attack the eastern or central portion of the wavy front line, since the weakest place was available on the left wing between Ljubar and Schepetowka, as well as on the far side of Schepetowka. The formations that had been intended to cover this weak point did not arrive on time or were, as was the case with *Kampfgruppe 'Wallonien'*, committed elsewhere. After the conclusion of the battle of the Tscherkassy *Kessel* the *Heeresgruppe* hastily ordered a series of armoured forces that had been freed up to the left wing of the 4th *Panzer Armee*. However, because of the lack of suitable railroad lines the movements had to proceed by road, and that under the road conditions then extant, so that the arrival of these formations at their intended sites of commitment and their readiness for action could not be expected before the middle of March. Nevertheless, in a event of a renewed enemy attack, they could be expected to maintain the situation at the front, but not to counter a broad enveloping movement around the western wing of this army.

The Balance of Forces

The *Heeresgruppe* evaluated its situation, as it had the previous month, such that the greatest danger was on the extreme left wing. Again it tried to get *OKH* (Hitler) to provide additional forces. A few numbers give evidence of the steady weakening of the *Heeresgruppe*. Intelligence results regarding the enemy indicated that the Soviets had received approximately 1,080,000 replacements during the period from July 1943 to January 1944, which probably approximated their losses during that period. During that same period, however, *Heeresgruppe Süd* had lost 405,000 dead, wounded and missing. Replacements had amounted to merely 221,893 men. That resulted in a change in the force ratio that was increasingly unfavorable to the Germans. Such a comparison of strengths must further consider that the combat-value of the freshly recruited infantrymen on the Soviet side was limited as the result of inadequate training. A meaningful comparison requires recognition of the Soviet reinforcement in armour and artillery – Stalin's hobby horse – especially the increase in ammunition supply for the heavy weapons.

According to the results of German intelligence the Soviets had received 2,700 new AFVs during the period under discussion, *Heeresgruppe Süd* received 872, including *Sturmgeschütze*. As the result of their short period of training, a mere eight weeks – wholly inadequate for service on the Eastern Front, the fitness for action of the recruits being sent to the German troops left much to be desired.

The inadequate personnel and matériel being sent to the German formations was in part, the result of Hitler's preference for creating new divisions instead of adequately caring for the old ones whose core cadres had been in active service in peacetime and now had experience on the Eastern Front. The men who were combed out of the labour force and the new recruits currently reaching the age for military service, as well as new production of guns and armour went to these newly activated formations. The Soviets did not make this same mistake to such a degree. In this time period they activated very few new artillery and armoured formations. Instead they supplied the fighting troops with adequate personnel and weapons replacements.

In addition to the superior Soviet outfit of artillery and armour, and better supply of ammunition was the superior mobility derived from the Studebaker lorries provided by the USA. These vehicles, with a total of ten gears and all-wheel drive, easily traversed the muddy terrain, whereas the German supply vehicles, typical of those used in civilian commerce, immediately got stuck. These vehicles that the Soviets used in such numbers served, at the same time, as tow-vehicles for light guns, especially the versatile 'Ratschbum' (7.62 mm antitank gun).

Hitler displayed notable – in part understandable – irresolution regarding von Manstein's constant demands for additional formations from occupied lands. German intelligence was still unable to clarify where the Western Powers intended to form their second front – other than the Italian front. The long coastline that had to be taken into account in considering an invasion, as, for example, in Greece and in the Atlantic, required overall occupation with combat-capable troops. In addition, there were possibilities for invasion in various other Europaean lands, even in neutral Portugal.

In support of his procrastination regarding taking troops from other occupied lands, Hitler pointed out that the muddy season was not yet completely over. As he saw it, this must significantly impact the effectiveness of Soviet formations, especially motorized and armoured units. He left out of his considerations the fact that Soviet AFVs had broader tracks, giving them greater mobility over soft ground than that of German armour. Hitler also hoped for the exhaustion of the Soviet forces. Above all, as Hitler saw it, the weather and terrain conditions must negatively impact any aggressive operations by wearing down the forces. He said that newly activated formations would be available in May. Disregarding the life-threatening danger to the left wing of the *Heeresgruppe*, Hitler refused to allow sufficient time for the evacuation of the Nikopol bridgehead and the frontal salient north of the lower Dnjepr, or for withdrawing the formations committed there. Instead, as a new reverse struck the overextended front of the 6th *Armee*, the *Heeresgruppe* had to give up additional forces to intervene with that *Armee*, namely the 3rd *Panzer Division* and 24th *Panzer Division*.

Precautionary Measures Taken by *Heeresgruppe Süd*

Intelligence revealed that the Commander in Chief of the 1st White Russian Front (Watutin) had shifted his command post to the area opposite the left wing of *Heeresgruppe Süd*. This measure suggested Soviet intentions in that area. Thereupon the *Heeresgruppe* immediately initiated a series of troop movements. Three of the infantry divisions promised by *OKH*, along with the 357th *Infanterie Division* and 359th *Infanterie Division*, ended up, finally, in the area of the 4th *Panzer Armee*. The 3rd *Panzer Korps* with the 1st *Panzer Division*, 11th *Panzer Division* and 16th *Panzer Division*, followed, as soon as possible, by the 17th *Panzer Division* and 18th *Artillerie Division*, were to be withdrawn from their former areas of operation with the 1st *Panzer Armee* and 8th *Armee* and assemble in readiness at Proskurow, behind the 4th *Panzer Armee*. In addition, the 7th *Panzer Division*, 1st *SS – Panzer Division 'Leibstandarte SS Adolf Hitler'* and *schwere Panzer Abteilung* 503 received orders to move to the area of the 4th *Panzer Armee*. They were to assemble at Tarnopol under the 48th *Panzer Korps* in order to prevent envelopment of the west wing of the *Heeresgruppe* via Tarnopol. Shifting the formations to the new area of action was difficult as a result of forces being tied up in the fighting at Berditschew and also because the mud-season had set in. The formations would not be able to complete their intended transfers before the middle of March.

See Map 41.

The *Heeresgruppe* again extended the individual *Armee* sectors, that of the 4th *Panzer Armee* toward the left wing, in particular, to take over command in the area between Tarnopol and Dubno that was now gaining in significance. At the same time the 4th *Panzer Armee* turned over its former frontline at Schepetowka to the 1st *Panzer Armee* and assumed command in the area east of Tarnopol – Dubno, where the 48th *Panzer Korps* was assembling and where, in addition, the 13th *Armee Korps* was already fighting around Dubno. In addition there was a police group at Kowel. The 1st *Panzer Armee* gained some relief by turning over the sector of the front north of Uman (7th *Armee Korps*) to the 8th *Armee*. This, in turn, gave the right wing *Korps* to the 6th *Armee*. Thus, there was a shifting of sector boundaries to the left.

These organizational measures show that the *Heeresgruppe* command continued to consider the danger to the left wing as far more threatening than that in the Kirowograd sector or with the 6th *Armee*. Even if the Soviets were to advance farther west along the Black Sea [*Schwarzmeer*] coast to the Bug, possibly with a simultaneous thrust from the Kirowograd area, that would be more endurable, regardless of the unfavorable supply possibilities through Bessarabia, than an advance on Lemberg with the supply arteries of the entire

Heeresgruppe Süd running through that city. These considerations entailed the necessity of a further pullback of the southern wing to the west in light of the far greater threat on the left wing of the *Heeresgruppe*.

Soviet behaviour regarding the front between Schepetowka and west of Berditschew, as well as after the conclusion of the battle of the Tscherkassy *Kessel* in the Winniza – Swenigorodka – Schpola area raised suspicions that the Soviets were preparing for further operations. The continuation of the fighting west of Berditschew did nothing to change the conclusions of reconnaissance that, among others things, indicated that the Soviets were shifting strong formations into the area west of Ljubar and Schepetowka. The German command must, accordingly, expect the *Schwerpunkt* of a new attack in that area and, even though it involved stripping other sectors of the front, and, regardless of the bad road conditions, set various divisions in march thereto. The command was fully aware of the danger of weakening the central front around Winniza. However, in the meantime, Manstein's conviction had prevailed that the *Schwerpunkt* would be on the left wing, with consequent neglect of the central front of the *Heeresgruppe*.

The expected Soviet attack at the start of March did not, however, begin simultaneously in all sectors of the front. A variety of assaults to feel out the German defense preceded the advance on the left wing at Schepetowka. Because of the extremely thin manning by the German forces in the central sector, no particularly strong Soviet preparations were required there. In the south, on the right wing of *Heeresgruppe Süd*, the front at that time was already in motion, so the Soviets needed no more than to carry on with their advance to the west.

13

Retreat of *Heeresgruppe* A

Evacuation of the Dnjepr Frontal Salient (6th *Armee*)

The defensive fighting on the right wing of *Heeresgruppe Süd* had, at the end of 1943, already brought about the gradual retrograde shifting of the German lines. Hitler, however, placed considerable emphasis on holding the frontal salient, especially the Nikopol bridgehead, in order to continue to be able to use the Manganese mines at Marganez and Scholochowo, as well as to hold open a route for the advance toward Perekop to establish a land-connection to the Crimea.

See Maps 26 and 28.

The balance of forces continually shifted farther in favour of the Soviets, who received constant personnel replacements and shipments of weapons, while the German formations gradually were bled white.

General Schörner reported to the *Armee* high command of the 6th *Armee* that the Soviets had absolute mastery of the air, which they utilized in full strength. The shortage of antiaircraft and 2 cm high-explosive shells complicated the defense. The Soviet mastery of the air also interfered with] the unhindered employment of artillery, and also of reserves. It crippled the effectiveness of German artillery by destruction of communications and interfered with command and supply of the troops. Low-flying enemy planes attacked individual motor vehicles and groups of men. The Soviets cleared the way for their infantry with steel and iron. The developing gaps could only be promptly closed where strong local reserves could be immediately on the spot or were assembled for counterattack. Schörner defended himself with this justification against the intended withdrawal of the 24th *Panzer Division* from its availability as the only mobile reserve behind the badly battered infantry formations. Nevertheless, the 24th *Panzer Division* received orders on 22 January to assemble in the Alexejewka area (20 kilometers west of Nikopol) for further march to the central sector of the southern front. During its 80 days of action the *Panzer* and *Sturmgeschütze*, as well as the *SPW* [lightly armoured half-tracked personnel carriers] of this division had already driven 2,000 kilometers per combat vehicle in their constant 'fire brigade' employment and, in light of the shortage of replacement parts, they had reached the limit of their service-lives.[1]

See Map 52 for geography.

Attack on the Dnjepr Salient

The 24th *Panzer Division* had barely started its march to the north and left its former operational area (28 January) when, on 30 January, the Soviets launched

---

[1] Infantry combat strengths of the 17th *Infanterie Division,* 111th *Infanterie Division,* 258th *Infanterie Division* and 3rd *Gebirgs Division* on 16 January 1944: 7,855 men total, 5,500 of which had been obtained by combing out the trains elements and formation of alarm units. The remainder were soldiers with Eastern Front experience.

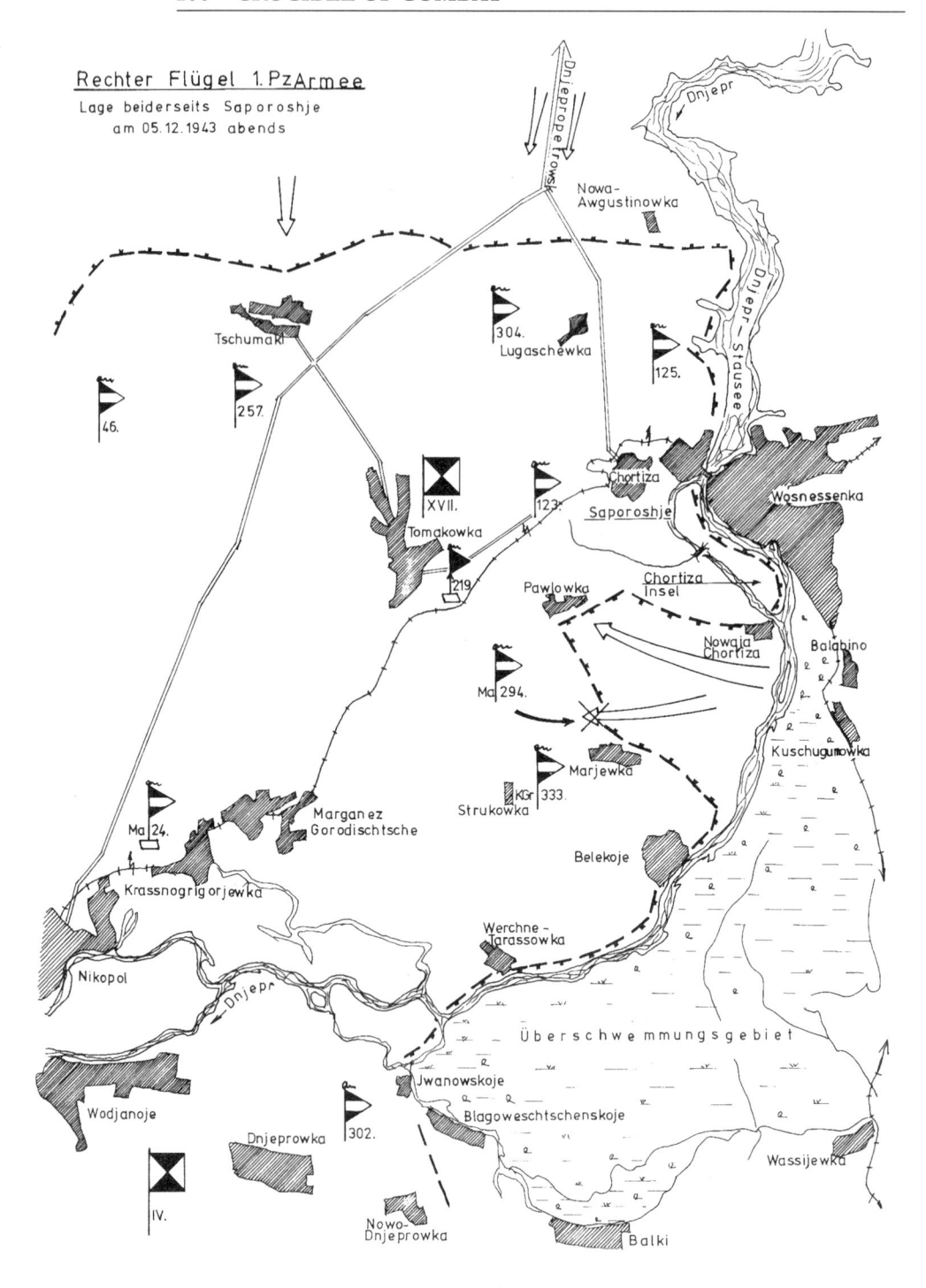

51. Right wing of the 1st *Panzer Armee*. Situation on both sides of Saporoshje on 5 December, 1943, evening.

their attack, initially against the weakened east front of the 17th *Armee Korps*. On 31 January, attacking from the north, they achieved a deep penetration into the main defensive area of the 9th *Panzer Division* . Regardless of the miserable weather and mud-bound roads, with the help of the *Ostland Schlepper*[2] and *'Maultiere'*[3] that the *Korps* had assembled in readiness to transport the infantry, the *Füsilier Bataillon*, the I./ 471, II./ *SfL Panzer Jäger* 258 and the I./ *Artillerie Regiment* 258 came up as reserves.

The Soviets reinforced the attack from east (Tomgajewski) to west, beginning shortly thereafter with a further attack by strong Soviet forces against the divisions of the 30th *Armee Korps*. Here they also achieved a breakthrough, which raised doubts about the previous conduct of the fighting in the 6th *Armee* sector. In the 30th *Armee Korps* sector the Soviets advanced on Scholochowo, which they apparently considered to be their primary objective in order to cut off the three *Korps* of *Gruppe Schörner*. This advance particularly endangered the vital supply routes of the formations in the Dnjepr salient, which may well have influenced Hitler's retrospective endorsement of Schörner's 2 February order to evacuate the Nikopol bridgehead. *See Map 52.*

On 1 February the Soviet attack was initially stemmed. Road conditions so delayed bringing up artillery that a counterattack could not be launched until 3 February. Following Schörner's 2 February order to evacuate the Nikopol bridgehead and to pull the Dnjepr salient back to the 'Ursula' position – line of the mouth of the Basawluk river (20 kilometers west of Nikopol), Kamenka – Dolinzewo (ten kilometers east of Kriwoi Rog) – formations first had to be committed from the forces that were exposed to encirclement to fight free the communications routes to the rear. That did not seem possible without losing terrain. Early on 2 February the Soviets had already broken into Scholochowo. They were stopped south of Scholochowo by *Feldersatzbataillon* 258 and *Feldersatzbataillon* 302.

Evacuation of the Nikopol bridgehead thus became extremely urgent. *See Maps 27 and 52.* This started immediately. First the 3rd *Gebirgs Division* crossed the bridge from Kamenka to Nikopol.[4] The 302nd *Infanterie Division* followed it as the last. Its rear-guard regiment, *Grenadier Regiment* 571 [302nd *ID*] was still engaged in heavy fighting in Wodjanoje and Kamenka. *Pioniier Bataillon* 302 then blew up the bridge over the Dnjepr at 2400 hours on 6 February 1944.

The first action required of the formations retreating out of the bridgehead was to form a defensive front facing west around Marinskoje (west of Nikopol) north of the Dnjepr. The 302nd *Infanterie Division* made it from Nikopol to Marinskoje, partly marching on foot, part with the last rail-transport. *Grenadier Regiment* 571 was still involved in heavy fighting with pursuing Soviets even as it entrained in the Nikopol railroad station.

---

2   Translator's note – The *'Ostland Schlepper'* was officially designated the *'Raupenschlepper Ost'*, a full-tracked vehicle capable of carrying personnel and modest loads and of towing a light field howitzer. Maximum gross vehicle weight was 4900 kilograms. Broad tracks gave it a low ground-pressure of 0.375 kg/ square cm, giving it good mobility over difficult terrain.
3   Half-tracked lorries.
4   Translator's note – The Kamenka referred to here is NOT the Kamenka identified on Map 52. The Kamenka bridge referred to here is shown on Map 27. It is also shown on the Map 52, between Nikopol and Wodjanoje, with arrows showing movement across it, but not identified.

Defense in the Line East of the Basawluk (Busuluk)

The German command now had to secure the retreat of the eleven to twelve divisions that were east of the Dnjepr. The Soviets were advancing to the Dnjepr from the north, both east of the Basawluk river from Scholochow and also west of this river to the Tok train-stop and Apostolowo. The intervals in bringing the formations back narrowed considerably. Initially the railroad was held open for transport to the rear. That required securing the bridge over the Basawluk, north of Gruschewka, near the Perewisskije farmstead.[5]

See Map 52.   To accomplish this the 3rd *Gebirgs Division* attacked the Soviets east of the Basawluk river, attacking toward the north with *Feldersatz Bataillon* 112 [*3rd Gebirgs* Division] and *Gebirgs Pionier Bataillon* 83 [*3rd Gebirgs Division*], supported by alarm units of *Kodina* 68 [probably *Kdr. Der Geb. Div. Nachschubstruppen* 68, which was under the 3rd *Gebirgs Division*] under the command of the 258th *Infanterie Division*. Hard fighting developed here with the loss of nearly half of the personnel committed. The Soviets advanced south from Scholochowo with strong forces to Alexandrowka and farther on the way to Perewisskije. Here *Gebirgs Panzer Jäger Abteilung* 95 [3rd *Gebirgs Division*] entered the fighting and knocked out several AFVs. The 1st *Kompanie / Feldersatz Bataillon* 112 on the left wing suffered particularly heavy losses because the fuses of the *Panzerfäuste* failed to function after lengthy storage in the mud. On 6 February the Soviet 24th Tank Brigade penetrated Perewisskije and turned the right wing of *Gebirgs Pionier Bataillon* 83. With the help of several *Sturmgeschütze,* which came to the assistance of the German defense, it was possible to regain the northern edge of Perewisskije in counterattack. *Gebirgsjäger Regiment* 138 [3rd *Gebirgs Division*] also joined in this fighting, and it was possible to form a continuous defensive front east of the Basawluk.

While this was taking place demolition squads blew up the factories and mine shafts in Nikopol. Elements of eight divisions struggled westward through the mud-bound roads between Nikopol and Perewisskije. Demolition squads blew up several thousand motor vehicles and guns that were left behind along the way.

On the left wing of this defensive front the *Armee* intended to initially recapture Scholochowo, while firmly holding existing strong points and utilizing the Ssolonja (Ssolenaja) sector as far as Kamenka, in order to counteract the Soviet advance west of the Basawluk river, with the help of a blocking position that was to be built east of Kamenka, thus north and, as

---

5   Formations committed in the Nikopol Bridgehead:
    29th *Armee Korps*
        335th *Infanterie Division*
        9th *Infanterie Division*
        97th *Jäger Division*
    4th *Armee Korps*
        17th *Infanterie Division*
        111th *Infanterie Division*
        24th *Panzer Division*
        258th *Infanterie Division*
        302nd *Infanterie Division*
        3rd *Gebirgs Division*
        79th *Infanterie Division*

RETREAT OF *HEERESGRUPPE* A

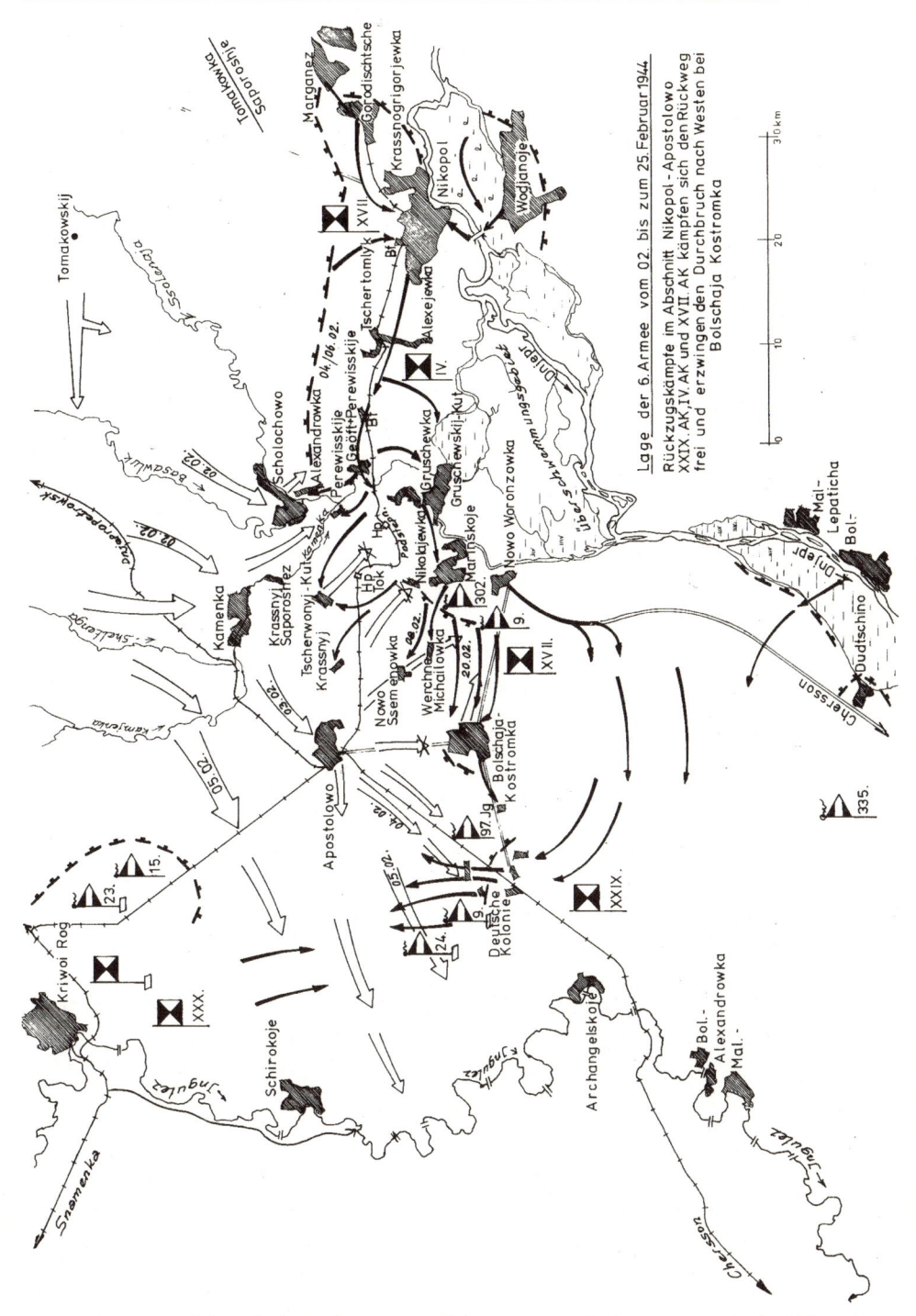

52. Situation of the 6th *Armee* from 2 to 25 February, 1944. Fighting retreat in the Nikopol – Apostolowo sector. 24th *Armee Korps*, 4th *Armee Korps* and 17th *Armee Korps* fight clear the route of retreat and force the breakthrough to the west at Bolschaja Kostromka.

a precautionary measure, southwest of Scholochowo and, if the opportunity permitted, regaining the *'Ursula'* position north and east of Kamenka. In the course of 4 February Soviet attacks on the front of this group were repulsed. However, the Soviet attack in regimental strength with armoured support from Scholochowo to the south proved embarrassing, especially considering the columns of vehicles streaming toward Perewisskije, for whom the Scholochowo crossing was the most favorable. These were forced to use a makeshift crossing west of the Perewisskije farmstead.

Schörner ordered that the motorized vehicles which had bogged down be ruthlessly burned in order to allow the foot-troops and the horse-drawn vehicles that were struggling painfully to pass through.

On this 4 February the railroad was still available and, to the extent that opportunities allowed entraining, provided important combat transport to the west. The *Gebirgsjäger* who were brought up by rail secured the railroad movements in that, at Tscherwonyj Kut, they forced back the Soviets advancing west of the Basawluk (Busuluk) southward from Kamenka.

Schörner, however, in a report to the supreme command, turned against continuation of the planned operations east of the Kamenka river. Such operations were no longer conceivable because, given continuation of the present weather conditions, they would involve the loss of 90% of all motorized elements. In the first line it therefore was a matter of bringing the foot-troops and horse-drawn weapons, along with the few remaining tracked elements, over to the west bank of the Kamenka river. Those elements that were already on the west bank of the Basawluk and Kamenka rivers and such as were available of the 29th *Armee Korps* were to secure the defense to the north and attempt to repulse the enemy forces advancing southward from Kamenka. In addition they were to restore contact with and onward through Apostolowo and, thereby, to secure the logistical elements east of the Kamenka river and the transport of wounded. Hitler immediately issued counter-orders to partially revoke the evacuation orders. Above all else, he demanded that the German Lepaticha bridgehead be held under any and all circumstances. In the event, the 29th *Armee Korps* still held two small bridgeheads on the far side of the Dnjepr at Lepaticha on the southern wing of this Basawluk – Dnjepr defensive front. The 29th *Armee Korps*, however, evacuated these during the night of 8/9 February and fell back across the river.

See Maps 52 and 53 for geography.

The road from Magarnez via Nikopol to Perewisskije-Balka was still full of immobile vehicles. Not even the urgently needed anti-tank weapons could get through. Communications equipment, especially radio stations, became stuck in the mud. The 17th *Armee Korps* moved to the *'Ria'* position and finally, in the course of this movement, evacuated Nikopol. The remaining formations crossed the Basawluk (Busuluk) to the west. There could be no clear picture at that time of the personnel and, above all, the matériel losses of these divisions. However, it could be expected that most of the motor vehicles and heavy weapons would be lost. In the event some divisions lost their entire outfit of anti-tank guns, artillery and infantry guns.[6]

The *Armee* still intended to hold a line around Gruschewskyj Kut and Marinskoje with firing direction facing east to receive the remaining columns advanced to the south. First, however, formations had to be brought up for that purpose. Only elements of *Grenadier Regiment* 570 [*GR* 570, 571 and 572 were under 302nd *ID*] and two artillery batteries were initially available for action. *Grenadier Regiment* 571 was still in Nikopol, *Grenadier Regiment* 572 and the main body of the division artillery was *en marche*. The 17th *Infanterie Division* supported the 302nd *Infanterie Division* for the ongoing action with *Grenadier Regiment* 95 [17th *ID*] and its artillery.

See Map 52.

The command had to particularly consider that the Soviets had built a bridgehead over the Dnjepr on both sides of Lepaticha. That raised the danger that the Soviets could advance from south to north to meet the Soviet formations attacking southward from Scholochowo east of the Basawluk (Busuluk) or the formations advancing on the west side of this river.

Northern Front of the *Kessel*

While the *Armee* concerned itself with extricating the eight divisions from danger of encirclement in the Dnjepr bend to the west across the line of the Basawluk (Busuluk) river, the necessity arose to secure this retreat against further Soviet advances farther west of Kamenka via Apostolowo toward Bolchaya – Kostromka. With the capture of these localities the Soviets would again be within a few kilometers of closing the ring.

See Map 52.

An operational reserve of the 9th *Panzer Division* initially delayed the Soviet advance in the sector of the 30th *Armee Korps*, until the Soviets went around both sides of Kamenka in the Kamenka position. The 9th *Panzer Division* operational reserve then fell back to Apostolowo, and, finally, had to fall back farther to the south. The 57th *Armee Korps*, adjoining the 30th *Armee Korps* on the left, held firmly against the attacks on its front, but had to pull back its right wing to prevent it from being rolled over and to protect the vital Kriwoi Rog transportation center. It was not, however, able to maintain contact with the 9th *Panzer Division*.

On 5 February the 9th *Panzer Division* had to evacuate Apostolowo. Its remnants fought their way back along the railroad line to Alexandrowka (in a southwesterly direction). However, the Soviets, not only advanced to Bolschaja – Kostromka via Apolstolowo but also moved in a parallel advance to the Tok train stop and past it, even to Nowo Ssemenowka, Werchne Machailowka and Nikolajewka.

---

6 Translator's note – In addition to the division's *Artillerie Regiment* with its three *Abteilungen* (battalions) of artillery, each German infantry regiment included, as its 13th *Kompanie*, an *Infanteriegeschützkompanie* with thee light infantry gun platoons (*leichte Infanteriegeschützzüge*) with two 7.5 cm light infantry guns and one heavy infantry gun platoon (*schweren Infanteriegeschützzug*) with two heavy 15 cm infantry guns. These infantry guns were lighter than those of the regular artillery and they could not use as heavy propelling charges as the regular artillery of the same caliber. They were accurate and effective and were to provide immediate support at the battalion level. Toward the end of the war they were in part replaced by medium and heavy mortars.

With the support of ground-attack aircraft, employing five regiments against the Tok train stop, alone, the Soviets had severed the railroad connection from Nikopol to the rear to Kriwoi Rog or Schirokoje. The fliers disrupted the approach of German artillery and trains elements on the muddy roads, but concentrated their attacks on the extraordinarily important railroad line that, in light of the road conditions, was so vital for bringing out German formations to the rear. One locomotive after another was hit and eliminated. Nevertheless, the railroad men were able to get the I. and III./ *Gebirgs Artillerie Regiment* 112 [3rd *Gebirgs Division*] back to the Tok train stop at night. With the help of the last locomotive the railroad also took the over-crowded hospital train that was waiting in Nikopol back to Podstepnoje. There, however, Soviet ground-attack planes attacked the wagons whose roofs were marked with great red-crosses on a white field. None of the wagons escaped damage. Three went up in flames. *Gebirgsjäger Regiment* 144 [3rd *Gebirgs Division*] provided pack animals and carts to transport wounded. Over 900 severely wounded, however, had to make their own way on foot to the south – a sad trek! Nevertheless, 2,000 wounded of all degrees of injury accumulated in Podstepnoje, Gruschewka and Gruschwyski Kut. Therefore the 3rd *Gebirgs Division* seized, mostly with use of force, vehicles from the formations streaming to the rear to bring out the wounded.

See Map 52.

Fighting Clear the Retreat Route

Initially the Command intended to secure the route of retreat in the northern section by advancing toward Kamenka after capturing Scholochowo, thereby attacking the advancing Soviet formations in the flank, cutting their line of march. The command maintained the same intention regarding the expected renewed capture of Bolschaja – Kostromka. This, however, could not be realized, for the 302nd *Infanterie Division*, which was initially intended for that operation, had only a few of its elements then available. The 17th *Infanterie Division* was ordered to support the 302nd *Infanterie Division* in that operation. The 9th *Infanterie Division* and elements of the 258th *Infanterie Division* also moved out toward Bolschaja – Kostromka, along with the 97th *Jäger Division*, in order to, at least, reopen the roads to the west.

To further these intentions, possibly also in hopes of, at the same time, in accord with the previously mentioned intent of the advance from Scholochowo toward Kamenka, of attacking the Soviets in the flank, the German thrust would regain the Tok – Nowo Ssemenowka line with a further advance into the Krassnyj area. If this operation succeeded, that would open the possibility of again making usable the railroad line to the rear. However, the chosen objectives of the attacks, Wechne Michailowka and Nowo Ssemenowka, were already deep in enemy held territory. Nevertheless the divisions' attack broke through, with the initial capture of Nikolajewka and Nowo Ssemenowka. That, however, triggered Soviet countermeasures. On 9 February the Soviet 8th Army launched counterattacks. At Tok Soviet armour rolled against the positions of the II. /*Gebirgsjäger Regiment* 144 and the I./ *Gebirgsjäger Regiment* 144, which were still arriving by rail. The Soviet attack foundered there.

However, the I./ *Gebirgsjäger Regiment* 144 was reduced to only six survivors in the course of that fighting.

Under heavy enemy pressure, especially from the Soviet airforce, the 125th *Infanterie Division* had to drop out of the advance toward Nowo Ssemenowka and Saporoshez – Krassny on 12 February and fall back to its jump-off positions. The strong Soviet attack forced the German command to abandon the operation in the Krassnyj – Apostolowo area in order to concentrate on fighting clear the Nowo-Woronzowka – Bolschaja – Kostromka road. The operation achieved its objective, in that the 17th *Armee Korps*, thanks to that day's heavy fog (lasting until 11 February), crossed the Basawluk (Busuluk) from Perewisskije to the west.

Recapture of Bolschaja – Kostromka

A prerequisite for the continued retreat of these formations was that Bolschaja – Kostromka had to be in German hands. The 302nd *Infanterie Division* launched the requisite attack early on 8 February with *Grenadier Regiment* 95 [17th *ID*] and *Grenadier Regiment* 570 [302nd *ID*] from Nowo – Woronzowka – with support from the 9th *Infanterie Division* – and captured Bolschaja – Kostromka in difficult, costly street and house-to-house fighting, except for a penetration site at its eastern edge. That opened the further route of retreat for the eleven divisions. However, that required the complete capture of the place, including its eastern edge. The 125th *Infanterie Division* was assigned that mission.

That attack started on 10 February with attached elements of the 302nd *Infanterie Division* and *Artillerie Regiment* 302. Bolschaja – Kostromka thus returned entirely to German control. Those elements of the 4th *Armee Korps* and 17th *Armee Korps* that had made it east across the Basawluk and that were still capable of marching and fighting could then continue their march to the west. However, the 125th *Infanterie Division* lost so heavily in this action that it had to be disbanded. The remnants of its *Grenadier* regiments then constituted '*Divisionsgruppe* 125'. Further consolidation of formations ensued: *Grenadier Regiment* 572 and *Grenadier Regiment* 571 of the 302nd *Infanterie Division* were consolidated into a single regiment. The newly activated 387th *Infanterie Division*, which had, just a year earlier, been formed from elements of the 298th *Infanterie Division*, 385th *Infanterie Division* and 387th *Infanterie Division* henceforth went into the 258th *Infanterie Division*. Artillerymen who no longer had guns, men combed out of the trains and logistical elements and stragglers were put together into alarm units, with, as experience showed, limited combat effectiveness and reliability. There was a disturbing shortage of pioneers and bridging equipment, which had, for the most part, remained stuck in the mud. Motorized formations proved limited in mobility and *Panzer* regiments had no armour fit for action.

Fighting after Securing the Breakout Route

The employment of, especially, the 125th *Infanterie Division*, 294th *Infanterie Division* and 17th *Infanterie Division* to fight free the route of retreat severely weakened these and other formations. Accordingly, the *Armeeoberkommando* considered how it could again form a continuous front to maintain contact between the 8th *Armee* and the Black Sea with the remnants of the three *Korps*. *General* Schörner contributed to these considerations with an extremely clear report on the condition of the troops in order to counteract the self-deception of the supreme command. He reported that some divisions no longer had a single anti-tank gun and that, to a large degree, the means of command [communications and administrative personnel and equipment] were lacking. The stock of infantry weapons was totally inadequate.

In actual fact, the urgent provision of heavy infantry weapons (machine guns, infantry guns and anti-tank guns) and artillery guns, *Sturmgeschütze*, vehicles capable of moving through mud and communications equipment, as well as close-quarters anti-tank weapons of all kinds was indispensable. The ammunition shortage, especially of infantry ammunition, was reaching a disturbing level that could not be met by airdrops from *Ju* 52s. The evident shortage of weapons, and especially of ammunition, at the front as contrasted with the repeated assurances of 'adequate' weapons and ammunition in propaganda significantly impacted the morale of the soldiers.

Regardless, the division remnants of the 4th *Armee Korps* and 17th *Armee Korps* that had made it back reformed themselves and formed a large blocking position around Marinskoje. On 15 February they cleaned up a Soviet penetration into the main line of resistance. Combat operations then slowed down for several days as the result of heavy snow. That, however, did not prevent the 97th *Jäger Division* and the 24th *Panzer Division*, which had, in the meantime, returned to the 6th *Armee*, from attacking from the area west of Bolschaja-Kostromka 20 kilometers deep to the northwest to fight free the Ingulez positions, an encouraging success, with the capture of 221 guns, 66 anti-tank guns and 62 machine guns.

However, in several sectors the *Armee* pulled the front line farther back to the southwest to gain reserves and time to organize its forces. It was possible to transport most of the wounded to the rear and again provide supplies, rations and – mail! The Soviets allowed the opportunity for this in that they only hesitantly followed the German withdrawals. Apparently they had to reorganize their own formations to change from a southward to westward direction of movement. The German command gained the impression that the Soviets intended to shift the *Schwerpunkt* of their attack farther to the north to the Kriwoi Rog and Kirowograd area, which could again determine the fate of the Dnjepr salient. The 6th *Armee* necessarily had to pay attention to the situation in the Kriwoi Rog area, thus carrying on its retreat.

The untimely retraction of the Dnjepr salient under enemy pressure led to losses nearly comparable with those in the Tscherkassy *Kessel* battle. Reports of the troop leaders stated that the troops were physically and morally overburdened, physically, numerically and materially fought-out. In light of the extreme shortage of officers and non-commissioned officers the inner structure of the fatigued formations were no longer, for the time being, capable of withstanding severe pressure.

It was no longer possible to recapture the manganese ore mines that were vital for the German armaments industry. In the future, the ore would have to

RETREAT OF *HEERESGRUPPE* A

be imported from Turkey. The Rumanian sources of oil that were indispensable for the mobility of armour, aircraft and U-boats now were exposed to attack by the Soviet airforce. Nevertheless, combat performance suffered less from doubts regarding the necessity, the justification and the likelihood of success of the battle than from the unavoidable excessive bodily and spiritual demands placed on the troops.

New Defensive Front Facing East

At the end of February the 6th *Armee* constructed a wavy but continuous line of defense between Chersson and Dutschino, running downstream along the course of the Dnjepr, and also from Archangelskoje to Losowatka and, finally, in further windings, with contact at Kirowograd to the 8th *Armee*, in the form of an inverted question mark. In the meantime, reconnaissance of the enemy revealed that the Soviets had already assembled six army corps with about 20 divisions, along with mobile formations of the 4th Guards Mechanized Corps, 23rd Tank Corps and troops of the 4th Guards Cavalry Corps. Clearly a new Soviet breakthrough operation to the south was imminent.

See Map 53.

The front of the 6th *Armee*, on the other hand, suffered from the fact that it was again echeloned forward about 80 kilometers to the east. The eastward salient should have immediately been retracted in order to free up formations for defense against the Soviets in the Schirokoje sector, the more so since two river crossing that could serve as obstacles, the Ingulez and the Ingul, lay to its rear, to the west. A Soviet advance from Schirokoje toward Nowyj Bug could again cost the *Armee* its basis of supply, particularly since, at that time, logistical support for the *Armee* came by rail from Kriwoi Rog via Schirokoje.

See Map 54 and, for geography, Map 55.

West of Apostolowo an open area extended as far as the Schirokoje – Kriwoi Rog railroad line. Therefore the 9th *Panzer Division* and 97th *Jäger Division* received orders to shift swiftly into this area to cut off the retreat route for the Soviet army corps that was already operating, in part, south of this line. This attack was in conjunction with the 30th *Armee Korps* advance to the southeast, from the opposite direction. The previously planned advance to the northwest in the area between Nowo Woronzowka and Bolschaja-Kostromka toward Krassny had the same objective.

Soviet Breakthrough at Kriwoi Rog

This concentration of strong Soviet formations in the area north of Schirokoje originated in the Soviet breakthrough at Kriwoi Rog. On 7 March the Soviets captured Kriwoi Rog and thrust on to the west at Schirokoje toward Nowyj Bug (60 kilometers west of Kriwoi Rog), reaching Nowyj Bug on 8 March. They then advanced southwest along the railroad toward Nikolajew. That day they reached Nowo Poltawa and, on 9 March, Baschtanka. A cavalry corps advanced west of the railroad, a motorized-mechanized corps on the left. On 10 March the Soviets were within 30 kilometers of Nikolajew, thereby threatening anew to encircle the 6th *Armee* and the Rumanian 3rd Army by advancing to the coast of the Black Sea. The advanced command post of the 6th *Armee* lost a portion of its communications equipment to the Soviet advance on Nowyj

See Maps 53 and 55.

210   **CRUCIBLE OF COMBAT**

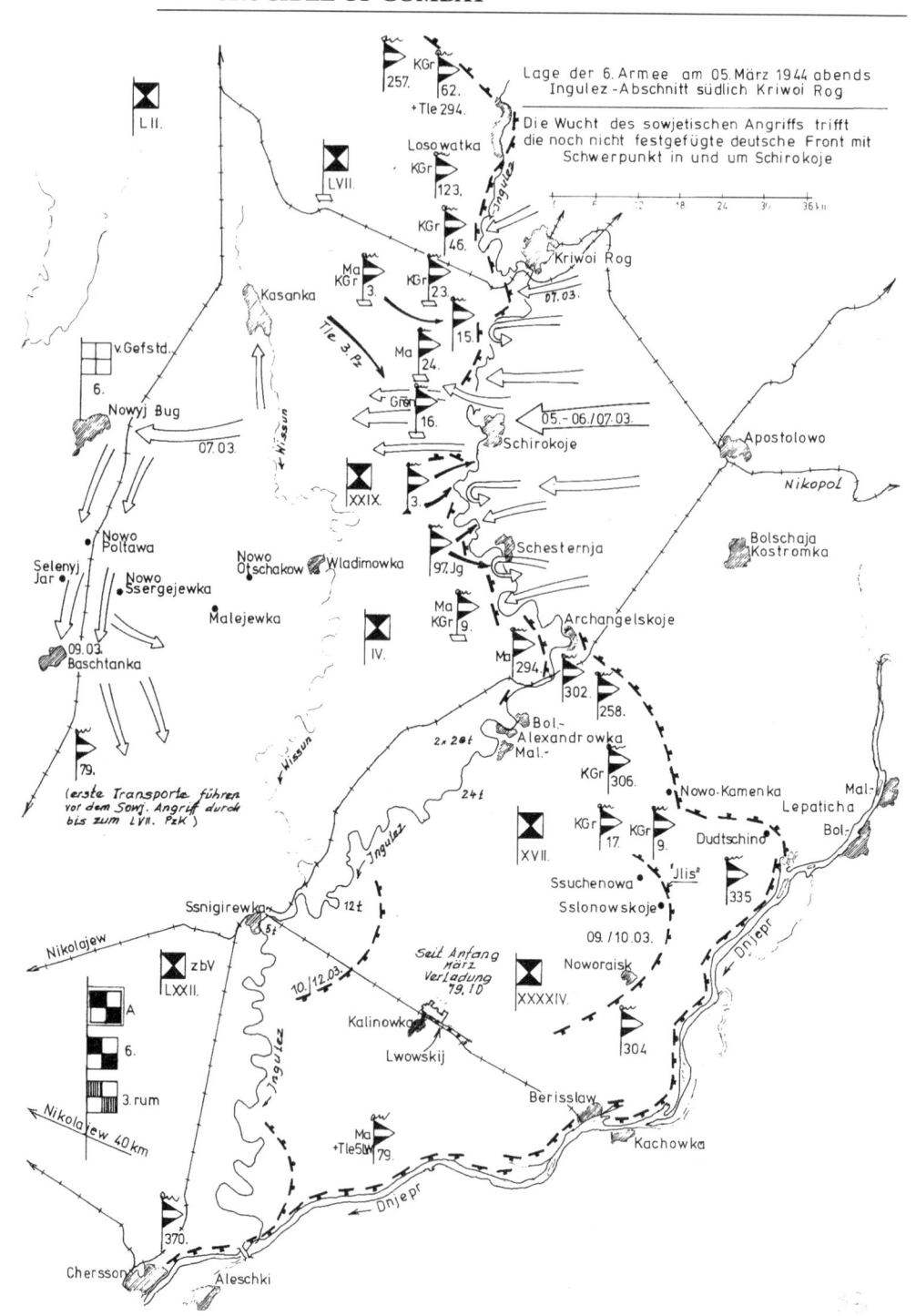

53. Situation of the 6th *Armee* on 5 March, 1944, evening. Ingulez-sector south of Kriwoi Rog. The weight of the Soviet attack hits the German front before it solidifies, with *Schwerpunkt* in and around Schirokoje.

RETREAT OF *HEERESGRUPPE A*

Bug because the second transport train with vehicles of the *Armee-Nachrichten Regiment* 549 could not continue its journey and had to be burned.

When, at the beginning of March, the Soviets launched their offensive in other sectors of the German defensive front, the southern wing of the front, namely *Heeresgruppe* A with the 6th *Armee* and the Rumanian 3rd Army was already in movement. In the Schirokoje area the 6th *Armee* immediately had a defensive position constructed, south of the locality, starting with the 97th *Jäger Division*, continuing from Gordowatka directly south of Schirokoje via the left-adjoining 3rd *Gebirgs Division* as far as the 16th *Panzergrenadier Division* – supported by elements of the 24th *Panzer Division*. Because of its meanders, the Ingulez river was not fully usable as a main line of resistance. A cordon position had to be built in the right section. The Soviets immediately utilized the six kilometer gap in the front that existed on 6 March at the 16th *Panzergrendier Division*. It was possible to stop the Soviets at Kamenka Gorka, Ukrainka and Selenyj Gai. However, the Soviets then reached Michailowka, scattering the train elements and falling upon the main dressing station. 181 wounded remained missing following this.

See Map 53 and, for geography, Map 55.

The *Armee* then gave up the northern front. The 79th *Infanterie Division*, 97th *Jäger Division*, 302nd *Infanterie Division* and 17th *Infanterie Division* ('*Kampfgruppe Wittmann*') prepared for a breakout attack to the west. The success of the costly defense against Soviet advances in the Schirokoje area may account for the fact that, after breaking through in the Schirokoje area, the Soviets divided their break-through forces. One portion continued to advance westward to the Bug (to Kasanka, 40 kilometers west of Kriwoi Rog), another portion to the south. That raised the danger that the northern wing of the 6th *Armee* might be rolled up. However, this split weakened the Soviet offensive forces. That, in turn, may have made it possible for the German defensive forces of '*Gruppe Wittmann*' to generally succeed in successfully withstanding the advance of the strongly superior Soviet forces in the Schirokoje area.

See Map 53.

Clearing the Way Again to the Ingul

Five German divisions were again encircled by the Soviets between the Ingulez and Ingul rivers. Three Soviet armies were exerting pressure between Chersson and Waldimirowka in the east. The pressure on the northern front of the 29th *Armee Korps* mounted. The Soviet 8th Guards Army stood in the west. Its spearheads were already fighting on the heights of Nikolajew on both sides of the Nowyj Bug – Nikolajew railroad line. Numerous Soviet divisions were there on the march to the south. It was now necessary to break through these Soviet forces on both sides of the Nikolajew railroad line to gain a route for retreat and, above all, a crossing over the Ingul.

See Map 55.

The attack of the 29th *Armee Korps* in the southern sector brought good initial success with 15 kilometers ground gain and capture of Nowo Otschakoff, west of Waldimirowka, Malejewko and, finally, Nowo Ssergejewka, near the Nowyj Bug – Nikolajew railroad line.

The 97th *Jäger Division* cut the Soviet route of advance when it crossed the railroad line and, on its far side, captured Selenyj Jar. Four divisions were then fighting on the Malejewka – Nowo Ssergejeska – Selenyj Jar line against the Soviet pressure from north to south in order to make possible the breakout to the west, namely the 3rd *Gebirgs Division*, 17th *Infanterie Division*, 302nd *Infanterie Division* and 97th *Jäger Division*. The *Korps* expected the 258th *Infanterie Division* as reinforcement but it arrived too late.

Screening this frontal position to the north, elements of the 97th *Jäger Division* likewise reached the railroad line 15 kilometers south of Selenyj Jar, but fought there in isolation.

After knocking out 32 out of 35 attacking Soviet AFVs, the 97th *Jäger Division* had to fall back from Selenyj Jar to the railroad line. The strong defense caused the 4th *Armee Korps* to decide to switch to a night attack with all the available divisions of *'Gruppe Wittmann'*. At the spearhead were the 3rd *Gebirgs Division*, elements of the 79th *Infanterie Division* and the 97th *Jäger Division*. Closely concentrated, the divisions broke through the Soviet infantry forces to the west, sometimes with a 'Hurrah', bringing along their wounded, heavy weapons and combat trains elements.[7] However, the *coup de main* of the *Jäger* at the Ingul bridge at Priwolnoje failed. Other formations reached the Ingul on 14 March on a broad front and crossed the Ingul farther to the south. They also captured the Gromkley bridge at Nowoja Trojizkoje on the Gromoklej River, clearing its junction with the Ingul. However, the 29th *Armee Korps* then swung to the southwest because, in light of the reduced combat strength and ammunition shortage a breakthrough farther west or northwest to Wossnessensk seemed to be ruled out. The *Armee Korps* now turned toward Gurjewka (northwest of Nikolajew).

Farther north, the 23rd *Panzer Division* and 24th *Panzer Division* also fought their way forward through muddy and swampy terrain onward to the west. The 23rd *Panzer Division* kept open a bridgehead over the Gromoklej river at Olgopol. This division and the 24th *Panzer Division* crossed the river in succession and then went into position south of the *Rollbahn* to stop approaching enemy forces before the crossing. The additional 20 kilometers to the crossing over the Jelanez proved especially torturous for these formations, through mud with clammy clothes and wet boots under enemy pressure. The battle with the enemy was easier to endure than the conflict with rain, mud and time.

See Maps 55 and 56.

The 258th *Infanterie Division* secured the blocking position east of the Jelanez river. On 17 March, however, the Soviets had already reached the Bug river at the mouth of the southwestwardly flowing Gniloy – Jelanez, the last bridgehead before Wossnessensk. That caused the formations to evacuate the east bank of the Gniloy-Jelanez during the night of 17/18 March to free up forces for the construction of a bridgehead and the defense of the Bug line, in hopes that the enemy would, initially, be held at Bug river. The 258th *Infanterie Division* and 384th *Infanterie Division* immediately shifted into the bridgehead while the 23rd *Panzer Division* and 24th *Panzer Division* covered the construction of the defense with the help of delaying tactics.

---

7   Translator's note – Both sides gave special recognition to attacks delivered with the attacking troops shouting 'Hurrah', as indicating a particularly ardent level of aggressiveness and having a particularly destructive effect on the opponent's morale.

After heavy night attacks to secure commanding hills and the route of retreat, under constant attacks by Soviet forces from the north and south, the remaining formations of this *Korps* reached the Wossnessensk bridgehead at the Bug where they initially completed construction of this position. Here there were a few days of quiet. The 24th *Panzer Division* immediately set its trains elements in march to Odessa. The other elements of this division reached Kischinew in Rumania by air, after a stop *en route* in Birsula at the headquarters of the 8th *Armee*.

Nevertheless, the 24th *Panzer Division* lost no less than 1,950 motor vehicles at Scholochowo, and another 710 vehicles in its further fighting retreat, amounting to one quarter of its former outfit. It had, thereby, also lost three 8.8 cm antiaircraft guns and 19 2cm antiaircraft guns, 14 7.5 cm anti-tank guns, 11 light and 22 heavy mortars, 445 machine guns, 43 field kitchens, as well as 13 light and heavy guns. The division lost 841 men (37 officers) in these actions – a total loss for the last quarter of the year totaling 3,590 men (125 officers). [See Map 52.]

The southern advance of '*Gruppe Wittmann*' also suffered in the ensuing days from the weather. It succeeded in breaking open a six kilometer gap in the Soviet bridgehead at Priwolnoje. The 258th *Infanterie Division*, in particular, slipped through this gap to cover to the north and northeast the crossing of other formations over the Ingul and Gromokley. The steady rain on 15 March softened the roads, causing traffic jams of vehicles, and that under constant fire of Soviet artillery. Snow finally followed the rain, and significant storms, which made the roads bottomless and complicated movement. [See Map 55.]

'*Gruppe Wittmann*' changed its direction of march from the south back to the north in order to build a defensive front at the Bug facing Nowaja Odessa, with the 294th *Infanterie Division*, 17th *Infanterie Division*, 258th *Infanterie Division*, 3rd *Gebirgs Division* and *Kampfgruppe* 97th *Jäger Division* in the main line of resistance. They repulsed various Soviet attempts to cross the Bug there and thereby forced the Soviets to a new concentration at the Bug-Front. [See Maps 55 and 56.]

A *Schwerpunkt* became evident on both sides of Nowaja-Odessa, presumably because a stretch of broad sandy shore on the west bank favored a crossing there. On 19 March five Soviet divisions crossing in succession built a bridgehead on the west bank. The 17th *Infanterie Division*, 294th *Infanterie Division* and 258th *Infanterie Division* attacked and, in three days of fierce fighting, forced the main body of the Soviet 33rd Guards Corps back over the river.

The 4th *Armee Korps*, however, did not limit itself to winning bridgeheads over the Bug at Wossnessensk and Nowaja Odessa, but attempted to do the same farther south at Trichaty. Granted, the bridges over the Bug had been destroyed. However, at Konstantinowka the formations discovered a dam that could be improved. *Gebirgs Pionier Bataillon* 97 [this may refer to *Pionier Bataillon* 97, which was under 97th *Jäger Division*] used timbers from the houses in Peski and Konstantinowkato make it usable as a river crossing. The march columns, however, reached clear to Swoboda – Selenyj Gai at the Gromokleij and from Nowo Troizkoje to Peski. The columns flowed toward the new crossing in forced marches. The 97th *Jäger Division* moved toward Peski. There was significant artillery fire on Konstantinoka, which caused the

Korps, regardless of heavy rain, followed by night-time snow, to build a new defensive front east of the Bug. During the night of 16/17 March Soviet armour and cavalry broke into the German lines at Peski. The III./ *Gebirgs Artillerie Regiment* 112 [3rd *Gebirgs Division*] saved only one gun by bringing it over the Ingul dam. Rear-guard action developed at Ostrowka and Mantschurija. On 17 March the elements of the 3rd *Gebirgs Division* that were in action crossed the railroad bridge at Trichaty. The pioneer military bridge over the Bug was blown up several days later.

The crossings farther south, particularly through Nikolajew, were available to the 3rd *rumanische Armee* for its retreat.

Employment of the 24th *Panzer Division*

See Map 55.

In the description of the fighting of the 6th *Armee*, the 24th *Panzer Division*, too, finally played a role again, which initially was supposed to establish contact with the 44th *Armee Korps* of *Heeresgruppe* A. Adjoining the 15th *Infanterie Division* on the left, it was, initially to receive the completely dispersed elements of the 16th *Panzergrenadier Division* (90 men under *Rittmeister Graf* von Hagen). The staff of the 16th *Panzergrenadier Division* attached itself to the 24th *Panzer Division*.

See Map 52.

The *Armee* then attached the 24th *Panzer Division* to the 57th *Panzer Korps*, which intended, with an attack from the south, to break through the enemy advancing against Andotjewka. In constant fighting against a closely pursuing enemy, the main body of the division fell back to the eastern edge of Nikolajewka (north of Marinskoje), while the Soviets were already feeling their way against Nikolajewka from the south, north and west. The foreign troops that were in Nikolajewka on the German side, were in disarray. Mobile equipment of the 24th *Panzer Division*, especially numerous vehicles, were demolished after their fuel had been drained for use in the remaining *SPW* [half-tracked personnel carriers] and *Selbstfahrlafetten* [self-propelled guns]. The staff mounted itself on *Panje* ponies [the tough little Russian peasant horses]. The night-time breakout from Nikolajewka proved extraordinarily difficult and costly. Many vehicles remained stuck in a swampy field. That was how the last radio station was lost.

Nevertheless, it was possible to fight open a gap and keep it open for the forces to march through. In this retreat the I./ *Panzergrenadier Regiment* 26 [24th *PzD*], alone, lost 20 *SPW*, ten lorries and three automobiles. Partly on vehicles, for the most part on foot, the march to Bredechina – Balka took more than two nights.

The further retreat, with delaying actions, required the commitment of the last fighting elements of the 16th *Panzergrenadier Division* and 24th *Panzer Division*. One day *Ju 52s* dropped fuel, some of which was lost, but the remainder restored mobility to the *SPWs*. During this time (11 March) the Soviets had already reached Nowyj Bug with the main body of their infantry formations (including the 15th, 20th and 28th Guards Rifle Divisions of the 37th Army), while the spearheads of their mechanized corps and cavalry formations advanced farther to the southwest in order to reach the lower course of the Bug river and cut off the 6th *Armee*. Strong enemy forces had turned to the south after reaching Nowyj Bug and turned the northern flank of the 6th *Armee* at Beresnogowadka and Ssnigirewka.

On 12 March strong enemy forces crossed the Ungul sector, took Olgopol and threatened to block the crossings over the Gromoklej sector. Thus it became necessary to attack to the south between these two rivers in order to block the Soviet *Rollbahn* from Nowyj Bug to Wosnessensk and thereby relieve the 6th *Armee*.

See Map 55 and, for geography, Map 56.

A *Kampfgruppe* consisting of elements of the 384th *Infanterie Division*, 23rd *Panzer Division*, 24th *Panzer Division* and 257th *Infanterie Division* assembled in the area north of Beresowja, crossed the Ingul during the night over the bridges at Korneitschenko and, on the following day, reached the Neu-Heim, Petropawlowka, Beresnogowadka assembly position area. After a brief artillery preparation, the *Kampfgruppe* took two important hills and thereby forced the Soviets to fall back to the Ingul lowlands.

The Soviets received constant supplementary forces by air and gliders, which required corresponding German precautionary measures. It now became necessary to secure the right flank of the 8th *Armee* to protect the formations from the looming envelopment by the Soviets. Withdrawn from that action, the fighting elements of the 24th *Panzer Division* made it by air behind the Dnjestr to build a new front there. With that, the 6th *Armee* lost the mobile reserve that it had, hitherto, employed with such great success. The time required for the Soviets to concentrate their forces granted the German formations several days of quiet. During these days personnel replacements and weapons arrived. Above all else, the divisions could organize and regroup their formations. The *Armee* initially organized to hold the Bug position for a lengthy period.

This readiness for defense, however, availed them little, for at the end of March the Soviets crossed the Dnjepr 200 kilometers to the northwest at Jampol and Soroca. On 25 March they were already at Balti on the Pruth. The *Armee* adjoining on the left (8th *Armee*) fell back farther to the west and southwest, thereby opening the left flank of the 6th *Armee*, so that it had to give up the Bug sector on both sides of Perwomaisk that it held. A new battle of encirclement loomed with the advance of the Soviets to the west. At the end of March the Soviets were already in the flank of the 6th *Armee* to a depth of 150 kilometers, so that the withdrawal of the entire *Heeresgruppe* A into a bridgehead position at the Dnjestr seemed inevitable.

See Maps 64 and 65.

Generalfeldmarschall von Manstein had already demanded this retreat to the Dnjestr without enemy pressure from Hitler at the Obersalzberg in mid-March. At that time the *Armee* was still in a frontal salient on the lower course of the Bug river that was echeloned far to the east. Therefore Hitler refused permission for the retreat.

On 26 March there was a change in the command relationships that shifted the 8th *Armee* and 6th *Armee* to the command of *Heeresgruppe* A. *Heeresgruppe Süd* had more important missions to attend to in the central and northern sector. Therefore it shifted its headquarters to Lemberg. The headquarters of *Heeresgruppe* A moved from Nikolajew to Tiraspol on the Dnjestr with a further move planned to Galatz.

See Map 57.

The Right Wing of the 6th *Armee*

See Maps 52, 53 and 55.

The description of the retreat of the 6th *Armee* and of the fighting involved would be incomplete without also looking at the events on its right wing. In light of the constant pressure from the north, on its left flank, the 6th *Armee* had to guard against losing its route of retreat to the west as a result of overhauling pursuit by the Soviets, not only with the initial advance southward from Scholochowo and west of the Basawluk to the south via Augustowo, but, above all, at the start of March with the breakthrough south of Kriwoi Rog to Schirokoje and thence to the west, and with several advances to the south. They finally advanced via Nowyj Bug toward Nikolajew.

See Maps 53 and 54.

As a result of the fighting retreat between Nikopol, Ingulez and Ingul, contact was broken within the front of the 6th *Armee* to its right wing at Dudtschino/Dnjepr. The formations that were still in the Dnjepr position between Dudtschino and Chersson under the command of the 44th *Armee Korps* – 335th *Infanterie Division*, 304th *Infanterie Division*, 370th *Infanterie Division* and elements of the 5th *Luftwaffe Feld Division* first received the warning order for the retreat during the night of 7/8 March, and that at a time when the Soviets were already at Schirokoje. According to the warning order these formations were to evacuate the Dnjepr line and occupy the *'Iltis'* position, farther to the west, resting on Ssolonowksoje and Ssuchanowa.

The *Armee* had squandered far too much time to secure a frictionless retreat of these formations. Only during the night of 9/10 March did the formations give up their previous positions. This was not, however, a matter of formations strong in personnel and adequately equipped with weapons. They had lost all of their anti-tank guns and numerous motor vehicles as well as most of their horse-drawn vehicles in the evacuation of the Nikopol bridgehead. Even the *Kfz* 15s of the division commanders were left, stuck in the swamp of the mouth of the Dnjepr. The troops had made themselves mobile using *Panje* horses and *Panje* wagons. Artillerymen without guns formed an alarm unit under the command of *Panzerjäger Abteilung* 335. At the Dnjepr there was no longer a continuous main line of resistance, merely a main defensive area with inadequately set up squad billets at intervals of 100 to 150 meters.

Loss of the Line of Defense at the Lower Dnjepr[8]

See Map 54.

The retreat led over field-roads totally softened by steady rain, at times right across the fields, toward the west. At the southwest exit from Dudtschino the rising terrain caused considerable difficulties, because the strength of the horses was insufficient to bring forward the loads they were given without time and strength-robbing additional multiple-teaming. There were no longer communications links to the division command post because the radio vehicles (*Kfz* 17) remained stuck in the mud of the Dnjepr lowlands. The radiomen brought their radio gear along on *Panje* wagons, but had to unload the equipment and set it up before they could operate it. Therefore, radio communications while on the move ceased. That situation did not last

---

8   Translator's note – As noted on Map 54, the following account of the retreat of the 335th *Infanterie Division* to the Bug serves to represent that of all the formations of the 6th *Armee*.

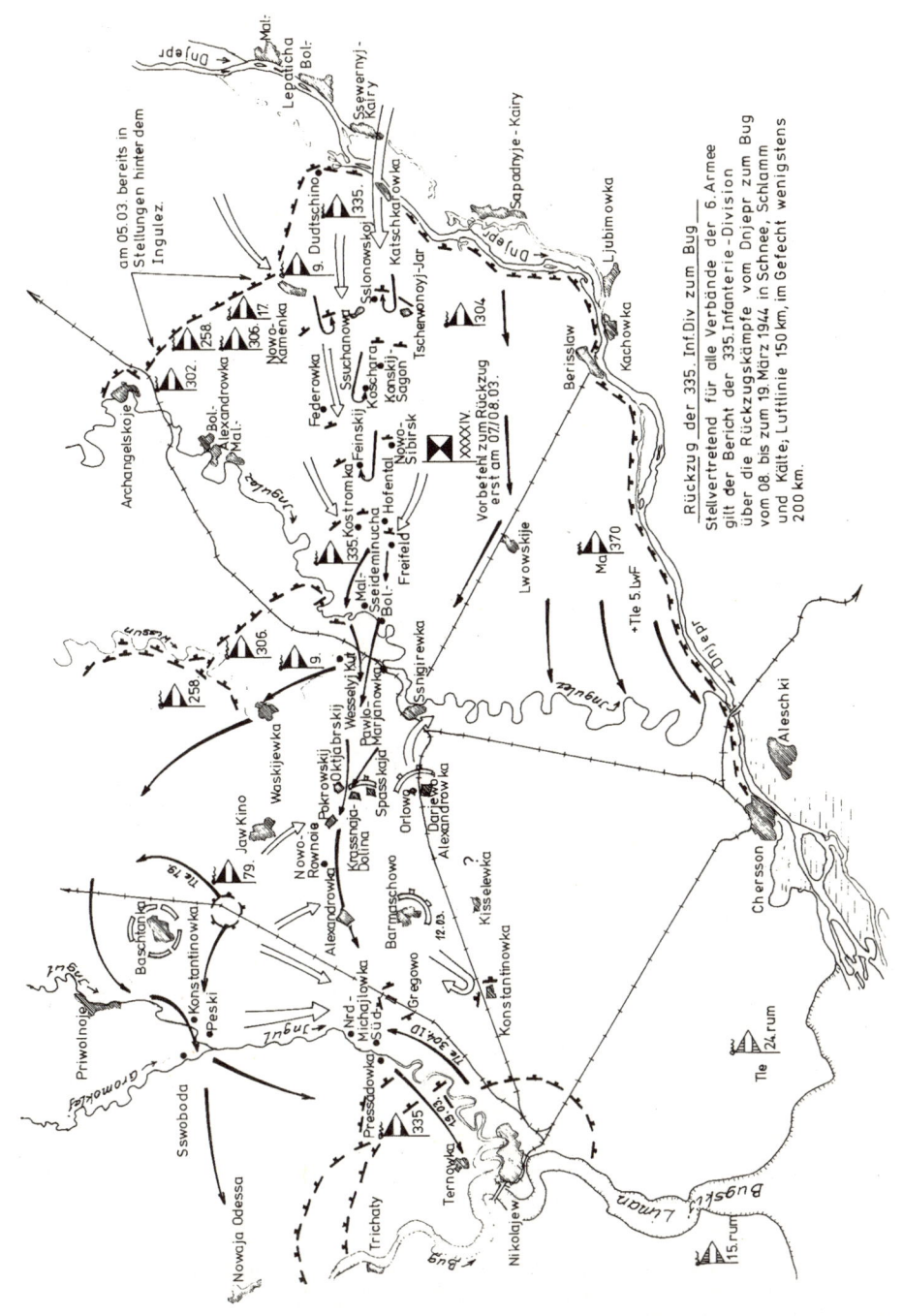

54. Retreat of the 335th *Infanterie Division* to the Bug. The report of the 335th *Infanterie Division* can represent the experiences of all the formations of the 6th *Armee* in the fighting retreat from the Dnjepr to the Bug from 8 to 19 March, 1944, in snow, mud and cold. The direct 'as the crow flies' distance was 150 kilometers, the distance as fought, however, at least 200 kilometers.

long, for, shortly thereafter, this radio equipment and the radio ciphers fell into Soviet hands. That further complicated command of the formations.

Next the formations moved from from Sslonowskoje – Tscherwonje Jar into the positions around Konskij, Sagon, Koschara and Fedorowka (11 March) under heavy pressure from pursuing enemy troops that had, apparently, crossed the Dnjepr at Katschjarowka. The retreat continued under direct enemy pressure on the rear guard to the 'Biber' position east of Feinshij, Nowo Ssibirsk. In each position the battalions had to immediately organize for defense to hold off the pursuing troops of the Soviet 5th Shock Army, as in the position east of Kostromka, Hofental – Freifeld.

In night-time forced marches the totally exhausted troops dragged themselves on through the mud-bound roads to the *'Wiesel'* blocking position or the *'Falke'* position east of the Ingulez (Sseideminucha.) There was no longer contact with the adjoining divisions on the right or left (304th *Infanterie Division* and 9th *Infanterie Division*, respectively). The situation of the retreating formations was most disturbing in that the Soviets advancing from the north had already severed the rearward connections of the 29th *Armee Korps,* 4th *Armee Korps* and 44th *Armee Korps*. Therefore the formations had to move westward by attacking but, at the same time, with their rear guards, despite rain and snow, to the rear of Kostromka, repulsing Soviets attacking, sometimes with 'Hurrah', in order, then, to reach the objective-position east of Sseideminucha over the mud-bound roads. In order to make possible the continued march to the west after crossing the Ingulez the 335th *Infanterie Division* had to secure the Wesselyj – Kut and Pawlo Marjanowko river crossings. From here on reconnaissance already reported north-south movements of Soviet armour toward Ssnigirewka.

See Map 54.

In Ssnigirewka six 7.5 cm anti-tank guns with prime movers were waiting to be picked up by the *Panzerjäger* of the 335th *Infanterie Division.* These factory-new weapons and machines fell into Soviet hands. From that time on the division had to organize for the retreat, preparing both for attack from the south and, at the same time, gain ground to the west to the 17 kilometer distant Oktjabrski and Krassnaja-Dolina or Spasskaja, respectively. There was no route, however, leading westward from Wesselyj-Kut, so the troops had to continue their march cross-country, initially favoured by the end of the rain and the start of sunshine on 13 March, with light frost.

The situation became ever more critical after enemy resistance appeared half way to Oktjabrski, along with Soviet aircraft that apparently supplied their spearheads with ammunition, as well as the sound of combat coming from the north. Nevertheless, with the help of anti-tank gun and artillery support it was possible to drive Soviet AFVs out of Oktjabrski and, in the course of the day, to gain possession of the entire locality. The capture of the two villages to the south, Krassnaja-Dolina and Spasskaja, failed in the face of strong enemy resistance. Nevertheless, in Oktjabrski the division received a march-battalion of about 350 men that was on its way to a *Gebirgsdivision*, a welcome reinforcement of the manpower of the *Grenadiere*. The retreat continued over a usable roadway to Pokrowsky and on toward Rownoie. From there on it went over miserable field roads 18 kilometers to Nowo-Alexandrowka.

RETREAT OF *HEERESGRUPPE* A 219

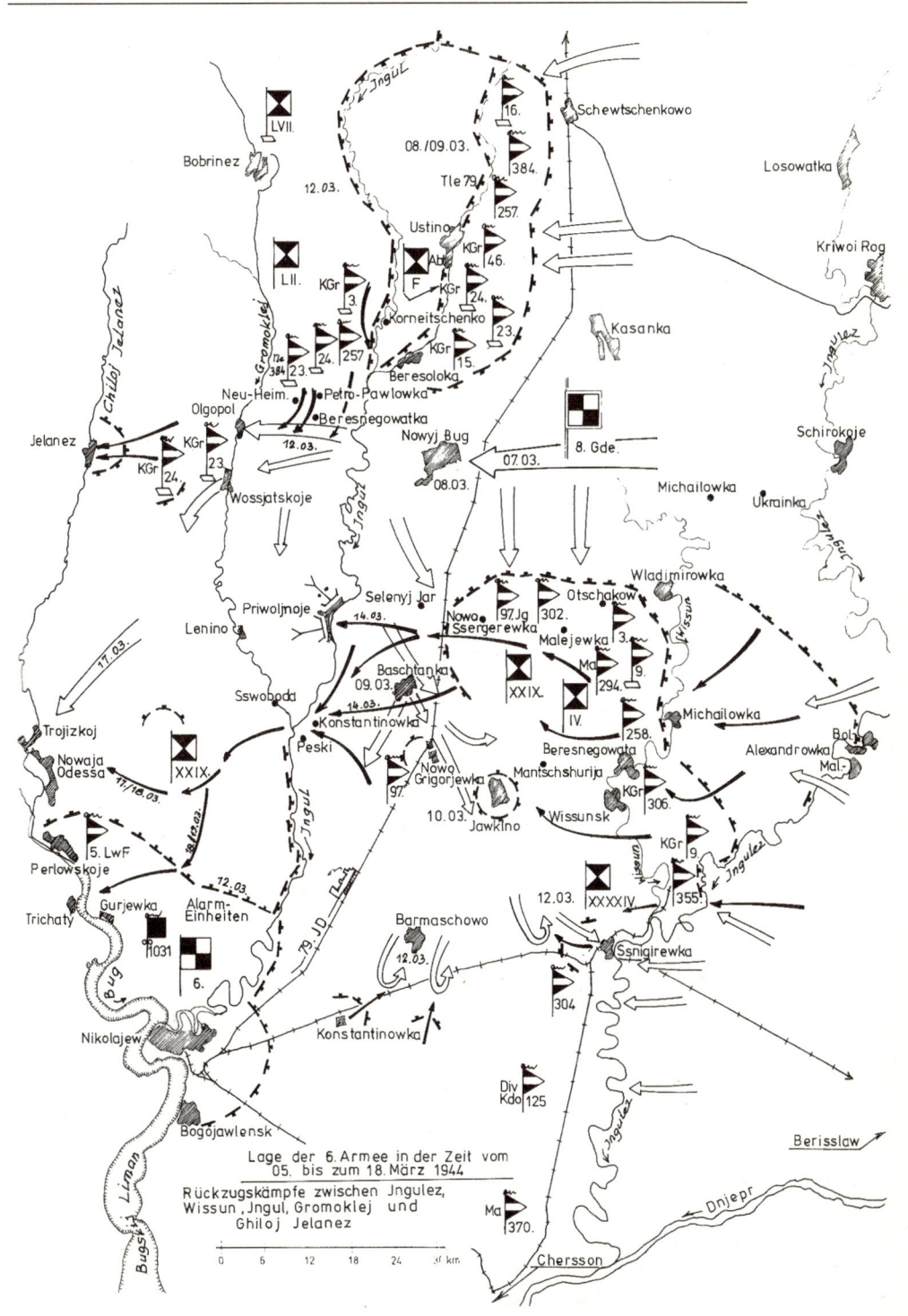

55. Situation of the 6th *Armee* during the period from 5 to 18 March, 1944. Fighting retreat between the Ingulez, Wissun, Ingul, Gromoklej and Ghiloi Jelanez.

The division, however, not only had to fend off attacks on the rear guard in the *'Wissun'* sector, some delivered with 'Hurrahs', but also repulse the various advances from Krassnaja – Dolina toward Oktjabrski (here by the I,/ *Artillerie Regiment* 335) . Furthermore, Orlowo and Barmaschowo were already in enemy hands. The division now had to see to securing the bridge over the Ingul at Peressadowka for its continued movement as quickly as possible, while its rear elements were still fighting against pursuing Soviets in the *'Wissun'* position.

The return of steady rain again made the march particularly difficult. The men marching to the rear sank ankle-deep in the mud, many vehicles to their axles. There was no time to pull them out, so various vehicles, including several guns, had to be destroyed and left behind.

From Peressadowka the division initially sent on *Panje* – wagon columns with wounded and all trains vehicles that were not absolutely necessary. There was no more contact to right or left.

See Map 54.

During the march to the Ingul the marching men watched Soviet armour, motor vehicles and mounted troops moving west at a good clip, apparently to overhaul the main body of the 335th *Infanterie Division*. It therefore became necessary to set up security both north and south of the railroad line at the Gregorowo railroad station using artillery. East of the Ingul the march column was favoured by terrain that dropped off in hollows that provided good cover. However, the softened ground of the open field led to loss of vehicles, including the last of the anti-tank guns and infantry guns. At Michailowka-South the marching formations came upon a chaos of destroyed vehicles. Here the Soviets had fallen on the march columns that came through earlier, especially the trains elements of the 335th *Infanterie Division*, and, according to a survivor, shot and beaten to death defenseless wounded and prisoners.

At the very moment of this discovery, 12 T 34 tanks attacked in wedge formation, charging forth from a wide-valley. The light field howitzers immediately set up to fire and thereby secured a way for the *Grenadiere* into a *Balka* [ravine] that started there, again, however, leaving behind the remaining vehicles, taking only the riding horses. The artillery pieces also remained behind, along with their crews, because the Soviets blocked the hollow anew with their T34s and thereby blocked the *Balka* for the last artillerymen.

The Ingul proved impassible on foot, too deep and extremely cold. There was no pioneer equipment available. Therefore the march column swung to the south through two-meter high reeds and bushes until the *Grenadiere* came upon a German outpost line. That, however, was not a bridgehead garrison supplied from the rear but a small defensive ring at Peressadowka that was held by a pioneer battalion of the 335th *Infanterie Division*.

A great deal of assorted dispersed troop elements with vehicles and weapons had gathered there, as well as several hundred Russian *Hilfswillige* [Russian prisoners who chose to work as unarmed volunteers for the German military] and prisoners of war and a herd of cattle that the Division still brought with it. It made quite a mass of men and equipment. At that point the Soviets must have suffered from a shortage of ammunition or they would have been able to make it a real bloodbath.

Crossing the Ingul

The first priority in the retreat between the Ingul and Bug for the formations gathered near Peressadowka was the capture of Michailowka, because there was a crossing there over the Ingul at the southern of the two places with the same name. The encircled forces repeatedly attempted to capture this bridge, also in a night attack, but to no avail. Without heavy weapons it was difficult to achieve anything against the Soviet forces estimated at three divisions with 25 AFVs.

In support of the breakout battle the 44th *Armee Korps* in *'Fester Platz'* ['fortress'] Nikolajew ordered the 304th *Infanterie Division* to advance northward from the Nikolajew bridgehead early on 17 March in a relief attack toward the northeast to relieve the retreating elements. An assault group of *Kampfgruppe Bartle* (*Pionier [Bataillon]* 335th *Infanterie Division* had broken through the Soviet ring of encirclement during the night of 15/16 March and brought a detailed sketch-Map showing the enemy situation to the division commander via the bridgehead – vital information for the relief attack.

Several *Staffeln* [squadrons] of German and Rumanian bombers supported this attack of the 335th *Infanterie Division* in breaking through the Soviet block. Shortly after 0800 hours Michalowka-South fell to the attackers, with the bridge in its southern part.

Now *Panje* – wagon columns with wounded and trains vehicles flowed across the bridge, including the prisoners, the *Hilfswilligen* and the herd of cattle. The retreat, however, was not undisturbed, for suddenly three T 34s broke into the village of Michailowka, but without the accompanying Soviet infantry, which were repulsed by the *Grenadiere*. The tanks rolled over the bridge in high gear and disappeared on the west bank. After the last formations had crossed, the rear guard destroyed the bridge and then set off toward Ternowka, the next assembly point of the division.

Again a long march stretched before them, regardless of over-exertion and poor nutrition – the field kitchens had long since been lost – the men were physically exhausted. The command therefore rated the 335th *Infanterie Division* as no longer fit for action, henceforth designating it as *'Kampfgruppe 335'*. There were essentially no more heavy weapons and vehicles. In the last few days about 50% of the personnel had been lost. In any case, the *Kampfgruppe* thus crossed the Bug.

Evacuation of the Bug Line

In the sector of the 6th *Armee* adjoining on the left the Soviets carried on their advance. The badly battered German formations there could no longer conduct a successful defense. The Soviets set as their highest priority objective gaining additional ground to the west, crossing the Pruth river and getting to the Carpathian Mountains in the sector adjoining the 8th *Armee* on the left, namely the 3rd *rumanische Armee*. On 26 March *Generalfeldmarschall* von Manstein gained permission from Hitler to give up the defense of the Bug.

During the night of 28/29 March the retreat began, this time with various intermediate positions determined in accord with general staff methods:

See Map 56.

Katherinental, Karlsruhe, Landau, Nowyj Speer, Waterloo-Siedlun, Rohrbach, Nowyj Worms, Lenintal – through numerous villages that had formerly been occupied by descendants of earlier German settlers – visible in the architecture of the houses and the names of the villages – parallel to the Trichaty (on the Bug)–Kudejamzewo railroad stretch, here with demolition of the railroad tracks. The Soviets disrupted the withdrawal movement at Beresowka, on the Tilikul River, with numerous AFVs and temporarily encircled individual battalions, which then had to fight their way through again. *Divisionsgruppe* 387 thereby lost heavily. All of the formations, however, were able to save themselves. Other divisions of the *Korps* repulsed the attacks directed against them, knocking out numerous enemy AFVs.

See Maps 56 and 57.

On the Bug the 6th *Armee* formed a line of defense between Wosnessensk and Trichaty, with contact at the Nikolajew bridgehead (44th *Armee Korps*). In the 29th *Armee Korps* sector, from right to left facing the Soviet bridgehead at Nowaya Odessa were the 294th *Infanterie Division*, *Kampfgruppe* 17th *Infanterie Division*, 258th *Infanterie Division* and again *Kampfgruppe* 335th *Infanterie Division*, 3rd *Gebirgs Division* facing Dmitrijewka, Beloussowka and the 97th *Jäger Division* as far as Wosnessensk with contact to the 30th *Armee Korps*. The days of quiet at the Bug line soon ended with the order to withdraw the troops to an Odessa–Grigorjopol bridgehead continuing further along the Dnjestr. A *Schwerpunkt* seemed apparent at Dmitrijewka – Beloussowka, with the Soviet 8th Guards Army and 46th Army including Mechanized Group Plijew, with the 23rd Tank Corps of the 37th Army farther north.

Earlier there had been shifts of German formations with the formation of the Bug defense. Accordingly *Kampfgruppe* 335th *Infanterie Division* had had to march from Petrowskoje through Trichaty and on to the north in order to take over its far-too-wide defense sector on the Bug. The order for the next retreat again placed significant demands on the troops that were marching on foot. The first B-Line required a march of 23 kilometers. In alternation the individual formations then had to occupy the next position, so that the second march-wave had to fall back 35 kilometers to the Michalowka railroad junction, farther to the west. From there it was 12 more kilometers to Kolossowka in the C-Line. There it was necessary to block the *Rollbahn* to Beresowka. Railroad pioneers not only blew up the Michalowka railroad station, but also the railroad tracks at 100 meter intervals. The Soviets, however, followed quickly with infantry loaded on lorries to Kryssowo. Cavalry and, finally, also Soviet armour approached the Rollbahn from the south. The march was favoured by the climate with dry and spring-like weather.

Step by Step Retreat

The C-Line served the purpose of blocking the Tiligul sector at Sawadowka, which was deeply incised into the terrain, and to Demidowka (to the D-Line).

After crossing the bridge in Sawadowka, the column marching toward Demidowka found that on 31 March endless columns of Soviet motor vehicles with half-darkened headlights were already rolling through Demidowka.[9] In

---

9   This was unusual. Even near the front, the Red Army usually drove its vehicles with headlights on high-beam.

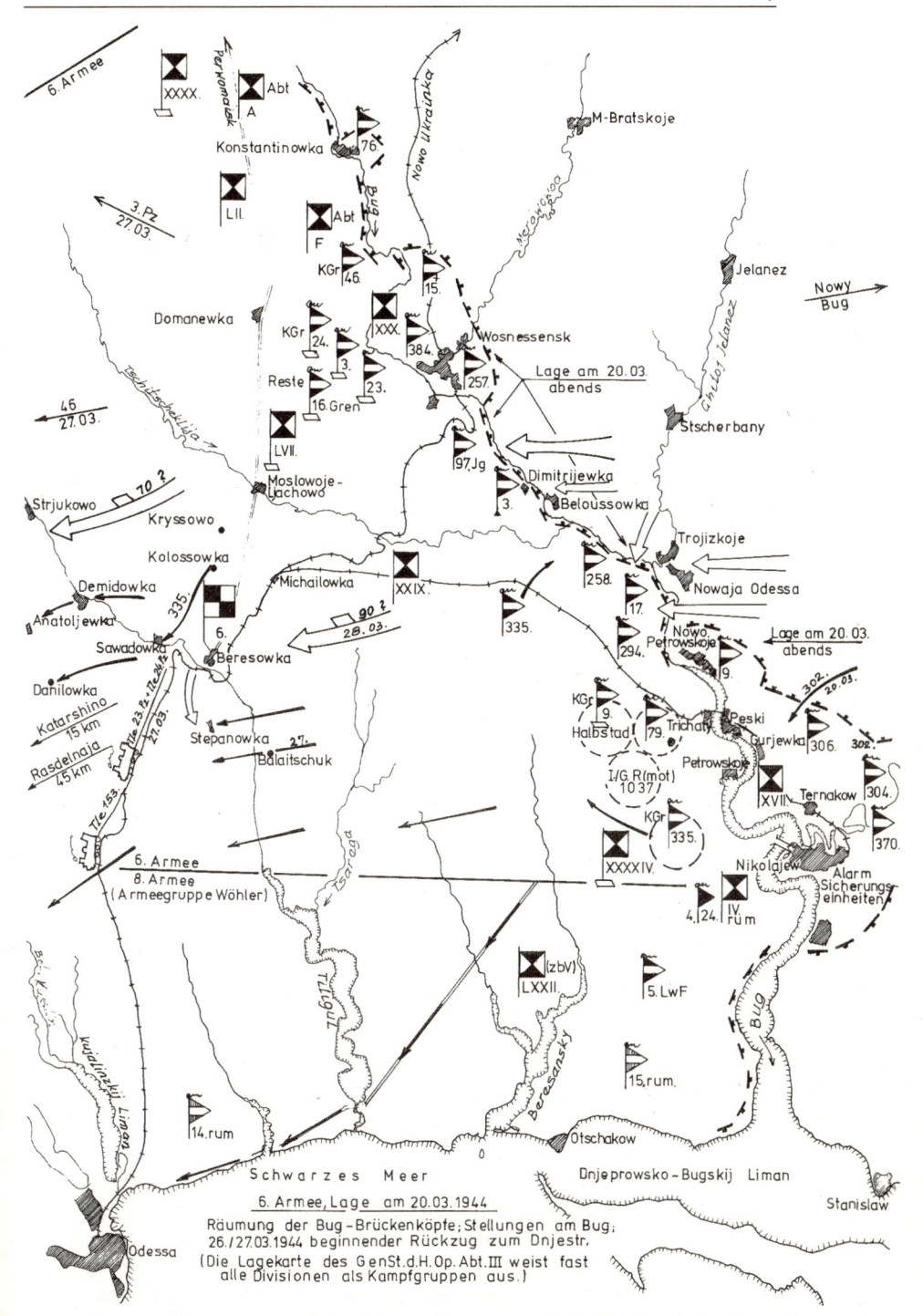

56. 6th *Armee*, Situation on 20 March, 1944. Evacuation of the Bug bridgehead; positions at the Bug; 26/27 March, 1944, beginning withdrawal to the Dnjestr. (The situation map of the General Staff of the *Heeres Operations Abteilung* III shows almost all the divisions as *Kampfgruppen*).

the dark *Grenadier Regiment* 683 was still able to conceal itself in the first portions of Demidowka. The division's rear guard crossed the bridge in Sawadowka, which the pioneers then blew up.

The retreat went on into the E-Line. Soviet pressure mounted. Facing the center of the *Armee* it was reckoned that 90 enemy AFVs were in the Beresowka area, 70 at Strjukowo. A Soviet *Schwerpunkt* was evident at Beresowka, made particularly obvious by the concentration of the 8th Guards – and 46 Armies, as well as the 4th Guards Mechanized – and 4th Guards Cavalry Corps, which were considered mobile and specialized attack formations.

See Map 56.

That forced the foot-marching formations to additional forced marches in order to occupy the intended E-Line between Danilowka and Stepanowka. Thus the regiment had to retreat over 105 kilometers on foot in three days, with additional distances within the position and in the fighting in the C-Line. To the left of this position ran the great *Rollbahn* employed by the Soviets via Katarshino and Rasdelnaja to Tiraspol.

This advance particularly affected the 3rd *Gebirgs Division* and the 97th *Jäger Division*, wherefor the *Armee Korps* set the two *Hornisse*[10] companies that were with *Kampfgruppe* 335th *Infanterie Division* in motion to the division adjoining on the left. An attack by 27 *Ju* 87 aircraft on Danilowka eased the situation for *Kampfgruppe* 335th *Infanterie Division*. Shortly thereafter, however, the Soviets attacked with armour, followed by lorries carrying infantry. With its last remaining rounds, the German artillery separated the Soviet infantry from their armour and vehicles, forcing them to continue their attack on foot. The German *Grenadiere* allowed the T34s to roll over them. Rudel's flying *Panzerjäger* also attacked the Soviet armour, crippling more tanks without loss to themselves. All in all, the troops counted 33 destroyed T 34s, six of which had clearly been destroyed by '*Panzerfäuste*'. During this fighting, which cost the Soviets a large number of dead and wounded, *Grenadier Regiment* 683 lost only one single wounded, However, Russian tanks ran over and crushed two of the three 8.8 cm wheeled anti-tank guns.

See Map 56.

Kampfgruppe 17 was also fired on at Balaitschuk (12 kilometers southeast of Stepanowka) and Onorjewka by the enemy tanks that had broken through *Kampfgruppe* 335th *Infanterie Division* and that rolled over the German main line of resistance to the west in front of Onorjewska. Two were knocked out. Forty AFVs attacked the 3rd *Gebirgs Division*. Anatoljewka was lost in the course of this fighting. The Soviets advanced to two kilometers west of Chutor Schutowa.

See Map 57.

On 1 April the troops evacuated the E-Line in order to reach the F-Line, 16 kilometers to the southwest extending on both sides of Bolschoi Kujalnik, before occupying the Odessa – Grigorjpol ('*Panther*') position, which it had been planned was to be held as the 'final' position. The night march again turned out be very difficult as the result of rain and the ensuing mud and water. The damp uniforms of the exhausted soldiers and water-filled boots proved, in light of the icy snow storm that came from the Carpathiens in the evening of 2 April, with temperatures of 10-15 Celsius degrees below freezing

---

10 Translator's note – Formerly called the '*Nashorn*', (rhinoceros), the '*Hornisse*' (hornet) , *SdKfz* 164, was a self-propelled anti-tank gun with an 8.8 cm *Pak* 43/1 L/71 on the *PzKfz* III/IV chassis.

[five to fourteen degrees above zero, Farenheit] to be extremely burdensome. The temperature precluded any resting in the terrain. As a result of lack of demolition or incendiary material the destruction of the Stepanowka bridge was inadequate. *Pionier Bataillon* 335 prepared the bridge over the Bolschoi Kujalnik directly west of Ssilowka for demolition, but apparently the Soviets captured it intact.

In this situation the *Hornissen* had to leave *Kampfgruppe* 335th *Infanterie Division*. The *'Ofenrohre' (Panzerschreck)*[11] had been used up, leaving no usable anti-tank weapons of any sort. One light field howitzer was all that was left to combat armour. The battle in the F-Line exacted substantial losses of personnel in the Nowo Nikolajewka area and Antonowka (three kilometers north of Ssilowka). The formations then broke off fighting in the F – Line and fell back to Olgino in the *'Panther'* Line (G-Position).

On 3 April the 258th *Infanterie Division* had to pull back its left wing to the Chutor – Losowij area, nine kilometers southwest of Katarschino. The Soviets took advantage of the resulting gap to advance toward Rasdelnaja. This advance served the obvious objective of an operative breakthrough with its *Schwerpunkt* the capture Tiraspol and Odessa. In order to prevent this, the 29th *Armee Korps* planned to free up the 294th *Infanterie Division* and *Kampfgruppe* 335th *Infanterie Division*.

The retreat, in a pitch-black night with snowstorm demanded the utmost from man and horse, the more so since the field howitzers of the artillery got stuck in swampy places or snowdrifts.

Fighting Through to the Dnjestr

In light of this Soviet advance it became necessary to secure passage of all formations through Straßburg and a bridgehead over the Turnutschuk river at Glinnoje. In the event, on 5 April enemy cavalry in at least division strength attacked Straßburg from the northeast. After hard fighting they took Straßburg and also Tschebrutscheweskij, west of Straßburg. They then turned their forces, east of the Kutschurgan Liman estuary, to the south. Earlier in Straßburg there was a fearsome confusion of stragglers and rear area services. A large portion of these, however, still reached the river-crossing that was in the direction of Glinnoje. The columns that were marching ahead secured the bridgehead in Glinnoje without interference from the Soviets. The bridge-officer collected stragglers and returned them to their units. He 'combed out' soldiers from the train elements that were not indispensable, allowing the rest to cross over the Dnjestr bridge at Rascaety to the west bank.

See Map 57.

By their capture of Straßburg, the Soviets blocked the retreat of the combat formations that were still east of Straßburg around Konstantinowka – Freidorf. Without tank-busting weapons it seemed impossible to force a breakthrough to the west through the strong Soviet formations that were marching from north to south through Straßburg. Initially the trapped formations intended to fight their way through via the Kutschurgan railroad station, but they ran

---

11 Translator's note – The *'Ofenrohr'* (lit. 'stovepipe') or *Panzerschreck* was the German equivalent of the American bazooka, a reusable infantry anti-tank weapon launching hollow-charge rockets. For details see the glossary.

into Soviet opposition there. Therefore they split up into small groups and made their way back north and south of the station over the railroad line, abandoning the vehicles, most of the horses and the heavy weapons. Thus, during the night of 5/6 April they got through the enemy advance. However, only about 200 men of the original 350 soldiers of *Regimentsgruppe* 683 came back.

Additional Formations Retreat from the Bug to the Dnjestr

See Map 56.

The formations fighting on the left suffered a similar fate. On 17 March the 3rd *Gebirgs Division* crossed the Trychaty railroad bridge. After the last forces had crossed this bridge was blown up, and vanished into the floods of the Bug. In quick march the division tried to reach its new combat area opposite the Soviet *Schwerpunkt* west of Nowaja Odessa – Troizkoje, where the Soviet 31st Rifle Corps was rapidly deepening its bridgehead on the west bank of the Bug. In three days of fighting the 97th *Jäger Division* and 3rd *Gebirgs Division* eliminated the bridgehead. The 3rd *Gebirgs Division* took over a swampy stream-ground, the Tschischikleja, with contact on the right to *Kampfgruppe* 335th *Infanterie Division*, on the left to the 97th *Jäger Division*. Here the formations took up a position favoured by the terrain on the steep west bank, 30 meters above the water level of the Bug, with an extensive system of trenches. As replacement personnel the divisions even received march battalions with men returning from leave and convalescence.

On 26 March the Soviet 27th Rifle Corps again undertook a river crossing with audacious assault troops. They clawed out a foothold at four places in the swampy lowland. They brought over reinforcements on makeshift ferries. Pioneers and alarm troops cleared the enemy out of Dimitrijewka, also taking Tscherwonyj-Majak and even Chutor-Rjuminskij. The *Gebirgs-Artillerie* [mountain artillery] sank several laden ferries with direct hits. In hard fighting the II./ *Gebirgsjäger Regiment* 144 [3rd *Gebirgs Division*] drove the Soviets out of captured Save and captured a complete radio squad with its radio equipment, thereby establishing voice-contact with the Soviet regiment. On the next day of the fighting the Soviets brought new troops in the swampy terrain to the west bank, in part over a plank-gangway. However, these to were forced back over the river, during which ferries and wooden rafts were sunk by gunfire.

Then, however, the Soviet advance farther north also forced the 97th *Jäger Division*, 3rd *Gebirgs Division* and *Kampfgruppe* 335th *Infanterie Division* to start their retreat to the Dnjestr. In twelve days they would put 300 kilometers behind them. After a forced march the 3rd *Gebirgs Division* traversed a substantial part of this stretch in two days, thereby sparing itself the A – and B – positions. It first went into position east of the villages of Lichtenfeld and Stalino (C-Line). Above all, the Soviets pushed especially hard against the left wing of the 3rd *Gebirgs Division* and the right wing of the 97th *Jäger Division*, the more so since the artillery had fired off its ammunition. At Bogo Roshdestwenka the formations passed through the burning village and crossed the Tiligul river to go into position in the D-Line. However, there were no anti-tank weapons. The 3rd *Gebirgs Division* still had all of two *Panzerfäuste*.

There were no *Sturmgeschütze* and anti-tank guns at all. Ammunition and rations did not arrive.

The Soviets alternated the locations of their thrusts, one time against the division adjoining on the right, then another time against that on the left. The soldiers moved out again to the E-Line level with Schutowa – Anatoljewka. The *Gebirgsjäger* had just reached this line when 80 to 90 Soviet AFVs rolled over the German front on both wings, advancing to Anatoljewka. There, for the first time, armoured personnel carriers emerged from the pack of T 34 tanks. Thereupon the 3rd *Gebirgs Division* formed islands of resistance with its batteries and battalions. Two guns of the 5th *Batterie* of *Gebirgs Artillerie Regiment* 112 were rolled over by tanks. At one place the Soviets even tried to capture the mountain guns by *coup de main* in German uniforms. At that moment Rumanian ground-attack places joined the fray and knocked out several AFVs. In several instances the petrol supply carried on the Soviet AFVs was set ablaze by gunfire.

This attack caused the command of the 29th *Armee Korps* to send the *Abteilung* of *Hornissen* that had been committed with *Kampfgruppe* 335th *Infanterie Division* to the 3rd *Gebirgs Division*. Within a short time 24 enemy AFVs were burning at Chutor Wesselyj. That helped the *Jäger* to put together a new blocking position at the level of Nitgidaigit. In the bitter fighting of that day the 3rd *Gebirgs Division* lost one third of its fighting strength. During the night of 2/3 April it crossed the Kujalnik (F-Line) east of the villages of Ssirotskoje – Jelisawetowka – Ssofijewka. At that point the Soviets shifted the *Schwerpunkt* of their armoured attack to the south to the sector of *Kampfgruppe* 335th *Infanterie Division* and also committed their cavalry there. In this way the Soviets reached Katarshino, thereby blocking the retreat route that had been planned for the 3rd *Gebirgs Division*. The division's mission read, to be ready the next morning for defense two kilometers farther south at Mal Kujalnik (G-Line). The approaching snowstorm reduced visibility to 50 meters, which gave the Soviet cavalry good opportunities to approach. Locally it developed into a free-for-all between Soviet and German march columns. In intense isolated fights the *Jäger* regiments crossed the Soviet route of advance. That held true not only for the formations of the 3rd *Gebirgs Division*, but also for the 258th *Infanterie Division*, 294th *Infanterie Division*, *Kampfgruppe* 17th *Infanterie Division* and *Kampfgruppe* 302nd *Infanterie Division*. The 3rd *Gebirgs Division* then reached the Nowo Ssuchomlinowo – Malachewskij – Shetewora sector and held this line for the next night.

See Map 57.

Encirclement loomed again when the 97th *Jäger Division* and the 257th *Infanterie Division* were forced back to the north by the Soviets. The other formations, especially the 258th *Infanterie Division*, however, were forced out of Losowoj to the south. Soviet armour and cavalry held Katarshino and also the other villages between Losowoi and Rasdelnaja to the southwest toward Straßburg. In Rasdelnaja the Soviet forces linked up with a tank corps that had penetrated the locality from the north. On 4 April the Soviets had already captured Straßburg and, in so doing, the last city before the mouth of the Kutschurgan river. The *Kessel* was compressed by pulling the front back to Chutor Wesselyj – Rostowzewo and, finally, to Bezilowka, without any contact

See Map 57.

with the encircled *Kampfgruppe* of the 335th *Infanterie Division* that had been cut off a bit farther to the south. This *Kampfgruppe* swung from the Belka area to the south in order to then attempt a breakthrough over the Kutschurgan toward Straßburg. The 97th *Jäger Division* and 257th *Infanterie Division* had reached the Kutschurgan in good time, so that merely the weakened 258th *Infanterie Division*, 294th *Infanterie Division*, *Kampfgruppe* 17th *Infanterie Division*, *Kampfgruppe* 302nd *Infanterie Division* and 3rd *Gebirgs Division* had to independently attempt a breakout to the west, consolidated into 'Korpsverbindungskommando Wittmann' [*Korps* contact-command *Wittmann*]. For this to succeed the ring around Freidorf, Bakalowo and Getmanzy had to be broken in order to reach the west bank of the Kutschurgan, 25 kilometers west of the ring of encirclement. In the intervening territory was the route of the Soviet advance to Rasdelnaja, so counterattacks by enemy armoured and artillery formations were to be expected.

'Gruppe Wittmann' Breaks Out

On 5 April the 3rd *Gebirgs Division* launched the attack to the northwest, followed, echeloned back to the right, by the 258th *Infanterie Divsion*, against the northern raised rim of the valley ground between Konstantinowka and Bakalowo. *Kampfgruppe* 302nd *Infanterie Division* attacked on the left, covering the valley against flank attacks from the south. *Kampfgruppe* 17th *Infanterie Division* and the 294th *Infanterie Division* formed the rear, behind the bulk of the trains elements. *Gebirgsjäger Regiment* 138 [3rd *Gebirgs Division*] took Bakalawo by storm. *General* Wittmann initially held up the attack there in fear that the 44th *Armee Korps* was still farther to the rear and in case the Soviets could prevent or delay the attack in their continued push to the south. In the event, Soviet armour, multiple rocket launchers and mortars attacked from all sides. Packs of 30 – 40 Cossacks penetrated the German lines. The German situation thus grew ever darker, so that *General* Wittmann immediately let the attack resume. At about 0230 hours the formations set out again and, in the gray light of dawn, reached the railroad line at Getmanzy.

See Map 57.

As the rear guards left the village of Bakalowo, the Soviets pushed into the village with a 'Hurrah'. They pushed especially hard against the right march group. Both then moved between enemy-held localities to the hill east of Tostucha. Further advance to Nakssija came to an initial halt 300 meters east of Nakssija before a Soviet block of heavy weapons. German batteries positioned west of the Kutschurgan also joined in this fighting. While the formations attacking from the east continued to fix the Soviets, two assault groups captured Nakssija from the south (II., III. / *Gebirgsartillerie Regiment* 112, *Gebirgspanzerjäger Abteilung* 95 and *Gebirgspionier Bataillon* 83 [all 3rd *Gebirgs Division*]). They took prisoners and booty. However, the crossings over the Kutschurgan that were held by the 97th *Jäger Division* and, especially, the 257th *Infanterie Division* were still several kilometers distant. This would have to be overcome in a last attack operation. This bridgehead was now the objective of the march, the more so since the route from Rasdelnaja toward Straßburg proved no longer free of enemy. In the meantime the main body of the formations was still marching northwest from the Bakalowo – Besilowka –

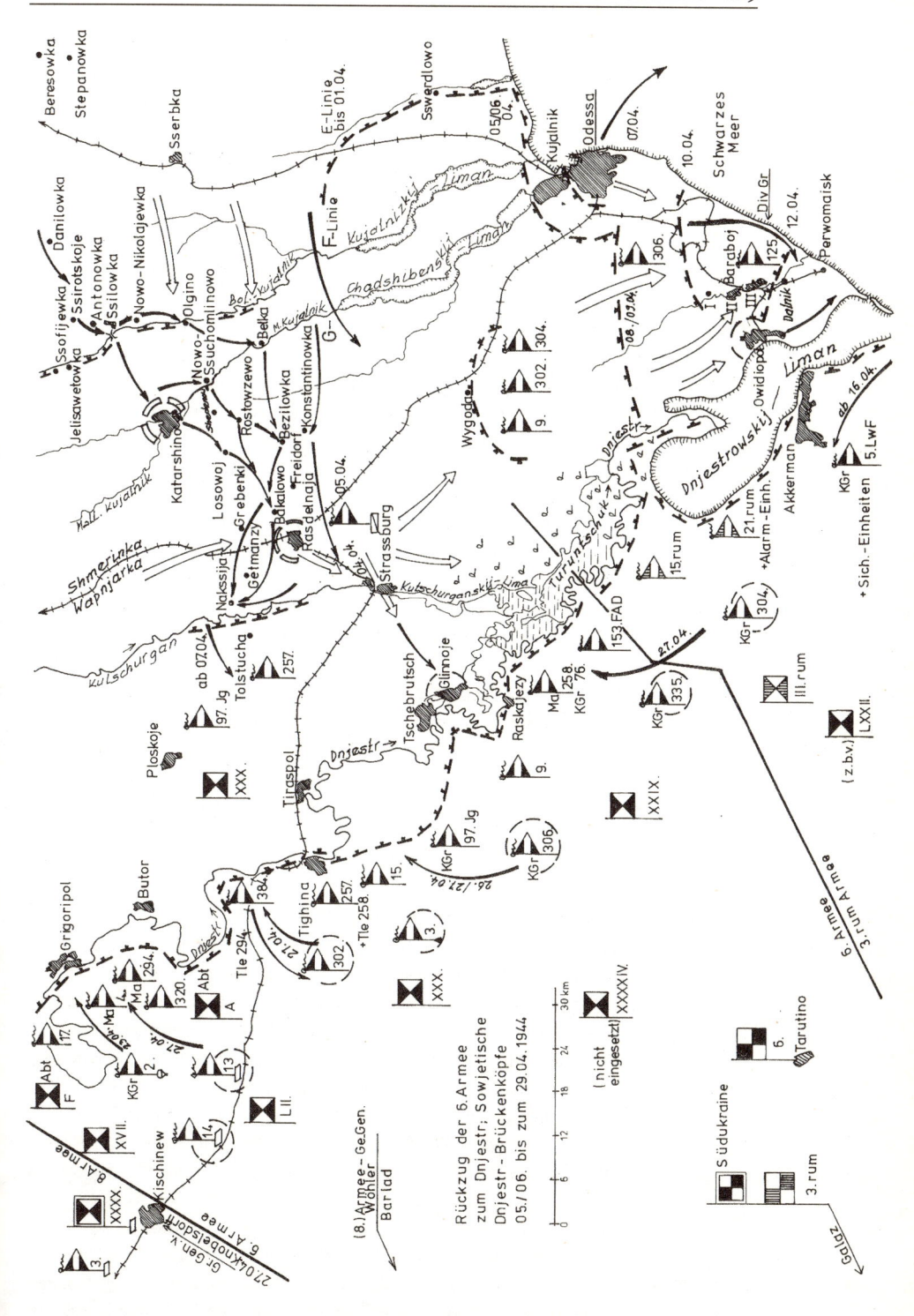

57. Retreat of the 6th *Armee* to the Dnjestr. Soviet Dnjestr bridgehead. 5 to 29 April, 1944.

Freidorf area and, northeast of Radelnaja, diagonally through the enemy. That was a different route than that of *Kampfgruppe* 335th *Infanterie Division*, but with the same objective, namely to reach the river crossing at Glinnoje, west of Straßburg.

On 6 April the formations marched, divided into two march-groups, three kilometers apart. On the left were *Kampfgruppe* 17th *Infanterie Division* and the *258th* Infanterie Division. On the right were the 294th *Infanterie Division* and the 3rd *Gebirgs Division*. The columns assembled at the northwest exit from Bakalowo, disregarding the fire directed at them by Soviet armour and artillery. On 7 April, despite catastrophic road conditions, the march columns safely crossed the Kutschurgan river.

On 8 April the march continued via Grebniki and Ploskoje. Once again, in the dark both march columns toiled through between enemy-held villages in which the Soviet soldiers were obviously doing well. 12,000 men, weapons, equipment and vehicles made their way into the 30th *Armee Korps* Nakssija bridgehead. The other elements that had broken through also reached this bridgehead that the 257th *Infanterie Division* had captured. The weather improved, so that the formations reached the stream area of the Dnjestr in sunny weather with dry roads.

Nevertheless, the formations had blocked the vital supply route for the Soviet 4th Guards Cavalry and a tank corps for over 24 hours. That must certainly have focused the interest of the Soviet troops on these *Kessel* formations. *Gebirgsjäger Regiment* 138 [3rd *Gebirgs Division*], along with *Feldersatz Bataillon* 112 and *Kampfgruppe* 17th *Infanterie Division* attacked toward the west. After an hour of hard fighting with guns and anti-tank guns in the extreme western line, they reached a decisive place for the breakout. The divisions provided security for the escaping traffic with separate assignments: the 258th *Infanterie Division* to the north, the 302nd *Infanterie Division* to the south, and the 294th *Infanterie Division* to the east. The remnants of these *Kessel* formations then crossed the Dnjestr three days later at Raskajezy.

The 302nd *Infanterie Division* On Its Own

See Map 55.

In the first days of March the divisions crossed the Ingulez at Bolschaja-Alexandrowka. Again and again it was a matter of defensive fighting and hasty counterattacks against the enemy troops advancing from north to south. While the formations marching at the front crossed the Nowyj Bug railroad line to the south and had to fend off armoured attacks there, the Soviets developed a pursuit attack against the 302nd *Infanterie Division* which was marching as rear guard. The division was able to repulse the attack.

As the six encircled divisions started the breakthrough over the railroad line about seven kilometers southeast of Nowyj Bug during the nights of 10/11 and 11/12 March, with two divisions beside each other or, behind each other, respectively, the 302nd *Infanterie Division* in the last rank alongside the 258th *Infanterie Division* on the right, after the forward divisions had already gone through, the 302nd *Infanterie Division* was hit by an enemy armoured thrust from the right flank that caused substantial casualties, especially in horse-drawn vehicles. Contact was lost with the other divisions. The division then turned, swinging out to the south behind the 258th *Infanterie Division*. Panic developed when it was again rolled over by Soviet armour until the 302nd *Infanterie Division* reached the dam across the Ingul at Konstantinowka. The 17th *Infanterie Division* secured the bridge site while the first four divisions crossed in the following night. The 302nd *Infanterie Division* took over a defensive position a bit to the north on the east bank in and around Konstantinowka and repulsed heavy enemy attacks, sometimes in street – and hand-to-hand fighting. On 16 and 17 March the last two divisions crossed the Ingul dam. Despite makeshift repairs, it was in poor condition. On the other side the 335th *Infanterie Division* laboriously held a blocking position at the river crossing.

This situation caused the division, also with the rear guard support, to evacuate the positions on the hills to the east during the night, at about 0100 hours on 17 March. 3,000 wounded, however, were left behind. Based on previous experience, every wounded man, and also every unwounded man, could picture their fate. A great deal of vehicles and military equipment were also lost.

That same day the division received a radio message that it was to drop out of the *Korps* formation and fight its way through to '*Fester Platz*' Nikopol independently. However, not all the elements of the 302nd *Infanterie Division* received this order, so one *Kampfgruppe* of this division continued westward in the *Kessel* with '*Gruppe Wittmann*'. See Maps 56 and 57.

Without rations, short of ammunition, constantly fighting against enemy troops that were pursuing or attacking from the eastern flank, the other elements of the division completed a four day retreat to Nikolajew. Exhausted, on 20 March the formations reached the northern front of the '*Fester Platz*' at Ternowka. Here the division came under the command of the 4th *Armee Korps* and had to close an existing gap in the northern front of the *Fester Platz*. Adjoining to the right, the 304th *Infanterie Division* held the position from Ternowka to the Ingul. South of the Ingul to the Bug *Liman* [estuary] was the 370th *Infanterie Division*. The evacuation of the '*Fester Platz*' took place during the night of 23/24 March. The 302nd *Infanterie Division* took up a blocking position on the west bank of the Bug through which the other divisions made a passage of lines, crossing over the old German pioneer-pontoon-bridge from 1918 after darkness fell. Demolition of the floating bridge that was held in place by several stacks of tree trunks was unsuccessful. The division then set off on its retreat to the Dnjestr independently from *Kampfgruppe* 302nd *Infanterie Division* that was marching farther to the north.

En route, at Owidiopol a Soviet cavalry brigade attacked and was completely smashed. The rear area services continued toward Odessa, the fighting elements of the division moved generally westward, north around the estuary (north of Odessa). The 302nd *Infanterie Division* and 304th *Infanterie Division*, along with the 306th *Infanterie Division* came under the command of the 29th *Armee Korps*. See Map 57.

During the first week of April, after difficult defensive fighting, these formations were again able to construct a continuous defensive front facing north, west of the Chadshibenskij estuary on both sides of the Wygoda railroad station. Strong enemy cavalry forces went around the left wing, forcing the *Korps* again to pull the *Korps* front back the evening of that day in order to gain the last possible crossing over the Dnjestr south of Akkermann to Bessarabia. With a combined, heavy, sudden concentration of artillery fire to conceal the German intentions, the formations were able to break contact with the enemy when darkness fell.

See Map 57. The division retreated to the south, reaching the railroad line east of Baraboi I. Together with *Divisionsgruppe* 125 the 302nd *Infanterie Division* took Baraboi I, while Baraboi III proved to be occupied by the enemy. Reconnaissance reported that strong enemy cavalry formations were moving south from Baraboi III back toward Owidiopol. *Grenadier Regiment* 570 immediately set out to block the northern edge of Owidiopol, with an artillery *Abteilung* in position west of Baraboi I, which opened fire on the cavalry, which was now flowing back at a gallop. *Grenadier Regiment* 572 swung out via Baraboi II to the southern edge of Owidiopol. A large part of the Soviet 10th Cavalry Brigade was cut off in Owidiopol and destroyed the following day. The remnants that broke out to the north fell into the hands of the 9th *Infanterie Division*, which wiped them out completely.

Enemy movements from Odessa to the south caused *Grenadier Regiment* 572 and *Divisionsgruppe* 125[12] to set off immediately to occupy a position at the railroad line from Baraboi III to Perwomaisk, south of Dalnik. The 9th *Infanterie Division*, which had arrived in the meantime, blocked facing north at Owidiopol.

In the Odessa area were so-called *Limane*, estuaries of the entering rivers that are, however, closed off in part by sandy spits as a result of the current of the Black Sea, rather like a *Nehrung*.[13] The original plan was that this *Liman* would be bypassed on the north. The Rumanian formations had received similar instructions, and had laid mines on these sand dunes, a tongue of land south of Akkerman. Rumanian formations had forcibly opened a route of retreat in front of the German march columns. Several German military policemen were found at the end of the tongue of land, shot at the side of the road.

While *Grenadier Regiment* 572 repulsed enemy attacks supported by armour on the east bank of the *Liman*, the other divisions of the *Korps* started crossing over the tongue of land and on the ferry south of Akkerman. The 9th *Infanterie Division* was next-to-the-last to cross the Dnjestr-*Liman*. Last to cross during the night of 15/16 April was the 302nd *Infanterie Division* with its *Divisionsgruppe* 125 as rear guard. During this time the narrow tongue of land was under constant enemy artillery fire. At 0400 hours in the morning the pioneers disassembled the sections of the military bridge that had been erected parallel to the tongue of land for crossing and brought the rearguard over in boats. By dawn the formations had all crossed.

---

12 *Divisionsgruppe* 125 belonged to the 302nd *Infanterie Division* as the third Grenadier regiment of the 302nd *Infanterie Division*, along with Grenadier Regiment 570 and Grenadier Regiment 572.
13 Translator's note – On the Baltic Sea coast the name *Nehrung* is used to describe such features, which are sometimes more in the nature of lagoons separated from the sea by a long sand-spit than estuaries.

The 302nd *Infanterie Division* then left its previous *Korps* and shifted to the 30th *Armee Korps*, which had crossed the Dnjestr farther north several days earlier and, with the 52nd *Armee Korps*, adjoining to its left, was engaged in bitter fighting to firm up the defensive front on the west bank of the Dnjestr, extending to the right from southeast of Tighina to about nine kilometers north of Thigina. Only opposite Tiraspol were the Soviets able to hold a deep bridgehead on the west bank.

Brought up in forced march via Akkerman, the 302nd *Infanterie Division* attacked this enemy bridgehead from the line of march and with such effect that, after two more days of fighting, even the commanding heights were firmly in German hands. The remaining Soviet bridgehead on the flat west bank proved too narrow and was under observation which prevented the Soviets from developing an attack from it. The front then congealed in this sector as of about 20 April.

See Map 57.

The Dnjestr Position

When Odessa fell, several days later, all elements of the 6th *Armee* were on the west bank of the Dnjestr. The troops organized there for defense against further attacks.

On 13 May the 9th *Infanterie Division* and 258th *Infanterie Division* smashed yet another enemy bridgehead.

The formations of the Rumanian 3rd Army, belonging to *Heeresgruppe* A, that were committed on the right of the 6th *Armee* extending to the Black Sea shared the fate of the 6th *Armee*, likewise reaching the lower course of the Dnjestr. However, *Heeresgruppe* A faced danger from Crimea. Up to this point the 17th *Armee* had started a costly retreat to Sewastopol. It had defended Sewastopol, and, finally the embarkation-head on the Chersonne peninsula (see below) with the last forces of the 50th *Infanterie Division*, the 98th *Infanterie Division*, the 73rd *Infanterie Division*, the 336th *Infanterie Division* and elements of the 153rd *Feldausbildungs Division* [field training division] of the 49th *Gebirgs Korps*.[14]

In light of the development of the situation of its neighbour on the left, *Heeresgruppe Süd*, the positions of the other elements of *Heeresgruppe* A on the mainland were no longer tenable. In March the Soviets were already in Jampol (140 kilometers north of Kischinew). They had crossed the Dnjestr and, shortly

See Map 65.

---

14 The following belonged to the Rumanian 3rd Army from right to left: The Rumanian Commandant of the Donau [Danube] mouth with marine infantry units, from the mouth of the Donau [Danube] to the mouth of the Dnjestr the Rumanian Infantry Brigade 110 with six battalions (3 infantry regiments), along the Black Sea coast from the mouth of the Dnjestr, security units of the 5th *Luftwaffe Feld Division*, 4th company of Rumanian Infantry Regiment 24, Rumanian 21st Infantry Division and alarm units, to the right sector boundary of the 6th *Armee* the Rumanian 15th Infantry Division. These were commanded by the Rumanian 3rd Army Corps and Rumanian 2nd Army Corps.

The 72nd *Armee Korps (zbV)* [zbV= *zur besonderen Verwendung*, for special use] was responsible for the German formations that were committed. In addition the 1st Slovene Infantry Division was on the right wing of the 6th *Armee*. It, however, like the Hungarian formations, could not be employed adjacent to Rumanian formations. In such a case German buffer-formations had to be inserted in between.

thereafter, also the Pruth in order to push forward toward the Carpathians and Galizien. By the end of March this front was already at the Carpathians.

The entire retreat of the 6th *Armee* had resulted in tremendous losses, a terrifying number of missing and killed. In addition there was the loss of weapons and equipment. When a division no longer has any anti-tank guns or has only a single light field howitzer one can well imagine how difficult it would be to bring up weapons and adequate replacement personnel via the new communications routes through Hungary, Siebenbürgen and Rumania. There was a shortage of both men and weapons in the *Reichs* territory because the factories were exposed to repeated aerial attack by the Western Powers. Regardless of these manufacturing problems and also the supply problems, and contrary to expectations of the divisions, thanks to effective support of the replacement troop elements, personnel replacements flowed in, so that the consolidated formations reached adequate trench strength. Thanks to the excellent logistical organization and, above all, the transport of the 'blue' *Reichsbahn* [the civilian railroad service wore blue uniforms, the military field railroad wore field-gray] and the '*feldgrauen*' railroad, and the incorporation of the Hungarian and Rumanian railroads, the formations received so many new weapons and vehicles that they could be rated as adequately refitted and, after some time, at least in this combination, ready for action.

Henceforth *Heeresgruppe* A was designated '*Heeresgruppe Süd-Ukraine*' and *Heeresgruppe Süd* became '*Heeresgruppe Nord-Ukraine*'.

14

Soviet Advance to and past Kriwoi Rog

The Situation of *Heeresgruppe* A

In the spring of 1944 the fighting retreat of the 6th *Armee* played the major role in the southern sector of the German Eastern Front. The Rumanian 3rd Army on its right necessarily had to conform to the movements of the 6th *Armee*. No special Soviet operations were needed against the Rumanian 3rd Army because its fate hung on that of the 6th *Armee*.

The consolidation of the formations already shows that there were fewer combat-ready formations, especially regarding *Kampfgruppen*, which, experience showed, had more complicated command, organization and logistical relationships, to say nothing of language difficulties.

The Soviet advance on Kriwoi Rog and on to the west – relating to the 6th *Armee* – with various advances to the south, was coordinated in timing with the Soviet 3 March offensive against the front of the 8th *Armee* and the central and northern wing of *Heeresgruppe Süd* – later *Heeresgruppe Nord-Ukraine*. *Heeresgruppe* A (6th *Armee*) found itself retreating. Therefore, in light of the development of the situation, it seemed comprehensible that the Soviets coordinated their assault in the sector adjoining to the north in order to block further routes of retreat for the 6th *Armee* to the west, northwest and north.

See Map 53.

Again and again, even though decimated, coherent formations of the 6th *Armee* had fought their way through to the west. Accordingly the Soviets had to attempt to finally get their hands on the formations of the 6th *Armee* with the advance from the Kirowograd area to Scholochowo, with several attempts to advance to the south, as well as to Nowyj Bug with further advance on both sides of the railroad to Nikolajewka. It also appears comprehensible that the Soviets could not, however, conduct these advances with the full force of their formations, but repeatedly had to divide them in order to set up new barriers farther west in the route of the 6th *Armee's* retreat, such as the advance on Olgopol, Jelanez, Bolschoje Ssolenoje in the direction of Wosnessensk at the Bug.

See Maps 18, 28, 52 and 53.

The surviving reports of German reconnaissance provide only poor information about what march routes with what troop strengths the Soviets chose at that time. Nevertheless it seems astounding that the formations of the 6th *Armee* not only ran into resistance in Nowaja Odessa, but also in the Trichany area, indeed, even around Konstantinowka. The Soviets even brought artillery that far, probably advancing along the Nowyj Bug – Nikolaew railroad in order to contest the approach to the Bug, not only from the north, but also from the south for the elements of the 6th *Armee* that had broken through to the west.

See Maps 55, 56 and 57.

Enemy Attack in the Kriwoi Rog Area

See Maps 16, 17, 18, 19, 20, 21, 22, 23 and, for geography, 28, 52 and 53.

The Soviets had already commenced their advance into the Kriwoi Rog area before the start of the new year, initially with unsatisfactory results. Accordingly on 19 December they attacked the positions of the 46th *Infanterie Division* southwest of Andrejewka with strong artillery support and armour. They got into the villages of Mendeljewka, Kolchose Rushba and Tscherwonyj-Tschumak. By the end of the year, however, they halted their attacks and only renewed them on 10 January, and that against the division adjoining on the left, east of Krassindorf.

See Maps 49 and 52, and for geography, Maps 15 and 16.

In conjunction with the evacuation of the Nikopol bridgehead position and the advance toward Apostolowo, an important railroad junction southeast of Kriwoi Rog, the Soviets increased their pressure in the Kriwoi Rog area, initially forcing the 46th *Infanterie Division* out of its positions to the area east of Kriwoi Rog. Pressure against the positions at Stalindorf mounted, leading to the front being pulled back to the eastern edge of Dolginzewo, with hard fighting around the Dolginzewo – Apostolowo railroad line. The German formations finally evacuated the city of Kriwoi Rog on 23 February without a fight and built a line of defense about two kilometers west of the city at the Ingulez, with a further retrograde movement of the 46th *Infanterie Division* into a line to the rear of Selenyj Gai – here with support by the 23rd *Panzer Division* (see below).

Advance to the Bug

For geography see Map 56.

From that moment on the great retreat to the Bug also began in this sector west of Kriwoi Rog, because the Soviets made good use of their targeted breakthrough to the west on both sides of Kriwoi Rog. Despite hard defensive fighting of the 46th *Infanterie Division* and 23rd *Panzer Division* as well as outflanking of the 11th *Panzer Division*, the Soviets reached the Bug on 25 March at Bugski–Höfe [farmsteads] south of Konstantinowka and crossed it. Without concerning themselves with other formations to be overcome, the Soviets marched onward toward the Dnjestr, however in a southwesterly direction of movement, to Dubossary, in order to gain the bridgehead. This direction of march showed that the breakthrough is also to be understood in relationship with the retreat of *Heeresgruppe* A in order, after breaking through various intended lines of defense of the formations of the 6th *Armee*, to provide the prerequisites for new blocking positions. The Germans simply lacked the formations to construct a continuous line of defense, or even to thwart the Soviet intentions by flank attacks.

See Maps 64 and 65.

In fact, on 5 April the 46th *Infanterie Division* still held a bridgehead at Dubossary, but had to evacuate it after heavy defensive fighting and fall back behind the Dnjestr. The severe winter weather with intense frost and deep snow drifts suddenly came to an end, giving way to summer weather that made it easier for the troops to march. They fell back to Kischinew (15 April), other elements toward Jassy, where the Soviets had already reached the ruth and were pressing from the north to the Jassy – Targul – Frumos – Pascan line. The front then initially stabilized in the right sector.

Fighting in Bessarabia

The crossing of the Dnjestr did not provide all the formations with an opportunity to rest and refit, filling out their ranks and equipping anew with weapons, for the recent weeks had been too strenuous an effort for the retreating soldiers, and for those who had to fight their way through. The Soviets repeatedly forced their pursuit. On about 14 April the Soviets crossed the Dnjestr in the sector of the 384th *Infanterie Division* and built a bridgehead around Tighina. A *Kampfgruppe* of the 3rd *Gebirgs Division* went into action there against the enemy penetration. The 4th *Gebirgs Division* and 306th *Infanterie Division* also had to fight defensively. On 26 April elements of the 302nd *Infanterie Division* and 14th *Panzer Division* launched a counterattack, constricting the Soviet bridgehead and capturing numerous guns. The front situation at Tighina then stabilized. Replacement personnel came from the homeland. Further supply of rations, ammunition and weapons initially remained scant.

See Map 57.

The troops closely watched the enemy movements on the other bank of the Dnjestr, observing general concentration on both sides of the Sereth river. The 335th *Infanterie Division* relieved the 97th *Jäger Division* so that the latter could, with the 9th *Infanterie Division*, clear out a Soviet bridgehead between Ziobirciu and Raskajezy and mop things up.

The End of the Movements

In the southern sector of the front west of the Dnjestr, except for skirmishing operations, the Soviets granted a quiet time for about two months. Either they also required a break to give the troops rest, fill out losses in personnel and matériel and build up supplies, or they already started at that time to shift offensive formations to the north for Operation 'Bagration' against *Heeresgruppe Mitte*. The rest was also good for the German formations, since it gave them a chance to organize the formations, absorb the personnel replacements and care for the remaining weapons. Logistical support, however, was not functioning properly. Initially even rations were scarce and, especially, ammunition. Above all the troops awaited replacements for the weapons they had on hand. Logistical support now had to come from the *'blauen Reichsbahn'* over the Hungarian and Rumanian railroads to Bessarabia. As a result of the differences between Hungary and Rumania passage of the trains caused occasional difficulties. The main problem had to do with extensive stretches of single-track secondary railroad lines that first had to be organized for effective traffic.

Replacement personnel came, and were greeted by the troops with open arms to make up the great losses. Nevertheless, there were problems in organizing the troops. Finally it was necessary to form combat-worthy formations. The previous consolidation of numerous divisions, regiments, battalions and companies did not, in itself, provide the cohesiveness required for a hard-hitting force. The prerequisite for an effective unit was that the men know each other in order to have the necessary feeling of comradeship and mutual responsibility. That, however, was lacking in motley outfits where the men did not know each other. Then there was the fact that every division had a different tone of command, so that many of the men had to adapt anew after the consolidation. In addition there was a superfluity of command staffs. A glance at the situation Map showed a great number of division and *Korps* numbers, which gave the impression that these had soldiers afoot. However, when one examines these *Kampfgruppen, Regimentsgruppen* or *Bataillonsgruppen* then one sees that, for the most part, they represented makeshift consolidations of decimated formations. An excess of *Korps* and division staffs could not make up for the personnel and matériel weaknesses of the formations committed and raise them to the effectiveness of a cohesive troop. Rather it led to friction regarding the limits of command as well as the responsibility, especially for provision and shifting of heavy weapons in order to make this conglomerate of remnant formations with high-sounding division and *Korps* designations fit for action.

As if that was not enough, a series of Rumanian formations had to fill the existing gaps. For the most part these were completely lacking in combat experience, especially experience on the Eastern Front. Initially they had no great combat value, especially for the Eastern Front. Some of these also lacked the requisite fighting spirit, which was still present in the German troops. The Rumanian formations repeatedly reported cases of defection, even in company and greater strengths.

With time the German remnant formations could at least be brought up to combat-worthy company strengths, the rations secured and the ammunition needs covered. Weapons, too, arrived sporadically. It was difficult to share them among the remnant formations that thirsted for them. Accordingly they were repeatedly shifted here and there according to the influence of the current division and *Korps* commanders. In any case, in the course of time, the troops established a makeshift readiness for defense that might stand up to the Soviet frontal attacks. It aroused concern that the Soviets were building their *Schwerpunkte* exactly opposite the newly brought in Rumanian divisions. Therefore individual German *Kampfgruppen* in platoon strength were committed within their sectors. In any case, initially a period of quiet set in for the 6th *Armee* and the Rumanian 3rd Army, and thus, the southern wing of the German front in the east.

15

Retreat in the Central Sector of *Heeresgruppe Süd*

Estimate of Soviet Intentions

The fighting retreat and withdrawal movements in the area of the 6th *Armee* of *Heeresgruppe* A can be described as cohesive military-historical events. However, in describing the extension of the combat area to the north (Kriwoi Rog and Kirowograd), the pressure of the Soviets in the Berditschew, Winniza, Uman area to the west, it is hardly possible to evaluate the Soviet intentions as having far-reaching objectives. Rather, the primary objective seems to have been to secure the formations advancing south from Kiew against German flank attacks. This advance to the south (Swenigorodka), in conjunction with the oppositely directed operation with two *Schwerpunkte*, the first from the Tscherkassy – Smela area to the west and the second north of Kirowograd to Schpola, pursued another objective, namely to cut off the Dnjepr '*Balkon*' of the 7th, 11th and 42nd *Armee Korps* from its rear connections. That was an independent operational objective.

See Maps 41, 42, 43 and 44.

See Maps 46, 47, 48 and 49.

Before the Soviets attempted to link up their forces at Swenigorodka, they advanced south from Berditschew toward Winniza and Uman, an operation that they abruptly abandoned after their spearheads were cut off in the Gaissin *Kessel*. This advance can be interpreted in two ways. Either the initial intention was less concerned with running into the spearheads of the formations advancing from Tscherkassy or, more likely, to assist the Soviet forces attempting the breakthrough at Kirowograd in moving forward to gain ground to the west or southwest. On the other hand, however, this advance pursued similar objectives to the advance from Berditschew to the west, namely flank protection against attacks from the west by German formations, in this case more from the northwest or north. This interpretation can be countered, however, by the fact that, just as initially in the Berditschew area, the Soviets initially had not identified or suspected any significant German offensive formations near Winniza and Uman. The southern explanation is favoured by the fact that involvement from the north would help the Soviet troops fighting against the 6th *Armee* by building new blocking positions farther to the west. That could have helped prevent the formations of the 6th *Armee*, which repeatedly slipped out of envelopments, from finally escaping. This perception is not discounted by the fact that the Soviets split off elements of their formations advancing in the Kriwoi Rog – Kirowograd area to go directly to the west, perhaps in the expectation that the troops advancing to the south would not achieve a final block of the 6th *Armee's* route of retreat. Such support for the Soviet formations attacking from the Kriwoi Rog – Kirowograd area assumed simultaneous attack in the Winniza – Uman sector.

See Maps 42 and 43.

This interpretation results in an explanation for the Soviet advance initially toward Winniza and Uman, as well as the later advance begun in this area after the breakout of the German forces that had been encircled in the Tscherkassy *Kessel*. According to this explanation there was hardly any intention initially that, in the event of success of the offensive formations pushing south and southwest, elements of them would later be turned to the west and finally to the north in order to get into the rear of the 4th *Panzer Armee*. Only an advance directly to the west to the Carpathian mountains would already contain the possibility of denying the German command an orderly supply of its southern front (essentially *Heeresgruppe* A), hitherto supplied over the good railroad line from Lemberg. Finally –the Soviets discovered this themselves in their advance in the entire southern sector with a great mass of motorized troops – a modern army requires substantial logistical support in order to supply offensive troops, and others, with adequate fuel and ammunition. That, however, applies in approximately the same degree to an army conducting a fighting retreat. The quantity of vehicles abandoned in its retreat by the 6th *Armee*, the number of German prisoners, captured wounded and unburied German dead must certainly have made it clear to the Soviets what an immense amount of replacements of matériel and personnel this army would need in the future in order to make it fully ready for action. The logistical worries of the German command would mount abruptly as soon as the railroad line through Lemberg was blocked. Logistical support would then have to come via Hungary –later Karpato-Ukraine to Tschernowitz or through Hungary – Siebenbürgen – Bessarabia over mostly single tracked railroads with numerous easily destroyed structures.

In addition there was another political motive that justified a further advance precisely in this area: Forcing the German front back to Bessarabia could make the states that were in a contractual relationship with the German *Reich* waver in their allegiance to the former 'Axis', now to the German *Reich*, and thereby impact the readiness of these states to provide troops for further participation in the war or to occupy the hinterland. The Soviet command may not yet have thought of capturing the oil fields at Ploesti that were so indispensable for the German conduct of the war, the more so since the synthetic-oil plants in the *Reichs* territory that manufactured petrol from coal were still operating after strikes by the allied bombing campaign.

The impressions gained during the retreat of the 6th *Armee* must have encouraged the Soviets to further advances, not only to the south, but also to the west. Thus it appears obvious that the Red Army initially committed all its resources to turn directly against the right sector of the German front, and also to sever that sector's supply routes. The 6th *Armee* had succeeded, granted, with losses of personnel and matériel, in breaking through all of the rings of encirclement. Therefore the Soviets must attempt to attain a hoped for, indeed, predictable, final success against a badly battered army, slowly marching westward – mostly on foot. Thus it appears understandable that, to the extent that it involved the central front at Winniza and Uman, in their 3 March attack the Soviets initially attacked toward the south, then also to the west. This area must have also seemed particularly suitable to the Soviets because the German command pulled forces out of this sector immediately after the conclusion of the battle of the Tscherkassy *Kessel* and [shifted them] to the left wing of the *Heeresgruppe*.

German Troop Redispositions

By the middle of February radio intercepts already indicated that something was imminent on the Soviet side. Therefore *Heeresgruppe Süd* undertook a fundamental shifting of forces to the left wing, also freeing up the 3rd *Panzer Korps* in its former combat area for transfer to the left wing of the *Heeresgruppe*. The 17th *Panzer Division* and 18th *Artillerie Division* were to follow this *Korps* as soon as possible to stand in readiness behind the 4th *Armee* at Proskurow. Road conditions, however, made it unlikely that these formations would arrive in combat-ready strength before the middle of March.

In actual fact, elements of the formations employed in the previous sector suffered such great losses in vehicles, especially prime movers, as a result of the extraordinarily miserable road conditions, that the 18th *Artillerie Division* lacked means of towing 14 light field howitzers, five heavy field howitzers and seven 15 centimeter cannon. The weather, shifting back and forth between frost and rain, had made the roads so bottomless that the prime movers were over-stressed, some of them no longer road-worthy. On 25 February the 18th *Artillerie Division* still had 95 tubes ready for action, as well as six *Sturmgeschütze* with the long 7.5 cm gun and one *Panzerbeobachtungswagen* III b [armoured artillery observation vehicle on a *PzKpfw* III chassis].

See Maps 41 and 49, and, for geography, Maps 43 and 44.

16

Soviet Attack against the Left Wing of the 8th *Armee*

At the end of February the Soviets prepared for a new assault on the German lines of defense. Their trench-strengths mounted by incorporation of the rear area services in the fighting troops. The filled the resulting gaps in communications, in offices, the medical service and transportation with women.

See Map 58.

On 3 March initial reconnaissance probes started on the left wing of the 8th *Armee*. More followed in the sector of the 2nd *Fallschirmjäger Division* southwest of Swenigorodka, stronger still in the sector of the 4th *Gebirgs Division*. The Soviets achieved a local penetration on its left wing. They then launched a strong attack with three-quarters of an hour of heavy artillery preparation in the sector of the 198th *Infanterie Division*, more against the front of the 2nd *Fallschirmjäger Division* and the 4th *Gebirgs Division* on a forty kilometer width, with the *Schwerpunkt* on the left wing of the 2nd *Fallschirmjäger Division* and the front of the 198th *Infanterie Division*.

The Soviets forced the line of defense of the 2nd *Fallschirmjäger Division* back three kilometers. A *Kampfgruppe* of the 14th *Panzer Division* and the 13th *Panzer Division* launched a counterattack, while the 4th *Gebirgs Division*, which had repulsed heavy attacks against its lines with exemplary steadfastness, cleaned up local penetrations in hasty counterattacks. However, the Soviets broke through the front of the 198th *Infanterie Division* on a broad front, which the Red soldiers used as darkness fell for the advance of an enemy armoured group from Risino to the west toward the stream sector of the Gornyj – Tikitsch at Buki. The front then had to be pulled back to a line six kilometers south of Swenigorodka, Onufrijewka, stream sector southeast and north of Buki.

See Map 58.

The German Lines are Broken

On 6 March the Soviets broke through at the inner wing of the 47th *Panzer Korps* and 7th *Armee Korps* with support of about 70 AFVs. Against bitter resistance, the Soviets broke through the German front line at several locations and, on the left wing of the 48th *Panzer Korps*, reached a locality 12 kilometers southwest of Swenigorodka. The counterattack of the 14th *Panzer Division* failed to break through. With support of about 50 AFVs the Soviets forced the 4th *Gebirgs Division* back in heavy fighting on both sides of Onufrijewka, without preventing it from establishing a new defensive front on the west bank of the sector on both sides of Buki. On the left wing the 75th *Infanterie Division* repeatedly repulsed concentric attacks west of Russalowka. Already, on the second day, of their attack conducted with vastly superior forces, the Soviets

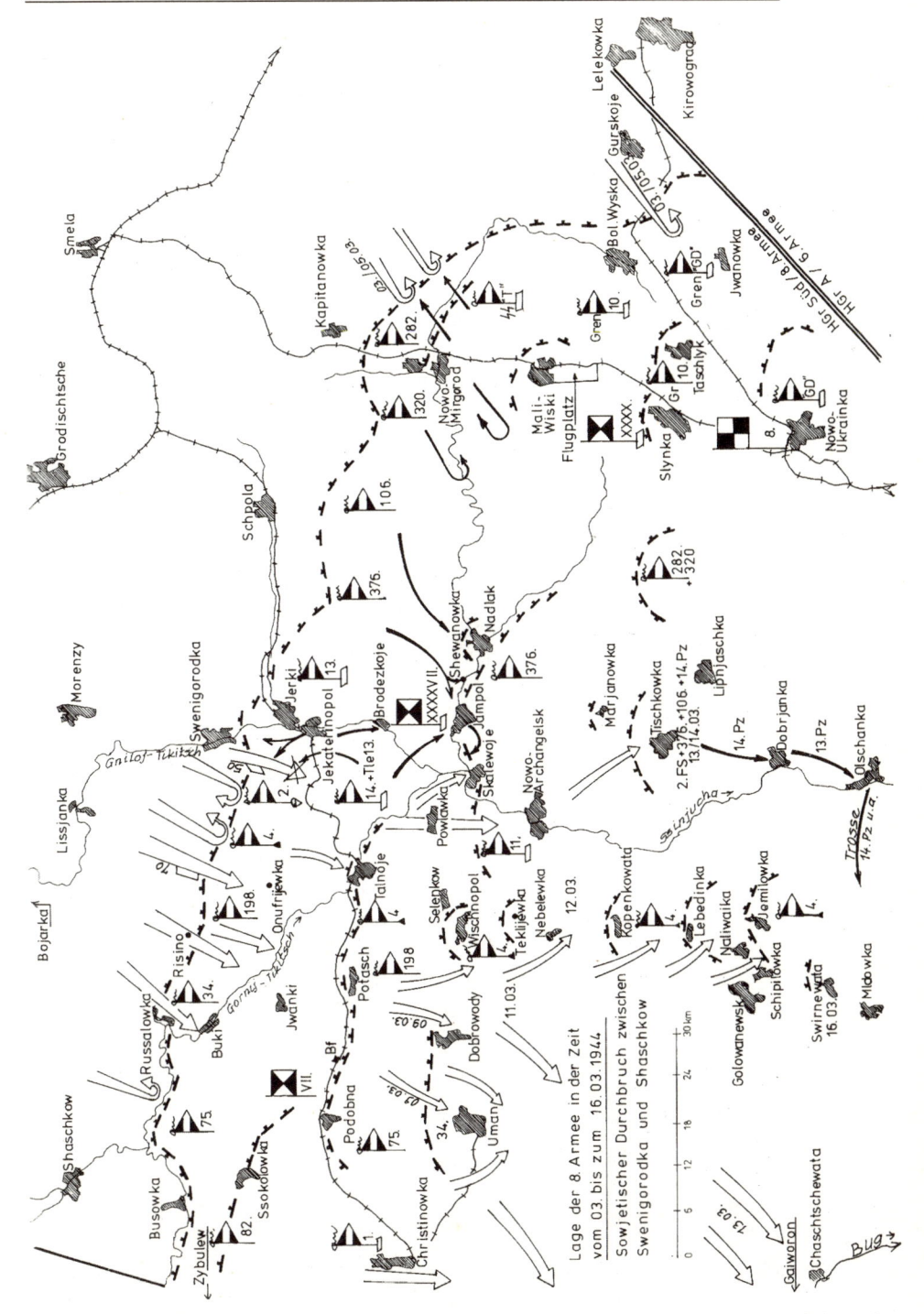

ATTACK AGAINST THE LEFT WING OF THE 8TH *ARMEE* 243

58. Situation of the 8th *Armee* during the period from 3 to 16 March, 1944. Soviet breakthrough between Swenigorodka and Shaschkow. Adjoined to the northwest by Map 69, to the west by Map 89, continues to the southwest on Map 60, adjoined to the south by Map 62.

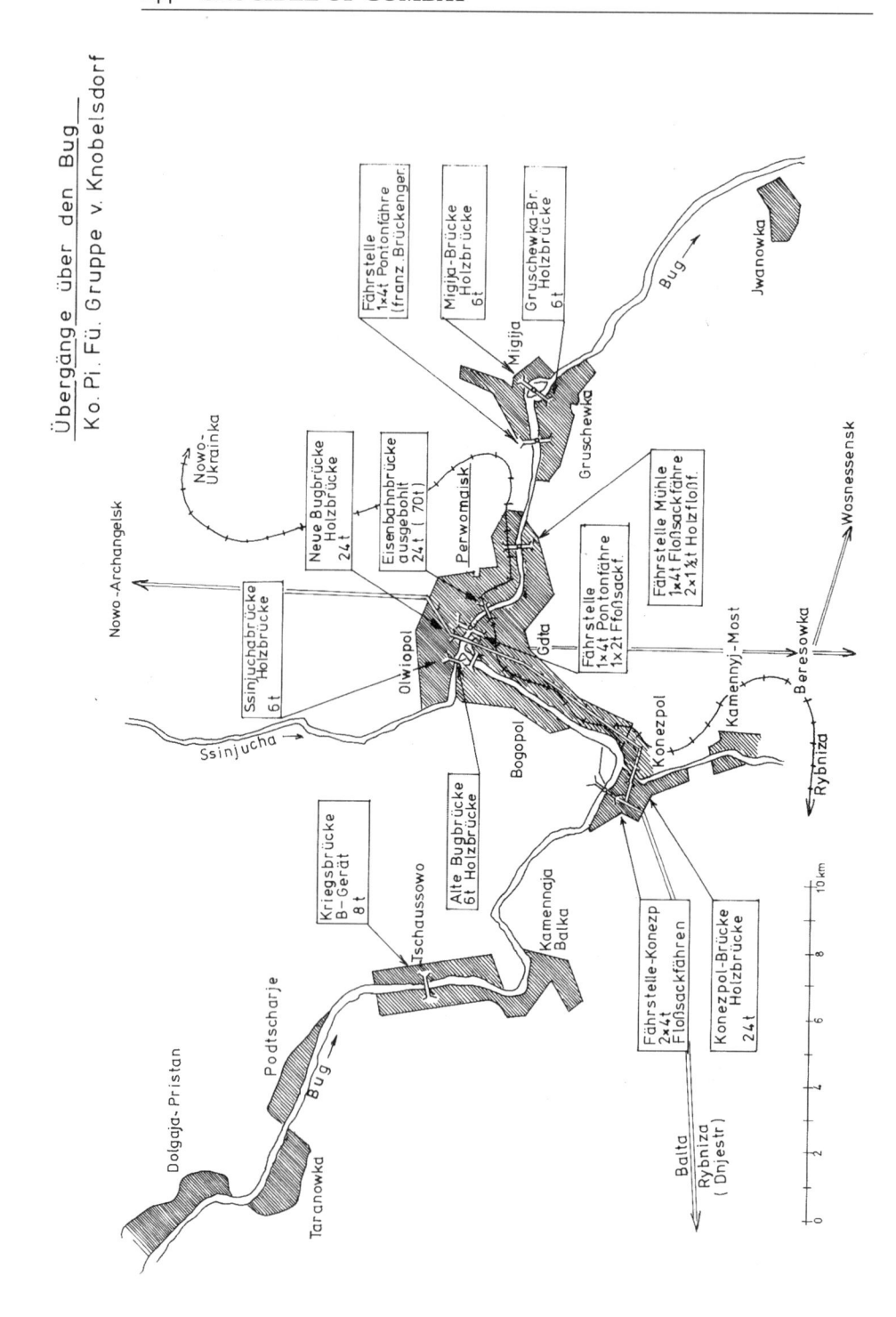

59. Crossings over the Bug. *KoPiFü Gruppe* von Knobelsdorf.

ATTACK AGAINST THE LEFT WING OF THE 8TH *ARMEE* 245

broke through the German lines with the breakthrough at the 4th *Gebirgs Division*. To relieve pressure in this combat sector the Soviets also attacked on the right wing of the 8th *Armee* in the sector of *Panzergrenadier Division 'Großdeutschland'* with strong infantry forces between the road and railroad after a heavy half-hour artillery preparation. This attack collapsed with heavy losses, as did the attack, delivered in the afternoon after artillery preparation in similar strength.

The Soviets carried on their attacks against the 47th *Panzer Korps* and 7th *Armee Korps* between the Gniloj Tikitsch and Gornyj Tikitsch rivers as well as west of the rivers with undiminished ferocity. Despite bitter resistance by the German formations that were so inferior to the Soviets in infantry and armour, fighting in a strongpoint defense, the Soviets forced them farther back to the south and southwest and advanced to the hills north of Talnoje and from Inwanki [Jwanki on the map] to the south, reaching the railroad line at the railroad station and village of Potasch, west of Talnoje. The number of 153 enemy AFVs knocked out in this sector gives an indication of the intensity of the fighting. *See Map 58.*

The next day the Soviets renewed their relief attacks, this time after an hour of artillery fire preparation against *Panzergrenadier Division 'Großdeutschland'* with three rifle divisions and support from 30 AFVs. Although this attack on the right wing failed, the Soviets attained a four kilometer deep penetration in the center of the division. The Soviets followed the withdrawal movement of the 282nd *Infanterie Division* on a broad front.

On the left wing of the 47th *Panzer Korps* the Soviets advanced to directly north of Pawlowka, [Powlawka on the map] which forced the northern front of the *Korps* to be pulled back and defense against attacks from the east and northeast against the Talnoje bridgehead. *See Map 58.*

In the 7th *Armee Korps* sector the Soviets gained about three kilometers of ground in the sector of the 4th *Gebirgs Division*. They broke through the 198th *Infanterie Division*, the 34th *Infanterie Division* and the 75th *Infanterie Division* and forced these formations farther back, the 198th *Infanterie Division* to Dobrowody-North, nine kilometers northeast of Uman; the 34th *Infanterie Division* to three kilometers north of Uman; the 75th *Infanterie Division* to directly west and four kilometers northwest of Podobna.

After repulsing several enemy attacks at Busowka, the left wing of the *Korps* was in motion to the rear to the line six kilometers southwest of Ssokolowka – Zybulew.

On 9 March the Soviets continued their relief attack against *Panzergrenadier Divison 'Großdeutschland'*, forcing a broad, six kilometer deep penetration south of Nikolajewka. The 282nd *Infanterie Division* in the front of the 40th *Panzer Korps* repulsed breakthrough attempts north of Nowi Mirogorod. In the penetration area southwest of Swenigorodka, however, the Soviets continued their breakthrough, employing newly brought-up cavalry formations as well as strong infantry and armoured forces, as well as an attack to the south toward Nowo Archangelsk, and also toward Uman. They took a part of the city of Uman with a double envelopment. *See Map 58.*

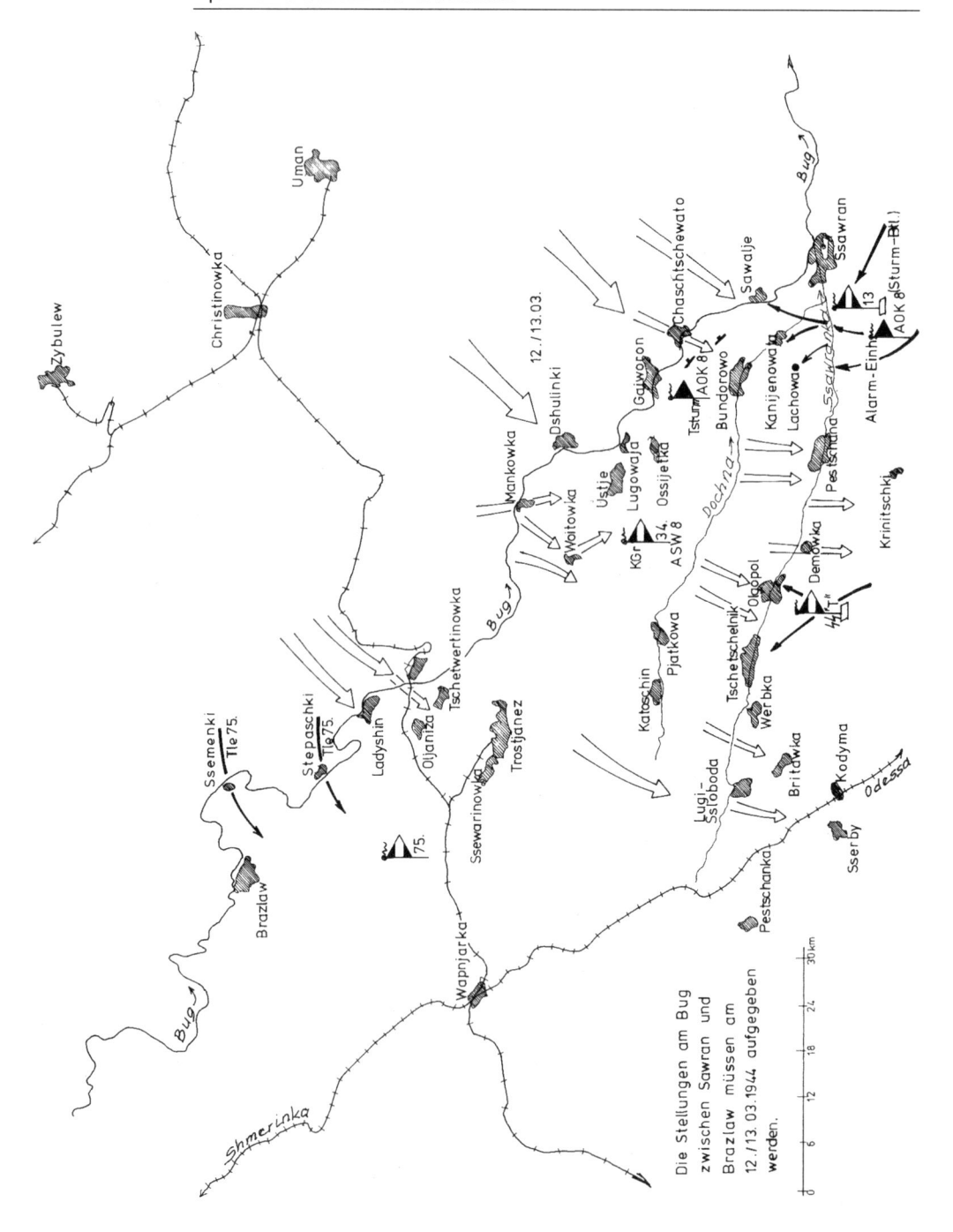

60. The positions on the Bug between Sawran and Brazlaw had to be evacuated on 12/13 March, 1944.

ATTACK AGAINST THE LEFT WING OF THE 8TH *ARMEE*

The Soviets likewise advanced against the weakened and exhausted formations holding the left wing of the 47th *Panzer Korps* with their *Schwerpunkt* via Pawlowka [Powlawka] to the south as far as the hills ten kilometers north of Nowo Archangelsk, after hard fighting against the 4th *Gebirgs Division* to Wichnopol to the hills north of Teklijewka.

In the 7th *Armee Korps* sector the Soviets captured Christinowka, then turned in to the west in order to gain the deep flank of the open left wing of the *Korps*. On that day 35 of 49 enemy AFVs remained, knocked out, on the field of battle.

See Maps 58 and 60.

The German Retreat

With that the Soviets had achieved the breakthrough to the south, southwest and also to the west. The German formations then had to attempt individually, without contact on either side, to 'sell themselves dearly' as possible, meaning to put up as much resistance to the Soviets as was possible and thereby delay their advance. The *Heeresgruppe* issued appropriate retreat orders. On 13 March the Soviets attacked anew the 40th *Panzer Korps*, striking the right wing of *Panzergrenadier Division 'Großdeutschland'*, also achieving a local penetration in the right wing of the 320th *Infanterie Division* There was no longer any discernible front line on the left wing of the 47th *Panzer Korps*. The security positions of the remnants of the 198th *Infanterie Division* were forced back about three kilometers to the southeast. The Soviets put in strong attacks against the Chaschtschowato bridgehead from the north, and captured the locality south of the Bug. West of Gaiworon the Soviets crossed the Bug, also in battalion strength, and advanced to the west on both sides of the railroad.

See Maps 58 and 59.

In the 7th *Armee Korps* sector the Red Army forced the remnants of the 34th *Infanterie Division* six kilometers back to the south. Attacking armour and infantry forces forced the troops in the bridgehead that remnants of the 74th *Infanterie Division* still held north of Gorejewka back to the west bank, which gave the Soviets the opportunity to cross the Bug south of there with strong forces. Also in the area of the 46th *Panzer Korps* of the 1st *Panzer Armee*, widening their attack, the Soviets crossed the Bug on both sides of Gaissin and achieved a roughly six kilometer deep penetration at the boundary between the 1st *Infanterie Division* and 254th *Infanterie Division*, additionally advancing south of the Lipowez – Winniza road to Woronowiza. In the 24th *Panzer Korps* sector it was possible to repulse the Soviets and to constrict the enemy's Janoff bridgehead. On the other hand, the counterattack to eliminate the Soviet Kurilowka bridgehead 15 kilometers west of Janoff failed.

See Maps 41 and 43 for geography.

Loss of Additional Ground – Loss of the Bug

The entire central front of the German formations in the Ukraine was thus in motion. The 40th *Panzer Korps* withdrew to the west under heavy enemy pressure on the 320th *Infanterie Division* and 282nd *Infanterie Division*. The formations of the 46th *Panzer Korps* were also forced back, as happened with the 75th *Infanterie Division* and 254th *Infanterie Division*, whereas the 1st *Infanterie Division* repulsed attacks against both of its bridgeheads. The Soviet forces that had penetrated from the south in battalion strength into Winniza

See Map 60 and, for geography, Map 62.

were thrown out in a hasty counterattack and attacks against the east front in this sector were beaten off. In the 24th *Panzer Korps* sector the Soviets widened their existing bridgehead west of Janoff by about three kilometers. However, an existing enemy bridgehead over the Bug 15 kilometers west-southwest of Chmelnik was eliminated.

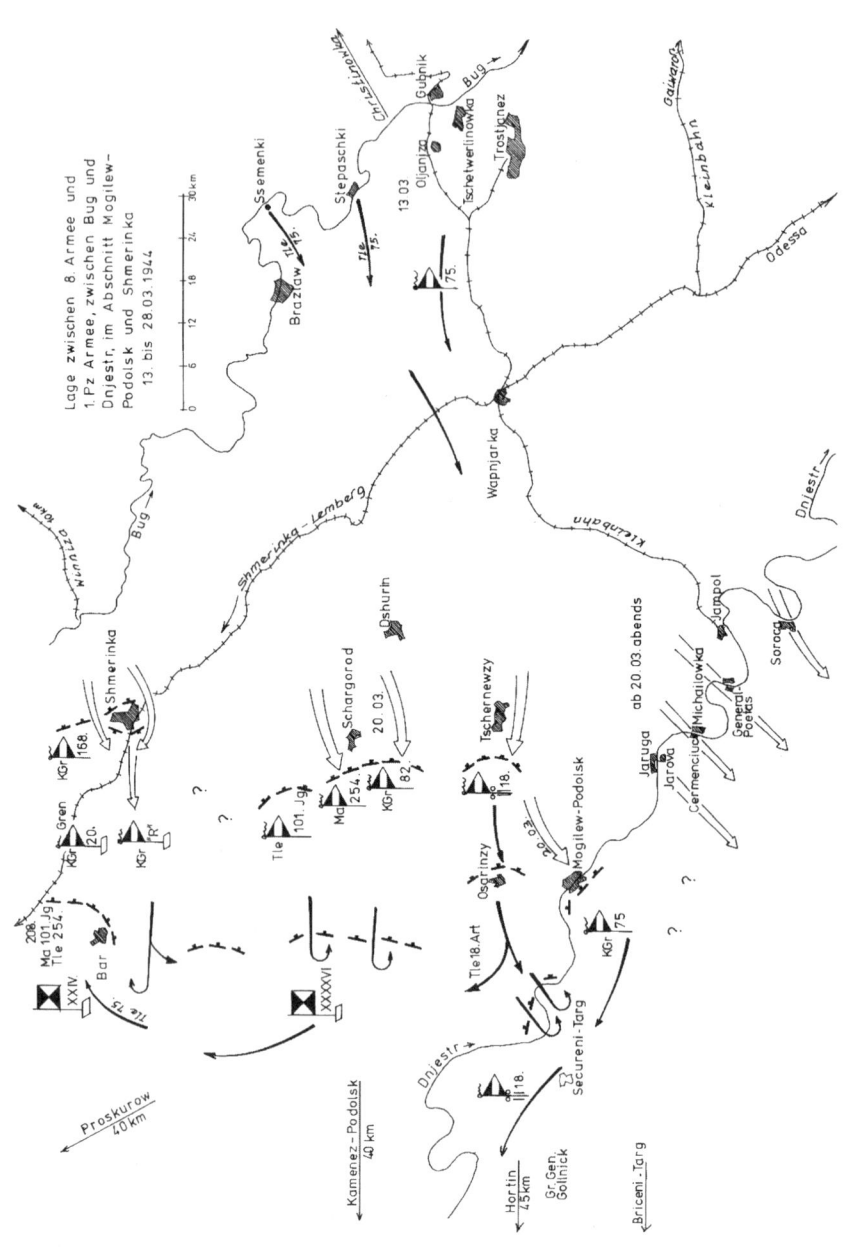

61. Situation between the 8th *Armee* and 1st *Panzer Armee* between the Bug and Dnjestr in the Mogilew-Podolsk and Shmerinka sector. 13 to 28 March, 1944. Map 90 of *Hube Kessel* overlaps this map and carries on to the west.

ATTACK AGAINST THE LEFT WING OF THE 8TH *ARMEE*

The general retreat continued in the ensuing days. The retreat of the 40th *Panzer Korps* went according to plan, aside from individual interruptions by enemy attacks, as with the 106th *Infanterie Division*, at the left wing of the 376th *Infanterie Division* and with the 2nd *Fallschirmjäger Division*. Elements of the 376th *Infanterie Division* and 2nd *Fallschirmjäger Division* fought their way through to the south in the Ssinjuchin Brod – Tschaussowo sector, while the 4th *Gebirgs Division* and remnants of the 198th *Infanterie Division* had to go back over the Bug in the sector on both sides of Goloskowo.

See Map 62.

On 18 March the 376th *Infanterie Division* of the 40th *Panzer Korps* felt its way forward from the area south of Ssinjuchin Brod toward the west against an enemy that was in the process of crossing the Bug at Tschaussowo and gained the Perwomaisk – Bolowanewsk road, 48 kilometers northwest of Perwomaisk in counterattack. The Soviets were able to build bridgeheads in the Bug meanders both at Tschaussowo as well as 15 kilometers northwest of Tschaussowo. They were also able to gain a foothold east of Pestschana on the south bank of the Ssawranka river. There were no German forces available for countermeasures, so there was no other alternative for the German remnant-formations than to retreat further to form a new line of defense, which had, initially, been intended at the Dnjestr.

See Maps 58 and 62.

On 19 March an enemy attack launched from the enemy bridgehead 21 kilometers northwest of Perwomaisk made no progress. The 282nd *Infanterie Division* repulsed weak enemy attacks. The 7th *Armee Korps* eliminated an enemy bridgehead at Petschana on the Ssawranka river (45 kilometers west of the mouth of the river in the Bug at Ssawran) and further constricted a bridgehead east of Olgopol (27 kilometers west of this mouth).

See Map 62.

Retreat to the Upper Dnjestr

With that the Soviets had already crossed the Bug in various places on a broad front and advanced to the Dnjestr. They first reached the Dnjestr in the sector of the 46th *Panzer Korps* and crossed the river in the Soroca – Jampol – General Pootas and Cremenoiuc sector with a breadth of 30 kilometers, without hindrance from the German formations there. Elements of the 75th *Infanterie Division* at Mogilew – Podolsk fell back to the south bank of the Dnjestr after blowing up the bridge. Elements of the 18th *Artillerie Division* that were west of Tschernowzy were forced back to Osarinzy by enemy forces attacking from the northeast, while attacks against elements of the 254th *Infanterie Division* and *Kamfgruppe* 82nd *Infanterie Division* that were south and east of Schargorod were unsuccessful. The Soviets closed up in the gap between Schargorod and Shmerinka in the general line between these two localities. Strong concentric attacks on Shmerinka ensued, cutting off the garrison of Shmerinka. Six kilometers west of Shmerinka a *Kampfgruppe* of the 2nd *SS-Panzer Division* 'Das Reich' of the 24th *Panzer Korps* advanced to the east. The 20th *Panzer Division* took Niskiwzy. Thus it was that it continued in the ensuing day, especially in an ever-widening sector of attack. Individual counterattacks, as by the 10th *Panzergrenadier Division* or the 3rd *SS-Panzer Division* 'Totenkopf' achieved limited success. Other formations, such as the weak elements of the 75th *Infanterie Division*, had to fall back before heavy enemy pressure. All

See Map 61 and, for geography, Maps 86 and 90.

counterattacks of the retreating German formations either failed outright or achieved no lasting effect. The German remnant formations could not hold fast against the strong pressure of far superior pursuing Soviet forces, so the retreat went ever further in the days that followed, with widespread crossing of the Bug and the Dnjestr. Again and again, with no contact on either side, German formations tried to compress Soviet bridgeheads in counterattacks and to hold the bridge-crossings east of the bridgeheads for as long as possible.

In this situation of fighting retreat a particular tactic of previous Soviet advance was not evident. Usually the Red Army attacked, alternating between two *Schwerpunkte*, as they had successfully done in advancing from Smela and Kirowograd on Schpola, whereby the German command constantly ran into difficulties due to lack of defensive formations. In this advance to regain the southern Ukraine the Soviets primarily concentrated on march-achievements that would fix the German formations and prevent building a continuous line of defense.

Further Retreat to the Pruth

See Map 61.

The retreating toops intended to use the Dnjestr as a line of defense. Thus the 18th *Artillerie Division* attempted to move over the Dnjestr with its light elements toward the southwest. However, other elements of the division had already been forced aside north of the river to the west, so the river crossing at Dzurin turned out to be extremely difficult. Individual enemy AFVs broke through to the approach road to the bridge and first had to be eliminated by the division staff at dusk.

Disruption of telephone communications already became evident, as the Soviets advanced everywhere and tapped into the cables, as with the question: '*Kluge? Kluge kaputt* [dead], *Njemen Soldat kaputt, Hitler kaputt,*' [Kluge? Kluge dead, German soldier dead, Hitler dead.]

See Map 90.

There was no effective way of stopping the Red Army at the upper Dnjestr given the unavoidably large defensive sectors. Therefore, south of the Dnjestr the 18th *Artillerie Division* withdrew farther to the west to the crossing at Hotin and then moved to the north to *Armeegruppe Hube*.

See Maps 65, 90, 93 and 94.

Elements of the 18th *Artillerie Division* attached to the 75th *Infanterie Division* of the 46th *Panzer Korps,* with four light batteries were to close a large gap between the 1st *Panzer Armee* and 8th *Armee* between Briczen, Sat and Lipkany, south of the Dnjestr. The gap was to be closed in the sector of the 3rd *Panzer Korps* at Bar. The commitment, however, was fragmented, inappropriate and dependant on others. On 24 March encircled elements foght their way through to the west. On 28 March a counterattack by *Gruppe Golnick* from the Briczen, Sat Hotin area to the north against the left wing of the Soviet 6th Tank Army forced the Soviets back to the northwest and east. Then, to regain contact with *Gruppe Breith*, came fighting north of the Pruth against the enemy that had already advanced to the west. The formations involved then ended up in the later Kamenez – Podolsk *Kessel*. Nevertheless, on 31 March, despite an extremely serious supply situation, they gained two bridgeheads over the Zbrucz river. The *Luftwaffe* brought ammunition, but could not bring the amounts that the troops needed. *Gruppe Gollnick* then

ATTACK AGAINST THE LEFT WING OF THE 8TH *ARMEE*

came under the command of *Korpsgruppe Breith* and, on 3 April, built a widely dispersed bridgehead over the Sereth, with the objective of reaching the Buczac area on the Strypa, north of the Dnjestr, in which the 2nd *SS-Panzer Korps* was expected.

On 5 April *Gruppe Gollnick*, with remnants of the 18th *Artillerie Division*, repulsed the attack of the Soviet 11th Tank Corps against the southern flank of the 3rd *Panzer Korps* at Uszcziecko, destroying 35 AFVs. On 6 April the 6th *Panzer Division* of the 3rd *Panzer Korps* took Buczac. These formations thereby got out of the impending encirclement at the same time that the gap north of the Dnjestr at the Strypa was closed.

See Map 96.

Fates of Individual Divisions

The Soviet superiority in motorized forces and, above all, in armour and artillery, left the *Panzer* divisions more than ever the effective *Schwerpunkt* of the defensive fighting. A report of the 4th *Gebirgs Division* from the first days of the new Soviet attack illustrates what a difficult situation infantry divisions without their own armour faced against the Soviet attacking forces.

Fighting Retreat of the 4th *Gebirgs Division*

The Soviets had used the days before the start of their second attack (5 March) to bring a great mass of artillery into position and supply it with adequate ammunition. Facing *Gebirgsjäger Regiment* 91 [4th *Gebirgs Division*] and *Gebirgsjäger Bataillon* 94, alone, were 100 to 150 AFVs at the time of the Soviet penetration into Ryschanowka and Kobyljaki. Wave after wave of enemy infantry supported them, so that the companies of the 4th *Gebirgs Division* that were committed there remained as weak little bunches of men, their batteries and anti-tank units soon out of ammunition. The last remaining groups were almost completely wiped out by the masses of advancing infantry and armour. It was the same story in other division sectors, as with *Gebirgsjäger Regiment* 13 [4th *Gebirgs Division*] and *Gebirgsaufklärungs Abteilung* 94 [*Aufklärungs Abteilung* 94 was under the 4th *Gebirgs Division*]. The change of position required as a result of the Soviet penetration placed new demands on the formations. Anti-tank and even mountain guns, complete with draft animals, sank into the glutinous, deep morass at Pawlowka. Indefatigably *Jäger* and cannoneers worked to get their guns and horses moving again. Many times while they were working in the impenetrably obscure weather they were surprised from all sides by groups of advancing Red soldiers. Sometimes they were able to repulse this enemy, sometimes they were able to blow up the guns, but that was not always possible, so several guns fell into enemy hands. Repeatedly the *Gebirgsjäger* had to charge the Soviets with cold steel because they were too short of ammunition. They received their first scanty supplies in Talnoje.

See Map 58.

By bounds, as ordered, the division retreated, forming a hedgehog at Teglijewka at the great road to Nowo Archangelsk, also at Nebelewka and Kopjenkowata. At Belaschki and Selenkoff the groups of *Jäger* found themselves already encircled and had to fight to open their retreat route. The *Luftwaffe*

See Map 58.

252 CRUCIBLE OF COMBAT

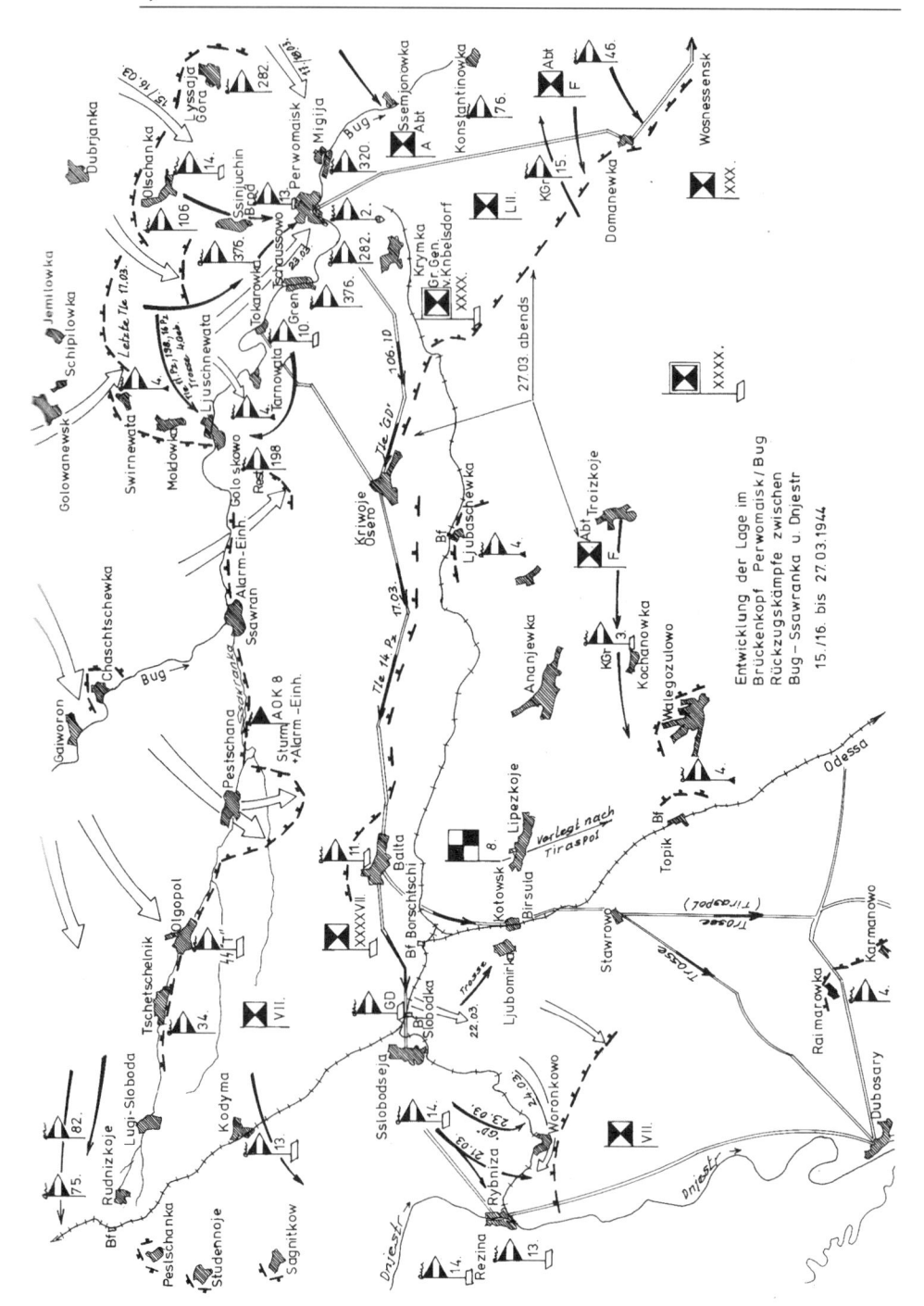

62. Development of the situation in the Perwomaisk/Bug brigehead. Fighting retreat between Bug – Ssawranka and Dnjestr 15/16 to 27 March, 1944. See Map 63 for 18-28 March, and for more details of the north-west quadrant of this map. Map 64 covers 26 March-3 April 1944. Map 60 adjoins and overlaps to the north.

ATTACK AGAINST THE LEFT WING OF THE 8TH *ARMEE*

dropped supply canisters with ammunition and rations. On 12 March the *Wehrmachtsbericht* mentioned this division.

This eventful fighting with enemy forces assembled in Goluwanewske attacking the positions held by elements of the division around Naljiwajka forced the battalions to break through via Schipilowka toward Alexandrowka and forced *Gebirgsjäger Regiment* 13 and *Gebirgsjäger Bataillon* 94 to hold the Jelinowka railroad station. Later they were able to break through the encirclement, force the Soviets back and, favoured by thick snow squalls, to withdraw in time.

On 16 March in Swinjewata, after the Soviets forced their way in, the batteries of *Gebirgsartillerie Regiment* 94 engaged in direct fire at extreme close range. However, after firing their last rounds the guns had to be blown up.

Gebirgsjäger Regiment 13 and *Gebirgsjäger Regiment* 91 fought as rear guards on both sides of the Alexandrowka – Oniolowo road. In the evening of 16 March they were in the bridgehead north of the Bug around Ljuschnijewata. The intense cold prevented the *Jäger* from digging into the frozen ground in the open fields. However, by holding the bridgehead they helped the last elements of the 198th *Infanterie Division*, and the 11th and 16th *Panzer Divisionen* to cross the Bug at that place on 17 March. See Map 62.

On 24 March the Division held the position on the south bank of the river between Tarnawata – Oniolowo – Krassenjenikoje. The Soviet river crossing at Wel, Metschetna and Tarnowata and the two bridgeheads they built during the night of 21/22 March compressed *Gebirgsjäger Regiment* 13 and *Gebirgsjäger Bataillon* 94 by the evening of that day into a small beachhead at Tarnowata.

Since the Bug position could not be held, the retreat had to continue toward the southwest via the Kodyma sector at Kriwoje Osero, the Ljubaschewka railroad junction, Welikoje and the Tobik railroad station where, for the first time, the Odessa – Winniza stretch of the railroad provided an opportunity to send off wounded. See Maps 62 and 63.

Muddy stream lowlands and icy snowstorms – the *Buran* [name given to that kind of weather] – immediately eliminated all tracks and limited vision to ten meters, which extraordinarily complicated defense against pursuing enemy forces.

The division held off the enemy for several days in the Karmanowo – Reimarowka (20 kilometers north of the Dnjestr) – Dubossary blocking position and repulsed all enemy attacks in the constricted bridgehead around Grigoriopol – Dorozkoje – Pogreby. *Gebirgsjäger Regiment* 91 continued to hold the bridgehead around Dorozkoje. With that, despite daily heavy fighting and the complications of the weather, in a total march of 300 kilometers, the Soviets had not succeeded, as was so often feared, in splitting up the division during the retreat. See Maps 64 and 65.

Actions of the 14th *Panzer Division*

The 14th *Panzer Division* at this time followed a nearly independent route. Initially it helped to eliminate the Soviet penetration between the 376th *Infanterie Division* and the 2nd *Fallschirmjäger Division* adjoining to the west by successfully counterattacking Olchowez and Petki. Thereupon the Soviets See Map 58.

launched an infantry attack with armoured support from Olchowez toward the southeast. That forced the III./ *Fallschirmjäger Regiment* 7 [2nd *Fallschirmjäger Division*] to fall back and endangered the deep flank of the 14th *Panzer Division*, causing the division to pull back to its previous jump-off position and to commit a combat-reserve group [*Einsatzgruppe*] of *Panzergrenadier Regiment* 108 [14th *PzD*] from Jekaterinopol to protect the threatened left wing. A new attack by the Germans in the morning of 7 March did not produce the desired effect. After initial success the attack ground to halt before a densely held anti-tank barrier. Here the armour provided no solution, because a portion of the AFVs stuck fast in the mud and therefore had to limit themselves to keeping the numerous enemy AFVs in check.

See Map 58. Reconnaissance revealed lively column traffic on the road from Olchowez toward Talnoje, including all sorts of weapons, which confirmed the suspicion that the main thrust of the Soviets targeted Uman and Gaissin, so that the attack on both sides of the Gniloi Tikitsch river sector toward Nowo Archangelsk and Jampol primarily served to screen the left flank. That included the danger that one day the advancing Soviets would turn in to the east and encircle the 14th *Panzer Division* and the formations that were still in the front facing north.

See Map 58. On 8 March in heavy snowstorms the sector-by-sector retreat of the fighting troops began. Again and again the Soviets tried to cut off individual formation, as by the advance of enemy armour over the hills south of Nowosselitza. That cost the Soviet infantry heavy losses, as also occurred in the Nowij Jekaterinopol sector. The German infantry also suffered losses due to freezing and wounds. In the haste of the necessary retreat, after salvage efforts failed, four AFVs that had churned themselves deep in the mud had to be blown up.

Isolated successful hasty counterattacks by armour and German artillery fire dampened the Soviet advance and reduced pressure on the continued retreat via Brodezkoje and Jampol toward the south in the direction of the west bank of the Ssinjucha river. Utilizing a gap in the front and thick ground-fog the Soviets built a bridgehead on the far bank of the river at Skalewoje. Lack of combat-capable formations precluded interference.

See Maps 58 and 61, and, for geography, Map 62. At that time Soviet formations gained considerable ground. In light of the large number of weak German formations they lost their fear of wide-ranging operations. Their spearheads were already before Gaiworon with the possibility of also crossing the Bug there. That appeared to put an end to the possibility of using the Bug as a line of defense.

Train Elements Sent to the Rear

See Map 58. The continued retreat, however, was difficult because the logistical services were unable to reach their prescribed march objectives due to terrain conditions and loss of vehicles. Due to damage the bridge in Nadlak had to be blocked, which resulted in the difficult assignment of extracting the jammed up march groups, one wagon at a time, and redirecting them to Jampol. The 1st *Batterie* of *Heeres-Flak-Artillerie Abteilung* 276 crossed the Wyss River at Shewanowka. On 11 March the main body of the train elements reached the Kalinowka and Marjanowka assembly points, with Lepnjashka as the next march objective.

ATTACK AGAINST THE LEFT WING OF THE 8TH *ARMEE*

The snowfall mixed with rain gave reason to avoid detouring over byways and to stick to the main *Rollbahnen*, despite the danger of increased threat from the air. These train elements therefore moved via Tischkowka and Dobrjanka toward Olschanka. Here, in order to avoid the Bug bridge at Perwomaisk, they crossed the Ssinjucha sector toward the west and reached Moldowka.

The choice of retreat routes, especially for the train elements, was influenced by the fact that logistical units and crews of straggling vehicles were 'combed out' by interception-parties at Goloskowo and consolidated into alarm companies.

Further Movements of the 14th *Panzer Division*

Despite the difficulties of the march that had to be overcome as a result of traffic jams on the road and deteriorating mud conditions on the *Rollbahn*, the division acted, for its own part, to increase its infantry forces by 'combing out' the trains elements and *Panzer* and armoured-car crews that exceeded their legitimate number of men. Regardless of these difficulties, the division worked its way farther back toward Perwomaisk and towed vehicles with the help of the last available prime movers, at least at the most important muddy and steep stretches.

On 16 March the main body of the *Kampfgruppe* arrived in Kriwoje Osero. The train elements, however, were still waiting before the Perwomaisk bridge, some firmly established in Golta, Kameni Most and Bereski. In the meantime the units that had remained behind, for example the *Heeres-Flak-Abteilung*, which had to tow its 8.8 cm guns with the few available prime movers shuttling back and forth from one locality to the next, were still at Olshanka. It still had the difficult steep slope at Kalmasowo ahead of it.   *See Map 62.*

The Soviets had finally built bridgeheads at Gaiworon and south of Gaisin and launched several armies in a thrust to Balta and Wapnaja, therefore endangering the last effective supply line, the Lemberg – Odessa railroad. Thereby they also impacted the possibility of using the last natural obstacle before Bessarabia, defending the Dnjestr sector.   *See Maps 62, 63 and 64.*

In its continued retreat via Jasenewa and Golma the division was able, on 18 March, to replenish its shrunken stock of ammunition and petrol at the Balta railroad station, and, in addition, to supply itself from a large army ration dump. However, north of Balta there was an uncovered area of 15 kilometers to the 3rd *SS-Panzer Division 'Totenkopf'*, in action to the west.

The Soviets were aided by the fact that German aerial reconnaissance concentrated on their formations advancing to the south instead of the combat groups striving for the Dnjestr, westward past the German security screen. The leading elements crossed the river between Soroki and Mogilew. Cavalry and armoured units came within a few kilometers of the Rybniza crossing point, wherefore the division – more or less in the rear of the Soviet southern group – continued its march on the Krutije – Jershew road, also towards Rybniza. That raised the possibility of stopping these enemy forces before they reached the Dnjestr. On 20 March there was a collision with the Soviet advance detachments. Several enemy AFVs that were firing on the bridge over the Dnjestr from elevated positions on the rim were knocked out by *Tigers* of   *See Maps 62, 63, 64 and 90.*

Panzergrenadier Division 'Großdeutschland'. Small groups of riflemen from the Rumanian infantry were fended off. On 22 March the division assembled west of the river in Rezina Targ. Now it was a matter of advancing to the northwest in order, in cooperation with *Panzergrenadier Division 'Großdeutschland'* and German infantry and *Jäger* formations, to stop the enemy that was advancing southward in a broad front after crossing the river in the first blocking position in the Soldanesti – Cotiogeni Maru – Floresti – Balti line.

Transfer of the 14th *Panzer Division* to its New Area of Operations

See Map 64.

On 27 March the division undertook a greater leap back into the area directly north of Zahorna. Since, however, the Soviets were advancing from the rear of the division along the Dnjestr toward Orhei, and also outflanked and bypassed the security barrier in the west by marching south in the Rautul valley, the division had to set a new objective in order to finally intercept the penetration while it was still north of the Orhei – Jassy line. The situation seemed favoured by the presence of a series of German formations that had, in the meantime, crossed the Dnjestr and which attacked the Russians, markedly slowing the tempo of the Soviet advance. Indeed, the farther south they advanced, the stronger resistance they could expect. For the Soviets the lengthening supply route was noticeably limiting, as evidenced by the fact that they primarily employed light, mobile cavalry and infantry units with few heavy weapons in the front, while the German *Kampftruppen*, on the other hand, still had a goodly amount of their heavy equipment.

The logistical units had, in part, enjoyed rail-transport as far as Balta. Others crossed the Bug bridge and, when the Soviets penetrated Perwomaisk on 23 March, most of the vehicles had already departed to the west in an adventurous conglomeration. Numerous guns and heavy vehicles in need of repair were assembled on the south bank of the river in the Golta section of the city. Even under bombing attacks and mounting artillery fire the logistical elements still loaded supply elements on the railroad and thus gained ground.

See Map 62.

In the course of this, on 22 March, one of the last trains, loaded with 8.8 cm guns, came under heavy fire from anti-tank guns and tanks. The German anti-aircraft guns took up the fight, firing broadside from the moving train, knocking out one tank and one anti-tank gun. Only a few of the trains elements that followed via Balta, marching on foot, reached the Rybniza crossing, because, on 22 March, the Soviets severed the railroad line and *Rollbahn* between the Borschtschi railroad station and Slobodka. Two days later they also captured Woronkowo. These train elements then had to detour through mud and, at times hindered by petrol shortages, via Bersula – Ljubonirka – Stawrowo to the Dubossary bridge. Several groups took the detour via Pawlowka, but there ran into endless treks of ethnic Germans and Rumanians from the Odessa area that hindered them with the herds of cattle they had brought with them and only moved forward grudgingly. All the march groups assembled in the Orincia area on the west bank of the Dnjestr on 28/29 March. The elements that had come by rail had to swing farther to the south and cross the river between Tiraspol and Tighina. Almost all of the

ATTACK AGAINST THE LEFT WING OF THE 8TH *ARMEE*

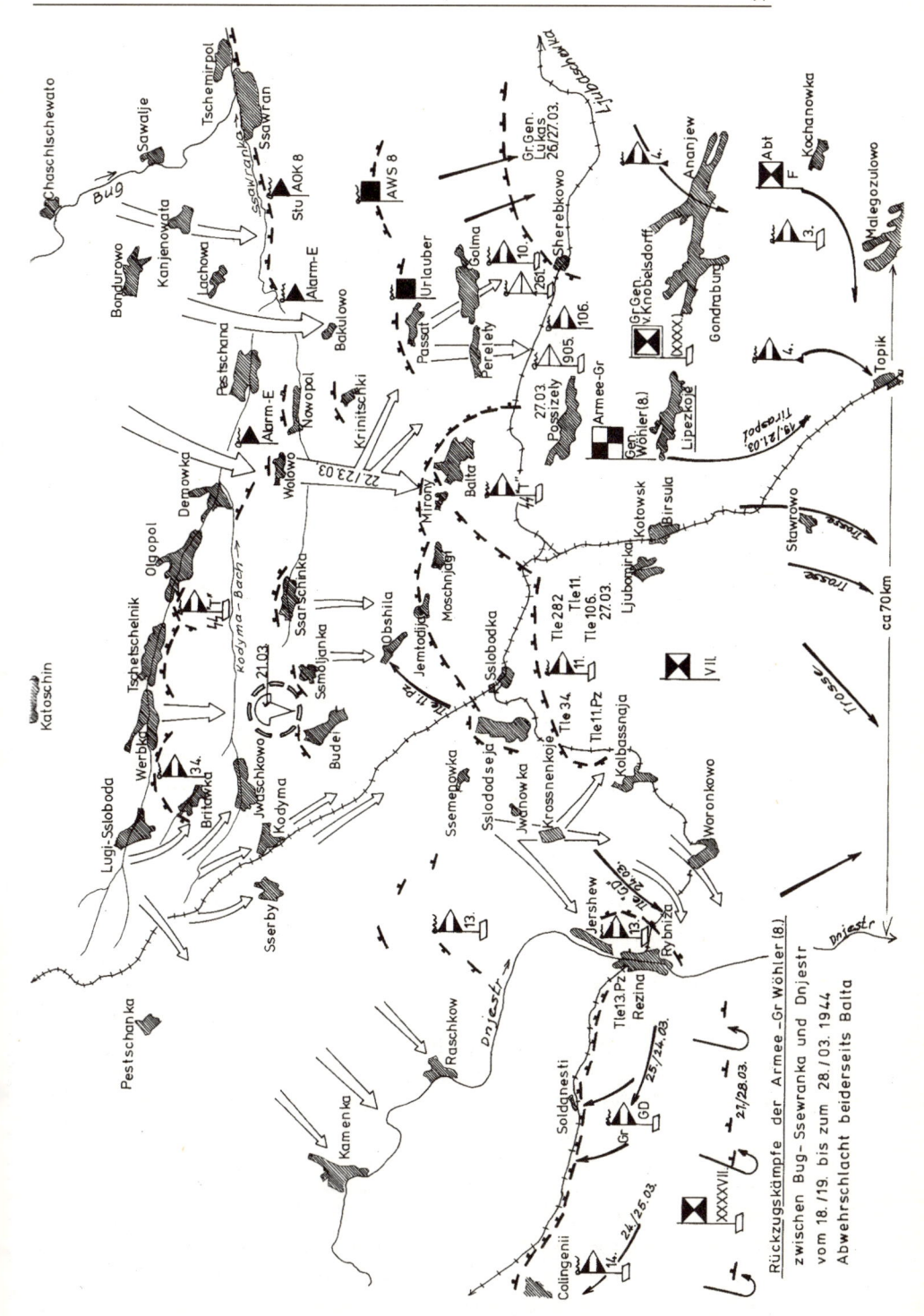

63. Fighting Retreat of *Armee-Gruppe Wöhler* (8th) between the Bug – Ssewranka and Dnjestr from 18/19 to 28 March, 1944. Defensive battle on both sides of Balta.

8.8 cm guns of the *Flak-Abteilung* were lost when a partisan group destroyed a locomotive by gunfire at the entrance to the Rasdelnaja marshalling yard.

Elements that were not fit for action marched via Hussy to Barlad and later via Vaslui to the Bacau area.

See Map 64.   The division shifted its security lines, step by step, to the south and, on 28 March, combat elements were on the hills close to Negureni and Banesdi.

Initial Fighting in the New Area of Operations

See Map 64.   On 29 March the III./ *Grenadier Regiment 36*, with a leave-battalion [*Urlauber Bataillon*], Cossack troop and infantry company of *Panzeraufklärungs Abteilung* 14 and two tanks, advanced to Mandresdi and Bacni. *Panzergrenadier Regiment* 108 advanced from Telenesdi via Mikalasa to Chiriseni and Chirova. The intention of the *Korps* to finally construct a firm defensive front led to pulling the positions back to the Cula sector.

Elements of the division, particularly the leave-battalion and *Panzergrenadier Regiment* 108, as well as *Füsilier Regiment 'Großdeutschland'* continued their attack westward from Chirowa. The mission of the division called for establishing contact with the 24th *Panzer Division* northeast of Jassy. It was not, however, possible to accomplish the mission, so the elements committed turned around in the night of 30 June/1 April and had to march back along the difficult route through the Cula valley and over the Duma – Hoginesdi hill-road, hindered by heavy snowstorms. Nevertheless they were able to drive off the enemy forces that had advanced along the south bank of the Cula stream and close the front at that location.

On 1 April, with two *Panzer* and the remaining *Sturmgeschütze*, *Panzeraufklärungs Abteilung* 14 took Chbravicea and repulsed a weak Soviet advance at Tibirica – undertaken by two wholly inadequately armed construction battalions.

See Map 64.   The commitment of *Kampfgruppen* of the 13th *Panzer Division* in the Vaprowa area finally brought relief. Together with *Gebirgsjäger* (4th *Gebirgs Division*) and *'Großdeutschland' Füsiliers*, they made it possible to build a new Moroceni – Mari – Valea Popii – Chbravicea – Meleseni – Tibirica line. At some places the Soviets had to give up land they had taken and fall back over the river with substantial losses. The German combat tactic at that time was to initially halt the Soviet advance with elastic defense by local position units and finally to throw the Soviets out with hastily assembled counterattack groups, However, the requisite stability was still lacking. The numerical inferiority could, in part, be compensated for by higher expenditure of ammunition. In that respect the loss of an effective logistical railroad line had a disastrous effect. The large supply dumps proved to have been emptied, so that the division only received a minute fraction of the requisite mass of ammunition, petrol and rations. However, transportation to the division also presented further difficulties, for the only paved road in this combat area ran on the enemy-held north bank of the Cula. The parallel road on the south bank proved to be impassable for extensive stretches and was open to Soviet observation and subject to fire from anti-tank guns for its entire length. During the nighttime hours the right wing of the division could be supplied over the direct road

ATTACK AGAINST THE LEFT WING OF THE 8TH *ARMEE*

from Orhei. Beyond that, every round, every canister of petrol, every can of rations had to be carried by lorry and *Panje* – wagon over the detour via Kishinew – Calarasi – Raciula – Frumosa to Bravica and redirected from there. The *Ju* 52 transport machines that had in earlier days landed in the front lines and brought supplies could not help at this time.

The Soviet intention of striving for a front line just east of Valea Popii with the stream-ground and the village of Saraseni was scuttled by powerful counterattacks from several *Grenadier* – and *Füsilier* – companies. A further action against the sector west of Hoginesti was smashed at the very beginning.

That made it evident that the Soviets had lost their zest for attack and had therefore chosen to wait for the arrival of armoured and artillery formations before delivering new blows. Granted, the Soviets still began with another wave of attacks. A few days of rest, however, restored the soldiers' fighting strength and provided an opportunity to organize the formations, which put them in a condition to survive the further defensive fighting until the beginning of August.

The 13th *Panzer Division*

The 13th *Panzer Division* experienced comparable action. After the Soviet attack, together with the 14th *Panzer Division,* it initially supported the left flank of the 2nd *Fallschirmjäger Division*. During the retreat numerous guns had to be blown up, as did the last 8.8 cm guns as the result of the loss of the heavy prime movers. Marching, for the most part, on foot, the *Grenadiere* reached Nowo Archangelsk, then made a forced march to Perwomaisk – Golta to screen the left flank. *Panzeraufklärungs Abteilung* 13 and *Feldersatz Bataillon* 13 had to undergo hard fighting before the Bug crossing. Next the division proceeded to the Kishinew area, where it could again organize its formations.

At that time the division was attached to the 52nd *Armee Korps* of the 6th *Armee* and had to fight defensively while *en route*. It thus undertook an attack with the 3rd *Panzer Division* to close a gap in the sector of the 320th *Infanterie Division*. After an initial rapid advance the entire line was hit by massed defensive fire that force the attack to be called off. The Soviets had brought up a great number of anti-tank guns and concealed them well in the underbrush in front of the anti-tank ditches, which resulted in 50% losses in the German armoured forces. Nevertheless. *Kampfgruppe Ehle* with the I./ 93 [*Panzergrenadier* Regiment 93, 13th *PzD*] and II./ 66 [*Panzergrenadier* Regiment 66, 13th *PzD*] gained a notable, if temporary success, in that the first named battalion took the anti-tank ditch in the first assault. Costly hand-to-hand combat ensued as the Soviets temporarily cut off the leading units, which then had to fight their way back to their jump-off positions. On the following day the I./ 93 and II./ 66 gained a firm foothold in the anti-tank ditches and rolled up the Soviet positions, one after another, with 'Hurrahs'. With *Panzeraufklärungs Abteilung* 13 and a few combat-worthy *SPW* of the I./ 66, three *Panzer* IV of the II./ *Panzer Regiment* 4 [2nd *PzD*] and four *Sturmgeschütze* of the *Sturmgeschütz* brigade of *Abteilung* 243, and after an effective *Stuka* attack, came a new advance. Repeatedly attacked by Soviet ground-attack planes, the attack formations ran under the defensive mortar and artillery fire at top speed, firing hand-held weapons and hurling hand grenades, and achieved a gratifying success. They rolled over several gun positions and brought in 600 prisoners, 15 light guns, 12 rapid-fire canon, 45 anti-tank guns, 16 mortars, 11 heavy and four light machine-guns.

Elimination of Two Soviet Bridgeheads

See Map 57.

The first item of business for *Heeresgruppe Südukraine* at the beginning of May was essentially the elimination of the Butor bridgehead. The intended surprise, however, failed. Nevertheless the 13th *Panzer Division* achieved a deep penetration into the enemy positions and, on the second day of the attack, attained the assigned objective of the attack, Serpeni on the Dnjestr. It thereby eliminated the Soviet Butor bridgehead. It then proceeded to the second Soviet bridgehead at Dubosari, where a weak *Kampfgruppe* of the 4th *Gebirgs Division* held a little bridgehead that had been compressed into a tiny area. At the time there was still a weak German bridgehead at Koschniza and at the ferry landing south of Dubosary. The attack force crossed at that point in order to reinforce *Gebirgsjäger Regiment 7*. In the course of the day the entire *Panzergrenadier Regiment 93* and the attached battalion of *Panzergrenadier Regiment 66* were put across the river with two available *VW-Schwimmwagen*, each *Schwimmwagen* with two inflatable assault boats in tow.

See Map 64 for geography.

Now the entire Dnjestr meander had to be evacuated, and something done to establish contact with the remnant of the *Gebirgsjäger* at Koshniza. The attack of units of the 14th *Panzer Division* (*Panzer Aufklärungs Abteilung* 14 and II./ 108 [*Panzergrenadier Regiment* 108, 14th *PzD*]) came to the aid of the formations here, which drove forward a corridor about one kilometer wide. After building a three-sided front – 14th *Panzer Division* with *Panzergrenadier [Regiment]* 103 [14th *PzD*]– took over the 13th *Panzer Division* front to the east, the 14th *Panzer Division* the same to the west. The enemy forces that had broken through were again compressed into the southern part. The Soviet airforce flew ceaseless missions. The Soviets employed heavy artillery to help their forces to the route of retreat.

A particularly strong sudden concentration of fire from Soviet multiple-rocket launchers during the night of 19/20 April was, apparently, the signal for the Soviet infantry to break through the German lines without firing a shot. This succeeded, but, thanks to the attention of the German security, only with heavy losses.

After evacuation of the two bridgeheads at Butor and Dubossari the Soviets desisted from further operations.

17

Soviet Attack against the Right Wing of the 8th *Armee*

Evacuation of the Area East of the Bug

For the formations committed farther south, mostly infantry divisions, the days after the successful Soviet breakthrough meant costly fighting and tremendous marches. The constant pursuit by Soviet forces that were aggressive, vastly superior and, above all, mobile because of motorization, resulted in losses in personnel and equipment. Because of their greater mobility and greater combat strength compared with the infantry divisions, the few *Panzer* divisions had the only prospect for successful resistance. The Soviets, too, however, were hindered in their movements in the early days of March as the result of rain, fog and mud, and, at times, initial successes were incompletely exploited. Their heavy weapons crews faced the same difficulties as the German artillerymen: their weapons, too, got stuck in the morass. Therefore the Soviet infantry, as a rule, went no further than the effective range of their artillery that was in position. Nevertheless, in light of the Soviet successes in the 6th *Armee* combat area and farther north with the 4th *Panzer Armee*, it became necessary to evacuate the hinterland as quickly as possible in order the provide freedom of movement for the fighting troops for mobile action.

The Situation

That also applied to the right wing of the 8th *Armee*, the Kirowograd – Kriwoi Rog combat area. The formations committed there put up stiff resistance against the Soviets. The Soviet advance in the Winniza – Uman area, however, forced the lines back, the more so since the 6th *Armee* to the right of the 8th *Armee* moved farther to the west.

See Maps 53, 58 and 88.

Of the divisions committed there, *Panzergrenadier Division 'Großdeutschland'*, with its armour and motorization, was able to put up the most substantial resistance. It, too, however, had to fall back (see below). The impression seems significant, however, that the attacking force of the Soviets in the sector of the 6th *Armee* and also the right wing of the 8th *Armee* gradually declined. In part that may be due to exhaustion of the foot-troops, but essentially it was due to the difficulties the terrain imposed on bringing up adequate logistical support. Granted, the combat troops of the Red Army had a major advantage in mobility over the German troops thanks to their outfit of all-terrain American lorries, but this advantage applied only to the combat troops, not the rear-area services. According to Soviet sources there were difficulties in the organization of the repair services as well as transport to the rear of damaged combat equipment and the provision of petrol and ammunition. The limited off-road mobility of the mobile repair shops prevented rapid repairs to the damaged tanks scattered widely over the terrain. The new combat equipment, fresh from the factories, was unloaded far from the combat areas where it was needed, resulting in delayed arrival in those areas. That particularly applied to the large number of AFVs that had to be provided as a result of the substantial losses. In 1943 the Soviets manufactured 24,000 tanks, assault guns and other AFVs (16,500 of these were medium and heavy tanks). In 1942 they had produced 24,668 AFVs, including 12,500 T 34 tanks. In addition the British provided Mark V tanks and the USA Sherman tanks. Organizational difficulties with the railroad may also have been the cause of these delays. The troops themselves had to set aside a number of AFVs to tow motor-vehicles carrying fuel or, themselves, bring up barrels of fuel and cases of ammunition, because the supply-vehicles could not make it due to miserable road conditions.

According to plans, at the start of the operation Soviet armoured formations were supposed to have 620 tanks and 189 assault guns for each tank army, with 46-48,000 men. However, as the result of losses in previous fighting, limited replacements and limited capability of the railroad, despite top priority to military transports, these numbers were not fully attained.

Consideration must also be given to the immense number of formations requiring logistical support, each with its own complement of AFVs, which were concentrated in a small area for individual aggressive operations. According to Soviet sources, the formations committed for the Shitomir – Berditschew operation were outfitted with a total of 876 AFVs (1st Ukrainian Front). The 2nd Ukrainian front had over 356 AFVs in action in the Kirowograd area. For the Korssun, Shewenkowitschi operation the 1st Ukrainian Front had over 669 AFVs. For Operation Proskurow – Tschernowitz the 1st Ukrainian Front had over 1,345 AFVs and, for the Uman – Butosany Operation the 2nd Ukrainian Front had 601 AFVs. That gives a total of 3,447 AFVs. These were numbers for the first three operations roughly at the start of the new year. The others were at about the beginning of March, 1944. The operations in the Shitmir –Berditschew area started with 900 tanks and assault guns. The operations in the Proskurow – Tschernowitz area started with about 730 tanks and assault guns, the operations in the 'second sector' with about 630 tanks and assault guns. The actual count of vehicles on hand varied continuously due the constant action of the formations and the associated continuing losses.

Such masses of AFVs, alone, – to which must be added the heavy weapons – required a substantial supply of fuel and ammunition, and of repair workshops. Rations came, in part, from captured stocks, as did fuel, but even that had to be brought forward, which, due to the miserable terrain, sometimes could not be done with wheeled vehicles, but required AFVs.

See Map 58.

The Soviet troops made slow forward progress in fighting against the 6th *Armee*, whose formations escaped every attempt to cut them off. In the south, on the right wing of the front, there were rivers whose courses ran across the direction of march, rivers which, in their lower courses, had significant breadth. For such reasons an advance against the left wing of the 8th *Armee* must have seemed far more promising of success. In its upper course the Bug completes a great bend from west to south, with the knee about at Perwomaisk,

ATTACK AGAINST THE RIGHT WING OF THE 8TH *ARMEE*   263

so that, farther north, no significant river barrier complicated the advance. The German command also recognized this, but could not bring formations into this area in timely fashion for the simple reason that they had none available. After the Soviet broke through the German line of defense in the Winniza – Uman area the German command issued retreat orders for the divisions that were farther east, in the Kirowograd area, the 10th *Panzergrenadier Division*, 282nd *Infanterie Division*, 320th *Infanterie Division*, 3rd *SS-Panzer Division 'Totenkopf'* and *Panzergrenadier Division 'Großdeutschland'*. The German command had considered withdrawing formations from this sector since mid-February. However, as long as these formations were fixed in action this intention could not be realized. There were no troops that could have taken over the positions.

In any case, there was no continuous main line of resistance, merely a series of strongpoints more symbolically designated as a line of defense. The danger of this thin manning was that the Soviets could slip through unhindered between the strongpoints into the rear area at night and in fog, and then threaten the lines from the rear. The thought occurred in one company of 3rd *SS-Panzer Division 'Totenkopf'* of filling these gaps with dogs that would be collected in the rear-area villages. Tethered in the gaps, these would simulate garrisons. However, instead of fulfilling their mission, they barked and thus betrayed to the Soviets, who quickly caught on to this trick, where there were no German garrisons. Therefore this practice had to be stopped.

Withdrawal of First Elements from the Kirowograd Area[1]

The Soviet breakthrough in the Winniza area forced the evacuation of the line of defense west of Kirowograd, in order to avoid exposing these formations to the danger of envelopment by Soviet forces. First the command strove to shift the 3rd *SS-Panzer Division 'Totenkopf'* in forced march to the Bug in order to construct a line of defense there. The withdrawal, however, ran into difficulties because the 320th *Infanterie Division* did not arrive on time to relieve *Totenkopf*, and also its sector then had to be extended around those of the 282nd *Infanterie Division* and 106th *Infanterie Division*. In addition, the sector of the 10th *Panzergrenadier Division* was to be occupied. The *Armee* pushed, since, otherwise, the construction of a line of defense at the Bug might be overtaken by events. The Soviets delayed the withdrawal of the 3rd *SS-Panzer Division 'Totenkopf'* with ongoing attacks. They did something else: They pounded the division's entire frontal sector of with extravagant artillery and multiple-rocket launcher fire, indicating a *Schwerpunkt* of their intentions.

See Maps 43, 46, 49 and 58.

With about 415 AFVs the Soviets attacked in the Gniloi – Tikitsch to Winniza – Uman area against the 2nd *Fallschirmjäger Division* and 4th *Gebirgs Division*, 198th *Infanterie Division* and 34th *Infanterie Division* of the 7th *Armee Korps*. They achieved such a rapid breakthrough here that withdrawal from the main line of resistance became pressing.

See Maps 58 and 88.

Under heavy enemy pressure, the individual elements of the 3rd *SS-Panzer Division 'Totenkopf'* withdrew from their former combat area in order to reach

---

1   3rd-*SS Panzer Division 'Totenkopf'*, 320th *Infanterie Division*, 10th *Panzergrenadier Division*, 282nd *Infanterie Division*, 106th *Infanterie Division*.

the A-Line. The Soviets put even heavier pressure on *Panzergrenadier Division 'Großdeutschland'* (see below) than they did on the 3rd *SS-Panzer Division 'Totenkopf'*. Here, too, they achieved penetrations, but their breakthrough attempt failed. Regardless of this development, the 3rd *SS-Panzer Division 'Totenkopf'* had to shift to the Nowo Ukrainka – Peschanyj – Brod area and attachment to *Armeeoberkommando* 8. The previously prepared demolition of the railroad line from Nowyj-Mirogorod to Mal-Wiski, as well as the Pleten Taschlyk railroad station could still be delayed in order to bring evacuation trains to that station.

See Map 62.
While, in the sector of the 7th *Armee Korps*, the *Kampfgruppen* of the 198th *Infanterie Division* and the 34th *Infanterie Division* were attacked from the side by enemy armour in the Gereschinowka, Grodsewo area and suffered substantial losses, the non-all-terrain vehicles of the 320th *Infanterie Division* and the tracked vehicles of the 3rd *SS-Panzer Division 'Totenkopf'* were entraining in Nowo Ukrainka and Kapustino. The command designated Balta as the goal of the movement. The railroad lines, however, did not always go in the desired direction, which meant that the trains had to cross the Bug at Perwomaisk, with an additional intermediate objective of Kriwoje Osero. The wheeled elements of the 3rd *SS-Panzer Division 'Totenkopf'* received corresponding march orders.

In the meantime the formations securing the withdrawal and evacuation repulsed heavy attacks, for example the II./ *Füsilier Regiment 'Großdeutschland'*, I. / 3rd *SS-Panzer Division 'Totenkopf'* and *Füsilier Regiment 'Großdeutschland'* east of Kwitka in the A-Line, but also the withdrawing formations of the 320th *Infanterie Division*. A Soviet advance into the artillery positions one kilometer northeast of Kwitka was sealed off by four *'Tiger'* of a *Kampfgruppe 'Totenkopf'*. In other sectors, too, the Soviets took advantage of the declining preparedness for defense due to the prevailing mood for breakout amongst the German formations to pursue closely, as at Raskobana-Grab-Nord. In the position sector of *Füsilier Regiment 'Großdeutschland'* and the I./ 3rd *SS-Panzer Division 'Totenkopf'* the German artillery and mortar fire in the enemy assembly position prevented the Soviets from deploying for further attacks.

See Map 58.
In the sector of the 320th *Infanterie Division*, too, the Soviets followed the withdrawal to the A-Line. *Grenadier Regiment* 585 [320th *Infanterie Division*], with attached *Füsilier Bataillon* 320 then relieved *Füsilier Regiment 'Großdeutschland'* with attached I./3rd *SS-Panzer Dsivision 'Totenkopf'* and II./ 3rd *SS-Panzer Division 'Totenkopf'* between Raskobana – Grab-Hügel [burial mound]-South, which then marched to Nowo Ukrainka to entrain.

See Map 62.
In the meantime *Pionier Bataillone* 56 and 666 secured the Bug crossings at Perwomaisk and Ljuschnewata, *Sturm-Bataillon AOK* 8 at Chaschtschewato. The 10th *Panzergrenadier Division* also joined onto the retreat to the west in

See Map 49.
order to support the left wing of the 47th *Panzer Korps* and also to screen the Perwomaisk crossing in the Olschanka – Dolgaja – Pristan line.

Withdrawal of *Panzergrenadier Division 'Großdeutschland'*

Panzergrenadier Division 'Großdeutschland' had been south of the combat sector of the 3rd *SS-Panzer Division 'Totenkopf'*, west of Korowograd, since the

ATTACK AGAINST THE RIGHT WING OF THE 8TH *ARMEE*

beginning of January. For a long time it had repulsed a series of Soviet attacks south and southwest of Kirowograd in cold and, at times, snowstorms. After the withdrawal of various formations and giving up the I./ *Panzer Regiment* 26[2] to the 11th *Panzer Division* in the Tscherkassy sector, in February the division went through a relatively quiet period – contact on the left to the 376th *Infanterie Division* with its own sector of the main line of resistance 16 kilometers wide.

On 7 March the Soviets in this sector exhibited aggressive intentions. On 8 March an artillery barrage with massive expenditure of ammunition opened on the entire sector of the division to a depth of almost 12 kilometers. The *Schwerpunkt* of the Soviet attack initially was not evident, until reports arrived from the southeast exit of Losowatka. At the moment the enemy artillery fire raised its impact area the first armour appeared, which immediately penetrated the artillery firing positions. The guns of the IV./ *Panzerartillerie Regiment 'Großdeutschland'* fell into enemy hands in hand-to-hand combat. Some of them were able to be blown up. The I./ *Panzerartillerie Regiment 'Großdeutschland'* also lost guns, and the grenadiers and pioneers particularly had losses due to the Soviet heavy weapons. In the fierce defensive fighting which, initially, seemed fruitless, the isolated squads of grenadiers grouped themselves around anti-tank guns, infantry guns or artillery pieces and thus built the backbone of the resistance. The intensity of the fighting died down in the evening, which provided an opportunity to collect the wounded and again concentrate the units. The Soviets penetrated deep into the German positions that day, up to five kilometers. Despite the destruction of entire companies, however, the Soviets did not achieve a breakthrough.

See Map 53.

On 9 March the Soviets continued their attack, leading to the loss of Dymio, Tscherwonyj and Nikolajewka. Hard fighting developed in Jelisawetka and Iwanowka. Again and again German formations launched hasty counterattacks in order, in isolated situations, to give the *Grenadiere* breathing space. In the end, however, the defensive battle was no longer worth while, since, after their penetration at Uman, the Soviets were advancing to the southwest, threatening to sever the supply route of the German formations fighting to the east, including *Panzergrenadier Division 'Großdeutschland'*.

See Map 58.

Under the impression of this larger situation the troops in this sector, too, were ordered to retreat to a shortened line of defense, that was initially to extend in a north-south direction roughly along the Bug. Now it became a matter of pulling out the German formations of *Heeresgruppe* A that were still east of the lower course of the Bug and at the Bug in front of the Soviet breakthrough south of Uman to the south. That, again, could only succeed if a

See Maps 57, 58 and 64.

---

2 Translator's note – According to Helmuth Spaeter in *Bd* II of his *Geschichte der Panzerkorps Großdeutschland'*. p. 431, "On 16 January the completely newly equipped and activated I./ *Abteilung/Panzer Regiment* 26, a *Panther-Abteilung*, commanded by *Major* Glaesgen, arrived in the Division area and was attached to *Panzer Regiment Großdeutschland* as a welcome reinforcement." In his *Germany's Panther Tanks*, Thomas Jentz says that the I/PzRgt. 26 was one of the additional *Abteilungen* converted to *Panther* tanks that was sent to the Eastern Front in 1944 and 1945, with a strength of 76 *Panther*. Jentz, Thomas, *Germany's Panther Tanks*, Schiffer, Atglen PA, 1995.; Helmuth Spaeter, *Die Geschichte des Panzerkorps Großdeutschland*, 3 volumes, Selbstverlag Hilfswerk ehem. Soldated für Kriegsopfer und Hinterbliebene e.V., Duisburg – Ruhrort, der Traditionsgemeinschaft Panzerkorps Grossdeutschland, 1958.

tenable front line facing north could be constructed as far forward as possible and as soon as possible. Thus it was important to bring the enemy advance to a halt farther to the west, north of Kishinew and north of Jassy.

See Map 62. On 10 March *Panzergrenadier Division 'Großdeutschland'* was already conducting a mobile fight, knocking out 43 enemy AFVs. On this day, however, the Soviets broke through into open terrain. House-to-house and street-fighting took place in the built-up areas. From the hills around Rownoje column after column of Soviets could be seen advancing to the southwest in the depths of the battlefield. This situation led the division to set all mobile combat elements in march to the west, or to the entraining station south of Rownoje, with their objective Rumania, especially damaged vehicles, workshops and the like. The combat elements received orders to withdraw into lines of defense A, B and C, the same [lines of defense that were ordered for the 3rd *SS-Panzer Division 'Totenkopf'* and other divisions, while delivering constant counterattacks]. The division prepared for its own retreat, with a crossing of the Bug at Migija, about eight kilometers southeast of Perwomaisk. Just as on the *Rollbahn* to the north, trains elements of all sorts, some in 'convoys' towed by prime-movers, toiled to the west, with herds of cows herded by *Hiwis* in between, and Ukrainian *Landespolizei* [Ukrainian local police force]. The vehicles that were not fit for driving were entrained at the Promoshnja railroad station.

See Map 61. On 12 March the rear guard reached the B-Line and, on 14 March, received orders to speed up the retreat via Petschenaja – Sacharewka, and then to go to the northwest: Gruscha, Schwtschenko, with Perwomaisk as the march objective. The division was to set up a line of defense at the Bug. However, Soviet armoured spearheads were already at Jampol on 18 March and, by their presence at that place, prevented utilization of the river barrier to build a new German line of defense.

Retreat to the Bug

The retreat came under increasing time pressure because the Soviets in the sectors between individual retreat areas advanced nearly unhindered to the west. They eagerly pursued, but in every case where they ran into German formations, they were repulsed, even though, at times, after achieving penetrations. Due to lack of time the formations no longer cleaned these up. It was far more important to gain ground to the west.

See Map 62. The Soviets attacked toward the railroad line to Perwomaisk, on which they observed the frantic movement of transports. The 3rd *SS-Panzer Division 'Totentkopf'*, alone, required 18 trains for the elements dispatched by rail from Nowo Ukrainka. The required number of trains, however, did not arrive, because the trains from Perwomaisk were immediately sent on to Balta, to the intended new area of action of the division. Individual trains initially accumulated in Kriwoje Osero. The railroad was short of rolling stock.

At that time the rear guards were already crossing the B-Line. In order to expedite their retreat, the *Luftwaffe* assisted with giant transport planes of the *'Gigant'* type from Nowo Ukrainka. The elements that were not being loaded there had to join the *Schlammschlacht* ['mud-battle'] of the *Rollbahn* traffic.

ATTACK AGAINST THE RIGHT WING OF THE 8TH *ARMEE*

On this march the units became thoroughly mixed with retreating elements of other divisions, such as those of the 320th *Infanterie Division*. This division relieved the repeatedly committed elements of the 3rd *SS-Panzer Division 'Totenkopf'* but sent its rear-area services on toward Perwomaisk in good time.

North of Golowanewsk the Soviets pressed against the 198th *Infanterie Division* which was there, and forced it back to the Krassnopolje – Grusskoje hill. The leading elements of the 11th *Panzer Division*, which was being brought up to Perwomaisk, arrived. The 13th *Panzer Divsision* proceeded via Puschkowo to screen the Ljuschnewata bridgehead.

See Maps 58 and 62.

The defense that had been built by *Korück* 558 [*Kommandant der Rückwärtiges Armee Gebiet*, Commandant of the Army Rear Area 558], however, proved from the very start to be extraordinarily scanty. At that time in the Perwomaisk bridgehead were:

See Map 62.

Elements of *Pionier Bataillon* 52
three 2-cm anti-aircraft alarm units of the 444th *Sicherungs Division*
and the II./ *Sicherungs Regiment* 571.

In the Ljuschnewata bridgehead:
Pionier-Bataillon 666 and
159 men of *Sicherungs-Bataillon* 571.

In *Sicherungsraum* [security area] Gologskowo – Koscharo:
A Rumanian construction battalion.

In *Sicherungsraum* Koschero – Dubino:
19th and 20th *Schwadron Ostreiter Regiment* 454

In *Sicherumgsabschnitt* [security sector] Dubino – Olschanka:
Pionier-Baubataillon [construction battalion] 119

In *Sicherungsabschnitt* Olschanka – Ssawran:
Pionier-Brücken [bridge] – *Bataillon* 144
Sturmboot-Kommando 905
elements *Landesschützen* [regional defense-] *Bataillon* 917 and
two 2-cm *Flak/Fla-Abteilung* 616.

In *Sicherungsabschnitt* Ssawran – Kasawtschin:
Armenisches Infanterie-Bataillon 810
II./ *Kuban* – *Kosaken-Regiment* 5.

The Soviets pressed hard against the west wing of the 8th *Armee*, where they strove for the Chaschtschewato bridge. They forced back *Fla-Abteilung* 616, which was committed in this bridgehead, so that it could not blow up the bridge. The Soviets immediately utilized this opportunity to send AFV after

See Maps 60 and 62.

AFV over the bridge. German dive-bombers scored a direct hit on the bridge at about noon.

See Maps 60 and 61.

Northwest of Gaiworon at Lugowaia the Soviets also crossed the river and pushed south to Ossitjetka, reaching Ustje at the same time. The *Armee* undertook a counterattack with *Kampfgruppe 'Bregenzen'* (fifty stragglers and 600 Rumanians). In the event, however, the counterattack was launched without the militarily worthless Rumanians, instead with a *Kampfgruppe* of the 34th *Infanterie Division* and *Armee-Waffenschule* [weapons school] 8th *Armee* to regain the line of the river at Mankowka. It reached the area south of Mankowka. The Soviets then also broke into Gubnik and Tschetwertinowka, dispersed the remnant elements of the 75th *Infanterie Division* that were there, which attempted to reach the west bank in small groups and then secured facing south at Oljaniza against enemy forces in Trostjanez and Ssewarinowka. *Grenadier Regiment* 222 [75th *Infanterie Division*] and the II./ 202 [*Füsilier Regiment* 202, 75th *Infanterie Division*] attempted to cross the Bug with makeshift means at Stepaschki and Ssemenki. In the afternoon of this day (13 March) there were no more German soldiers at the Bug from Chaschtschewato to Gubnik.

See Map 62.

This development shows how quickly the last formations east of the river had to attempt to get back over the Bug in order to avoid being cut off and, instead, to assemble on the south bank. Both the B-Line and the C-Line, and even the Bug line proved no longer tenable. The Soviets advanced too rapidly to the west, apparently in order to reach Rumanian territory as quickly as possible. They showed special interest in the railroad junction southwest and west of Balta, the march objective of the 3rd *SS-Panzer Division 'Totenkopf'* and *Panzergrenadier Division 'Großdeutschland'*.

Concentration of the Withdrawn Elements West of the Bug

See Maps 60, 62 and 63.

This retreat movement of the formations that had remained east of the Bug came under the substantial pressure of the development of the situation in the area north of the upper Bug. In this area the Soviets advanced with armour and motorized infantry along the Bondurowo – Pestchana road toward the Ssawranka – sector. At the same time they closed up with strong forces in the Berladinka sector. Aerial reconnaissance identified 500 vehicles and cavalry moving south on the Mankowka – Woitowka road. The Soviets replaced the Chaschtschewato bridge that the *'Stukas'* destroyed with a pioneer's bridge, thereby making it possible to send forward additional combat formations.

See Maps 60, 62 and 63.

In the meanwhile, the division remnants that had made their way back through the morass-like roads proved to have no significant combat effectiveness, so that even regaining the area that had been lost northeast of the upper Bug seemed to be out of the questions. Therefore the 7th *Armee Korps* resolved on building a line of defense behind the Dochna – sector Pjatkowa – Bondurowka line.

The division command of the 3rd *SS-Panzer Division 'Totenkopf'*, which had arrived in Balta, concerned itself with the arrival of the transport trains. Up to that point thirteen trains had unloaded in Balta. Others were standing in Krimoje – Osere. *SS-Sturmgeschütz Abteilung* 3 was still awaiting transport

ATTACK AGAINST THE RIGHT WING OF THE 8TH *ARMEE*

by rail in Nowo-Ukrainka. The II./ *SS-Panzergrenadier Regiment 6 'Theodor Eicke'* reached Ogopol, with march objective Katoschin in the Dochna sector with the help of the immense *'Gigant'* transport airplanes. The leading elements of the wheeled elements of the 3rd *SS-Panzer Division 'Totenkopf'* that were in land-march, along with nearly all of the rear-area services, first crossed the Bug at Perwomaisk at a time when the division command that had arrived in Balta was concerned with unloading the trains that had arrived there and with bringing up additional transport trains that were waiting in Krewojesero.

In the meantime, the march of the endless columns on the *Rollbahn* from Nowo-Ukrainka to Perwomaisk proved to be an exhausting operation. Muddy roads reduced driving to a crawl. Soviet bombers repeatedly attacked the columns. Without any German air defense the armoured Soviet *'Schlachter'* ['Butchers'] (Ilyushin II) had easy game, hunting along the *Rollbahn* and dumping their bombs on and strafing the German 'vehicle-worm', slowly creeping along below. *Balkas* [ravines] and valleys caused additional jams of hundreds of vehicles. There was no trace of unified command. In addition came a sudden snowstorm that complicated this last bit of the route to the Bug. Vehicles that were left lying as a result of engine trouble or broken axles had to be blown up. There were no means of towing or any sources for replacement parts. Precious medical material, including an operating-room vehicle and valuable workshops with complete technical outfits were lost. The 3rd *SS-Panzer Division 'Totenkopf'* suspected that it lost about 50% of its stock of supply vehicles.

The apparently bottomless mud of the *'Rollbahn'* presented the foot and horse-drawn troops with the same problems that it caused for the motor vehicles. The narrow wheels of the heavily-laden *Heeres* vehicles sank under the weight of the loads into the mud and doubled the effort required of the harnessed horses. The same was true for guns, usually drawn by six horse teams, now, in part, as during the advance in the fall of 1941, requiring twelve horse teams.

In addition was the fact that the transport or, as the case might be, march to the rear, became ever more urgent. In the area of penetration at the 302nd *Infanterie Division*, south of the Kirowograd–Nowo-Ukrainka railroad line, the Soviets advanced to Taschlyk, without, however, achieving the breakthrough to Nowo Ukrainka. This, however, was at a time when formations that were supposed to entrain at the Nowo Ukrainka railroad station were still waiting there for their transport. A railroad accident northeast of Perwomaisk had temporarily put that stretch of track out of service, so that the departure of the trains, some of which were already loaded, was put off for nearly 24 more hours.

See Map 58.

Evaluation of the Situation

See Map 56.

In light of this situation one could only hope that the Soviets suffered from the same supply difficulties as the German formations. Even though their troops at the front drove forward with all-terrain vehicles and tracked vehicles to achieve success through mobility and surprise, one hoped it was without sufficient forces available to undertake an orderly attack. In any case, the German command still suspected that the Soviets who had broken through here would turn to the southeast in order, in cooperation with the forces advancing in the breakthrough-gap at the 6th *Armee*, to Wosnessensk, to cut off the 8th *Armee*. Accordingly, as a precautionary measure, the command concerned itself with securing the Bug crossings while the 40th *Panzer Korps* and '*Gruppe von Horn*' occupied the C-Line on the hills west of Gruskaja, east of Nowo Ukrainka, west of Pleten-Taschlyk, south of the Glodassy – Scochoj – Taschlyk sector. As suspected, after regrouping their forces, the Soviets attempted to break through from the Plethen Taschlyk area to Nowo Ukrainka.

See Map 62.

At this time there was no prospect of the columns getting through the mud east of Perwomaisk. Individual prim movers that had been brought in worked to gradually tow, one by one, vehicles stuck in stretches of bottomless mud or up steep slopes. A massive jam of vehicles developed. Individual columns turned aside to Migija, in order to use another bridge location. Formations of the 14th *Panzer Division* came to the marching columns as the road conditions continued to worsen. The rain continued, which left no hope for improvement of conditions for the marching columns.

Further Evacuation East of the Bug

The rail transport to evacuate the formations that were east of the Bug did not materialize in the desired sequence and rapidity, because the Rumanian rail service blocked the lines with their own evacuation transports. Therefore the *Heeresgruppe* command demanded that the railroad immediately be placed under German command. On 15 March elements of the 3rd *SS-Panzer Division 'Totenkopf'* were still waiting in Nowo Ukrainka for the last trains to move out toward Perwomaisk after restoration of that stretch of rails.

See Maps 58 and 62.

The condition of the roads as the result of rain mixed with snow and also of rain, itself, led repeatedly to decisions no longer to use byways, because these appeared to be even more bottomless than the '*Rollbahn*' and, instead of using the byways, to stay on the *Rollbahn* under constant aerial attack on that muddy way. Individual march elements were redirected to the Ssinjuchin – Brod bridge crossing. There they ran into columns coming from the north, especially those of the 14th *Panzer Division*. Since rumour had it that the Soviets were already at Olschanka, the march columns continued toward Dolgaja – Pristan, until a messenger called them back, again to march for Perwomaisk.

See Map 62.

The Soviets then grouped their formations to thrust on to Perwomaisk. The 376th *Infanterie Division* held the Olschanka bridgehead. In the Ssinjucha – Bug triangle the Soviets advanced to the southeast with strong forces and forced the 2nd *Fallschirmjäger Division* back. Elements of the 10th *Panzergrenadier Division* had to stand ready for commitment to intercept the developing enemy advance on Bogopol (western section of the city of Perwomaisk, north of the Bug). *Kampfgruppe Wartenberg* (11th *Panzer Division*) blocked northwest of Perwomaisk with elements of *Pionier Bataillone 52*. In the meantime the withdrawal movement of *Gruppe 'von Horn'* (376th *Infanterie Division*, 2nd *Fallschirmjäger Division*, *Kampfgruppe* 4th *Gebirgs Division*, 198th *Infanterie Division*) was completed more quickly than planned. *Gruppe 'von Horn'* fell

ATTACK AGAINST THE RIGHT WING OF THE 8TH *ARMEE*

back to the Ossjanka – Rokoschna line. The 4th *Gebirgs Division* fought its way out of a double envelopment to the south to the Odai – Rasdol line. *Panzeraufklärungs Abteilung* 13 on the left fell back to the Moldowka – Delfinowka line. *Gruppe 'von Horn'* was then to hold the Ljuschnewata bridgehead position until elements of the 10th *Panzer Division* arrived to take over the defensive sector on the south bank at Goloskowo.

Above all else, the 14th *Panzer Division,* which had advanced via Nowo-Archangelsk to Tischkowka, finally Dobrjanka to Olshanka, in order from there to initially be thrown in to the west toward Moldowka, was committed against the Soviet advance from the north toward Perwomaisk. Here, starting immediately without completely assembling the march groups the division set out toward the Goloskowo bridge over the Bug. The division was supposed to prevent the advance via the Ljushnewata bridgehead toward Boloskowo. Before it got that far, however, the division received orders to march back over the Ssiniucha to Olshanka and Ssinjuchin-Brod, presumably because at Goloskowo, an 'interception-commando' was collecting the crews of dispersed individual vehicles to form alarm companies. The troops did not want to be exposed to that possibility. Therefore the division went on toward Perwomaisk with the intention of getting to Balta via Kriwoje-Osero. *See Map 62.*

During these movements the division command of the 14th *Panzer Division* attempted, in any case, to consolidate the available remnants into a battalion-strength formation, this while, likewise, forming an alarm company from members of the trains elements and surplus *Panzer* and armoured-car crews, with a remnant outfit that was still combat-capable of two *Sturmgeschütze*, one command tank and one *SPW*. The strong rain, however, softened the roads so greatly that the division with its main body initially was stuck at the exit of Perwomaisk and then concerned itself with gradually dragging the vehicles through the worst muddy stretches with the remaining prime movers. The higher command pushed for expediting the march movement to the west toward Balta and Wapnaja. On 18 March the leading elements of the march reached the Balta railroad station, where they were able to replenish their shrunken supplies of ammunition and fuel, and also rations. *See Maps 61 and 62.*

In the 47th *Panzer Korps* sector, elements of the 3rd *Panzer Division* extended the German bridgehead at Ssawran to the northeast to the general line Sawalja – Kamjenowata – Lachowa. *Radfahr Straßenbau Pionier Bataillon* 507[3] repulsed enemy attacks against Baibusowka. *See Map 62.*

Especially the formations east of the Bug that formed the rear guard achieved defensive successes. These provided another opportunity for formations east of the Bug, in both the 6th and 8th *Armee,,* to cross the river. Reconnaissance, however, reported that the Soviets were concentrating their formations on the north bank of the Ssawranka, therefore farther to the north. In any case, the Soviet advance, here, appeared to be stopped, at least for the time being.

---

3   Translator's note – Bicycle Road Construction Pioneer Battalion 507. Yes, that does mean a road-construction pioneer battalion riding bicycles! Could there be a better commentary on the state of the German war economy?!

18

Soviet Advance into the Vacant Area Between the 8th *Armee Korps* and 1st *Panzer Korps*

See Maps 59, 60 and 61.

The 47th *Panzer Korps* intended to close the gap between the 8th *Armee* and the 1st *Panzer Armee*, farther to the north, where, among others, the 75th and 82nd *Infanterie Division* had been split off to the north. In this entire intervening space there was no organized resistance. The Soviets took advantage of this situation to drive strong formations forward to the west. According to the results of German reconnaissance, a Soviet troop concentration was brewing in the Gaisoron – Dshulinski area, which would result in additional pressure to the southwest. Anyhow, there were eight military bridges, alone, in construction over the upper Dnjestr, along with twelve river crossings that were already in use. The elements of the individual divisions that were assembling southwest of the Bug therefore received appropriate missions, as, for elements of the 10th *Panzergrenadier Division* and *Kampfgruppe Wartenberg* (11th *Panzer Division*) to intercept a developing enemy thrust aimed at Bogopol. However, precautionary measures also had to be taken in the Perwomaisk area against the Soviet advance from north to south. Elements of *Pionier Bataillon* 52 of the Perwomaisk *Kampfkommandant* [Perwomaisk city commandant given special powers and duties for the battle. Note, below, that Perwomaisk was elevated to the status of '*Fester Platz*', thereby requiring a *Kampfkommandant*.] were therefore to block along the Orljanskije – Tschaussowo line. From Podtschorje upstream, nearly everywhere, the Soviets were already at the Bug. The Tokarowka bridge had been destroyed by the direct hit of a bomb. The Ljuschnewata bridge suffered the same fate on 17 March after *Panzeraufklärungs Abteilung* 3 and the 4th *Gebirgs Division* had already evacuated the bridgehead. While *Gruppe 'von Horn'* with the main body of the 10th *Panzergrenadier Division*, *Kampfgruppe* 4th *Gebirgs Division* and the 198th *Infanterie Division* took over securing the Bug as far as Dubinowo, the Soviets occupied the entire north bank of the river opposite Goloskowo to Ssawran.

See Maps 62 and 63.

The Soviets made further use of the gap between the left wing of the 8th *Armee* and the right wing of the 1st *Panzer Armee*. There were no significant obstacles facing the Soviets in this area. The next significant barrier facing the Soviets was the Bug, for which reason the elements of individual German divisions gathering southwest of the upper course of the Bug, running from the northwest to the southeast, received appropriate orders, as did the formations of the 3rd *SS-Panzer Division 'Totenkopf'* that were arriving to detrain in the Balta railroad station. Immediately on detraining they were to move out against the Soviet spearheads and build a bridgehead at Pestschana. The shortage of infantry was to be ameliorated with a *'Urlauberregiment Balta'* [Leave-Regiment Balta] activated by the *Kommandant* of the *Armee* – *Waffenschule AOK* 8th *Armee* from leave-men of the 8th *Armee* arriving from Transnistrien [part of Moldavia east of the Dnjestr]. Elements of the 10th *Panzergrenadier Division* and *Kampfgruppe Wartenberg* of the 11th *Panzer Division* were ordered to intercept a developing enemy thrust to Burgopol.

Perwomaisk was declared a *Fester Platz'* and attributed significance of a knee in the projected German line of defense. From Perwomaisk it would no longer run to the north, but would follow the course of the Bug to the northwest, finally turning to the west.

The 11th *Panzer Division* occupied Perwomaisk in the face of the Soviet pressure on the Bug position from the east. In the meantime the 2nd *Fallschirmjäger Division* moved toward Welikaja – Mtschetna, *Panzeraufklärungs Abteilung* 13 on the left moved to Ljuschnewata and, farther left, the 3rd *Panzer Division* to the Bug front at Tschemirpol. The 3rd *SS-Panzer Division 'Totenkopf'*, as well as the 14th *Panzer Division*, along with *Panzergrenadier Division 'Großdeutschland'* and the 24th *Panzer Division*, which were approaching in transport, all had orders to transfer into the area farther to the left. The Soviets could advance from there to the south without having to cross rivers and with more favorable railroads and roads running in the direction their advance. In addition, a later advance to and into Bessarabia could cut the German formations there off from their rear connections.

See Map 62.

Despite complicated logistical support on the German side as the result of extended railway connections via Budapest, through Siebenbürgen and Bukarest, or through Slovakia, all sorts of logistical support, especially weapons, arrived, so that the formations, also including *Panzergrenadier Division 'Großdeutschland'*, could extensively make good their losses in heavy weapons. For the *Panzer* division the arrival of fuel was particularly important. That was evidenced by the fact that, on the road, a *'Panzer IV'* required 300 liters of petrol, a *'Panther'* 365 liters, a *'Tiger'* 782 liters. On the terrain these amounts doubled, and in mud, tripled. The Soviets were better off in this regard. The T 34 required only 180 liters on the road, the JS II 210 liters, with similar increases in consumption on the terrain, particularly in mud.

The Soviets now started their advance to the south from the Kusmin – Jampol bridgehead with strong infantry formations and, shortly thereafter, reached the Rybniza – Balta railroad line west of the Dnjestr at Hartrop – Floresti and Alexandreni–Tg. The 14th *Panzer Division* was ordered, regardless of the difficult terrain conditions, to advance north against the Poiana – Unicheste – Hartrop line in order to prevent further enemy impace on the railroad line. Logistical support of the German formations caused difficulties in this combat situation. Lack of lorried-column space and totally inadequate aerial supply resulted in a logistical bottleneck. In addition, behind the Bug and the Dnjestr there had been no precautionary establishment in preceding years of supply dumps. The Rumanians had carried away the existing stocks of rations.

See Maps 61, 64 and 65.

The Situation Between the Bug and Ssawranka

It is not clear from the records available how far the Soviet advance had gone at that time in conjunction with the advance southwest of Tschepetowka against the front of the 1st *Panzer Armee*. Should it dissipate the German forces or should it turn against the left flank of the 8th *Armee*? Or should they finally prepare the destructive encirclement of the 8th *Armee* and 6th *Armee* that the Soviets had striven so long for? The strong concentration of troops against the left wing of the 8th *Armee* argues for the last choice.

See Maps 59, 62 and 64.

The Soviets advanced toward Balta from both north and south, as also from the east via Perwomaisk to the west. This last pressure from the east to the west after crossing the Bug at Perwomaisk, and also over a newly erected bridge at Dolgaja-Pirstan, served the purpose of supporting the advance from north to south toward Balta, where there was a lack of adequate German formations.

See Map 63.

The Soviets also used a gap in the front west of Demowka to advance to the south. The attempt to narrow this gap in the front during the night of 20/21 March failed. On both sides of Olgopol the Soviets increased their commitment of artillery against *SS-Panzergrenadier Regiment* 6 'Theodor Eicke'. The limited combat strength of the companies made it impossible to prevent the Soviets from breaking into the security lines along the south bank of the Ssawranka at several places.

See Maps 62 and 63.

On 22 March reconnaissance reported Soviet preparations for an attack between Tokarowka and Ssawran from north to south. The attack that started on 22 March against the front of the 7th *Armee Korps* intensified the situation for this *Korps* within a few hours. The Soviets reinforced their commitment with artillery that they had brought up in the meantime, as well as by involving their air force. *Feld Ersatz Batillon* 13 and *Panzergrenadier Regiment* 110 [11th *Panzer Division*] initially intercepted the enemy thrust toward Balta, occupying security positions northwest of Krinitschki, *Panzergrenadier Regiment* 110 southeast of Krinitschki.

Defense Facing North between the Bug and Dnjestr

See Map 63.

Knowing the weakness of the German left wing, the Soviets turned the left wing of the 34th *Infanterie Division* with their 41st Guards Rifle Division via Lugi-Ssloboda and broke into Britawka and Owaschkowo. They thereby cut the supply road of the 34th *Infanterie Division* and linked up with the partisan group at Kodyma.

A *Kampfgruppe* of the 34th *Infanterie Division* ('Hochbaum') was engaged in defensive fighting on both sides of Werbka against numerically far superior enemy forces. They were threatened, just as were the security forces of *ArKo* 124 [*Artillery Kommandeur* 124, the *Korps* artillery commander] that were committed on the extreme left wing of the *Korps*, both by the Red Army and by the partisan bands operating behind the front. Such a partisan group fell on a supply stretch of the 34th *Infanterie Division* between Werbka and Kodyma. A 200 man-strong partisan band, in German uniforms, no less, launched a surprise attack on the Kodyma strongpoint and forced its way into

SOVIET ADVANCE INTO THE VACANT AREA

the northern part of the town. They threw the German security forces in the town out to the southeast. The same happened to the Sserby outer guard.

In support of this advance the Soviets also came from the east, namely from the bridgeheads they had gained on the Bug between Tschaussowo and Ljuschnewata west of Perwomaisk, advancing toward the west, but, from there on, also to the south, apparently to roll up the Bug front as far as Perwomaisk. *See Map 62.*

For the first time a *Kampfgruppe* of the 11th *Panzer Division* set out to clean up the penetration at Mirony, and, similarly, southwest of Moshnjagi. A *Panzergruppe* of the 11th *Panzer Division*, with elements of the 282nd *Infanterie Division*, launched a counterattack from the woods north of Sslobodka against Obshila and forced the Soviets back to the north bank of the Kodyma stream. *See Map 63.*

On 21 March the Soviets dropped paratroopers northwest of Smoljanka (combat elements of the 6th Guards Airborne Division) with the mission of reinforcing the partisan bands and, among others, to capture the Smoljanka strong point.

'Kampfgruppe Rose' (ArKo 124) was forced to fall back to the southwest. These elements were attached to the 11th *Panzer Division* to support the west wing of the 7th *Armee Korps* to prevent a Soviet breakthrough between Ssawranka and Dnjestr in a southeastward directions. Elements of the 282nd *Infanterie Division* that had been freed up at Perwomaisk were brought in by air. The II./ *Panzergrenadier Regiment* 66 was brought in from the assembly area of the 13th *Panzer Division* at Ssarashinka. These occupied positions in the Budei – Smoljanka area. Additional elements of the 11th *Panzer Division* were to transfer from the Sslobodka area to the Abamelekowo railroad station area to block the path of the Soviets advancing along the Kodyma – Sslobodka railroad line. *See Map 63.*

To the left of the 3rd *SS-Panzer Division 'Totenkopf'* was a *Kampfgruppe* of the 34th *Infanterie Division*. Several enemy reconnaissance attempts foundered on it. The command diverted the 376th *Infanterie Division*, which had been intended for commitment northwest of Balta in the Golma – Passat area, in order to employ it against the new enemy bridgeheads. In the Ssabotinowka – Tschernipol area the 376th *Infanterie Division* broke into the Soviet preparations to cross the Bug. The 47th *Panzer Korps* received orders to take over the sector to the line Balta (inclusive) – Demowka (inclusive) and relieve the elements of the 7th *Armee Korps* that were committed there ('Kampfgruppe Lukas', Panzergrenadier Regiment 110, Feldersatz Bataillon 13, elements of the 3rd *SS-Panzer Division 'Totenkopf'* – including *SS-Panzerpionier Bataillon* 3 and the III./ 'Totenkopf'). However, the Korps had to be sparing with its forces in order to be able to hinder the enemy from gaining further footholds on the south bank of the Bug.

'Kampfgruppe Lukas' took Rakulowo by surprise, capturing numerous enemy weapons. In the Krinitschki area the Soviets continued their attack southeast against the security front of *Panzergrenadier Regiment* 110, also shoving farther to the south in the Schljachowo penetration area. The poorly equipped *'Urlauber Regiment'*, 322 of whose men had to remain in Balta without weapons, went into action northeast of Passat. *See Map 63.*

Two Soviet regiments broke out of the Wolowa area, hoarsely shouting 'Ooray'. They advanced south and broke through the German security on both sides of Nowopol. They then linked up with the forces advancing via Schljachowo to Krishowlin. They then attacked from Krinitschki and Krishowlin to the southwest and west, penetrating the lines of *Feldersatz Bataillon* 13 and *Panzergrenadier Regiment* 110 at several places. That evening, however, the Soviets were halted 500 meters south of Wolowa, thereby sealing off the penetration area in makeshift fashion. Between *Feldersatz Bataillon* 13 and *Panzergrenadier Regiment* 110 a four kilometer wide gap yawned in the right wing, which a battalion arriving by rail was supposed to fill.

See Map 65.

In the ensuing days the situation continued to develop until there was fighting around Balta – always with the Soviets advancing over the line of defense that ran nearly east – west. Again and again individual localities had to be recaptured and Soviet spearheads beaten back. Despite the German inferiority to the Soviets in manpower and weapons, the Soviets were unable to break through. Locally there was considerable back and forth, and confusion – especially at night. One time the Soviets attacked in hand-to-hand combat, at which they were very good. Shortly thereafter they ran off as quickly as their legs could carry them. The Soviet 'Ooray', that they screamed in their attack, was muffled in the 'Hurrah' of the attacking German formations. In the darkness this shout helped in orientation as to who was friend, who foe. The pressure of the Soviet infantry, mixed with partisans who were familiar with the terrain, increased constantly. The Soviets followed hard on the heels of the at-times leaderless German battalions as they fell back after suffering losses. The steadily dwindling strength of the German formations made it undeniably clearer from one day to the next that the security lines would have to be pulled back father to the south. It was difficult for the high command to gain a clear picture of the situation in this fighting, since each sector of the front was involved in independent, eventful combat, generally against greatly superior forces with poor logistical support of the German troops.

In any case, *Armeeoberkommando* 8 reported that, in light of the enemy *Schwerpunkt* formation and the steadily declining combat strength and lack of heavy weapons, as well as lack of adequate supply for the German formations, it could no longer guarantee secure holding of the line of defense between the Bug and Dnjestr as well as along the course of the upper Dnjestr – a line whose existence was more theoretical than actual. Respecting the looming danger on the left wing, especially the Soviet breakthrough farther north through the lines of the 1st *Panzer Armee* between Zbrucz and Sereth, with Kamenez – Polosk and Hotin as objectives and with an additional assault wedge toward Tschernowitz – the command had to accept the risk to the right wing of the *Armee* and, as soon as possible, bring the last formations over the Bug and send them on toward the Dnjestr and then onward over the Dnjestr and to the west.

The Situation

See Maps 62 and 63.

On 24 March the situation between the Bug and Dnjestr markedly worsened. The Soviets attacked on a broad front northeast, north and northwest of Balta with nine rifle divisions and one armoured formation. Several enemy reconnaissance forays also foundered during the night of 23/24 March on the left hand of the *Kampfgruppe* 34th *Infanterie-Division* that was committed by the 3rd *SS-Panzer Division 'Totenkopf'*. The Soviets broke through the security of the 282nd *Infanterie Division* between Stremba and Abamelekowo railroad station. Similarly, they also reached the Ssobodka – Kodyma railroad line. After breaking through weak Rumanian security (5th *Sicherungs Division*) the Soviets advanced toward Rybniza and entered Jershew with armour. However, the Soviets also constantly introduced fresh forces into the area of the penetration on the left wing of the 3rd *SS-Panzer Division 'Totenkopf'*. The *Kampfkommandant* of Balta attempted to construct a defensive front in the line Bensari-hills northeast and north of Balta with *Panzergrenadier Regiment* 110, *Urlauber-Rückkehr* [returning leave men]-*Regiment 'Balta'*, *Feldersatz Batillon* 13 and the 3rd *SS-Panzer Division 'Totenkopf'*. Elements of the 3rd *SS-Panzer Division 'Totenkopf'* were cut off north of Balta. The division commander broke through to the south with these elements.

During the retreat from the Bug line from Ssawran and farther south, the Soviets followed hard on the heels of the German troops, repeatedly attacking into the retreat movement.

Penetration near Perelety
East of Balta the Soviets advanced with strong forces against the Perelety railroad station grounds and crossed the tracks toward the south with 500 men, two T 34 tanks, anti-tank guns and mortars, thereby crippling rail traffic between the Sherebkowo railroad station and Balta. East of Sherebkowo six railroad trains were still standing on the rails waiting to continue their journey to Balta, including a hospital train with 600 wounded, a train with the entire communications park of the 8th *Armee* and a transport with the remaining elements of the I. *SS-Panzergrenadier Regiment* 5 *'Thule'*. Suddenly a German armoured train (*Panzerzug* 70) appeared, armed with 7.5 cm guns, 3.7 cm anti-aircraft guns and machine guns. The *Kommandant* of the train believed that he would be able to assist at least the hospital train full of wounded to continue its journey. About 300 meters from the railroad station the locomotive took a direct hit from an anti-tank gun but was still able to move the train back.

See Map 63.

The railroad line through Perelety had to be fought clear again from Sherebkowo. *Grenadier Regiment* 849 of the 282nd *Infanterie Division* was available for that from Sherebkowo, along with the II./ *Grenadier Regiment* 239 of the 106th *Infanterie Division*. The *Kommandant* of Sherebkowo (commander of the 12th Batterie of *Artillerie Regiment* 107 [106th *Infanterie Division*]) received orders to work his way east with a *Kampfgruppe* from Balta toward *Grenadier Regiment* 849 [282nd *Infanterie Division*], coming from the opposite direction. In the meantime, intense house and street fighting was already taking place in Balta, so that the infantry of *SS-Panzergrenadier Regiment* 5 *'Thule'* was unable to take part in the Perelety operation.

Above all, west of Balta the Soviets thrust hard to the south toward the Borsztschi rail triangle southeast of Woliadinka and attempted to gain the Dnjestr crossings west of the Sslobodka – Rybniza railroad line. East of Rybniza, too, the Soviets were already feeling their way forward to the Andrejewka –

See Maps 62 and 64.

Rybniza rail line. Only a few of the divisions of the 47th *Armee Korps* that were fighting west of the Bug reached the Rybniza crossing over the Dnjestr. The others had to set out on the detour to Dubossary.

See Map 63.

The Soviets extended their penetration east of Balta via Perelety. The Soviet 16th and 3rd Tank Corp stood there with the infantry of the Soviet 52nd Army following them to launch the breakthrough in the Jassy area. Two Soviet tank armies seemed intended for the further thrust to the west.

As *Gruppe 'Scheffel'* held the Ananjew sector, at Kapustjanka. *Kampfgruppe 'Lukas'* was to the west as far as Golma (east of Perelety), into which the Soviets penetrated with armour. The II./ *Grenadier Regiment* 239 [106th *Infanterie Division*] and *Grenadier Regiment* 949 [359th *Infanterie Division*] came under the command of the 10th *Panzergrenadier Division*. On 27 March a new counterattack of *Grenadier Regiment* 849 [282nd *Infanterie Division*] started from Sherebkowo against the Soviet forces that had gotten into the Perelety train station to cleanse the railroad southeast of Balta. The attack made only slow progress, held up especially in the woods east of the railroad station. According to reports from fliers, the Soviets reinforced their forces around the station, itself. The 3rd *SS-Panzer Division 'Totenkopf'* set out from the southern part of Balta and from the Balta train station to the east, toward *Grenadier Regiment* 849 and the II./*Grenadier Regiment* 239 coming from the opposite direction. An armoured *Gruppe* of *'Tiger'*, SPW and *'Hummeln'* [15 cm *Panzerhaubitze* 18 (M) on *PzKpfw* III/IV chassis, *'Hummel'* (Sd. Kfz. 165.) 15 cm self-propelled gun.] of the I./*SS-Panzeraufklärungs Abteilung* 3 and two *Panzer* IV of only limited combat capability (with damaged final drives and little fuel) supported the operation. The *Grenadiere* stormed up the slope and captured a Soviet 7.65 cm battery with the help of which they beat back a subsequent Soviet hasty counterattack. In the meantime the Soviets advanced west of the Perelety railroad station and fell upon an artillery *Abteilung* of the 106th *Infanterie Division* at Pssizely, also occupying the town. However, they had to fall back again before the counterattack of *Grenadier Regiment* 240 in the evening.

See Map 63.

West of Balta the III./ *SS-Panzergrenadier Regiment* 5 *'Thule'* advanced south of Jewtodija. Other elements held the railroad knee northeast of the Balta station. Balta itself was in enemy hands. The Soviets shoved additional forces through the Sslobodsejy – Dnjestr gap in the front, especially into the Iwanowka area. Elements of the 11th *Panzer Division* narrowed the penetration area by attacking from Sslobodseja to the southwest. After hard fighting they took Kolbassnaja at the Woljadinka – Rybniza rail stretch, as well as Domniza. Southwest of Kolbassnaja, however, there were already strong enemy forces. The 13th *Panzer Division* attacked from Rybniza toward Krassnenkoje, but their attack did not break through. Therefore the *Kampfgruppe* fell back to Michailowko. With their continued advance the Soviets cut off the retreat route through Rybniza for the elements of the 8th *Armee* that were still east of the Dnjestr. Therefore the 11th *Panzer Division* was assigned the mission, on the following day, to break through to Woronkowo with an armoured group, bringing along the elements that had been relieved by the 34th *Infanterie Division* and establish contact with the Rybniza bridgehead garrison. That happened at a time when the Soviets cut off the German 1rst *Panzer Armee* farther to the north (*Hube-Kessel*).

On 28 March, supported by two *Sturmgeschütze* and two self-propelled guns of *SS-Sturmgeschütz Abteilung* 3, elements of the 3rd *SS-Panzer Division 'Totenkopf'* attempted, yet again, starting from near Balta, to advance via the Perelety railroad station to the south to Possizely in order to take the enemy in the flank. They reached the general line railroad-knee three kilometers northeast of the Balta railroad station – Kodyma (south bank) to the east exit of Balta and broke through to Possizely with two self-propelled guns, established contact with the security of *Grenadier Regiment* 849 – without, however, freeing up the railroad line.

19

Defense toward the Northeast and East

Fighting in the Area Between the Dnjestr and Pruth

See Maps 62 and 63. According to the situation evaluation of *Gruppe von Knobelsdorf*, on 26 March there was no longer a continuous defensive front, merely four independently fighting sections with locally uncovered intervening spaces of 15 to 20 kilometers. The 106th *Infanterie Division* was to attempt to close the 'hole' between Sslobedseja and Rybniza and to hold a bridgehead there. The elements of the 10th *Panzergrenadier Division* that were *en route* were to close the gap east of Balta and, on 27 March, fight free the railroad west of the Perelety railroad station. Bringing up additional elements of troops caused difficulties, as did the fact that the elements of the 376th *Infanterie Division* that were fit for action could, at most, achieve only 20 kilometers march per day due to the condition of the terrain and the ground, and the state of exhaustion of man and horse. The roads east of Ljubaschewka via Sherebkowo to Ananjew were filled with jams of slowly moving motor vehicles and numerous horse-drawn columns. Von Knobelsdorff considered that there was no chance of fighting free the Ljubaschewka – Rybniza railroad line.

See Maps 63 and 66. The Soviets gained a foothold in the northern part of Kriwoje Osero through the many gaps they had broken through the German line of defense. South of Kriwoje Osero the 14th *Panzer Division* regained terrain formerly held by the enemy. In the sector of the 10th *Panzergrenadier Division* on both sides of Jassinewo I and II, two Soviet regiments forced their way into Sherebkowo from the Golma area to the northwest. They were thrown out in resolute counterattacks and went back into the wooded terrain north of the town. Security forces of *Grenadier Regiment* 20 of the 10th *Panzergrenadier Division* moved into the gap in the front to the west, north of Ossipowka, That same day the gap between Ossipowka and the right wing of *Grenadier Regiment* 849 of the 282nd *Infanterie Division* north of Strutinka was closed.

In the meantime a new gap opened from Gonorata to the right wing of the 34th *Infanterie Division* at Jurkowka North. The 34th *Infanterie Division* repulsed several enemy attacks in the position it had taken during the night from Jurkowka to Kolbassnaja. The 11th *Panzer Division* counterattack launched from Kolbassnaja narrowed the area of the enemy penetration and reached the area two kilometers east of Woronkowo. A link-up with the garrison of the bridgehead southeast of Rybniza got no further than establishing visual contact with the elements of the 13th *Panzer Division* advancing from the bridgehead.

Evacuation of the Balta railroad station ran into difficulties when, during the work of loading the trains, the Soviets attacked and knocked out

DEFENSE TOWARD THE NORTHEAST AND EAST 281

a locomotive, which resulted in losses of weapons and vehicles. The 47th *Panzer Korps* finally gave up its plans of regaining the bend in the Bug and of cleansing the area northwest of Rybniza and of pushing security forces north to the Dnjestr. There was a lack of formations fit for action that could counter the Soviet advance. Granted, elements of the 13th *Panzer Division* and the first *Kampfgruppe* of *Panzergrenadier Division 'Großdeutschland'* arrived in Rybniza to provide support. These were immediately committed to regain the Botschoi – Molokisch sector. On the left wing of the 47th *Panzer Korps* the 14th *Panzer Division* was engaged in fighting around Unichesti, and elements of *Panzergrenadier Division 'Großdeutschland'* south of Hartrop – Guara – Camenca.

On 29 March elements of the III./ SS-*Panzergrenadier Regiment* 5 *'Thule'* were still fighting their way back in bitter fighting in the Kutowsk – Birsula area south of Possizely, with two *Sturmgeschütze* and two self-propelled guns. During the preparations for closing the gap in the front between the 106th *Infanterie Division* and the 11th *Panzer Division* the Soviet air force repeatedly attacked the Dnjestr bridge at Dubossary. The Rumanian anti-aircraft withdrew so that German anti-aircraft forces had to move in to protect the bridge from further aerial attack and keep it in service. During the night of 29/30 March the Rybniza railroad bridge was destroyed and the bridgehead east of the river was evacuated.

See Map 63.

In the meantime, on 31 March the forces marching to the rear east of the Bug were already in the C-Line. *Gruppe von Knobelsdorff* prevented an enemy penetration between the Birsula – Rasdelnaja railroad line and the Dnjestr to Grigoriopol – Dubossary, in order, with the help of the formations to be sent from the 6th *Armee* (*Korps-Abteilung* F, *Kampfgruppe* 46th *Infanterie Division*, *Kampfgruppe* 3rd *Panzer Division*) as well as the 10th *Panzergrenadier Division*), to attack the east flank of the enemy advancing south to Dubossary. *Korps-Abteilung* F reached the Walegozulowo area in the evening. *Kampfgruppe* 46th *Infanterie Division* received orders to move forward from Walegozulowo to the neighbourhood of the Perekrostowo railroad station.

See Map 64 and, for geography, Map 62.

The efforts to cut off or force back the Soviet forces that were advancing, nearly unhindered, through the gaps in the defenses east of the Dnjestr continued, with daily loss of ground. Gradually *Armeegruppe Wöhler* gradually pulled the formations back to the west bank of the Dnjest, the 3rd *SS-Panzer Division 'Totenkopf'* crossing in Dubossary. Individual battalions delivered successful counterattacks, bringing in prisoners and captured weapons. The prisoners showed surprising confidence in victory, which they expressed by saying *'Njemetzki* [Germans] *kaput'*.

Bringing up German motorized and armoured formations, however, proved difficult, because the railroad was short of rolling stock. Only as one vehicle or one train at a time did these units arrive. Therefore the German defensive formations had to be thrown into the fighting individually and endure defensive fighting and also launch counterattacks without mutual support and contact. Thus the fighting in the area east of the Dnjestr took form as defensive combat against an extraordinarily superior enemy, and that with motley formations, wholly inadequately outfitted with personnel and

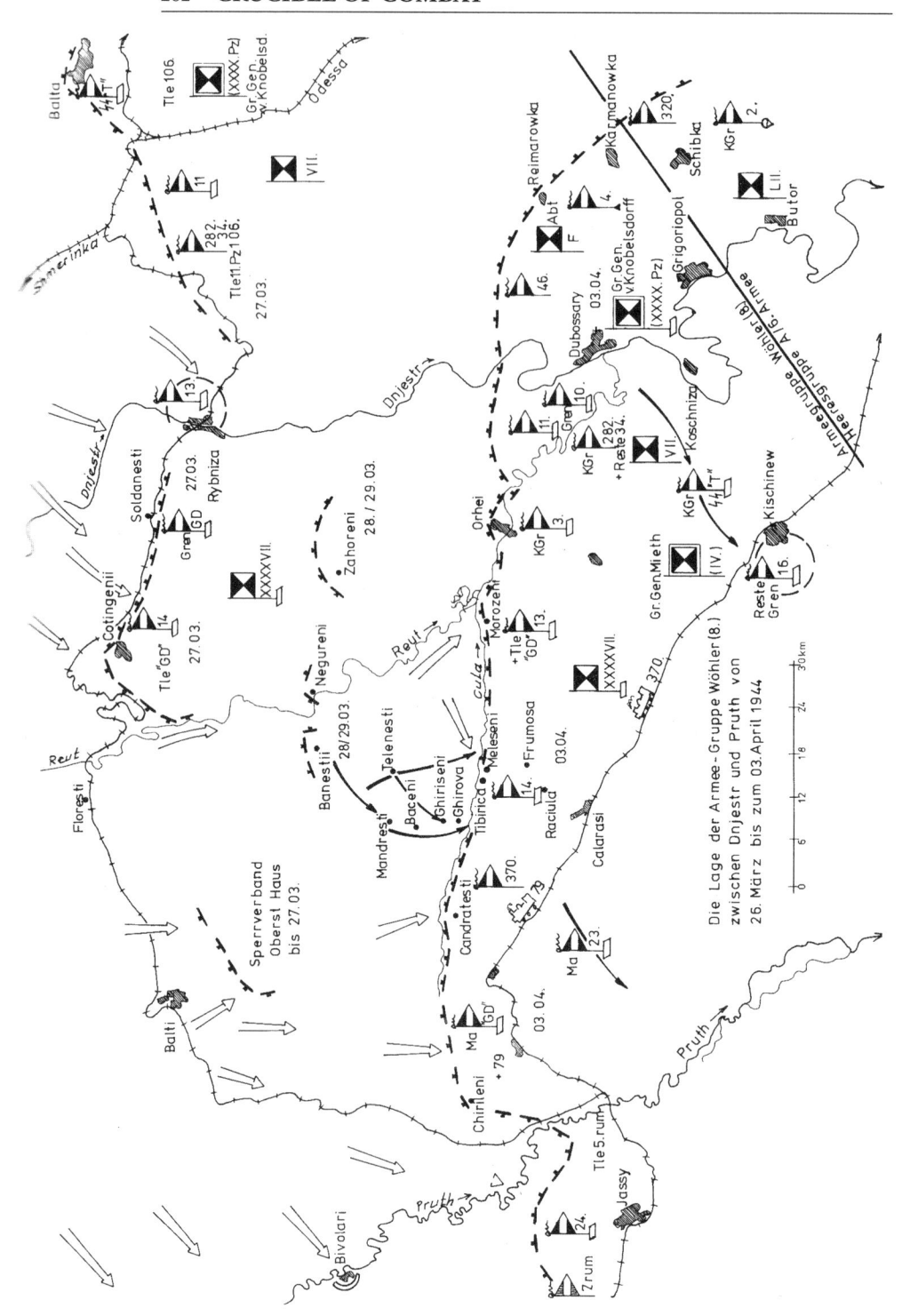

64. The situation of *Armee-Gruppe Wöhler* (8th) between the Dnjestr and Pruth from 26 March to 3 April, 1944.

DEFENSE TOWARD THE NORTHEAST AND EAST

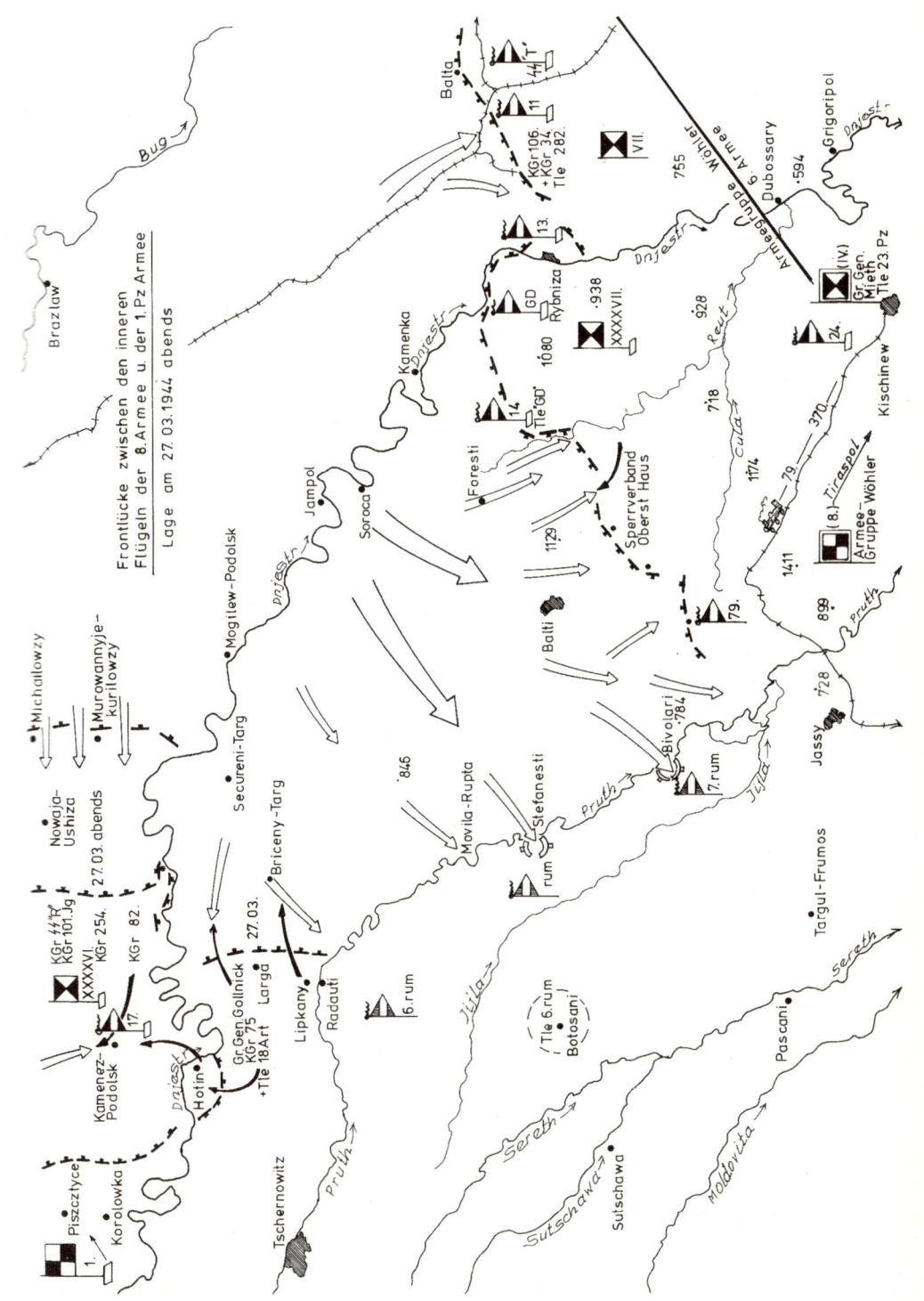

65. Gap in the front between the inner wings of the 8th *Armee* and the 1st *Panzer Armee*. Situation on 27 March 1944, evening. Map 90 overlaps northern portion as of 27 March 1944.

matériel. All they could attempt was to attack the Soviet advancing forces in the flank or to stop them frontally.

See Map 64.

Troop movements suffered from the weather conditions and the resultant condition of the unpaved roads. Nevertheless, the elements of the 14th *Panzer Division* and the 370th *Infanterie Division* that were already over the Dnjestr beat back the enemy attack against the Cula line and forced the enemy, four divisions strong, that had broken in during wild storms and snow, back to the north. They recaptured two localities south of the Cula sector. An attack of the 14th *Panzer Division* against the enemy Carpiti bridgehead south of Sculeni failed. The 24th *Panzer Division* attacked the enemy advancing from the bridgehead from the south and west.

See Maps 65 and 66.

Korps-Abteilung F, elements of the 3rd *Panzer Division*, 46th *Infanterie Division* and the 376th *Infanterie Division* were available for defense against Soviet forces from the east. Farther to the west, however, a great danger was brewing in the Jassy – Targul Frumos area.

Change of Command

See Maps 65, 66, 89 and 90.

In the meantime, farther to the north, the Soviets had already captured Tschernowitz, the capital city of Bessarabia. With that the situation arose that *Generalfeldmarschall* von Manstein had so long foreseen. The 6th *Armee* was isolated at the lower Dnjestr and broken through in several places by the 3rd Ukrainian Front. The 8th *Armee* was smashed, and was still fighting only as isolated *Kampfgruppen*. The Soviets had encircled the 1st *Panzer Armee* with 22 divisions in a giant *Kessel* (Hube-*Kessel*) between the Pruth and Dnjestr, separated from the 4th *Panzer Armee* by an 80 kilometer gap. In addition, the 4th *Panzer Armee* was torn apart and had been forced back to the west.

The proposals of the Commanders in Chief of *Heeresgruppe* A, *Generalfeldmarschall* von Kleist, and of *Heeresgruppe* Süd, *Generalfeldmarschall* von Manstein, to pull back endangered sectors of the front in time and free up troops, thereby eliminating risks, were not received well by Hitler, but, instead, resulted in the relief of the Commanders in Chief of both *Heeresgruppen*. *Generalfeldmarschall* Model, formerly in command of *Heeresgruppe Nord*, assumed command of *Heeresgruppe* Süd, *Generaloberst* Schörner assumed command of *Heeresgruppe* A. In the future *Heeresgruppe* A became *Heeresgruppe Südukraine*, *Heeresgruppe* Süd became *Heeresgruppe Nord-Ukraine*. Both *Heeresgruppen* were cut off from direct logistical support from Lemberg, for at that time the 1st *Panzer Armee* to the north was already encircled in the Hube-*Kessel* and sought to gain ground to the west and break out.

Rearguard Combat of Individual Formations

See Map 65.

The situation worsened appreciably. Aerial reconnaissance reported that the Soviets had crossed the Dnjestr with forces of the 2nd Ukrainian Front on a breadth of over 100 kilometers between Kamenka and Mogilew – Podolsk. These forces had to have the mission of reinforcing the forces that were already advancing against the left wing of the 8th *Armee* after crossing the upper Bug heading south, in order, thereby, to undertake the thrust to the south in cooperation with the attacking forces of the 3rd Ukrainian Front

DEFENSE TOWARD THE NORTHEAST AND EAST

against the 8th *Armee* and, finally, *Heeresgruppe* A. The distant objective could be to continue to advance to the southwest over the Pruth to the southern Carpathian mountains, in order thereby to prevent construction of a defensive front at the Carpathians. The Soviets could thus compress the forces of the 8th *Armee* and *Heeresgruppe* A into the bottleneck between the Black Sea and the Carpathians, with the possible remote objective of reaching the Ploesti oilfields.

For the German command the most urgent mission remained that of stopping the enemy forces advancing from north to south between the Bug and the Dnjestr, in order to enable the German forces east of the Dnjestr to get back over the river.

Moreover, it was also vital to halt the southward advance of the Soviets west of the Dnjestr. On the other hand, it was also important to reinforce the ever lengthening west wing in hopes of striking the Soviets between the Dnjestr and Pruth or Pruth and Carpathians and, if possible, to force them back to the Bug, or even across it.

In its newly assigned combat area *Panzergrenadier Division 'Großdeutschland'* prepared itself, in accord with the results of reconnaissance of the enemy, for a difficult defense against a superior enemy. The pioneers erected barbed wire and laid mines, especially on terrain that was hidden from observation and difficult to reach with heavy weapons. That did not, however, exhaust the German defensive preparations. Additional troop formations would have to be brought into this area that was clearly slated for future Soviet offensive operations on a large scale.

Renewed Commitment of the 24th *Panzer Division*

After aerial transport of the remnants of the division on 22 March, with a stop *en route* at Birsula, this division reached the Kishinew bridge location and enjoyed a few days rest there for reorganization and reequipping. Then, however, it had to build a lasting line of defense at the Dnjestr and Pruth, which meant the division had to immediately make itself fit for action. With the help of the train vehicles that had been brought forward to Odessa the combat elements of the division that had been brought up by air again became mobile, regenerating themselves during the coming days with captured vehicles that they found and vehicles left behind by other formations. Those elements of the division that had come under the command of other formations during the fighting retreat returned to the division.

See Map 65 and, for geography, Map 63.

Initially there were differences of opinion between the German command and the commanders of the Rumanian formations regarding the future employment of the division. The Rumanians wanted to give up the Targul – Frumos – Jassy road and let the main line of resistance run south of the old *'Trajan'* or *'Strunga'* position, with favorable terrain conditions throughout. While the German command, however, with the German formations that had arrived there, constructed an advanced main line of resistance to protect the above-named road, there were inactive Rumanian formations to the rear in the *'Trajan'* position. They then moved forward, a bit at a time, into the line the

Germans had intended. Their combat value, however, continued to be judged as minimal.

See Map 66.

The 24th *Panzer Division* initially was ordered to reach the Jassy area and to hold itself in readiness for commitment north of the city. While it had to cover the open right flank of the 8th *Armee* in march, it increasingly moved to its open left flank. The *Armee* was afraid of losing Jassy and thereby being outflanked to the north. The foremost *Kampfgruppe* of the I./ *Panzergrenadier Regiment* 26 [24th *Panzer Division*] and *Panzeraufklärungs Abteilung* 24, as well as the II./ *Panzergrenadier Regiment* 21 [24th *Panzer Division*] with three guns, set out from Ungheni-Targ, the bridgehead east of the Pruth, to the north and forced the Soviets back to Petresti, thereby clearing the road in this area. On 31 March the Soviets overran the weak infantry that had, in the meantime, been committed, and forced their way forward to Sameni, where, attacking from the line of march, the *Kampfgruppe* again forced them back.

The following operation of the *Kampfgruppe* on 1 April developed into a complete success, with three troops advancing along the road on foot, while the armoured group with one *SPW* troop, two *Sturmgeschütze*, one 'Panther' and two command tanks attacked west of the road. At the edge of Parliti Sat they ran into enemy resistance. The *Kampfgruppe* broke the enemy resistance in a valiant attack and captured Parliti Sat by 1400 hours. The armoured group, which was to envelop the place to the west, ran into strong anti-tank and armoured opposition between Parliti Sat and Todiresti. One troop of *Panzeraufklärungs Abteilung* 24 advanced on foot into Parliti Sat with the troops that had thrust through Parliti Sat to the northwest and knocked out four AFVs and four heavy anti-tank guns in the Soviet group that was fleeing to the north before the fire of the German armoured group.

Further successful counterattacks ensued – in part impacted by hurricane-like snowstorms – initially to Vulturol, Moisesti and Epureni, until snowdrifts barred further movement. On 4 April enemy forces that had advanced past Vulturol were beaten back at Dorobantu, six kilometers in front of Jassy. Rumanian soldiers then occupied the line that was thereby attained. North of Vulturol, Rumanian infantry fled to the rear, whereupon *Panzergrenadier Regiment* 26, supported by three tanks, regained the old line, knocking out six enemy AFVs in the process.

On the next day, too, the Soviets repeatedly attempted to advance to the south and again crossed the road to Targul Frumos west of Jassy, moving south. *Panzergrendier Regiment* 21 took Letcani on foot in an enveloping attack, destroying the enemy forces that had advanced, knocking out ten guns.

On 12 April the Soviets advanced from their strongpoints at Vulturol to north of Podul Iloaei. An armoured group of the 24th *Panzer Division* attacked the flank of the penetration area and destroyed all the enemy AFVs. In addition it thrust across the German lines into the remaining enemy forces and dispersed them without any losses to itself (see below).

On 13 April German infantry started to arrive, which then, on 13 April, north of Podul Iloaei, while the enemy guns were screened by smoke, helped to force back enemy forces that had broken in and recapture the locality they

DEFENSE TOWARD THE NORTHEAST AND EAST

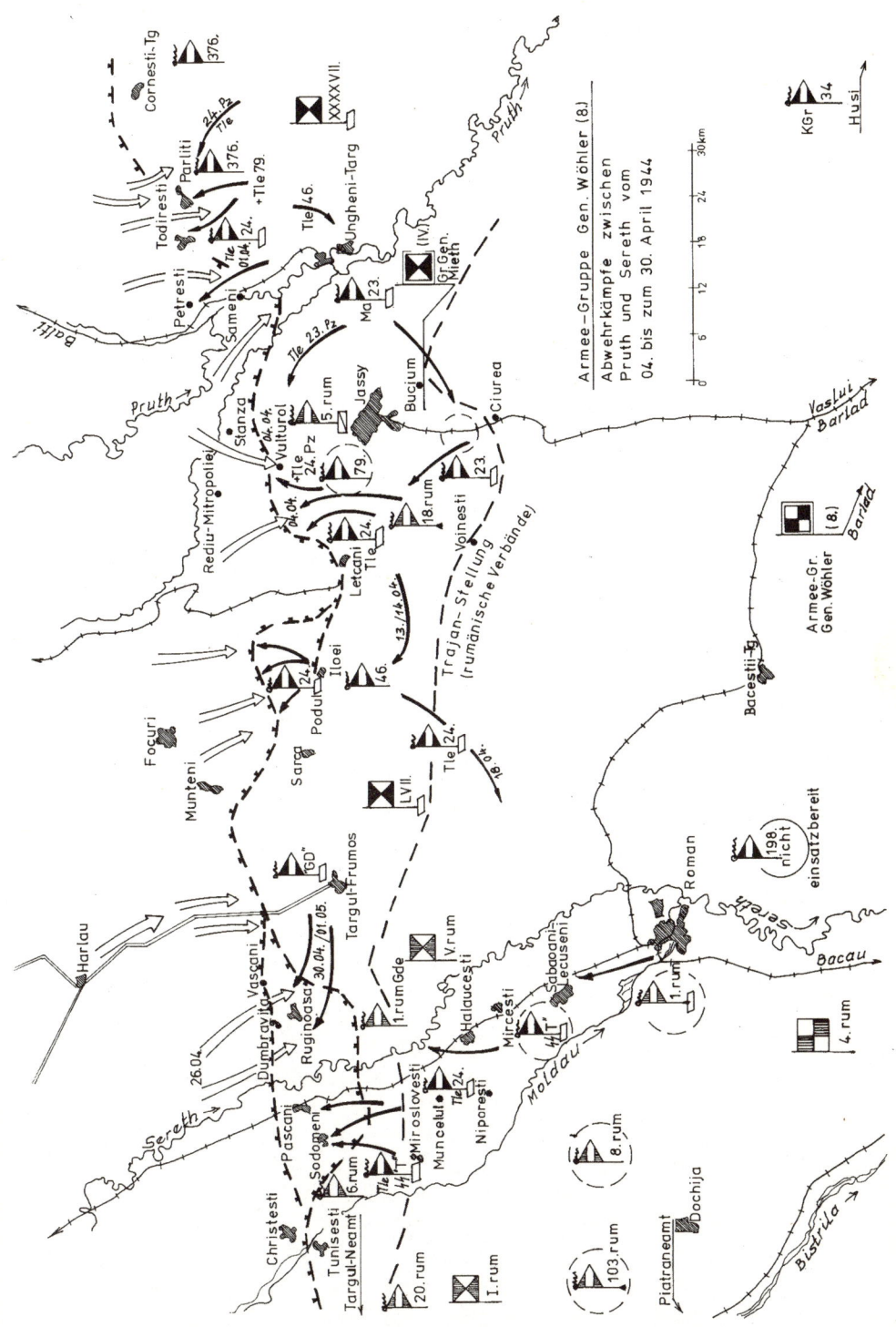

66. *Armee – Gruppe General Wöhler* (8th). Defensive fighting between the Pruth and Sereth from 4 to 30 April, 1944.

had occupied. The Soviets broke in again the next day, but were, again, beaten back with the destruction of most of the forces that had broken in.

20

Battle of Targul-Frumos

The formations that had been sent into the new combat area, whose leading elements had already arrived, had to set up for hard defensive fighting, just as the 3rd *SS-Panzer Divison 'Totenkopf'* was engaged in bitter fighting in the Balta area. The same was true for the 24th *Panzer Division* in the Jassy area as also with the arriving elements of *Panzergrenadier Division 'Großdeutschland'*. At that time *'Großdeutschland'* again had three *Abteilungen* of artillery, which coupled its fire to that of the heavy infantry guns. The *Flak-Abteilung* of *Panzergrenadier Division 'Großdeutschland'* again had four batteries, three of which had 8.8 cm guns. One of these was employed in anti-tank mode. To the right of *Panzergrenadier Division 'Großdeutschland'* was the 46th *Infanterie Division*, with the 24th *Panzer Division* alongside it.

In the Ruginossa sector in the left part of the area of *Großdeutschland's* positions reaching to the Sereth river was a Rumanian brigade, abundantly outfitted with German models of automatic weapons and anti-tank guns, as well as artillery. Nevertheless, they had limited combat value, to the extent that the German division commanders found these Rumanian formations to be a burden. The Soviets, too, had a realistic picture of the Rumanian combat effectiveness. Accordingly, one expected that the *Schwerpunkt* of the Soviet attack would be in their sector.

The Situation

During this time period the Soviets reorganized. The main body of the Soviet 6th Tank Army was in the bridgehead north of Jassy, the Soviet 2nd Tank Army north of Targul-Frumos, a large formation on the Brotesani, Harlau, Cristesti road west of the Sereth. The Soviets repeatedly attacked the Jassy bridgehead with strong artillery support. The 24th *Panzer Division* was there, and held off the Soviets.

The Soviet advance on the west bank of the Moldau river, however, caused the 57th *Panzer Korps* to have the 24th *Panzer Division* relieved by the 46th *Infanterie Division* in order to have the 24th *Panzer Division* move into the Saboanie – Lecusene area and the 3rd *SS-Panzer Division 'Totenkopf'* hold itself in readiness for commitment toward the northwest on short notice. The Rumanian 6th Infantry Division, in a hasty counterattack out of Tunisesti and into the woods to its southwest were able to force back weak enemy forces advancing over the Moldau toward the southwest. Therefore the 3rd *SS-Panzer Division 'Totenkopf'* sent additional forces from the assembly area west of Roman to reinforce its reserve group at the Halauceste – Pascani road and in the Tnisporesti neighbourhood.

The threatening concentration of the enemy main force between Jassy and Targul-Frumos raised expectations of an impending advance to the south to

See Map 66.

get into the rear of the Dnjestr front, *Armeegruppe Wöhler*. Therefore it became important to strengthen the center of the west wing and its right wing by fortification.

On 20 April a reserve group of the 3rd *SS-Panzer Division 'Totenkopf'* was on call in the Mircesti – Muncelul – De-Suis – Dhalaucesti area.

Further preparations were complicated by necessary negotiations with the Rumanians. The Rumainian 6th Infantry Division received orders to attack on 24 April at 1400 hours and to take Sodomeni. However, they did not do so.

While the 24th *Panzer Division* launched its advance into the Soviet assembly positions on 25 April, the reserve group of the 3rd *SS-Panzer Division 'Totenkopf'* was assigned the mission to advance to the west bank of the Sereth to reconnoiter the enemy situation between the Sereth and Moldau and, finally, went into action toward Pascani. It therefore had to assault a heavily mined defensive front with strong anti-tank defenses. In the meantime the division received substantial additional supplies from the stocks of other *Waffen-SS* divisions. 100 men with lorries, 25 *SPW*, 16 eight-ton prime movers, ten 12-ton prime movers and three eighteen-ton prime movers.[1] The members of the adjoining formations could only dream of such matériel additions.

See Map 66.

In the meantime the Soviets attacked the sector north of Vultur (elements of the 79th *Infanterie Division*) and, later, the sectors adjoining to the east and west of the Rumanian 5th Cavalry Division, the Rumanian 18th Mountain Division and the east wing of the Rumanian 3rd Infantry Division. The 79th *Infanterie Division* repulsed all attacks between the Jassy, Stancha – Jassy and Rediu Mitropoliei roads, destroying from 12 to 14 AFVs, while the Soviets penetrated the Rumanians. The 23rd *Panzer Division* and elements of the 79th *Infanterie Division* launched a counterattack to intercept the enemy that was pushing sharply to the south. On the next day, too, the Soviet attacks to conquer the Jassy area with the *Schwerpunkt* north of the city were repulsed. On the left, too, on 26 April the Soviets broke through *Panzergrenadier Divison 'Großdeutschland'* into the Vascani – Dumbravita hill-terrain and penetrated into Vascani and Dubravita, losing 18 AFVs in the process.

On 23 April the 24th *Panzer Division* regained several kilometers of ground that had been lost in the Jassy combat area. While that was happening, *Panzergrenadier Division 'Großdeutschland'* repulsed Soviet attacks supported by armour.

The terrain between the Dnjestr, Pruth and Sereth rivers must have been particularly significant to the Soviets for a further advance into Rumania. That was evident from the Soviet refusal to give up on attacking in the Jassy area. They shifted the main body of their forces into the Sereth sector and escalated their attack preparations east of the Sereth river before the east wing of the Rumanian 4th Army, also, especially, before the defensive sector of *Panzergrenadier Divison 'Großdeutschland'*.

The concentration of strong infantry and armoured formations along the Pascani – Cristesti line toward the front that was reported by aerial reconnaissance suggested Soviet intentions to extend the wing of their

---

1 Translator's note – Prime movers were rated by the number of tons they could tow.

attack, if possible, to the Moldau. Far to the northeast of Cristesti strikingly strong enemy artillery was going into position. The 24th *Panzer Division* was available to defend against the major attack in the right sector. The formations of *Panzergrenadier Division 'Großdeutschland'* and *3rd SS-Panzer Division 'Totenkopf'* that were adjoining to the left (in the Letcani – Pordul – Iloaei area) received orders from *Armeegruppe Wöhler* to thrust northwestward via Sarca into the flank of the enemy forces that were attacking toward Targul-Frumos. An operational reserve group of the *3rd SS-Panzer Division 'Totenkopf'* moved forward during the night of 30 April/1 May from their assembly position area around Harlaucisti on the west bank of the Sereth into the Targul-Frumos area, while the Rumainian 1st Armoured Division closed up in the Halauceste area.

Preparations for the Battle of Targul-Frumos

The German command intended to anticipate the Soviet offensive that aerial reconnaissance indicated was imminent, consequently *Panzergrenadier Division 'Großdeutschland'* attacked into the presumed assembly positions, especially in the area of the Dumbravita hill, with its *Schwerpunkt* with the II. And III./ *Panzergrenadier Regiment 'Grodeutschland'*. At 0415 hours after a short concentrated artillery preparation they moved out of their foxholes and drove the Soviets before them in wild flight. The anti-tank guns destroyed 31 heavy Soviet anti-tank guns and three enemy AFVs. Farther to the left along the *Rollbahn* to Pascani, *'Tiger'* and *'Panther'* of *Panzer Regiment 'Großdeutschland'* also reached their objective despite substantial enemy defense, especially by anti-tank guns and armour. The significance of this operation was that the attack had hit actual enemy assembly positions, which provided definite clarity regarding the expected *Schwerpunkt* of the Soviet attack.

See Map 66.

The terrain of the fighting proved especially favorable for an armoured attack, which probably caused the Soviets to select this terrain. On 27 April tanks and *Sturmgeschütze* of *Panzergrenadier Division 'Großdeutschland'* undertook an new thrust into the enemy assembly positions on the high ground between Pascani and Dumbravita.

Inspection of knocked-out Soviet armour showed, however, that these had a new 12.2 cm main gun. The Soviets were employing here a new type of 'Josef Stalin' tank with stronger armour, a significant factor to be considered in preparation for defensive fighting.[2] The division feverishly prepared its defense, with switch-positions for the artillery, alternative observation posts, construction of radio lines (two-station nets), blocking positions in the depth of the battlefield, obstacles against armour, and employment of anti-aircraft troops.

The troops expected the offensive to start on 1 May. This however, did not take place. Perhaps the attacks into the enemy assembly positions caused this delay. Aerial reconnaissance continued to report substantial concentrations of armour as well as a multitude of new artillery positions in the already suspected

---

2 JS II tanks.

Schwerpunkt areas. *Major* Rudel and his *Stukas* concerned themselves with attacking Soviet arour in the assembly position.

The Offensive Opens

Early on 2 May, at 0420 hours, the hurricane of fire began, lasting over 60 minutes. In the mist of the early morning, AFV after AFV, including a large number of new types, advanced in the thick clouds of dust between the impacts of the artillery fire that was slowly lifting toward the German rear. The terrain proved to be generally navigable for armoured vehicles, and, what is more, with a wide field of fire. There were favorable positions for German observation posts, anti-tank guns and artillery, the vegetation offering good opportunities for camouflage. A blue sky, clear nights and sunny, spring weather simplified combat operations.

After the fire preparation ended, the *Grenadiere* of *Panzer Divison 'Großdeutschland'* locally allowed the Soviet armour to roll over them in order to turn the prey over to the 8.8 cm anti-aircraft guns dug-in at the northern exit of Targul-Frumos. Most of the attacking armour – about 25 AFVs – became victims. The remainder, about ten AFVs, burst into the assembly positions of the *'Großdeutschland' Panzer* regiment and were destroyed there. In the adjoining sector, too, 30 Soviet AFVs tried to reach a height of ground at high speed. There, too, the infantry allowed them to roll over them. At a range of 300 meters the *Sturmgeschütze* knocked out and set ablaze all of the attacking AFVs. Some exploded into tiny fragments, all without any German losses.

Another Soviet tank company drove through the positions that the Rumanians had abandoned in single file. They then ran into a company of German tanks, which destroyed every one of the intruders. Then a new wave of Soviet armour followed the first. The new type of Soviet tank whose armour could withstand the long-range fire of the *Tiger*, also joined the fight. Accordingly, the *Tiger* had to close the range to 1,800 to 2,000 meters. Four of these new Soviet AFVs burnt right off. Three left the battlefield, then to fall victim just east of Ruginorasa to German *Panzer* IV tanks that approached under cover to about 1,000 meters and fired on the enemy tanks from the rear. The Joseph Stalin II tank, the heaviest Soviet tank, had up to 16cm of armour and a lower profile than the *Tiger*.

By 1100 hours about 250 enemy AFVs lay on the battlefield, destroyed. Granted, many more AFVs were visible in the enemy hinterland, but these only fired from long range without getting involved in the fighting.

Alarming reports arrived from *Panzerfüsilier Regiment 'Großdeutschland'*. 32 Soviet AFVs forced their way into a village held by that regiment. 24 of the Soviet AFVs were destroyed in close-quarters fighting after the infantrymen had allowed them to roll over them and separated the Soviet infantry from their armour. Therefore the division broke off the armoured battle in the sector west of Targul-Frumos, merely leaving one *Abteilung* of *Panzer* V *['Panther']* and *Panzer* VI *['Tiger']*. One company of *Panzer* IV were moved to the right wing, where, in short order, they knocked out about 30 Soviet AFVs. After crossing the front line, the remaining enemy AFVs wandered around in the rear position area of the regiment.

BATTLE OF TARGUL-FRUMOS 293

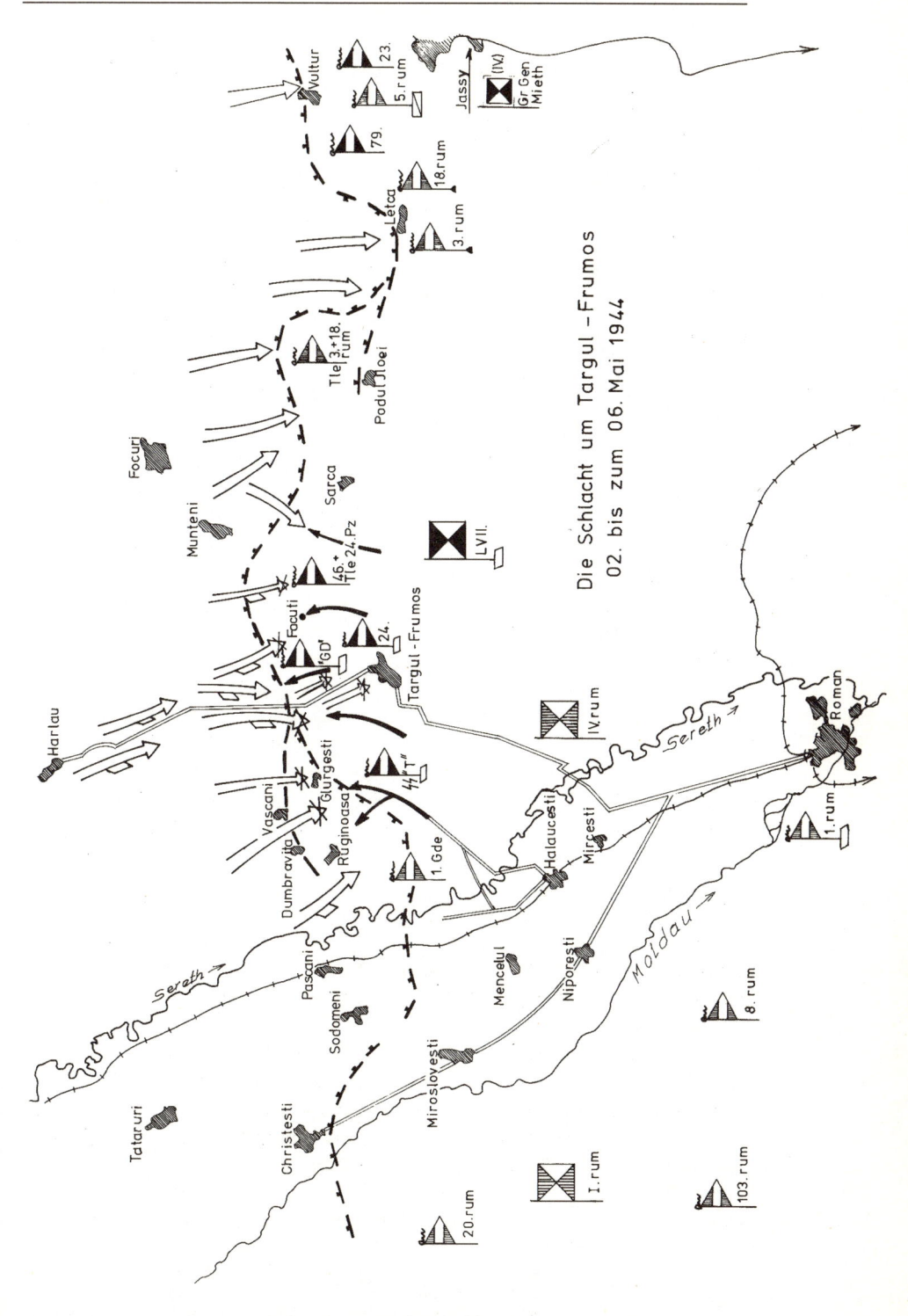

67. The Battle of Targul-Frumos 2 to 6 May, 1944.

See Map 67.

In the left combat sector of *Panzergrenadier Division 'Großdeutschland'* two Soviet armies and six Soviet rifle divisions started moving south on that morning (2 May), with the objective of taking Targul-Frumos as the base and jump-off point for future breakthrough operations. Farther to the left, at the boundary with elements of the 3rd *SS-Panzer Division 'Totenkopf'* Soviet armour rolled over and through the foremost positions of the I./ *Panzergrenadier Regiment 'Großdeutschland'* along and on both sides of the *Rollbahn*. The company that had been rolled-over could no longer disengage. From the distance it could be seen that individual *Grenadiere* raised their arms in the hopeless situation, but were simply shot or beaten to death. The Rumanian liaison command [*Armeeverbindungskommando*] and observation positions had changed positions at the start of the Soviet artillery preparation, leaving the German company in the lurch. The artillery had withdrawn to positions farther to the rear.

The first enemy armour reached the east edge of Dumbrovita, where *Sturmgeschütze* engaged them and immediately set seven heavy AFVs ablaze. Nevertheless the Soviets advanced to within 30 meters of the firing positions of the *Werfer* [*Nebelwerfer*, German multiple-rocket launchers], which supported the German infantry that had been rolled over further forward with their fire. Here the *Sturmgeschütze* set three more Soviet AFVs ablaze with a few rounds, but then had to withdraw after they had expended their ammunition, along with the *Werfer*. Two Soviet AFVs, however, broke through. Four *Schützenpanzerwagen* [*SPW*] then took over the security of the four kilometer open flank.

Suddenly four more T 34 appeared directly in front of the *SPW*. At the last minute *Panzer* and *Sturmgeschütze* of the 3rd *SS-Panzer Division 'Totenkopf'* joined the fray. Before a single T 34 had aimed its main gun, all of them took direct hits. Then a mighty armoured battle began in no-mans-land. The *Stukas* (*Ju 87*) of *Oberst* Rudel dived incessantly and showed the *Panzer* the way. The four *SPW* of the 2nd *Kompanie* followed these directions and found abundant work. The Soviet infantry seemed to have followed their armour by the thousands and suffered substantial losses under the fire of these *Sturmgeschütze*.[3]

The Soviet breakthrough was thereby scuttled in this sector, too, though with the loss of one company of the I./ *Panzergrenadier Regiment 'Großdeutschland'*.

In the adjoining sector of the III./ *Panzergrenadier Regiment 'Großdeutschland'* one 7.5 cm anti-tank gun knocked out seven enemy AFVs in less than 20 minutes, until the gun, itself, received a direct hit.

The battle also raged before Giurgesti. The 5th *Kompanie* of the II./ *Panzergrenadier Regiment 'Großdeutschland'* had to abandon its positions after the enemy penetrated them with AFVs. Anti-tank rounds finally brought these to a halt. Farther to the rear, however, were 26 more enemy AFVs with

---

3 Translator's note – The author's wording, in all the excitement, is, perhaps, a trifle unclear. By way of clarification, note that tanks and *Sturmgeschütze* had joined with the four *SPW*, so German tanks, *Sturmgeschütze* and the four lightly armoured *SPW* were all involved, all assisted and guided by *Oberst* Rudel's *Stukas*.

more than 300 infantry. Here, too, however, *Stukas* suddenly brought aid and dived upon the packs of enemy armour. The old main line of resistance was successfully reestablished in counterattacks.

The other companies of *Panzergrenadier Regiment 'Großdeutschland'* also had to withstand bitter fighting, defending themselves against Soviet AFVs with *Haft-Hohlladungen*.[4] In the sector near Bals the Soviets rolled forward to Nicolne, where the guns of the 1st *Batterie* of *Panzerartillerie Regiment 'Großdeutschland'* immediately destroyed five enemy AFVs in direct fire, which gave the 2nd and 3rd/ *Panzerartillerie Regiment 'Großdeutschland'* a chance to change positions. As Soviet armour attacked from the right, *Panzer,* armoured cars and *SPW* of the 24th *Panzer Division* rolled before Facuti and pursued the Soviet armour, which had taken flight. The II./ *Panzerfüsilier Regiment 'Großdeutschland'* won back its old positions in this manner.

13 enemy AFVs, including several Stalin tanks, got through at Targul-Frumos. Others were left knocked-out or blown to bits. *'Tiger', 'Panther'* and *Panzer* IV did this slaughter. The last of the Soviet AFVs were the victims of the 8.8 cm anti-aircraft troops at the edges of the city. None of the enemy AFVs made it back to their jump-off positions.

By 1100 hours of this day about 250 AFVs were counted, knocked out on the battlefield. The Soviet losses, however, were yet higher. It was estimated that the Soviet losses for the entire day, including losses to bombers amounted to about 250 AFVs, with about 200 more damaged.

In this battle the old armoured tactic had again proved successful, of setting tank against tank, in contrast to the Soviet practice of dividing the armour up and employing it as a support weapon for the infantry.

The Second Day of Battle

Despite this defensive success, on 3 May the Soviets continued their attack. Numerous AFVs rolled against the, in part, new positions of the *Grenadiere*, built up their *Schwerpunkte* and vanished after traversing the German lines, which they left behind them. There, however, *'Tiger'* and *'Panther*, as well as *Sturmgeschütze* awaited them in ambush positions. Anti-aircraft and anti-tank guns targeted them. Again there was a slaughter of armour, with strong aerial activity on both sides. *Ratas* circled and fired on identified targets. *Il* 2 spewed cannon and machine gun fire onto the battlefield. *Stukas* dived, sirens screaming, on identified targets, releasing their bombs at low altitude with great accuracy. Other *Stukas* were active with anti-tank guns mounted under their wings.

The Third Day of Battle

On 4 May the Soviets attempted to achieve a breakthrough only at a few points, concentrating strong infantry and armoured forces and pouring

---

4 Translator's note – *Haft-Hohlladung, 3 kg,* three kilogram magnetic anti-tank demolition charge. The shaped charge of 1.47 kg of explosive had a steel casing with three powerful horseshoe magnets attached to the plywood or plastic base to hold it to and at the right distance from the armour. A penetration of 110 mm of armour was reported. There were two models with time delays of four seconds and seven seconds from the time the friction igniter was pulled. (Chamberlain, Doyle and Gander, *Deutsche Panzerabwehr*).

artillery, mortar and *Stalinorgel* [Stalin Organ – truck-mounted multiple rocket launchers that the Russian soldiers called *Katyushas*] fire on these areas to wipe out any expected resistance. Armour and massed infantry attempted to roll down the last surviving *Grenadiere*.

A dominating hill position, Point 256, named *'Kalmü'* had a special attraction for both combatants. It was in no-man's-land. *Sturmpioniere* [assault pioneers] of *'Großdeutschland'* stormed it several times and were, each time, thrown back out of their positions. Finally they stormed it with flame-throwers and close-combat materials and captured it, this time to hold. The other battalions improved their positions with attacks with short-range objectives.

Conclusion of the Battle

5 May was, finally, quieter than the preceding days. The Soviets had obviously expended their strength without gaining due reward.

The II./ *Panzergrenadier Regiment 'Großdeutschland'* thrust anew toward Giurgesti. Because of greatly reduced combat strength, however, the battalion had to be disbanded and distributed among other units.

In the early morning hours of 6 May the *Panzerfüsiliere* and *Panzersturm-Pioniere*, supported by 2cm anti-aircraft guns on self-propelled mounts, penetrated to Nicolne and finally, on 7 May, captured the *'Kalmü'* hill, after a sudden barrage by artillery and *Nebelwerfer* and use of flame throwers and close-combat materials with support by *'Panther'* and *Sturmgeschütze*. The 24th *Panzer Division* then took over this sector. However, the *'Kalmü'* changed hands several more times. On 11 May, finally, calm fell on this position in the front.

21

Situation at the Beginning of May

The behaviour of the Soviets in the ensuing period may, initially, have been due to exhaustion after such a long approach march, but, essentially, could be attributed to the tremendous weakening of their formations. In other sectors, too, the Soviets allowed calm to prevail.

It seems almost inexplicable how the Soviets had managed to bring such a mass of armour into this sector in such a short time. After the evacuation of Odessa. which had only taken place on 10 April, they did not yet possess a significant transport fleet in the Black Sea for bringing up armour. The railroad line leading north from Odessa first became available in full on 23 February. On the other hand, the Soviets could not, in any way, have brought such a huge mass of armour over 100 kilometers to the site of the combat under its own power, especially given the unavoidable wear and tear to fully-tracked vehicles, the more so given the sometimes muddy, sometimes frozen subsoil. As if that wasn't enough, there was the associated necessity for the supply of an immense amount of fuel. It is presumed that the Soviets, as they did later on the Orscha – Smolensk – Molodeczno – Lida stretch, used captured German railroad rolling stock to bring such a mass of armour to the west, keeping, for the time being, the Europaean standard gauge on the single-tracked railroad leading west from Uman.

For all that, in their advance to the west the Soviets had already reached the Carpathian mountains and gained terrain favorable for armour in the Targul-Frumos and Jassy area for possible further advance. For a further thrust to the south they need cross no significant river obstacles. Likewise, roads and railroad were available for matériel logistical support to the south. If they had no intentions in this direction the Soviets probably would not have brought such masses of troops, especially armour, into this sector. The fierce defense, especially by the 3rd *SS-Panzer Division 'Totenkopf'*, *Panzergrenadier Division 'Großdeutschland'* and the 24th *Panzer Division,* but also infantry formations, including the 46th *Infanterie Division* and 34th *Infanterie Division*, had probably sufficed to effectively cripple the offensive force of these formations, so that the Soviets in this area were quiet, for the time being. That encouraged the German formations to engage in small counterattacks that served to gain more favorable lines of defense. Only at the beginning of June did the enemy start limited attacks in small sectors, probably not to demonstrate their interest in this combat sector, but to provoke the German defense.

The Big Picture

The end of the presentation of the fate of the 8th *Armee* gives occasion for a review of the other sectors of the front. It is a perpetual source of wonder how the emaciated German formations were able to delay, and finally to halt, the Soviets with their immensely superior forces. Certainly they were assisted by difficulties that also affected the Red Army, for such large formations, motorized and with strong artillery, required a significant mass of supplies. In addition, certainly, was the fact that in the summer of 1944 the Soviet troops, too, were, to a certain extent, weary.

Initially the Soviets had attempted to outflank the 6th *Armee* and cut it off from its connections to the rear. When this failed, they undertook ever more advances to the north with the intention of drawing a new noose around the 6th *Armee*, in which additional regions of the front would be drawn into the operations of the Red Army. That renders the advances at Kriwoi Rog comprehensible, as, later, at Kirowograd and, finally, at Winniza – Uman. The Soviet advance southwest from Schepetowka and finally to the south toward Proskurow also fits into this strategy.

This viewpoint is supported by the fact that the Soviets conducted their advance from the Schepetowka area, not to the west toward the *Generalgouvernement*, where it would certainly have found the German defense even more sensitive, but toward the southwest, and then turning toward the south, thus in direct conjunction with the operations first against the 6th *Armee* and later also against the 8th *Armee*.

Regarding this connection of the fighting of the so-called 'Second Blow' against the 1st *Panzer Armee* with the simultaneous attacks at the start of March farther south, it would be advisable to extend the discussion to the actions of the 1st *Panzer Armee*. At the same time as the attacks against the 1st *Panzer Armee* there were also thrusts farther north into the Tarnopol area and, yet further north, in the area around Rowno – Dubno and, finally, Kowel.

The emphasis of the Soviet advance, however, did not lie in this left wing region of *Heeresgruppe Mitte*, but in the attack southwest of Schepetowka against the 1st *Panzer Armee*. With that in mind, it seems appropriate, initially, to examine the fighting on the left wing of *Heeresgruppe Süd*.

22

The Battle of Tarnopol

The Situation in the Sector of the 1st and 4th *Panzer Armee* (Kirowograd – Winniza – Uman)

The 4th *Panzer Armee* had to care for far too broad a sector, thus the staff of the 1st *Panzer Armee*, after being relieved by the 6th *Armee* in the southern sector, took over the right wing of the 4th *Panzer Armee*. Further sector shifts proved necessary afterwards, such as broadening the sector of the 1st *Panzer Armee* to include that of the 46th *Panzer Korps*. The staff of the 1st *Panzer Armee* finally moved on 1 February 1944 from Letitschew – Winniza to Brody.

At the start of March the Soviets launched a new offensive, not, however, limiting themselves to the area west of the position of the breakout of the troop remnants from the *Kessel* of Tscherkassy – Korssun, after the withdrawal of the staff of the 1st *Panzer Armee* against the left wing of the 8th *Armee* and right wing of the 1st *Panzer Armee*. Instead, they extended their attack into the Winniza – Uman area farther against the formations of the 4th *Panzer Armee* to the north. Finally, the Soviet enemy intelligence had determined with a probability bordering on certainty that the German command attributed the greatest significance in their evaluation on the dangerous situation on the left wing of *Heeresgruppe Süd*, and, therefore, shifted a series of formations, such as the staff of the 1st *Panzer Armee* to that point. Otherwise it would hardly seem possible to break through the German lines only two days after the start of the attack in the Winniza – Uman area (5 March) and start the advance to the south, but also to set out to the west.

See Map 68.

At that moment the foremost strongpoint-type German line again exhibited a unique curvature. From the jutting bastion west of Kirowograd the main line of resistance of the 8th *Panzer Armee* extended northwest on both sides of Uman, and then, with the right wing of the 1st *Panzer Armee*, to develop into a front facing to the northeast with the right wing of the 1st *Panzer Armee* until just west of Schepetowka. At that point the more or less continuous German main line of resistance came to an end.

See Maps 53, 58, 80, 88 and, for geography, 41, 43 and 85.

In light of the success of the Soviet success in battle against *Heeresgruppe* A and the next day's success in the area west of Winniza – Uman against the left wing of the 8th *Armee*, the point jutting to the right west of Kirowograd could not hold, although the formations committed there, especially *Panzergrenadier Division 'Großdeutschland'* offered fierce resistance to the Soviets.

Elements of the formations attacked in the Winniza – Uman area finally ended up, in the context of the westward retreat, in the sector of the 4th *Panzer Armee*, as did elements of the 18th *Artillerie Division* (other elements of that division were committed with the 254th *Infanterie Division* forward of Winniza with the 46th *Panzer Korps*).

300   CRUCIBLE OF COMBAT

See Maps 69 and 80.

The Soviet advance from the area west of Tscherkassy to the west, however, could only gain significance with a simultaneous advance against the left wing of the 4th *Panzer Armee*. Above all, it was advantageous to the Soviets that the German lines ended just west of Schepetowka. There were as good as no German troops in the entire sector reaching as far as the right wing of *Heeresgruppe Mitte*. Terrain limitations essentially eliminated the Pripjet area from consideration for major Soviet operations. To its south, however, the terrain was favorable for armoured operations, as for an advance on Rowno, with the danger of a further advance to Lemberg and Lublin.

In light of the enemy forces concentrated in the Shitomir area – facing the free sector to the left of the 4th *Panzer Armee* – the Soviets initially preferred an advance in this area rather than a possible advance on the extreme left wing of the *Heeresgruppe*.

The German command was entirely in the clear about this danger. They had to reckon with certainty on an advance of the strong Soviet forces concentrated around Shitomir into such a sector that had been almost completely stripped of German troops. For that reason the *Heeresgruppe* shifted all available formations from the area west of Tscherkassy to the west wing of the 4th *Panzer Armee*, as the 3rd *Panzer Korps* with the 1st *Panzer Division*, 11th *Panzer Division* and 16th *Panzer Division*, later followed by the 17th *Panzer Division* and, finally, the 18th *Artillerie Division*, while the command of the 48th *Panzer Korps* ordered the 7th *Panzer Division* and 1st *SS-Panzer Division 'Leibstandarte SS Adolf Hitler'*, as well as *schwere Panzer Abteilung* 503 to Tarnopol.

Gap in the Front Southwest of Schepetowka

See Maps 69, 80, 86, 88, 89 and 91.

In this area the 1st Ukrainian Front was facing the German 4th *Panzer Armee* with the 24th *Panzer Korps*, 59th *Armee Korps*, 13th *Armee Korps* as well as the 48th *Panzer Korps*. The 24th *Panzer Korps* operated southeast of Schepetowka and south of the city. From its left wing at Horyn to Jampol, to the right wing of the 13th *Armee Korps* at Kremjanez yawned a gap of 40 kilometers. To the left of the 13th *Armee Korps* the 48th *Panzer Korps* adjoined immediately to the northwest. From its left wing – *Gruppe von dem Bach*, which was attached to the *Korps* in the Kowel area – stretched a 100 kilometer gap in the front, the so-called *'Wehrmachtsloch'*, between the two *Heeresgruppen*.

The hope that, as they had done in past years, the Soviets would hold off on major operations during the mud-season proved illusory. By this time the Soviets had gained mobility even in swampy or muddy terrain that was far superior to that of the German motorized formations, most of which were equipped with standard commercial type vehicles, through the provision of all-terrain American Studebaker lorries – in six figure quantities.

See Maps 68, 69 and 70.

In addition to the forces that had been transferred to the 4th *Armee* in the Proskurow – Tarnopol area in light of the unequal force ration, the 7th *Panzer Division*, attached to the 48th *Panzer Korps* and employed in the Lusk area, received orders to pull out and shift into the gap between the 59th *Armee Korps* and 13th *Armee Korps* at Zbaraz (18 kilometers northeast of Tarnopol).

Commitment of the First German Formations

One of the first formations of the 3rd *Panzer Korps* to arrive in its specified assembly position area at Tarnopol was a *Divisions-Kampfgruppe* of the 1st *SS-Panzer Division 'Leibstandarte SS Adolf Hitler'*, additionally the 7th *Panzer Division* and *schwere Panzer Abteilung* 503. Tarnopol had an important railroad line with a river crossing that was significant to bringing up additional German forces for their logistical support. In addition, if Tarnopol were lost it would open the railroad and roads to the west for the Soviets. Finally, on 9 January the Soviets had already briefly cut the railroad to Lemberg, which impacted German supplies.

See Maps 68 and 69.

Lack of German reconnaissance meant that as February ended and March began, the 1st *Panzer Armee* was poorly informed about the enemy situation on its west wing. Accordingly it ordered reconnaissance to the west and northwest, as well as from Krasiloff, 20 kilometers north of Proskurow, and also from Stary Konstantinow, 40 kilometers north of Proskurow as far as the Poljakowa – Teofipol line. An additional mixed reconnaissance group with armour received orders on 3 March to relocate to the Basilija area. Aerial reconnaissance revealed that Soviet infantry forces were already in Swieriec and Wierbowica (60 and 40 kilometers, respectively, northeast of Tarnopol). That suggested that the Soviets in this area were initially feeling their way forward from village to village, possible still unaware of the minimal German occupation of this area. Enemy contact came directly south of Teofipol.

See Maps 68 and 89.

Reconnaissance then reported 100 enemy AFVs advancing to the southeast from Jampol, wherefore the 1st *SS-Panzer Division 'Leibstandarte SS Adolf Hitler'* received orders to move to Basilia via Bokijewka – Pisarewka – Kupel, attached to the 48th *Panzer Korps,* and to launch an attack east of the Tarnopol – Jampol railroad line. The 7th *Panzer Division* had to move forward as quickly as possible into the area northeast of Zbaraz (50 kilometers west of Basilija), because the *Armee* suspected that the Soviets were attempting to get in the flank and rear of the 59th *Armee Korps* via Teofipol.

See Maps 68, 70 and 89.

Also, while considering the formations of the 59th *Armee Korps*, a yawning gap of over 50 kilometers opened between the *Korps* left wing and the right wing of the 1st *SS-Panzer Division 'Leibstandarte SS Adolf Hitler'*. With time, the various advances gave an overview of enemy intentions. The enemy route of advance led through Mal. Sherebki to the south. Therefore a German *Kampfgruppe* with 30 *Sturmgeschütze* and 40 men attacked Sherebki in the early morning, reached the south bank of the Sslutsch/Szluss and temporarily occupied the town, thereby blocking the Soviet route of advance to the west. The *Kampfgruppe* reconnoitered further toward Mecherinzy. The Soviets then felt out the occupation of the approaches, employing the same tactic that the Germans used.

See Maps 80 and 89.

Reconnaissance of the Soviet intentions, in itself, was not going to halt their advance. Nor were there enough formations to maintain such vigilance. Only in small, isolated operations was it possible to knock out individual enemy AFVs, and, thereby, to capture Galtschinzy. The appearance of strong enemy armoured formations forced the evacuation of individual localities. First the *Kampfgruppen* that had been committed had to fight to clear the retreat

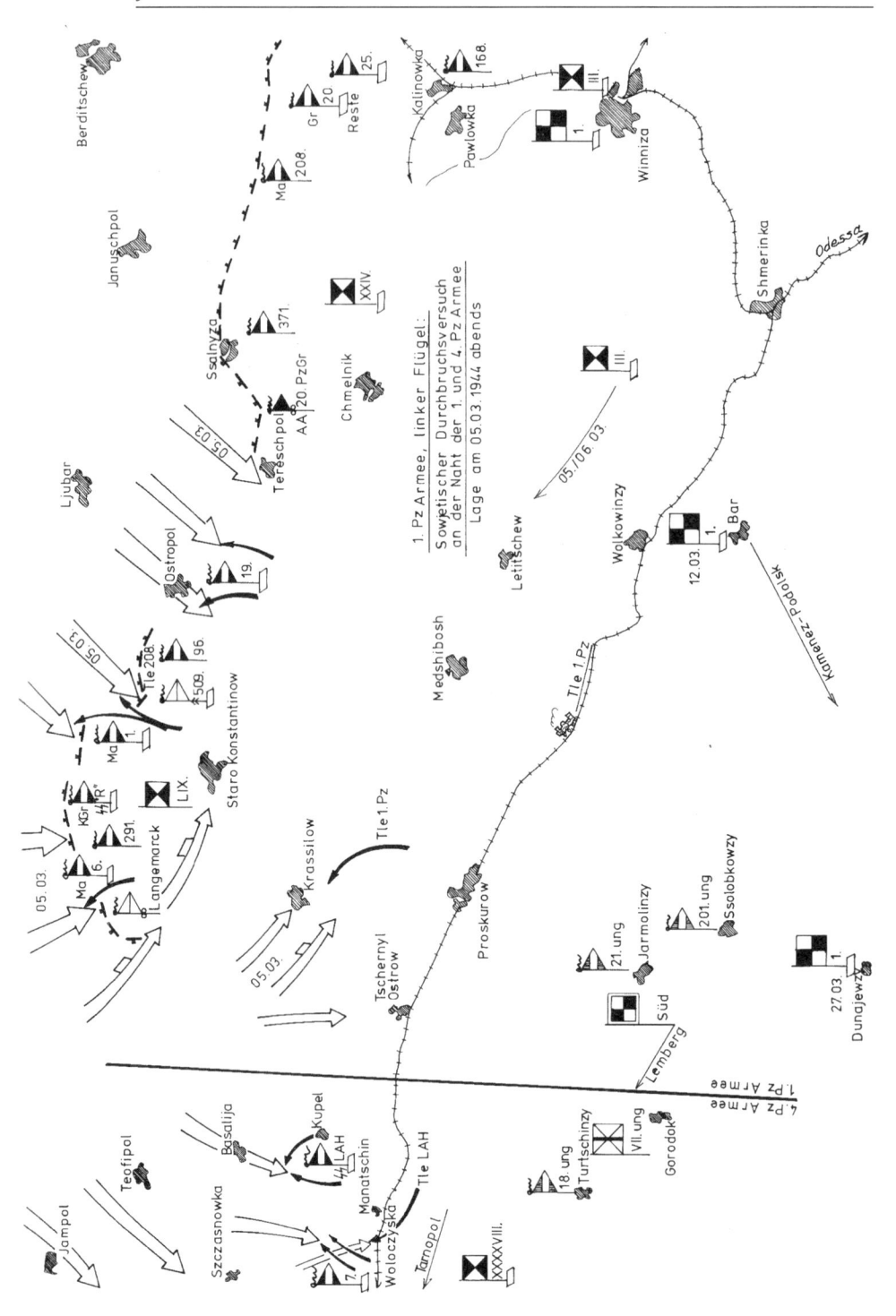

68. *1st Panzer Armee*, left wing: Soviet breakthrough attempt at the boundary between the 1st and 4th *Panzer Armeen*. Situation on 5 March, 1944, evening.

THE BATTLE OF TARNOPOL 303

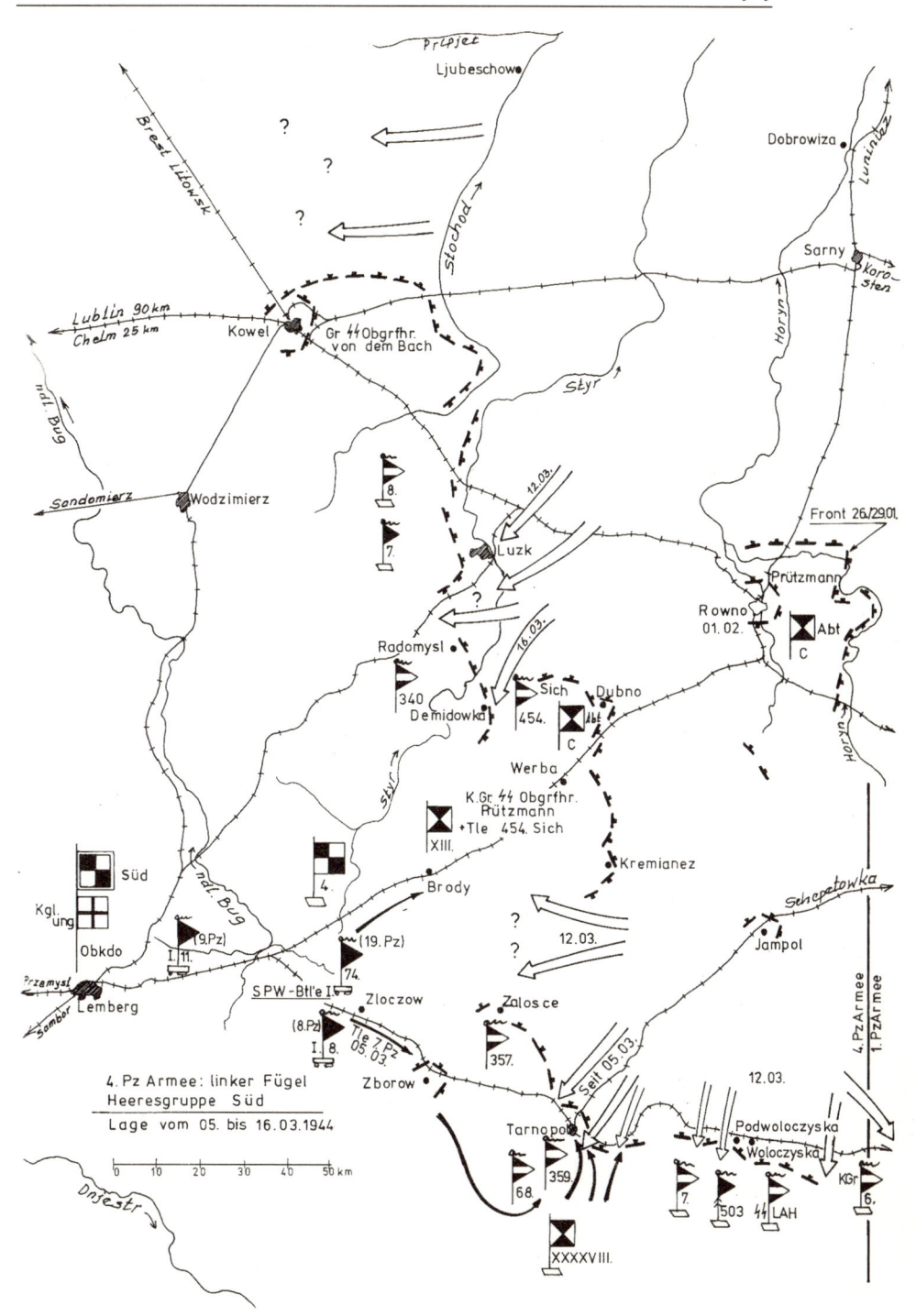

69. 4th *Panzer Armee*, left wing, *Heeresgruppe Süd*. Situation from 5 to 16 March, 1944. See Map 80 for 27 January-18 March 1944. Map 70 shows Tarnopol, 2-12 March 1944. Map 68 adjoins to the lower right. Map 79 shows Rowno, 26 January-1 February 1944.

route from Basilija to the south. The 1st *SS-Panzer Division 'Leibstandarte SS Adolf Hitler'* assembled an 'armoured train' in the Woitowzy railroad station on its own, consisting of a locomotive and a few flatcars on which were loaded *Panzer* IV that were could no longer be driven but could still shoot. Some of the wagons were coupled in front of the locomotive, some behind.

Just as there was no continuous front on the German side, there was no continuous aggressive front on the Soviet side. Nevertheless, enemy forces pushed farther forward to the west in small advances, as east of Kupel. Endless enemy columns reinforced the advanced spearheads of the attack. In Cholodez and Wojkiw they received constant reinforcement. The German command realized the importance of Cholodez because of the paved road there from Kupel to Wojtowzy.

23

Operations in the Tarnopol Area

Finally the Soviets launched a massed attack against the lines of the 7th *Panzer Division* and, on 9 March, attempted to take Tarnopol in a *coup de main* with armour. This was prevented. The situation east and southeast of Tarnopol, however, remained unclear. The 357th *Infanterie Division* was able to eliminate the enemy Czerniechow, Pleszkowce and Zalosze Szare bridgeheads in the sector north of Tarnopol. Nevertheless, the advance of strong enemy forces to the south and southwest with the direction of the advance toward the Rumanian border and the Carpathians raised fears that Tarnopol would be cut off. Accordingly, on 10 March the 1st *SS-Panzer Division 'Leibstandarte SS Adolf Hitler'* was assigned the mission by attacking to the west to reestablish contact with the 7th *Panzer Division*, which, for its part, would attack towards the *Leibstandarte* thrust from the Balkowzy – Korostowa area.

See Maps 69, 70 and 72.

The shortage of combat-capable formations forced another combing through of the rear area services, the workshop and bakery personnel and stragglers, in order to come up with makeshift garrisons for the various localities, and, above all, to keep open the communications between them. Everywhere there was a lack of combat-worthy troops that would have made it possible to effectively halt the Soviets.

To the extent that the Soviets ran into opposition, they bypassed such places, attempting to cut off their contact with the west so that the German formations would then be forced to evacuate the locality and fall back to the west. Thereby, each time, the Soviets gained ground to the west and southwest. It was not always possible to keep open the German supply routes. The division security company [*Divisonssicherungskompanie*] of the 1st *SS-Panzer Division 'Leibstandarte SS Adolf Hitler'* defended Woitowzy, but had to evacuate the place under heavy enemy pressure. That resulted in blockage of the division's supply road to the north. *Kampfgruppe 'Rentrop'*, hastily formed from stragglers, prevented further Soviet advance to the south. *SS-Panzergrenadier Regiment 'LSSAH'* 2 of the 1st *SS-Panzer Division 'Leibstandarte SS Adolf Hitler'* then cleaned the enemy out of Losowa.

See Map 72.

Starting on 6 March the Soviets reinforced their operations against the *Korps* sector, apparently with the objective of getting possession of the Tarnopol – Proskurow *Rollbahn* and railroad stretch in the Woloczyzka – Kaitowzy area on a broad front, thereby blocking it, thus extending their successes to the south. Despite initial success, isolated operations of the 1st *SS-Panzer Division 'Leibstandarte SS Adolf Hitler'* and the 7th *Panzer Division*, which were fighting in the right-hand *Korps* sector failed. Nevertheless, they ran into four mobile Soviet corps (10th Guards Tank Corps, 6th Mechanized Corps, 9th

See Maps 70 and 72.

Mechanized Corps, 6th Guards Tank Corps) as well as the rifle divisions of the 60th Army that had rapidly been brought up to the 4th Guards Tank Army and 3rd Tank Army. The German 1st *SS-Panzer Divison 'Leibstandarte SS Adolf Hitler'* and the 7th *Panzer Division* had to go through a hard, extraordinarily unequal defensive battle.

In order to screen off the German *Schwerpunkte* on both sides of the Zbrucz the Soviets tried again to advance to the southeast via Ibaras and to take Tarnopol in a *coup de main*. Thanks to mobile conduct of the fighting of the weak German formations in and south of Ibaras it was possible to delay the enemy advance for several days.

First Battle of Tarnopol

At this time the Soviets appeared to turn against the Tarnopol area with reinforced strength. Repeatedly enemy forces that had broken through were destroyed, and weak enemy forces forced back from the west bank to the east bank of the Sereth. Interrogation of prisoners revealed that the Soviets had brought up additional rifle divisions with the presumed *Schwerpunkt* north and south of the city. These formations were at full combat strength. Nevertheless, the enemy troops were predominately freshly drafted and inadequately trained civilians from the recaptured territories with reduced combat value. The Soviet armoured formations lost 150 AFVs in these days of the battle in the Tarnopol area. They also suffered losses as a result of the bad road conditions, but still received unhindered logistical support by road and rail.

See Map 72.   *OKH* did, indeed, promise more troops. Their approach, however, suffered from the same road-complications that hindered the movements of the fighting troops. The 1st *SS-Panzer Division 'Leibstandarte SS Adolf Hitler'* conducted a withdrawal to the Bowenez sector. The next day reconnaissance revealed that Widawa and Motschulinzy were held by the enemy. Further enemy movements to the south were expected from there. Reconnaissance to the west proved that Tarno-Ruda, Korzyzka, Kanewka, Orzeckowice, Golochwasty and Nemirinzy were enemy held. In individual villages the fighting partisan bands made themselves evident, ambushing isolated *Wehrmacht* vehicles and arousing unrest by gunfire even before the arrival of the Red Army.

'Fortress' Tarnopol

Hitler then ordered that Tarnopol be held as a *'Fester Platz'* ['fortress'] and that the appointed *Kampfkommandant* build fortifications around the city. Such a measure, which Hitler obviously believed would strengthen the defense, did nothing to increase the defensive will of the formations, since they were already performing beyond what could normally be expected from troops of their strength. Above all else, such a decree took away the freedom of decision from the troop leaders at all levels. In the future, no division commander could move his troops through Tarnopol because the formations would immediately come under the command of the *Kampfkommandant*, and the division commander would thereby lose his formations.

Führerbefehl [Führer Order] *Nr.* 11 was the basis of the mission-statement of the *'Feste Plätze'*. They were to fulfill the same mission as former fortresses.

They were to prevent the enemy from capturing these strategically significant places. The formations that were present had to allow themselves to be encircled and, thereby, tie down the greatest possible amount of enemy forces, thus making it possible to conduct successful counter-operations.

In addition to the concept of the *'Fester Platz'* under its *'Kommandant des Festen Platzes'*, Hitler ordered the creation of several more *'Ortsstützpunkte'* ['Locality Strong Points'], similarly under *Kampfkommandanten* and, indeed, in the event of an enemy breakthrough, they, too, had the mission of defending these strong-points in the depth of the combat area. By inclusion in the main line of resistance they were to provide the backbone of the defense, and, if the enemy broke through, they were to form the hinge-points and cornerstones of the front and, further, to be the jump-off points for counterattacks. According to *Führerbefehl*, the commander of *'Fester Platz'* Tarnopol was immediately subordinate to the Commander in Chief of the *Heeresgruppe*.

Anlage 1 [Appendix 1] to *Führebefehl Nr.* 11 provided 'Guidelines for the *Kommandant* of a *'Fester Platz'*. The entire garrison was to be divided into a *'Sicherheitsbesatzung'* ['Security Garrison'] which had to continually garrison the *'Fester Platz'* and the *'Gesamtbesatzung'* ['Total Garrison'], which, depending on the opportunities, would be sent to the *'Fester Platz'* and, if the enemy attacked in a planned manner, would occupy the defensive positions, but also had to conduct breakouts.

According to these guidelines, the defense was to prepare by blocking important roads, preparing to blow up bridges and other demolitions, with the emphasis on defense against armour. Following the various guidelines and individual directives for the *Kommandant* of the *'Fester Platz'* assumed adequate types and amounts of combat-ready formations and anti-tank guns, as well as heavy weapons, as well as the requisite supplies. The significance of Tarnopol in its municipal architecture and appurtenances was primarily economic, firstly because of its favorable transportation situation north of the Carpathians and, secondly, as a significant industrial center. The city proved quite unsuitable for the intended defensive role, not only in light of its unsuitable architectural layout, but also because of its surroundings that were devoid of cover.

Soviet Advance to the West and Southwest

The systematically advancing formations of the hostile 60th Army, especially the 4th Guards Tank Corps, thrust west past Jampol and took Klepieszowka (one kilometer northwest of Jampol) and Pankowce (three kilometers southwest of Jampol), then Jampol, itself, on 2 March. They reached Lanowce (20 kilometers southwest of Jampol) and, on 31 March, Wierzbowiec (35 kilometers southwest of Jampol). That made the Soviet intentions unmistakably clear, particularly severing the Proskurow – Tarnopol railroad line and capturing the city of Tarnopol itself. *OKH* announced more infantry divisions, the 68th *Infanterie Division*, 357th *Infanterie Division* and 359th *Infanterie Division* that were to be attached to the 48th *Panzer Korps* in the Tarnopol area.

As its essential mission, the 48th *Panzer Korps* was to prevent the envelopment from the west of the 59th *Armee Korps*, and also establish contact

See Maps 68, 70 and 72.

with the 13th *Armee Korps*. In light of the significance of Tarnopol, the command also shifted the sector boundary between the 24th *Panzer Korps* and the 59th *Armee Korps*. The Ljubar – Tschepetowka area came under the command of the 1st *Panzer Armee*.

Offensive of the 1st Ukrainian Front

The offensive of the 1st Ukrainian Front from the area on both sides of Jampol burst into the midst of the regrouping of the 48th *Panzer Korps* that had been ordered for 4 March, thus, for the German command, coming at a markedly unfavorable time. At this point the 7th *Panzer Division* was still on the march to its new combat location, as was the main body of the 1st *SS-Panzer Division 'Leibstandarte SS Adolf Hitler'*. Therefore the intended closure of the gap between the 1st and 4th *Panzer Armeen* which had been planned could not be carried out. The Soviet 3rd Guards Tank Army and 4th Tank Army thrust on through to the south and achieved deep penetrations, while the 60th Army advanced to the southwest.

See Maps 70 and 72. The rapid Soviet advance on 5 March east of Podwoloczyska (armour with mounted infantry) that reached the Proskurow – Tarnopol *Rollbahn* (*Durchgangstraße* IV [through-route IV]) and blocked it for several hours, led to the proposal by *Generalfeldmarschall* von Manstein that the 7th *Panzer Division* be redirected from Tarnopol toward Podwoloczyska rather than via Zbaraz, to concentrate in this area and, with it, to keep the enemy forces distant from the road and railroad, as well as to prevent further advance of the enemy to the south.

See Maps 68, 70 and 72. The two formations that were committed in the *Schwerpunkt* of the Soviet advance, the 7th *Panzer Division* and the 1st *SS-Panzer Division 'Leibstandarte SS Adolf Hitler'* were completely isolated and, on 7 March, initially had to fall back to the Kupel – Manatschin line. In order to avoid being cut off, the divisions daily fell back farther to the south. Initially, however, it was not possible to establish contact between the two formations. The 1st *SS-Panzer Division 'Leibstandarte SS Adolf Hitler'* had to defend itself in a bridgehead position north of Podwoloczyska against superior Soviet armoured forces that received further support from the Soviet 8th Rifle Division and 251st Rifle Division. In the meantime, on 8 March, enemy infantry advanced to the southwest on a broad front from the area around Awratyn and reached the Bogdanowka – Jankowce line, thereby blocking the railroad and *Durchgangstraße* IV between Podwolczyska and Tarnopol at Kamionki. On the next day they reached Chmeliska and Kolodciejowka as far as Skalat (10 March). The two divisions that were in action [7th *Panzer Division* and *'LSSAH'*] were thereby exposed anew to the threat of encirclement.

On the next day elements of the Soviet 351st Rifle Division made it east of Frydrychowka to the south and from southeast of Frydrychowka to the southeast to Woloczyska (three kilometers east of Podwoloczyska), thereby splitting the 7th *Panzer Division* into two parts. In order to avoid exposing both divisions to destruction, they were ordered – designated *'Absetzbewegung* [withdrawal movement] *Bleiken'* – to fall back effective 11 March behind the Bowenez — Zbrucz river line, which was an obstacle to armour, while the 7th

OPERATIONS IN THE TARNOPOL AREA 309

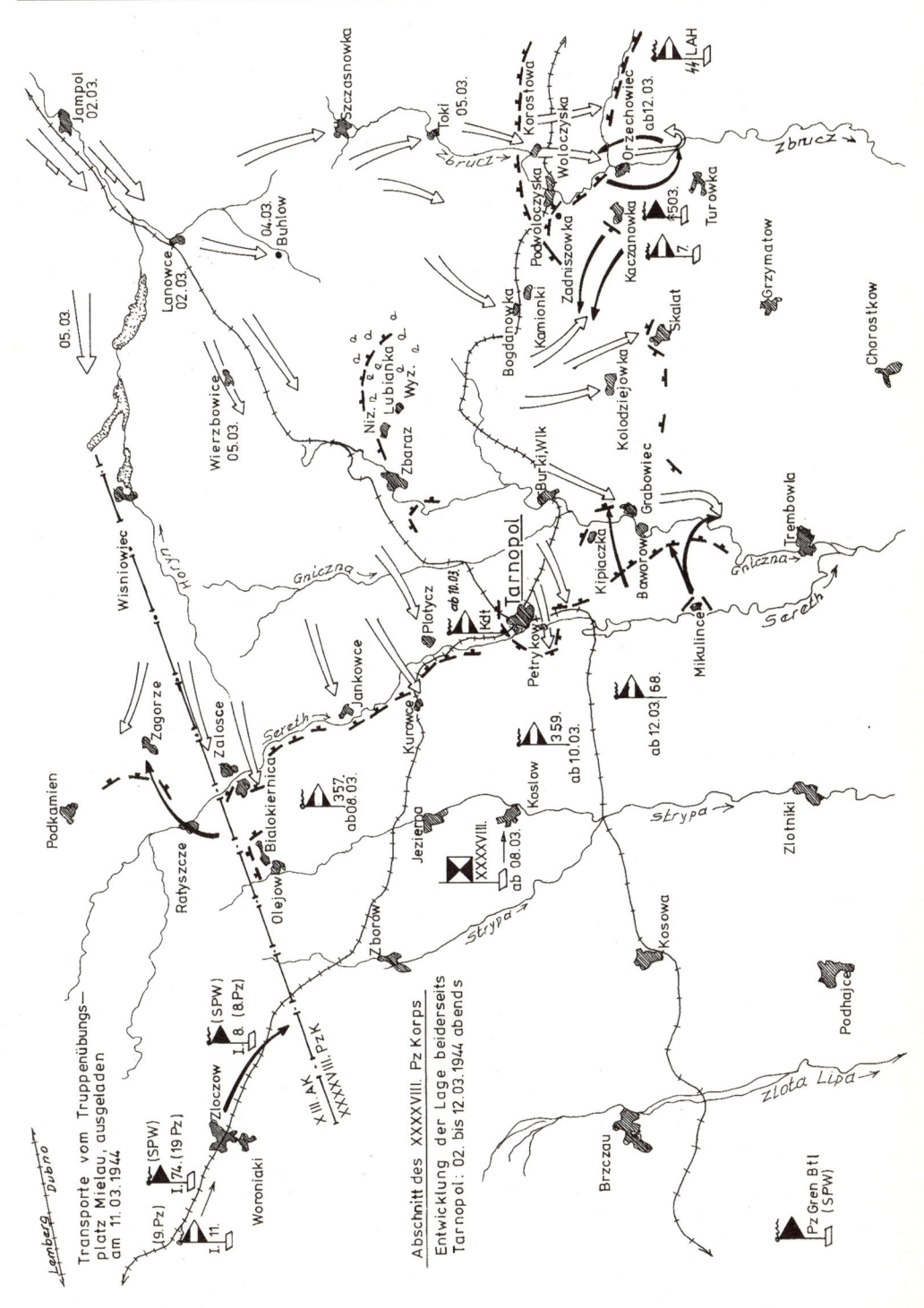

70. Sector of the 48th *Panzer Korps*. Development of the situation on both sides of Tarnopol, 2 to 12 March, 1944, evening. Map 68 adjoins to the right.

Panzer Division continued to hold with its left wing at Zadniszowka, in order to restore contact between these two divisions. That, however, meant that the two formations could no longer carry on the role of a 'functioning bridge' in the midst of the Soviet advance.

The Soviets thereby gained one of their important attack objectives in a few days, namely blocking the great railroad and supply lines north of the Carpathian mountains from Lemberg to Odessa, between Proskurow and Tarnopol. At that moment the German command had the impression that the Soviets were not planning to immediately build upon their great success, rather initially to drive forward the attack that the 2nd Ukrainian Front had launched farther south in the Winniza – Uman area. The *Schwerpunkt* of the Soviet intentions in this area, however, was around Tarnopol, which the Soviets had gradually enveloped on both sides in the shadow of their massed commitment of the Ukrainian Front to the south. On 5 March the Soviets reached Sieniawa – Rosnoszynce (ten kilometers northeast of Zbaraz). The penetration of enemy armour into Sieniawa and the constant artillery fire caused the *Korps* command post to transfer from Zbaraz to Tarnopol. The Soviet troops occupied Zbaraz in the evening of that same day and moved on further toward the southwest, reaching the eastern part of Czernichowce (14 kilometers northeast of Tarnopol) where *Panzer Pionier Bataillon* 50 and the 1st *Kompanie* of *Pionier Bataillon* 327 held a small bridgehead.

24

Fighting in the Tarnopol Area

A series of thrusts by small German formations, as in the area north of Tarnopol, and also south of Tarnopol, were intended to prevent the encirclement of the vital transportation crossroads. The Soviet forces, however, proved to be too strong to stop. On 7 March they reached Jankowce, where they built a bridgehead across the river that included Czerniechow (20 kilometers northwest of Tarnopol). They crossed the Sereth farther to the north at Reniow – Zalosce (15 kilometers northwest of Jankowce) and advanced from there to the south, feeling their way forward by 9 March to the Pleszkowce – Bzowica line. From there the column turned to the southeast toward Malaszowce on the east bank of the Sereth.

See Maps 70 and 72.

The commitment of a *Füsilier* battalion from the Demba troop-training ground proved impossible, since the Soviets advanced from Lozowa between Tarnopol and Iwaczow Gorny to Czystylow and Plotysz on the Sereth.

Three kilometers south of the city the Soviets forced their way through to the Sereth at Petrykow and crossed the river, establishing themselves firmly in the Czarny Las woods. At the same time they attacked *'Fester Platz'* Tarnopol on 8 March with ground-attack planes, thereby temporarily cutting Tarnopol off for the first time from its connections to the rear. In light of this situation, the 357th *Infanterie Division*, which was *en route* to strengthen the defense of Tarnopol, had to detrain at Jezierna in order to immediately attack the enemy frontally.

In the course of 9 March, with *Grenadier Regiment* 944 [357th *Infanterie Division*], after breaking the enemy resistance in Czernichow, Pleszkowce and Zalosce Stare, this division regained the Sereth river and pushed forward German security into the Nosowce Bialoglowy Bialokiernica stream sector northwest of Tarnopol. The division also recaptured Reniow and thereby secured the Jezierna – Tarnopol road connection.

Reinforcement of the 'Fortress' Troops

Thus *Sturmgeschütze* and anti-tank guns could be sent in to the *'Fester Platz'* in order to throw out the enemy that had already penetrated the city. Nevertheless, enemy armour that had broken in with mounted infantry reached the western edge of the city at the Sereth and shelled the Zagrobela suburb from there. They could not, however, accomplish any more, because the outer defense prevented any supply and reinforcement, knocking out five tanks and one enemy assault gun.

See Maps 71 and 72.

On 10 March Soviet troops succeeded in penetrating the northeast edge of the city and captured the supply dump that was located there, then continuing their thrust into the city with armour and infantry. They also thrust toward Biala from the north and secured the east edge of the lake formed there by the Sereth, losing four AFVs in the process. Simultaneously they penetrated the city from the south. After ten AFVs were knocked out, the Soviets fell back again from the northern part of the city, only retaining their hold on the supply dump.

After reinforcements were sent, the entire northern and northeastern parts of the city were back in German hands, cleared of far superior enemy forces. These 'fortress' formations regained the old main line of resistance, knocking out six Soviet tanks and one assault guns, as well as two guns, and counted 400 enemy dead.

The *'Fester Platz'* did not just receive troops, as those of the 444th *Sicherungs Division*, staff of *Artillerie Kommandeur* 144, staff *Feld-Kommandantur* 675, which were to conduct additional thrusts north and south of the city. The 359th *Infanterie Division* set out to the east from the bridgeheads south of Tarnopol. The 68th *Infanterie Division*, which had been hastily brought up, assembled in the Myszkowce – Mikulince bridgehead to advance in the same direction. The two divisions were then supposed to turn to the north and northeast against the Podwoloczyska – Tarnopol road and close the gap to the 7th *Panzer Division*. In the event, against stubborn resistance, the 359th *Infanterie Division* reached Toustolug, Kipiaczka and Zastawi on the Gniczna with elements of *Grenadier Regiment* 947 and 948 [both 359th *Infanterie Division*].

In the days that followed the two divisions that had been brought in were able to relieve the situation around Tarnapol in the face of tough Soviet armoured opposition and, with that, build a continuous front line from the left wing of the 359th *Infanterie Division* to Tarnopol. The 69th *Infanterie Division* took Borki Wielki, the 359th *Infanterie Division* Stupki and Smykowce, so that the *Rollbahn* between Stupki and Tarnopol was again usable for German formations. The Soviets built a proper *'Panzerfront'* against these two divisions, which prevented a further advance, which also, however, excluded the intended clearing of the *Rollbahn* between Podwoczyska and Stupki. Thus contact was not established with the 7th *Panzer Division*. That objective was served by the attack on 18 March with the capture of Kolodziejowka and, on 20 March, the link-up with the left wing of the 7th *Panzer Division* north of Skalat. With that a nearly continuous line of the divisions of the 48th *Panzer Korps* was established on the right wing. Contact, however, was still absent between the 13th *Armee Korps* and 48th *Panzer Korps*.

See Maps 72 and 73.

In light of the strength of the enemy on the east bank an advance of the 357th *Infanterie Division* committed on the north, to support the 359th *Infanterie Division* and 68th *Infanterie Division* attacking from the south no longer appeared likely to succeed. Therefore the *Armee* ordered exclusively that bridgeheads be built on the east bank of the Sereth, but not to cross the river with the main bodies of the formations. That way, in any case, the river-barrier of the Sereth would be used against the enemy advance. The command also decided to build a bridgehead at Zalosce (30 kilometers northwest of Tarnopol) and to establish contact with the 13th *Armee Korps* after an attempted crossing by the II./ *Grenadier Regiment* 944 [357th *Infanterie Division*] failed, on 11 March. The new attempt on the following day at Ratyszcze, eight kilometers further north, by the II./ *Grenadier Regiment* 946 [357th *Infanterie Division*] succeeded in cooperation with a crossing operation from Zalosce Stare to Zalosce Nowe, this including occupation of a series of additional localities. On 15 March the II./ *Grenadier Regiment* 946 finally linked up with the 13th *Armee Korps* (*Sicherungs Bataillon* 226) at Zagorce – Seretec.

Envelopment of 'Fortress' Tarnopol

During the night of 12/13 March the Soviets used the gap existing between Tarnopol and the 359th *Infanterie Division* to cross the Sereth anew at Petrykow with forces of the 336th Rifle Division, with the mission, enveloping Tarnopol to the south, to attack from the west and gain possession of the Sereth river-crossings, getting to Zagrobela, directly west of the city. *Füsilier Bataillon 'Demba'* was able to destroy these forces in the Czarny Las woods. Soviet elements that fell back to the east suffered the same fate at the hands of *Grenadier Regiment* 949 [359th *Infanterie Division*], belonging to the Tarnopol garrison. *See Maps 72 and 73.*

A group of armoured vehicles that were in Tarnopol (five tanks, one *SPW* platoon, the 1st *Batterie* of *Sturmgeschütz Brigade* 301) undertook an attack to the southeast with one company of *Grenadier Regiment* 949 from the south part of the *'Fester Platz'* to establish contact with the 359th *Infanterie Division*. This was exposed to attacks of the Soviet 336th Rifle Division delivered from the north and northeast. The II./ *Grenadier Regiment* 948 [359th *Infanterie Division*] established contact with the armoured group of the *'Fester Platz'* when it reached the Podwoloczyska – Tarnopol railroad line. *See Map 73.*

A further attack of *Grenadier Regiment* 949, with support of the II./ *Grenadier Regiment* 948 (from the left wing of the 359th *Infanterie Division*) on the next day led to the capture of several localities east of Tarnopol, but was then brought to a standstill before Soviet armoured spearheads. The 68th *Infanterie Division* advancing north from Chodaczkow Maly had similar results. An operation of *Sturmgeschütz Brigade* 311 with the II./ *Grenadier Regiment* 948 on the left wing of the 359th *Infanterie Division* experienced the same outcome.

The formations belonging to the garrison of Tarnopol and the divisions committed both north and south of the city launched attacks in all directions with the objective of breaking out little bits of the enemy front, a chunk at a time, and thereby improving the German situation and distracting the Soviets. The 68th *Infanterie Division* took Borki Wielki, Stupki and Smykowce. On 17 March, with *Grenadier Regiment* 188, it took Romanowka, which, however, was lost again to a counterattack with about 50 Soviet AFVs.

These German attacks served to prevent the encirclement of Tarnopol, but led to the realization that the Soviets were bringing up a strong armoured front east of Tarnopol that prevented a further shifting of the attack-front to the east. *See Map 74.*

During the period from 13 to 18 March the Soviets crossed ever stronger forces into their Iwaczow Gorny bridgehead, which, with strong artillery support, would attain the breakthrough that would lead to the final encirclement of Tarnopol. The attacks of the 165th Rifle Division, mostly in regimental strength, could be repulsed, however, until, on 18 March, contact with the 13th *Armee Korps* was torn open in the sector of *Sicherungs Bataillon* 226. After about five days it was possible to restore a nearly continuous line on the east bank of the Sereth between Zalosce Nowi and Ratyszcze, but not contact with the 13th *Armee Korps*.

Final Encirclement of Tarnopol

On 21 March the Soviets launched their decisive attack on Tarnopol, with the *Schwerpunkt* east of the city between the Sereth and Zbrucz, with the 1st Tank Army and 4th Tank Army with over 200 AFVs and the Soviet 16th Army northwest of Tarnopol. The Soviets immediately inserted new forces (the 165th Rifle Division) into the gap they attained.

In the sector of the 68th *Infanterie Division* east of Tarnopol elements of the Soviet 1st Tank Army attacked with about a hundred AFVs and several infantry regiments, resulting in the loss of Kolodziejowka and Chodaczkow Maly. The 68th *Infanterie Division* lost most of its anti-tank defense during this heavy fighting. In order to assure unified command, the *Korps* consolidated remnants of the 68th *Infanterie Division* with the 1st *SS-Panzer Division* 'Leibstandarte SS Adolf Hitler' and the 7th *Panzer Division* into a *Kampfgruppe* 'Maus', which, located south of Podwolocczysk and Ssatanow at the Zbrucz, no longer had contact with the 48th *Panzer Korps* and, thus, no longer had contact with the 4th *Panzer Armee*. On 24 March the *Heeresgruppe* therefore attached it to the 1st *Panzer Armee*.

See Map 74.

The Soviet tank army (10th Tank Corps) advanced with over seventy AFVs and infantry formations of the 336th Rifle Division and 148th Rifle Division against the 359th *Infanterie Division,* which was in action west of the 68th *Infanterie Division*. On the first day they captured Stupki and Borki Wielki. West of Smykowce they broke through the German main line of resistance. A few hours later the Soviet armour reached the Sereth in the east part of Berezowica Wielki and outflanked the south wing of the 359th *Infanterie Division*, also getting to the Sereth at Miszkowice. Thereupon the 359th *Infanterie Division* pulled its main line of resistance back to the Sereth in the evening of 23 March.

See Map 74.

The Soviets succeeded in breaking through to the south from their bridgehead at Jankowce – Horodyszcze and go past Tarnopol on the west. Despite the arrival of *schwere Panzer Abteilung* 507, the 357th *Infanterie Division* was unable to clean up the situation at Korowce due to lack of infantry, nor was it able to build a security line along the railroad. On 23 March enemy infantry and armoured forces thrust much more into the retreat movement, dispersing *Grenadier Regiment* 945 [357th *Infanterie Division*], and continued on to the south toward Chodaczkow Wielki. The 359th *Infanterie Division* now found itself enveloped from both sides and had to fall back extremely quickly to the course of the Strypa river and ist Wosuszka tributary between Kupczynce – Denysow – Mlynier – Horodyszcze – Kozlow. The 357th *Infanterie Division* completed a similar movement, falling back to the bow-shaped length of the course of the Lobuszanka around Olejow and Bialokiernica.

The withdrawal movements during the night of 23/24 March to the Strypa – Wosuszka line brought about the final encirclement of Tarnopol. The Soviet spearheads coming from the north and south on the west side of Tarnopol linked up at Chodaczkow Wielki.

The Battle for 'Fortress' Tarnopol

The entire encircled area was divided into four defensive sectors corresponding to the four cardinal points of the compass.

On the following day (24 March) the Soviets made several attempts to capture what its situation made the only possible jump-off point for the garrison of the *'Fester Platz'* to break out to the west or, as the case might be, the objective of possible relief operations. In the course of the day Zagrobela

See Map 71 and, for the 'big picture', Map 93.

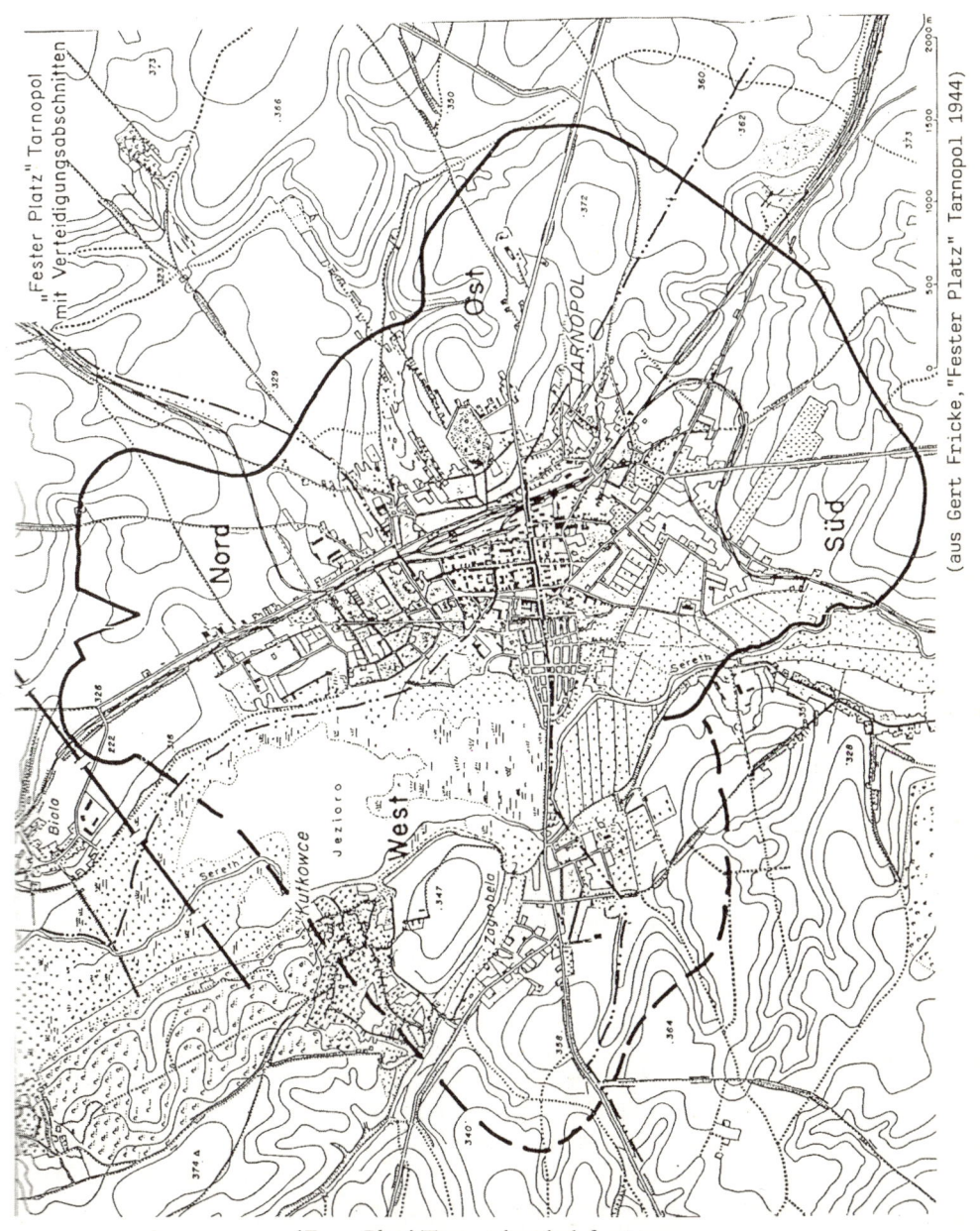

71. *'Fester Platz'* Tarnopol with defensive sectors.

changed hands repeatedly, but evening found it back in German hands, regardless of further attacks from the north and south on the opposite bank. That day a *Parliamentaire* demanded the surrender of Tarnopol. There was no answer to this demand. In any event the *'Fester Platz'*, though with a wholly inadequate stock of ammunition, could withstand another day of major fighting.

See Maps 74, 75 and 76.

The 4th *Panzer Armee* planned for 25 March the advance of an armoured formation from the Jezierna area along the Jezierna – Tarnopol road to get a supply convoy through to Tarnopol. The force involved was a combined *Kampfgruppe* of the 8th *Panzer Division* under *Oberst* Friebe (8th *Panzer Division*).

First Relief Attempt

See Maps 74 and 75.

Preparation of the supply convoy, however, involved difficulties: 40 tons of ammunition, five ambulances – the more so since the loads of supplies that were to be carried through to Tarnopol first had to be loaded in Lemberg. In light of the danger that the Soviets would immediately set up a strong anti-tank-front in this sector, the Friebe formation started immediately, without waiting for the arrival of the supply convoy.

Starting from Jezierna the armoured formation broke through several lines of resistance constructed at the road. As it approached *'Fester Platz'* Tarnopol, of course, the Soviet resistance mounted. Four kilometers west of Zagrobela the attack formation ran into a strong defensive position with artillery support from the east bank of the Sereth and flanking artillery fire from both north and south. The Red Air Force also joined the fray, so that the attack was brought to a standstill and, even after regrouping and swinging out the south, it foundered on strong dug-in anti-tank gun and tank-fronts. At that point a breakout of the 'fortress garrison' would, in all likelihood, have been successful. Hitler, however, refused permission for that.

Since, even if it succeeded through further efforts, the supplies could not have been brought in with the armoured vehicles, the 4th *Panzer Armee* cancelled the operation at about 1300 hours with the order to return to the former main line of resistance with all salvageable armoured vehicles. A substantial portion of the failure was attributed to the fact that no aerial reconnaissance preceded the endeavor.

On 26 March *Panzerverband* [armoured formation] *Friebe* smashed the enemy forces that had broken through between the 359th *Infanterie Division* and the 357th *Infanterie Division,* which were before the northern wing of the 359th *Infanterie Division*, with an attack from north to south. At other locations at Cecory and Taurow the Soviets pulled formations that had advanced back across the Wosuska to the east. Hitler still refused permission for a breakout from the *'Fester Platz'*, placing far more hopes on the commitment of a newly activated combat formation (the 2nd *SS-Panzer Korps*) which would initially launch a thrust toward the east-northeast, and then turn southeast in the general direction of Czortkow. The 48th *Panzer Korps* advanced with a group of forces from its southern wing to the east in order to prevent a shift of enemy forces from its front to the south. *'Fester Platz'* Tarnopol, however, gained no relief from the armoured advance of *Angriffsgruppe* [attack group] *Hausser* (2nd *SS-Panzer Korps*).

The 48th *Panzer Korps*, however, gained relief. It established contact with the 1st *Panzer Armee* at Buczacz with the 10th *SS-Panzer Division 'Frundsberg'*. For the time being the Soviets no longer attacked the 48th *Panzer Korps*, initially seeming to limit themselves to securing the *Kessel* of Tarnopol.

Situation of the 'Fortress'

On 25 March the Soviets advanced with 17 AFVs and infantry in the northern sector of the *'Fester Platz'*. The advance of *Panzerverband 'Friebe'* had been of no use to the garrison of the *'Fester Platz'*. On the next day the Soviets delivered uncoordinated attacks against individual sectors of the defensive front of the *'Fester Platz'*. Attacks on the morning of 27 March could also be repulsed, although the defensive power of the defenders suffered from a shortage of ammunition.

Granted, the *Luftwaffe* dropped ammunition, but the quantities were inadequate: Over five days they dropped 44 containers with 144 high-explosive rounds for light infantry guns, 111 rounds for tank main guns, 25 rounds for 7.5 cm anti-tank guns, 112 for light field howitzers and 18,000 rifle cartridges. Due to heavy Soviet anti-aircraft defenses the drops were from above 600 meters, so that only one third of the ammunition dropped could be recovered. On account of the strong anti-aircraft defenses drops of supplies failed to achieve the desired success, consequently now gliders brought supplies into the city.

The heavy Soviet artillery fire especially impressed the soldiers of *Grenadier Regiment 949*, freshly drafted 18 year-olds with wholly inadequate training and without experience at the front. Finally the line of defense had to be pulled back to the edge of the city. Losses of the defenders' men and matériel increased, the more so since enemy weapons and assembly positions could not be engaged due to shortage of artillery ammunition.

On 31 March, after an hour of artillery preparation with support from ground-attack planes, the encircling forces launched a concentric attack and forced their way to the Tarnopol railroad station. They captured the east part of the city. The north and south sectors also had to be pulled back to the edge of the city. The next day the Soviets achieved penetrations into the southern and eastern parts, as well as into Zagrobela to the west. In the east a heavy field-howitzer battery repulsed an attack with direct fire. Except for five containers, the entire night-drop of supplies failed to reach its objective because the circumference of the *'Fester Platz'* had already been so constricted.

See Map 71.

After the east and south wings of the line of defense of the *'Fester Platz'* had been crushed, the garrison fell back to a line to its rear in order to avoid being split up. Calling in the last reserves, the garrison repulsed an attack with armoured support against the heart of the city, knocking out ten enemy AFVs.

Signs of disintegration under the impression of strong enemy superiority began to appear within the garrison, as among elements of the *Waffen-SS-Freiwilliger Regiment 'Galizien'*, which was committed in the northern sector. An effective *Stuka* attack balanced the loss of individual blocks of houses that resulted from the retreat of the demoralized elements of *'Galizien'*.

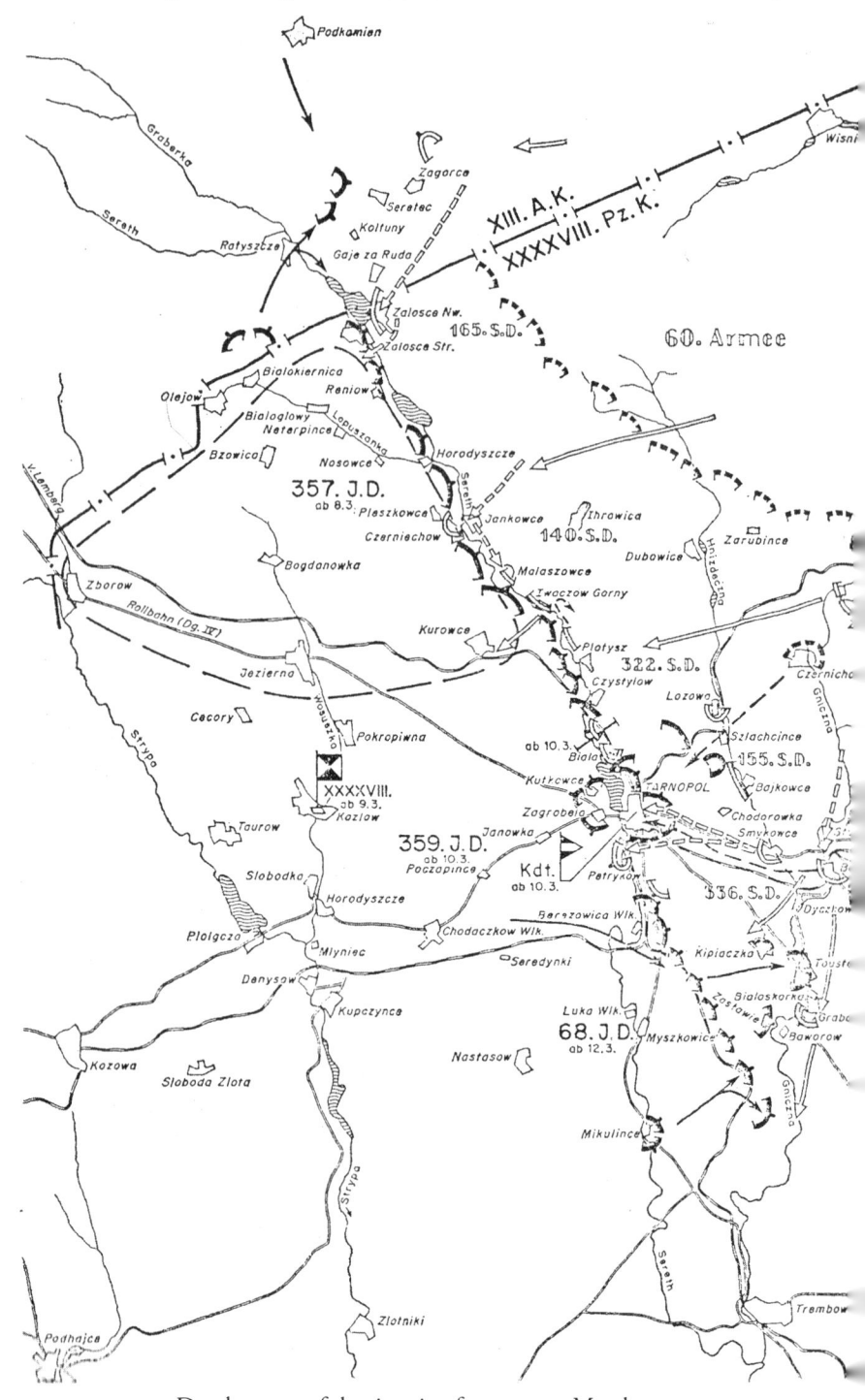

72. Development of the situation from 5 to 12 March, 1944

FIGHTING IN THE TARNOPOL AREA

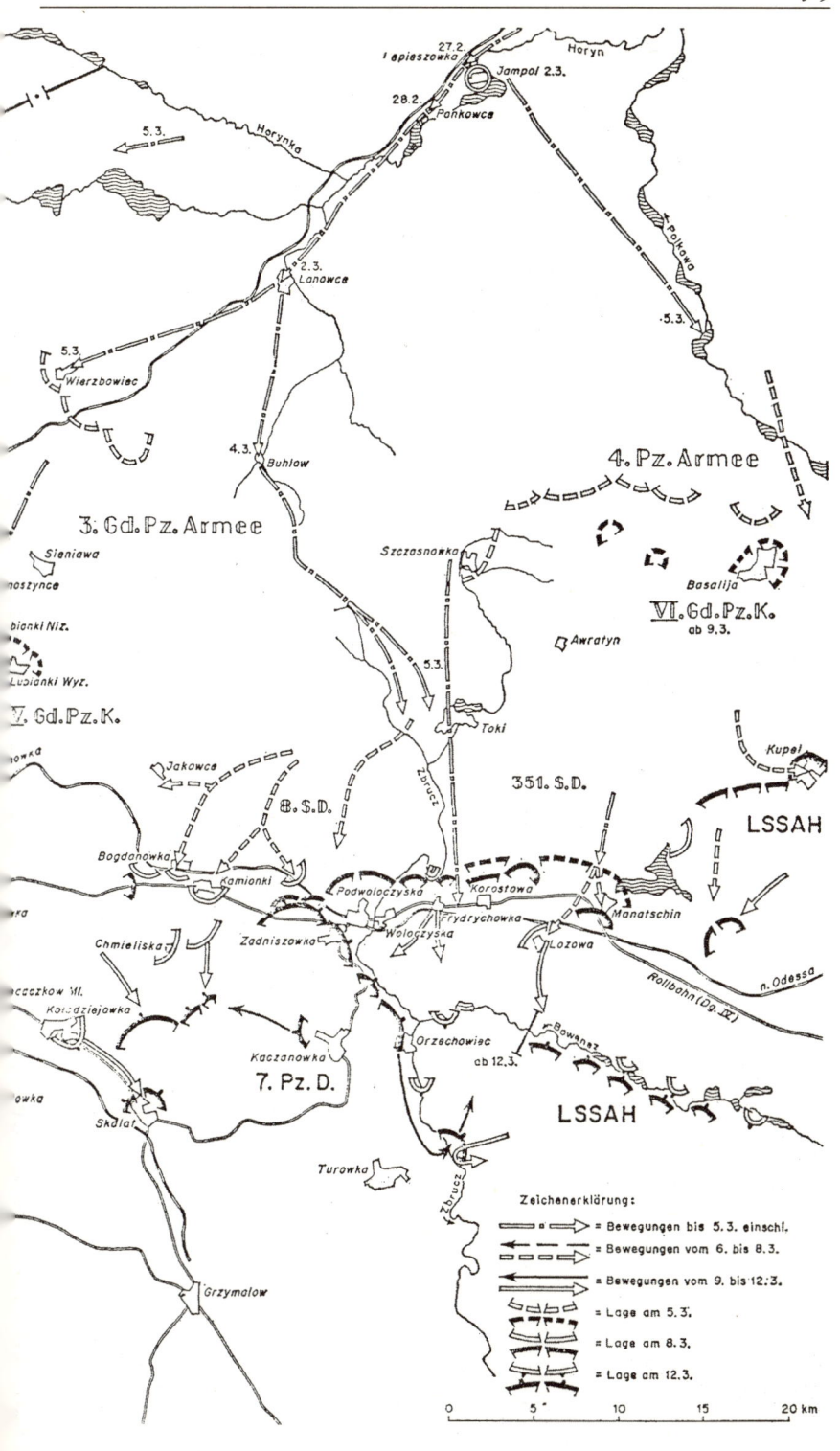

CRUCIBLE OF COMBAT

Entwicklung der Lage vom 13.3. bis 20.3.1944

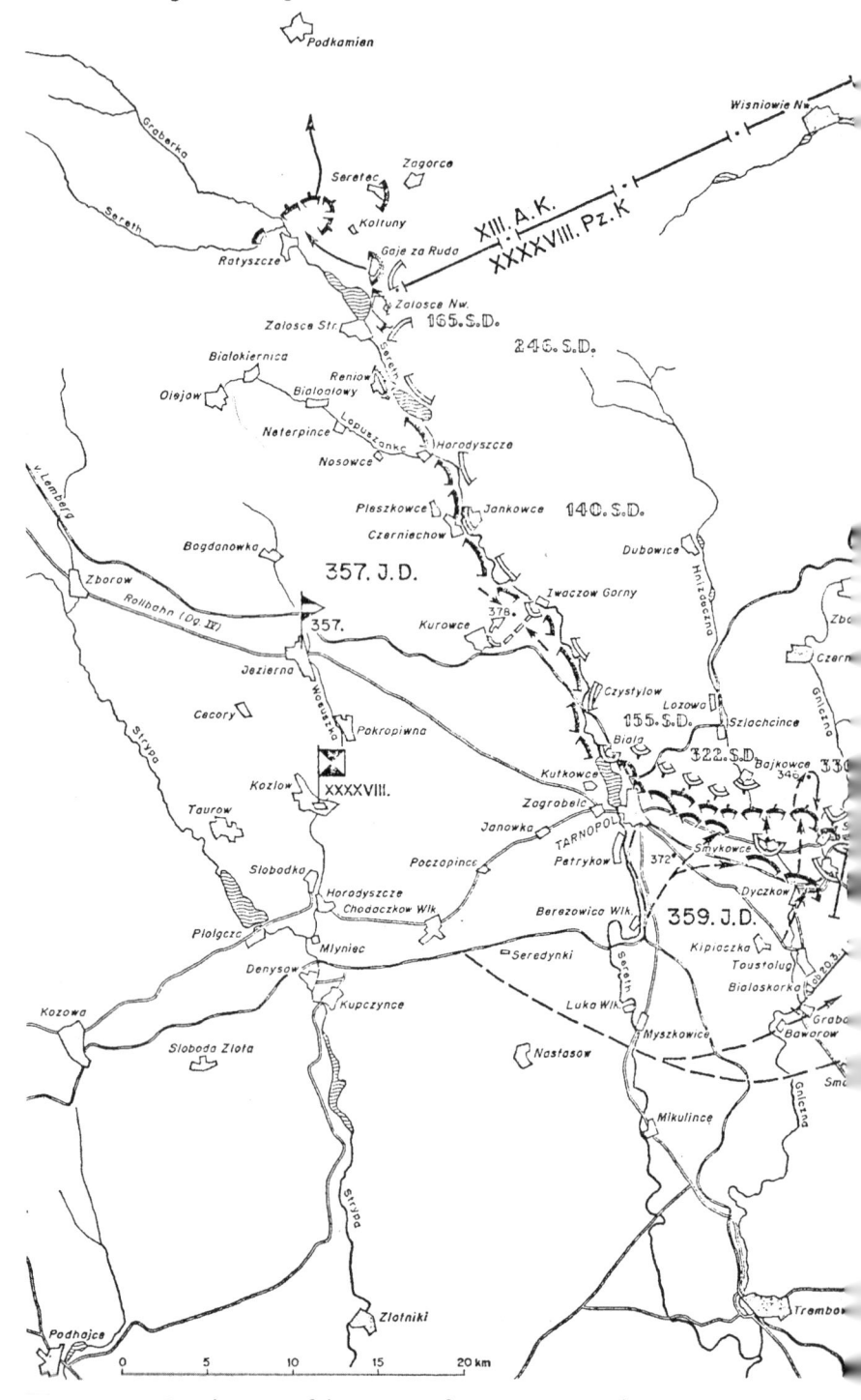

73. Development of the situation from 13 to 20 March, 1944.

FIGHTING IN THE TARNOPOL AREA

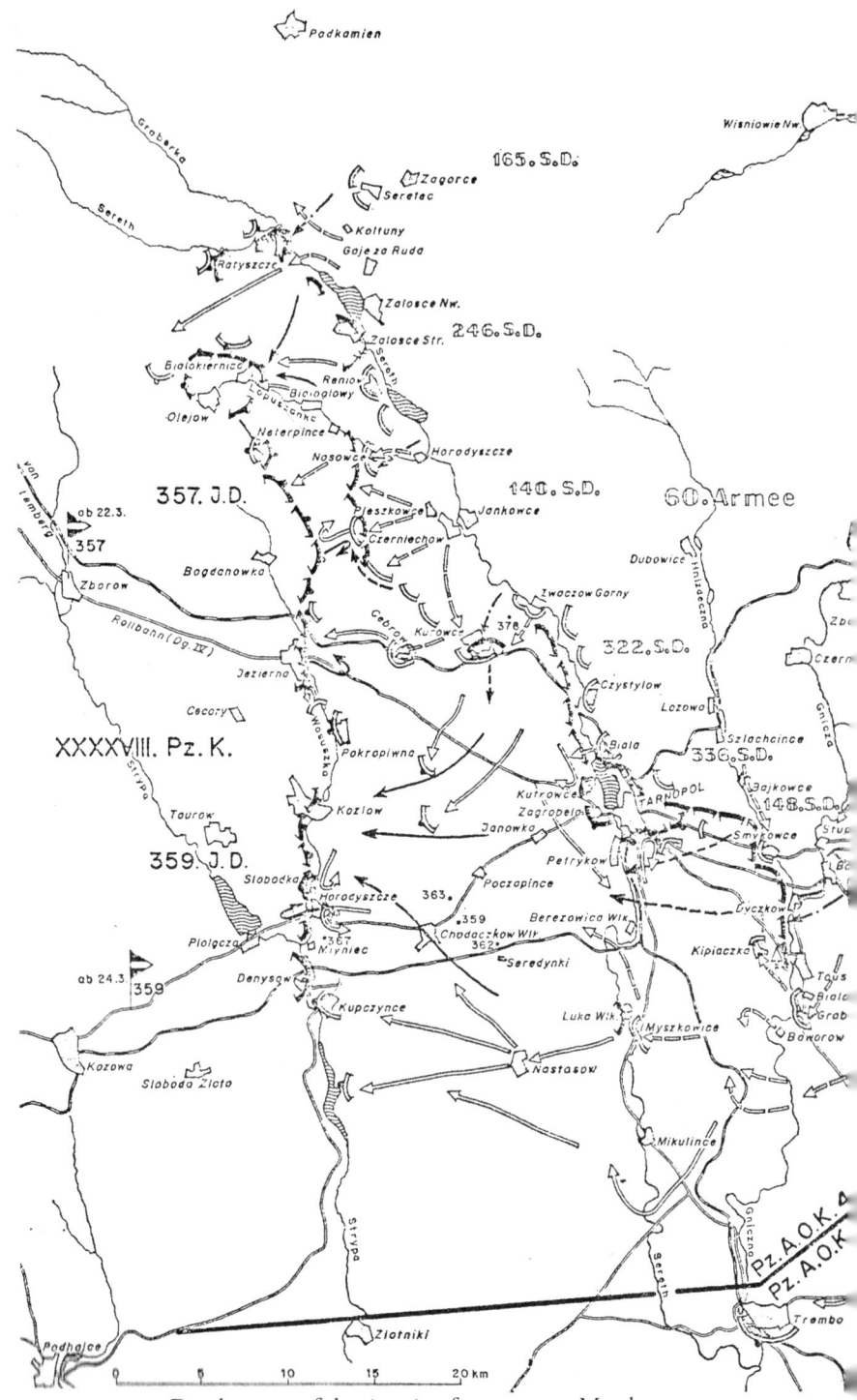

74. Development of the situation from 21 to 24 March, 1944.

FIGHTING IN THE TARNOPOL AREA

75. The Thrust toward Tarnopol on 25 March, 1944 by *Panzerverband Friebe*.

FIGHTING IN THE TARNOPOL AREA

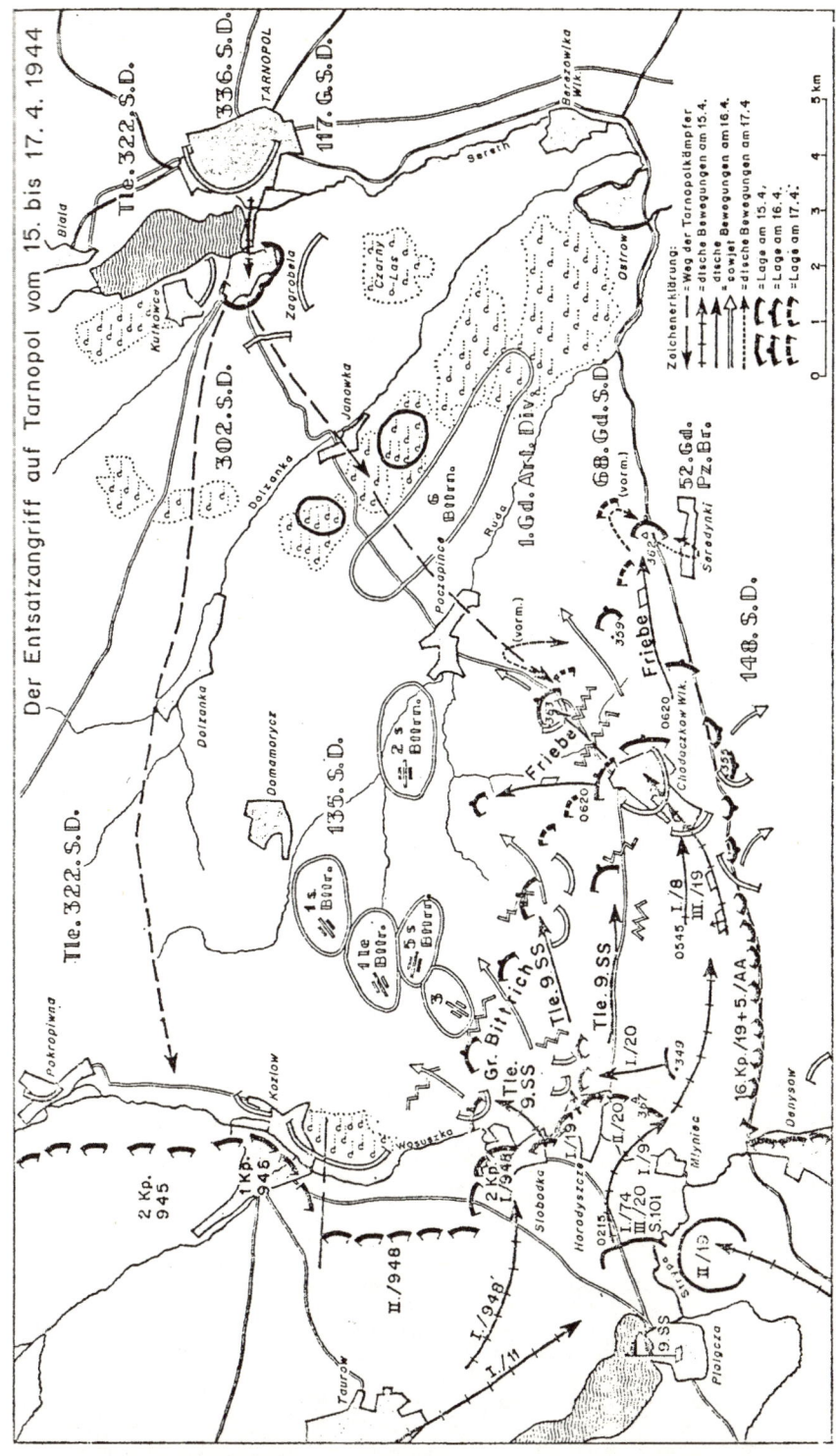

76. The Relief Attack toward Tarnopol from 15 to 17 April, 1944.

On 4 April over 1,000 wounded already lay in the cellars of Tarnopol, without medical supplies or personnel. On this day the attacker suddenly eased up in the western sector and, instead, concentrated all his efforts on the portion of the city that was on the east bank. Another deep penetration in the north was intercepted by commitment of *Stukas*, but forced renewed shortening of the front. The *Heeresgruppe* again prohibited breakout operations by the *Kommandant* of the *'Fester Platz'*. Preparations were made on 5 April in the hope that a planned advance of the 100th *Jäger Division* would provide relief for the troops of the *'Platz'*.

On 5 April the Soviets covered the entire city with fire of all calibers. Ensuing infantry attacks, however, were again repulsed. The *Kommandant* had to face the question of how long his troops could stand up to that kind of burden.

During pauses in the artillery fire the Soviets used loudspeakers with German melodies, interspersed with demands to give up the fight. They sent back German prisoners repeatedly to the troops with similar demands.

Further Relief Attempts[1]

For the necessary 'Big Picture', see Maps 93, 94 and 95. See also Maps 76 and 82.

In the afternoon of 6 April the 10th *SS-Panzer Division 'Frundsberg'* succeeded in advancing to Buczacz and establishing contact with the attack-spearheads of the 1st *Panzer Armee*. Accordingly, the 9th *SS-Panzer-Division 'Hohenstaufen'* was ordered to remain with its main body in its former concentration area to the rear of the 48th *Panzer Korps*, but to push elements forward to Kuzowa, in order to advance from there to the southwest and cooperate on the far bank of the Strypa with the 10th *SS-Panzer Division 'Frundsberg'*. *Panzerverband 'Friebe'* was also to take part in the relief of the *'Fester Platz'*. Plans for the opertion went back and forth. It turned out, however, to be difficult to carry out a relief operation from the west, because the Soviets had reinforced their forces there to an extraordinary degree. The 9th *SS-Panzer Division 'Hohenstaufen'* was to move out of the Horodyszcze area and *Einsatzkommando* [special command] *'Friebe'* from the Kozlow area, then cross the Strypa and fight on through to Tarnopol.

See Maps 74 and 76.

In the morning hours of 11 April, after lengthy preparation, the advance of *Panzerberband 'Friebe'* started, with 24 *Panzer* V [*'Panther'*], 9 *Panzer* VI [*'Tiger'*] and 101 *SPW*. It forced the crossing at Kozlow over a subsidiary branch of the Wosuzka, but then came to a standstill. A new attempt to cross the river to the east also remained without success at noon. The enemy defense proved stronger than originally expected. The Soviet command had expected

---

1 Translator's note – Hinze appears to base much of his treatment of Tarnopol on Fricke's monograph, *'FesterPlatz' Tarnopol*. Although Fricke's monograph is generally detailed and accurate, historians of the II. *SS-Panzer Korps* take issue with Fricke's treatment of that *Korps'* relief attack. For highly readable, excellent accounts from the viewpoint of the men who fought in the Waffen-SS 9th and 10th *SS-Panzer Divisionen 'Hohenstaufen'* and *'Frundsberg'*, see Wilhelm Tieke's *Im Feuersturm letzter Kriegsjahre*, a history of the 2nd *SS-Panzer Korps*, which is also available in English translation as *In the Firestorm of the Last Years of the War*, published by Fedorowicz, and Herbert Fürbringer's massive history of the *'9th SS-Panzer-Division 'Hohenstaufen'*, published by Heimdal, in a dual-language edition in French and German.

an advance on Tarnopol and prepared a strong defense before the sector of the front between Jezierna and Denysow, and blown all the bridges.

The 9th *SS-Panzer Division 'Hohenstaufen'* set out against Horodyszcze with 30 *Panzer* IV and 30 *Sturmgeschütze* and captured it against stubborn opposition. It was possible to build a small eastward bridgehead at the demolished road bridge. A few kilometers to the south, the I./ *SS-Panzergrenadier Regiment* 20 [9th *SS-Panzer Division 'Hohenstaufen'*] together with the I./ *Grenadier Regiment* 947 of the 359th *Infanterie Division* crossed the Wosuzka river at Mlyniec on inflatable rubber rafts and advanced further to capture Hill 367. The I./ *Grenadier Regiment* 947 forced the enemy that was directly east of the Strypa back to the Denysow – Tarnopol railroad line. That established a jump-off position south of Horodyszcze for the advance to Tarnopol.

See Map 76.

The pioneers immediately undertook construction of a bridge at Mlyniec. However, as the result of hours of cloudbursts, the bridging apparatus was delayed in its arrival, forcing initial postponement of the bridge construction. The pioneer's bridgehead at the demolished highway bridge at Horodyszcze was lost under heavy enemy pressure. As the result of command problems within the 9th *SS-Panzer Division 'Hohenstaufen'*, which lacked experience at the front, and inadequate briefing of the command over the conditions of combat that existed at the time, all operations on 12 and 13 April proved pointless. Only in the morning hours of 14 April were the pioneers able to have a military bridge ready at Mlyniec so that the relief operation could start.

At 1000 hours the thrust to Tarnopol began against the Soviet 135th and 148th Rifle Division. The III./ *SS Panzergrenadier Regiment* 19 of the 9th *SS-Panzer Division 'Hohenstaufen'* got off to a delayed start. Because of that the attack had to be held up and then, after an hour's interruption, continued. That, however, gave the Soviets warning. At noon the German *Panzer* spearhead had only reached the area southwest of Chodaczkow Wielki. The Soviets put up stubborn resistance at the edge of the built-up area. On the other hand, capture of the Tarnopol – Dynisow railroad line in order to screen the southern flank succeeded.

General Balck directed the attacking formations, after the capture of Chodaczkow Wielki, to continue the attack, even by moonlight, without delay, in order to reach Zagrobela. However, the attack could not continue without first receiving resupply with ammunition and petrol. After fierce fighting *Kampfgruppe 'Friebe'* then took territory east of Chodaczkow Wielki and hills north of Seredynki, as well as additional hills 1.5 kilometers east of Chodaczkow Wielki. Tarnopol was still eleven kilometers distant.

Final Battle in the 'Fortress'

On 14 April the Soviets split the defended area of the *'Fester Platz'* in two, the one portion in Tarnopol, the other in Zagrobela, separated by the Sereth river. The bridge and the Sereth dam provided the only link between the two parts, and they were under observed fire. The main body of the defenders that were in the east, about 1,300 men, crossed the Sereth during the night at the Zagrobela crossing. Small elements still remained on the east bank in order

See Maps 71, 74 and 75.

to hold that section in whose cellars lay the wounded who were incapable of marching.

During the night of 14/15 April the *'Fester Platz'* had to evacuate its bridgehead on the east bank of the Sereth, leaving 700 severely wounded to their fate. Rations were scant, because the ration-stock on the east bank was in Soviet hands. In the afternoon of 15 April the report arrived of the death of the *Kommandant* of the *'Fester Platz'*. Henceforth there was no radio contact because the apparatus had been destroyed by gunfire.

On 16 April, after *Oberst* von Schönfeld had assumed command, at about 2000 hours the last of the *'Fester Platz'* fighters, divided into two groups of about 700 men each, along with the walking wounded, launched a breakout. They broke through the immediate ring of encirclement around Zagrobela. The Soviets appeared to be surprised. One group set out to the west, the other, led by the *Kommandant*, set out to the southwest. This group made it over the hills southwest of Zagrobela and past Janowka into the woods south of this place where there were enemy heavy artillery and anti-tank gun positions without significant losses. The crews of the guns were dispersed and, in part, wiped out. The Soviets, however, attacked the group from its rear and from both sides, forced it out of the woods and, once west of the woods, totally dispersed it. All of the officers were killed, including *Oberst* von Schönfeld. The survivors split up into smaller groups and attempted, continually weakened by constant losses, to reach the German lines. Only a few succeeded.

Fifty men made it within shouting distance of the German lines at Kozlow but could not make it to the lines because the Soviets suppressed every movement. Towards evening five men of this group reached the German lines and salvation. On 18 April two men from a group that had broken out of Zagrobela to the west made it to the German lines. Ten men reached *Panzer*-spearhead *'Friebe'* on 16 April. All in all, a grand total of 55 men made it from *'Fester Platz '* Tarnopol to the German lines – the outcome of Hitler's order to defend Tarnopol as a *'Fester Platz'*.

The benefits that were intended to come from this *'Platz'* had not materialized. It was true that the *'Fester Platz'* had temporarily drawn three or more Soviet divisions to it and brought about a degree of quiet at the Strypa and Wosuszka line since the beginning of April. It is possible to attribute to it the delay of the Soviet 48th Tank Corps offensive expected for the end of March. In light of the strength of the Soviet formations, however, tying down individual divisions at Tarnopol cannot be considered a serious hindrance for the Soviets. It is possible that they halted in this area initially in order to await the results of their advances farther south toward Bessarabia. In any case, it could have caused the Soviets no problems when it came to carrying on their attack, if they wished, aside from tying up a few formations around Tarnopol.

Withdrawal of the Relief Forces

Strong enemy counteraction from the south, southeast, east and northeast prevented continuation of the attack by *Gruppe Friebe* on 17 April. The formations had to fend off strong attacks. Therefore they could not attend to their objective of receiving additional Tarnopol fighters. The relief operation from the Mlyniec bridgehead had already cost 1,200 men and 18 AFVs, and was now pointless.

The formations that had now been forced back to the main line of resistance were exposed to strong Soviet attacks east and northeast of Chodaczkow Wielki, but were able to repulse these attacks.

25

The Situation on the Left Wing of *Heeresgruppe Süd*

Events in the Shitomir combat area, later Berditschew, then Tscherkassy and also the battles of *Heeresgruppe* A diverted attention from the fate of the northern wing of the *Heeresgruppe*, namely the 13th *Armee Korps* and 59th *Armee Korps*. In light of their badly battered condition, these were in no position to restore a continuous line to the right wing of *Heeresgruppe Mitte*, but were forced again and again to fall back to avoid being outflanked.

See Maps 31, 36, 39 and 40.

After the fighting around Korosten, with initial loss of the city and its later recapture, the troops conducted a staged fighting retreat. Regular Soviet troops infiltrated through the gaps where there were no German field troops and there linked up with the locally operating partisan bands. The central command of the partisans was in Emiltschino, 60 kilometers west of Korosten. Well-equipped and strictly commanded bands controlled the entire rear area, with the exception of those places garrisoned by German troops. While these bands had previously only engaged in harassment, they now undertook railroad demolitions, cutting telephone lines, sabotage of logistical facilities and ambushing isolated vehicles and soldiers. It was conspicuous that the bands appeared in temporal and geographical conjunction with operations of the Red Army at the front. They prepared the areas that were not garrisoned by German troops for the advance of the Red Army, holding the west bank in time to ease the Soviet crossings, provided guides who were familiar with the localities and terrain and preparing cross-country routes for the advance.

Despite all this, it was possible to prevent the Soviets from attaining an operational break-through on the highly exposed front of the northern wing of *Heeresgruppe Süd* until the end of 1943 and the start of 1944. Now, however, they had the opportunity to advance further in the so-called 'land-bridge', the 60 kilometer wide movement-corridor north of the left wing of the 59th *Armee Korps* as far as *Heeresgruppe Süd* on both sides of the great Kiew – Shitomir – Rowno – Lemberg road. This through-route even had a certain kind of protection provided by the nearly impassable wood and swamp terrain on both sides.

See Map 40.

The German defense on the Korosten front could no longer stand up to the strong Soviet attack on 28 December and fell back to the line west of Uschomir (ten kilometers west of Korsten). On 31 December the *Korps* was approximately at the Bondarewka – Osatpy line 6 – 25 kilometers north of Belka.

See Maps 69 and 83. Gorodniza is shown in the upper part of Map 85.

On the extreme northern wing on both sides of the Sarny – Kowel railroad line the Soviets drove rapidly farther to the west against the isolate German fighting formations that were there (elements of the 454th *Sicherungs Division* and police units). In this retreat elements that had been cut off had to fight their way back through partisan occupied and harassed localities, such as Gorodniza and Kurtschizy. However, the troops were able to bring all their heavy weapons with them and to keep the artillery ready at any time to support the weakened infantry forces.

The troops, themselves, described their retreat as the way 'from *Kessel* to *Kessel*'. Supply of the formations with petrol and ammunition took place at that time, in part, from the air.

On 4 January the last elements of *Korpsabteilung* C crossed the Slucz river at Gorodniza to the south and, on 5 January, secured at the Korczyk and Slucz southwest of Gorodniza, the main body of the 291st *Infanterie Division* in Koezec. On 6 January *Korpsabteilung* C surrounded Korzec in a wide arc (6 – 10 kilometers) from the southeast to northwest. With that the line had been shifted back about 110 kilometers from Korosten to Korzec. On 11 January the Soviets renewed their westward drive in this sector. During the night of 12/13 January *Korpsabteilung* C with the 454th *Sicherungs Division* fell back to the Hoszcza bridgehead. Here it was possible, despite heavy Soviet attacks, to build a new defense at the Hoszcza and Tuczyn bridgehead. The straight-line distance between Korzec and Hoszcza amounted to 35 kilometers. *See Maps 78, 80 and 85.*

In the meanwhile, a 50 kilometer 'hole' gaped between them and formations in the south at Schepetowka. To the north the great 'Wehrmachtsloch' [*Wehrmacht's* gap] stretched to *Heeresgruppe Mitte*. *See Map 80.*

Advance on Rowno

The Soviets pressed with superior forces and armour against the Hoszcza bridgehead and forced back the German security. It was possible to blow up the great bridge over the river in time. There was no great combat activity of any sort until the end of January, when, on 27 January, the Soviets renewed their attack against the 13th *Armee Korps* and 59th *Armee Korps,* with the *Schwerpunkt* at the 13th *Armee Korps* at and south of the Korzec – Rowno road, against Rowno. In the 59th *Armee Korps* sector the Soviets took Schepetowka after enveloping it from the east and north. The southern wing of *Korpsabteilung* C was particularly exposed to the main enemy pressure, with repeated Soviet attempts, utilizing gaps in the front, to envelop the elements fighting in the front on both sides and to push their advance through to Rowno. On both sides of the Sarny – Kowel railroad line the Soviet 1st and 6th Guards Cavalry Corps advanced to the southwest on Luzk and west on Kowel. It is not possible at present to determine how far these cavalry forces gained ground to the west at that time. The resistance of the 13th *Armee Korps* was being severely tested. With the fall of Rowno, the Kowel – Rowno – Brody railroad line was no longer available for logistical support. *See Maps 78, 80 and 83.*

In the event, the Soviets took possession of the entire west bank of the Horyn southwest of Hoszcza and, for a short time, gained a foothold on the west bank directly north of Hoszcza. *Korpsabteilung* C was the only truly combat-worthy formation there. Otherwise there were only police forces under the command of *SS-Obergruppenführe* von dem Bach-Zelewski (*SS-Kavallerie Regiment* 17, II./*SS-Polizei Regiment* 17, *Sturmgeschütz Abteilung* 118, *Heeres-Pionier-Bataillon* 50 (horse drawn) and *Heeres-Pionier-Bataillon* 662 (horse drawn)), and also *Polizeigruppe 'Prützmann', Füsilier Bataillon* 217, which the *Korpsabteilung* had annexed to itself on the march and elements of the artillery of *Korps Abteilung* C (II./ *Artillerie Regiment* 219) to come to the rescue.

At this point the High Command declared that Rowno was a *'Fester Platz'*. All that the *Kommandant* had available for its defense were four *Landesschützen* [regional defense] companies (400 men) and two alarm units (265 men). North of the place Soviet cavalry formations attacked, armoured forces to the south. Here *Korpsabteilung* C prevented a breakthrough.

Battle of Rowno

On 1 February the troops defended in the Sdlobuno – Tajcury – Zytyn Maly – east of Kustyn line. On that day the northern wing was already enveloped. The Soviet 8th Guards Cavalry Division attacked the rear of Rowno from the northwest. Even so, it was still possible to prevent the Soviet cavalry from penetrating into the city.

Korpsabteilung C continued in action south of Rowno, the 454th *Sicherungs Division* at the eastern front of the city. *Gruppe 'Prützmann'* was to defend the northern front and fight free the northern flank. The command of this formation suffered extraordinarily under the designation of Rowno as a *'Fester Platz'* in that the commander had to prevent any of the formations attached to his command from touching the city boundary of Rowno so that they would not be seized by the *Kampfkommandant*.[1]

Korpsabteilung C had great difficulties occupying the Uscie river sector south of Rowno. The men's felt boots disintegrated in the moist soil, so that, despite the cold, many infantrymen went barefoot.

From the 454th *Sicherungs Division*, *Sicherungs Regiment* 375 and *Landesschützen Batillon* 465 (combined combat strength 700 men) fought on the eastern edge of Rowno, as well as the II./ *Artillerie Regiment* 219 from *Korpsabteilung* C with nine tubes. Several police battalions and *Gendarmerie* platoons fought on the northern and northwestern edge (combined combat strength 350 men). *Gruppe 'Prützmann'*, and *Landesschützenkompanie* along with the II./ *Reserve Artillerie Abteilung* 257, with eight German and four Soviet tubes also saw action in the vicinity. The police units were unsuited for combat, inadequately prepared and equipped for such assignments.

See Maps 79 and 80.

On 2 February the last German formations had to evacuate the southern part of the city and closed up to the defense of the Uscie sector, firm again in a line directly south of Rowno. *Gruppe 'Prützmann'* (two battalions of *Regiment König*) fought its way back out of the area north of Rowno. Combat-worthy elements of the 13th *Armee Korps* were unavalable for defense against the enemy cavalry threat in the deep west flank. Therefore the 7th *Panzer Division* received orders to send a *Kampfgruppe* into the area west of Rowno at the Lemberg – Dubno railroad line.

---

1   Translator's note – One of the powers granted to the *Kampfkommandant* was the right to attach any and all troops and troop elements that entered his designated command area to his command.

SITUATION ON THE LEFT WING OF *HEERESGRUPPE SÜD*

Fallback to the Dubno Area

With that, Luzk, Rowno, the 'Stolbuno' railroad junction in the Lemberg direction and, on 11 February, already Schepetowka were in enemy hands. It seems conspicuous that the Soviets paid particular attention to capturing the railroad lines and rail junctions, because these offered them better opportunities for reinforcement and logistical support during the mud season that the muddy roads through the land.

See Map 80.

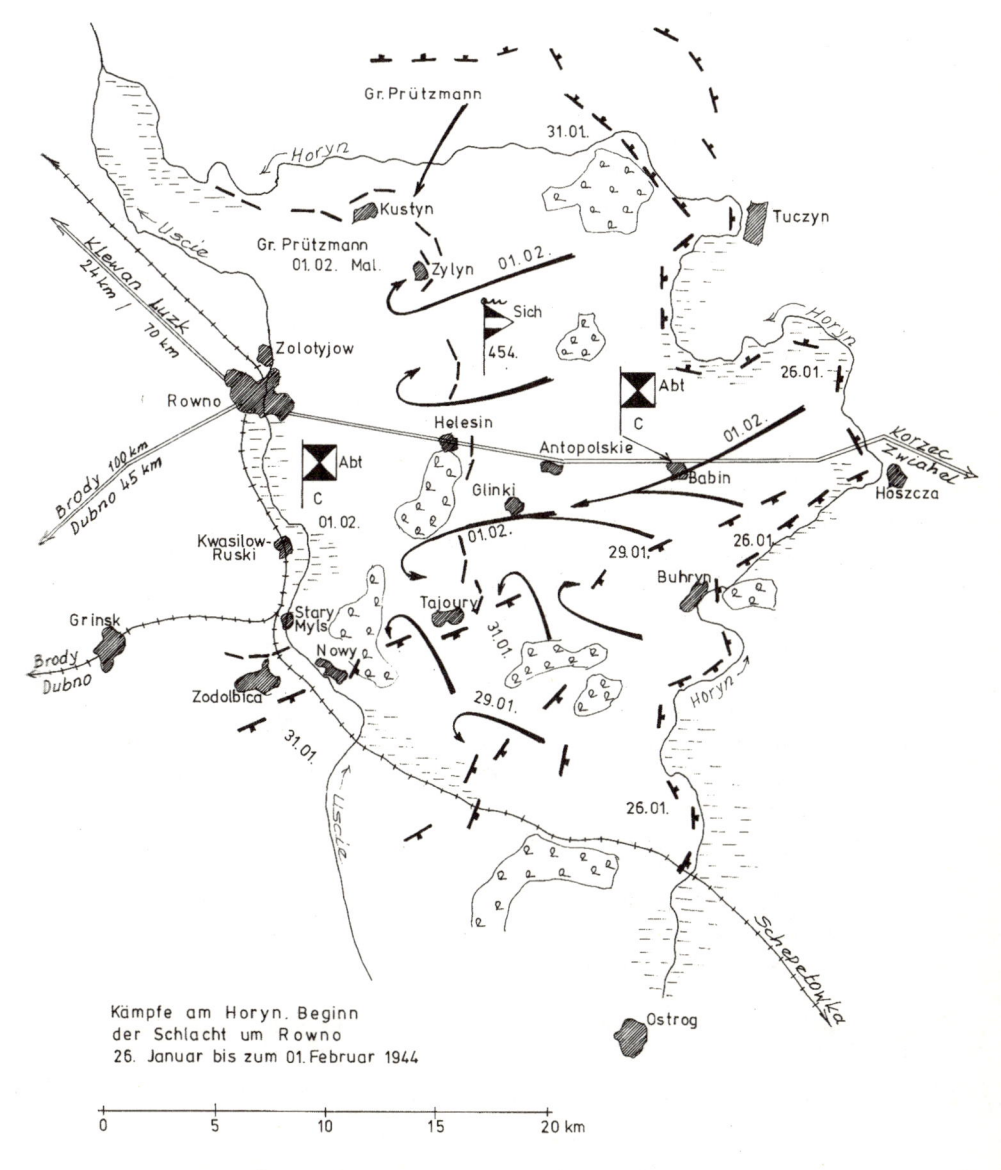

79. Fighting at Horyn. Beginning of the battle of Rowno, 26 January to 1 February, 1944. See Map 80 for larger picture.

The 13th *Armee Korps*, which, at this time still had over 2,444 infantrymen, including formations made up of Eastern peoples [*Ostvölker-Verbände*], was exposed to attack by at least four rifle divisions of the Soviet 13th Army and two to three divisions of the 6th Guards Cavalry Corps. Thrusts by a *Kampfgruppe* of the 7th *Panzer Division* could bring only temporary relief. Because of the catastrophic condition of the roads, they were limited to the firmest of the roads and, therefore, for the time being could only be directed to the north and northeast, while the enemy had a free hand south of the Dubno – Rowno road to continue his advance unhindered.

Nevertheless, the *Kampfgruppe* of the 7th *Panzer Division*, with eleven *Panzer*, one command *Panzer* and 25 self-propelled guns assisted with its thrusts northwest of the Rowno-Dubno *Rollbahn* the withdrawal of *Korps-Abteilung* C into the Dubno area in three stages, each 6 – 10 kilometers. For artillery support *Panzerzug* [armoured train] 71 was available on the right wing.

See Map 80.

Henceforth *Gruppe 'Prützmann'* was in the Kremianez area, *Korps Abteilung* C around Dubno and, northwest of it, the again-independent 454th *Sicherungs Division* with attached *Polizei Regiment 'König'*. The 7th *Panzer Division* secured the deep north and northwest flank in the area 20 to 30 kilometers west-northwest of Dubno.

At this time there was a gap of over 70 kilometers to the left flank of the 59th *Armee Korps* in the Schepetowka – Saslaw area, northward to *Polizeiverband* von dem Bach-Zelewski. There was another 60 kilometer gap from about 30 kilometers southeast of Kowel to the foremost elements of the 7th *Panzer Division*, the *'Wehrmachtsloch'*.

The German command recognized the danger that the Soviets now had the opportunity to eliminate the 13th *Armee Korps* and gain the area around Lemberg that was decisive for the conduct of later operations. That would also lend military emphasis to a political relaxation in the former Poland favorable to the Polish resistance movement. The Soviets had recognized that the German force-situation allowed commitment of even weak forces with widely set objectives at no risk.

Again and again in ensuing days individual attacks with armoured support were delivered on the spot against German formations. There was no continuous line of defense. The 13th *Armee Korps* held the city of Dubno as the key point of the German defense. The garrison of the city of Dubno (*Divisionsgruppe* 217 / *Korps – Abteilung* C) achieved defensive successes in hard fighting, destroying 30 enemy AFVs, but at the price of heavy German personnel losses.

On 14 February the Soviet attacks ended. Instead, they displayed transparencies lettered, 'German soldiers! Resistance is pointless! Save your lives and come to us!' Similar appeals followed over loudspeakers.

26

The Soviet 'Second Blow' Against the German Lines

After the start of the Soviet attack in the Tarnopol area the attacker decided to also advance farther to the north, and attempted to unhinge by envelopment the powerful Kremianez and Dubno strongpoints, which were favoured by the terrain. The operations against the 13th *Armee Korps* could also act as diversions from the attack against the 1st *Panzer Armee*. The German forces in this area, however, remained extraordinarily weak, so that there was danger of collapse of the line of defense in the event of a hard attack on both flanks.

See Map 80.

At the same time as this attack the Soviets also advanced against Luzk and Kowel, farther north, which they surrounded on 17 March. An advance via Luzk entailed the danger of reaching Lemberg by turning to the south.

See Maps 80 and 83.

On 15 March in the Dubno sector the Soviets strengthened their attack against the lines of the 13th *Armee Korps* and penetrated at the 340th *Infanterie Division* between Smordwa and Radomysl. With that they forced the 13th *Armee Korps* to an orderly evacuation of the Dubno combat area.

See Map 81.

The ensuing retreat of *Korps-Abteilung* C took place in difficult terrain. As the result of close pursuit by the Soviets the situation of the 13th *Armee Korps* worsened significantly on 17 March. In the locations of the penetrations north and northwest of Kozin, the German defensive forces brought the Soviets to a halt at Demidowka and forced them back to the north and northeast.

The enemy forces advancing southwest of Kremianez were pushing against the main body of the 361st *Infanterie Division* in concentric attacks from the Dunajow and Podlesi areas (localities southwest and west of Kremianez). On 17 March *Divisionsgruppe* 183 counterattacked Wokowyje (In the sector of the 340th *Infanterie Division*) and, on 18 March broke through to the south out of an enemy envelopment. *Korps-Abteilung* C captured the village of Kozin and two adjoining localities by attacking from the southeast. By attacking north of the Plazowka sector it threatened the flank of the Soviet advance, thereby limiting their advance to the southeast – which would provide some relief to the enemy forces in the Tarnopol area. The German formations brought to a halt a counterattack from the north supported by 29 enemy AFVs, knocking out ten enemy AFVs, and held the line that had been attained, though with substantial German losses.

See Map 81.

Granted, according to the results of German reconnaissance, the Soviets had not committed anything like as strong forces as they had to south, in the Tarnopol area, but, still, there was one tank corps with four rifle divisions and elements of two cavalry corps.

336 CRUCIBLE OF COMBAT

80. 4th *Panzer Armee*. Development of the situation between Schepetowka and Luzk; Battle of Rowno, Dubno and Brody. 27 January to 16/18 March, 1944. See Map 69 for 5-16 March, Map 81 for 16-26 March, Map 82 for 7-16 April 1944. Map 85 adjoins to lower right.

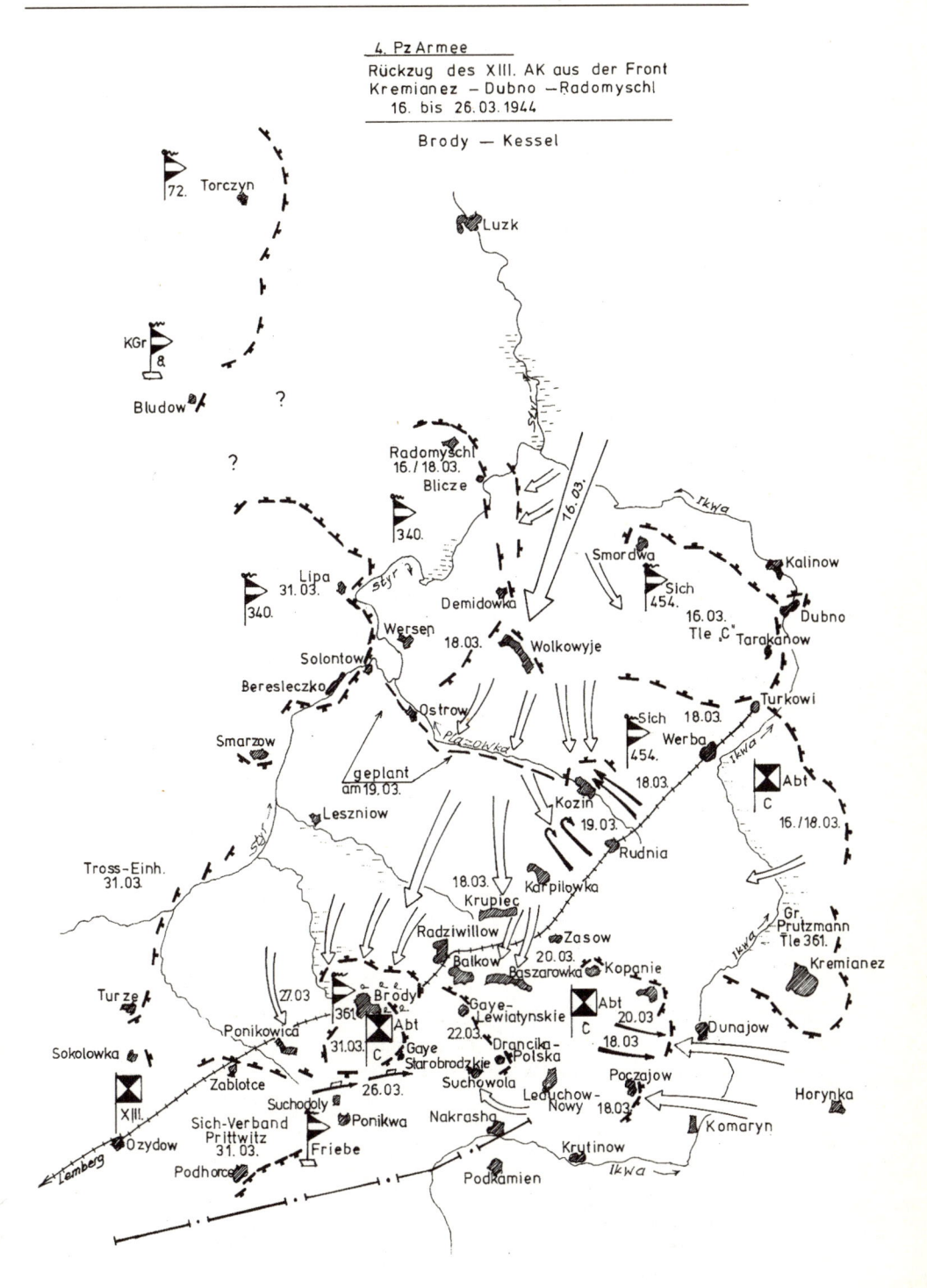

THE SOVIET 'SECOND BLOW' AGAINST THE GERMAN LINES

81. 4th *Panzer Armee*. Retreat of the 13th *Armee Korps* from the front Kremianez – Dubno – Radomyschl 16 to 26 March, 1944. Brody *Kessel*. Map 82 adjoins lower left corner.

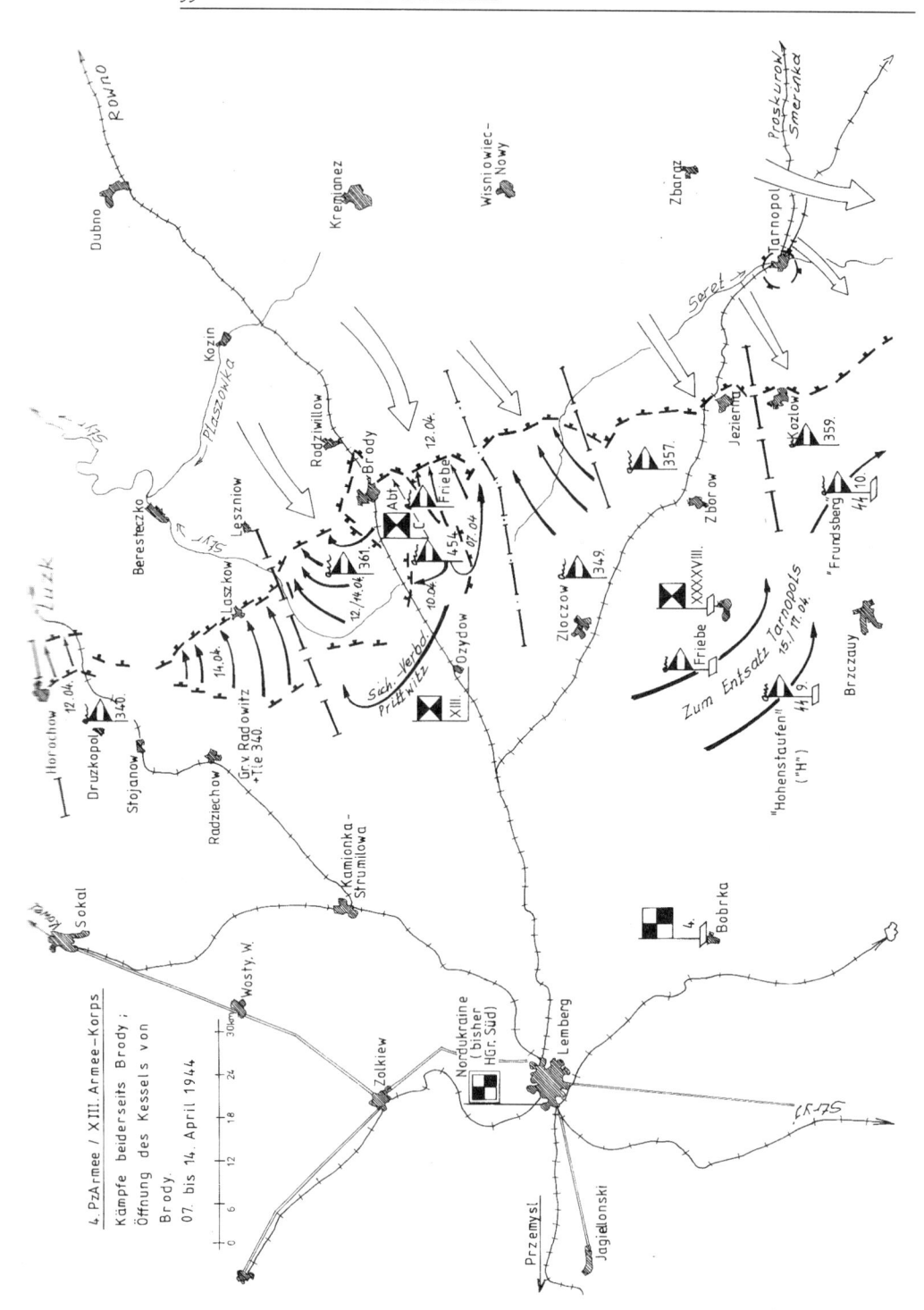

82. 4th *Panzer Armee* / 13th *Armee Korps*. Fighting on both sides of Brody; Opening of the Brody *Kessel* 7 to 14 April, 1944. Map 81 adjoins upper right corner.

THE SOVIET 'SECOND BLOW' AGAINST THE GERMAN LINES

The forces of the 13th *Armee Korps* could not stand up to this pressure, the more so when the Soviets broke through in the area southeast of Radziwillow and also captured Kremianez. The 13th *Armee Korps* therefore shifted its lines behind the Ikwa in the Komaryn – Dunajow sector, south of Werbe – Kozin – Plazowka – Ostrow – Solontow – Lipa, southwest of Radomysl. The 13th *Armee Korps* was reinforced by the arrival of the 361st *Infanterie Division*, which, in cooperation with *Korps-Abteilung* C, helped offensively to constrict the area of the Soviet penetration southwest of the Plazowka sector. After initial successes the formations ran into a Soviet counterattack supported by 28 AFVs. 12 Soviet AFVs were left lying on the battlefield. However, the German forces had to return to their jump-off positions.

See Map 81.

The next day the Soviets attacked at several locations, each time alternating with armoured support, as in the Ikwa lowlands against *Landesschützen-Bataillon* 528. Expected additional counterattacks did not take place because the 13th *Armee Korps* issued retreat orders to avoid destruction by envelopment on both sides.

In the ensuing days six enemy attacks were repulsed and penetrations cleaned up in hasty counterattacks, particularly with the help of the artillery and *Werfer-Brigade* 6.

Brody Surrounded

On 27 March the Soviets attacked the German forces in the immediate Brody area from the east, north and west with support from 35 AFVs in order to close a ring around Brody at Suchowola from the southeast. In the meantime two Soviet divisions with 30 AFVs attacked the forces of *Korps-Abteilung* C. About one to three kilometers of ground were lost to the west in bitter fighting on the right wing and in the center. However, in the deep left flank the Soviets were in the Ponikowica area, eight kilometers southwest of Brody, thereby nearly cutting off the Brody combat area.

See Map 81.

Brody was then declared a *'Fester Platz'*, even though this area did not fulfill the prerequisites for a breakwater against the waves of the Soviet attack, neither operatively nor tactically, especially with regard to the surrounding terrain.

On 28 March *Panzerverband 'Friebe'* provided relief by fighting free the Brody – Podhorce road with a security formation made up of elements of the 454th *Infanterie Division*. By a thrust south of Brody to the east into the depth of the Soviet main defensive area it also gave perceptible easing of the pressure on the reinforced *Korps-Abteilung* C.

On 29 March the Soviets attacked *Korps-Abteilung* C with four rifle divisions and the reinforced 25th Tank Corps, which, by this time, led to a serious crisis. The enemy forces broke through the main line of resistance. Gaje – Starobrozkie was lost.

At this point *Panzerverband 'Friebe'* had only three combat-worth AFVs left. Nevertheless 16 Soviet AFVs were knocked out in those days, seven of them by the infantry. A total of seven rifle divisions of the Soviet 3rd Army and the 1st and 4th Guards Cavalry corps (southeast and southwest front), the

See Map 81.

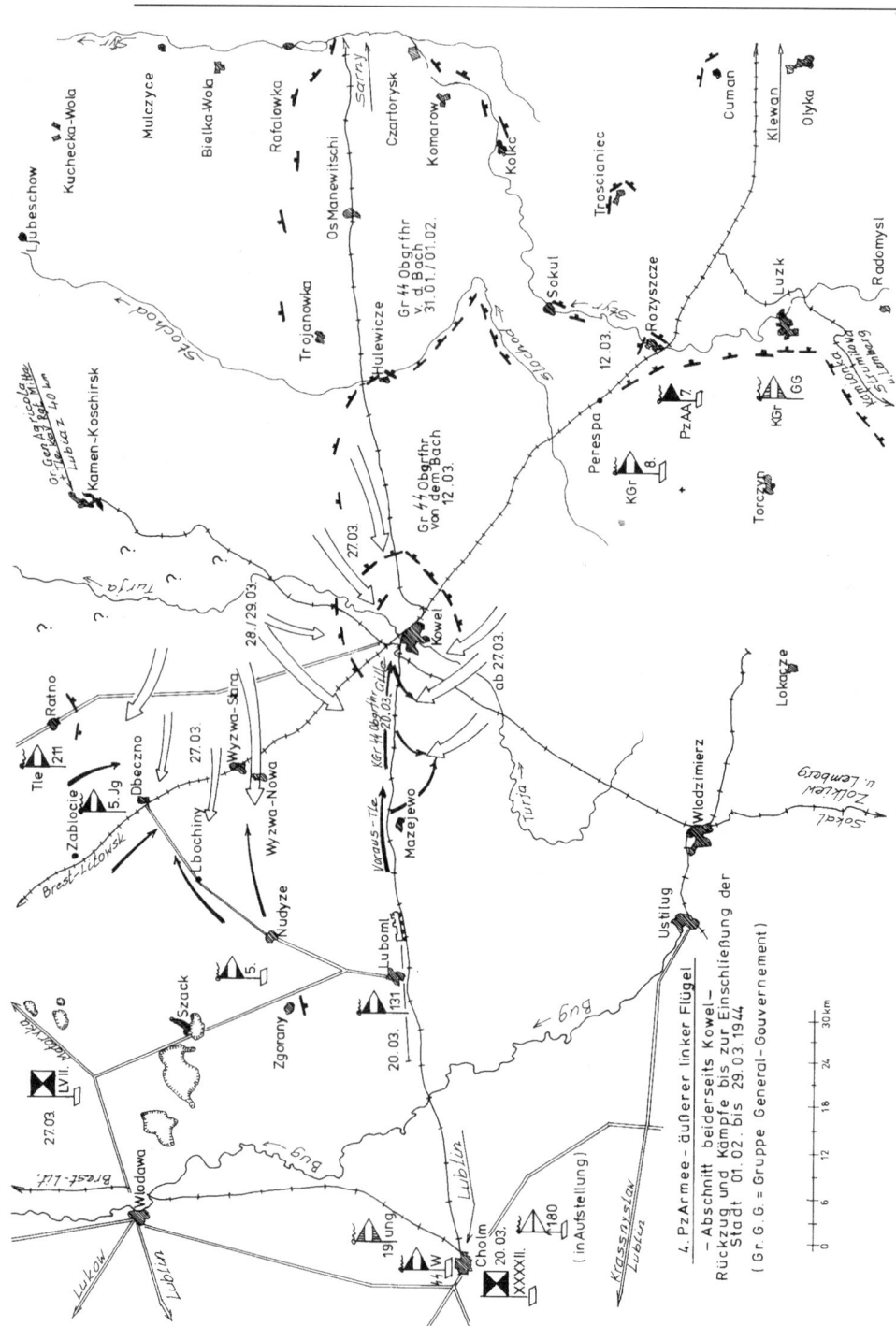

83. 4th *Panzer Armee* – Extreme left wing sector on both sides of Kowel. Retreat and fighting until encirclement of the city, 1 February to 29 March, 1944. See also Map 84 which extends farther northward.

25th Tank Corps and the 150th Independent Tank Brigade were in the Brody combat area facing *Korps-Abteilung* C and the 361st *Infanterie Division*.

The Brody *Kessel*

The *Korps-Abteilung* C front enclosed the city of Brody and the woods that were north of the city on the east, north and northwest as well as the woods southwest of the city. With the support of *Panzerverband 'Friebe'* in the ensuing days the division[1] repulsed enemy attacks delivered southeast and east of Brody, even fighting free the *Rollbahn* for a brief period. In the Suchodoly area *Panzerverband 'Friebe'* was able to bring an armoured convoy with supply vehicles in to the encircled troops in Brody, though with the loss of five *'Tiger'* to land-mines in the road. 700 wounded who were awaiting transport out of Brody were successfully taken out during the night of 30 March/ 1 April by the same route.

The *Kessel* had a diameter of about five kilometers. The elements of the 454th *Infanterie Division* that were attached to *Korps-Abteilung* C were released from their attachment at the end of the month 'and left the *Kessel* by night and in fog with the return of one of the supply transports that had come to the *Kessel*. They then took over the mission of *Sicherungs Regiment* 375 in and south of the Suchodoly area. *Sicherungs Regiment* 375, in turn, then had to repulse the strong partisan bands and Soviet forces that had broken through in the area about 30 kilometers west of Brody.

See Map 81.

The Situation Around Brody at the Beginning of April

The 13th *Armee Korps* was assigned the mission of keeping the area around Brody open. The newly provided 349th *Infanterie Division* was supposed to close the gap at the left wing of the 48th *Panzer Korps* (eight kilometers southwest of Zalosze) between it and the right wing of the 13th *Armee Korps* (at that time at Podhorce) by attacking in the area east of Zloczow to the northeast to Podkamien. Such a thrust would have given *Korps-Abteilung* C quite some relief, especially in the deep right flank.

See Map 82.

In the next two weeks there was a lot of back-and-forth attacking and counterattacking. The situation stabilized, however, despite the ongoing enemy artillery and mortar fire on the Brody area. There seemed, however, to be lasting cause for concern that the 13th *Armee Korps* had, in part, police forces in action that were not experienced in combat, let alone as conducted on the Eastern Front. These also fought without support of their own heavy weapons. For several days the 454th *Sicherungs Division* held the *Rollbahn* open to Brody. Nevertheless, encirclement of Brody seemed inevitable. Lack of forces prevented pushing the main line of resistance to the east. The 4th *Panzer Armee* had no forces available for such a purpose. It first had to concern itself with the relief of Tarnopol.

---

1   Translator's note – The author is referring to *Korps-Abteilung* C, which had approximately the strength of and functioned as a division. *Korps-Abteilung* C ran up an admirable record as a fighting formation which is described in detail (see bibliography) in a German military-historical study that is accompanied by excellent, detailed maps.

On 10 April it appeared that the Soviets were abandoning the encirclement of Brody, which *Korps-Abteilung* C used as an opportunity to shove its own lines father to the east. However, the land-mines that the Soviets had laid first had to be disarmed under heavy artillery fire. *Infanterie-Pionier-Zug* [platoon] 217 alone lifted 465 mines.

The presumption that the Soviets had abandoned their aggressive intentions in this area due to the heavy losses they had suffered – about 250 AFVs – seems downright optimistic. Possibly the Soviets shifted their offensive formations to the area south of Tarnopol.

27

Review of the Situation

The formations under attack were, in part, police formations, *Verband 'von Prittwitz'* and *Verband 'Prützmann'*, later *'Brenner'*. In light of the weakness of these formations the 13th *Armee Korps* was constantly concerned with aerial reconnaissance, because only that offered the possibility of identifying enemy intentions in time to shift the German defense forces to the expected hot-spots. *Korps-Abteilung* C built up its own division *Panzer* platoon from five captured T-34 tanks, manning them with *Panzerjäger* personnel.

The defense of encircled Tarnopol to the right of the Brody area ended in mid April. North of the 13th *Armee Korps* north of Horochow the 42nd *Armee Korps* received orders on 10 April to assume command of the 214th *Infanterie Division* and 72nd *Infanterie Division*. Farther to the north the garrison of the encircled city of Kowel fought for and, on 5 April, gained its freedom. With the help of the newly-arrived formations there was a continuous front and loose contact with *Heeresgruppe Mitte*. With that the gap that existed in the fall of 1943 north of Kiew between the two *Heeresgruppen* was closed for the first time.

See Maps 82 and 84.

Reconnaissance revealed that the Soviets in the Tarnopol area had withdrawn their forces after the fall of Tarnopol. The forces committed in the area around Brody, especially the 1st Guards Cavalry Corps, had merely been pulled out for a few days refitting, but were then back in the front line. Nevertheless, there seemed to be regrouping on the Soviet side with the result that the Soviets were quiet for a few days. However, it was expected that, with the end of the mud season, The Soviets would bring up additional forces for a new initiative.

Soviet intentions remained unclear to the German, whether they now intended to advance across the Bug to Lublin and the Weichsel in the combat area of the 13th *Armee Korps* and 42nd *Armee Korps* or whether they would advance from the Tarnopol area (48th *Panzer Korps*) toward Lemberg. It is uncertain whether on not at that moment the Soviets considered cooperation of the strong formations that were concentrating in the area southwest of Schepetowka with the successful advance on the left wing of the 8th *Armee* to the Carpathians.

The formations of the 42nd *Armee Korps* and 13th *Armee Korps* then enjoyed several weeks of calm, which they urgently needed after five and a half months of unbroken action. The lines however, remained extraordinarily thinly held. The 13th *Armee Korps*, with about 80 kilometers of front, had merely 13 machine guns, 0.6 anti-tank guns, 1.3 light artillery tubes and 0.4 heavy artillery tubes per kilometer.

Since 4 November *Korps-Abteilung* C was composed of remnants of the 183rd *Infanterie Division*, the 217th *Infanterie Division* and the 339th *Infanterie*

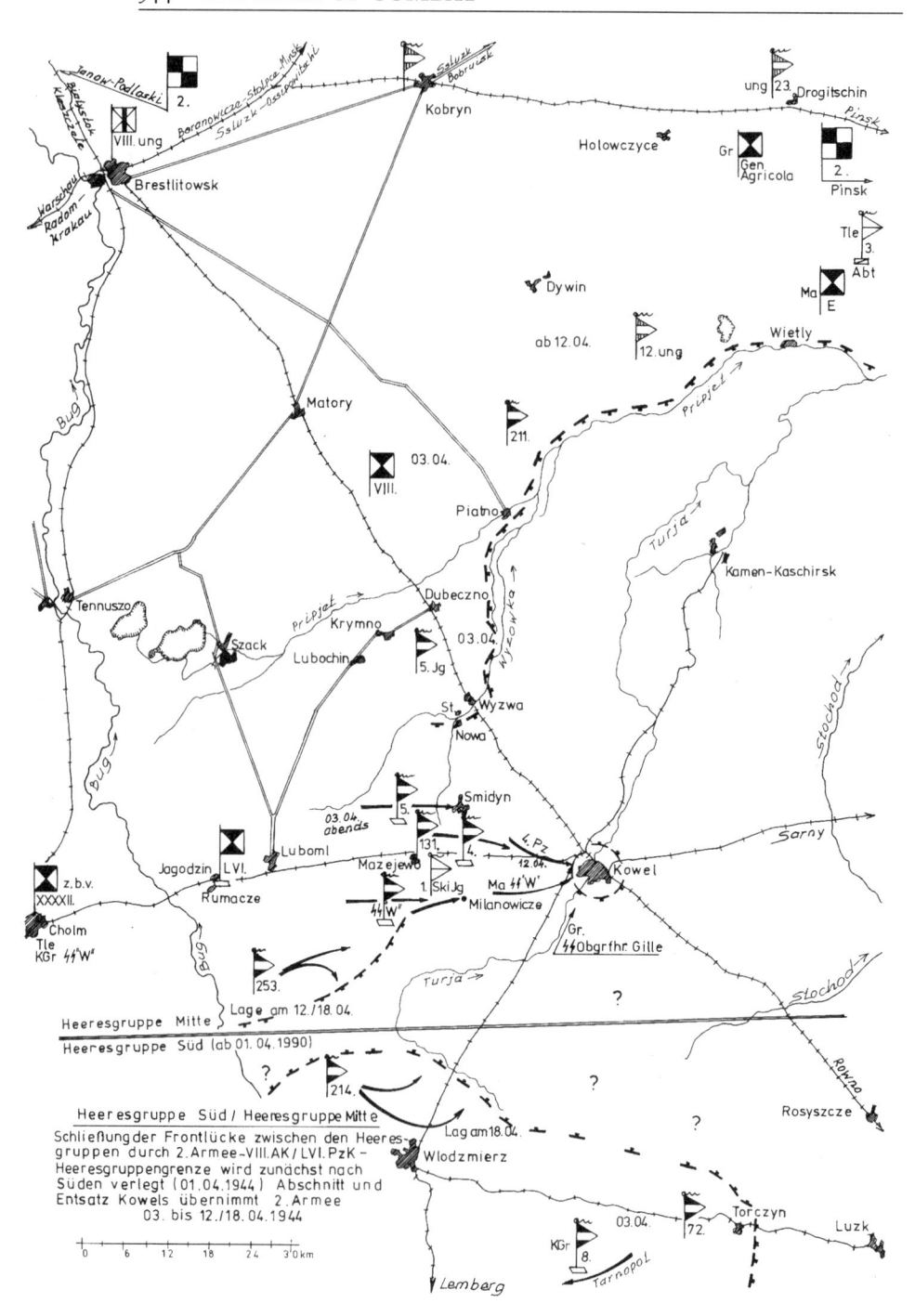

84. *Heeresgruppe Süd / Heeresgruppe Mitte.* Closure of the gap in the front between the *Heeresgruppen* by the 2nd *Armee* – 7th *Armee Korps* 56th *Panzer Korps. Heeresgruppen* boundary was initially shifted to the south (1 April, 1944). The 2nd *Armee* took over the Kowel sector and action. 3 to 12/18 April, 1944.

Division. It corresponded to an infantry division with normal organization., The infantry regiments were designated *'Divisionsgruppe (DivGr)'*. The infantry battalions were called *Regimentsgruppe (RgtGr)'*. Both retained their old division or regimental numbers. The heart of the *Korps-Abteilung* consisted of seven *Kampfbataillone*: six *Regimentsgruppen* and the *Füsilierbataillon* of the 217th *Infanterie Division*. During the fighting retreat elements of the 454th *Sicherungs Division* were attached for a time as was a *Kampfgruppe* of the 361st *Infanterie Division* in the Brody sector. The *Aufklärungs Abteilung, Pionier Bataillon, Panzerjäger* and *Nachrichten Abteilung* were given the number 219. *Korps-Abteilung* C continued its existence until 12 August 1944.

In the meantime personnel replacements arrived, as did weapons, so that the artillery was brought up to 32 light field howitzers, 22 heavy field howitzers, along with ten light infantry guns, three heavy infantry guns, nine light anti-tank guns, one medium anti-tank gun, 25 heavy anti-tank guns (*Ratschbum*) [Russian 76.2mm field guns], two heavy 8.8 cm anti-tank guns and nine 2 cm anti-aircraft guns.

The Soviets remained quiet in this area, training recruits without combat experience, just as were the Germans. The way the German front line was held as a series of strong points provided the Soviets with the opportunity to employ what was later christened the *'Piesel'* tactic, whereby individual solders, on foot or mounted, infiltrated through the gaps between the German defensive strongpoints by night or in fog and then assembled in the German rear or joined up with partisan bands, which were, at that time, quite active.

The second great *Kessel*-battle around Brody started on 13 and 18 July 1944, so that it seemed, so far as reports were concerned, to begin in the broader combat area southwest of Schepetowka.

28

Advance Against the 1st *Panzer Armee*

The situation of the southern wing of the German Eastern Front gave rise to ever increasing concern. The right wing of *Heeresgruppe* A, the 17th *Armee*, was on the Crimean Peninsula facing extraordinarily strong, superior enemy forces in a bitter defense and fighting retreat. Finally came the evacuation of Sewastopol and Cherssone Peninsula with the transfer by sea of a portion of the troops – abandoning their guns and vehicles – first to Odessa and later to Konstanza (Rumania). The last elements of the fleet that the navy used to evacuate the German formations came under heavy Soviet defensive artillery fire and attack by Soviet aircraft and were unable to enter the bay of the Cherssone Peninsula, so that the last formations defending there went into Russian captivity. Several divisions were sacrificed in this fighting: the 50th *Infanterie Division*, 73rd *Infanterie Division*, 98th *Infanterie Division*, 111th *Infanterie Division* and 336th *Infanterie Division*, along with the Rumanian 2nd Mountain Division, Rumanian 10th Infantry Division, Rumanian 1st Mountain Division, Rumanian 19th Cavalry Division, Rumanian 3rd Mountain Division and Rumanian 6th Cavalry Division.

See Maps 64, 65, 66 and 67.

In the sector of the 6th *Armee* on the mainland, the situation stabilized after reaching the Dnjestr, apparently, among other reasons, as the result of a necessary breather for the Soviet offensive forces. In the area of the 8th *Armee*, after the failure of their attack in January and February in the Kirowograd area, the Soviets advanced in the Winniza – Uman area. After their breakthrough with mobile formations gained ground to the west, they continued in their intention of outflanking the 8th *Armee* and thereby rolling up the entire lines of the 8th *Armee* and, finally, also the 6th *Armee*. The left wing of the German main line of resistance extended ever farther over the Bug to the Dnjestr, to Pruth, to the start of the Carpathians, due to hasty shifts of the troops of the 8th *Armee* to its left wing. Thus the Soviets were denied the opportunity to get into the rear area of the 8th *Armee* without a fight. The Soviets shifted powerful offensive formations with great masses of armour into areas that appeared favourable to them on the left wing of the 8th *Armee* in hopes of getting ahead of the German troop shifts. After hard fighting against the 3rd *SS-Panzer Division 'Totenkopf'* they advanced southward via Balta, and, finally, to Jassy, against the 24th *Panzer Division* and, at last, against *Panzergrenadier Division 'Großdeutschland'* in the Targul-Frumos area across the Targul-Frumos – Jassy road. Here the Soviet surprise attempt failed and forced the Red Army to systematic preparations for attack.

See Maps 41, 42, 43 and 68.

In addition to the advance to the southwest and, finally, south, the advance from the Winniza – Uman area also provided the Soviets with the

ADVANCE AGAINST THE 1ST *PANZER ARMEE*

possibility of an advance to the west toward Tschernowitz and the margin of the Carpathians. This advance exposed the German formations of the 8th *Armee* and the 1st *Panzer Armee* located north of the area of the breakthrough. Granted, there was no reason to think that, from the beginning, the Soviets had linked an intention to outflank the lines of the 1st *Panzer Armee* with their advance. What is more likely is that some of the advancing troops were diverted toward Kamenez – Podolsk to take advantage of a situation that was extraordinarily favorable for the Soviets. However, they were soon far into the hinterland of the German formations of the 24th *Panzer Korps* and 46th *Panzer Korps* that were still west of Winniza. Those German formations now received orders to retreat on account of the dangerous situation, as had those south of the area of the penetration.

The Soviet Attack

The advance in the Winniza – Uman area did not take place right at the left boundary of the 8th *Armee* but in the center of its sector of the front. The Soviets forced back to the south the divisions of the 8th *Armee* against which their major thrust was aimed – the 4th *Gebirgs Division*, 198th *Infanterie Division* and 34th *Infanterie Division*. On the other hand elements of the 75th *Infanterie Division* and the 82nd *Infanterie Division* initially remained in their positions, as did the formations of the right wing of the 1st *Panzer Armee* (24th *Panzer Korps* and 46th *Armee Korps)*, for example the 1st *Infanterie Division*, 254th *Infanterie Division*, 18th *Artillerie Division* and 101st *Jäger Division*.

See Maps 58 and 88.

However, a gap in the front soon formed within the retreating formations of the 1st *Panzer Armee*. A few days after the Soviet breakthrough *Kampfgruppe* 82nd *Infanterie Division*, two-thirds of the 254th *Infanterie Division*, elements of the 18th *Artillerie Division* and the 1st *Infanterie Division* were north of Mogilew – Podolsk. Between them and the formations farther to the north there was an uncovered intervening space around Kopai-Gorod. Elements of the 254th *Infanterie Division*, 168th *Infanterie Division*, 101st *Jäger Division* and 208th *Infanterie Division* were around Shmerinka.

See Maps 61, 88, 90 and 91.

At this time the Soviets had already reached and crossed the Dnjestr at Mogilew-Podolsk . They had also found crossings farther south at Soroca and Kamenka. A split in the Soviet formations already began to appear imminent, for the greater part of the Soviet combat groups passed through this latter interval between Kamenka and Mogilew-Podolsk over the Dnjestr and on to the southwest, while undisturbed possibilities for advance for mobile Soviet forces beckoned between Murowanyje-Kurilowzy and Shmerinka toward Kamenez-Podolsk and the west.

See Map 61.

The retreat of the German formations took place as in the other area of the 8th *Armee* farther to the south, over deeply thawed, apparently bottomless roads under rain, sometimes snow – and under substantial pressure from the developing situation. In addition to that was the fact that the formations had only limited mobility after the losses of vehicles they had sustained in the previous fighting to relieve the Tscherkassy *Kessel*. The 18th *Artillerie Division* had reported earlier (20 February) that 14 light field howitzers, 15 heavy field howitzers and seven 15 cm guns were immobile either due to lack of prime movers or lack of repair parts for the prime movers. According to its most recent strength-report, at the start of the fighting this division still had over 25 artillery tubes, six *Sturmgeschütze, 7.5 cm lang* [with the long 7.5 cm gun] and one *Panzerbeobachtungswagen* IIIb [armoured artillery observer's vehicle on *PzKpfw* III chassis].

<small>See Maps 86 and 90.</small>

When the three Ukrainian fronts attacked in this area west of Winniza on a front of 180 kilometers with 37 to 40 rifle divisions and 11 tank and mechanized corps, the 1st *Panzer Armee* faced them with only eight infantry divisions and the 18th *Artillerie Division*.

<small>See Maps 89, 90 and 91.</small>

Soon after the start of the Soviet penetration the German line of defense took on a unique nose-shape, with the point west of Winniza, then extending to the northwest toward Medshibosh, so that it must have seemed easy to the Soviets to divert a portion of their formations out of the main body of the offensive troops advancing to the west toward the north in order to advance into the rear area of the formations of the 24th *Panzer Korps* of the 1st *Panzer Armee*.

<small>See Maps 88, 89 and 90.</small>

In recognition of this situation, a few days after the start of the attack the 1st *Panzer Armee* issued further retreat orders for this sector, the more so since they endeavoured to bring up additional formations out of the area of the Soviet advance from Uman toward Tschernowitz for defense against the attack in the Schepetowka area. At this point it was not yet possible to anticipate how far the Soviets would succeed in their advance in the area of the 8th *Armee*. The formations of the 8th *Armee* that had been split off toward the north ended up in the rear area of the 1st *Panzer Armee*, initially with missions assigned to the divisions and *Kampfgruppen* to halt the Soviet advance. In addition they were to take advantage of river-barriers and deliver local counterattacks where opportunities presented themselves. In order to strengthen the will to resist, Shmerinka was declared a *'Fester Platz'*, as was Jampol on the left wing. Finally the *Armee* assigned the formations the objective of securing the Kamenez-Podolsk bridgehead (at the Ssmotritsch, a tributary of the Dnjestr), which was highly significant for the logistical support of the 1st *Panzer Armee*. In addition they were to secure the river crossing at Hotyn.

<small>See Maps 61, 90, 93 and 94.</small>

The 18th *Artillerie Division* attempted to gain ground over the Dnjestr to the southwest. However, the Soviets forced elements of the division off north of the river to the west before they could accomplish this mission. The river crossing at Dzurin turned out to be quite difficult. Individual enemy AFVs broke through to the bridge on the access road and first had to be eliminated in the dusk. After a difficult river crossing the main body of the division fell back farther to the west until they made it over to the north side of the river again at Hotyn and were attached to *Armeegruppe* Hube. The rear area services of this division received retreat orders in good time and were continuing their march to Bessarabia.

29

The 'Second Blow' from the Area Southwest of Schepetowka

1. Time of Preparation

After the retreat from Shitomir the 48th *Panzer Korps* with the 2nd *SS-Panzer Division 'Das Reich'*, *SS-Brigade (motorized) 'Langemarck'*, 8th *Panzer Division*, 19th *Panzer Division* and, on the left wing, the 7th *Panzer Division* initially brought the Soviet advance to a halt. At first the Red Amy held off on major attacks, even though the German formations could not occupy a continuous line of defense due to lack of sufficient forces.

See Maps 39 and 43.

In order to close the gap to the adjoining *Korps*, the 96th *Infanterie Division* rolled down out of the sector of *Heeresgruppe Nord* and took over the right wing of the 59th *Armee Korps*. However, it could not close the gap to the 7th *Panzer Division* with its own forces.

See Maps 85 and 86.

After the withdrawal of the 48th *Panzer Korps*, which, at the beginning of February, was to strengthen the front of the 13th *Armee Korps*, the 59th *Armee Korps* assumed command in this sector and had to close the substantial gap to the 19th *Panzer Division* by regrouping with its own means. The threat of envelopment of the *Korps* from the west resulted in the loss of Schepetowka.

See Map 86.

The gap to the right wing of the 13th *Armee Korps* at the Ssaslaw – Ostrog – Stary-Mylsk (directly south of Rowno) road, in which Soviet cavalry was already feeling its way forward and where partisan bands were already at work, grew on 31 January to a width of about 45 kilometers.

See Map 85.

The 96th *Infanterie Division*, which had been ordered in to plug the gap at the left wing of the 19th *Panzer Division*, rolled, little by little, from *Heeresgruppe Nord* and finally, in part, arrived in the Tarnopol area, so that the left flank remained open. Other elements of this division arrived later and went into action at the right wing of the 19th *Panzer Division*. The approach march of additional intended reinforcements suffered from the snow and, thus, road conditions, which, however, also impacted Soviet mobility. Thus it was possible to construct a thinly-held new line of defense in the sector of the 59th *Armee Korps*.

The 17th *Panzer Division* was to be committed to the right of the 19th *Panzer Division* for the same reason. In order to distract Soviet attention from the current weakness in this sector, the 19th *Panzer Division* attacked with *Stuka* support and gained ground, initially thereby depriving the Soviet advance of its force. The 19th *Panzer Division*, however, no longer had its full complement of heavy weapons. The artillerymen who were thus freed were employed as infantry, as, among others, in *Kampfgruppe 'von Mitzlaff'*, which was attached at various times to several divisions, and also in the division's own *Panzergrenadier* regiments.

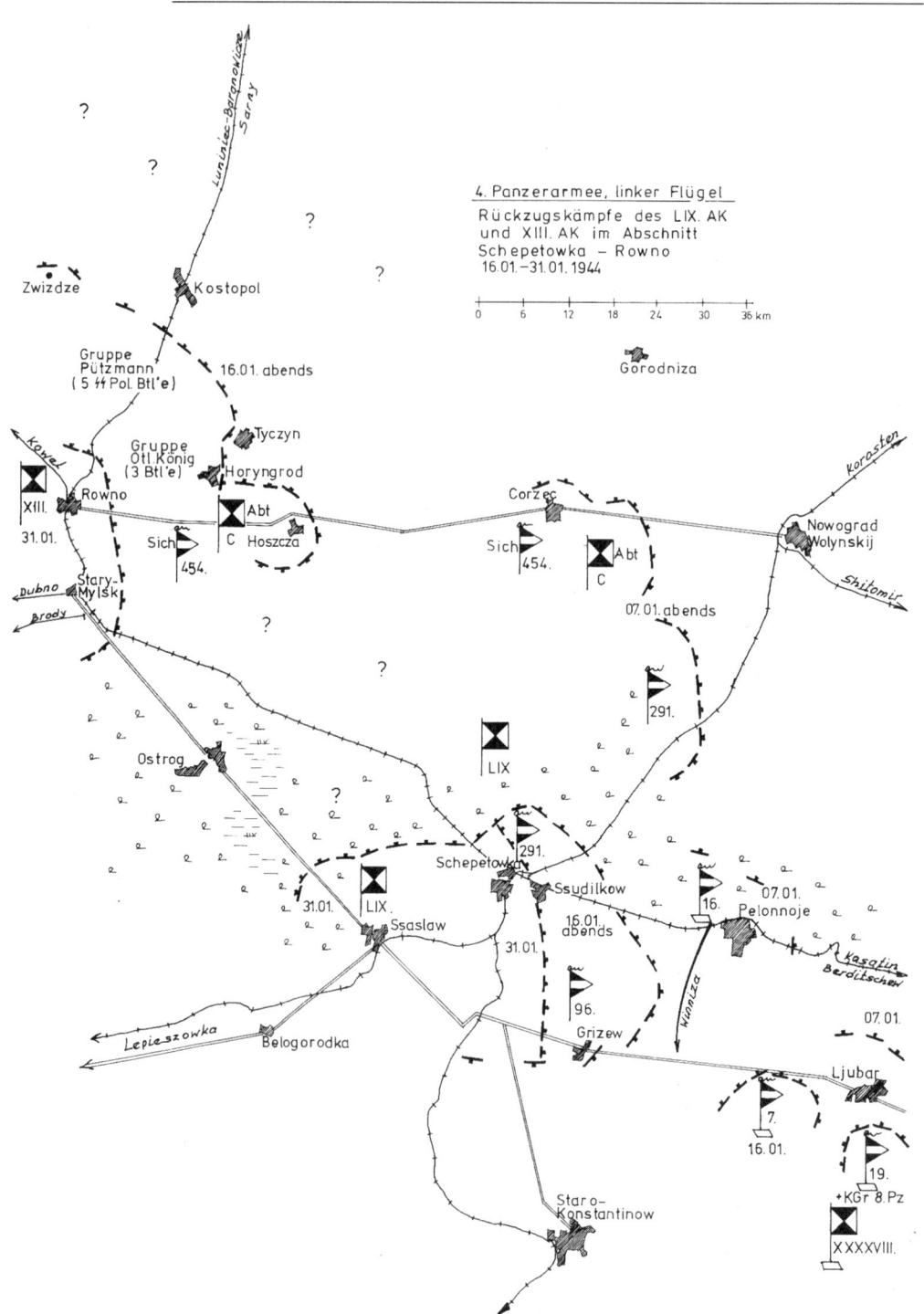

85. 4th *Panzer Armee*, left wing. Fighting retreat of the 59th *Armee Korps* and 13th *Armee Korps* in Schepetowka – Rowno sector 16 – 31 January, 1944. See Map 87 for 7 January-29 February 1944. See Map 89 for 4-12 March 1944, overlaps this map. See Map 68 which adjoins to the right.

SECOND BLOW FROM SW OF SCHEPETOWKA

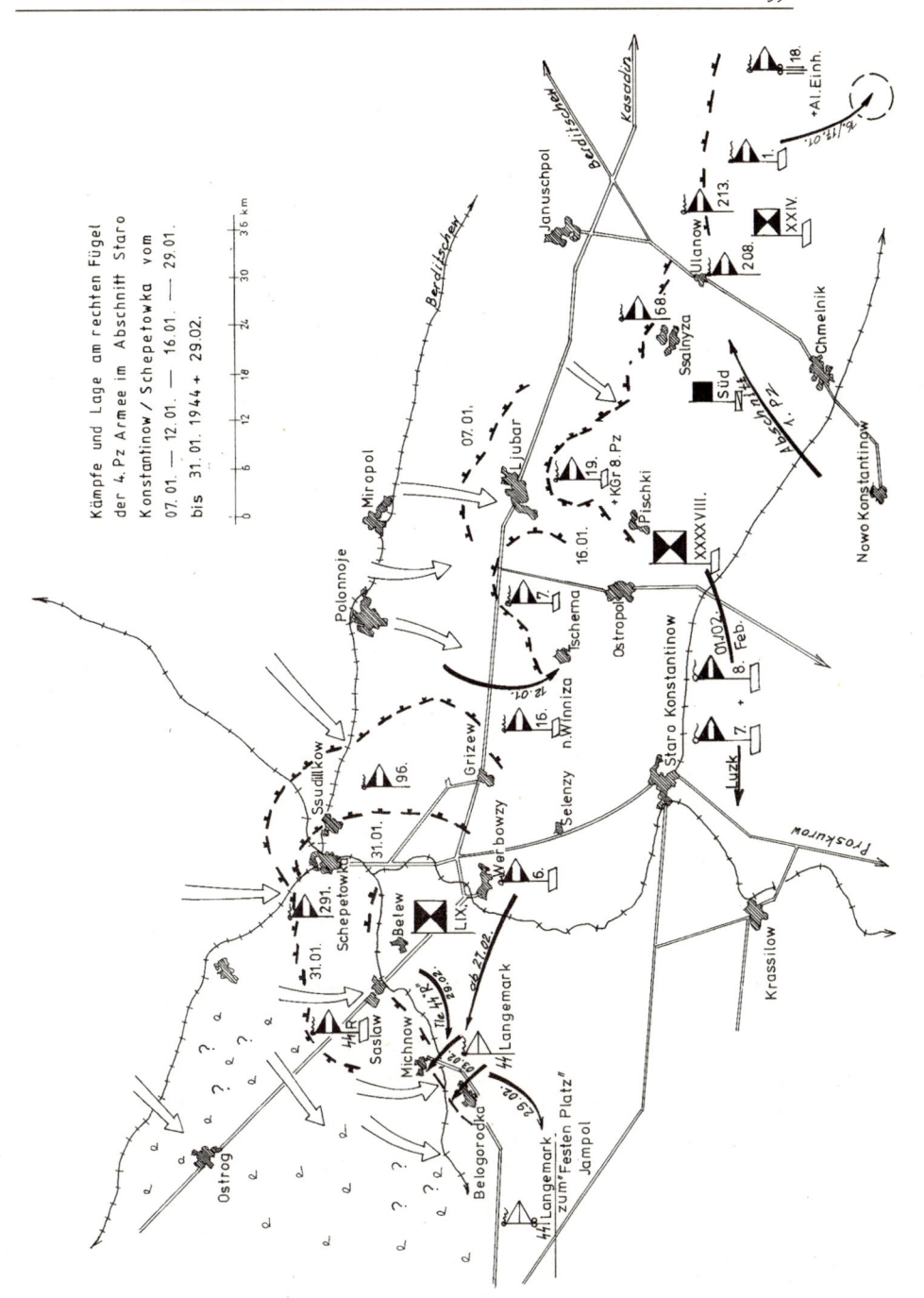

86. Fighting and situation on the right wing of the 4th *Panzer Armee* in the Staro Konstantinow / Schepetowka sector from 7-12-16-29-31 January, 1944 plus 29 February, 1944. See Map 41 for 7-16 January, Map 85 for 16-31 January, Map 87 for 19 February 1944 near Ljubar and Tscherna. Map 88 adjoins to the right. Map 91 for 12 March 1944 adjoins bottom, and Map 90 for the Hube *Kessel* overlaps.

However, the massive Soviet superiority in strength compared to the German formations was not only the result of the German shortage of heavy weapons and supply difficulties – especially of ammunition, but also, especially, resulted from the activity of the partisan bands that included members of the regular army operating in the German hinterland. These attacked the German supply lines or in the rear of the front-troops out of the forests and localities that were not held by the Germans with infantry weapons, and, in part with small groups equipped with mortars and anti-tank guns, without allowing the formation of any comprehensive picture of their strength, equipment and mission. The German formations committed in the main line of resistance – and this was especially true for the firing positions set up behind the lines – had to remain constantly alert for attacks from all points of the compass.

With both the partisan bands and also elements of the regular troops employed at the front, in addition to Russians who had infiltrated there were Ukrainians from the regions formerly occupied by the *Wehrmacht*. These were familiar with the customs of the German troops and understood the German language. One group even wore German *Feldgendarmerie* [military police] uniforms, stopped vehicles driving in the rear of the main line of resistance and shot the drivers. On the other side, however, there were Soviet volunteers in the *Bataillon 'Alexander'* attached to the 2nd *SS-Panzer Division 'Das Reich'* in action in the German main line of resistance against the Soviets. They proved themselves in night-patrols with their knowledge of the Russian language, and also in tracking the partisan bands in action to the rear of the main line of resistance.

The force-ratio between the German and regular Soviet troops arose also from the lack of personnel replacements, as well as supply difficulties on the German side as contrasted with the Soviet troops that were constantly filled out with newly-drafted men as well as arriving replacements. In major attacks these exhibited a strikingly massive superiority in guns, especially in ammunition. In addition they seemed to have an inexhaustible supply of armour, whereas the German divisions preserved their last available AFVs to employ them as 'corset stays' at exposed positions in the front.

2. Preparatory Attacks Southwest of Schepetowka

See Maps 68 and 86. In January, for the time being, the Soviets gave no rest in the frontal area of the 4th *Panzer Armee*. Repeatedly they launched attacks with limited objectives against the positions of the 19th *Panzer Division* and the 2nd *SS-Panzer Division 'Das Reich'* to its right. Finally, however, the situation calmed down again.

See Map 41. The troops observed, instead of the above activity strong march movements on the road from the east to Ljubar, which understandably disturbed them and gave rise to conclusions about the future intentions of the Red Army.

See Maps 68 and 86. On 20 January the 2nd *SS-Panzer Division 'Das Reich'* received orders with the *Legionsbataillon 'Alexander'*, which belonged to *Division 'Brandenburg'*, elements of the 19th *Panzer Division* (*Panzergrenadier Regiment 73* and *Regimentsgruppe von Radowitz*) to withdraw, following its own relief by *Grenadier Regiment 670* of the 371st *Infanterie Division*, while, however,

SECOND BLOW FROM SW OF SCHEPETOWKA 353

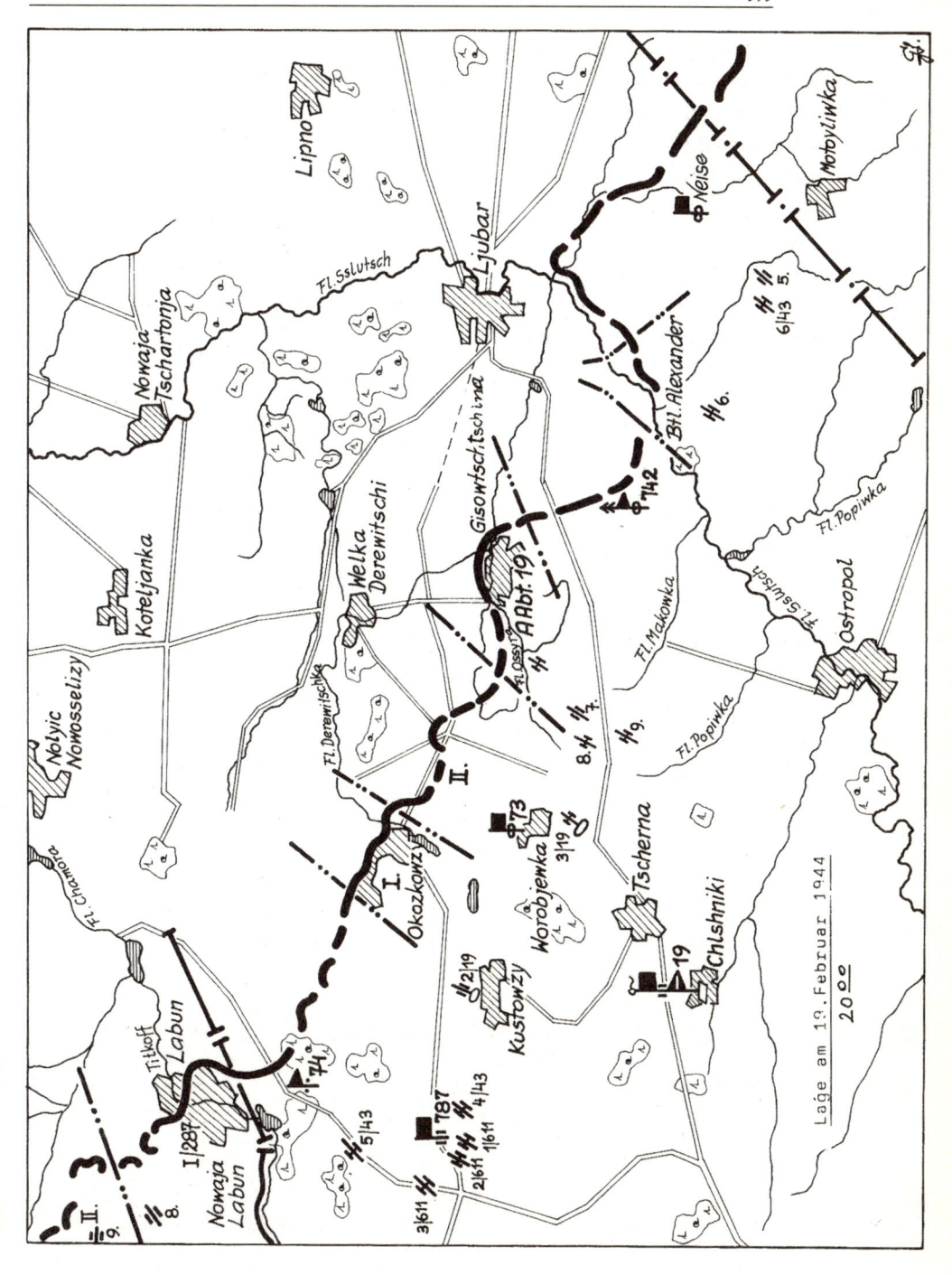

87. Situation on 19 February 1944, 20 00 hours.

continuing to hold the sector hitherto held by *SS-Freiwilligen-Brigade 'Langemarck'*. The troops repulsed Soviet harassing attacks against the movements in the sector of the 2nd *SS-Panzer Division 'Das Reich'* in Koran for the time being with concentrated fire of heavy weapons before they attained the Sslutsch sector. A *Zug* [platoon] *'Tegethof'* of the 2nd *SS-Panzer Division 'Das Reich'*, consisting of five *'Tiger'*, was attached to the 19th *Panzer Division* as mobile combat reserve, because the latter division no longer had any armour of its own in service. Additional elements of the 2nd *SS-Panzer Division 'Das Reich'* were ordered to withdraw from their former sector and move to the Belew – Saslaw combat sector in order to scuttle the Soviet plans to advance west of Tarnopol to the west or southest and thereby cut off the main body of the 4th *Panzer Armee* (effective 1 / 2 March, 1st *Panzer Armee*) from its rear connections.

See Maps 68 and 86.   The vehicles worked their way over snow-drifted roads via Pischki – Ostropol – Tscherna – Staro Konstantinow to Belew. This area held special significance because the command feared that, after their advance to the west in the Belew – Ssaslaw (Issjaswal) area, the Soviets could turn south. With the help of the automatic-anti-aircraft weapons and heavy infantry guns, anti-tank guns and artillery fire, the III./ *Panzergrenadier Regiment 'Das Reich'*[1] of *Kampfgruppe 'Das Reich'* recaptured Ssaslaw from the Soviets.

The mainly symbolic main line of resistance could only be held as a series of strongpoints, some of which were held by members of the combat train elements. The Flemish *Sturmbrigade 'Langemarck'*, alone, held a 32 kilometer sector with fire-support from the 3rd *Würfer-Batterie*. On 3 February, with armoured support, they undertook a successful operation toward Michnoff. The Belgorodka railroad station changed hands several times. The German strong points in this loosely held line were, in places, at intervals of 400 to 800 meters. The *'Grillen'* (15 cm self-propelled heavy infantry guns) repeatedly displaced themselves in order to simulate heavy firepower in the entire sector by changing position. The 2-cm anti-aircraft guns did likewise.

On 29 February, after the relief of *Brigade 'Langemarck'* by *Bataillon Persch* (II./*Panzergrenadier Regiment 'Das Reich'*), the Soviets attacked in strength of two battalions out of the woods northwest of Pokaschtschewka, Beleshinzy and Dworez as well as toward the Belogorodka railroad station. The Soviets advancing on the Belogorodka road to Okopi were held down by heavy weapons fire. After its relief *Brigade 'Langemarck'*, with support by a *Sturmgeschützbrigade* took over the defense of *'Fester Platz'* Jampol. However, the *Rollbahn* east of Jampol remained blocked, as before.

---

1   Translator's note – According to Bender and Taylor, vol. 2 p. 83, "On December 12,1943, an advance staff was sent from *'Das Reich'* to Stablack in East Prussia for the purpose of reestablishing the Division as a *Panzer Divison*. In early February 1944, portions of the Division were transferred from the Eastern Front to their new training center in Bordeaux, southwest France, while the remainder of the Division fought on as *Kampfgruppe 'Das Reich'*, (unofficially known as *Kampfgruppe 'Lammerding'*)." Effective January 1944 *SS-Panzergrenadier Division 'Das Reich'* became the 2nd *SS-Panzer Division 'Das Reich'*. During the period currently under discussion in the text *Kampfgruppe 'Das Reich'* fought on with the former two *Panzergrenadier Regimenter* consolidated to a single *Panzergrenadier Regiment 'Das Reich'*.

On 2 March the formations committed in the area south-southeast of Schepetowka (forward of Staro Konstantinow), especially *Kampfgruppe 'Das Reich'*, launched an attack into the Soviet assembly positions. More than 30 *Stukas* took part, dropping bombs. The Soviets had organized against armoured attacks, as evidenced by their strong outfit of anti-tank guns. Therefore the German armour finally had to fall back to its own lines with the loss of two *'Tiger'* and three *'Panther'*.

The troops were to repeat such an attack on 3 March. However, the Soviet spring offensive (the 'Second Blow') came first (see below).

See Map 89.

3. Preliminary Attack against the line of the 19th *Panzer Division*

In the days before the start of the offensive the snowstorms let up and the sun brought about thaws and mud. That caused the Soviets to launch preliminary attacks. Engine noise and registration of heavy artillery prepared for the attack. One such started at 0945 hours on 29 February on a broad front. The troops believed that it was probably the expected offensive. In fact this attack merely served as armed reconnaissance with the objective of identifying the positions of infantry weapons and artillery and their blocking barrage areas and ranges.

German reconnaissance revealed the concentration of strong armoured forces and numerous enemy batteries, which led the troops in this sector, especially the 19th *Panzer Division*, to expect the offensive, the so-called 'Second Blow' of the Soviets on 1 March, to be introduced by a feared concentration of artillery fire as well as ensuing armour and infantry attack. Neither took place, which, while a relief to the *Grenadiere* in the foremost positions, was still nerve-wracking.

After two postponements of the expected start of the attack, on 2 March at 1415 hours the artillery preparation opened on the entire width of the 19th *Panzer Division* sector. The Soviets achieved limited initial successes with the ensuing attack. Therefore on 3 March at 0645 hours they repeated the same extravagant bombardment, which was costly to the German troops. The infantry attack that followed it came to a standstill in the blocking barrages fired by the batteries.

4. Additional Formations Brought Up

The force ratio between the Soviet forces standing by for the attack and the German formations that were gradually arriving, bit by bit, proved so unequal that the command had to expedite bringing additional formations into the combat area.

a) 1st *Panzer Division* brought up

From its last area of action west of Winniza, regardless of the miserable road conditions, the 1st *Panzer Division* had more than 200 kilometers to cover in order to get to the area specified in its orders, the Krassiloff area (south of Schepetowka). The main body of the division arrived in the assembly area at Proskurow by 2 March. The matériel losses, particularly as the result of vehicle breakdowns, had reduced the combat readiness of individual elements of the division to 55%. *Panzer Pionier Bataillon*

See Maps 68, 86 and 89.

37 [1st *Panzer Division*] was still missing almost two-thirds of its motor vehicles after the action at Lissjanka on 28 February. *Panzergrenadier Regiment* 1 was at 50% readiness for action. Heavy weapons and prime movers, tracked vehicles and *SPW* were still lying along the roadside, especially those of *Panzergrenadier Regiment* 113 [1st *Panzer* Division] and *Panzerartillerie Regiment* 73 [1st *Panzer Division*] . The latter was missing forward observers and observation-post officers ['*B-Offizieren*'], radiomen, telephone men and cannoneers, as well as lorries and prime movers. The IV./ *Panzerartillerie Regiment* 73 was completely immobilized for lack of prime movers. The repair services and workshop companies worked feverishly to restore mobility to the formations.

The tracked elements of the division (1st *Panzer Division*) were spared the march over the muddy roads thanks to transport by rail. Their first elements only arrived in Proskurow by 5 March, after the start of the offensive. The *Panzer* regiment received 23 new *Panzer* V (*Panther*) there. Thus, at the start of the first day of major fighting the division was not ready for action, but could only enter the battle later.

See Map 89.

The division set out from the assembly area around Proskurow for Staro Konstantinow with the mission, in cooperation with *schwere Panzer Regiment 'Bäke'*, of intercepting the enemy that was advancing to the south in the gap in the front southwest of Schepetowka and forcing him back to the northeast, thereby restoring contact with the *Korps* adjoining on the left.

For geography see Map 86.

This movement bogged down totally in the mud of the bottomless roads, especially in Proskurow. The *Grenadiere* therefore dismounted and continued their march to the assembly position area with their equipment on foot. *Kampfgruppe 'Richter'* and elements of *Panzergrenadier Regiment* 113, elements of *Panzerjäger Abteilung* 37 [1st *Panzer Division*] and elements of *Grenadier Regiment* 337 of the 208th *Infanterie Division* held a blocking position north of Selenzy on both sides of the *Rollbahn* to Staro Konstantinow. Here there was contact with *schwere Panzer Regiment 'Bäke'* and the command echelon of the 1st *Panzer Division* (elements of *Heeres-Flak Abteilung* 229 and the *Divisions-Begleit-Kompanie* [division escort company, part of the division headquarters troops]. They occupied blocking positions on both sides of the Schepetowka – Konstantinow road.

Panzergrenadier Regiment 113, behind *Kampfgruppe 'Nierle'* (reinforced *Panzergrenadier Regiment* 1 and elements of II./ *Panzer Regiment* 1) had to march more than 20 kilometers into the area around Tscherna in order to concentrate there for a counterattack with elements of other Panzer divisions. That, however, did not take place because during the night of 4/5 March the *Grenadiere* arrived in a new area of commitment, though without a single heavy weapon. *Kampfgruppe 'Nierle'* occupied a security line on both sides of the *Rollbahn* facing northeast about 25 kilometers northeast of Staro Konstantinow in order to seal off an enemy penetration in the sector of the 19th *Panzer Division* still north of the Slucz sector. A combat echelon of the I./ *Panzer Regiment* 1 reached the area northeast of Selenzy on 5 March, initially with 15 AFVs, later with an additional 23 AFVs, where it supported the 6th *Panzer Division*.

b) 6th *Panzer Division* Brought up

This division also received march orders to march from the area west of Winniza to Staro-Konstantinow. To the extent that the movement took place by rail, the last trains arrived on 27 February at the Tschertyrboki detraining station northwest of Staro Konstantinow, *Panje* – columns of the division's commander of logistical support. The II./ *Panzer Regiment* 11[6th *Panzer Division*] had over 23 *Panzer* IV. In addition the division had six heavy anti-tank guns on self-propelled mounts. The first combat unit to arrive was the I./ *Panzergrenadier Regiment* 4 [6th *Panzer Division*] which arrived on 27 February in Belgorodka at the *Rollbahn* to the west, and went into position there. Enemy assembly positions were before them to the northwest. Next came the I./ *Panzergrenadier Regiment* 114 [6th *Panzer Division*] from the division's concentration area around Grizew – Werbowzy – Dratschi – Mal.-Schkarowka. On 28 February the artillery was ready to fire on the expected enemy in the Gisowschtschine – Tadeuschpol area.

See Maps 68 and 86.

The fighting elements of the 6th *Panzer Division* prepared themselves adjacent to the *Rollbahn* to move out to the east, north or northeast, depending where the Soviet *Schwerpunkte* developed. Uncertainty regarding the *Schwerpunkte* of the expected Soviet attack led to fragmented commitment of the 6th *Panzer Division* on the west wing of the 59th *Armee Korps*. During the Soviet attack on 2 March at 1500 hours the division was at the north and northeast front as operational reserve. *Panzergrenadier Regiment* 114, II./ *Panzer Regiment* 11 and the 1st *Kompanie* of *Panzerpionier Batillon* 57 [6th *Panzer Division*] and the I. And II./ *Panzerartillerie Regiment* 76 [6th *Panzer Division*] were in the Belogorodka – Bissowotschka area.

The II./ *Panzer Regiment* 11 and the I./ *Panzergrenadier Regiment* 114 set out for Gulewzy, but were unable to prevent demolition of the bridge over the Horyn River. Elements of the *Panzeraufklärungs Abteilung* had, however, reached another bridge over the Horyn at Kemelinzy and built a bridgehead to the west and north. The I./ *Panzergrenadier Regiment* 4 [6th *Panzer Division*] was supported by an armoured group of *Kampfgruppe 'Das Reich'* in an attack on Dworez and, despite strong anti-tank gun and artillery defense, carried the attack to within 500 meters of Dworez.

The Soviet attack on the 19th *Panzer Division* had not yet led to a change in the 6th *Panzer Division's* commitment. The *Korps* command intended to leave the 6th *Panzer Division* to the west as long as the situation permitted in order to clean up the area north of Belogorodka. It would seem to have been desirable to assemble reserves behind the 19th *Panzer Division*. *Generalfeldmarschall* von Manstein, however, required the employment of the entire 6th *Panzer Division* to the west, the more so since he felt that he had to accept risks in the combat area of the 19th *Panzer Division*.

On 3 March, after an artillery preparation, the II./ *Panzer Regiment* 11 with the II./ *Panzergrenadier Regiment* 114 took Ssossnowka and, with armoured support, Hill 275. On the following day the division moved out to eliminate the enemy forces around Ssinjutki – Gulewzy.

See Map 89.

With that elements of the 6th *Panzer Division* were already fully committed on the first day of major fighting in the left flank of the 59th *Armee Korps*. A costly battle developed around Bissowka. Six German AFVs fell victim to the heavy armoured and anti-tank gun fire. The remaining *Panzer* could not carry out their mission alone and fell back to Bissowka. When the Soviets crossed the *Rollbahn* on a broad front with seven T 34 tanks the German armour knocked out two of them. The rest turned away. Bissowka then remained enveloped from the east and west. Therefore the troop was ordered to withdraw via Christowka – Antoniny to Staro Konstantinow. The *Kampfgruppe* could not fully carry out this mission because the intended intermediary locality was already in enemy hands. They reached Staro Konstantinow with the last drop of petrol. Their day's success included the destruction of eleven T 34s and eight anti-tank guns. They had, however, themselves lost a total of 13 *Panzer* IV and three more damaged.

On 4 March the east-west *Rollbahn* was thereby lost, so that now the north-south *Rollbahn* was exposed between Staro Konstantinow and Proskurow. The situation west of Staro Konstantinow and the depth of the enemy breakthrough to the south were still unclear. Therefore, south of Staro Konstantinow the 1st *Panzer Division* advanced to the west and, at Krassilow, ran into the T34s following from north to south. A *Kampfgruppe* of this division that was fighting northeast of Staro Konstantinow had to withdraw.

30

The Offensive

The account of the fates of these two divisions has already led us into the events of the two days of heavy fighting. The attack that started, following an extravagant artillery preparation on 3 March when the dawn first permitted aiming was brought to a standstill in the blocking barrage of the German batteries, which did not prevent the Soviets from starting a similarly extravagant preparation, this time, however, not only with attacking infantry but also with armoured support. The *Schwerpunkt* of the Soviet attack soon became evident, namely on the two wings of the *Korps*, therefore, on the one side in the sector to the right of the 19th *Panzer Division* and, on the other side, in the sector of the 6th *Panzer Division* and of *Kampfgruppe 'Das Reich'* on the left. While the 96th *Infanterie Division* and 291st *Infanterie Division* to the right of the 19th *Panzer Division* generally held their positions in heavy fighting against continuing fixing or simulated attacks or regained them in counterattacks, on the left wing and, later, also on the extreme right wing, the Soviets attained deep penetrations through use of massed infantry and armour. In the Gisowschtschin and Labun sectors on the one side and the Belogorodka sector on the other, the Soviets tore open the German front and thrust especially into the gap to the neighbour on the left, where no resistance could be offered, with strong forces. That immediately revealed the enemy's intentions, by continuing and broadening his breakthrough-attack to smash the German forces south of Schepetowka and push on through to the Tarnopol – Shmerinka railroad line. The rapid breakthroughs on both of the *Korps'* wings with concentric advance on Staro Konstantinow exposed the 59th *Armee Korps*, with the main body of its elements in the area between Schepetowka and Staro Konstantinow, to being cut off.

See Maps 68, 86, 87 and 89.

Defensive Fighting on the Wings of the 59th *Armee Korps*

First Day of Major Fighting (3 March)

West of the Slucz river a gap was soon torn all the way to the Sseweriny – Posselok – Lenin – Kustowzy line northeast of Kratschanowka, with the danger of a further Soviet advance into the depths. The troops formed a new defensive front in the Dubrowaya – Ssassanowka – Mikulion line and attempted to reseal the breach between Tscherna and Dubrowaya. In the 96th *Infanterie Division* sector, in repeated attacks, the Soviets merely penetrated into one portion of Mikulino until the counterattack forced them back out to the east and captured a hill that had been lost at the southern edge of Labun. The 291st *Infanterie Division* repulsed strong attacks that were supported by armour and cleaned up individual penetrations with hasty counterattacks. In

See Map 68.

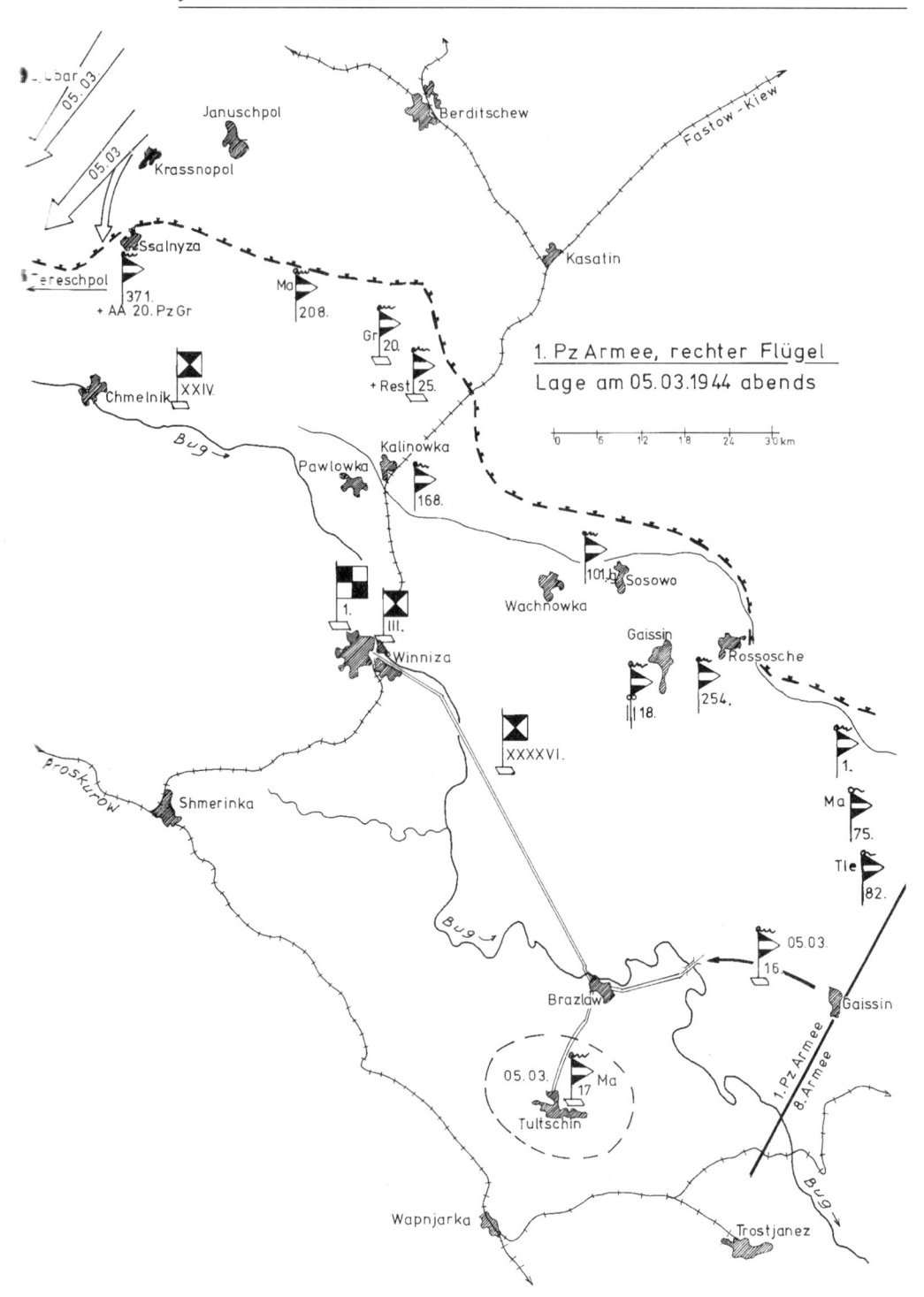

88. 1st *Panzer Armee*, right wing. Situation on 5 March, 1944, evening. Map 89 shows the left wing. Maps 89, 41 and 43 adjoin to the left. Map 58 shows lower right and adjoins.

particular it forced enemy forces that had temporarily advanced over Hill 305.3 to the Schepetowka – Ssaslaw road back to their jump-off positions.

The situation in the sector of *Kamfgruppe 'Das Reich'* and of the 6th *Panzer Division* on the left wing of the 59th *Armee Korps* underwent especially critical and inscrutable developments. Initially the fire of the three *'Tiger'* forced the waves of Soviet infantry to ground, thereby temporarily halting the attack. A Soviet armoured attack then followed with mutual losses. Ten to twelve of the 60 attacking T 34s were knocked out. That caused the others to turn away, but they then advanced to the left of the stationary wing to get into the rear of the line of German armour. This maneuver forced the German armour to fall back and the 6th *Panzer Division*, in light of this developing situation, to halt its ongoing attack on Ssinjutki. The 6th *Panzer Division* attempted to recapture from the west Belogorodka, which had been lost. At that moment a hitherto undetected mass of 70 enemy AFVs attacked the German attack group, smashing and dispersing it so that only remnant elements were able to fight their way back to Christowka.

On the extreme left wing 100 enemy AFVs with lorries and mounted infantry advanced in the general direction of Teofipol and Kartschewka. With that it became evident that the left flank was wide open. Elements of the 6th *Panzer Division* fought their way through to the southeast.

The enemy envelopment operations also forced *Kampfgruppe 'Das Reich'* to fall back with the armour. To the extent that opportunities existed for loading them, they took the wounded back with them. However, the Soviets soon blocked the retreat route toward Semjelintzy, the former assembly area of the armour. A single bridge there offered the only possibility of crossing the upper course of the meandering Horyn river. Semjelintzy, however, was already in enemy hands. Pursued by Soviet armour, the *Panzer* reached the bank of the Horyn but could not cross the river there. Therefore they resolved to violently break through Semjelintzy to the bridge there (Michnow). Another group with light tanks was to follow along downstream, but got hopelessly bogged down in a swamp. From there on, walking wounded had to attempt on their own to reach the German main line of resistance over the frozen river and the adjoining hills to the south.

The heavy *Panzer* drove right through the midst of Soviet columns toward Semjelintzy, even through the battery position of a horse-drawn enemy anti-tank gun company. One *'Tiger'* took a direct hit, whereupon the enemy armour concentrated its fire on the last *'Tiger'* until that, too, took a direct hit and caught fire. The fire was successfully extinguished and [the *'Tiger'*] regained the bank of the Horyn at top speed. That was as far as it got. A new fire in the tank forced the crew to bail out. The operational reserve was standing by at the east edge of Semjelintzy at the road from Saslaw to Jampol. The remaining crew and the wounded had to work their way back to that point under heavy fire on foot. Although they had knocked out 31 enemy AFVs, it was at a loss of 12 German AFVs, and that hurt them more than the Red Army suffered from its losses.

Situation in the Central Sector (19th *Panzer Division*)

The development of the situation on the left wing of the 59th *Armee Korps* (6th *Panzer Division, Kampfgruppe 'Das Reich'*) forced the *Korps* to pull back the 96th *Infanterie Division*, 291st *Infanterie Division* and, finally, also the 19th *Panzer Division* on the right.

See Maps 86 and 87.

The troops had, indeed, just as on the left wing, figured on a strong Soviet superiority in forces, but not on such an overwhelming superiority as had never until now been experienced. There was no way of discerning how great a mass of armour the Soviets employed here. They seemed, however, to have an inexhaustible supply of armour. It was estimated that there were at least five Soviet tanks committed for each German *Panzer*, and that was merely considering AFVs committed in action, not those that were available. As for artillery, the force-ratio at that time was even worse, particularly considering the available and ready-to-use stocks. The troops determined that the Soviets placed more and more emphasis on the employment of heavy weapons (armour, artillery and anti-tank guns). They were extremely cautions with their 15.2 cm guns, positioning them so far behind the lines that they were out of the more limited range of the German batteries. This superiority in heavy weapon altered the Soviet tactics. They used individual attacks exclusively, with strong artillery preparation and armoured support. The Soviet attack according to the 'Brussilow Tactic' of the First World War, or as was still practiced in 1941/42, exclusively with huge masses of infantry in deep waves, one after another, appeared to be a thing of the past.

Large-scale reorganization of the German side involving better weapons and larger amounts of ammunition foundered on personnel grounds on the one hand, and, on the other, because the requisite logistical support was lacking. Even the best weapons are of little use without an adequate supply of ammunition. Nevertheless, the German command learned from previous mistakes. Rear area services that had clustered at crossroads because of danger from partisan activity had to spread out among the villages on both sides of the supply roads, which noticeably interfered with the activity of partisan bands and also limited the effects of Soviet aerial attacks.

With the help of pioneer units the *Grenadiere* strengthened their positions, digging in during the days before the attack and, in the same way, used columns of civilian workers to construct new lines of defense to the rear. The artillery set up a widely branched network of observers to secure the area of the front with mutually flanking, overlapping blocking barrage areas.

Since the extravagance of the Soviet artillery preparations before their attacks had eliminated whole chains of artillery forward observers, the *Korps* ordered the painstaking construction of a second chain of forward observers, especially since observed fire was of even greater significance as contrasted with pre-planned blocking barrages in light of the limited supply of ammunition. The 19th *Panzer Division* did the same.

In their preparatory attacks the Soviets merely tested the defensive power of the individual German sectors. The artillery blocking barrages prevented the intended successes. Soviet employment of artillery now forced the Germans to echelon their defense. In the first line the *'Hummeln'* [self-propelled 15 cm heavy

THE OFFENSIVE 363

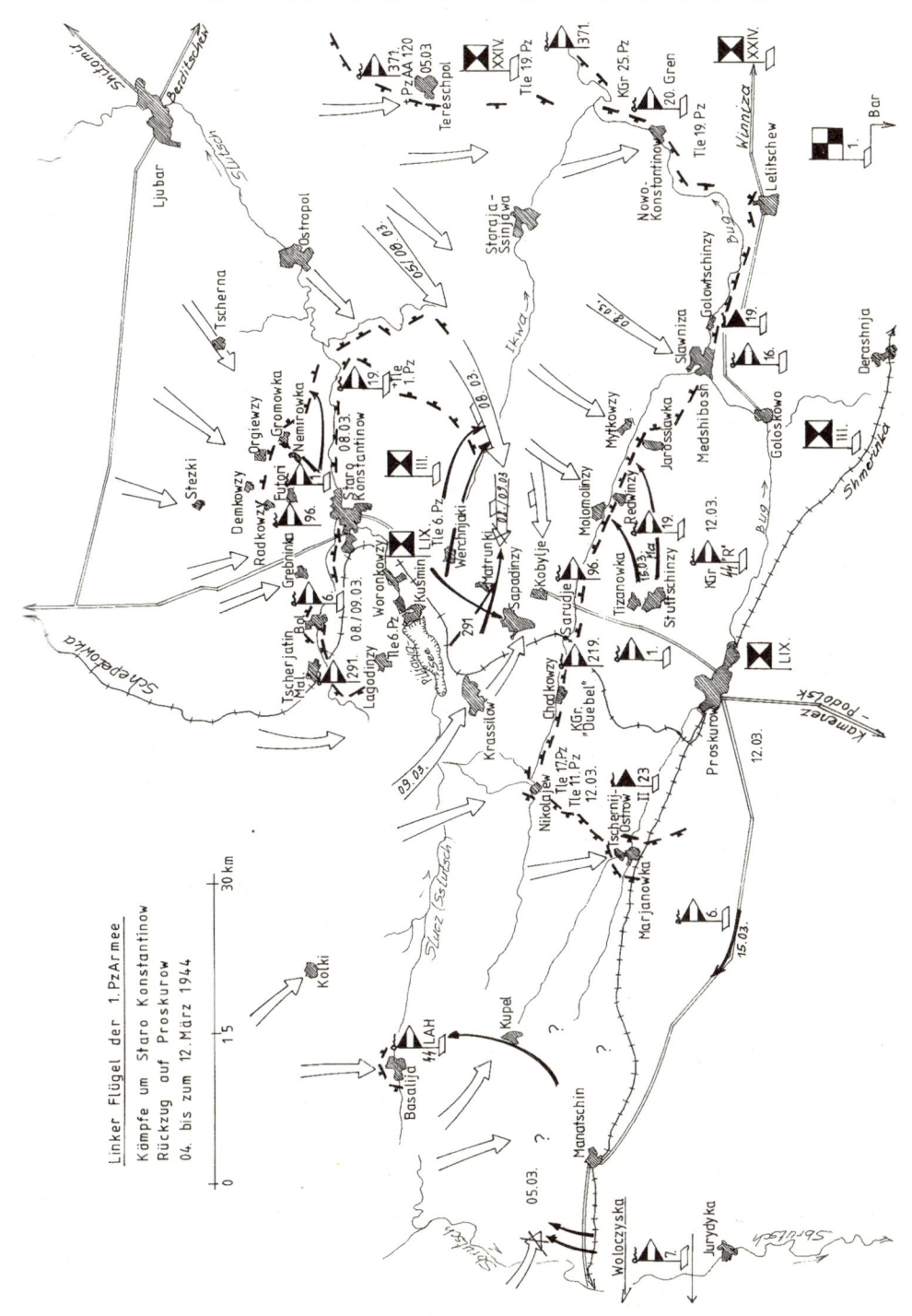

89. 1st *Panzer Armee*, left wing. Fighting around Staro Konstantinow. Retreat to Proskuros, 4 to 12 March, 1944. Map 88 shows right wing, adjoining to the right. Map 61 overlaps the lower right corner. Map 41 covers 7-16 January 1944, Map 86 7-29 January.

field howitzer] and *'Wespen'* [self-propelled 10.5 cm light field howitzer] stood, ready for action, behind the foremost line of *Grenadiere*, while the towed guns (light and heavy field howitzers) were in a second position farther to the rear – to attentively support the *Grenadiere* who, due to the lack of armour, were yet more dependent ton artillery support.

The Second Day of the Offensive

On 4 March the Soviets again pounded the entire width of the front with an artillery preparation from a yet greater number of tubes with massive expenditure of ammunition, this time with echeloned impact area. Above all else, they concentrated on the firing position of the batteries whose blocking barrages had scuttled the attacks of the preceding day. The Soviets came on in strong waves of infantry and forced their way into the foremost German positions regardless of the fire of the German heavy weapons whose fire was weakened by the simultaneous Soviet counterbattery fire. Nevertheless, they did not initially achieve any breakthrough, despite the fact that the personnel replacements the *Grenadiere* had received were freshly trained recruits, still lacking in experience at the front.

After their heavy losses in infantry during the first attack, the Soviets now attacked in the sector of the 19th *Panzer Division* with a larger number of AFVs, which, understandably, complicated the German defense. On 4 and 5 March no less than 104 Soviet AFVs were knocked out in the *Korps* sector. Thereby the 19th *Panzer Division*, however, lost its last *Panzer* that had been put in action after repairs, the *Grenadiere* thus losing the effective fire support provided by these 'mobile fortresses'. The melting snow and muddy, slippery terrain made the fighting extremely difficult, complicating the employment of motorized vehicles.

For geography, see Map 86.

In order to avert the threat resulting from being outflanked to the right for the center of the *Korps* formations, especially for the 19th *Panzer Division*, the *Korps* ordered a *Regimentsgruppe* [reinforced regiment] of the 1st *Panzer Division* to advance along the road to Ljubar and regain the former main line of resistance on both sides of Okazkowzy.

See Map 89.

Still on 4 March the 19th *Panzer Division* reported enemy forces advancing on Posselok Nina and Matyniwka. Although this division had no combat-capable armour at that time, it was ordered to halt the enemy advance with all possible means in the second 'yellow line' [*'gelben Linie'*] until additional forces arrived. By afternoon of that same day the division had to pull its right wing back to another fortified position north of Sseminiwka. The 96th *Infanterie Division* and 291st *Infanterie Division* were also ordered to retreat. The 59th *Armee Korps* communicated with the 24th *Panzer Korps* to determine the common boundary for the new line of defense.

During the night of 4/5 March the formations – 19th *Panzer Division*, 96th *Infanterie Division*, 291st *Infanterie Division* – carried out the withdrawal as ordered. During the course of 5 March the 1st *Panzer Division*, split into two *Regimentsgruppen*, took over the Belezk – Mikulino sector. While elements of the 19th *Panzer Division* were relieved by *Grenadier Regiment* 337 [208th *Infanterie Division*] the gap that still yawned between Belezk and Dubrowaja was to be closed. Weak elements of the 6th *Panzer Division* in the Teleschinzi area were to pass through the lines of *Kampfgruppe 'Das Reich'*, while the other elements of the 6th *Panzer* Division assembled in Staro Konstantinow for later commitment against the enemy forces advancing from the west. After it was split, the left flank of the 6th *Panzer Division* was wide open. Here *Kampfgruppe 'Das Reich'* knocked out 22 of the total of 30 destroyed T34s. German losses, however, amounted to seven *Panzer* IV and three *Panzer* VI ['*Tiger*'].

The 59th *Armee Korps* was ordered to seal off the breakthrough between the left wing of this *Armee Korps* and the right wing of the 48th *Panzer Korps* and to prevent enemy forces from getting through there.

The 19th *Panzer Division* reported heavy enemy pressure on the right wing. Considering the expected additional Soviet advance in this area, the boundary to the 24th *Panzer Korps*, the German forces tried to get the lines shifted to the rear. Initially the formations were to hold the *'Adler-Stellung'* ['eagle position']. Further retreat to the *'Chomora – Stellung'* remained reserved only if ordered from above. *Generalfeldmarschall* Model, however, declared that he was in agreement with that, but only if there was no other alternative.

Fighting to Prevent the Encirclement of the 59th *Armee Korps*

The 6th *Panzer Division* was ordered to attack to the west in order to take the pressure off of Staro Konstantinow. In the meantime, in the midday hours of 5 March the Soviets reached Kamenka (two kilometers west of Staro Konstantinow) with about 15 AFVs and mounted infantry. At that time it was not possible to tell how far enemy combat forces had advanced to the south from the Jampol area. It was evident, however, from their movements, that the Soviets intended to cut the *Korps* off from its rear connections. In the meantime the pressure on Staro Konstantinow from the west continued to mount. Elements of the 6th *Panzer Division* intercepted enemy forces at Kamenka. The 59th *Armee Korps* therefore decided to fall back during the night of 5/6 March to the next line of defense, behind the Chomora sector, in order to take into account the enemy advance in the east and in the deep west flank.

In order to prevent the 59th *Armee Korps* from being cut off, the formations received additional supplementary missions to withdraw in an orderly fashion behind the Sslutsch river east of and at Staro Konstantinow, as well as east of the Ikoott sector west of the city. It appeared vital to prevent the Soviets from cutting off the German forces north of both sectors before they could get to the crossings at Staro Konstantinow.

The German forces that were west of the city fell back behind the Sslutsch. The 59th *Armee Korps* pulled its northern front back behind the Chomora sector. A new security line was to be constructed from Ladygi west via Kisseli to Grizew. In the meantime the Soviets again attacked in the sector of the 1st *Panzer Division* and the 96th *Infanterie Division*, especially at *Grenadier Regiment* 113 [106th *Infanterie Division*]. A German counterattack by *Grenadier Regiment* 337 [208th *Infanterie Division*] stalled northwest of Wel. Mazewitischi.

The Situation of the 59th *Armee Korps*

See Maps 69, 86 and 89.

On the first two days of major fighting the German reserves had already proven everywhere to be too weak. The available formations merely delayed the enemy advance to the southwest without bringing it to a halt. According to the results of the *Armee's* reconnaissance, at this time the Soviets intended to advance via Staro Konstantinow to Proskurow. In order to attain this objective they continued to advance on both sides of the Schepetowka – Staro Konstantinow line with the intention of cutting off the formations of the 59th *Armee Korps* that were in action in this area. It was not, at that time, possible to ascertain what depth the Soviet advance west of this line had reached. Reconnaissance thrusts from Krassiloff to the northwest toward Tscherneleska were to provide some such information. A patrol identified T 34s rolling in from the north, but then went missing, itself. 13 kilometers west of Krassilow near Tschernelewka and also Jaworowzy flank security was engaged in heavy fighting against strong enemy armoured forces advancing toward the south.

See Map 77.

'Kampfgruppe Nierle' was fighting in the right-hand area of the advance on both sides of Scherna, south of the Ljubar – Schepetowka *Rollbahn*. With two light batteries of *Panzerartillerie Regiment* 73 [1st *Panzer Division*] it repulsed heavy attacks of the Soviet 1st Guards Army. As a result of the lack of anti-tank protection, enemy armour moved freely around behind the strongpoints of the *Grenadiere*.

Because of the Soviet advance via Belogorodka to the south and also at the boundary between the 59th *Armee Korps* and 24th *Panzer Korps* the situation of the 59th *Armee Korps* –favoured on the right by thick fog – gave increasing cause for concern. The German lines of defense could only be held as a series of strongpoints. The Germans could expect no further troop reinforcements.

31

Fighting Retreat of the 59th *Armee Korps*

A few days after the start of their attack the Soviets pressed from all sides on Staro Konstantinow, as, on 7 March, from the east and northwest (6th *Panzer Division*) while the northern front (96th *Infanterie Division*, 291st *Infanterie Division*) reported nothing unusual on that day. The Soviet pressure was increasingly directed at the flanks in order to gain depth there and encircle Staro Konstantinow. Accordingly they repeatedly attacked Staro Konstantinow with infantry, sometimes with armoured support, from the north, northeast and southeast. These attacks were beaten off with limited losses of terrain in bitter fighting. Aside from assault-troops and patrols, the Soviets then were quiet, from which the command concluded that the Soviets were regrouping their forces for the next day.

See Map 89.

Staro Konstantinow Bridgehead

Ground and aerial reconnaissance identified a 15 kilometer-long enemy column with infantry-vehicles towing guns of all sorts on the road leading south from Ostropel. Radkowzy was lost. The 1st *Panzer Division* recaptured Ogijewzy. The 6th *Panzer Division* recaptured several localities west of Staro Konstantinow. In the meantime, after it was relieved, as ordered, the leading elements of *Kampfgruppe 'Das Reich'* reached Staro Konstantinow and went into the eastern front of the Staro Konstantinow bridgehead. The Soviets continued to advance southward and southeastward from Ostropel with strong motorized forces.

For detailed map of Staro Konstantinow area see Maps 77 and 89.

According to orders from the *Führer* [*Führerbefehl*] Staro Konstantinow was to be held under any and all circumstances, even under threat of encirclement. Therefore the 59th *Armee Korps* issued orders to build a bridgehead on the north bank of the Slucz around the city, with the commander of the 1st *Panzer Division* as *Kommandant* 96 March). For the time being the withdrawal was only to go as far as a Krassnosselki – Nemirowka – Futori –Popowzy – Greneninka bridgehead position south of Tschernjatin.

See Maps 77 and 89.

The 6th *Panzer Division* was ordered to build the bridgehead, to capture Malyi Tschernjatin and to destroy the bridge there. After forcing back the enemy at Demkowzy, the 1st *Panzer Division* was to hold the Gromowka – Stezki (inclusive) line and commit elements that were freed up to reinforce the eastern wing. The regiment of the 96th *Infanterie Division* that was on its way was to be committed to construct a blocking position on the especially exposed eastern front. The 96th *Infanterie Division* and 291st *Infanterie Division* remained, as ordered, in the Staro Konstantinow bridgehead. The 1st *Panzer Division* with elements of the 19th *Panzer Division* (later also *Kampfgruppe 'Das*

See Map 89.

Reich') was to take over protection of the east flank south of the Sslutsch with the objective of establishing contact with the 24th *Panzer Korps*. *Kampfgruppe 'von Bernuth'* (6th *Panzer Division*) was responsible for protection of the west flank in the Lagodinzy area.

Completion of these measures suffered from the miserable condition of the roads, for which reason formations that were expected to pass through Staro Konstantinow accumulated in a traffic jam south of the city. Accordingly orders were issued to hold up any traffic north from Proskurow at Sapadinzy and ruthlessly clear the road from north to south.

The danger of the *Korps* being cut off shifted ever further to the rear toward Proskurow. In the meanwhile troop-movements continued over the bridge in Staro Konstantinow, even though complicated and delayed by the road conditions. However, exactly that made it necessary to hold the bridgehead and, on the other side, stimulated the Soviets to strengthen their attacks against the bridgehead-front, especially with *Schwerpunkt* from the east and southeast against the arc of the 19th *Panzer Division* front. Despite establishment of a traffic-control staff and commitment of construction forces to improve damaged sections on the *Rollbahn* from Staro Konstantinow to Proskurow, the troop movements fell short of what was desired. This also affected the east-west and west-east traffic between the two flanks of the bridgehead, as well as transfers to the northern front. However, all of the Soviet attacks were repulsed in bitter fighting, though, at places, with limited losses of terrain.

See Map 89.   Finally the 10th *Panzer Division* and 1st *Panzer Division* continued to cover the right flank south of the Sslutsch, the 96th *Infanterie Division* on both sides of Staro Konstantinow, the 291st *Infanterie Division* adjoining to the west until the *Korps* boundary at Bulajewka, with a strong reserve echeloned to the left rear. *Panzergruppe Bernuth* (6th *Panzer Division*) was in the Werchnjaki area as an attack group. For the night of 7/8 March the command planned to pull the northern front back at least into the bridgehead position, for it was necessary to employ *'Panzergruppe von Bernuth'* elsewhere, at the east front of the bridgehead where the Soviets attempted to outflank the lines of the 19th *Panzer Division* to the south (east and southeast).

In the evening of 7 March Hitler authorized that the bridgehead line be pulled back on the Sslutsch to Bulajewka and the evacuation of the part of the city of Staro Konstantinow that was north of this line. The 1st *Panzer Division*, 96th *Infanterie Division* and 291st *Infanterie Division* were to fight a delaying action north of this sector until the bulk of the vehicles had crossed the bridges to the south. The 59th *Armee Korps* had to pay particular attention to the area south of the Sslutsch to the southeast toward the Ikwa sector, in order to prevent a further Soviet advance there to the southeast.

On 8 March the formations continued their retreat through Staro Konstantinow, though falling behind the intended plan of march. Despite strong Soviet attacks against the north and northeast front of the bridgehead with armour and ground-attack planes the Soviets were unable to crush the bridgehead. The northwest front withdrew to the Ikopot sector as planned, secured by weak rear guards left north of the Ikwa. Armoured elements of the 6th *Panzer Division* set out from Werchnjaki to the east to support and

FIGHTING RETREAT OF THE 59TH *ARMEE KORPS*

relieve the hard-struggling 19th *Panzer Division*. The 1st *Panzer Division* pulled elements out of the northern front and committed them on the exposed northeast front. *Stukas* helped soften the pressure of the Soviet attack with, among others, attacks on a sugar factory that was in an advanced location. The enemy troops, however, had strong support from Soviet fighters and ground-attack planes that strafed and bombed the main line of resistance, the *Rollbahn* and Staro Konstantinow, as well as localities in the hinterland.[1]

In the meantime Hitler rescinded the order to hold Staro-Konstantinow so that the withdrawal behind the Iwa Sector – Pilawa-*See* [lake] at Kusmin (inclusive) could continue.

During the evening hours of 8 March the Soviets repeatedly exerted strong pressure from the north and northeast against the bridgehead front and against the deep eastern flank of the *Korps*, penetrating into Matrunki and blocking the *Rollbahn* to the south. This development of the situation caused the Command to immediately evacuate Staro Konstantinow.

Evacuation of Staro Konstantinow

The first orders to evacuate the bridgehead came out on 9 March. Thereupon the main body of the formations had to fall back to the intermediate position at the Slucz [Sslutsch] and leave rearguards in the former positions. The 6th *Panzer Division* was ordered to attack the enemy that had advanced to Pogerelaja – Matrunki and force him back to the east in order to provide relief to the 19th *Panzer Division*, which was still involved in heavy fighting. The 6th *Panzer Division* and 291st *Infanterie Division* threw the enemy out of Matrunki during the night and fought the *Rollbahn* free, carrying on their attack farther to the east.

In the early morning hours of 9 March the Soviets attempted to intensify the situation by attacking anew from the west to reach and block the *Rollbahn* south of Staro Konstantinow. Strong enemy forces were approaching Krassilow. Therefore the 291st *Infanterie Division* was ordered to accelerate its withdrawal and immediately attack Krassilow south of the lake with the forces that were freed up . The 1st *Panzer Division* cleaned up a Soviet penetration and withdrew to the south bank of the Ikopot sector. The north bridge in Staro Konstantinow was blown up. Two regiments that had previously been cut off (including *Grenadier Regiment* 287 [96th *Infanterie Division*] and *Grenadier Regiment* 337 of the 208th *Infanterie Division*) fought their way through to Kamenka. In the meantime the 19th *Panzer Division* secured the east flank southeast of Staro Konstantinow the entire night through under extremely heavy enemy pressure and while notably short of ammunition and petrol.

See Map 89.

These costly failures apparently caused the Soviets to end their attacks against the formerly targeted sector and advance farther to the south with the objective of blocking the *Korps* from the crossings over the Bushok sector. In light of the march elements that were still flowing through to the south, the 1st *Panzer Division* continued to hold Staro Konstantinow. The 96th *Infanterie Division* and 291st *Infanterie Division* fell back on both sides of Woronkowzy

---

1 Numerous localities and river names are taken from 1:50,000 scale maps, but may not be shown on larger scale maps at scales of 1:100,000 or 1:300,000.

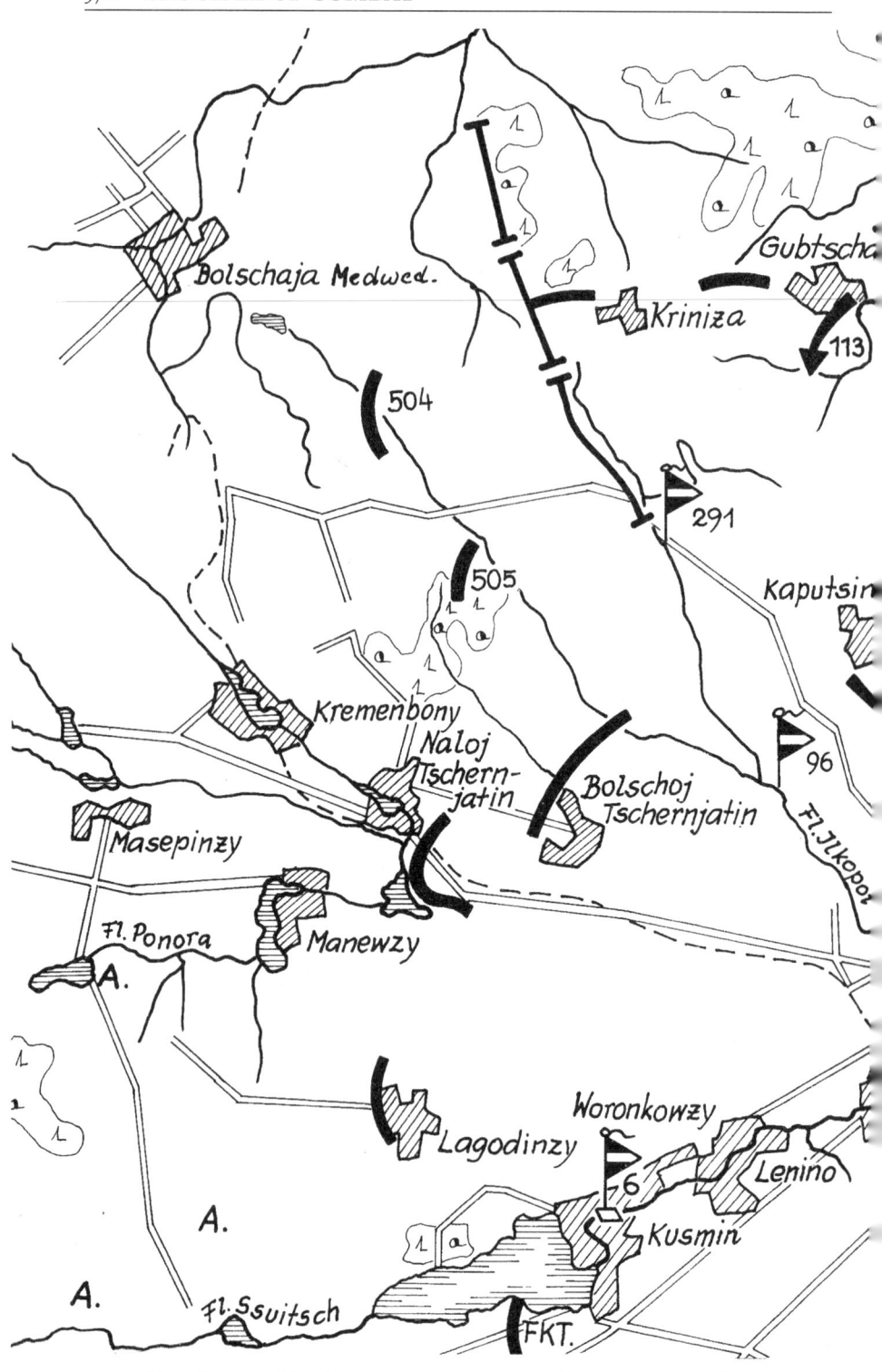

77. Situation on 7 March, 1944, 1000 hours. Staro Konstantinow Bridgehead

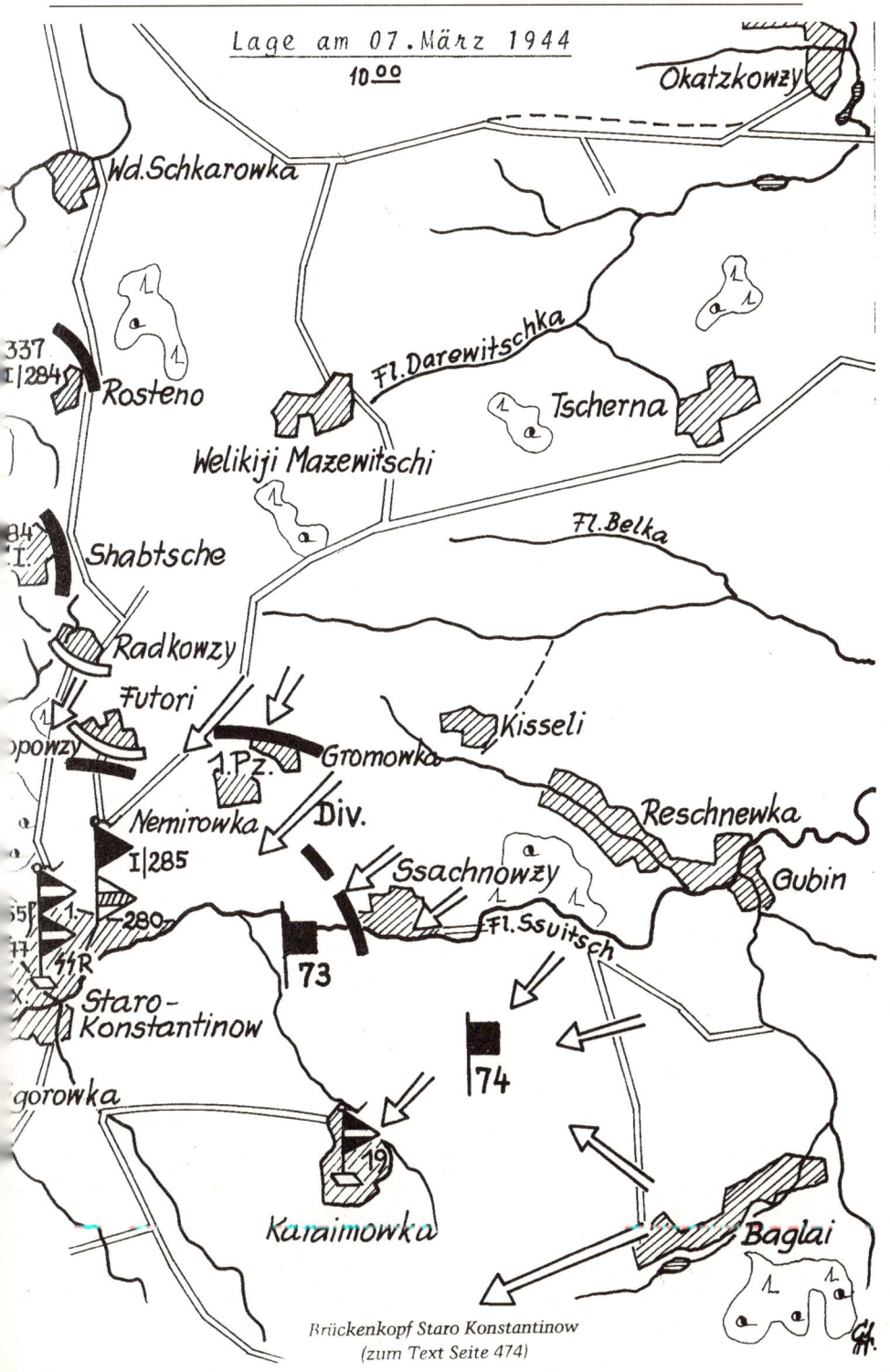

FIGHTING RETREAT OF THE 59TH *ARMEE KORPS* 371

Lage am 07. März 1944
10.00

Brückenkopf Staro Konstantinow
(zum Text Seite 474)

behind the Slucz sector. The 6th *Panzer Division* eliminated an impending threat from the east by recapturing Byshaja – Pogerelaja, regardless of pressure from the *Korps* to expedite its withdrawal or, as the case might be, to fight its way through to the south behind the Ikwa sector.

Further Retreat of the 59th *Armee Korps*

See Map 89.

With the evacuation of Staro Konstantinow, the 59th *Armee Korps* fell back by stages to the Bushok line. The 19th *Panzer Division* was to force back enemy forces that had crossed the Bushok sector at Redwinzy with a thrown-together '*Panzerkampfgruppe* 3rd *Panzer Korps*'. The other formations withdrew, sector by sector, toward the new line with orderly evacuation of the city of Staro Konstantinow and the areas on both sides of the *Rollbahn*. Enemy forces with armour and infantry pushed into the construction of the western front by the 291st *Infanterie Division* from the southern end of the lake by Kusmin as far as Mitinzy. Fighting kept up there throughout the entire day.

The withdrawal of the *Korps* suffered from enemy interference at various places along the *Rollbahn*, indeed, from both sides as well as from the air – and, in addition, from the complete blockage of the *Rollbahn* by traffic jams from the intersection south of Bushok to Proskurow. In order to guarantee the passage in both directions of at least the combat echelons, motor vehicles that were not participating in the battle were, by orders, pushed into the roadside ditches in order to clear the *Rollbahn* for the movement of the fighting formations.

Grenadier Regiment 287 and *Grenadier Regiment* 337, which had made it back to the *Korps*, were immediately attached to the 96th *Infanterie Division*. During the night of 10 March a night-time enemy armoured attack dispersed the division staff of the 291st *Infanterie Division*.

See Map 89.

Reconnaissance of the enemy indicated that the Soviets were advancing to the south with strong forces at Redwinzy and Mytkowzy. This information caused the 3rd *Panzer Korps* to urge the 19th *Panzer Division* to accelerate its march to Redwinzy. This commitment was expedited with regard to the Soviet intentions to block the *Rollbahn* anew from east and west. In order to prevent that, Sapadinzy had to be taken. As the result of constant fighting and wearisome marches on the muddy *Rollbahn* the troops were seriously exhausted. In addition there were the repeated, unavoidable combat commitments against the unending attempts of the Soviets to block the *Rollbahn* at one of the exposed points. The withdrawal behind the Bushok sector thereby fell behind the plans of the *Panzer Armee*.

North of the Bushok the 19th *Panzer Division* had to hold its bridgehead until the elements of the 96th *Infanterie Division* and 291st *Infanterie Division*, as well as the 6th *Panzer Division* had passed through to the south. They were then to assemble in the Stuftschinzy and Tiranowka area for later attack toward Redwinzy. While holding a small bridgehead, the 96th *Infanterie Division* occupied a new line and also took over the sector of the 19th *Panzer Division*. The formations completed their withdrawal according to plan on 11 March, despite all the terrain complications and disruption by enemy operations.

FIGHTING RETREAT OF THE 59TH *ARMEE KORPS*

At this point the danger of encirclement of the 59th *Armee Korps* by attacks on the right wing and an armoured thrust into the open left flank seemed to have ended.

The Bushok Line

The withdrawal movement was supposed to come to an end with this development. The *Armee* hoped that it would succeed in forcing minor elements of the enemy that had already crossed the Bushok back over the river. With this in mind the *Korps* attacked these enemy forces on 12 March, threw them back across the river and built a defensive front on the south bank of the Bushok, initially with contact with the 16th *Panzer Division* at Jarosslawka and, at Chodkowzy, with *'Kampfgruppe Duebel'*. After repulsing several enemy attacks and destroying both bridges, the 19th *Panzer Division* evacuated the bridgehead north of the Bushok on 11 March. There were no more *Korps* formations north of the Bushok. The Soviets were not content with this development, as was evident from the high activity of enemy aircraft and the repeated attacks in various sectors. Thereby advanced enemy forces showed up in the area south of the Bushok – with the exception of the bridgehead at Redwinzy – primarily as troops that had been defeated. Farther to the east and in the west flank, however, the Soviets had gained depth to the south and that seemed to abolish hopes of continued holding the Bushok line. Far more, the danger loomed anew of an envelopment and encirclement, not only of the 59th *Armee Korps* and 3rd *Panzer Korps*, but also of the right wing of the 1st *Panzer Armee* (24th *Panzer Korps* and 46th *Panzer Korps*).

[See Map 89 and, for geography, Maps 88 and 90.]

In order to counter this threat to the left flank, the 3rd *Panzer Korps* was ordered to stop an envelopment by the enemy by offensive operations. To accomplish this it was to destroy the enemy that had advanced into the gap between the 59th *Armee Korps* and 48th *Panzer Korps* of the 4th *Panzer Armee* with single blows, with the final objective of establishing contact with the 48th *Panzer Korps*. The 96th *Infanterie Division* carried out night attacks, while the 291st *Infanterie Division* repulsed Soviet forces that had advanced in the left flank over the former railroad bridge toward Sarudje and then held the south bank of the Bushok in its sector. In any event, the 3rd *Panzer Korps* succeeded in narrowing the gap to the 48th *Panzer Korps* which had, in the meantime, fallen back with its foremost lines to the west after the encirclement of Tarnopol.

[See Map 89.]

In the right flank, *Stukas* and ground attack planes effectively supported the eastward directed attack of the 6th *Panzer Division* and 19th *Panzer Division* toward Tereschewzy and Arkadejewzy, and also against the Redwinzy bridgehead (12 and 13 March). Although the Soviets attacked here with armoured support, reconnaissance indicated that the Soviets were pulling forces whose strength could not be ascertained back to the north. These movements were covered by heavy artillery fire on Stuftschinzy and Arkadejewzy. South of Molmolinzy, too, they were pulling back to the north, presumably to shift these formations into the left flank of the 59th *Armee Korps*.

[See Map 89.]

This short-term easing of the situation gave the commanding general of the *Korps* occasion to express his gratitude to the 6th *Panzer Division* and 19th

Panzer Division for their service and to arrange for mention of the divisions in the *Wehrmacht* report.

Attempts to Close the Gap in the Front to the 48th *Panzer Korps*

The attempt of the 3rd *Panzer Korps* on 14 March to gain ground from the enemy that was advancing farther to the south in the western flank failed. The result was more that the Soviets took back a number of the localities that they had lost the day before. With that the danger again mounted of an envelopment and encirclement of the *Korps*. Therefore the *Panzer Abteilung* of the 1st *Panzer Division* was attached to the 3rd *Panzer Korps* in exchange for the 16th *Panzer Division*, which was attached to the 59th *Armee korps*.

The German operations, especially shifting of troops from the east flank sector to the west flank sector, or the reverse, and the accomplishment of a variety of operations, were delayed by sluggish supply of petrol. Nevertheless, on 14 March the 19th *Panzer Division* reached the northern edge of Redwinzy. *Stukas* bombed and destroyed the bridge the Soviets were using over the Bushok. On 15 March the enemy bridgehead south of the Bushok was no longer in its former dimensions, being reduced to no more than a small bridgehead garrison directly at the site of the bridgehead. Due to the lack of adequate infantry in the wooded terrain, initially it was not attacked. There were no forces available to fight enemy forces in approximately regimental strength in the woods east of Golowtschinzy. The daily report particularly praised the efforts of the 7th *Kompanie* of *Panzergrenadier Regiment* 64 [16th *Panzer Division*] and the 16th *Panzer Division*, as well as the remnants of *Panzerpionier Bataillon* 19 [19th *Panzer Division*]

The 3rd *Panzer Korps* received further reinforcement through provision of *Tiger-Abteilung* 509, *schwere Panzerjäger Abteilung* 88 and *Sturmgeschütz Brigade* 276 for additional offensive missions along *Durchgangstraße*.IV west of Proskurow. Reconnaissance that revealed that the enemy forces mission was to advance via Parchomowzy to Jarosslawka and build a bridgehead there.

In accord with their initial intention, the Soviets continued to alternate their pressure between the boundary separating the 59th *Armee Korps* and 24th *Panzer Korps* on the one hand, and the left flank sector, with further advance into the depth of the rear areas of the 1st *Panzer Armee*. It seemed conspicuous that, on 16 March, the Soviets remained relatively quiet in the left sector and pressed forward all the stronger in the right sector, and that from Nedshibosh to Letitschew, Blibotschanskije, the thrusts in both sectors coordinated in their alternation. The increasing pressure in the right sector led to the 16th *Panzer Division* and 19th *Panzer Division* being assigned the mission of shifting farther to the right following their relief by the 96th *Infanterie Division* and 291st *Infanterie Division*.

See Map 89.

The 19th *Panzer Division* utilized its march to the east to cleanse the Bachmatowzy – Dawydkowzy forest area of additional enemy remnants. Regardless of renewed enemy shifting of forces to the west that was expected as a result of intercepted Soviet telephone messages, the German command still reckoned on strong enemy attacks on the right wing between Letitschew and Medshibosh. Nevertheless, the formations could not be spared to counter them. The only remaining reserve that the *Panzer Korps* had for this service was merely the 19th *Panzer Division* with attached elements of *Kampfgruppe 'Das Reich'*, all in all with a combat infantry strength of about 1000 men, but with a mere three *Panzer*. Therefore this division was given the last remaining *Sturmgeschütz Brigade* in the *Korps*, with all of four *Sturmgeschütze* fit for action. On the other side of the coin, the 19th *Panzer Division* had to give *Kampfgruppe 'Das Reich'* formerly attached to it over to the 24th *Panzer Korps*, adjoining it on the right. The forces remaining to the 59th *Armee Korps* were now to prevent a breakthrough at this boundary position west of Letitschew until the 24th *Panzer Korps* pulled its front back behind the Tribuchowzy – Proskurow Bug sector upon receiving the code-word *'Amanda'*. Proskurow was designated as a *'Fester Platz'* with attachment of a *Grenadier* regiment, as well as an *Artillerie-Abteilung* of the 291st *Infanterie Division* under the command of the *Platzkommandant*.

The *Armee* also ordered that the entire male population between 12 and 65 years old was to be seized and transported to prevent later recruiting by the Red Army.

32

Development of the Situation of the 1st *Panzer Armee*

See Maps 89 and 90.

At this point the following situation existed: The 59th *Armee Korps* was in the center of the Soviet attack. The Soviets had not been able to dent its front, only force it back. The strength of the attack in this sector did not permit the assumption that the Soviets merely intended to fix the German forces in this sector so as later to be able to encircle them by a deep thrust into the flanks. It seemed far more likely that the Soviet actions obviously were intended to dent the front and break through along the main Staro Konstantinow – Proskurow *Rollbahn* to the south.

The ground gained, however, in the boundary area between the 59th *Armee Korps* and 24th *Panzer Korps*, as well as on the left flank of the 59th *Armee Korps* to the 48th *Panzer Korps* gave the Soviet command reason to change their plan so as not to break through at the 59th *Armee Korps* –which had failed–, or to cut the 59th *Armee Korps* off from the other formations of the 1st *Panzer Armee* – to date also a failure, but to draw the circle wider around the entire 1st *Panzer Armee*. This, too, had concerns about its right wing.

See Map 90 and, for geography, Map 91.

There was no contact with the left wing of the 8th *Armee* to the south. A gap of over 100 kilometers yawned there. The *Heeresgruppe* saw no possibility of closing it in the foreseeable future. The troops simply were lacking. Merely *Kampfgruppe 'Das Reich'*, formerly attached to the 19th *Panzer Division*, received orders to transfer to Bar in order to relieve the garrison of *'Fester Platz'* Shmerinka and to receive them when they broke out – in the expectation that the garrison of the *'Fester Platz'* would be able to hold the place until the permitted breakout. The 17th *Panzer Division* was, likewise, to set out for there, which did not come to pass because the *Schwerpunkt* of a Soviet attack in the Medshibosh – Lettitschew area gave rise to fears of an advance to the southwest toward Proskurow.

See Map 90 and, for geography, Map 91.

On 17 March the 24th *Panzer Korps* was still in action east of Chmelnik in the midst of the 1st *Panzer Armee*, thus, not only east but actually northeast of the sector of the 59th *Armee Korps*. That day the Soviets deepened their penetration by about four kilometers, later, with the commitment of two divisions despite a counterattack, to a depth of eight kilometers and a breadth of two kilometers on over the Bug to the southern edge of Strishawka. Therefore the 16th *Panzer Division* shifted to the boundary between the 59th *Armee Korps* and 24th *Panzer Korps* and fought free again the road between Letitschew and Medshibosh. In the meantime the 20th *Panzergrenadier Division* repulsed enemy attacks 15 kilometers northeast of Letitschew, while *Kampfgruppe 'Das Reich'*, which had been attached to the 24th *Panzer Korps* advanced eastward

THE SITUATION OF THE 1ST *PANZER ARMEE*

from the Bar area to about six kilometers west of Shmerinka. Brailow, located north of Shmerinka, returned to German hands.

While the 3rd *Panzer Korps* on the left wing of the *Armee* repulsed attacks against the northwest front of the 1st *Panzer Armee* at Nikolajew, the 6th *Panzer Division* undertook a successful local thrust to the east, the Soviets forced back the 46th *Panzer Korps* in the right sector of the 1st *Panzer Armee* so that there was now danger of the *Panzer Armee* also being cut off from the south. The security forces of the 75th *Infanterie Division* and 254th *Infanterie Division*, as well as the 18th *Artillerie Division* were forced back to the Tschernowzy – Dshuryn line. On 21 March the Soviets advanced in the sector of the 46th *Panzer Korps* between Kamenka and Mogilew Podolsk even farther over the Dnjestr to the west, to ten kilometers southwest and 20 kilometers west of Jarowa. *See Map 90 and, for geography, Map 91.*

The situation seemed to grow ever more critical. While, in the 3rd *Panzer Korps* sector, the 19th *Panzer Division* and 16th *Panzer Division* were in a bitter fight in a general line six kilometers west of Proskurow – Felschtin and six kilometers southwest of that location, the gap to the right wing of the 48th *Panzer Korps* of the 4th *Panzer Armee* broadened, which would certainly encourage the Soviets to send additional armoured formations through to the south via Kusmin. Finally, several *Panzer* were just west of Jarmolinzy, a locality through which not only the supply line ran from Kamenez-Podolsk to Proskurow, but also where a railroad line from the west ended. On 22 March the 3rd *Panzer Korps* gained essentially no ground against extremely tough enemy resistance. *See Map 90.*

The repeatedly assigned mission for the 3rd *Panzer Korps* to advance to the north corresponded to the repeatedly assigned mission for the 48th *Panzer Korps* to advance to the south, this to be done with 'Gruppe Maus' (7th *Panzer Division*, 1st *SS-Panzer Division 'Leibstandarte Adolf Hitler'* and *Kampfgruppe* 68th *Infanterie Division*), specified for that task. 'Gruppe Maus' repeatedly pressed to the south against enveloping enemy attacks, but not through to the east to the 1st *Panzer Armee*. Leading elements reached the railroad line ten kilometers northwest of Gussjatin. According to their observations, after passing through the gap between the 1st *Panzer Armee* and the 4th *Panzer Armee*, the leading enemy armoured spearheads were already in the bend of the Dnjestr at Ljanskorum (30 kilometers northwest of Kamenez-Podolsk and at Zaleszczyki. With that the encirclement of the 1st *Panzer Armee* was immediately impending. *See Map 90.*

Apart from this, unusual sector-situations developed. While, in a stable front each *Korps* occupied its sector, within the framework of other *Korps* sectors, in a broad front. However, the 'wandering *Kessel*' of the 59th *Armee Korps* had already resulted in the fact that the 3rd *Panzer Korps* was, for the most part, behind the 59th *Armee Korps*, the 59th *Armee Korps* with its defense assignment facing north, the 3rd *Panzer Korps* with its offensive missions to the west. This situation developed yet more uniquely as, in the course of the next day, the 24th *Panzer Korps* took over the east front of the 'wandering *Hube-Kessel*', while the 3rd *Panzer Korps* and 59th *Armee Korps* advanced offensively to the west. *See Map 90.*

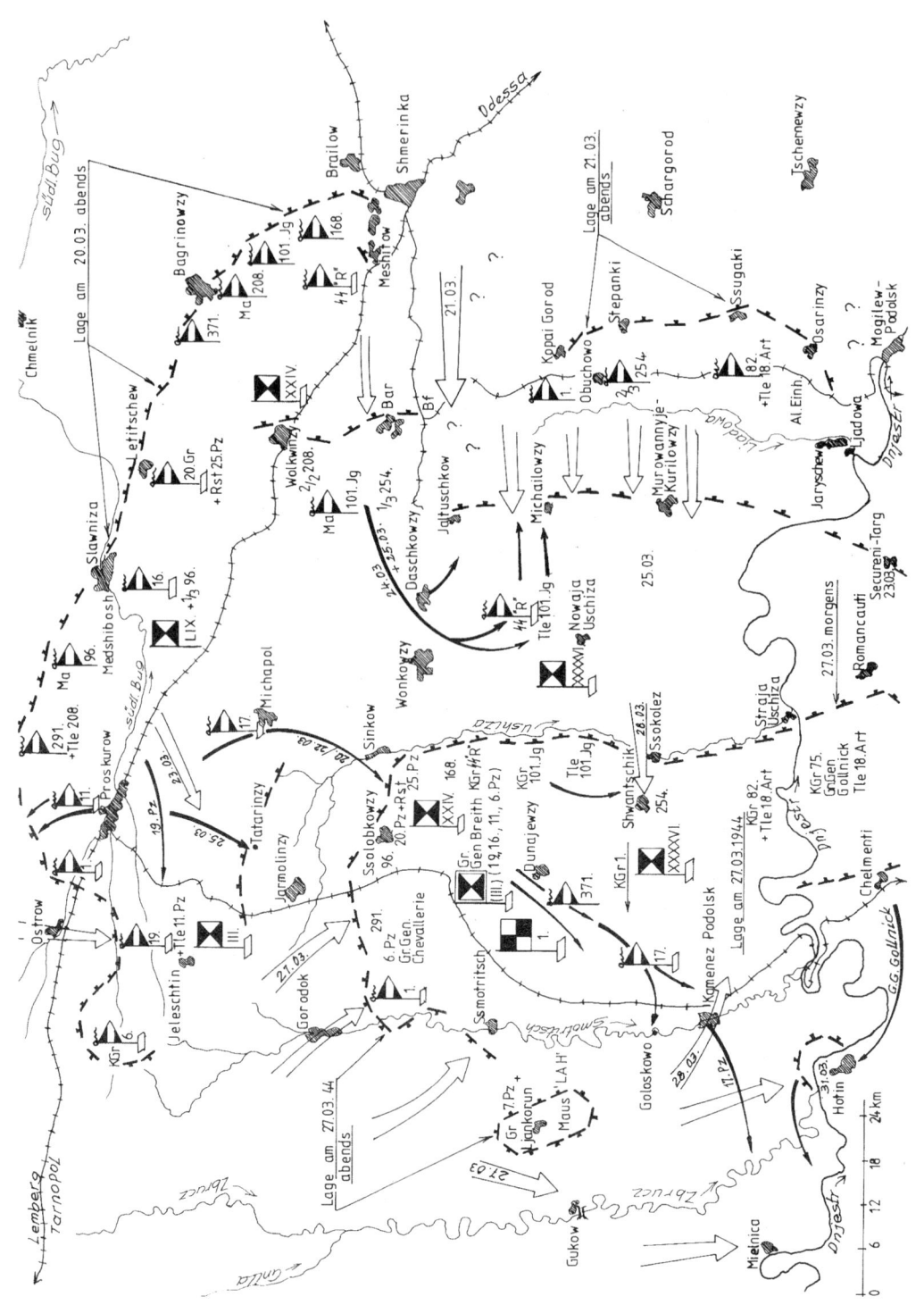

90. The Hube *Kessel*. Situation 20-27 March 1944. Map 65 overlaps bottom for 27 March. Map 61 overlaps to the right, 13-28 March.

THE SITUATION OF THE 1ST *PANZER ARMEE*

'Gruppe Maus' of the 48th *Panzer Korps* pushed forward from the north, coming parallel to the Soviet advance, and so far to the south that, on 25 March, it came to cooperation with the orderly withdrawing 46th *Panzer Korps*. On the other side, 'Gruppe Maus' attempted to establish contact with the forces of the 3rd *Panzer Korps*. In the reverse direction, this order had armoured elements of several *Panzer* divisions attempting to establish contact with 'Gruppe Maus', which was advancing in the Gussjatin area, but they only advanced a few kilometers westward from Jarmolinzy.

The 1st *Panzer Division* had to withstand heavy fighting with armour-supported enemy forces. It had to evacuate Gorodok again and fall back on Tschernowody. That did not prevent 'Gruppe Maus' from moving farther to the southeast as far as the area south of Tschermorowzy, where it ran up an admirable score in knocking out enemy AFVs and brought in booty and prisoners.

For the 1st *Panzer Armee*, in this situation, it became a matter of securing the supply lines to the rear with the forces of the left wing. Therefore it ordered 'Gruppe General von Waldenfels' (with elements of the 6th *Panzer Division*, 19th *Panzer Division* and 11th *Panzer Division*) to advance from the northeast, and the 16th *Panzer Division* from the west to the Kamenez-Podolsk – Proskurow railroad line in order to thrust into the flank of the enemy forces that were advancing at and south of Frampol and to force them back. It reached the area northeast of Frampol and captured Frampol. In the meantime 'Gruppe Oberst Maus' formed a hedgehog position [organized for 360 degree defense] on both sides of Dunajawzy. That did not prevent the Soviets from advancing east of Frampol farther to the south and to force the German garrison out of the city of Kamenez-Podolsk. Therefore the 1st *Panzer Armee* had the 17th *Panzer Division* attack these enemy forces to again fight free the supply route via Hotin and Kamenez-Podolsk. Leading elements of this division reached the area seven kilometers northeast and north of Kamenez-Podolsk but were unable to reconnoiter the situation to the south and west. With that it became evident that the 1st *Panzer Armee* was cut off from its connections to the rear, except for isolated lorries that got through more-or-less by accident.

See Map 90.

Organization of Formations

Until 5 March the 1st *Panzer Armee* was responsible for a sector of about 200 kilometers, stretching about 100 kilometers to the right and to the left of the command post. This front was divided among four *Korps*, the 46th *Panzer Korps*, 24th *Panzer Korps*, 59th *Armee Korps* and, finally, the 3rd *Panzer Korps*.

See Maps 88 and 89.

As the east front of the 1st *Panzer Armee* approached Kamenez-Podolsk the gradual encirclement began from the north and west, with simultaneous pressure against the Dnjestr. The depth of the *Kessel* to the east remained generally under 30 kilometers, the north-south dimension general 40 kilometers, therefore only 15 to 20 kilometers from the command post (a distance that was, in each case, greater at the start of attacks from north, northwest or west).

See Maps 91, 93, 94, 95 and 96.

The area for the four *Korps* grew ever smaller. The lost communications equipment could not be replaced. With shorter communications links, fewer staffs, which served as possible sources of errors, were needed. Therefore the

3rd *Panzer Korps* was consolidated with the 46th *Panzer Korps* as *Korpsgruppe unter General* Breith, and the 24th *Panzer Korps* was consolidated with the 59th *Armee Korps* as *Korpsgruppe unter General* von de Chevallerie.

See Map 90.

The 1st *Panzer Armee* now had to fend off attacks, especially from the north and east, and find a way out of this encirclement. The 19th *Panzer Division* reached the Klinkowzy-*Süd* south to Malinitschi line west of Proskurow, while the 16th *Panzer Division* and the 96th *Infanterie Division* were responsible for preventing an enemy advance west to the *Rollbahn* between Bushok and the Bug as well as between the Bug and Ploska toward Proskurow. The 1st *Panzer Division* advanced north from the Gorodok area, while the 24th *Panzer Korps* and 46th *Panzer Korps* received permission to carry out the '*Amanda*' retreat.

See Maps 89 and 90.

On the east front of the *Kessel* there was still fighting at Redwinzy, with a penetration at Iwankowzy. The 1st *Panzer Armee* placed less emphasis on this front and far more on holding open the Proskurow – Jarmolinzy supply route, the last remaining *Rollbahn* for supplying the 59th *Armee Korps* and its withdrawal movement within the combat area of the 1st *Panzer Armee*. At that time, if needed, the 1st *Panzer Division* was available for such an assignment, but could not banish the growing danger alone, the more so since its complement of armour constantly shrank. The 19th *Panzer Division*, also without armour, could only achieve adequate combat effectiveness if provided with reinforcements. Those, however, would only become available after completion of the '*Amanda*' movement.

Transporting the formations required for that action involved additional difficulties because no more trains came through via Kamenez-Podolsk to Jarmolinzy or Proskurow. Therefore shortages of petrol immediately became evident. The miserable road conditions and stretches of slow driving demanded yet more quantities of petrol. The 1st *Panzer Armee* was forced to consider separate supply by air for the 1st *Panzer Division* at Gorodok. Soviet armour blocked the road between Jarmolinzy and Gorodok.

In order to economize on petrol the *Armee* issued instructions to collect local *Panje* – vehicles in order to use these as combat vehicles for the fighting troops. The *KoPiFü* [*Korps Pionier Führer*, commander of the *Korps* pioneers] received precautionary orders to establish crossings over the Ushiza between Bielowoce and Sinkow and to reconnoiter corresponding possibilities over the Dnjestr. The *Armee* assigned 40 *AFVs* to the 1st *Panzer Division*. The 1st *Panzer Division* had to repulse concentric attacks on Gorodok after temporary penetration of enemy armour into the Jarnolinzy railroad station (24 March). As ordered, the 11th *Panzer Division* set out to the Jarmolinzy area in support.

The *Armee* advised the *Gruppe* on new tactics of the enemy forces, namely the arrival of Soviet soldiers in civilian dress in localities that were still occupied by German troops. Anew, partisan bands dressed as *Heere* sentinels had also stopped motor vehicles and killed their occupants.

'*Fester Platz*' Proskurow

By mid-March the defensive fighting on the northern front proved difficult because, in light of the road conditions, these formations were no longer adequately supplied with ammunition and petrol. Accordingly, the *Armee* had

THE SITUATION OF THE 1ST *PANZER ARMEE* 381

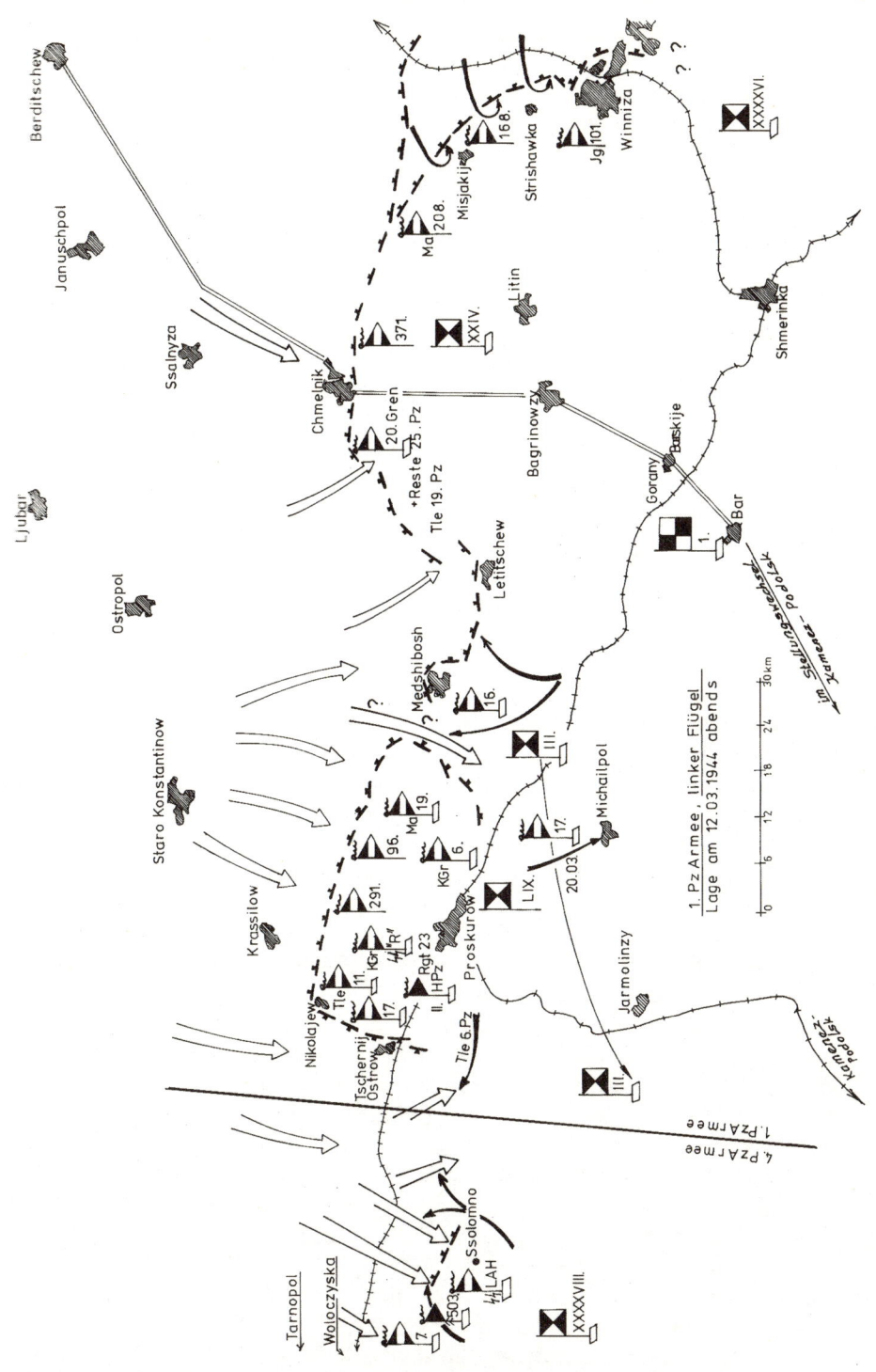

91. 1st *Panzer Armee*, left wing. Situation on 12 March 1944, evening.
Map 86 adjoins to the north for 7 January-29 February 1944.

to accept withdrawal of the northward-extending points of the 59th *Armee Korps*.

See Map 89.

Initially the Bushok line was evacuated. Rear-guard formations held on until the combat elements of the formations committed there could slip away to the south. To be sure, on 11 March the *Armee* was still ordering, as usual, that the current lines were to be held. Further withdrawal movements, however, had to be planned in good time, initially with a retreat to the Paszutinzy bridgehead position. The Soviets immediately interfered with the withdrawal movement, attacking Sapadinzy and Sarudje from the north. The *Armee* attempted to hurl back the enemy forces advancing over the Bushok to the south. In the meantime, south of the Bug the Soviets attacked to the northwest toward Gretschany and occupied Oleschin. In Sarudje the demolition failed to completely destroy the bridge, which meant that the bridgehead position had to be recaptured yet again so that the bridge could be destroyed.

See Map 91.

The situation for *'Fester Platz'* worsened, not only due to the above, but also as a result of the enemy advance between Letitschew and Medshibosh. The *Armee* had withdrawn too many forces for service in other sectors, as, for example, *Kampfgruppe 'Das Reich'*, and the gap between the 24th *Panzer Korps* and 46th *Panzer Korps* had, in the meanwhile, grown to 30 kilometers wide.

The first withdrawal of the 24th *Panzer Korps* planned on using Letitschew as its hinge point (17 March), the second, Proskurow. The sector between Goloskowo and Tribuchowzy proved to be too weak, which resulted in the urgent demand for additional forces for this section and for the bridgehead that was to be built at Proskurow. The 59th *Armee Korps* could spare no additional forces. Above all, the withdrawal movement suffered in the ensuing days from lack of deliveries of petrol. In any case, in the meantime the Proskurow railroad station ceased to serve as a base of supply.

The road conditions to the rear of Proskurow required reconsideration of the plans, wherefore the 19th *Panzer Division* did not set out, as intended, toward Bar, but was hurriedly transferred to the sector west of Proskurow in order to relieve the 17th *Panzer Division*, until the orders to withdraw behind the Bug finally came out, simultaneously with carrying out the *'Amanda'* withdrawal by the 24th *Panzer Korps*.

See Map 90.

Above everything the Command had to prepare for the shift of Soviet forces from the right flank sector to the left flank of the northern front. In addition Proskurow gained significance as the pivotal point of the front. Therefore, on 21 March, orders were issued for a counterattack in this sector to keep the enemy forces distant from Proskurow, the more so since execution of the *'Amanda'* withdrawal had been delayed by miserable road conditions. Such operations suffered in part from the fact that various formations lacked artillery ammunition to engage enemy movements.

Nevertheless, on 22 March the 59th *Armee Korps* prevented enemy breakthroughs to the south to Proskurow. *'Fester Platz'* Proskurow was still to be held for further withdrawal movements of the 24th *Panzer Korps* that were expected to take place during the night of 22/23 March, for which reason the *Kommandant* was assigned a reinforced regiment for the defense of Proskurow

THE SITUATION OF THE 1ST *PANZER ARMEE*   383

(*Grenadiere Regiment* 504 [291st *Infanterie Division*] and *Füsilier-Bataillon* 291 [291st *Infanterie Division*]).

The plans of the *Armee*, however, changed at the moment that enemy armour appeared at Jarmolinzy. The Jarmolinzy – Proskurow railroad had, in any case, ceased to function. That left the remaining road through Jarmolinzy as the only transportation-artery for further withdrawal of formations of the 59th *Armee Korps* from the Proskurow area to the south. Therefore the *Armee* now had to commit forces to secure the road south of Proskurow.

On 23 March the Soviets sent strong infantry and armoured forces down the Proskurow – Jarmolinzy road, but also on the Jarmolinzy – Gorodok road. The formations that were tied up in Proskurow could not flow back so quickly, wherefore the 96th *Infanterie Division* occupied the Bug sector with all its elements, *Grenadier Regiment* 504 [291st *Inanterie Division*] occupied the bridgehead position north of Proskurow until the start of the evacuation, pulling the garrison back to the edge of the city. *See Map 90.*

The Proskurow *Kampfkommandant* received permission to pull the bridgehead back to the south bank of the Bug until, for 24 March, the *Armee* ordered the Proskurow garrison back to the Karpowzy line, with attachment of the fortress garrison by order to the 291st *Infanterie Division* while simultaneously revoking the designation of Proskurow as a *'Fester Platz'*. During the evening hours of 25 March the force evacuated Proskurow in accord with the withdrawal movement of the 291st *Infanterie Division* to Tatarinzy.

Situation of the 1st *Panzer Armee* to the Time of its Encirclement

The retreats and the change of various formations from one sector to another left the *Armee Korps* rather in the background, replaced by the *Korpsgruppen* which, at the time, consisted of two *Armee Korps*. Also, at a lower level of command, changes resulted from the formation of the stronger or weaker *Divisionskampfgruppen* appropriate to the current demands. South of the Dnjestr stood *'Korpsgruppe General Gollnick'*, which moved on 27 March via Ianauti to Chelmenti. In the meantime, *'Gruppe Breith'*, to which the 17th *Panzer Division* belonged, repulsed strong enemy attacks from the south and took Goloskowo (six kilometers north of Kamenez-Podolsk) to fight free the retreat route. It also built a bridgehead there. Then there was *'Gruppe General de Chevallerie'*, which withdrew to the Malejewzy (six kilometers east-southeast of Mizowzy) – Frampol line, with the mission of covering the north flank of the *Armee*. In addition *'Gruppe General von Waldenfels'* had to establish contact within the *Armee* to the 1st *Panzer Division*. In many instances neither the *Korps* nor the divisions had contact with each other, so that *Divisionsgruppen* or, as the case might be, *Korpsgruppen* operated independently under these designations under the direct control of the *Armee*. *See Map 90.*

This shows, already, the significance of the Soviet advance in the gap to the 8th *Armee* to the right of the 1st *Panzer Armee* in addition to the Soviet advance in the gap to the 48th *Panzer Korps*.

Defensive Battles of the 24th and 46th *Panzer Korps*

See Map 90.

On 21 March the Soviets advance reached the Mogilew – Podolsk – Bar railroad line on a broad front through the gap in the front between the 24th Panzer Korps and 46th Panzer Korps, capturing the Bar railroad station and encircling the Shmerinka rail hub. With zealous aerial reconnaissance the Soviets sent their infantry forces through the gaps in the front and over the Dnjestr between Kamenka and Mogilew-Podolsk, initially with weak forces, to ten kilometers southwest and 20 kilometers west of Jaruga and built a bridgehead west of Mogilew-Podolsk. To the north the 46th Panzer Korps held at the Ljadow sector to east of Murawanyje Kurilowy and won back territory that had been lost west of the Ljadowa sector in counterattacks, thereby delaying the Soviet advance. An attack to eliminate the enemy bridgehead six kilometers west of Mogilew-Podolsk the next day failed. Rather, the right wing of the 82nd Infanterie Divisio was forced back by strong enemy forces to the northwest. However, in a counterattack the enemy was forced back from a village ten kilometers west of Jaryschow on the hills directly east of the Ljadowa sector to about nine kilometers north of Jaryschow. The 168th Infanterie Division had to withstand defensive fighting, as did the 254th and 1st Infanterie Divisionen.

See Maps 65 and 90.

On 23 March the 75th *Infanterie Division* forced the Soviets back from the south bank of the Dnjestr to the area east of the railroad triangle eight kilometers southeast of Secureny Targ, while the 46th *Panzer Korps* repulsed enemy attacks north of the river and, on the next day, carried out the planned withdrawal.

On 24 March contact between the two *Korps* (24th *Panzer Korps* and 46th *Panzer Korps*) was established on the general line Samechoff – Jaltuschkoff by attack of the 101st *Jäger Division* and the 168th *Infanterie Division*. However, considering the overall development, not much was gained.

See Map 93.

On 28 March Soviet armoured forces took Tschernowitz and thrust south toward Sereth, as well as with armoured spearheads to the southwest to Storojiniti, while *'Gruppe General Breith'* held the German lines against weak enemy forces. Merely at Shwantschik the Soviets concentrated their forces to achieve a deep penetration into the area west of Shwantschik. A counterattack by the 101st *Jäger Division* failed to completely seal off the penetration. In the Kamenez-Podolsk area the fighting surged around the city.

In the meantime, on 28/29 March north of the Dnjestr a group of the 17th *Panzer Division* and 371st *Infanterie Divison* thrust past to the north of the city and captured the Kamenez – Podolsk airfield, knocking out seven enemy AFVs. On the south bank of the Dnjestr *'Gruppe General Gollnick'* withdrew toward Hotin. On 31 March, operating from the Hotin bridgehead to the west against enemy armour it built a bridgehead over the Zbrucz.

New Defensive Front in the Pruth Valley

See Map 93.

The existing gaps in the front enabled the Soviets to advance farther to the west without running into any significant opposition. Thus they entered the Pruth valley, where the right wing of the Royal Hungarian 7th Army Corps was building a line of defense. Two Soviet divisions immediately attacked the 201st Royal Hungarian Light Division, thereby losing two out of five attacking

THE SITUATION OF THE 1ST *PANZER ARMEE*

AFVs, but dispersing this division which evacuated Kolomea by the end of the month. The 21st Royal Hungarian Division repulsed individual attacks supported by armour at Czortowiec and south of Luka. The 7th Hungarian Army Corps no longer was attacked to the 1st *Panzer Armee*, but directly to the *Heeresgruppe*.

The Soviets pressed forward with armour carrying infantry against the right wing of the Royal Hungarian 7th Army Corps and dispersed the 201st Hungarian Light Division, advancing via Delatyn, Nadworna to the southwest edge of Stanislau, from which German forces forced the Soviets back via Bohrodezany, knocking out four AFVs. In the 7th Hungarian Army Corps sector *'Gruppe Puechler'*, with the help of intercepted leave-men, occupied a line at the south edge of Stanislau – Marjampol, while the front remained at the Dnjepr between Niznrow and Halicz.

This group then advanced east from Stanislau and dispersed an enemy mechanized brigade at Tysmienica, knocking out six enemy AFVs and 15 heavy anti-tank guns, and bringing in a great deal of booty and 50 prisoners. A leave-battalion and alarm units that were sent in later forced weak enemy forces back to the southeast and blocked the access roads to Tysmienica from both north and south. Remnant elements of Soviets with armour fell back northwest of Tysmienica to the north, later attacking toward Stanislau.

'Gruppe Gollnick' delayed the enemy advance in the area west of Levinti, but could not prevent further Soviet advance that penetrated into Tschernowitz farther south with armoured forces and thrust to the south toward Seret and, to the southwest with armoured spearheads to Storojuneti. *'Gruppe General Breith'* intercepted enemy attacks north of Comarova and west of Shwantschiuk – Dunjajewzy. In counterattack the 101st *Jäger Division* cleaned up a deep Soviet penetration in the Kamenez-Podolsk area. At the end of the month the situation around Kamenez-Podolsk remained unclear. The airfield was back in enemy hands. *See Map 90.*

The Wandering 'Hube *Kessel*'

Named for its Commander in Chief, the 1st *Panzer Armee* was now surrounded on all sides and had to defend itself, not only from enemy attacks from the north and east, but also against a reinforcement of the ring of encirclement south and also west of the combat area. Geographically the area of the *Kessel* was characterized by the transportation lines running from north to south, particularly by the Proskurow – Kamenez-Podolsk railroad line with a branch-line westward from Jarmolinzy. The roads were essentially governed by the terrain and ran in the same direction as the Smotritsch, Zbrucz, Seret and Strypa rivers. Between these, running from north to south, the land rose, with few local stands of trees, therefore with little opportunity for cover. Therefore the 1st *Armee* initially strove to stop the Soviet advance from north to south with the 1st *Panzer Division* at Gorodok. Otherwise, in general, it conformed to the same movement to the south. Accordingly, *'Gruppe Maus'* (7th *Panzer Division*, 1st *SS-Panzer Division 'Leibstandarte SS Adolf Hitler'* and elements of the 68th *Infanterie Division*), attached now to *Korpsgruppe 'de Chevallerie'* and, likewise, moving from north to south, was ordered to advance farther to the *See Maps 90 and 93.*

south in order to hold the Gussiatyn [Husiatyn on the map] bridges open for the crossing of German forces. In the meantime *'Gruppe de Chevallerie'* was ordered to cover the northern flank of the *Armee*, however, with the mission to simultaneously gain ground to the west in order to be able to fall back before the pressure on the eastern front. The north-south running streams offered favorable defensive positions for this against further attacks from the east.

See Map 90.

The varying Soviet thrusts and the usual uncertainties about enemy intentions in such cases required an extraordinary sensitive command system,

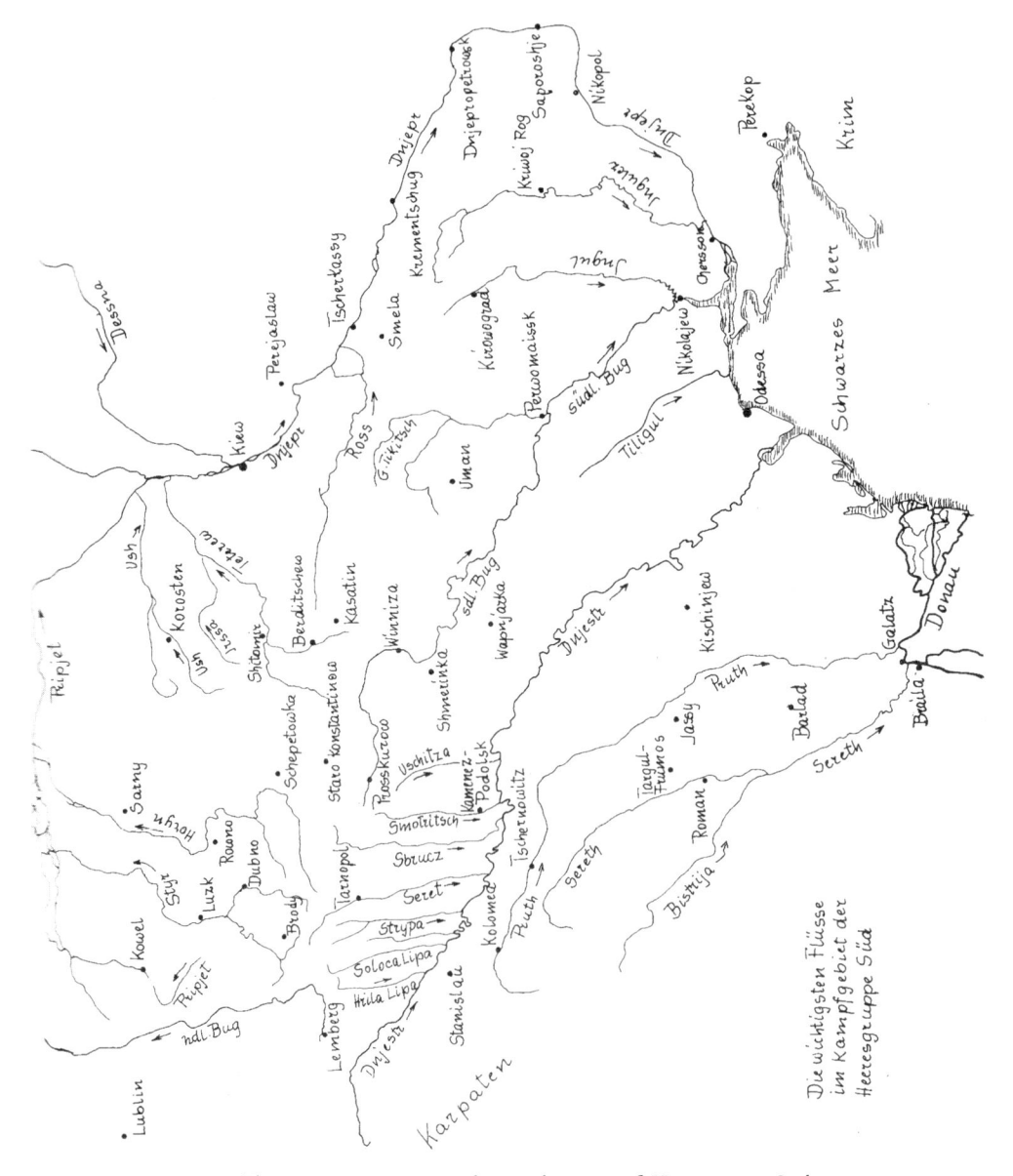

92. The important rivers in the combat area of *Heeresgruppe Süd*.

THE SITUATION OF THE 1ST *PANZER ARMEE*

and especially the deployment and shifting of the formations, as well as the heavy weapons. Again and again there was reorganization within the individual *Korps*. *'Panzergruppe Waldenfels'* (6th *Panzer Division*, 11th *Panzer Division* and 19th *Panzer Division* – later, also the 1st *Panzer Division*) received the mission of gaining additional ground to the west, the 24th *Panzer Korps* defending to the west, while, itself, slowly withdrawing. *'Gruppe Waldenfels'* took over flank protection to the north with the 96th *Inanterie Division* and 291st *Infanterie Division*. The 6th *Panzer Division* had to relieve the 1st *Panzer Division* which was involved in heavy defensive fighting around and cut off in Gorodok and, when darkness fell on 25 March, recaptured the Jarmolinzy railroad station. However, south of this place in the Ssolobkowzy area the Soviets were already within three kilometers of the *Rollbahn*. Reconnaissance reported the arrival of strong enemy forces and occupation of the Gorodok – Gussiatyn road.

The Commander in Chief of the *Armee* notified the formations on 25 March that the *Armee* was now exclusively dependent on supply from the air and, above all, was entirely on its own resources regarding a breakout attempts. No help was in the offing from the west. The 1st *Panzer Armee* planned anew to gain contact with the 4th *Panzer Armee* at Klimbowka on its own. The road conditions, however, gave rise to the fear that, if the weather continued as it was, it would hardly be possible to force another river-crossing to the west (Seret).[1] This knowledge impacted considerations regarding the prospect of a breakout to the west. Between the Zbrucz and Seret reconnaissance had already identified 13 – 14 enemy rifle divisions, with an additional 2 –4 rifle divisions of the Soviet 1st Tank Army to the south which were in march to the Dnjestr. The Soviets had diverted one tank corps against the 1st *Panzer Armee* in the Kamenez-Podolsk area, which now meant that it was necessary to fight free the route to the south via Kamenez-Podolsk.

See Map 92 showing major rivers in the *Heeresgruppe Süd* combat area.

All such plans, however, foundered on the realities of road conditions and on the fact that the Soviets had destroyed the highway bridge at Kamenez-Podolsk. The road from Dunajewzy to Kamenez-Podolsk was jammed with motor vehicles. Only four-wheel-drive and tracked vehicles had any chance, under the existing terrain conditions, of getting through. Therefore the Commander in Chief expressed his conviction that only the *'Süd* [south] – *Operation'*, thus, breakout to the south, had any chance of success, which he then prepared for under the codeword *'Litzmann'*, in memory of *General* Litzmann's breakout at Brzecziny in the First World War.

Appropriate orders went out to all the formations of the 1st *Panzer Armee*. According to them the 1st *Panzer Division* was to turn to the south, the 16th *Panzer Division* was to move out from Ssolobkowzy to Frampol with arriving elements, while the 6th *Panzer Division* advanced and cleaned up the place, but was unable to advance further due to lack of infantry ammunition.

In agreement with the German plans, the Soviets, too, figured on the *'Hube Kessel'* breaking out to the south. That was evident from the troop movements from north to south as well as the movement from east to west on the right flank of the 1st *Panzer Armee*. Hitler also insisted on the breakout to

---

1 It is necessary to distinguish between two rivers, the Seret (without an 'h') north of the Dnjestr and the Sereth (with an 'h'), south of the Dnjestr.

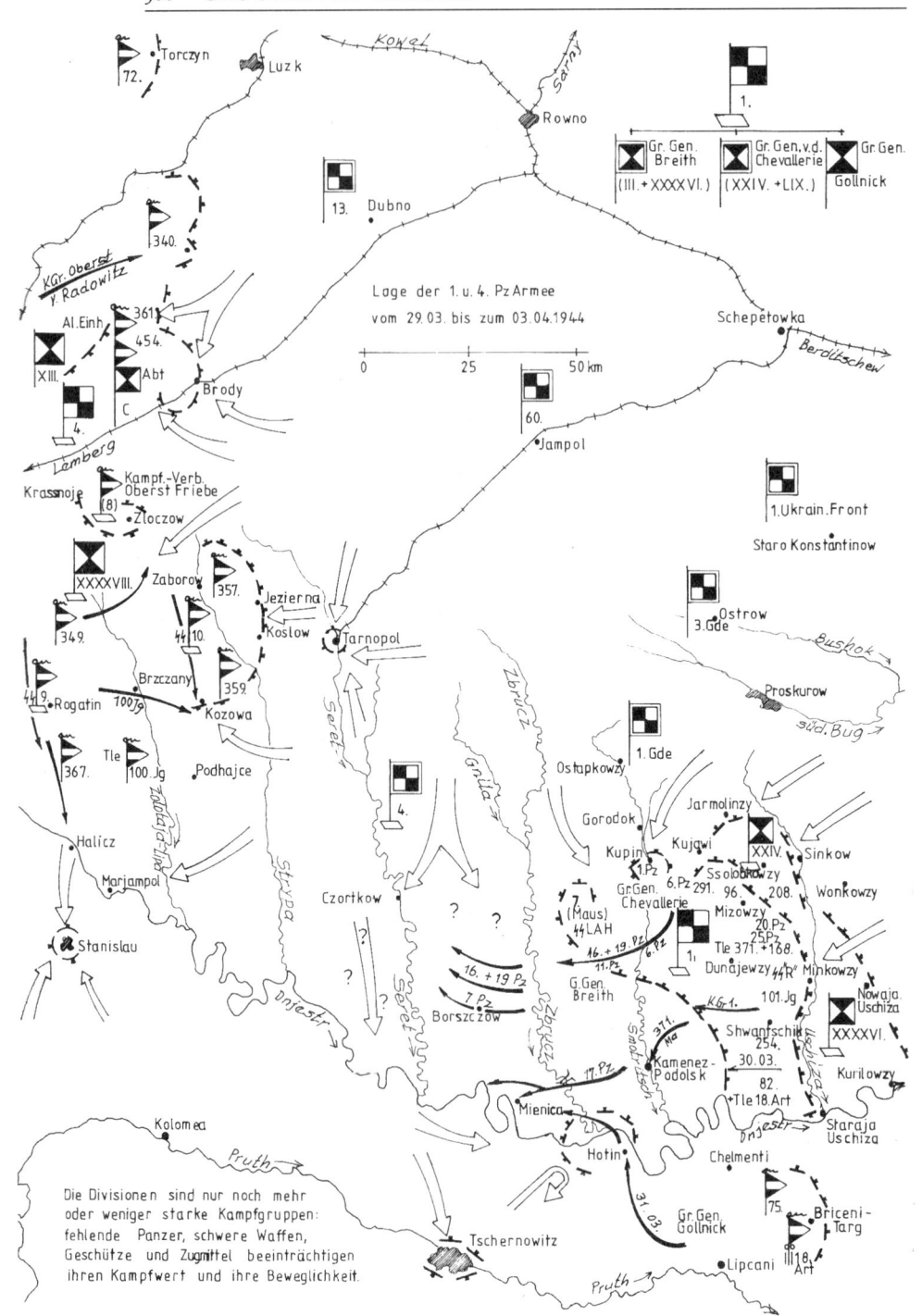

93. (upper center) Situation of the 1st and 4th *Panzer Armee*n from 29 March to 3 April, 1944 (lower left) The divisions are neither more nor less than strong *Kampfgruppen* lacking armour, heavy weapons, guns and prime movers, which impacts their combat effectiveness and their mobility.

the south. Any military judge of the situation would, even today, consider the further advance of the 1st *Panzer Armee* in that direction necessary, indeed, considering the terrain, as downright essential. *Generalfeldmarschall* von Manstein, however, had something else in mind. He proceeded to Obersalzberg in order to dissuade Hitler from his plan for the breakout to the south and get permission to break out to the west. It took a great deal of persuasion by von Manstein to gain Hitler's agreement to such a divergent plan. Von Manstein apparently based his argument on the fact that anyone observing the situation would expect the breakout to the south. The Soviets would, accordingly, be prepared to prevent such a breakout. On the other hand, a breakout to the west across two river barriers, contrary to all military understanding, would offer a degree of surprise that might well promise success. *Generalfeldmarschall* von Manstein resolved on this course of action.

Detailed orders were first prepared, at times in open radio traffic, for Operation 'Litzmann', the breakout to the south, for purposes of disinformation, while the new plans for breakout to the west remained limited to personal conversations with the commanders in chief. In retrospect that proved advantageous.

Crossing the Zbrucz

The *Armee* now had to gain ground to the west, and, indeed, first with mobile forces to build and secure a bridgehead to Skala. The *Armee* sent the following formations to accomplish this:

See Maps 90 and 93, and, for geography, Map 94.

A) 'Korpsgruppe Breith'
B) 'Korpsgruppe de Chevallerie' with the 1st *Panzer Division*, 6th *Panzer Division*, 19th *Panzer Division*, 16th *Panzer Division*, 20th *Panzergrenadier Division*, Kampfgruppe 11th *Panzer Division*, 96th *Infanterie Division*, 291st *Infanterie Division*, 208th *Infanterie Division*,'Gruppe Maus' with the 7th *Panzer Division* and elements of the 1st SS-Panzer Division 'Leibstandarte SS Adolf Hitler'.
C) 'Gruppe Gollnick'.

'Kampfgruppe von Waldenfels' moved out immediately and took Alexinez-Polyj on 26 March, knocking out 32 AFVs. 'Korpsgruppe Maus' formed a hedgehog position and held the crossing over the Seret open at Ljanzkorun – this against strong enemy pressure from the south and west.

In keeping with the weather conditions – snowstorms – the *Armee* command did a certain amount of rearranging missions of the individual formations. 'Panzergruppe von Waldenfels' was disbanded and attached to the 19th *Panzer Division*. This, in the meantime, arrived in Frampol. Kampfgruppe 11th *Panzer Division* was attached to the 16th *Panzer Division*.

The attack to the southwest was carried out by the following formations:

A) the 291st *Infanterie Division* on the right, reinforced with *Sturmgeschütz Brigaden* 276 and 280

B) the 16th *Panzer Division* in the center with attached *Kampfgruppe* 11th *Panzer Division* and 19th *Panzer Division*
C) the 20th *Panzergrenadier Division* on the left.

Additional withdrawals followed the plan *'Amalia'*, namely *'Barbara'*, *'Cäcilie'* and *'Dorothee'*. The *Korps* had to reach the Zbrucz as rapidly as possible, there to hold bridgeheads east of the river with the 208th *Infanterie Division* and 96th *Infanterie Division*, reinforced with *Grenadier Regiment* 337 [208th *Infanterie Division*] until the last German formation had crossed the river.

On the left wing of the formations advancing to the southwest, the 20th *Panzergrenadier Division* proceeded to Tschertsch and built a bridgehead there. At that point this division, too, complained earnestly about supply of ammunition for the heavy artillery. Therefore the order was issued to destroy the guns after firing off the ammunition and to destroy vehicles that were not all-terrain in order to save petrol so as to keep the combat vehicles mobile.

See Map 90 and, for geography, Maps 93 and 94.

The 16th *Panzer Division* gained the Ssmotritsch bridgehead without enemy contact and continued toward Ljanzkorum, while the 24th *Panzer Division* evacuated Dunajewzy on the eastern front. The leading elements of the 16th *Panzer Division* finally reached Ljanzkorum, thereby opening the way to the next river crossing. These movements took place under pressure of reinforced pursuit by the Soviets from the east, and also from the north against the 96th *Infanterie Division*. The *Armee* therefore issued the directive that the area of the *Kessel* occupied by the 1st *Panzer Armee* was not, under any circumstance, to be reduced. The movements to the west, however, had priority, in order to gain ground in this direction before the Soviet command reacted. In order to accomplish this it necessarily required concessions on the northern and eastern fronts. The 16th *Panzer Division* reached the Zbrucz sector at Shrish during the night of 29 March and built a bridgehead there on the west bank. In the meantime, the 19th *Panzer Division* repulsed repeated enemy attacks as it secured the north flank.

Change in the Direction of the Breakout

See Maps 93 and 94.

In the meantime the *Armee* command suspected that the Soviets might well have become aware of the change of the German breakout-plan from the south to the west. This suspicion was based, among other things, on the 29 enemy AFVs that were reported in the Bireshanka – Süd sector. Therefore haste seemed desirable. Accordingly, early on 29 March at 0530 hours the 7th *Panzer Division* (*'Gruppe Maus'*) moved out of the Rusha area with the objective of reaching the Zbrucz at Skala and building a bridgehead there. During the evening hours the *Gruppe* gained such a crossing in a vigorous thrust. The town, itself, finally also fell into German hands. In the meantime, other elements of *'Gruppe Maus'*, and *'Gruppe Scheuerpflug'* (the 68th *Infanterie Division* and elements of the 1st *SS-Panzer Division 'Leibstandarte SS Adolf Hitler'* secured in the line Kugajewzy – Andrejewka – Sakrinzy, where enemy reinforcements, including the arrival of armour, became evident. On the left wing of the thrust to the west the 20th *Panzergrenadier Division* reached the Ljanzkorun – Stefanowka – Tschertsch line and advanced further to the south, less to broaden the breakout-wedge of the 1st *Panzer Armee* to the west, than to deceive the Soviets regarding the change in the direction of the breakout, and also to shield against the movement of Soviet forces from the Dnjestr area.

On the west bank of the Zbrucz there were no signs of either strengthening of the natural terrain features or of digging, which suggested that either the Soviets had not yet recognized the change in the German plans to breaking out to the west rather than to the south or that they had not yet reacted to it. Reconnaissance results that day caused the *Armee* command to believe that the Soviets still believed in a breakout to the south. In the meantime individual formations were ordered to reconnoiter to the Seret without making it evident to the Soviets what were the actual breakout intentions. In any case, the area between the Zbrucz and Seret proved very weakly held by the enemy, which caused the 1st *Panzer Division* to accelerate its advance to the west. During the night of 31 March/ 1 April the thrust would reach the Seret, with *'Gruppe de Chevallerie'* screening the northern flank.

See Maps 94 and 95.

In the meantime the withdrawal of the 24th *Panzer Korps* continued as planned over the *'Barbara'* line to the *Cäcilie* line, as did the advance to the west. The Sbrish and Skala bridgeheads were extended.

See Map 94.

Finally reconnaissance indicated that the Soviets had recognized the change in German plans. They did not, however, change the movement of their Soviet 4th Guards Tank Corps from north to south. It evidently had the mission, while continuing in accord with the former evaluation of the situation, of preventing a possible German breakthrough to the south over the Dnjestr. Observations, however, indicated that the Soviets were now sending strong forces from the north, including from the area west and southwest of Frampol, thereby in the area of the breakout of the 1st *Panzer Armee*, with the Soviet 17th Guards Rifle Corps as a new addition. 70 – 80 enemy AFVs were identified before the front of the 68th *Infanterie Division*. This situation gave sufficient reason to widen and fortify the Skala bridgehead. In the meantime the 24th *Panzer Korps* continued to carry out by night its *'Cäcilie'* withdrawal movement, with the mission, on withdrawing from the *'Dorothee'* position of holding an adequate bridgehead on the east bank.

Observation of the enemy made it clear that, while maintaining the frontal pressure against the eastern front (*Schwerpunkt* toward Ssmotritsch) with mobile elements swinging out via Gussiatyn, the Soviets intended to thwart the further advance of the *Korpsgruppe* to the west, not only by advancing from the north, but also from the south, to prevent the breakout. This intention had to be effectively met, which called for building a bridgehead over the Niczlawa sector. In order to strengthen the infantry combat force it was again necessary to destroy motor vehicles and collect the drivers into alarm units.

On 31 March, despite strong enemy pressure against the eastern defensive and covering front of the *Kessel*, the offensive troops made good progress to the west. In hard house-to-house fighting they captured Kociubinzy and Gusztyn in concentric attacks, this while destroying at least six T34s and 20 heavy anti-tank guns. There was heavy fighting in Kosiacz. The formations advanced by *Kampfgruppen*, *'Kampfgruppe Back'* from the Debowka area to the northwest, *'Kampfgruppe Hesse'* forced its way forward to just east of Wola Czanokoniezka.

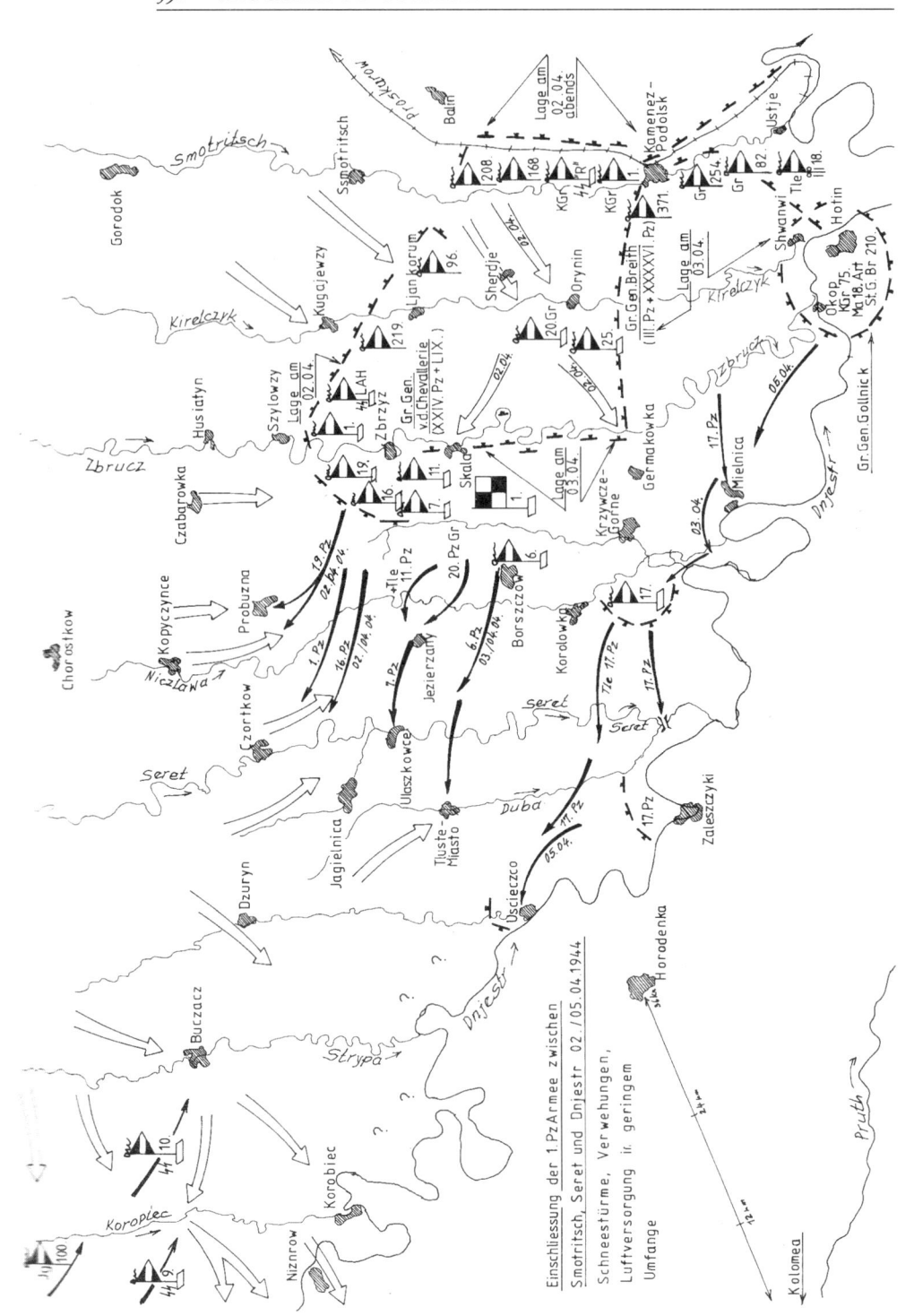

94. Encirclement of the 1st *Panzer Armee* between Smotritsch, Seret and Dnjestr 2 to 5 April, 1944. Snow storms, drifts, air-dropped supplies to a limited degree.

THE SITUATION OF THE 1ST *PANZER ARMEE*

The 7th *Panzer Division* captured Borsczow and the Wierzchiakowce in a fast-moving thrust and got into the Gleboczek area. It next had to capture and secure the bridges at Lisowce after another swift thrust.

Further Advance to the Seret

The advance of the 1st *Panzer Armee* to the west also made good progress on 1 April, despite sudden onset of heavy snow-squalls and the resulting miserable road conditions. During the night of 31 March/1 April the 7th *Panzer Division* reached the Seret and built a wak bridgehead at Kapuscine. In the meantime the 24th *Panzer Korps* took the *'Dorothee'* line at the Zbrucz under close pursuit of, in part, mounted (cavalry) formations.

The weather, however, impacted aerial supply. On 1 April the quartermaster reported the landing of merely four *Ju* 52 with four cubic meters of petrol. The *Ju* 52s took about 60 wounded back with them on their return. Despite this the movement had to continue.

In the meantime the Soviets increased their pressure from the north and east, carrying out another thrust from the south from the direction of Orynin to Skala. For the 1st *Panzer Armee* top priority went to effectively securing the north flank, extending to the west, in order to gain further undisturbed crossings over the Zbrucz.

See Map 94.

In the meantime the Soviets pressed especially hard from the east, thereby impacting maintenance of the timetable set for the *'Dorothee'* operation. The 208th *Infanterie Division* fought its way through to the specified line and took Sherdje. It was impossible to know, however, whether all the German formations had already crossed the Zbrucz on that day. In addition, the 24th *Panzer Korps* was ordered to mine all of the fords through the Zbrucz.

In the meantime the shortage of petrol significantly interfered with the movements of the *Kampfgruppen*, so that on 2 April the order went out anew to destroy all vehicles that could possibly be spared. If the mobile formations were immobilized, that would have led to a halt of the entire breakout operation. In any event, the infantry formations had to carry out forced marches in order to gain ground to the west, and these had to be conducted off to the side of the roads jammed with vehicles in order to leave these free so that supplies could be got moving for the mobile formations.

Enemy infantry forces moved out from Husiatyn toward Czortkow in pursuit with the intention of overhauling and enveloping the German force. Therefore it was necessary to destroy the bridge over the Seret at Czortkow. In the early morning hours of 2 April the 7th *Panzer Division* took Dezierzany [Jezeriany on the map], which was strongly secured with anti-tank guns and armour, and, in a *coup de main*, captured two 60-ton bridges, undamaged, at Ulaskowce. On the other hand, the 6th *Panzer Division* had to halt its advance from the Lisowce bridgehead to the west via Swidow to Tluste Miasto because of unusually heavy snowstorms.

See Map 94.

Other formations, however, were again successful, such as the 7th *Panzer Division* with the capture of Jagielnica and the 20th *Panzergrenaderi Division* with its advance from Gleboczek toward Konstanzia.

Advance to the Strypa

See Map 95.

The Soviets attempted, by means of overhauling pursuit and bringing up elements of their 1st Tank Army to the area south of Horodenka, to anticipate and counter the breakout efforts of the German 1st *Panzer Armee*, moving in the opposite direction south from Czortkow. Therefore the 1st *Panzer Division* had to blow up the three bridges in Czortkow. After hard fighting, in which it destroyed eight T 34s, only the southern bridge could be blown. The *Stukas* effectively took care of the other bridges. The 7th *Panzer Division* and 1st *Panzer Division* pushed farther forward to the northwest via Jagielnicka, took Pauszowka and thrust on toward Dzuryn, to the next river crossing (Strypa). The leading elements of the formations there could already hear the sound of fighting from the Przewloka area, probably from the 2nd *SS-Panzer Korps* which was, in the meantime, attacking from the west.

Reconnaissance of the enemy led to the conclusion that the Soviets planned a security line facing east at the Strypa or in the Koropiec sector, in order to counter the breakout of the 1st *Panzer Armee* to the west, supported by a thrust east of the Seret from north to south in order to block strong formations from escaping to the west. At the same time they exerted more pressure on the northern and eastern fronts of the *Armee*.

On 4 April petrol arrived via the Jagielnicka airfield, which had been placed in service, and the Borszczow airfield. On 5 April the troops captured a railroad train loaded with diesel fuel. However, with the exception of the *Kfz* 76, all of the fighting vehicles required petrol.[2] During the night of 4/5 April 60 *Ju* 52s arrived at the airfield north of Glebotschek, alone, mostly with petrol, but also with infantry ammunition. For this night the *Luftwaffe* planned two flights, each consisting of 60 *Ju* 52s and 55 *Heinkel* landings. The most critical concerns about fuel seemed, thereby, to have been taken care of. The formations could continue their advance. The 7th *Panzer Division* took Jagielnica – Stara and Dzuryn.

Korpsgruppe 'de Chevallerie' had to extend its line of defense to the north toward Czortkow – Dzuryn after its successful further advance to the west. Corresponding to the ground gained to the west, the 24th *Panzer Korps* also shifted, as, on 6 March, to the Miczlawa sector and was to reach the Seret on 7 April, that, again, as had been done at the Zbrucz, with the establishment of several bridgeheads on the east bank. The Soviets again interfered by thrusting strongly into these withdrawals, especially those of the 208th *Infanterie Division*.

The 20th *Panzergrenadier Division* also was successful in its advance to the west. In knocked out several anti-tank guns and three T 34s at Muchawka and captured ammunition and fuel. It fought free the Janielnica – Tluste-Miasto supply road.

---

2   Translator's note – The *Kfz 76 Beobachtungskraftwagen* (artillery observation vehicle) was one of a series of 6x6 standardized diesel lorries whose *Kfz* numbers varied with the special-use body. Büsing-Nag, Magirus, Borgward, FAUN, Man, Henschel and Krupp manufactured the standardized diesel lorries which included the *Kfz* 76.

THE SITUATION OF THE 1ST *PANZER ARMEE* 395

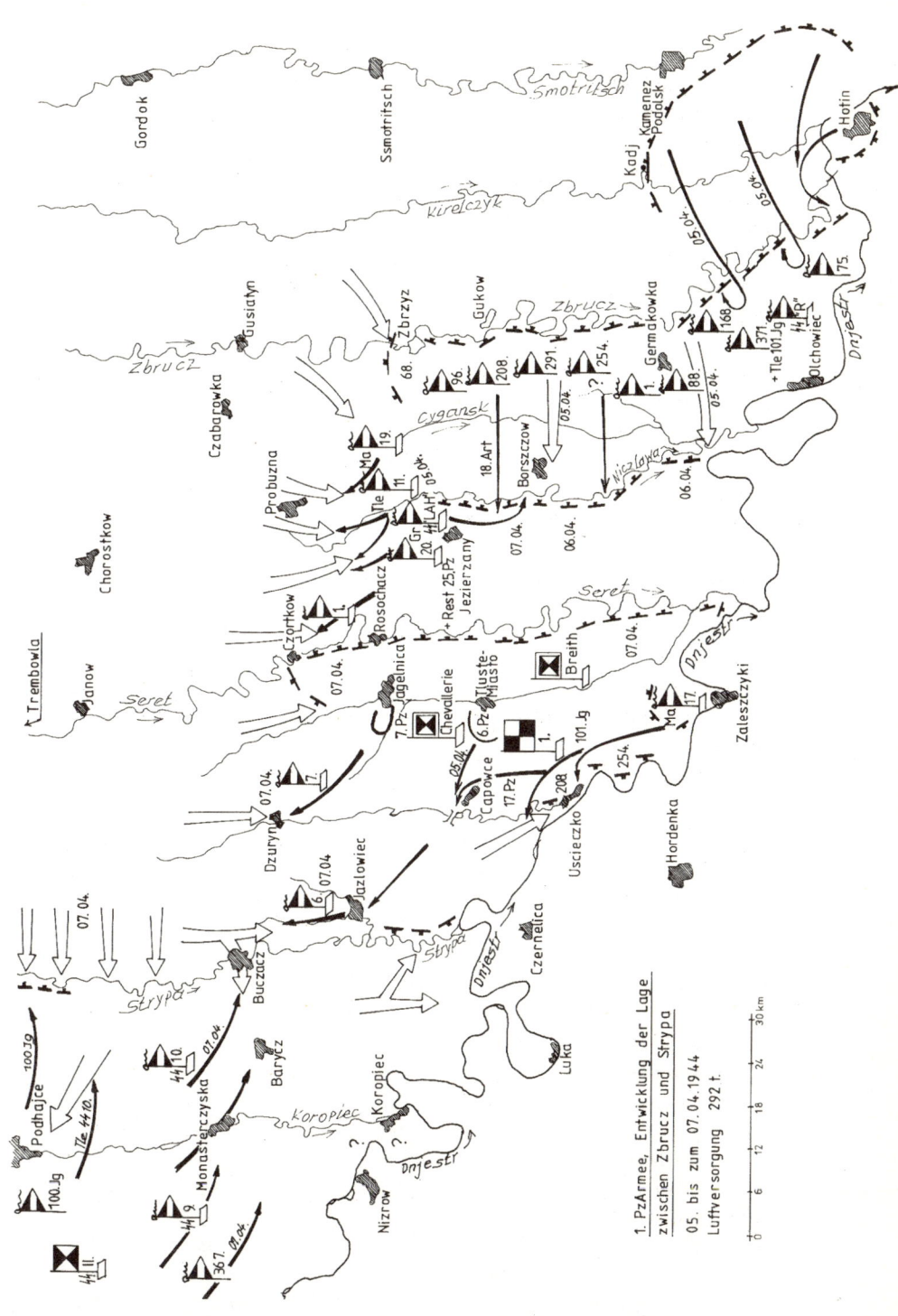

95. 1st *Panzer Armee*, Development of the Situation between the Zbrucz and Strypa, 5 to 7 April, 1944. Air-dropped supplies, 292 tons.

33

The Breakout of the 'Hube Kessel'

See Maps 95 and 96.

In the breakthrough sector the formations of the 2nd *SS-Panzer Korps*, the spearheads of the 10th *SS-Panzer Division 'Frundsberg'*, cleaned up the area six kilometers northeast of Buczacz (on the Strypa). That caused the Soviets to oppose this advance with the objective of diverting the direction of the 2nd *SS-Panzer Korps* thrust to the north.

See Maps 95 and 96.

Simultaneously the Soviets attempted to force the *Kessel* formations that were advancing from the southeast toward Buczacz away to the south. They attacked Dzuryn, south of Czortkow and southwest of Kalinowczczyna. Infantry forces attacked the lines of the 7th *Panzer Division* on a broad front. It seemed conspicuous that the Soviets initially committed no armour, whereas it was usual for every attack to have armoured support. The Soviets pushed their pursuit from the east over the Seret in order to prevent the construction of an organized German defense.

The fighting against the northern flank of the *Kessel* proved quite costly for the Soviets, especially in the Dzuryn area in the German elimination of a previously achieved Soviet penetration. At first the Soviets lacked heavy weapons. Gradually, however, they brought up artillery of all calibers and multiple-rocket launchers. Finally, armour also arrived in this area. Its initial absence seemed miraculous to the German troops. The delay in its transfer from the area north of Proskurow to the area northeast of Buczacz was probably attributable to terrain difficulties.

However, the troops still had to wait for the breakout to the west. First the Buczacz – Trybuchowce road had to be fought free. In addition, despite further advances of four kilometers to the east, the 10th *SS-Panzer Division 'Frundsberg'* remained stalled before a strong Soviet anti-tank gun and mine barrier. This attack, however, by diverting the Soviets, conferred advantages on the 16th *Panzer Division* that was attacking out of the *Kessel* with respect to local improvements in positions.

The mission of achieving the breakthrough finally fell to the 6th *Panzer Division*, which, at the end of the month, shifted its attachment from the 24th *Panzer Korps* to the 3rd *Panzer Korps*.

Preparation for the Breakthrough

The 6th *Panzer Division* incorporated battered elements of the 96th *Infanterie Division* and, on 1 April, received orders to advance via Borszczow Gorolowka and build a bridgehead over the the Seret in the Bilcze (*Schwerpunkt* here) – Kasperowce sector. Already in the evening of this day they reached the assigned objective. At that time the Soviets still did not know exactly where

THE BREAKOUT OF THE 'HUBE KESSEL'

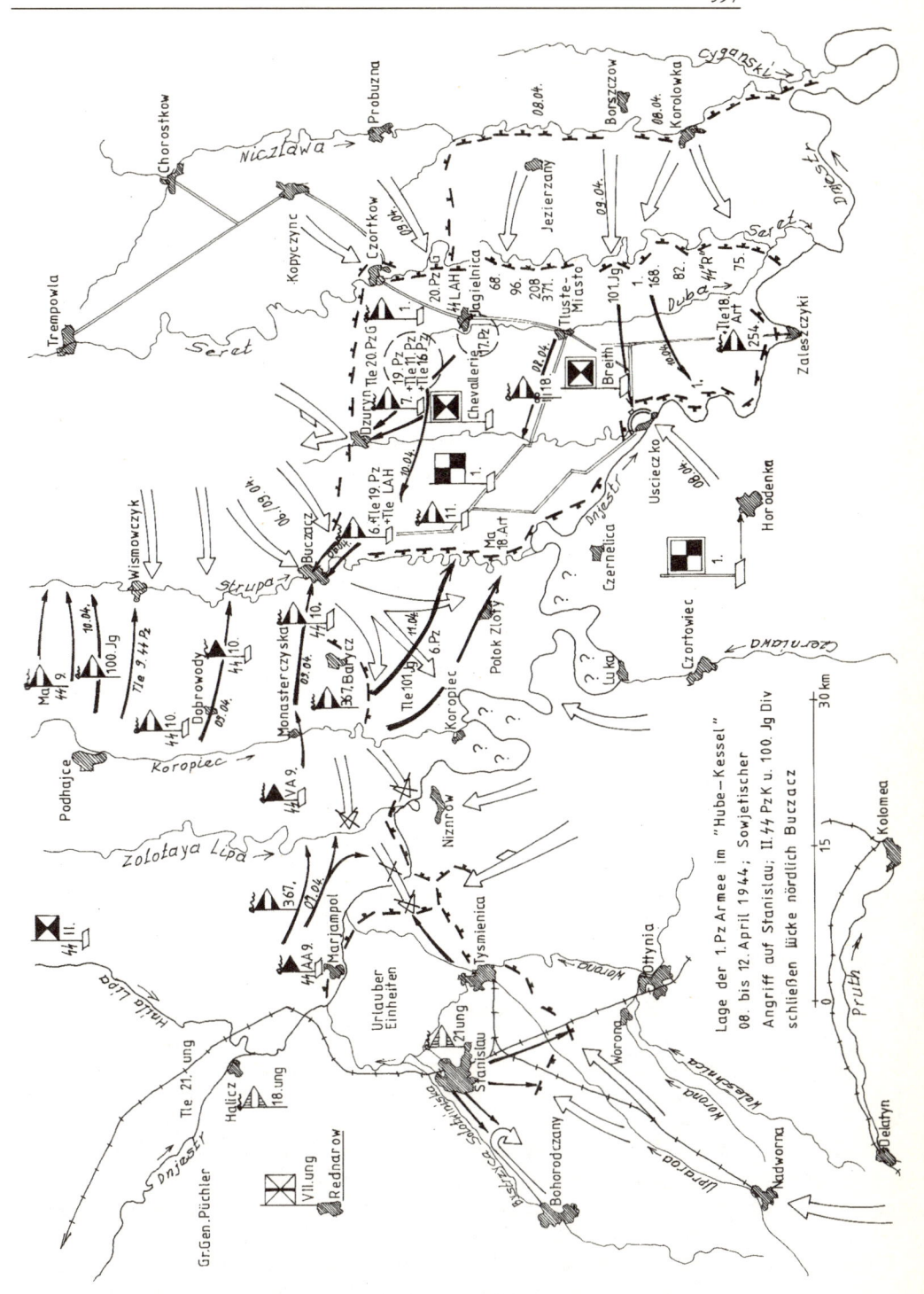

96. Situation of the 1st *Panzer Armee* in 'Hube Kessel' 8 to 12 April, 1944; Soviet attack on Stanislau; 2nd SS-*Panzer Korps* and 100th *Jäger Division* close gap north of Buczacz.

the breakthrough was planned. To that extent, the Germans held the initiative. The enemy formations, which were struck in the flank by the 6th *Panzer Division's* thrust to the west, demonstrated that they were not prepared for this thrust. These Soviet formations were clearly under orders to march and attack to the south, but not to make a front to the east and counter the breakout attempt.

Early on 4 April the division – filled out with men from the train elements – captured Tluste Miasto from the Soviet 206th Infantry Division until the shortage of petrol again took effect. Therefore the further advance took place entirely on foot, with limited support from the few roadworthy heavy weapons.

See Map 95.

On 4 April *Korpsgruppe Breith* was ordered to win crossings over the Strypa and, in an emergency, to open the crossings to the south at Buczacz . Regardless of Soviet relieving attacks from the north and south against the 1st *Panzer Division* at Chortkow, the 6th *Panzer Division* reached the east bank of the Strypa southeast of Buczacz where, however, in accordance with orders, it had to stay put. Officers of the 6th *Panzer Division* undertook a patrol to just short of Buczacz in order to discover the strength of enemy forces there. This scouting then provided the information that *Panzergrenadier Regiment* 114 [6th *Panzer Division*] later used to attack Buczacz from the south.

On 6 April the 6th *Panzer division* captured Buczacz in a *coup de main*. However, in their advance from the east towards Buczacz, other elements of the division, such as *Panzergrenadier Regiment* 4, ran into strong enemy forces that blocked the road from a system of positions that stretched from the Strypa to the northwest part of Trybuchowce. After reconnaissance showed that the embankments of the river bed were free of enemy, an assault in the dusk, with 'Hurras', into the flank of the totally surprised enemy forces succeeded. The enemy forces fell back to the north. The northern portion of Trybuchowce fell into German hands. After bitter fighting, an additional thrust to the north reached the Medwedowce – Podzamczek line, so that the road from the east to Buczacz was again free of the enemy.

See Map 96.

The 6th *Panzer Division* then sent additional reconnaissance to the west without enemy contact and had a patrol remain for several days about two kilometers west of Buczacz. That was where first contact took place with the *Waffen-SS* formations advancing from the west. The Commander of the 10th *SS-Panzer Division 'Frundsberg'* suddenly appeared at an *SPW* that had run onto mines. The *Waffen-SS* ostensibly had a 'supply package' ready, lorries with 600 tons of supplies for the 1st *Panzer Armee*. That, however, did not reach Buczacz. The 6th *Panzer Division* was ordered to hold the Buczacz – Trybuchowce road open against menacing enemy pressure for the expected German relief forces expected from the west to the northwest. Considering the strong Soviet interest in preventing contact between the 1st *Panzer Armee* and the relief forces and, later, in breaking such contact, the 6th *Panzer Division* was ordered to hold a 30 kilometer wide sector.

On 8 April the breakthrough was accomplished and *Generalfeldmarschall* Modell greeted the commander of the 1st *Panzer Armee* Hube at the 6th *Panzer Division* command post.

Breakout to the West

With this meeting the breakout to the west was not yet secured. The Soviets attempted with repeated attacks, especially upon the march route to Dzuryn, to disrupt the preparations for the breakout. They built a bridgehead over the Seret to the west at Bilcze. There was another penetration southeast of Jagielnica. Enemy assault troops attempted to disrupt the Jagielnica – Polowce and Jagielnica –Stara supply routes in the *Armee* rear area, but were driven off by *Kampfgruppen* committed for that purpose.

See Map 96.

In the meantime the 2nd *SS-Panzer Korps* had to repulse heavy enemy attacks northwest of Buczacz in order to secure the area of the breakthrough. To accomplish this the west bank of the Seret had to be cleansed of enemy at Kujdanow (14 kilometers north of Buczacz). These attacks helped the 3rd *Panzer Korps* to gain more ground, to capture Potok with the 6th *Panzer Division* and 101st *Jäger Division* in a joint thrust to the west and, from there, to advance about eight kilometers to the south. The right wing of the 101st *Jäger Division* penetrated into a place eight kilometers northwest of Potok and took a locality about three kilometers northeast of it.

Nevertheless, the Soviets forced a crossing over the Strypa at the left wing of the 10th *SS-Panzer Division 'Frundsberg'* and built a bridgehead, thus gaining ground farther to the west. They delivered attacks supported by armour from the north against Zielona, northwest of Buczacz, but were halted there in the defensive fire of the 7th *Panzer Division*. Attacks against the bridgehead on the left wing of the 2nd *SS-Panzer Korps* only gained ground slowly. The German bridgehead north of Wisnowczyk on the east bank of the Strypa had to be pulled back. On the other hand, the 3rd *Panzer Korps* held a Nizniow bridgehead that was extended to the west, south and southeast despite stubborn enemy resistance, with the destruction of seven Soviet AFVs. The 101st *Jäger Division* cleaned up an enemy penetration into the bridgehead east of Dolina, thereby capturing one AFV and several guns and knocking out four AFVs.

The march out of the *Kessel* was then to follow on 11 April. The road out, however, was under fire. Therefore initially it was necessary to regain the northern point at Dzuryn, which had been lost, with the help of pioneers and *'Panther'*. In addition reconnaissance reported strong enemy concentrations of forces at Slobodka. In the early dawn light of the second day of Easter *Stukas* attacked these and smashed the concentration. That same day the 2nd *SS-Panzer Korps* launched an attack with fifty AFVs from the west against Slobodka, while the *Kessel* troops attacked at the same moment from the east toward Slobodka.

While the Soviets diverted *SS* formations by attacks from the north, the 19th *Panzer Division* advanced on Slobodka in the gray dawn light of 12 April expending its remaining ammunition and advanced anew to Dzuryn, capturing several anti-tank guns and hunting down AFVs. The surprise succeeded. The *Rollbahn* from Czortkow to Buczacz was again free of the enemy, the march route no longer under enemy observation. It was no longer commanded by the Soviets, march movements could no longer be disrupted by ground-based weapons. With that the breakout and the march out were secured.

The March Out

See Map 96.

In unbroken succession the encircled formations now marched out of the *Kessel* through Buczacz and passed through the lines of the formations of the 2nd *SS-Panzer Korps*. The trench-strength [*Grabenstark*, actual number of men at the sharp end, doing the fighting] of the formations had significantly diminished. The 19th *Panzer Division* filed a report indicating that, even after the *Grenadiere* had been filled out with drivers of non-working vehicles and gunners without guns, they had a trench-strength of 200 men. As for guns, there were two *Hummeln,* two *Wespen,* six light field howitzers, four heavy field howitzers and two 10-centimeter guns.

The drive, or as the case might be, march through Buczacz also turned out to be not entirely a simple matter, because the streets were jammed with abandoned and bombed vehicles of the 4th *Panzer Armee* from the fighting of weeks gone by. The 19th *Panzer Division* secured by placing guns in position on both sides of the through route of march. Now there was a new front east of the Strypa that reached as far as an enemy bridgehead five kilometers north of Osowce on the west bank of the Strypa.

In other sectors, however, the Soviets still attacked, as, on 12 April, in regimental strength south of Tluste Miasto, and forced German forces back. An attack with its *Schwerpunkt* south of Jagielnica was repulsed. North of Dzuryn the Soviets achieved another penetration, but could no longer stop the march-out of the entire 1st *Panzer Armee*.

The march led toward Czechow and Monastercyska. The drive of the *Kessel* formations toward the rear finally overcame all difficulties of the route. Individual combat units branched off the retreat road to the left and right in order to take over protection of the eastern front at the Strypa, thereby reducing the traffic. In all haste units were consolidated and supplied with required weapons from the disbanded companies and batteries, in order to then build another defensive front at the Strypa front facing east. Above all it was necessary to clear the area west of the Strypa to the south from enemy forces. This mission was essentially that of the formations of the 24th *Panzer Korps*, but also involved elements of the 3rd *Panzer Korps*, which shifted to the south toward Stanislau and Kolomea.

The Situation after the Breakout

The Soviets disrupted the march movements of the *Kessel* troops at night by repeated employment of their *'Nebelkrähen'* ['hooded crows', Russian night bombers], which dropped parachute flares and series of small bombs. The Soviet forces that had concentrated were not happy with the breakout of the 1st *Panzer Armee*. On 15 April they crossed a bridge that had not been destroyed in time in Bobulince to the west bank of the Strypa and build a bridgehead that was five to six kilometers deep. The bridge even supported the weight of armour. Therefore several of the formations of the 1st *Panzer Armee* that had just broken out immediately had to move out for commitment at this bridgehead, including the 19th *Panzer Division* with remnants of *Panzergrenadier Regiment* 73 [19th *Panzer Division*], *Panzerjäger Abteilung* 19, elements of *Panzeraufklärungs Abteilung* 19 and two batteries of the II./

Panzerartillerie Regiment 19. With the help of 22 factory-news *'Tiger'* tanks that were made available, it was possible to narrow the bridgehead in the face of strong artillery and Stalin Organ [multiple rocket launcher] fire, especially from the east bank. The German success was probably attributable to the fact that the Soviet formations were in the process of assembling for an attack and fell into disorder when surprised by the German advance. In any case, the German troops reached the river, captured a lot of prisoners and captured weapons. However, they did not entirely eliminate the bridgehead.

After its relief north of Buczacz by an infantry division as *Korps* reserve in an area 20 kilometers west of Buczacz, the 7th *Panzer Division* shifted again on 21 April to a refitting area south of Stanislau. Only on 25 April did the division again go into action attached to the Royal Hungarian 7th Army Corps, this time at the passes of the Carpathian Mountains, until, on 2 July, after the arrival of personnel replacements and new armour, the division was transferred by rail via Lemberg to new service in the *Heeresgruppe Mitte* sector.

The 1st *Panzer Division* initially had to take over covering the rear of the 1st *Panzer Armee* to the east during the march out. Two days after its breakout, however, it was already back in action, at Medwedowce, six kilometers northeast of Buczacz in order to relieve a *Panzergrenadier Regiment* of the 10th *SS-Panzer Division 'Frundsberg'*. A new enemy armoured *Schwerpunkt* had developed there with strong concentration of artillery. The *Grenadiere* allowed the enemy armour to roll over them, thereby separating the escorting infantry from the tanks (T 34 and 'Stalin' tanks), which they then engaged with mines, magnetic charges and *Panzerfäusten* at close range. After the loss of Medwedowce and Polawa the Soviet thrust was halted and an impending breakthrough averted. Finally an armoured group of the 10th *SS-Panzer Division 'Frundsberg'* came to the aid of the 1st *Panzer Division* and elements of the 20th *Panzergrenadier Division* with an *SPW* battalion, *Jagdpanzer* and *Panzer* IV. It advanced against the Soviet forces that had penetrated with *Panzergrenadier Regiment* 6 [7th *Panzer Division*] and the *Aufklärungs Abteilung* of the 7th *Panzer Division*. Despite the extravagant Soviet blocking barrages it was possible, with the help of the *SS-SPW* battalion to advance past Pilawa, mounted, regain the old main line of resistance and get through to the I./ *Panzergrenadier Regiment* 1 in Pilawa. After bitter house-to-house fighting and destruction of several AFVs, Medwedowce was also recaptured. At 2100 hours the old main line of resistance was back in German hands. The next day the Soviets attacked anew with a change of *Schwerpunkt*. The front, however, remained at the Strypa and, indeed, with contact to the southern wing of the 4th *Panzer Armee*. At the end of April the 1st *Panzer Division* also assembled its formations in the rear area of the *Armee* and transferred to the area around Lemberg for reconstitution and personnel replenishment.

On 7 June the 1st *Panzer Division* marched into the later area of the 1st *Panzer Armee* west of Brody – Tarnopol, where a new Soviet offensive was expected.

The remnants of other divisions similarly were committed in the protection of the west bank of the Strypa. Then, however, more restful days of positional warfare followed. After four weeks of interruption mail from home arrived. The train elements that had been sent to the rear in good time via Kamenez-Podolsk found themselves back with their parent units, in part, over the Carpathians in Siebenbürgen, the remainder over the Dnjestr in the *Generalgouvernment*.

It was only in the area north of Buczacz that the situation remained active. However, danger also existed on the right wing of the new defensive front with the Hungarian 7th Army Corps, because this formation was composed of soldiers with no combat experience at all. Therefore elements of the 19th *Panzer Division* again shifted farther to the south to prevent further Soviet advances between Stanislau and Kolomea. With artillery support from the Hungarian formations and also from German artillery they attacked north of Thumacz, but had to break off the advance as the result of heavy Hungarian losses.

Here, too, a defensive position was set up, to so called 'Adler-Stellung'. Finally the 19th *Panzer Division* turned over its entire outfit of weapons and combat vehicles to the 1st *Panzer Division* and 8th *Panzer Division* and marched on foot to Reichshof in the *Generalgouvernment*, entraining there for reconstitution in Holland.

The remaining divisions, to the extent that they were not immediately withdrawn from service, had time during the ensuing days without combat action to reconstitute, re-equip with weapons and vehicles and incorporate personnel replacements.

Final Conclusion

With that the Soviet offensive from the summer of 1943 to the summer of 1944 had freed the Ukraine from German occupation, though the fighting was costly to the Soviets, too, utilizing the former German military tactics of the breakthrough and the overhauling pursuit, with the intention of getting behind enemy forces to cut them off from their connections to the rear. This had led to local successes, as at Tscherkassy, but not to total success as had been the case at Stalingrad. Again and again the German formations had fought their way out, though, at Tscherkassy, with the loss of all their matériel.

There must be notable significance for the science of troop command in this kind of defensive fighting of an ever-weakening force against an attacking force that had immense personnel and matériel superiority, with the constant possibility of bringing up supplies of personnel and matériel, of exchanging formations and, above all, which had greater mobility due to motorization, with no real concerns about fuel.

34

Situation of the 17th *Armee*, Evacuation of Crimea

The description of the fighting retreat of the German southern front in the USSR would have to remain incomplete, especially regarding the actions of *Heeresgruppe* A, if it did not include a description of the right wing, namely the 17th *Armee,* which had crossed from the Kuban bridgehead to the Crimean Peninsula.

On 9 October, 1943, the successful evacuation of the Kuban bridgehead ended with the transport of 177,355 German and 50,139 allied soldiers, as well as 55,942 *Hiwis,* work brigades and civilians, large amounts of weapons, vehicles, horses, ammunition, fodder essentially to Kertsch. With that the 17th *Armee* could initially feel secure from immediately impending combat operations in the knowledge that between the Soviets and the German troops were the straits of Kertsch (*Asowsches Meer,* [Sea of Asov]).[1]

In the meantime, however, on the mainland the Soviets had continued to gain ground, so that *Heeresgruppe* A urgently needed troops in other sectors. At the time of the evacuation of the bridgehead, fighting was already raging around the Dnjepr bridgehead at Saporoschje, later also against the *Wotan – Stellung* leading to the south via Melitopol.

There were, certainly, contradictory views at the command level regarding the question of whether Crimea should be held, and the corollary question of whether the formations that were there were adequate to conduct an effective defense, or whether it would be wiser to reinforce the mainland formations of the 6th *Armee* by transferring troops from Crimea to the mainland. According to the available sources it appears that the Commander in Chief of Crimea expressed the opinion that, with the unavoidable transition from the offensive to the defensive, the Crimea no longer had any significance as the starting point for a new advance to the east, and that, with the formations that were available, its defense appeared difficult. Initially the 17th *Armee* counted five German and seven Rumanian divisions under its command. A number of formations were, however, immediately transported to the mainland by air from Wladislawowka or by rail via Perekop to the mainland. A short time afterward

---

1   The evacuation of Crimea represented an organizational *tour de force.* On 14 July the aerial-cableway from Jenikale to the Tschuschka peninsula was available with a daily capacity of 1,000 tons, along with naval landing craft with a capacity to carry 3,500 tons per day across the straits. *Organization Todt* had been directed by Hitler on 1 May, 1943, to build a five kilometer long road and railroad bridge across the straits. After construction of ten bridge piers, however, the work was halted on 5 September. The evacuation of the Kuban bridgehead reached beyond transporting soldiers, prisoners of war and civilian personnel, as well as weapons, vehicles, ammunition and rations, also including narrow-gage matériel. 109 locomotives and 1,450 wagons were brought back over the straits; the track and bridges, so far as possible, were previously demolished. Only the demolition of the tunnels north of Noworossisk remained incomplete.

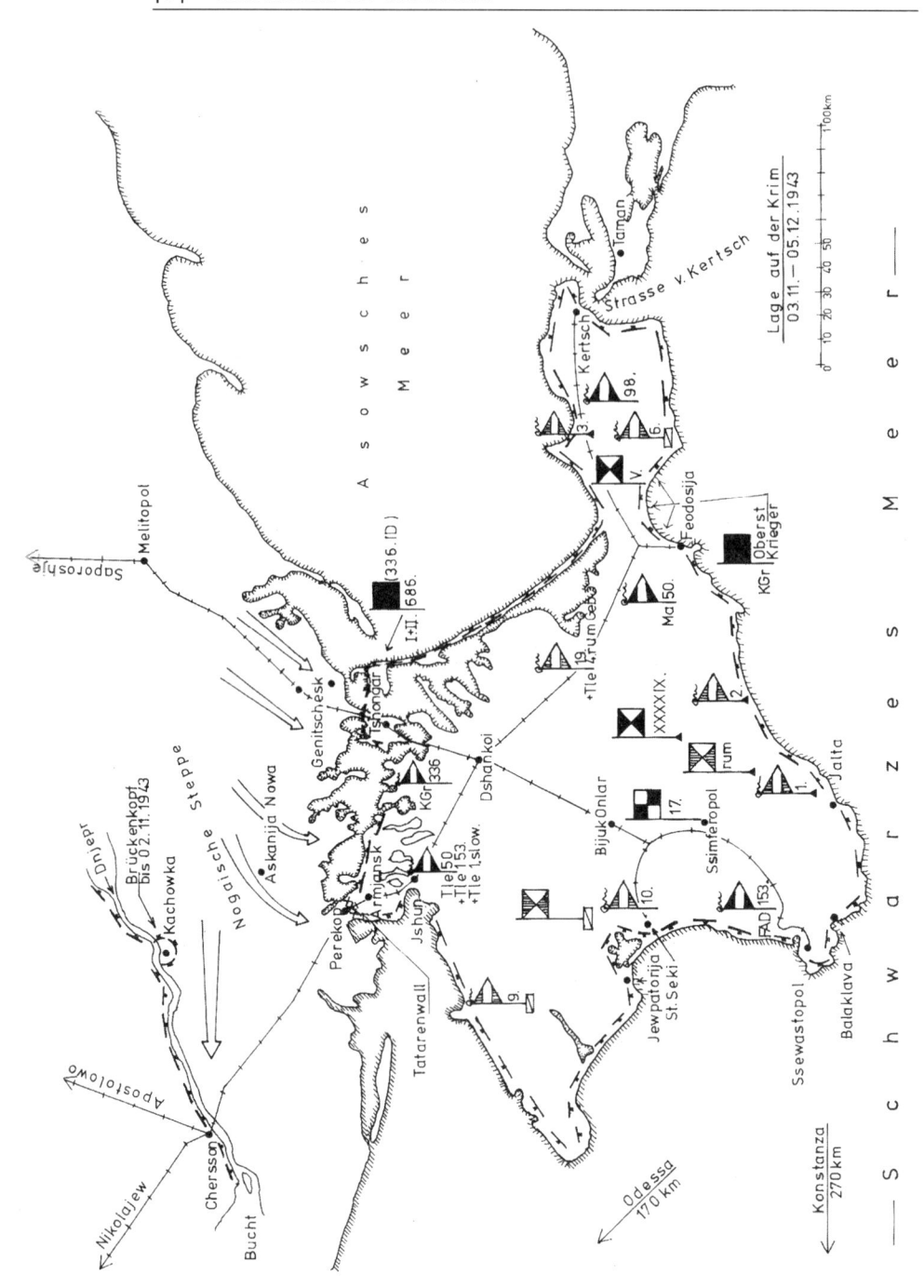

97. Situation on the *Krim* [Crimean Peninsula] 11 March to 12 May, 1944. [*Schwarzes Meer* = Black Sea; *Asowsches Meer* = Sea of Asov; *Strasse f. Kertsch* = Straits of Kertsch.]

the 39th *Gebirgs Korps*, which had to secure the Perekop isthmus, no longer had any German formations under its command, only Slovak, Rumanian and similar eastern volunteers [*Ostfreiwilligen*]. In the eastern sector of Kertsch, after the withdrawal of the Rumanian 10th Infantry Division, the 5th *Armee Korps* had only the 98th *Infanterie Division* in a roughly 100 kilometer long stretch of coastal front on both sides of Kertsch, this initially still supported by *Heeres* – and *Marine* [naval] – artillery forces as well as anti-aircraft formations. The Rumanian 6th Cavalry Division was also attached to the 5th *Armee Korps*. The Rumanian 3rd Mountain Division served as the *Korps* reserve.

On the south coast the 50th *Infanterie Division* was in the sector on both sides of Feodosia with the mission of organizing the installations of the *Parpatsch-Stellung* for defense facing east. Attached to this division were foreign ethnic formations [*fremdvölkische Verbände*] such as the *Aserbeidschanische Bataillon* 806, as well as German troop remnants of *Pionier Bataillon* 71, I./ *Grenadier Regiment* 121, and IV./ *Artillerie Regiment* 150 of the 50th *Infanterie Division*. Extending to the west in the coastal sectors of the II. and III./ *Grenadier Regiment* 121 were *Marineeinheit* [naval unit] *Hossfeld* and several naval coastal batteries which, however, not only had to secure to the south, but, at the same time, defend against the partisan-infested Jaila mountains. *Grenadier Regiment* 122 [50th *Infanterie Division*] followed to the west as far as Tschuds*kap* [Cape of Tschud] with a Turkish battalion, I./ *Grenadier Regiment* 370 [Croatian, 369th *Infanterie Division (kroat,)*] and the II./ *Artillerie Regiment* 150. There were also several more smaller elements, such as *Sicherungsgruppe* 'Marienfeld' with *Aufklärungs Abteilung* 150 [50th *Infanterie Division*].

See Map 97.

Initially the formations left on the Crimea had to organize the defense of the long coastal sector and could, for the time being, certainly count on the immediate landing of enemy forces on the Crimea. Reconnaissance reported construction of landing-craft piers on the Taman peninsula, as well as the arrival of heavy, long-range Soviet guns, the concentration of means of crossing at the Kossa Tschuschka opposite Kertsch and in the *Bucht* [bay] of Taman and increased commitment of Soviet air force formations against the German artillery and infantry positions. The 17th *Armee* could, however, expect that the Soviets would initially need adequate preparation time for a crossing operation that would, in all likelihood, be linked with their advance on the mainland. On the other hand, one could presume that the Soviets needed troops on the Melitopol front and would transfer such from the Kuban area. Those would then be lacking for a crossing to the Crimea.

On 23 October on the mainland formations of the Soviet 4th Ukrainian Front broke through the *'Wotan' Stellung* and captured Melitopol, which led to further pulling back of the lines and, finally, to the Soviet advance to the mouth of the Dnjepr. With that the Soviets gained the Perekop isthmus and also direct access to the Crimean peninsula. From that point on the 17th *Armee* had to expect attacks from the north.

Shortly before the rail connection via Perekop was severed, the German transport of troops to the mainland continued, as with the first elements of the 50th *Infanterie Division*. At the same time, due to the need for haste, half of *Grenadier Regiment* 123 [50th *Infanterie Division*] had already reached the area of the 6th *Armee*, flying from Wladislawoka on *Ju* 52s. Additional forces, including the III./ *Artillerie Regiment* 150 entrained in good time with the reinforced *Regimentsgruppe* 123 and assembled around Kschowka, east of Bereslaw. Additional transports of the 50th *Infanterie Division*, however, failed to make it out via Perekop.

The situation caused the 17th *Armee* – *Generaloberst* Jänicke – and also the Commander in Chief of *Heeresgruppe* A, *Generalfeldmarschall* von Kleist, to propose the evacuation of the Crimea to Hitler. The 17th *Armee* had already prepared such an evacuation under the codeword '*Michael*', with the objective of establishing contact, by force, if necessary, with the 6th *Armee* via Perekop. There were, however, a variety of considerations against such a solution in the *Führer* headquarters, because the Soviets would thereby be able to command a large part of the Black Sea (*Großadmiral* Dönitz). Göring described the Crimea as a kind of 'aircraft carrier'. On the other hand, Rumanian Marshal Antunescu demanded the evacuation of the Crimea from Hitler. Hitler mollified him in a written reply with the promise of reinforcing the German combat forces.

Hitler directed that the evacuation of the Crimea that had already been prepared according to the plan '*Michael*' must be stopped immediately. In any case, carrying out the plans of the 17th *Armee* seemed, at this point in time, no longer to promise success in light of the development north of Perekop with the further advance of the Soviets to the west. In addition, this concentration of troops could by no means be moved with available rolling stock and the available stock of vehicles in the few days that were planned, certainly not while bringing along the assembled supplies.

See Map 97.

On 30 October Soviet armoured spearheads appeared at the Tartar Wall [*Tatarenwall*] near Perekop. A few days later the first Soviet AFVs advanced south to Armjansk at a time when the defense of the Perekop bottleneck was the responsibility of a few *Ostbatillonen* and *Flak-Kampftruppen* of the 9th *Flak Division*.

Defense of the Kertsch Peninsula

Until the closing of the of Perekop isthmus a large part of the German formations that had been brought back from the Kuban bridgehead were, after the evacuation of the bridgehead and transport to the Crimea, in the process of further transport to the mainland. The 98th *Infanterie Division* took over the defense of the east coast of the Kertsch peninsula.

In the meantime Soviet preparations for embarkation on the eastern side of the Straits of Kertsch progressed. The crossing of the channel was imminent and could be anticipated at its narrowest place to the nose of Kertsch, namely north of Kertsch. The concentration of shipping in the Bay of Taman, as well as the repeated attacks by Soviet aircraft on the fixed German batteries of long-barreled guns finally appeared conspicuous. These observations resulted in feverish construction of positions, erection of barriers, and the holding in readiness of transportation to move the operational reserves.

See Map 98.

On 31 October three large boats set out from the Taman harbour under strong Soviet air protection. German artillery dispersed this group. The boats soon disappeared in a smokescreen. The first warning for the German defensive

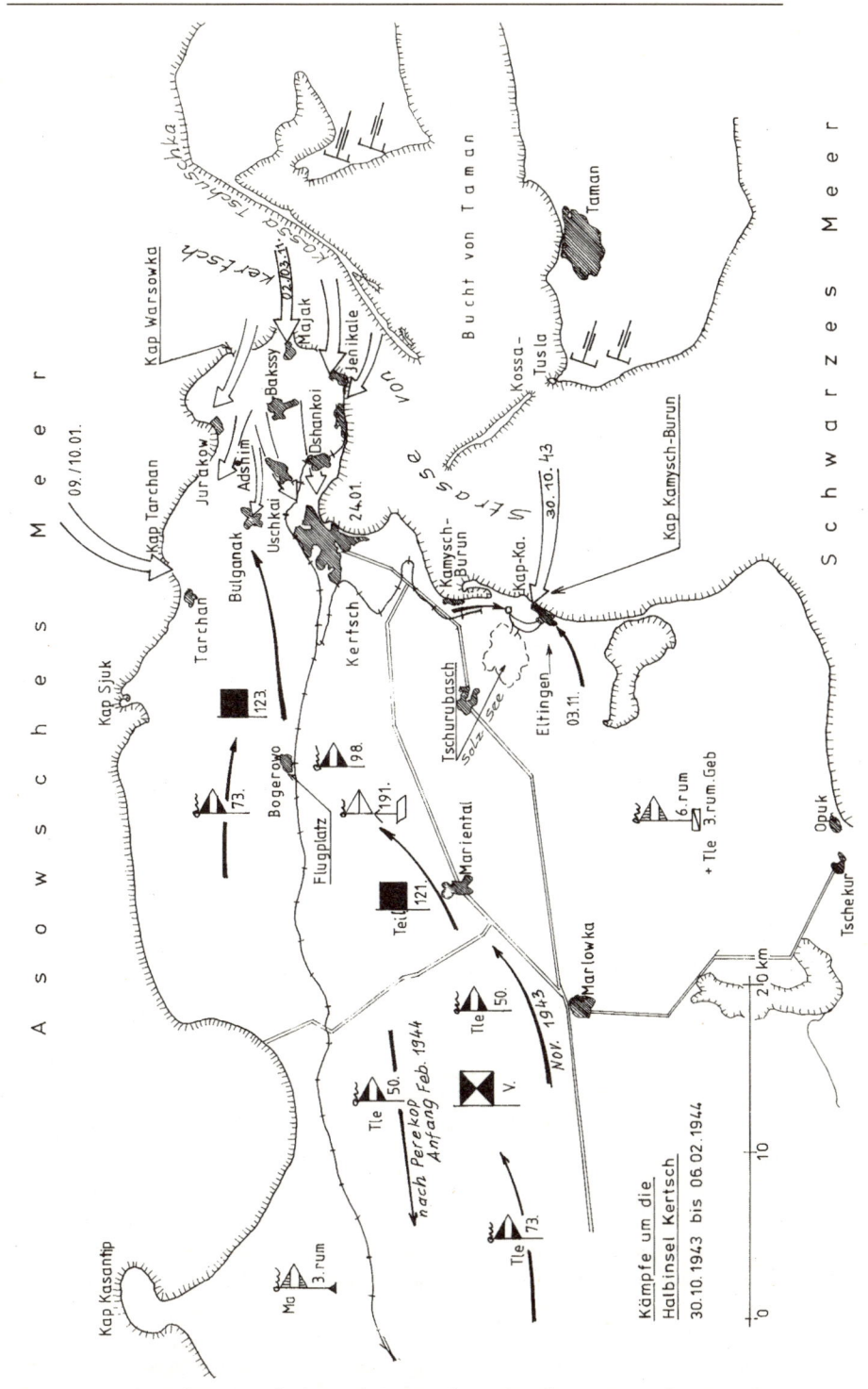

SITUATION OF THE 17TH *ARMEE*, EVACUATION OF CRIMEA 407

98. Fighting on the Kertsch Peninsula 30 October 1943 to 2 June 1944.

formations, however, did not yet make clear where the Soviets planned to land. This first attempt might have been directed at the northeast coast, but could also have been a deception maneuver.

Enemy Landing at Eltingen

See Map 98.

That same day one hour of heavy caliber Soviet artillery fire fell on Jenikale at Kertsch and Eltingen. The target area of this artillery fire still did not allow unconditional identification of the intended landing place. The first Soviet forces then landed south of Kamisch-Burun, after artillery preparation, surprising the security forces of the Rumanian 6th Cavalry Division there. A nearby battery, the 3. *Artillerie Regiment* 198 [98th *Infanterie Division*], set up for direct fire after the Rumanians had abandoned their positions. The Red soldiers fell back before the artillery, and also infantry, fire. This action involved the Soviet 386th Naval Infantry Battalion, which also came up against the German I./ *Grenadier Regiment* 282 [98th *Infanterie Division*] at the northwest corner of the Eltinger landing area. Light *Flak-Abteilung* 89, stationed in the area of the shore, destroyed ten and damaged additional Soviet landing craft in the early dawn light.

The I./ *Grenadier Regiment* 282, which had been brought up, occupied a blocking position at the south shore of the Tschurabaschka salt lake [*Salz See*]. In a counterattack it forced the Soviet naval infantrymen back to the rim of the hill at Eltingen. The next morning the extent of the landing became evident. The German command now had to recognize the *Schwerpunkt* on the northern flank of the beachhead, where the counterattack of the I./ *Grenadier Regiment* 282 had not broken through.

In the following night the Soviets reinforced the forces they had landed and simultaneously attempted to widen their beachhead. The I./ and II./ *Grenadier Regiment* 282, as well as *Pionier Bataillon* 46, attempted to eliminate the beachhead. With the help of *Sturmgeschütz Bridgade* 191, which was brought in by rail, it was possible to considerably reduce the size of the beachhead. The 3rd *Räumboot* [mine-sweeper] *Flotille* and the 1st *Schnellboot* [E-boat (torpedo boat)] *Flotille* attacked the Soviet landing and supply convoy despite its strong support by the Soviet Air Force, finally blocking the supply of the formations in the beachhead.

On 3 December 80 artillery tubes were standing by to eliminate the beachhead, supported by two batteries of *Sturmgeschütz Brigade* 191. The 2nd battery of *Sturmgeschütz Brigade* 191 attacked from south to north, the 1st battery from west to east.[2] They broke into the Soviet positions against tough enemy resistance. However, the Rumanian infantry did not follow after them so that the initial success remained under-utilized. The German sea-blockade did not prevent reinforcement of the Soviet forces ashore and their supply with ammunition and anti-tank weapons. The Soviets also received support from their heavy artillery on the Taman peninsula.

---

2   Translator's note – Despite their mobile employment on the battlefield in support of infantry, and, on occasion, employment as if they were tanks, *Sturmgeschütze* were considered as artillery rather than as a form of tank and were, accordingly, designated as batteries. They were also equipped and trained to fire in indirect fire, when that was needed, as artillery.

Additional Landings

As usual, the Soviets were not satisfied with one offensive sector, but prepared a second. This operation could not have arisen from the knowledge that the landing at Eltingen had been contained and was, to date, unsuccessful. It is certain that the Soviets had begun preparations for this additional landing a long time before, as was determined both from observations, especially from the air, and also from statements by prisoners. With that the northeast coast of Kertsch had to be considered as immediately endangered. The landings took place after two hours of artillery preparation and bombing attacks on Kertsch, Jenikale and Majak, as well as the five kilometer wide east coast during the night of 2/3 November. As the artillery fire ended, the landing force came ashore and captured ground both at Jenikale, against the II./ *Grenadier Regiment* 290 [98th *Infanterie Division*] and also the II./ *Grenadier Regiment* 290, adjoining to the north. The situation forced the division command immediately to occupy the hills east of Baksy and Dshankoj during the night. Baksy was significant because of a usable road running from there to Kertsch, whose acquisition appeared desirable for the Soviets.

About 800 meters south of Majak the 8th *Batterie* of *Artillerie Regiment* 198 [98th *Infanterie Division*] was in well-constructed firing positions, with two batteries of *Marine Artillerie Abteilung* 613 in front of it. Although the personnel of the latter had been dispersed by artillery fire, the 8th *Batterie* of *Artillerie Regiment* 198 resisted in their position, which was fortified for 360 degree defense, despite a direct hit in the ammunition and personnel bunker. This bastion located in the center of the coastal sector that the Soviets had selected caused the Soviets considerable difficulties. The battery received immediate infantry reinforcement from the regiment's pioneer platoon, as well as a *Kampfgruppe* formed from train elements of the I. and III./ *Grenadier Regiment* 290. The 2nd and 3rd *Kompanien* of *Pionier Bataillon* 198 set out for Hill 175, north of Majak in order to reinforce the remnants of the 9th *Kompanie* of *Grenadier Regiment* 290 and battery troops of *Artillerie Regiment* 198 that were defending there.

The Soviets initially failed to attain their objective. The II./ *Grenadier Regiment* 290 built a new line of defense between Dshankoj and Kapang in which they withstood all attacks with a division battalion that had been brought up and the 1st *Kompanie* of *Pionier Bataillon* 198. On the north coast Hill 106 at *Kap* [Cape] Worsoka remained in German hands. A company of *Feldausbildungs* [field-training] *Regiment* 218 [153rd (*Feldausbildungs*) *Division*] took position between Hills 106 and 175 during the night.

Early on 3 November the Soviet disembarkation went on at full speed, covered by a rolling commitment of the Red Air Force. The battle raged on a five kilometer front, though without a continuous German line of defense. That same day two Soviet divisions landed on the Kertsch peninsula.

The 8th *Batterie* of *Artillerie Regiment* 198 south of Majak continued to hold out and engaged the Soviet landing craft. Finally the battery fired off its last rounds and blew up its remaining two intact guns. The concentrated fire of artillery to the rear provided the survivors with an opportunity to fight their way through to the west.

The main Soviet assault was directed against Baksy and Hill 175, but also against the Dshankoj Hill 102. The Soviets stormed both hills, which meant that the villages of Baksy and Dshankoj, which were in their field of fire, had to be evacuated, as did Hill 106 by the I./ *Feld Ausbildungs Regiment* 218 at *Kamp* Worsowka on the northern wing.

West of Baksy the pioneers held Hill 129.6, south of Baksy; the I./ *Grenadier Regiment* 290 and the arriving *Sturmgeschütze* of *Sturmgeschütz Brigade* 191 held their positions. However, the Soviets tore apart the I./ *Feldausbildungs Regiment* 218 at Hill 144.1 and forced it back, thus the Rumanian 11th *Jäger* Battalion occupied a blocking position west of Jurakow Kut on Hills 106.6 and 154.4. By the evening of 3 November the Soviet 56th *Armee* had gained an eight kilometer wide and five kilometer deep beachhead at Baksy, this with a 20:1 superiority in forces. On the German side *Grenadier Regiment* 290 had lost heavily, but so had the Soviet attackers, so that they did not launch a new attack for several days.

Defensive Fighting North of Kertsch

On 9 November the Soviets continued their offensive at Baksy. German artillery helped to deny the Soviets success. They, however, therefore shifted their *Schwerpunkt* to the sector of the Rumanian 11th *Jäger* Battalion, which they forced back. On 10 November the division reserve of the 98th *Infanterie Division* which was immediately brought in, with one battery of *Sturmgeschütz Brigade* 191, retook the line that the Rumanians had given up.

In the morning of 11 November three Soviet divisions attacked another time from the Baksy area, got to Adschim Uschkoj and turned in toward Kertsch.

The situation caused the elements of the 50th *Infanterie Division* (*Grenadier Regiment* 123) that had already been flown to the mainland to be brought back by *Ju* 52 to the island, landing in Bagorowo. They were immediately transported by lorry to Bulganak. The I./ *Grenadier Regiment* 123 recaptured Hills 113.3 and 125.6 by storm and established contact with the III./ *Grenadier Regiment* 290 in the north and the II./ *Feldausbildungs Regiment* 218, thereby scuttling the attempt to roll up the German front to both sides. *Sturmgeschütz Brigade* 191 was the backbone of the German defense. Another *Sturmgeschütz Brigade* (279) was in transport to Crimea. Additional elements of *Grenadier Regiment* 123 and also the I./ *Grenadier Regiment* 121 [50th *Infanterie Division*], which had also been flown in, were committed in the Bulganak area. Elements of the 98th *Infanterie Division* were committed in the Eltingen area after their replacement by Rumanians in their previous area of commitment.

On 12 November the Soviets attempted anew to break through the German front at Bulgana. The I./ *Grenadier Regiment* 121 was able to improve the German position in counterattack. On 14 November yet another attack came in with great packs of Soviet AFVs, with its *Schwerpunkt* at Bulganak. The III./ *Grenadier Regiment* 123, which had, in the meantime, been flown in, brought the Soviet attack to a standstill where it had been inserted between the I./ *Grenadier Regiment* 123 and the I./*Grenadier Regiment* 121, knocking out nine enemy AFVs. In the meantime the German *Luftwaffe* attacked targets in

Baksy, targeting arriving troops and the crossing site where the troops were landing.

After several unsuccessful intermediary attacks the Soviets started a new offensive early on 20 November, at 0405 hours, after an artillery preparation of about 10,000 shells in one hour, this with support from 40 AFVs. The latter rolled over the German main line of resistance southeast of Bulgnak and pushed into the town, which they then had to back out of with the loss of ten AFVs. South of Bulgnak 20 enemy AFVs stood opposite the German main line of resistance, but they hesitated to go any further forward. Yet again 35 *Stukas* and 26 *Me* 110s attacked the enemy armour south of Bulganak and nailed the Soviet armoured spearheads down tight. The II./ *Grenadier Regiment* 282 advanced in conjunction with the aerial attack eastward from the bend in the railroad at Kertsch. Elements of the I./ and II./ *Grenadier Regiment* 123 attacked from Bulganak and closed the existing gap in the front, while knocking out a series of enemy AFVs. During this period of time the German formations received personnel replacements. All leaves were blocked for the 17th *Armee*.

35

Attack against the Isthmus near Perekop

The calm that had set in at this point in the encircled beachhead at Eltingen and the front at the Kertsch nose gives occasion to consider the other battlefields. The last trains with the elements of the 50th *Infanterie Division* that had been ordered transferred to the mainland could no longer cross the Perekop isthmus, because the sudden arrival of Soviet armoured spearheads there prevented continuation of the journey. The elements of the 50th *Infanterie Division* that had thus arrived, including the staff of the division, went into action at Perekop attached to the 39th *Gebirgs Armee Korps*.

This isthmus proved extremely difficult terrain for defense against an attack from the north. Alongside the firm land with the rail and road connections this sector had swamps, islands and the like. Above all else there were no adequate forces available to repulse the Soviets. There was merely a Slovene training battalion with no combat experience, as well as the III./*'Bergmann'*(*As erbeidschaner*), *Bau* – [construction] *Pionier-Kompanie* 288 and the 8th *Batterie* of *Flak-Abteilung* 257 of the 9th *Flak-Division*. In addition a *Flak* armoured train arrived from Woinka.

On 30 October *Flak* batteries engaged the Soviet armoured spearheads that emerged in the flat terrain near Perekop and stopped them. The arriving *Flak* armoured train consisted of several goods wagons surrounded by planks with light and heavy anti-aircraft guns on them.

See Maps 97, 99 and 101.

The 50th *Infanterie Division* assumed command in this sector and, indeed, for the narrows of the isthmus at Perekop, Tschongor and Genetschesk, with the following units: on the right was the 336th *Infanterie Division*, which had been badly battered in the fighting around Melitopol, now consisting only of infantry battalions without heavy weapons. Therefore one battery of the II./*Artillerie Regiment* 42 was attached. In addition there was the Rumanian 10th Infantry Division, formerly attached to the 59th *Gebirgs Armee Korps*, with the right sector of the Siwasch front, the Rumanian 19th Infantry Division at the Tschogary-Damm [embankment-type dam or embankment] and on the Arabat peninsula, as well as the Rumanian 9th Cavalry Division as coastal protection at the west coast, the latter supported by naval landing craft of the 5th *Landungsflotille* of the *Marine*.

See Map 99.

The Soviet armoured forces attacked on 31 October at the Tartar Wall. The *Flak* armoured train '*Muhr*', which had arrived, in the meantime, and the anti-aircraft batteries that were in position knocked out several Soviet AFVs. The armoured train had to drive back under concentric fire from Soviet artillery, so that in the evening the Soviets crossed the Tartar Wall with 16 AFVs and escorting infantry and got to the north edge of Armjansk, where the

ATTACK AGAINST THE ISTHMUS NEAR PEREKOP

II./ *Artillerie Regiment* 42 and the III./ *Artillerie Regiment* 150 [50th *Infanterie Division*], which had just detrained, stopped them. The Soviets dispersed the infantry elements committed there, which had no combat experience. The commander of the 50th *Infanterie Division* first had to reassemble them

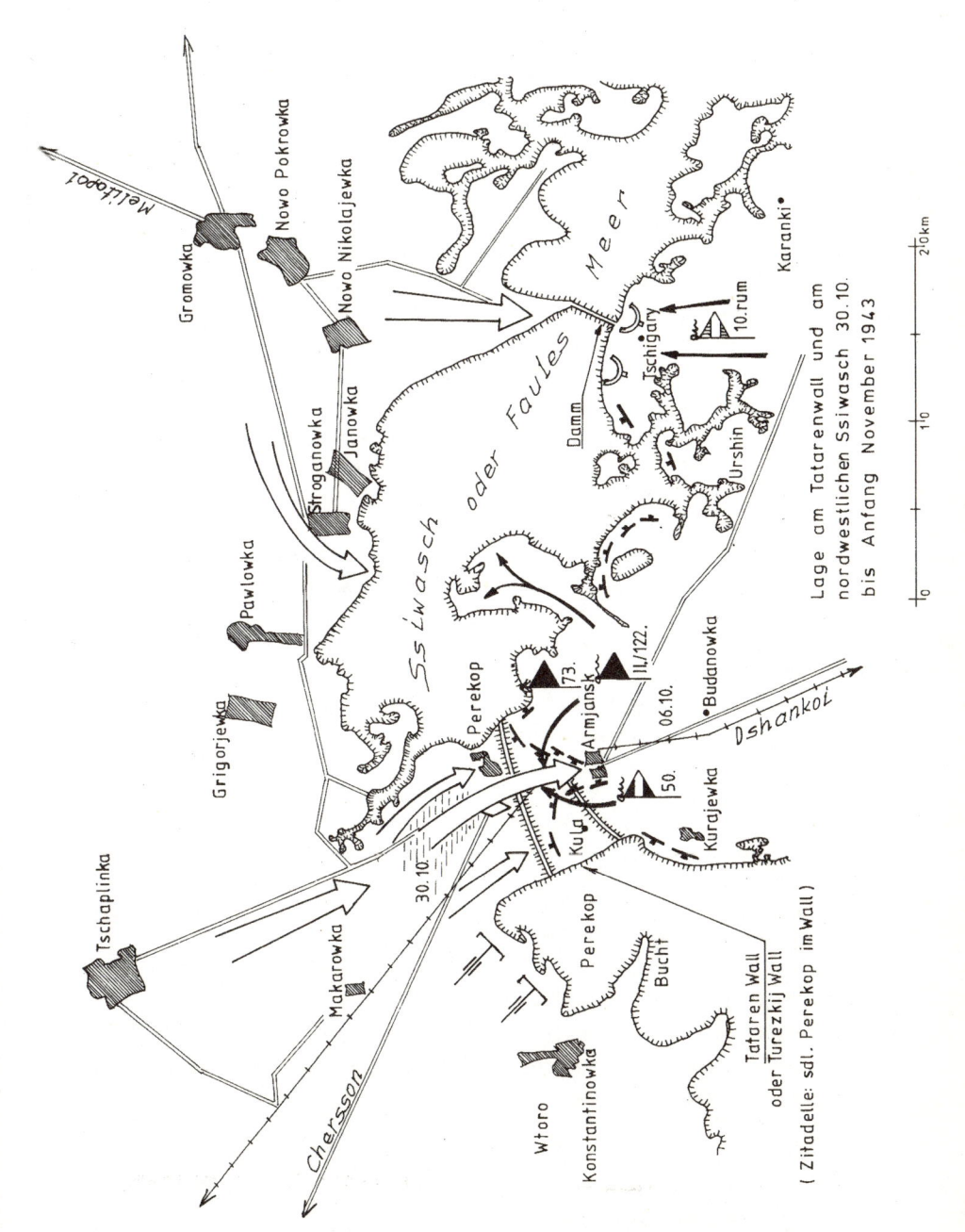

99. Situation at the Tartar Wall [*Tatarenwall*] and at the northwestern Ssiwasch from 30 October to the start of November, 1943. See also Map 6.

in order to direct them into the new defensive positions. Nevertheless, the Soviets finally overran the firing positions of the II./ *Artillerie Regiment* 42, until the III./ *Grenadier Regiment* 122 [50th *Infanterie Divsion*] arrived in the night in Armjansk and immediately regained the lost artillery position in a hasty counterattack. The division then built a new line of resistance north of Armjansk. However, a Soviet penetration remained beyond the Tartar Wall.

The Germans then received reinforcements – this as the advantage of holding the 'interior line'– namely the II./ *Sturmgeschütz Brigade* 191, brought in from Kertsch and elements of *Panzerjäger Abteilung 150*. On 1 November, however, the Soviets tried to take advantage of the currently uncertain situation on the German side. They were met, essentially, by armoured train '*Muhr*', which rolled up again and here knocked out its 24th AFV. In addition *Sturmgeschütz Brigade* 191 joined the fighting and, shortly thereafter, *leichte Flak Abteilung* 86, ordered in as reinforcement from Feodosia.

However, an extraordinary number of gaps remained in the German defense. Therefore another armoured train, '*Michael*' rolled in, consisting of captured Soviet armoured gun-wagons and normal passenger cars. The train unloaded infantry to the rear in order to bring them to the combat area. Nevertheless, on 2 November, against additional elements of the 50th *Infanterie Division* that were arriving, the Soviets attempted to deepen their three kilometer deep penetration beyond the Tartar Wall. However, the attack, supported by 25 AFVs, foundered in the fire of anti-aircraft, anti-tank and artillery fire of the armoured trains, as well as of the *Sturmgeschütze*, which restored the situation in a decisive counterattack. Two battalions of *Grenadier Regiment* 121 stiffened up the German main line of resistance in the eastern part of the Tartar Wall.

See Maps 99 and 101. Thereupon the Soviets crossed the three kilometer broad and flat swamp area of the Siwasch with three companies and took Karanki, Aschkadan and Tarchan over the limited resistance from elements of the Rumanian 10th Infantry Division, with the mission of reaching the road and railroad to the rear at Ishun and Woinka. Therefore the formations that were already in Woinka and that were intended for transfer to the Tartar Wall, had to detrain in Woinka in order to deliver counterattacks in the narrow terrain of Tarchan and Tomaschewka. Both routes were ideal for the Soviet flanking thrust to the south. In addition, however, an advance via Urshin offered the possibility of advancing to the west, directly into the rear of the German line of defense at the Tartar Wall.

New Front at the Siwasch

See Maps 99 and 101. The German formations immediately advanced via Tomaschewka to Karnaki, until they ran into Soviet troops. A *Kampfgruppe* of the I./ *Grenadier Regiment* 122 with the 3rd *Kompanie* of the *Pionier Bataillon* and one 2 cm anti-aircraft battery made good initial progress advancing via the Tarchan bottleneck, recapturing Tarchan and the hills north of it. Finally this *Kampfgruppe* went over to the defensive.

This evasive movement over the Siwasch forced the German command to postpone the planned counterattack north of Armjansk in order initially to eliminate the Soviet bridgehead on the Tschigary peninsula. On the right flank it was possible to take the hill four kilometers south of Karnaki, with support from a Rumanian *Panzer Kompanie* 53 it was also possible to take Karnaki and the to close narrow area north thereof. Fortune thus favored halting the Soviet forces at this place north of Tarchan and also at Urshin. On the other hand, the further concern to recapture the Tschigary beachhead failed, impacted by the new Soviet diversionary attacks north of Armjansk. Armoured trains *'Michael'* and *'Muhr'* as well as anti-tank guns, artillery and anti-aircraft guns, along with the 2nd *Batterie* of *Sturmgeschütz Brigade* 191 thereby knocked out 27 Soviet AFVs. This attack forced the German command to halt, for the time being, the advance to the Tschigary – *Damm* in order, first, to eliminate the 'boil' at the Tartar Wall north of Armjansk. For that the command brought in 2,500 infantry and pioneers as well as 70 guns, the two armoured trains and the 2nd and 3rd *Batterien* of *Sturmgeschütz Brigade* 191. Facing them were three Soviet rifle divisions with two cavalry divisions behind them. This troop concentration and its organization made it clear that the Soviets intended to initially break through with infantry forces and then advance with cavalry forces into the depth.

Fighting at the Tartar Wall

The German operation began early on 6 November at 0300 hours, with an assault from both sides against the 'boil' in the main line of resistance in the Tartar line north of Armjansk. The I./ *Grenadier Regiment* 122 attacked from the west with *Pionier Bataillon* 71[50th *Infanterie Division*] and two training battalions. *Pionier Bataillon* 73 and the II./ *Grenadier Regiment* 121 attacked from the east. Both attacking forces had one common objective, the citadel in the Tartar Wall. The latter *Pionier Bataillon* took the citadel by storm, while the attack of the group advancing on the left came to a standstill at the railroad cut through the Tartar Wall, so it was not possible for the forces to link up.

A third *Kampfgruppe* II./ *Grenadier Regiment* 122 with *Feldersatz Bataillon* 94 (4th *Gebirgs Division*) and *Füsilier Bataillon* 336 [336th *Infanterie Division*] as well as the III./ *Grenadier Regiment* 257 [83rd *Infanterie Division*] was supposed to push out of the Armjansk area against the Tartar Wall after the other two *Kampfgruppen* had linked up. Its attack was delayed and came under Soviet flanking fire, so that the attack had to be broken off, though with the destruction of 30 Soviet AFVs. After repulsing several Soviet counterattacks the German formations halted their attacks.

In mid-November the 50th *Infanterie Division* repeated a similar operation, again divided into three groups. On the right were the II./ and III./*Grenadier Regiment* 121 as well as three battalions from outside the division. In the center (northern edge of Armjansk) were six non-division battalions. On the left were the I./ and III./ *Grenadier Regiment* 122, *Feldersatz Bataillon* 150 and a battalion from outside the division, this later relieved by *Aufklärungs Abteilung* 150. In the meantime two non-division battalions were at the Siwasch front. They later smashed a Soviet landing group. At the west coast were the *'Bergmann' Bataillon* and the *Kosaken-Schwadron* [Cossack cavalry troop] *'Bohlschlag'*, as well as the Rumanian 9th Cavalry Brigade. At the year's end the *Slowakische Infanterie Regiment* 20 arrived.

416 CRUCIBLE OF COMBAT

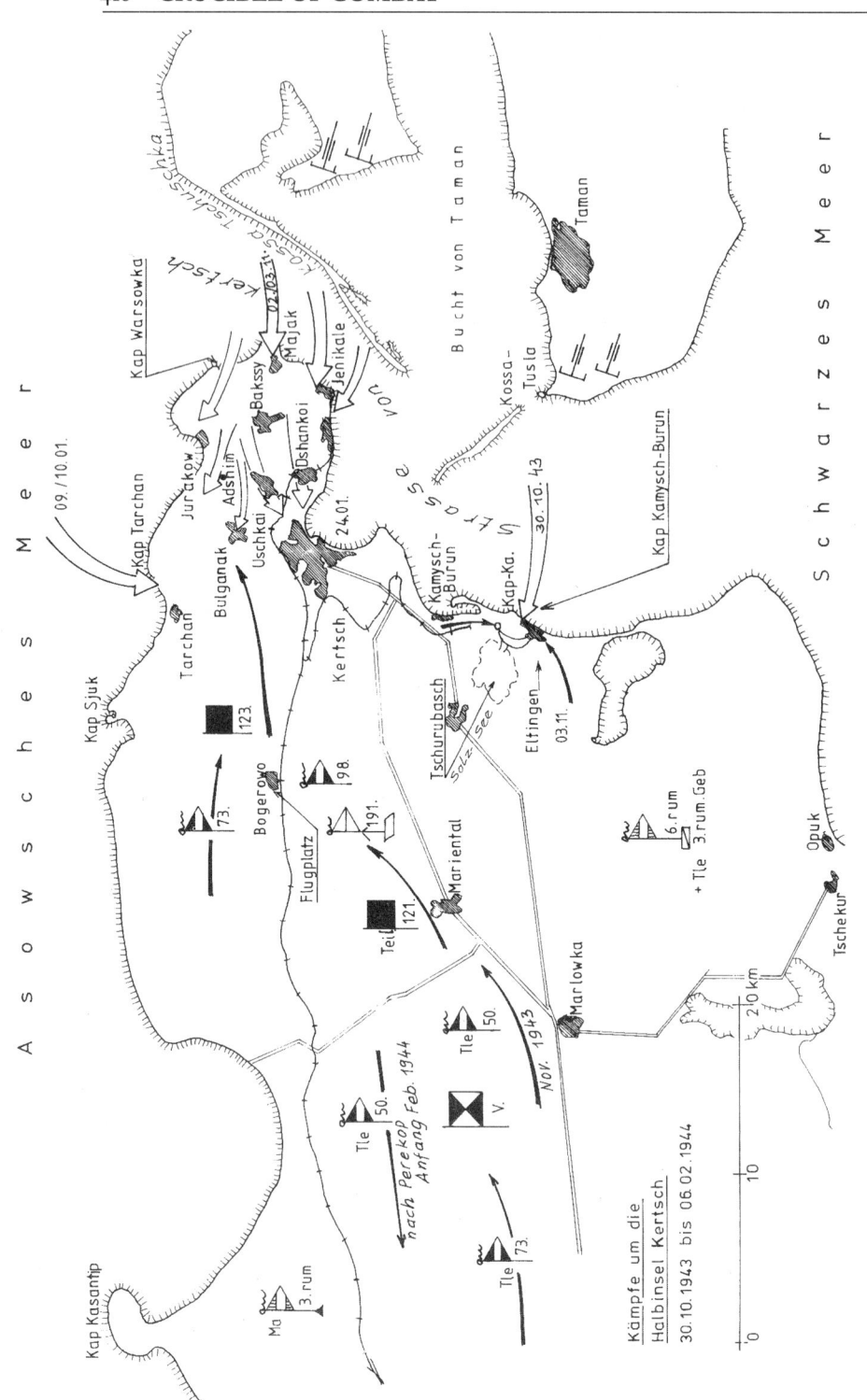

100. Fighting on the Kertsch Peninsula, 30 October, 1943 to 6 February, 1944.

ATTACK AGAINST THE ISTHMUS NEAR PEREKOP

At the Perekop front and at the coast, then, were: *Artillerie Regiment* 150, *slowakisches Artillerie Regiment* 20, *Küsten* [coastal] *Artillerie Abteilung* 114 and *Marine Artillerie Abteilung* 614, a total of 28 batteries, while the II./*Sturmgeschütz Brigade* 191 moved back to Kertsch. In mid-November the Soviets forced back the Rumanians who were north of Tarchan. With that, the rail line supplying the Perekop front was again threatened with being severed. On 27 November German and Rumanian forces therefore regained the old line north of Tarchan in a counterattack.

At the end of the month the Soviets attacked at the Tartar Wall yet again, initially with the objective of cutting off the east portion of the woods position of *Grenadier Regiment* 121. A few days later they repeated the same attempt against the west wing of the Tartar Wall (27 November to 4 December). The last assault did, indeed, achieve a penetration, which *Grenadier Regiment* 122 closed again on 4 December.

In mid-December the Soviets renewed attacks at the Siwasch front. The 50th *Infanterie Division* turned over this sector to the adjoining 336th *Infanterie Division* and then defended the 18 kilometer length of the Tartar Wall front with 17 battalions, only ten of which had combat experience. At the end of the year the German formations organized to defend the achieved line, because elimination of the Soviet bridgeheads at the Tartar Wall and on the Tschigary peninsula no longer seemed possible due to shortage of forces.

The 17th *Armee* tried anew for permission to evacuate the Crimea, which Hitler refused. He sent *General* Schmundt, who informed himself of the situation at Perekop. The unit leaders briefed him on the hopelessness of defending longer, and also on the fact that the loss of the German Nikopol bridgehead freed up ten Soviet divisions that could now be committed at the Tartar Wall. The effort to take advantage of the so-called 'advantage of the interior line' would have to founder at the moment when the Soviets could attack simultaneously in both sectors. The repeated shifting of individual companies and batteries back and forth between the Kertsch front, Perekop front and the Siwasch front according to the results of reconnaissance of the enemy was already extraordinarily sensitive.

36

Fighting at the Kertsch Front, Eltingen and Mitridat

After the Rumanian attack against the Soviet Eltingen beachhead on 3 December failed to achieve the desired results, the Rumanians launched a new concentric attack on 7 December with substantial support from *Sturmgeschütz Brigade* 191. In three days of fighting the Soviet beachhead was eliminated and 2,000 prisoners were taken. The seagoing force operating out of Kamisch-Burun (three naval landing craft, six minesweepers and five torpedo boats) took a major part in this success, with a total of 355 missions. During this siege they sank 41 Soviet seagoing craft and damaged another 22. Three motor-gunboats, 24 landing craft and 24 motor launches and cutters fell into German hands on the beach at Eltingen.

During the night before the German attack against the Eltingen beachhead several hundred Red Army soldiers filtered out of the northern part of the beachhead front in the darkness, probably due to the inattention of the weak Rumanian security forces there, and broke out into the open terrain to the north. West of Kamisch-Burun they ran into a light *Flak* platoon, whose sentries they surprised and whose crew they killed in their tent-covered foxholes. Due, probably, to inattention, these had not recognized the approaching Soviets in time. A nearby heavy *Flak* battery had gained no enlightenment from the relatively limited sound of fighting and felt no danger.

The group that had broken out reached the commanding Mitridat hill, south of the city of Kertsch, surprised the observation post located there, and organized themselves on the hill for defense with light weapons.

An enemy group that broke away to the west from this march group ran into a battery (I./*Heeresflak Abteilung* 279) and was wiped out by it. The Mitridat group held out several days and, finally, was no longer very far from the leading elements of the Soviet land forces that advanced from the beachhead north of Kertsch after its extension on 17 November. *Aufklärungs Abteilung* 150 and elements of the *Füsilier Bataillon* and *Pionier Bataillon* of the 98th *Infanterie Division* advanced against the garrison of the Mitridat hill, but got no further. The 2nd *Batterie* of *Sturmgeschütz Brigade* 191, brought in from Etlingen, could accomplish little with their guns in the rocky land there, only prevent further support from the sea. On 10 December this brigade supported the action against the Red soldiers, dismounted, with the machine guns that they had dismounted from their *Sturmgeschütze* and, that day, regained the peak of the Mitridat hill. Still, however, they were unable to prevent a portion of this Mitridat garrison from falling back into the ruins of Kertsch toward the harbour, where they were picked up by Soviet torpedo boats.

THE KERTSCH FRONT, ELTINGEN AND MITRIDAT 419

A few days later, in zero-visibility weather, the Soviets undertook a new assault with torpedo boats against the Kamisch-Burun harbour, escorted by five enemy ground-attack planes. One airplane fell victim to anti-aircraft fire. One torpedo boat exploded as the result of a direct anti-aircraft hit. The objective of this operation was hard to discern. Possibly the Soviet command hoped to rescue more Red soldiers who had escaped in this sector.

37

The Situation of the 17th *Armee*

The quiet days of Christmas provided an opportunity to evaluate the situation. Granted, the limited seaborn logistical support and personnel supply was, for the time being, secured. The *Armee*, however, had to expect new landings in other sectors of the coast at any time, especially on the northern front, from the Soviet bridgehead on the Tschigary peninsula at the Siwasch. German forces were not adequate to clean up these enemy penetrations. The *Armee* could not, in any way, risk the limited number of mobile armoured guns of the *Sturmgeschütz* units, because the defensive power of the infantry forces depended on their preservation. Moreover, the Soviets at the Siwasch had a substantial amount of artillery north of the Siwasch. When the surface of the Siwasch froze over the Soviets would have an easy opportunity to reinforce and extend their beachhead. The 17th *Armee* therefore abstained from further counterattacks and limited itself to the construction of defensive positions, including positions to the rear, even in the area of the Sewastopol fortifications.

The 17th *Armee* prepared plans for the event of a broader Soviet attack, with retreat to Sewastopol. However, the corresponding evacuation movement required permission of *OKH*. After working out the corresponding study '*Gleitboot*', the command tried again to obtain permission. This, however, remained denied. At the start of the new year 270,000 German and Rumanian soldiers were still in the Crimea, with fighting strengths at Perekop and Kertsch of 32,293 Germans and 30,218 Rumanians, a total of 62,500 men.[1]

Fighting Continues in the 'Nose' North of Kertsch

See Map 98.

The improvement of the weather on 9 January permitted the Soviets, on 10 January, after a brief but heavy sudden concentration of artillery fire to successfully attack the positions of the III./ *Grenadier Regiment* 290 [98th *Infanterie Division*] between Hill 125.6 and the Asov coast. They strove to destabilize the northern wing of this front, to gain ground parallel to the coast of the Sea of Asov toward Tarchan. That would provide a later opportunity to block the Kertsch bottleneck with a thrust to the south. To support this operation the Soviets landed forces during the night at *Kap* [cape] Tarchan, which immediately took possession of several commanding hills. When it grew light Soviet ground-attack planes joined in the fight. The breakthrough that was achieved there through the German main line of resistance at Hill 125.6 exposed Hill 113.3, which *Feldersatz Bataillon* 125 with the newly brought in III./ *Grenadier Regiment* 123 nevertheless held. The I./ *Grenadier Regiment* 290 also held its positions around Hill 95.1, regardless of eventful fighting, thereby

---

1 These numbers are from Tieke, *Kampf um die Krim*.

THE SITUATION OF THE 17TH *ARMEE*

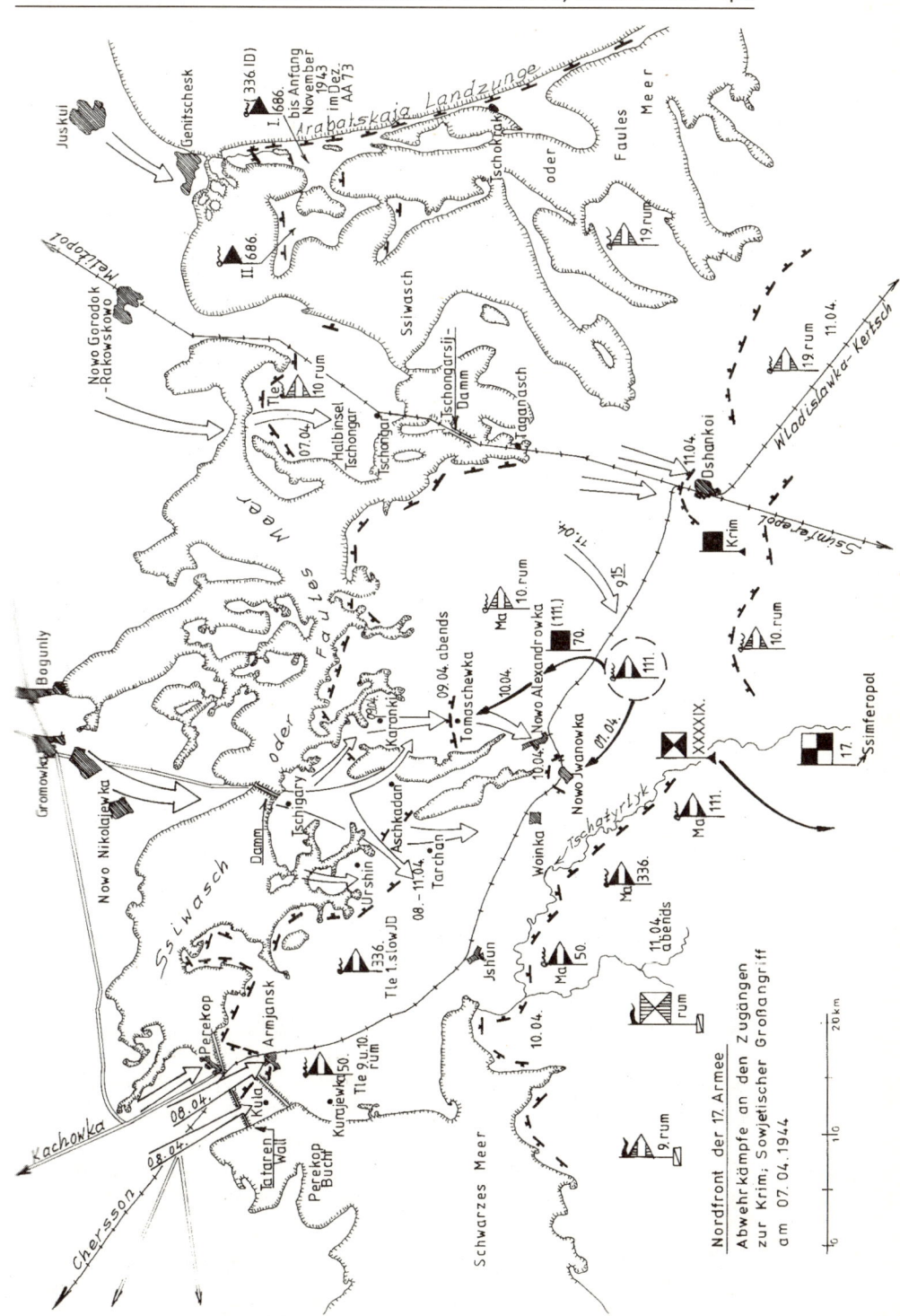

101. Northern Front of the 17th *Armee*. Defensive fighting at the entrances to the Crimea; Soviet offensive on 7 April, 1944.

preventing the Soviets advancing from the east to the west from linking up with the forces that had landed at Tarchan. The commitment of additional German forces that were brought in to a counterattack, and that with *Füsilier Bataillon* 198 and the *Korps* reserve, as well as guns of *Sturmgeschütz Brigade* 191, led to the recapture of the ridge at the Sea of Asov. With the exception of Hill 115.5, all the other hills were back in German hands.

Thereupon the Soviets repeated their attack with armour and strong support by ground-attack planes on 12 January. They gained ground from the II./ and III./ *Grenadier Regiment* 290. Both battalions lost about two-thirds of their combat strength. The I./ *Grenadier Regiment* 290, however, held onto Hill 95.1. With the help of two Rumanian *Jäger* battalions that were inserted during the night, the remnants attempted to build a new line of resistance, with support by the II./ *Sturmgeschütz Brigade* 191. With the destruction of five enemy AFVs and the loss of one *Sturmgeschütz* the old main line of resistance was restored. The fighting also raged on the following days with *Schwerpunkten* at Hills 133.3 and 165.5. Soviet attacks alternated with German counterattacks. It was a struggle, but the German main line of resistance held.

This fighting, however, gnawed away at the forces of the 98th *Infanterie Division*, which caused the commander to point out in his report that the bounds of human capability and the maximum endurable attrition of the troops had been reached. The companies were at the end of their strength. The *Armee Korps*, however, emphasized the importance of regaining Hill 115.5 because that would allow shortening the northern wing of the main line of resistance that was hanging back. The 5th *Armee Korps* received orders to utilize the forces that would be freed up to carry out the penetration to Hill 115.5. The I./ *Grenadier Regiment* 282 [98th *Infanterie Division*], which had been pulled out of the harbour of Kertsch when relieved by Rumanian formations and the I./ and II./ *Grenadier Regiment* 123 [50th *Infanterie Division*] that had been intended for transfer to Perekop, thereupon undertook the operation under the cover-name 'Seestern', again with support by the I./ and II./ *Sturmgeschütz Brigade* 191 on 21 January 1944, doing so from Hill 165.5, from the west. Simultaneously *Füsilier Bataillon* 198 attacked from the south. It reached the southern slope of Hill 115.5, but then foundered in Soviet defensive fire with heavy losses. A Soviet relief attack brought Hill 133.3 back into Soviet hands. On the next day, however (22 January) Hill 133.3 was recaptured.

In their usual tactic of changing *Schwerpunkt* the Soviets landed troops again east of Kertsch at about midnight of 21/22 January under cover of fog, overran the III./ *Grenadier Regiment* 282 that was stationed there and landed in the harbour of Kertsch behind the south wing of the III./ *Grenadeir Regiment* 282. The entire southern wing of the German front in the Kertsch land-protrusion collapsed. The Soviets got into the eastern part of Kertsch. With that, the door to the Crimea was open to them. However, they did not utilize this success.

The 73rd *Infanterie Division* moved via rapid rail transport from the quiet Dnjepr position at Melewoje to Nikolajew and then by *Ju* 52 to Odessa and on in close formations by air to the Crimea. The I./ *Grenadier Regiment* 186 and *Pionier Bataillon* 173 immediately continued by lorry to Kertsch. This arrived there in time to prevent a catastrophe. Both formations immediately entered the battle in the morning of 22 January and, with remnants of *Grenadier Regiment* 282, built a new line of resistance along the course of the north-south axis and still held this on the following day. Additional reinforcements failed to arrive in time from the mainland because of bad weather conditions, which forced the Perekop and Siwasch front formations at the Kertsch front, two battalions of *Grenadier Regiment* 685 of the 336th *Infanterie Division* to give up ground.

On 24 January the Soviets attacked with their coastal army and forced the Rumanian forces committed in the Kertsch harbour area back to the south. With that the eastern part of the city of Kertsch was also lost. Granted, two battalions of *Grenadier Regiment* 685 again arrived by dribs and drabs and built a new German defensive front from the harbour mole along the railroad embankment of the Kamisch-Burin rail siding to the brickyard.

The German lines, however, proved to generally be too weak in relation to the Soviet superiority of forces. Nevertheless the Soviets failed to take advantage of this situation on 25 January for a decisive breakthrough, so the German formations were able to reinforce their line of defense and to repulse the ongoing attacks on 26 January.

See Map 98.

Additional elements of the 73rd *Infanterie Division* moved by air from Odessa to Dshankoi and Bagarowo, several battalions continuing by lorry to Kertsch. The Rumanians sent heavy artillery over the Black Sea. The train elements of the 370th *Infanterie Division* that had been forced aside into the Crimea in the Fall serviced the elements of the 73rd *Infanterie Division* that had been flown in.

On 6 February, in light of the losses suffered by the 98th *Infanterie Division*, all elements of the 73rd *Infanterie Division* were attached to the 5th *Armee Korps* in the Kertsch area. During the time from 1 November, 1943 until 31 January, 1944, the 98th *Infanterie Division* lost 12,363 men and received only 6,045 men of all ranks in replacements.

Preparations for an Attack on the Crimea

The evacuation of the Nikopol bridgehead by the 6th *Armee* on 6 February ended hopes for a German relief attack from there to the Crimea. Far more evident was the danger of the transfer of the Soviet formations that had been freed up to the Perekop front, consequently *Grenadier Regiment* 123 again shifted to this front. In ensuing days all fronts became quiet until mid-March, which the Soviets used to bring in new forces, both from the north to the Perekop front and also from the east over the isthmus of Kertsch.

Finally the fears were substantiated of a Soviet advance against the Crimea after the evacuation of Chersson and, thereby, of the area to the mouth of the Dnjepr at the Black Sea (13 March). With that the Soviets freed up additional forces to use against the Crimean front. In fact, two Tank Corps were ready facing the Perekop front (Tartar Wall and Siwasch front) and, in addition, the Soviet coastal army that had crossed into the Kertsch bridgehead.

Except for limited amounts, the reinforcements for the troops in the Crimea that Hitler had repeatedly promised never arrived. As the old year turned to the new *Sturmgeschütz Brigade* 279 moved by naval landing craft from Nikolajew to Eupatoria to the Crimea. Aside from men returning from leave, the troops could expect no further reinforcements. With the evacuation of the Nikolajew harbour it was easy to see that the imminent loss of the Odessa supply harbour would further complicate logistical support. The Rumanian Marshal Antonescu therefore renewed his demand for the evacuation of the Crimea, which Hitler refused.

After the new organization of the German southern front, namely into *Heeresgruppe 'Nord-Ukraine'* and *Heeresgruppe 'Süd-Ukraine'*, along with the recall of *Generalfeldmarschall* von Manstein and *Generalfeldmarschall* von Kleist, *Heeresgruppe Süd-Ukraine* with the 17th *Armee* on the Crimean Peninsula (*Generaloberst* Jänicke) was now under the orders of *Generaloberst* Schörner.

Before the revival of Soviet offensive operations the 111th *Infanterie Division* and remaining elements of the 73rd *Infanterie Division* moved by air and sea from Odessa to Eupatoria and the Crimea, along with ten *Sturmgeschütze* for *Sturmgeschütze Brigade* 279 and 12 *Sturmgeschütze* for *Sturmgeschütz Brigade* 191. Several motor vehicles, *Nebelwerfer* and light field howitzers followed. The battered formations, such as the 98th *Infanterie Division* received no significant replacement personnel or matériel support.

The Soviets finally faced the Perekop front (49th *Armee Korps*) with a concentration of 400-500 AFVs, the coastal army with 12 divisions and 100 AFVs ready to attack in the Kertsch bridgehead – both armies with support from an air-army totaling 2,000 aircraft.

Attack on the Northern Flank (Perekop and Siwasch Front)

See Map 101.

The Soviet offensive began on Good Friday, 7 April, with a local attack supported by strong Soviet aerial forces in the sector of the Rumanian 10th Infantry Division in the Karanki isthmus. German fighter planes and anti-aircraft shot down 29 aircraft. In weeks of work the Soviets had erected a causeway across the Siwasch whose surface, for concealment, was a few centimeters below the surface of the water. Over this causeway the Soviets brought motorized forces into the Karanki bridgehead, Tarchan and Urshin without difficulty, regardless of repeated disruption by German artillery and *Stuka* attacks. The advance in this eastern region brought with it the possibility of getting behind the German defense in the Tartar Wall line and cutting off its logistical support at Ishun. The Soviets gained ground around Karanki by successive landings east of Ashkadan. The 3rd *Batterie* of *Sturmgeschütz Brigade* 297 supported the Rumanians there, knocking out several Soviet AFVs.

The Soviet offensive opened on 8 April against the Perekop front, after strong preparation by artillery, mortars and multiple-rocket launchers, with its *Schwerpunkt* in the southernmost projection in the Soviet line north of Armjansk, the 'boil' in the front that projected across the Tartar Wall. Despite a temporary collapse of the infantry line, the Soviet advance was stopped by the *Sturmgeschützen*. North of Armjansk anti-aircraft, anti-tank and artillery knocked out 26 enemy AFVs, here, again, with participation by the railroad anti-aircraft train '*Muhr*'. A bypassing landing maneuver on the west coast foundered on the resistance of the German – Rumanian coastal security forces. However, the Soviets forced their way into the western part of Armjansk.

The German forces wanted to recapture this middle section in a counterattack with support from four *Sturmgeschützen*, one anti-tank platoon on self-propelled mounts and the railroad armoured train *'Michael'*. The II./ and III./ *Grenadier Regiment* 117 [111th *Infanterie Division*] as well as *Aufklärungs Abteilung* 150 and one pioneer company attacked, receiving later support from elements of *Grenadier Regiment* 123 and the I./ *Grenadier Regiment* 687 [336th *Infanterie Division*] from the east. The *Grenadiere* fought their way into the center of Armjansk by dark, but then were halted by a Soviet counterattack shortly before the Armjansk railroad station.

The Soviets simultaneously attacked on the Tschigary front (Karanki), this time against the Rumanians, without success. A hasty counterattack by the Rumanians on 9 April, with support from *Sturmgeschütze* did not get through and resulted in the loss of several *Sturmgeschütze*. The command pulled back the left wing of the Tartar Wall front back to the fortified Armjansk blocking position in order to shorten the line of defense. The Soviets immediately pressed their pursuit during the night into the sector of *Feldersatz Bataillon* 159 and the III./ *Grenadier Regiment* 122 until they ran into an anti-aircraft battery at Kula and *Sturmgeschütze*, which halted them. Immediately after the Armjansk blocking position was manned, the Soviets renewed their attack on Easter Sunday, with the *Schwerpunkt* against the Tuschulga – and Armjansk-blocking position. With powerful artillery support it was possible to repulse the Soviet attacks. Immediately two fresh Soviet regiments attacked west of Armjansk and now broke through the blocking position until a counterattack of the III./ *Grenadier Regiment* 122 forced the Soviets back and regained the lost artillery positions of the I./ *Artillerie Regiment* 150 and made possible the building of a new defensive front at Tschulga.

Armoured train *'Michael'* joined the battle several times and helped the troops that were already stretched thin. However, as the result of total Soviet superiority in the air, it took a direct hit from a bomb in the ammunition wagon, which put it out of service for several days. *Grenadier Regiment* 50, which had been brought in as reserve, helped strengthen the western sector. A Soviet attack from Armjansk to the east forced the withdrawal of the eastern wing, which was still jutting forward. The Rumanians also fell back at the Karanki front and left the *Sturmgeschütz Brigade* in the lurch. It then had to fight its way back to Tomashewka, to the rear, where *Grenadier Regiment* 70 of the 111th *Infanterie Division* built a blocking line. The 17th *Armee*, however, had to hold this isthmus at least as long as the 5th *Armee Korps* held the bridgehead front at Kertsch. The renewed evacuation proposal of the Commander in Chief of the 17th *Armee*, *Generaloberst* Jänicke, was again turned down by Hitler.

Further Soviet Advance

The further Soviet advance via Karanki – Tomashewka exposed at Nowo Alexandrowka the supply railroad for the formations farther to the west at Tarchan and Ishun. On 11 April the Soviets were already at Nowo Alexandrowka, thus at the Dshankoi – Armjansk railroad line. An immediate counterattack,

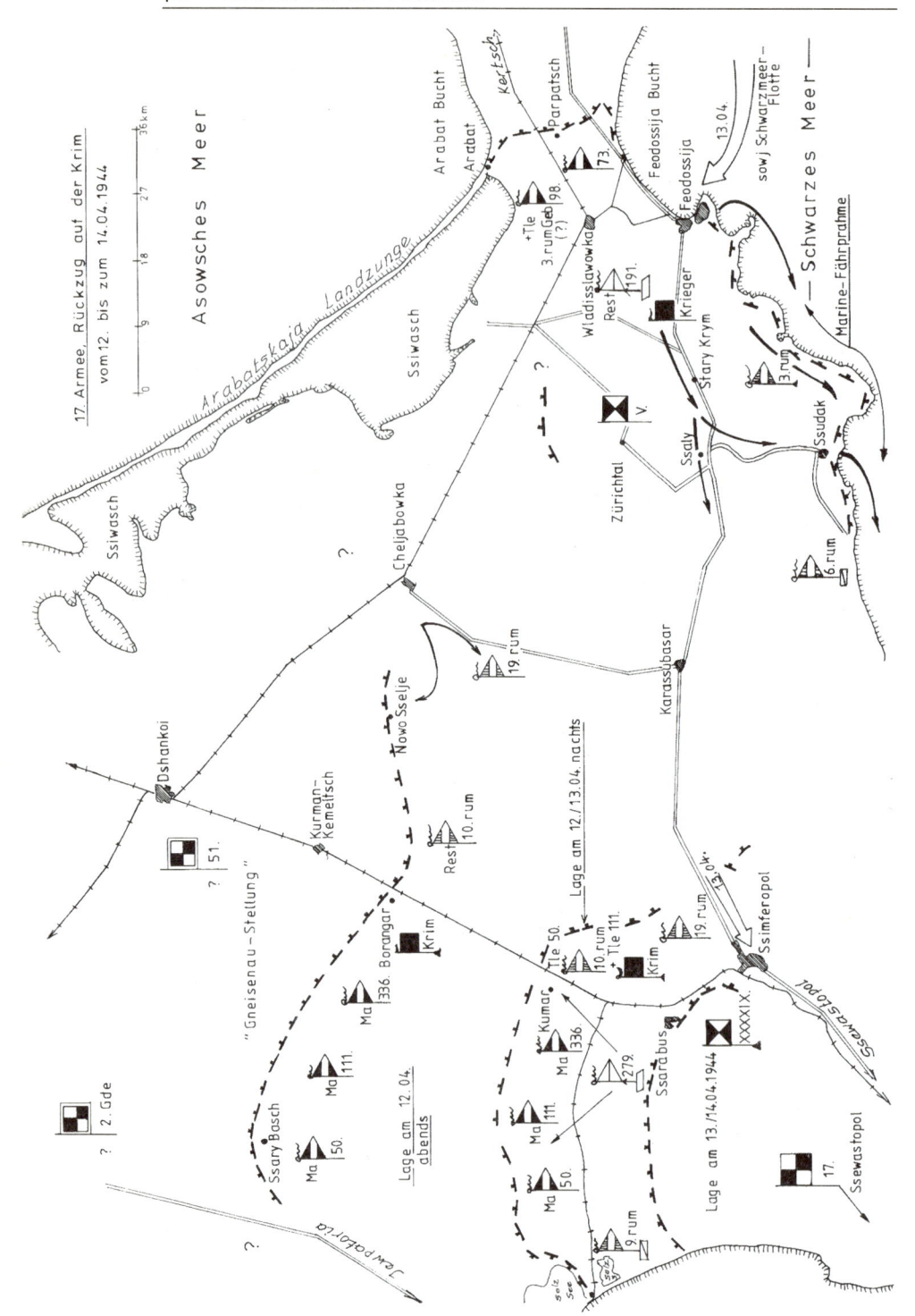

102. Withdrawal of the 17th *Armee* in the Crimea from 12 to 14 April, 1944. [*Sowj. Schwarzmeer-Flotte* = Soviet Black Sea Fleet].

however, came to a halt after gaining three kilometers of ground. Thus the way into the Crimean Peninsula east to Nowo Alexandrowka and beyond lay open for the strong formations that the Soviets had previously held back. This obviously threatened the evacuation plan for the 17th *Armee*.

Regardless of Hitler's attitude and without permission from *OKH* the 17th *Armee* immediately started the evacuation of the Crimea that had been planned under the cover-name 'Adler'. This could only be executed to the extent that it was possible to delay the Soviet advance at the northern front, and, indeed, where it appeared possible, namely at Ishun. For the formations that were in action there was a series of crisis situations. Regardless of the resistance put up by the 50th *Infanterie Division,* the 336th *Infanterie Division* and the 111th *Infanterie Division*, Soviet formations pushed into the Ishun bottleneck after the breakthrough at the Rumanian 10th Infantry Division to Dshankoi, then some turned in to the west in order to strike the Ishun defense from the rear. The endeavor of the formations to block the Tomashewka bottleneck with commitment of all *Sturmgeschütze* and mobile anti-aircraft batteries failed. The German forces proved no longer strong enough to carry out a counterattack. Hitler, however, refused to allow the northern front to be pulled back. At that moment this seemed justified in light of the formations of the 5th *Armee Korps* that were committed at the Kertsch front, which would first have to pass through the bottleneck north of Feodosia (Parpatsch – *Stellung* [position]).

See Map 101.

As ordered, the troop remnants retreating from the northern front built a makeshift new defensive front south of the straits. The situation became serious for *Grenadier Regiment* 121, because this regiment that had been temporarily cut off by the Soviets first had to fight its way back to Ishun in order to then slip into the Tschatyrlyk position.

The *Schwerpunkt* of the fighting, however, was again on the eastern wing of the northern front at Nowo Alexandrowka. Both armoured railroad trains repeatedly took part in this battle until the report arrived that the Soviets were closing in on Dshankoi. Both armoured trains then had to be immediately pulled back in order to avoid losing their route of retreat through this railroad junction.

At 0915 hours of that day the Soviets were already west of Dshankoi, whose railroad station was significant for transport to the rear from the Kertsch area. The 17th *Armee* therefore ordered the immediate occupation of the 'Gneisenau' position. While the Soviets pushed into Dshankoi, at the southern edge of the town the *Sturmgeschütze* of the 2nd *Batterie* of *Sturmgeschütz Brigade* 191 were being unloaded from the training and going right into action at the railroad station. However, locomotives that had steam up in the railroad station could no longer get out of the railroad station. Thereby the vital railroad junction fell into Soviet hands.

At this point Hitler's permission finally arrived to evacuate the Crimean Peninsula as far as Sewastopol. That granted the command of the 17th *Armee Korps* greater freedom of movement. If permission had been granted sooner the retrograde movement of the formations committed north of Kertsch could have taken place safely. Now, however, it was necessary to hold the northern front until all the Kertsch formations had made it past the Parpatsch

Holding the Northern Line

See Map 101.

Gebirgsjäger Regiment 'Krim', consisting of several *Feldausbildungs* [field-training] formations such as *Feldausbildungs Regiment* 23, *Feldausbildungs Regiment* 94 with *Jäger* – and artillery elements of the 4th *Gebirgs Division*, along with a bunch of local volunteers, was dispersed with substantial losses. Only 30 kilometers south of Dshankoi, at Kurman, the retreating remnants of the formation halted. The first troop remnants of the 5th *Armee Korps* that had been brought out of Kertsch were incorporated into the new defensive front.

After arriving, the remnants of the 49th *Armee Korps* occupied the Tschatyrlyk position, however with an open right flank. 30 – 40 kilometers south of this position the troops prepared a makeshift intermediate position with weak forces. Already in the morning of 12 April a serious crisis developed in the Tschatyrlyk position, consequently the troops commenced the retreat to the next *'Gneisenau'* position.

See Maps 101, 102, 103 and 104.

Thus, the 17th *Armee* retreat-plan *'Adler'*, which foresaw the evacuation in five stages, could no longer be executed and the troops had to attempt to oppose the Soviet advance by waves, so that the formations at the west wing of the northern front could retreat toward Sewastopol, as also for the retreating elements of the 5th *Armee Korps* south and north of the Jaila Mountains. The original Plan *'Adler'* had allowed six to seven days for the withdrawal. The troops, however, still had about 420 kilometers to go to reach Sewastopol.

See Map 101.

During the evacuation of the Tschatyrlyk position *Grenadier Regiment* 122 of the 50th *Infanterie Division* came into dire straits. Two battalions evacuated the position. The III./ *Grenadier Regiment* 122 fended off a Soviet attack at the mouth of the Tschatyrlyk, was cut off in the process, then broke through to the south and thus regained contact with German forces. As *Grenadier Regiment* 123 saw the adjoining regiment withdraw, it found itself prevented from evacuating the position because of an immediately impending enemy attack. To the rear was steppe, offering little cover. Therefore *Grenadier Regiment* 123 set up a hedgehog position around Woronzowo and broke through to the south during the night.

On the right wing of the 50th *Infanterie Division* in the river-bend near Dolinka was *Grenadier Regiment* 121, which was also falling back to the south under constant flanking fire with the last elements of the 336th *Infanterie Division* that had crossed its lines. At the east wing of the *Korps*, near the railroad to Sinferopol, the regiments of the 111th *Infanterie Division* marched to the south, *Grenadier Regiment* 50 on the west, *Grenadier Regiment* 117 in the center and *Grenadier Regiment* 70 to the east. Pursuing Soviet formations attempted to outflank these on both sides.

Considering this threat, the *Korps* offered the immediate continued movement into the *Gneisenau* position, which the formations of the 49th *Gebirgs Korps* reached by the evening of 13 April – in part with the help of columns of lorries.

The 5th *Armee Korps* Withdraws

Orders for the evacuation of the position and for individual formations to move out, leaving protective rear guards, arrived so suddenly that they did not reach all the formations simultaneously and completely. Thus various formations began to blow up their bunker positions and fire off or blow up the remaining ammunition, thereby revealing to the Soviets ahead of time the intention to withdraw, which stimulated them to immediate pursuit that same evening with armour and infantry.

One problem was that numerous artillery and anti-aircraft batteries did not have their own prime movers, but had to depend on the assistance of a transport group, which could not, however, carry out all the transports at the same time. A series of guns were entrained, later detraining in Seitler and then being sent on with tractors that had been brought there in the meantime. Other formations had to set out on foot.

The Rumanian 6th Mountain Division had the most favorable retreat route, utilizing the southern coastal road. However, it then had to deal with all the winding of this road caused by the shoreline, resulting in a longer march than that of the formations marching directly west from Kertsch. *See Map 103 and, for geography, Map 100.*

During the night a series of companies of the 73rd *Infanterie Division* and 98th *Infanterie Division*, as well as *Feldersatz Bataillon* 85 became intermingled and were dispersed or wiped out by the pursuing Soviet forces. With daylight the ground-attack planes strafed the march columns and Soviet armour pursued.

The evacuation plan intended that the formations would initially set up a defense in the *'Marienberg'* position. However, they arrived there in complete disorder, their timing disjointed so that there was no organized defense. Some of these formations met their fates in the Bagarowo and Dscheilow area, only a few of their soldiers later getting through to the west. The Soviets smashed *Grenadier Regiment* 213 [73rd *Infanterie Division*] as it resisted an armoured attack on Alexejewka. Here, too, only remnants reached the Parpatsch position. *Grenadier Regiment* 282 [98th *Infanterie Division*] and the 198th *Infanterie Division*, with support from the III./ *Artillerie Regiment* 198 reached the *Marienberg* position nearly entire. At the defensive *Schwerpunkt* at the railroad line at the Taschlyjar railroad station the Soviets thrust through between the 73rd *Infanterie Division* and 98th *Infanterie Division* in order to cut off the regiments. There they smashed the 8th *Kompanie* of *Grenadier Regiment* 282. Although the *Marienberg* position was not fully occupied, the Soviets zealously fired into it, especially around the Taschlyjar railroad station. The forces committed there received orders to withdraw further into the Parpatsch position. The III./ *Artillerie Regiment* 198 covered the further retreat, especially the displacement of the artillery of the I./ and II./ *Artillerie Regiment* 198 to the rear – to the extent that their ammunition allowed. When they, however, wanted to move to the rear and the limbers arrived, Soviet AFVs shot these to pieces so that the last guns had to be blown up and the artillerymen attempt to reach the Parpatsch position on foot along with *Grenadier Regiment* 282. *See Map 103.*

The further retreat followed on rutted and muddy stretches. Vehicles that got stuck were set on fire. At Katerles they were directly threatened by Soviet

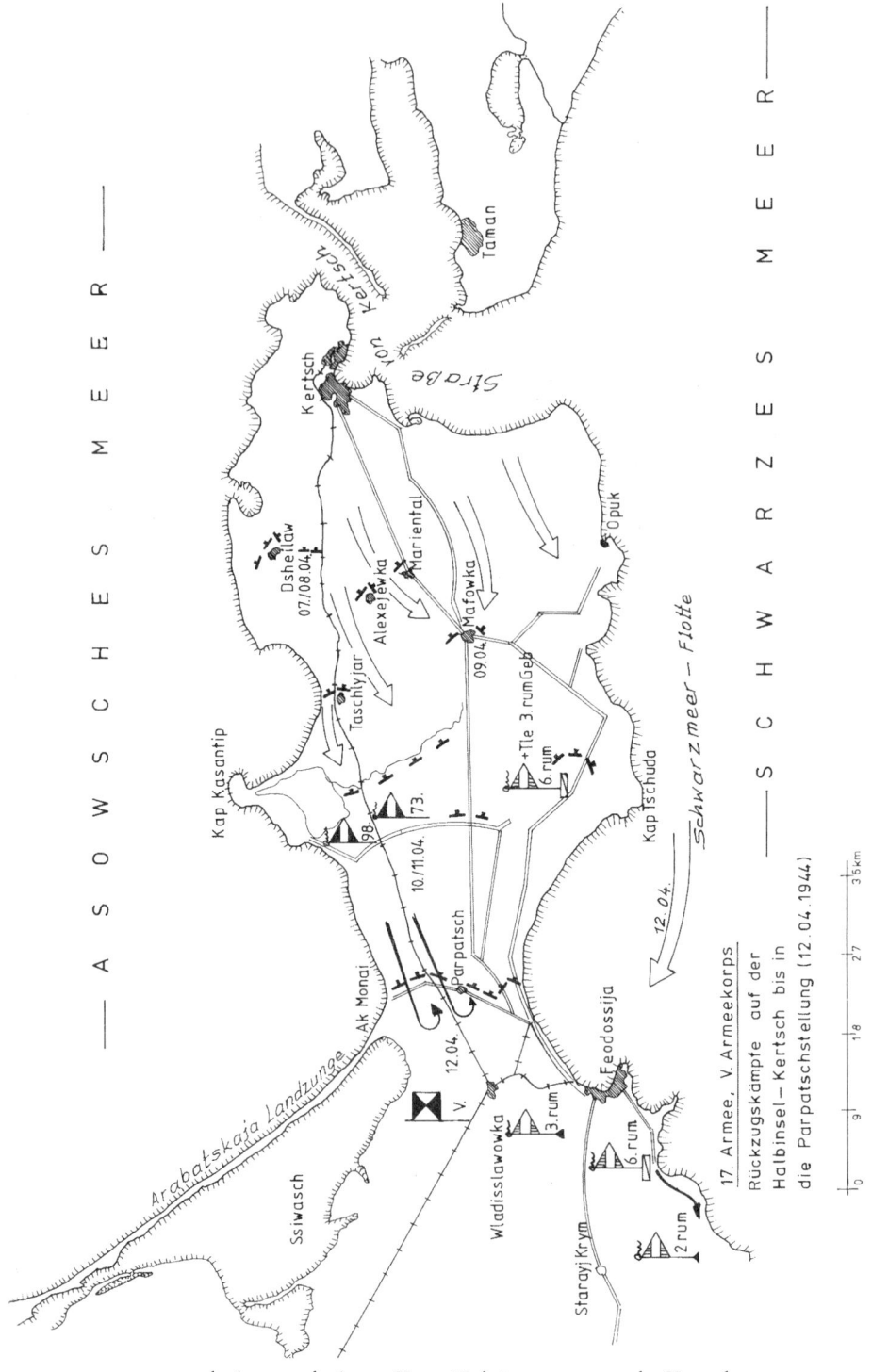

103. 17th *Armee*, 5th *Armee Korps*. Fighting retreat on the Kertsch peninsula to the Parpatsch position (12 April, 1944).

armour and thereby brought at night into total disorder. With daylight the Red Air Force strafed the column of march. One of the columns of lorries sent to bring back the formations from Bagaro came under fire from Soviet armour.

Under these circumstances the intended occupation of the intermediate position (A 2) behind the little Ssolarmi river failed, which forced an immediate continuation of the march to the Parpatsch position. Covered by the rearguard formed by *Sturmgeschütze Brigade* 101 remnants of *Grenadier Regiment* 282 and *Grenadier Regiment* 290 [all 98th *Infanterie Division*], as well as *Grenadier Regiment* 289 arrived in the Parpatsch position during the night and in the morning of 12 April. The last guns of the III./ *Artillerie Regiment* 198 served as the backbone of the resistance to cover the further withdrawal to the rear. The II./ *Artillerie Regiment* 198 knocked out 12 enemy AFVs in quarry terrain southeast of AK Monay. These batteries, too, had to finally blow up their guns.

The retreat route was more favorable for the Rumanian 3rd Mountain Division, with numerous Siebenbürger-Schwabians under command of the ethnic-German *General* Schwab. Elements of it were able to use the coastal road along the southern edge of the Crimea, undisturbed by the partisan bands that dominated the Jaila Mountains. By blowing up bridges to their rear they were able to prevent pursuit by enemy forces following them. That took place later, as yet other elements of the 5th *Armee Korps* used this march route.

See Maps 103 and 104.

The Formations of the 5th *Armee Korps* Retreat

The formations that came into the *Gneisenau* position, more or less disorganized, were merely those that reached Dshankoi or Seitler by rail or foot or by vehicle and, from there, marched to the south or west. Other formations fleeing the Parpatsch position to the west via Zürichtal – Karassubar strove toward Sinferopol. Soviet forces, however, bypassing *Gruppe Sixt* that had 'hedgehogged' in Sarabus, which it had been holding, had already reached Sinferopol in the evening of 13 April, thereby blocking the retreat route from Karassubasar to Sinferopol. Accordingly, the elements of the 5th *Armee Korps* that were initially marching, and also straggling elements tried the Ssyla – Ssudak mountain road through the Jaila Mountains in order to get to the southern coastal road. Involved were, among others, the trains elements of the 98th *Infanterie Division* and 73rd *Infanterie Division* and the 2./ *Sanitäts Abteilung* 173, which were attacked while marching west in Karassubasar, not only by regular troops but also by partisan bands.

See Map 102 and, for geography, Map 104.

Additional elements of the 73rd *Infanterie Division* of the 5th *Armee Korps* marched out of the Parpatsch position to the south toward Feodosia. Naval landing craft of the 1st *Landungsflottille* – covered by the 3rd *Artillerie-Träger-Flotille* there loaded whatever the ships could carry for transport to Balaklawa. In the gray dawn of 13 April, however, forces of the Soviet Black Sea Fleet landed there, which led to immediate evacuation of the Feodosia harbour and also of the city. Those march columns for whom the route to the coastal road was thus blocked had to follow the route via Stary Krim to Ssaly, north of the Jaila Mountains, where the paved Barguba – Stary Krim road lay open to them. They had to bypass the latter place, since it was already held by the enemy. Other formations of the 73rd *Infanterie Division* struck out to the southwest from the *Marienberg* position directly to Ssaly, in order to cross the Jaila Mountains from there toward Ssudak. They arrived in Ssudak with the logistical support columns that were flowing to the rear from Krassubasar, and also with units arriving via Barguba and around Stary Krim. Initially they formed a blocking line around Ssaly in order to secure the crossing over the mountains. This mission was undertaken by elements of the 98th *Infanterie Division*, with elements of the 73rd *Infanterie Division* to the east. One gun of *Panzerjäger Abteilung* 198 knocked out nine enemy AFVs there, thus preventing the Soviets from advancing into the first stretch of the road over the pass.

See Map 104.

Gruppen Schmidt (98th *Infanterie Division*) and *Graben* (73rd *Infanterie Division*) held the northern approach to the pass open until late afternoon, then followed the march groups of the 282nd and 290th [98th *Infanterie Division*], and remnants of *Grenadier Regimenter* 170, 186 and 213 [all three 73rd *Infanterie Division*] over the pass-road to the south. They arrived there after the Rumanian 3rd Mountain Division and Rumanian 6th Cavalry Division had already marched off to the west and left Ssudak. In Ssudak, too, naval landing craft embarked some of the marchers and carried them to Balaklawa. One blocking group, supported by *Sturmgeschütze*, held the area around Ssudak until the evacuation of the harbour, shortly before Soviet naval forces landed there. The march went on to Aluschta, again covered to the rear by the 1st *Batterie* of *Sturmgeschütz Brigade* 191 as rear guard. In Aluschta the march column met columns of lorries, which transported additional elements of the 98th *Infanterie Division* and 73rd *Infanterie Division* to Sewastopol. Also in Aluschta German naval landing craft again embarked elements and stragglers of the 98th *Infanterie Division*, but were fired on by Soviet armour as they departed.

The remaining march columns cleared out the rations warehous in Jalta, constantly sought out by aerial attack and fired on by partisan bands, until they, too, reached the mainland from Sewastopol. Units of the Rumanian mountain corps that had been sent ahead secured this area until the arrival of the rest of the 5th *Armee Korps* on 16 and 17 April –however, the latter troops arrived with almost no heavy weapons and no heavy equipment.

Retreat of the 49th *Gebirgs Armee Korps*

See Map 104.

During this time the 49th *Gebirgs Armee Korps* carried out its retreat from Dshankoi to Sinferopol. The Soviet pursuit essentially followed both sides of the railroad line. For the German formations it became a matter of delaying this pursuit, particularly to win time for the additional formations striving to reach Eupatoria. The *Sturmgeschütze* received the mission of repulsing the Soviet mass of armour. On 12 April they succeeded in doing this in a defensive position 20 kilometers north of Sarabus until the threat of being outflanked forced them to retreat to Sarabus. The *Luftwaffe* helped in forcing back the enemy armour that had penetrated the place with bombing by *Kampfgeschwader* 27 from the Sarabus airfield. The counterattack against the advancing Soviet armoured spearheads resulted in knocking out 44 Soviet AFVs and clearing the enemy from Sarabus.

This place was considered the eastern pillar of the *Gneisenau* position. Therefore it had to be held until the last straggler arrived from the direction of Eupatoria. In the meantime the western wing of the 49th *Gebirgs Armee Korps* strove in forced marches on 13 April to reach the *Gneisenau* line that was fixed around Sinferopol to Eupatoria. In the meantime the Soviets launched a major attack on Sarabus, initially from the north, then from the east and west. In accord with their mission, the German troops formed a hedgehog position, thereby allowing the *Luftwaffe* to fly the last wounded out of the Sarabus airfield. Armoured train *'Michael'* rolled off to Sinferopol. The *'Muhr'* anti-aircraft train, however, remained. *Kampfgruppe 'Sixt'* which had been fighting in a hedgehog position then broke out to the west and, with the 2nd *Batterie* of *Sturmgeschütz Brigade* 191 as its spearhead, broke through via Bulganak to the German lines.

One *Schwerpunkt* of the Soviet advance became evident around Kambary between Ssaki and Karatscha-Kangi, where the Soviets broke through the center of the *Gneisenau* position to the west toward Kara Tobe, blocking the retreat route from Eupatoria to Ssaki. Simultaneously an enemy group thrust forward from Eupatoria by Temesch toward Ssaki behind the *Gneisenau* position, where encountered *Aufklärungs Abteilung* 150. The 49th *Gebirgs Armee Korps* thereupon ordered all formations to take the retreat route to Sewastopol via several intermediate positions near Ssaki, where *Artillerie Regiment* 150 again stopped a Soviet armoured spearhead, with the loss of several guns. The first units of the 49th *Gebirgs Armee Korps* reached the old positions of the former 'Fortress Sewastopol' during the night of 13/14 April.

See Map 104.

Remnants of the regiments of the 49th *Gebirgs Armee Korps* marched through the Alma valley, other formations through the Belbek valley in order to keep the retreat route along the coast free of the enemy. The regiments of the 336th *Infanterie Division* and 111th *Infanterie Division* reached the line of the Sewastopol fortifications by forced marches in the evening of 14 April while the rear guards were still slugging it out with the pursuing Soviets.

38

The Battle of Sewastopol

The Situation before the Battle of Sewastopol

Despite feverish construction work it was impossible in so short a time to restore the defensive installations of the former Fortress Sewastopol that had been destroyed when the fortress was stormed in 1941. In order to screen the construction of positions the command initially hoped to stop the Soviet forces before they reached the lines of the fortress, and to do so with two infantry battalions, six anti-aircraft batteries, the remnants of *Sturmgeschütz Brigaden* 191 and 279 as well as the anti-aircraft-armoured-train *'Muhr'*. The defense began on the hill position north of Bachtschissary, where the defensive forces achieved successes on 15 and 16 April, knocking out nine enemy AFVs. This initially brought the Soviets to a halt and granted the retreating regiments of the 49th *Gebirgs Armee Korps* and 5th *Armee Korps* a valuable head start. That denied the Soviets fulfillment of their intentions of reaching the fortress area of Sewastopol before the arrival of the German formations.

The command and troops, however, had to organize for further defensive fighting, because Hitler ordered that Sewastopol be held. That proved hopeless from the start, in light of the weakness of the formations that had made it back to the fortress. 30 percent of the artillery and nearly 75 percent of the anti-tank weapons of the retreating forces of the 17th *Armee* were lacking. It was thanks to the navy and its landing craft that the remaining anti-aircraft and artillery pieces were saved. During the retreat they had transported nearly 10,000 men with weapons and equipment from the harbours of the south coast to Balaklawa. On the other side, during the fighting retreat in Crimea, according to German reports, the Soviets had lost 464 AFVs and 232 aircraft. These losses may well have caused them to initially make systematic preparations for the attack on Sewastopol and to bring up reinforcements.

The manpower of the 17th *Armee* had significantly diminished, according to rations reports, from 235,000 men on 9 April to 124,233 men on 18 April (78,000 Germans and 46,000 Rumanians). During the period from 12 to 20 April the Navy and *Luftwaffe* transported 67,000 men to Rumania, including 36,000 Germans, 16,000 *Ostlegionäre*, 3,800 prisoners, 1,600 civilians and 9,600 Rumanians. German losses during that period amounted to 13,131 men (1,253 killed, 4,125 wounded, 6,987 missing, 763 ill) and 17,652 Rumanians.[1]

On 16 April the fighting strength of the Sewastopol formations amounted to only 9,231 German and 10,360 Rumanian soldiers, or the strength of about two divisions. The personnel shortages of the German divisions included 22% of the 50th *Infanterie Division*, 79% of the 73rd *Infanterie Division*, 43% of the 98th *Infanterie Division*, 67% of the 111th *Infanterie Division* and 23% of the

---

1   Numbers from Tieke, *Kampf um die Krim*.

336th *Infanterie Division*. During the Soviet defense of the fortress, when it was in good condition, in the summer of 1942 the Soviets had eight divisions with several independent brigades, totaling about 100,000 men – this in comparison with the more recent German strengths. Moreover, the German defense had to be conducted from the old Soviet positions with destroyed works. Therefore men worked feverishly to construct a new line of defense. In any case, there was no way that the defensive forces could attain the strengths of the 1942 Soviet defense.

After the return of the remnants of the 5th *Armee Korps* the line of defense around Sewastopol consisted of the 73rd *Infanterie Division* in the right front sector, adjoined by the 111th *Infanterie Division*, then the 98th *Infanterie Division*, together with *Kampfgruppen* of the Rumanian 3rd Mountain Division, Rumanian 19th Infantry Division, Rumanian 6th Cavalry Division and Rumanian 9th Cavalry Division. In addition there were the *Kampfbataillone* of the *Luftwaffe*. The 49th *Gebirgs Armee Korps* held its lines with the 336th *Infanterie Division* and 50th *Infanterie Division*, these together with hastily formed *Kampfgruppen* of the Rumanian 1st and 2nd Mountain Divisions, the Rumanian 10th Infantry Division and corps troops of the Rumanian 1st Mountain Corps, as well as naval *Kampfbataillonen*.

Regardless of this limited manning of the front, reserves had to be ready in order to launch immediate counterattacks in the event that the German lines were penetrated. A series of motley alarm companies of various arms of service stood by for this purpose.

Although, as a former fortress, Sewastopol enjoyed a certain reputation, without adequate manpower and armament it did not appear defensible against the superior Soviet forces. The Rumanian Commander in Chief, Antonescu, and the Commanding General of the Rumanian *Gebirgs Korps*, Schwab, therefore pressed anew for transport of the Rumanians to Rumania, the more so since, according the reports of the 17th *Armeeoberkommando*, their defensive strength was shaken.

The Battle of Sewastopol

The Command of the 17th *Armee* directed the defense of Sewastopol down to the tiniest detail, especially the consolidation of all soldiers that were in any way dispensable, whether they were *Luftwaffe*, *Marine* or *Heere*. The orders that were prepared, however, made no reference to any later evacuation of Sewastopol and the transport of troops to Rumania. That was what the troops were hoping for, especially after the example of the successful evacuation of the Kuban bridgehead.

Preparatory attacks ensued on 14 and 15 April, stronger attacks on 16, 17 and 18 April against the northern front. Despite active aerial reconnaissance and attacks by Soviet ground-attack planes, the Soviets gained no successes. Artillery fire on Sewastopol *Flugplatz* [airfield] III, however, forced the transfer of the German fighters to Cherssones. Anti-aircraft and fighter planes shot down 12 enemy aircraft on 17 April. Reconnaissance revealed systematic Soviet concentration. Strong enemy aerial reconnaissance suggested intensive preparations. The German fighters shot down 36 enemy aircraft on 19 April.

German *FW* 190 fighter-bombers destroyed 23 enemy aircraft on the Sinferopol airfield and bombed Soviet supply links.

The Soviet 51st Army Offensive

On 23 April the awaited offensive of the Soviet 51st Army began, initially against the northern front, with strong support from artillery and from the air. Heavy fighting developed at the 'High Road' at the south edge of the Belbek valley and around the *'Ölberg'* ['Mount of Olives'], which changed hands several times in the ensuing days. However, the Soviets achieved a deep penetration in a sector held by the Rumanians with anti-aircraft support and *Aufklärungs Abteilung* 150, as well as the III./ *Grenadier Regiment* 122. Reserve groups regained the old main line of resistance in a hasty counterattack. The artillery of armoured train *'Michael'*, which hid in a railroad tunnel and emerged for action, joined in the battle for the Belbek heights, the *'Ölberg'* and the *'Bunkerberg'* on 24 April. The hill positions were regained in heavy fighting.[2]

While the Soviets kept receiving constant reinforcements in the northern sector, the Germans lacked usable reserves. On 27 April the hotly contested *'Ölberg'* changed hands twice and remained, in the evening of that day, held by the Germans.

That same day the Soviet coastal army also joined the fighting, where the remaining 20 *Sturmgeschütze* of the two *Sturmgeschütze Brigaden* 191 and 279 provided valuable support for the 73rd *Infanterie Division* in the battle against attacking Soviet armour. On that and the following day (28 April) the line of defense held, with the loss of ten German *Sturmgeschütze*. The Soviets failed to achieve any penetration into the Sapun-hill position against the remnants of the 73rd *Infanterie Division,* 111th *Infanterie Division*, 98th *Infanterie Division* and three Rumanian *Gebirgsjäger* regiments.

A new presentation of *Generaloberst* Schörner and *General* Allmendinger at the *Führer* Headquarters failed to bring about the desired decision from Hitler. He merely promised reinforcements and provision of more weapons. Sewastopol would have to hold about eight weeks, until the expected impending western invasion had been repulsed. The Commander in Chief of *Armeeoberkommando* 17, *Generaloberst* Jänicke, complained to *Heeresgruppe Süd-Ukraine* by teletype that only a morsel had arrived of the four promised battalions, which in no way matched the ongoing losses.

Hitler, however, stuck by his *'Nein'*. *Generaloberst* Jänicke, himself, flew yet again to Berchtesgaden to persuade Hitler. Hitler however decided that Sewastopol would have to be held to the last man who could be brought in. On his way back to Crimea Jänicke found his discharge orders and prohibition that he return to Crimea.

Regardless of Hitler's attitude, *Armeeoberkommando* 17 continued to prepare for the evacuation of Sewastopol (*Studie 'Leopard'*), which involved the *Luftwaffe* and the *Marine*. According to this plan the ships that brought

---

2   Translator's note – Many of the names of fortifications and significant locations come from the days of the Crimean War of 1853 to 1856 between Russia and Great Britain, France, The Ottoman Empire and Sardinia, where the Siege of Sewastopol was the center of world interest.

the daily 600 tons of supplies to Sewastopol were to take back with them unnecessary personnel. Upon the arrival of permission to evacuate Sewastopol, within 24 hours the *Marine* was to carry out the evacuation by sea. The plan also planned details of the conduct of the fighting around Sewastopol, initially with the evacuation of the northern front and the retreat of the 5th *Armee Korps* to the Cherssones position, while embarking the units that were freed up for sea transport. In the last stage 26,000 men were to leave Crimea by sea, 4,500 men by air.

The Final Soviet Offensive

In the meantime the Soviets prepared a new offensive, which, unfortunately, led to the replacement of several German commanders just before its start. The Germans expected the *Schwerpunkt* of the attack to be northeast of the Kamyschly ravine in the southern sector at the road-saddle and on the Sapun heights. As for the promised replacements, by 30 April only 2,647 men had arrived, against the departure of 4,836 wounded. By 12 May another two march battalions with 1,300 men had arrived, along with 15 heavy anti-tank guns, ten howitzers [210 mm or larger, *Mörser*], four heavy field howitzers and several mortars and infantry guns. Thereupon the Red Army set up a blockade of the fortress area, which led to the loss of 15 enemy aircraft over the sea and 19 over the fortress area. The German *Marine* mourned the loss of seven lighters and tugs. That, however, did not significantly impact the traffic by sea.

The Soviets opened 5 May with an extravagant artillery preparation from 400 tubes with support from 400 multiple-rocket launchers upon the sector of the main line of resistence between the *'Ölberg* and the *B-Stellen-Berg* [Observation-Point Hill], primarily against the hill position of the motley 336th *Infanterie Division*. The Red Air Force kept 40 aircraft constantly in the air for support.

The *'B-Stellen-Berg'* was finally lost. The next night the Soviets also broke through to the *'Bunker-Berg'* until a counterattack allowed construction of a blocking front between the *'B-Stellen-Berg'* and the *'Bunker-Berg'*. An enemy attempt to break through with armour in the ravine east of the *'Ölberg'* collapsed with the destruction of seven Soviet AFVs. The commitment of the Red Air Force mounted on the following day with up to 60 aircraft constantly in the air, of which German fighter planes shot down 34, anti-aircraft ten. The massed firepower of the Soviet artillery and air force, however, together with repeated attacks against the northern sector, led to the melt down of German infantry defensive strength to one-third of its establishment.

On the morning of 7 May, after a hail of about 80,000 artillery shells, the Soviet coastal army also attacked with infantry and armour, supported by ground-attack planes. The main thrust was directed along the Kamary – Nikolajewka road to the road-saddle at the south foot of the Sapun Heights. A series of hill positions, the *'Adlersdorf'* [Eagle's Village] and *'Adlerhöhe'* [Eagle Hill] held. Farther south, however, the Soviets achieved a penetration of *Grenadier Regiment* 186 [73rd *Infanterie Division*] and *Grenadier Regiment* 213 [73rd *Infanterie Division*], also north of the *'Adlershöhe'* at *Grenadier Regiment* 70 of the 111th *Infanterie Division*. They forced the German defensive forces

438 CRUCIBLE OF COMBAT

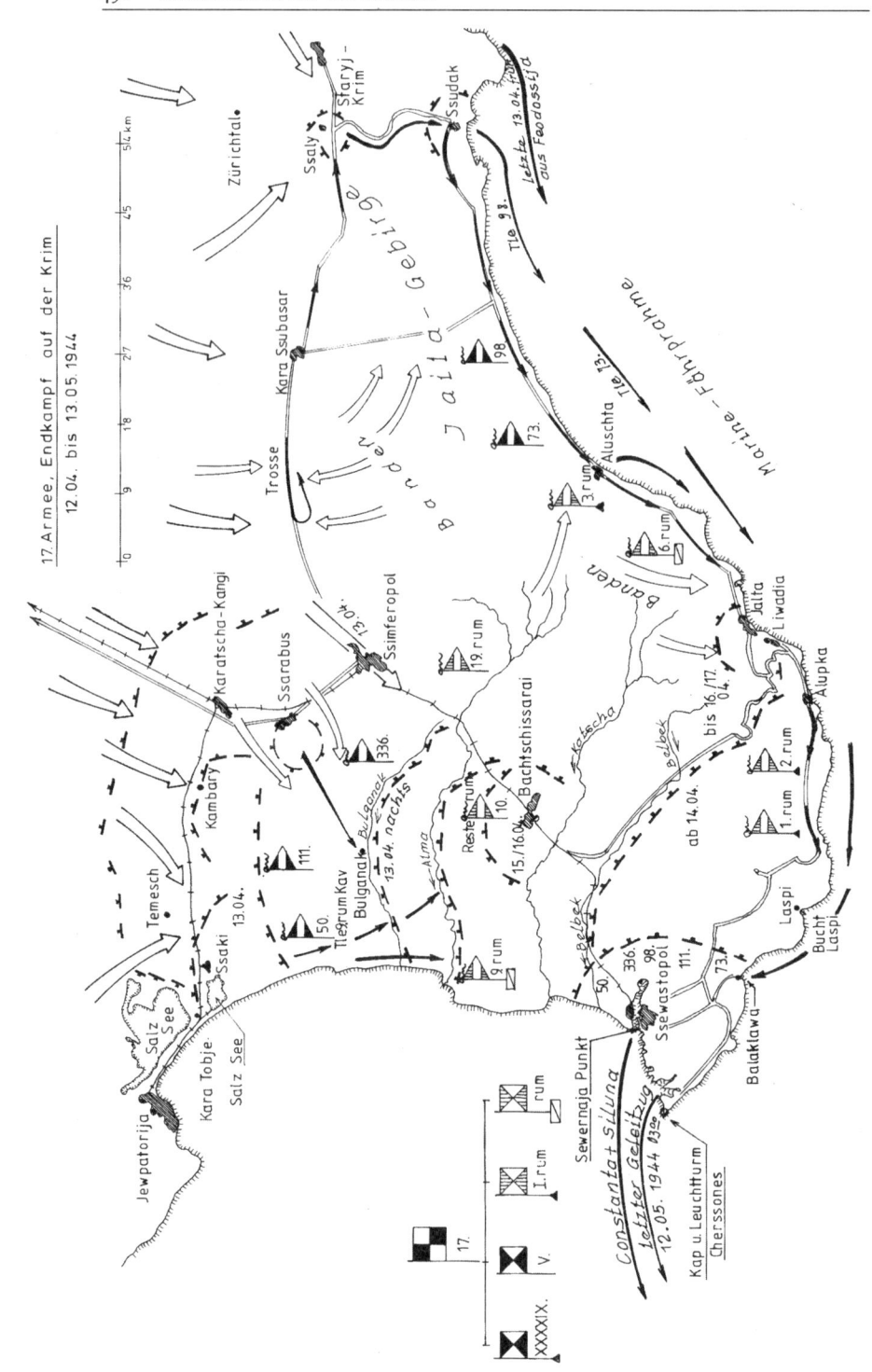

104. 17th *Armee*, Final Battle in the Crimea, 12 April to 13 May, 1944. [*Letzter Geleitzug* = last convoy; *Kap u. Leichtturm* = cape and lighthouse; *Tal* = valley].

gradually back. Regardless of the repeatedly formed blocking positions, as at the *Serpentinen* [Winding Road] and between the *Serpentinen* and Sewastopol, the Soviets kept pressing forward in other sectors, as at the English Cemetery and at the Jalta Road, and finally forced back the German lines at the *Serpentinen*. A hasty counterattack delivered with reserves in the afternoon of that day failed.

The Soviets captured the *'Hohe Batterie'* [High Battery] at the Balaklawa Bay on the right wing, until their attack foundered east of Karan. *Grenadier Regiment* 170 continued to hold out on the *'Adlerhöhe'*, though enveloped on both sides. The Soviets gained a dangerous penetration over the *'Kalkberg'* [Chalk Hill] directly west of Kadykowka toward the *'Straßensattel'* [road-saddle]. This breakthrough raised the danger of the German line of defense being rolled up from both ends. With the help of the last *Sturmgeschütze* of *Sturmgeschütz Brigaden* 191 and 279 the reserves of the 73rd *Infanterie Division* closed the front again at the southern foot of the Sapun Heights. At the road-saddle, too, the reserves that were committed locally reached the old main line of resistance. The Soviets, however, bypassed the advanced islands of defense, *'Adlerhöhe'*, *'Windmühle'* [windmill] and *'Bügelberg'* [Stirrup Hill], so that, in light of the diminution in German forces the final Soviet breakthrough had to be immediately impending.

Evacuation of the German Positions

In the sector of the 49th *Gebirgs Armee Korps* there were similar *Schwerpunkte* to the Soviet advance on 7 May around the *'Buhse-Bunker'* and *'Ölberg'*. The Red Air Force was again in action on a large scale, resulting in 123 Soviet aircraft being shot down on 7 May. However, there were no more German reserves available in this sector. One march battalion arrived by sea that day at Sewastopol, which, however, could not alter the situation. The command of *Armeeoberkommando* 17 therefore decided to pull back the northern front in order to use the formations that would thereby be freed up against the impending breakthrough on the southern front. This took place in two phases under the cover-name *'Wildkatze'*. The *Marine* opposed this movement because it would result in the loss of the loading installations in the harbour of Sewastopol and the *Marine* would have to load at the makeshift facilities in the bay of the Cherssones Peninsula. Hitler likewise opposed execution of this operation. *Generalfeldmarschall* Schörner nevertheless reported to *OKH* that the front of the 5th *Korps* had collapsed and the Commander in Chief of the 17th *Armee*, *General* Allmendinger, had therefore ordered execution of Operation *'Wildkatze'*. In order to avoid the collapse of the entire defense of Sewastopol, the Sapun Heights, with their opportunities for observation of the Cherssones Peninsula had to be retaken and naval ships set in motion to transport about 20,000 men to Rumania.

The optimistic evaluation of the situation by *Heeresgruppe Süd* prevented further preparations for evacuation of the entire garrison of the Sewastopol area.

On 8 May *'Adlerhöhe'*, which had been held until then by remnants of *Grenadier Regiment* 170, was lost. The survivors were taken prisoner. The

Soviets bypassed the *'Windmühle'* and *'Bügel-Berg'.* The remnants of *Grenadier Regiment* 186 [73rd *Infanterie Division*] that had been holding these positions fought their way through to the German lines with losses. The same was true for *Grenadier Regiment* 50 [111th *Infanterie Division*] at the *Serpentinen*.

On 8 May the 50th *Infanterie Division* evacuated the harbour-protection position at the north edge of the Sewernaja Bay after laying mines on the north shore and destruction of the harbour facilities.

As the result of errors in instructions, several ships proceeded into the harbour of Sewastopol. The *Marine* was unable to warn them in time and redirect them in the heavy fog. Soviet artillery destroyed them.

On 9 May *Generalfeldmarschall* Schörner tried again to get permission from Hitler for the immediate evacuation of Crimea. This permission finally arrived, but, again, with conditions that made it difficult to execute. These required that the Cherssones position must be held and, if possible, the Nikolajewka position in order to avert enemy influence on the embarkation points. The *Armee* command had to continue to win time for the arrival of the evacuation fleet, which had to traverse 400 kilometers by sea from Rumania.

At that time all that were facing the 24 Soviet rifle divisions, one rifle brigade, eight armoured formations and three artillery division with 1,100 tubes were the remnants of five former divisions with 200 tubes, half of which were without ammunition. The outcome was, thus, predictable. The Soviet Air Force, however, held back on 9 May, probably as the result of the heavy losses of the preceding days. Nevertheless, is still had 56 planes shot down. The hoped for recapture of the Sapun Heights failed, so that the intended objective of Operation *'Wildkatze'* could not be attained.

On 9 May 120 anti-aircraft and artillery tubes were available, with a scanty supply of ammunition. From the high ground around Karan and from the *'Windmühlen-Berg'* [Windmill Hill] the Soviets could observe the southern part of the Cherssones Peninsula. A German counterattack to recapture the Nikolajewka position between the *'Englischer Friedhof'* ['English Cemetery'] and *'Weingut Nikolajewka'* [Nikolajewka Vineyard] merely led to regaining the vineyard, but came to a standstill at the edge of the cemetery. Soviet heavy weapons dominated the cemetery area. In the afternoon the Soviets attacked to the west from the cemetery. Defense seemed hopeless against their strong forces, so the German remnants fell back through the tank-ditch ravine. In other sectors the situation was similar. Similarly, the concentrated defense at the south shore of the Sewernaja Bay collapsed against enemy forces that landed. In the south the blocking position at the Giorgiewskiy Cloister collapsed. With that, on 9 May the entire German defensive front was in movement, which led to a costly state of confusion.

After the collapse of the front of the 5th *Armee Korps* the 49th *Gebirgs Korps* assumed command in the Cherssones position and finally held this against the pursuing Soviets. The Cherssones airfield then came in range of the Soviet artillery, whereupon the last German fighter planes had to head for the mainland. Henceforth the troops lacked fighter protection. A Soviet bombing attack transformed the Cherssones airfield into a crater-field during the night of 9/10 May. Only bold *Ju*-52 pilots could still land and take out wounded.

Embarkation of the Last Formations

The 17th *Armee* command pressed for immediate dispatch of additional shipping space for 35,000 men. Shipping for only 20,000 men was then at sea and was to arrive before Cherssones during the night of 9/10 May. The prerequisite for embarkation of the last formations was gaining time and, for that purpose, holding the Cherssones position. Additional convoys set out on 9 May from Konstanz and Sulina with space for 25,000 men. The earliest that these could arrive before Cherssones would be during the night of 10/11 May. Four more convoys followed on 11 May. With that, German and Rumanian warships and commercial cargo ships were at sea with a carrying capacity of 87,000 men. Soviet long-range reconnaissance identified these convoys promptly. German long-range fighter formations could only provide fighter cover to about 100 kilometers short of the Crimean coast. The Soviet Air Force ruled this intervening space uncontested.

During the night of 9/10 May foul weather suddenly set in with force 7–8 winds, scattering the convoys and forcing smaller ships to turn back. The first transport group arrived before the Cherssones Peninsula in the morning hours of 10 May. It stood by two sea miles offshore, beyond the range of the Soviet artillery. *Siebel* ferries [landing craft constructed on two pontoons serving a wide variety of functions, sometimes heavily armed] and pioneer landing craft commenced the embarkation. The Red Air Force did not miss this opportunity. They attacked the German craft in the offshore area with 30 to 40 bombers and torpedo planes, 25 times in 13 hours. Several ships that were already loaded took direct hits and ran aground. These losses forced the *Marine* to greater caution, which delayed the embarkation. Therefore, during the night of 10/11 May, only a few forces were embarked.

In the meantime the Cherssones front still held with 50 tubes – poorly supplied with ammunition – while the Soviet artillery covered every point in the five kilometer deep Cherssones bridgehead, with particular concentrations of fire on the embarkation points. Due to the delays the troops were ordered to hold the position an additional 24 hours against the substantial Soviet pressure. With the help of anti-aircraft guns a *Kampfgruppe* of the 73rd *Infanterie Division* knocked out 20 AFVs. The strength of the troops on 10 May was estimated at 30,000 men. Initially rear area services, staffs and the like were transported out. *Ju* 52 transports brought back over 1,000 waiting wounded from the grievously damaged Cherssones airfield during the night of 10/11 May.

On 11 May troop remnants in the Cherssones position repulsed no less than seven Soviet attacks. Soviet artillery fire on the German positions intensified, finally also including the hinterland of the peninsula. The remnants of the 98th *Infanterie Division* repulsed a subsequent attack, whereupon the Soviets stopped further attacks for the time being.

At about 2130 hours of that day the first groups withdrew from the Cherssones position and went for embarkation at the bay. At that time there were adequate ships in the roads to embark all the troops. The transports, however, did not find the way into the bay as a result of the loss of the navigation system and an unintended smokescreen resulting from the artillery fire, made worse by the loss of the beacon on the Cherssones point.

442 CRUCIBLE OF COMBAT

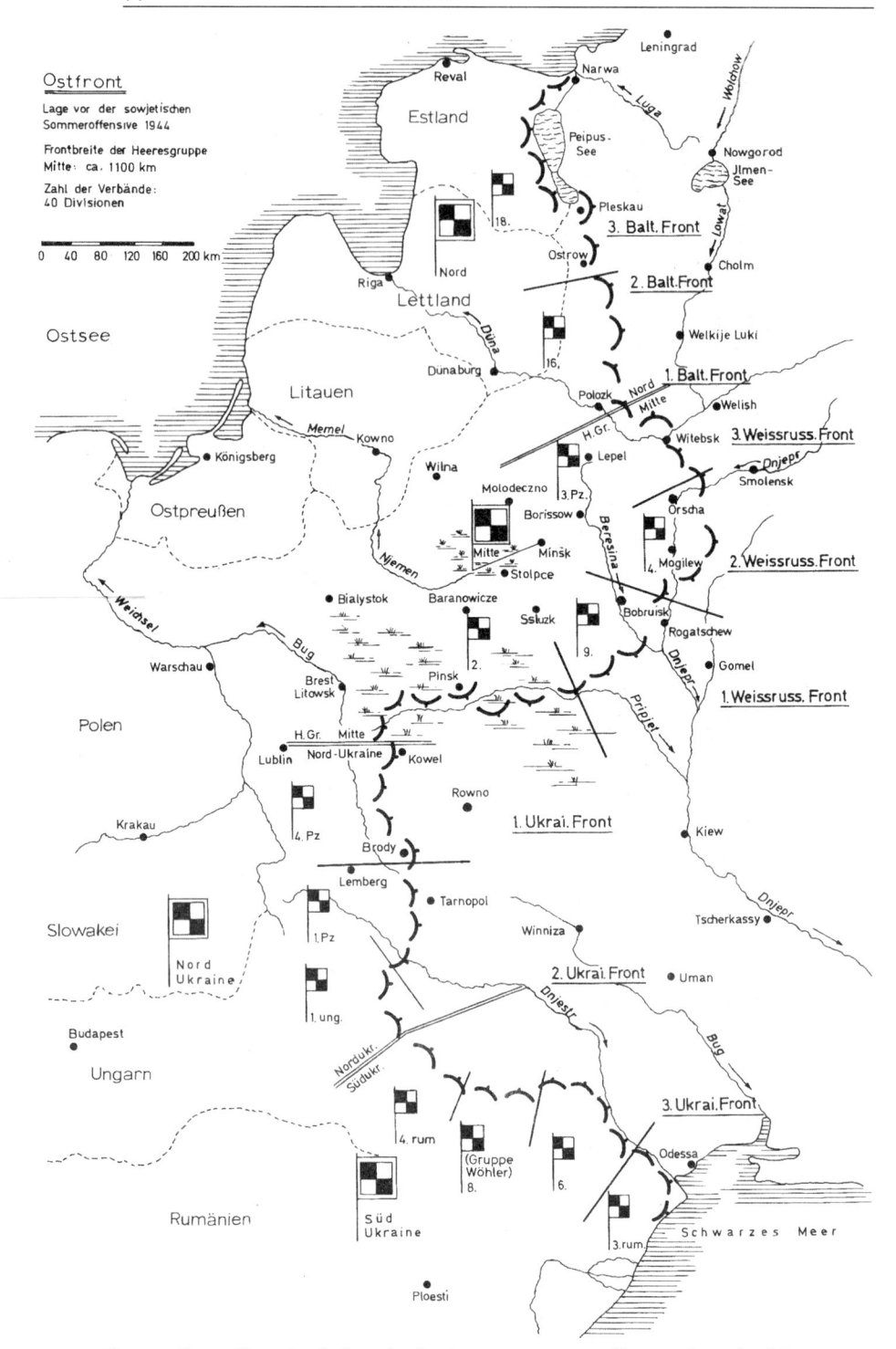

105. Eastern Front. Situation before the Soviet 1944 summer offensive. Length of front of *Heeresgruppe Mitte*: about 1,100 kilometers. Number of formations: 40 Divisions.

Artillery and *Nebelwerfer* in the Cherssones position delivered a powerful sudden concentration of fire to demonstrate to the Soviets the defensive force that was still there, and then joined to march to the embarkation points.

In the morning of 12 May *Siebel* ferries and naval landing craft and assault boats landed again and embarked troops to the limit of their capacity. They had to halt their activity, however, due to the Soviet aerial attacks to be expected when it became light. At that point it became necessary to re-occupy the Cherssones position, but that was no longer possible.

The *Marine* issued orders that all convoys that arrived off Sewastopol after 0200 hours were to turn around and perform only rescue-at-sea. This was due not only to the fear of Soviet artillery fire on the transports but also a result of the Soviet aerial attacks that could be expected in the roughly 100 kilometer zone where German fighters could not provide cover. The last convoy departed the Cherssones sea area at about 0300 hours on 12 May. This convoy also lost a steamer to Soviet aerial bomb and torpedo attacks. Torpedo boats of the 1st *Schnellboote-Flotille* followed at 0330 hours. A damaged sub-chaser sank itself. Another steamer hit by bombs was towed to Konstanza. A Soviet submarine that broke through the naval security line torpedoed a steamer.

The great attack that was expected from the Soviet Air Force against the landing fleet and the bridgehead on 12 May, however, failed to take place. Now, however, no more German ships arrived, which left the German troop remnants no alternative but to raise the white flag.

The 50th *Infanterie Division* still defended its embarkation point and repulsed the last Soviet attack at about 0900 hours. Guns of *Artillerie Regiment* 150 and two self-propelled anti-tank guns knocked out two Soviet AFVs at about 1000 hours. Two hours later these groups, too, stopped fighting at about 1200 hours.

Isolated troops fought their way through to the extreme end of the point and hid themselves in caves and scree. German long-range aerial reconnaissance identified such groups at the installations at about 1500 hours. Torpedo boats rescued another 82 men from Cherssones during the night of 12/13 May. These survivors had hidden at the coast, some shoving off on makeshift rafts. Further attempts in the ensuing nights proved fruitless.

Conclusions

According to the *Wehrmacht* reports during the period from 9 April to 12 May the Soviets lost 604 aircraft, 196 AFVs and 113 guns. During the period from 4 to 14 May, alone, 262 Soviet aircraft were shot down against German losses of nine machines. However, 76 German aircraft that were not ready to start had to be destroyed when the airfield was evacuated.

More important than the losses of matériel on the Soviet and German sides was the loss of men. For the entire period from the end of 1943 to May 1944 the Soviets reported 26,000 prisoners. According to German reports, the total of dead and missing from 8 April to 13 May was 57,500 men (31,700 German, 25,000 Rumanians). Of the 230,000 men determined to be in the 17th *Armee* in April, 130,000 Germans and Rumanians were transported out by sea. 21,457 were flown out by the *Luftwaffe*. Precise figures cannot be determined. By comparing the entire personnel complement of the 17th *Armee* at the start of April 1944 with the figures for those transported out and the reported losses, there still remains an unexplained number of 80,000 men missing.[3]

Such numerical summaries sound like statistical presentations, but conceal the personal fates of the individuals involved. The fighting men did their duty to the final moment and held the positions so that rear-are services, staffs and the like could embark. The rear guards, themselves, however, then fell into enemy hands. It remains to be mentioned that according to the knowledge then current among the soldiers at the front, Soviet prisoners were regularly put to death in despicable fashion, meaning that prisoners were not taken. The fact that a small percentage of German soldiers would return from Soviet captivity many years later was not known at that time. The defenders therefore fought to the last with the courage of drowning men, not only to hold their position, but also for their own lives. What disillusionment they must have then suffered at the embarkation bay!! Certainly there was no way of knowing that, on 12 May, the Soviets would not repeat their aerial attacks on the ships and that the sea would remain calm. Nevertheless, it would have been appropriate in relation to the desperate commitment of the soldiers in holding the last positions on the Cherssonese for the ships to have accepted the risk of artillery fire and of aerial attack as they did in April and May of 1945 at the embarkations at Pillau and, above all, in Hela and the roads before Hela, disregarding artillery fire and aerial attack, to the point of independent action.

It appears lamentable, again, in this context, that the situation evaluation of the military commander in chief found so little consideration at the highest command level of *OKH* (Hitler), as if the combat successes of the troops merely depended on their good will.

---

3   Tieke, op.cit.

Epilogue

Many participants in the events of that time may miss presentation of individual, even harder actions. Such an overall outline of the events must, of necessity, limit itself generally to the *Schwerpunkte* battles. Their selection, however, at this stage of the war no longer rested with the German command, but with the Stavka of the Red Army.

The endeavours of the troops may, for a participant in the events described, stir old memories with their exhausting marches through bottomless mud, lack of rest and any possibilities for cultivation, days and nights without sleep under acute effects of engine noise, gun fire and incoming rounds. The significance of this comprehensive presentation lies less, however, in refreshing the memories of former participants and much more in the determination of the events and, thereby, the immense endeavours of the troops under the physical and psychological demands put upon them, often, indeed, by themselves, which had hitherto been considered impossible and, thereby, unreasonable.

This description, therefore, is essentially for later generations. Whether the outline is now successful so that it makes clear the situation of the troops for those who were not there seems uncertain to the author, though that has been his goal. Every reader will ask how troops, inferior in personnel and armament and without hope of victory in a fighting retreat could have brought forth such endeavours.

Certainly contributing to the immense endurance and will to fight was the fact that it was a matter of keeping distant from Europe Stalin's version of communism, whose effects had become familiar in the advance into – and during the years of occupation of – the Soviet Union. If the Red Army was not kept far from the borders of the *Reich*, such a system would mercilessly break into Europe, establishing the same soul-destroying system in our own homeland. In addition was the fact that the Red Army took no prisoners. From the start of the war in the East the troops had seen that comrades whom they had seen to be alive when they were captured were later found shot, frozen, stabbed or killed in other ways when localities that had been lost were later recaptured. The troops did not know at the time that the Red Army allowed a small percentage of the prisoners they had taken at Stalingrad to survive. The promises repeatedly made by the Red Army and also from the *'National-komitee Freies Deutschland'* over loudspeakers had never, to that point, been kept, meeting well-founded mistrust. Therefore no German soldier could fall into Soviet hands because then his fate seemed certain, even without any predictability of the manner of his dying.

The demands that were placed on the troops took a variety of forms. The majority of the infantry divisions found themselves far inferior in mobility to the Red Army soldiers with their great number of vehicles provided by America. Therefore they had to achieve correspondingly greater performances of marching in order to reach the march objectives set by the command and demanded by the situation. Above all, the infantry divisions lacked organic protection in the form of armour, mobile anti-tank guns on self-propelled mounts and artillery on self-propelled mounts such as the *Panzer* divisions had. Therefore they repeatedly proved inferior to the Soviet attacks that were regularly supported by armour, which they had to combat with infantry weapons and close-combat materials such as *Panzerfäusten*, magnetic anti-tank hollow charges and the like. The *Grenadiere* of a *Panzer* division, with their own mobile heavy weapons behind them, were blessed with greater self-confidence because their unit could better protect itself against the strong Soviet attacks.

The force ratio between the Red Army and the German formations became ever more unequal during the course of the fighting retreat because the Soviets could constantly feed new weapons, especially armour and artillery, into the battle while the German formations received totally inadequate supply of weapons of such sort and ammunition. The Soviets drew personnel from all parts of the Soviet Union, especially from the territories formerly occupied by the Germans, in the form of young Ukrainian men who had attained military age whom they could now draft into their forces. On the other hand, the Germans received only the most scanty, wholly inadequate supply of personnel, so that the personnel complement of the German formations rapidly dwindled, the divisions shrinking to the strength of *Kampfgruppen*, some to no more than that of weak battalions.

Therefore the soldiers had to see what they could make of the situation. Day in and day out, they defended against attacks, marching again at night to take up new positions to the rear and then, on the next day, without any sort of rest, again fending off the hotly-pursuing Soviet forces.

To the observer after the fact the conduct of the war at that time must seem irresponsible. The *Reich* did, finally, have to send personnel and matériel to several fronts, such as the southern front in Italy that was so wasteful in troops and matériel, and the formations involved in fighting partisan bands in Yugoslavia. Furthermore, preparations had to be made for the expected invasion by the Western Allies, the more so since one could not know where this landing would take place, whether in Greece, or on the Belgian or English Channel coasts. In addition, came the withdrawal movements of *Heeresgruppe* E from the Mediterranean islands and, finally, from Greece. The troops therefore had a certain understanding of why they did not receive the requisite supply of matériel and personnel that would have been needed to contest the battle, let alone to establish parity with the Red Army.

Questions regarding the practicality, indeed, the responsibility of the actions of *Heeresgruppe Süd* in the time period described must remain outside of consideration, because a soldier, no matter what his rank, has no influence on that. The political and strategic decisions were made in the *Führer* headquarters. *Generalfeldmarschall* von Manstein repeatedly attempted to persuade Hitler to accept his proposals, but he got no more than partial agreement, and that too late. Hitler significantly restricted the commanders at the various levels of command in their freedom of decision by direct instructions so that the only remaining way out was to place further demands on the troops, to engage in extremely sensitive reconnaissance and to lead, especially to devise new tactics at the upper, middle and lower levels, to test them and to introduce them.

It appears lamentable that the *Bundeswehr* has, under the influence of 'Reeducation', taken such a negative role in maintenance of tradition, in contrast with the Austrian *Bundesheer*. The action of the soldiers had nothing to do with the ideology or political motivation of the leadership of the *Reich*. A soldier fulfills the duty assigned him and, understandably, expects recognition of his service from the community of the people or a state.

Such has generally been denied to the German soldiers of the Second World War. It seems unwise to lose sight of the combat experience gained in hard fighting, as also experiences with climatic and organizational difficulties. Granted, we hope that peace will continue to be maintained. Nevertheless, a *Bundesheer* will be retained so as to defend the territory of the nation in the event of an attack. In such a case the soldiers must, of necessity, refer to previous experience, unless one expects the troops to have to gain all the difficult and costly experience yet again.

Photographic Essay

Generalfeldmarschall Erich von Manstein (CO *Heeresgruppe Süd*). (Private collection)

Generalfeldmarschall Walter Model (CO *Heeresgruppe Nord/Nordukraine*). (Private collection)

Generalfeldmarschall Ewald von Kleist (CO *Heeresgruppe* A). (Bundesarchiv 183-1986-0210-503)

Generalfeldmarschall Ferdinand Schörner (right) (CO *Heeresgruppe A/Südukraine*) with *General der Infanterie* Otto Wöhler (CO 8. *Armee*). (Bundesarchiv 183-2007-0313-500)

Generaloberst Hans-Valentin Hube (CO 1. *Panzer-Armee*). (Bundesarchiv 146-2009-0114)

Generaloberst Erhard Raus (CO 4. *Panzer-Armee*). (Bundesarchiv 146-1984-019-28)

Generaloberst Karl-Adolf Hollidt (CO 6. *Armee*). (Bundesarchiv 146-1972-007-23)

Generaloberst Erwin Jaenecke (CO 17. *Armee*) (centre of photograph). (Bundesarchiv 183-J17694)

A German field car on a muddy road in the Ukraine, late 1943. (Bundesarchiv 101I-708-0252-33)

A German SdKfz 250 half-track in the Ukraine, autumn 1943. (Bundesarchiv 101I-708-0258-39)

German infantry in a shallow trench, southern Russia, late 1943. (Bundesarchiv 101I-708-0256-15A)

German *Gebirgsjäger* stand before a knocked-out Soviet heavy tank, southern Russia, autumn 1943. (Bundesarchiv 101I-708-0270-09A)

A conference in the field for the *Panzertruppen*, southern Russia, 1943/44. (Bundesarchiv 101I-708-0298-36A)

A French tank – a Char B1bis - now in German hands being used as a flamethrower in southern Russia, 1943. (Bundesarchiv 101I-708-0293-14)

Junkers Ju 52 transport aircraft on the ground, Ju 87 Stukas are overhead, at Korsun, during the fighting for the Cherkassy pocket. (Bundesarchiv 141-1280)

German *Gebirgsjäger* officer, the Ukraine, autumn 1943. (Bundesarchiv 101I-708-0298-19)

A German PzKpfw IV tank and crew, Ukraine, 1943/44. (Bundesarchiv 101I-708-0298-28)

Soviet prisoners, southern Russia, winter 1943/44. (Bundesarchiv 101I-708-0299-21)

Two German PzKpfw IV tanks, southern Russia, 1943/44. (Bundesarchiv 101I-708-0299-01)

A VW field car is helped through mud at the Nikopol bridgehead, late 1943. (Bundesarchiv 101I-709-0301-38)

The commander of a German *Sturmgeschütz* views Soviet positions through his binoculars, Nikopol bridgehead, late 1943 (Bundesarchiv 101I-709-0303-12)

A German soldier with a *Panzer*faust anti-tank weapon, Ukraine, 1944. (Bundesarchiv 101I-709-0337A-10A)

A German soldier demonstrates the firing of a *Panzer*schreck anti-tank weapon, Ukraine, 1944. (Bundesarchiv 101I-709-0338-26)

A soldier of the *Panzer*truppen, southern Russia, 1943/44. (Bundesarchiv 101I-708-0300-17)

German troops ride on a PzKpfw IV, southern Russia, 1943/44. (Bundesarchiv 101I-708-0300-35)

A column of German SdKfz 251 half-tracks in the open terrain typical of southern Russia. (Bundesarchiv 101I-711-0410-33)

A good impression of the horrendously muddy conditions encountered in southern Russia 1943/44 – even this half-tracked *Raupenschlepper Ost* is struggling. (Bundesarchiv 101I-709-0347-35)

German infantry and a SdKfz 250 half-track, southern Russia, spring 1944. (Bundesarchiv 101I-711-0446-21A)

Signals troops from *Panzergrenadier Division 'Grossdeutschland'* during the battles for Targul Frumos, spring 1944. (Bundesarchiv 101I-712-0494-13)

Oberleutnant Dr. Bold and another officer from *Panzergrenadier Division 'Grossdeutschland'*, Targul Frumos, spring 1944. (Bundesarchiv 101I-712-0497-24)

An *Oberleutnant* from *Panzergrenadier Division 'Grossdeutschland'*, Targul Frumos, spring 1944. (Bundesarchiv 101I-712-0494-37)

A German veteran from *Heeresgruppe Südukraine*, 1943/44. (Bundesarchiv 101I-709-0350-15)

Appendix

Orders of Battle

Schematische Kriegsgliederung
Stand: 15.10.1943

Divisionen	Korps	Armeen	Hgr	zV OKH	
	Befh.West-Taurien			Zahlenmäßige der Divisionen	Übersicht
Ma.1.slow. Ma.153.F.A.D.+Tle.1.slow. 4.Geb.	XXXXIX.Geb.Korps	17.		Pz.Div. Inf.Div. Jg.Div. Geb.Div.	2 11 2 2
1.rum.Geb. 2.rum.Geb.	rum.Geb.K.	9.rum.K.D. Ma.10.rum.			17
50.+Gr.Oberst Krieger 6.rum.K.D.+Tle.10.rum. 98. 3.rum.Geb. 19.rum.	V.		A	Sich.Div. Feldausb.Div. Lw.F.D. fremdl.Verb.	1/3 1 2 10
24.rum.+Tle.4.rum.Geb.+Kav.Rgt.Süd K.Gr.336.+Tle.Radf.Sich.Rgt.4+Ma.4.rum.Geb. 79.+Tle.17.Pz. 111.+Tle.15.Lw.F.D.+Tle.370.	XXXXIV.	6.			
79. 17.+Tle.5.Lw.F.+Tle.15.Lw.F.+Tle.13.Pz. 9.+Tle.13.Pz.	XXIX.	Ma.370.(i.Antr) 97.Jg.(i.Antr.)			
K.Gr.258. 3.Geb.+Tle.302.+Tle.5.Lw.F. Ma.17.Pz.+Tle.5.Lw.F. 101.Jg. Ma.302.	IV.				
335. 333.+Reste K.Gr.294. 123. 16.Pz.Gr.+125. 304.	XVII. XXXXPz.				
257. 46. 387. 15.	XXX.	1.Pz.			
2/3 62.+K.Gr.38. K.Gr.328. 355.+K.Gr.161.+K.Gr.293.	LII.				
306. "Gr.D."+Tle.6.Pz. Ma.SS-K.D.+Tle.6.Pz. K.Gr.9.Pz. 23.Pz.+1/3 62. Ma.K.Gr.6.Pz.+Tle.SS-K.D.	LVII.Pz.		Süd		
106.+K.Gr.39+Tle.SS-"T" Ma.SS-"T" K.Gr.282. K.Gr.198.	XI.				
320. Tle.11.Pz. 389. K.Gr.167.	XXXXVII.Pz.			376.(i.Antr.) 24.Pz.(i.Antr.)	
K.Gr.168.+K.Gr.223. SS-"W" 57.+1/3 88. 3.Pz.	III.Pz.	8.		Pz.Div. Pz.Gr.Div. Inf.Div.	9 7 44+1/2
K.Gr.112.+K.Gr.255. 20.Pz.Gr. 19.Pz. 72. Ma.11.Pz. Ma.SS-"R"	XXXXVIII.Pz.			Sich.Div. Res.Div. fremdl.Verb.	60+1/2 3 2 4
10.Pz.Gr.+Tle.SS-"R" K.Gr.34.	XXIV.Pz.				
2/3 88.+1/2 213.Sich. 75.+1/2 213.Sich. K.Gr.323.	VII.				
82.+Tle.K.Gr.327.+1/2 340. 208. 1/2 340. 68.	XIII.	4.Pz.			
183. K.Gr.8.Pz. 217. 291. 339. 7.Pz.	LIX.				

Schematische Kriegsgliederung
Stand: 26.10.1943

Divisionen	Korps	Armeen	Hgr	zVOKH	
333.+K.Dv.294. 123. 125. 2/3 304.	XVII.	1.Pz.		1.Pz.(i.Antr.) 384.(i.Antr.)	
257.+1/3 304. 46. 387 Tle.15.	XXX.				
62.+K.Gr.38 K.Gr.306.+K.Gr.328.+Reste 355.+K.Gr.161.+ K.Gr.293. „Gr.D."+Tle.23.Pz. K.Gr.9.Pz.+Ma.SS-,K.D." } Gr.Gen. +Tle.15. } Buschenhagen 16.Pz.Gr	L II.			Pz.Div.	11
				Pz.Gr.Div.	7
				Inf.Div.	45+1/2+1/3
					63+1/2+1/3
Tle.23.Pz.+Tle.15. 11.Pz.+Tle.SS-,T."	LVII.Pz.			Sich.Div.	3
24.Pz 376. 14.Pz. Ma.SS-,T."	XXXX.Pz.			Feldausb.Div. (Res.Div.!)	2
				fremdl.Verb.	4
2/3 167. 6.Pz.+Tle.SS-,K.D." 106.+K.Gr.39 282.	XI.	8.	Süd Kav.Rgt Süd		
198. 389. 320.	XXXXVII.Pz.				
168.+1/3 167.+K.Gr.223. SS-,W." 57.+1/3 88. 3.Pz.	III.Pz.				
K.Gr.112.+K.Gr.255. 20.Pz.Gr. 19.Pz. 72.	XXXXVIII.Pz.				
SS-,R." 10.Pz.Gr." 34.	XXIV.Pz.				
1/3 82.+1/2 213.Sich. 2/3 75.+1/2 213.Sich. 1/3 88.+1/3 82.+K.Gr.323. K.Gr.68.+1/3 88.+1/3 75.	VII.	4.Pz			
K.Gr.208. 340.+K.Gr.327. 212 K.Gr.183.	XIII.				
K.Gr.339. 291.	LIX.	2.Pz. 8.Pz.			
454.Sich.	XXXXII.				

Schematische Kriegsgliederung
Stand: 8.11.1943

Divisionen	Korps	Armeen	Hgr.	z.V.OKH	
9.rum.Kav.Div.	rum.Kav.Korps			zahlenmäßige Übersicht	
10.rum.		XXXXIX. Geb.			
Ma.50.+Tle.K.Gr.336+ Tle.153.F.A.D. Tle.1.slow. Ma.K.Gr.336.+Tle.1.slow. } Gr.Gen.Weber	Gr.Gen.Lt. Sixt	17.		Pz.Div. Inf.Div. Jäg.Div. Geb.Div.	2 5 1 1
1.rum.Geb. 2.rum.Geb.	rum.Geb.Kps.				9
Ma.6.rum.K.D. 98.+Tle.153.F.A.D. 3.rum.Geb. 19.rum. Gr.Oberst Krieger+Tle.6.rum.K.D.	V.		A	Feldausb.Div. Lw.F.D. fremdl.Verb.	1 2 10
370. 4.Geb 13.Pz. 101.Jg.+Tle.50. K.Gr.73. 24.rum. 4.rum.Geb. Stab 5.Lw.F.D.	XXXXIV.	6.			
17.Pz. Tle.153.F.A.D. Tle.1.slow.(Stab) Stab 15.Lw.F.D.	Befh.West-Taurien				
	Befh.H.Geb.A				
K.Gr.111. 97.Jg. 9. 335. K.Gr.17.	XXIX.			Pz.Div. Pz.Gr.Div. Inf.Div. Jäg.Div. Geb.Div.	13 8 50+1/2+1/3 1 1
K.G.79 258. 3.Geb. 302. 24.Pz.	IV.	XXXX.Pz. Henrici			73+1/2+1/3
				Sich.Div. Res.Div. fremdl.Verb.	2 2 2
294.+K.Gr.333. 123. 125. 304.	XVII.				
257. 46.+Tle.11.Pz. 387.+Tle.15.	XXX.	1.Pz.			
Ma.62+K.Gr.38.+ Ma.16.Pz.Gr. K.Gr.306+K.Gr.328+ } Gr.Gen.Lt.Schwerin Reste 355+K.Gr.161+ K.Gr.293 „Gr.D."+Tle.15 K.Gr.9.Pz.+Tle.SS-„K.D" } Gen.Lt.Buschenhagen Stab+Tle.62.+1/315 K.Gr.23.Pz. 14.Pz. Ma.11.Pz.	LVII.Pz.				
76 384. SS-„T."	L II.		Süd		
376. 2/3 167. 6.Pz.+Tle.SS-„K.D." 106.+Reste 38. 282.	XI.	8.	Kav.Rgt.Süd		
389. 320.	XXXXVII.Pz.	1/2 SS-„A.H." 1.Pz.			
K.Gr.72.+1/3 167. SS-„W." 57.	III.Pz.				
3.Pz. 112.+K.Gr.255. 19.Pz. 168.+Reste 223. 10.Pz.Gr. 34.	XXIV.Pz.				

Stand: 8.11.1943

Divisionen	Korps		Armeen	Hgr.	z.V. OKH
82.+ 1/2 213.Sich. 2/3 75.+ 1/2 213.Sich. SS-"R." 25.Pz. 198.(i.Zuführ.)	XXXXVIII.Pz.				
2/3 88. 20.Pz.Gr. 7.Pz. K.Gr.68.+1/3 88.+1/3 75.	VII.		4.Pz. 1/2 SS-"A.H." 4.Pz.(i.Antr.)		
8.Pz. K.Gr.208. 340.+ K.Gr.327.	XIII.				
K.Abt.C (183., 217., 339.) 291.	LIX.				
454.Sich.	XXXXII.				
444.Sich.(Stab)		Kdr.Gen.d. Sich.Tr.Süd	W.B. Ukraine		
21.ung. 201.ung.	Kgl.ung.VII.				
143.Res. 147.Res.	LXII.Res.				

Schematische Kriegsgliederung
Stand: 20.11.1943

Divisionen	Korps		Armeen	Hgr.	zVOKH	
9.rum.K.D.	rum.Kav.Kps.				Zahlenmäßige Übersicht der Divisionen	
10.rum.						
Ma.50.+Tle.K.Gr.336.+Tle. 153.F.A.D. } Gr.Gen.Weber 1.slow.(Tle.) Ma.K.Gr.336.	Gr.Gen.Lt. Sixt	XXXXIX. Geb.	17.		Pz.Div. Inf.Div. Jg.Div. Geb.Div.	1 5 1 1
1.rum.Geb. 2.rum.Geb.	rum.Geb.Kps.					8
Ma.6.rum.K.D. 9B.+Tle.153.F.A.D.+Tle. 50. 3.rum.Geb. 19.rum. Gr.Oberst Krieger	V.			A	F.A.D. fremdl.Verb	1 10
370. 4.Geb. 17.Pz. 101.Jg. 73.	XXXXIV.		6.			
Reste 1.slow. 4./24.rum. Stab 5.Lw.F.D.+Tle.153.F.A.D. Stab 15.Lw.F.D.	Befh.West-Taurien					
	Befh.H.Geb.A					
K.Gr.111 97.Jg. 9. 335.	XXIX.	XXXX.Pz. Gr.Gen. Eberbach			Pz.Div. Pz.Gr.Div. Inf.Div. Jäg.Div. Geb.Div.	13 6 50+2/2+V 3 1 1
K.G.79. K.Gr.17 258. 3.Geb. 302. 24.Pz.	IV.					73+2/2+1/3
294.+K.Gr.333. 123. 125. 304.	XVII.		1.Pz.		Sich.Div. Res.Div. Lw.Verb. fremdl.Verb.	2 2 1 2
257. 46. K.Gr.387.	XXX.		13.Pz 14.Pz			
K.Gr.306.+Reste 328.+ Reste 355.+K.Gr.161.+ } Gr.Gen.Lt. Reste 293. Schwerin 16.Pz.Gr. "G.D." } Gr.Oberst Sperl 9.Pz.+Ma.SS-,K.D." 15. 62.+K.Gr.38. 23.Pz.	LVII.Pz.			Süd		
SS-„T"+1/376. 2/376. 384.	LII.					
376. 2/3 167. 106.+Reste 39 282.	XI.					
389. 320.	XXXXVII.Pz.		8.			
72.+1/3 167. SS-„W." 57. 11.Pz.(i.Zuf.) 6.Pz.+Tle.SS-„K.D."6 Zuf.) SS-Freiw.Stu.Bc.„Wallonien"	III.Pz:					
112.+K.Gr.255. 168.+Reste 223. 34. 3.Pz. 10.Pz.Gr.	XXIV.Pz.					
82. 75. 198. SS-„R."	VII.		4.Pz. 2.Fallsch.Jg(i.Antr.)			
25.Pz. 19.Pz. SS-„A.H." 1.Pz. 7.Pz.	XXXXVIII.Pz.					

Stand: 20.11.1943

Divisionen	Korps		Armeen	Hgr.	z.V. OKH
K.Gr.68.+ K.Gr.323. Gr.213.Sich.+ Rest 88. K.Gr.340.+ K.Gr.327. 8.Pz. K.Gr.208. Kav.Rgt.Süd	XIII.	Armee- Abt. Matten- klott			
K.Abt.C (183., 217., 339.) 291. Ma.454.Sich. 1/3 147. Res.	LIX.				
Tle. 454.Sich.					
444.Sich.(Stab)			W.B. Ukraine		
21.ung. 201.ung.	Kgl.ung. VII.A.K.				
143. Res. 2/3 147. Res.	LXII.Res.				

Schematische Kriegsgliederung
Stand: 3.12.1943

Div.	Korps		Armeen	Hgr.	z.V. OKH		F.A.U.
9.rum.K.D. 10.rum.	rum.Kav.Kps.		17.				
Ma.50.+Tle.K.Gr.336.+Tle.153.F.A.D. Tle.1.slow	Gr.Gen.Lt.Sixt	XXXXIX.Geb.					
Ma.K.Gr.336 1.rum.Geb 2.rum.Geb	rum.Geb.Kps.						
Ma.6.rum.K.D 98.+Tle.50 3.rum.Geb. 19.rum Gr.Oberst Krieger	V.			A	Zahlenmäßige der Divisionen	Übersicht	
3.70 4.Geb 17.Pz 10.1 Jg. 73. Tle.153.F.A.D (Stab)	XXXXIV.		6.		Pz.Div. Pz.Gr.Div. Inf.Div. Jäg.Div. Geb.Div.	1 — 6 1 1 9	
Reste 1.slow (Stab) 4/24.rum Stab 5.Lw.F.D	Befh West-Taurin				Sich.Div. Feldausb.Div. fremdl.Verb.	— 1 10	
Tle.153.F.A.D	Befh d dtsch Tr in Transnistrien				= = = =	= = = =	
97.Jg. 9. 335.	XXIX.	XXXX.Pz. Gr.Gen. Schörner					
17.+K.Gr.79. 2/3.111 258 3.Geb.+1/3.111. 302 24.Pz	IV						
Ma.294.+Reste 333.+Tle.304 123 125	XVII.		1.Pz.				
K.Gr.306.+Rest.328 +Rest.293 } Gr.Gen.Lt 16.Pz.Gr } Schwerin Gr.D 9.Pz. } GrOberst 15 } Sperl 62.+K.Gr.38 23.Pz.+Reste 355.+K.Gr.161.+Tle.294	LVII.Pz.		13.Pz				
SS„T" 76 384	LII.						
Ma.304 257 46 387	XXX.						
376. 11.Pz 14.Pz.+Tle.167	XI.			Süd			
6.Pz.+Tle.SS„KD" 106.+Reste 39.+Tle.167 282 389 320	XXXXVII.Pz.		8. 10.Pz.Gr				
72.+Tle.167.+Tle.SS„W" 3.Pz Ma.SS„W".+SS Fr.w.Stu.Br.„Wallonien" 57	III.Pz.				Pz.Div. Pz.Gr.Div. Inf.Div. Jäg.Div. Geb.Div.	13 8 50+2/2+1/3 1 1 73+2/2+1/3	
112.+K.Gr.255 168.+Reste 223 34	XXIV.Pz.						
82 75 198.+Reste 88	VII.				Sich.Div. Res.Div. Lw.Verb. fremdl.Verb.	2 2 1 2	
25.Pz 19.Pz. SS„R" 2.Fallsch.Jg. 7.Pz.+K.Gr.20.Pz.Gr 8.Pz	XXXXII.		4.Pz.				
1.Pz SS„AH" K.Gr.208.+Kav.Rgt.Süd	XXXXVIII.Pz.						
K.Gr.68.+K.Gr.323. Gr.213.Sich. K.Gr.340.+Reste 327	XIII.						
K.Abt.C (183.,217.,339.) 291. 1/3.147.Res.	LIX.						
454.Sich.							

Kriegsgliederung - Stand 15. 04. 1944

Heeresgruppe Süd-Ukraine
    Zur Verfügung Ma 1. Geb.(OKW-Reserve)

17. Armee
    Zur Verfügung: 1. Rum. Geb. Div, Rum. KavK. 73 und Reste 3. Rum. Geb. Div. und Rum. Kav.Div.

V. AK
    98. und Reste 111. und Reste 19. Rum. und Reste 9. Rum. Kav. Div.

49. Gebirgskorps
    336. und Reste 1. Rum. Geb.Div., 50. und Reste 2. Rum. Geb.Div. und Reste 10. Rum. ID

Armeegruppe Generaloberst Dumitrescu (3. Rum.)
    9. Rum.,   der Donaumündung (Marine-Inf.-Einheiten)

6. Armee
    Zur Verfügung Kampfgruppe 302.- ID und Divisionsgruppe 125. ID, Kampfgruppe 9. ID, 1. Slowenische ID

3. Rum. Korps
    Rum. Donaustab, 21. Rum. ID

72. AK (ZBV)
    Kampfgruppe 304, KGr. 5. ID, Luftwaffen-Feld-Div., Teile 24. Rum. ID

44. AK
    Alarmeinheiten, 15. Rum. KGr. 306

29. AK
    153. Feld-Ausbildungs-Div., 76. ID, KGr. 335. ID und Kampfgruppe 258. ID

30. AK
    KGr. 97. Jäg.Div., KGr. 15. ID, 257. ID, 384. ID und KGr. 3. Geb.Div. und 14. PzD

52. AK
    Korpsgruppe A (Divisionsgruppen 161. ID, 293. ID, 355. ID), 320. ID, KGr. 294. ID, Ma 4. Geb.Div., Teile 13. ID

17. AK
    KGr. 17. PzD, KGr. 2. Fallsch.Jäg.Div. und Teile 4. Geb.Div., Kompanieabt. F (Divisionsgruppen 123. ID, 62. ID, 38. ID)

Armeegruppe General Wöhler (8.)
    zur Verfügung: 7. AK, Kgr. 46. ID (im Antransport) Reste Kampfgruppe 34. ID, 22. PzD "T", II./Rum. Panzerverband, 20. Rum. ID (im Antransport), 1. Rum. ID, 2. Rum. ID, 3. Rum. Geb.Div., 5. Rum. ID,

    11. Rum. ID, 13. Rum. ID.

8. Armee
    40. PzK, KGr. 282. ID und KGr. 198. ID, 10. Pz-Gruppe, KGr. 3. PzD, 11. PzD

47. AK
    14. Rum. ID, KGr. 106. ID, 370. ID

4. AK
    79. ID, KGr. 376. ID, Ma 23. PzD, 5. Rum. Kav.Div und Teile 3. Rum. ID, Teile 23. PzD

57. PzK
    24. PzD, PzD "GD"

4. Rum. Korps
    18. Rum. Geb.Div., 3. Rum. ID, Teile 7. Rum. ID

5. Rum. AK
    4. Rum. ID, 3. Rum. ID, Garde-Division, im Antransport 1. Rum. Kav. Div., 8. Rum. Kav. Div. und

4. Rum. Armee
    zur Verfügung Gren. Rgt. (mot) 1030

1. Rum. AK
    6. Rum. ID, 3. Rum. ID, Divisionsverband Sereth und Teile 3. Rum. Geb.Div.

78. AK (ZBV)
    3. Grenz-Rgt., Grenadier-Rgt. (mot) 1029

Heeresgruppe Nord-Ukraine:

1. Ung. Armee
    zur Verfügung 201. Ung. leichte ID, Ma 2. Ung. Geb. Brig.

11. AK
    Teile 1. Geb.Div, 1. Ung. Geb.Brig., Teile 2. Ung. Geb. Brig., 2. Ung. PzD

Gruppe General Püchler (7. Ung.)
    16. Ung. ID, 21. Ung. leichte ID, 18. Ung. leichte ID

9. Ung. AK
    20. Ung. ID, 23. Ung. ID, 27. Ung. leichte ID

1. Panzerarmee
    zur Verfügung 24. PzK, KGr. Waff-S-PD "AH", Kgr. ?

3. PzK
    Kampfgruppe 1. ID, Ma 367., KGr. 17. PzD, KGr. 6. PzD, KGr. 18. Art. Div, KGr. 101. Jäg.Div., Teile 367. ID

The following units belonged to 6. *Armee*:

```
4./24. Rum. ID
Teile 5. LwFDiv.
Masse 370. ID
Sich Kgr.
Teile 370. ID
79. ID
304. ID
335. ID
Kampfgruppe 9. ID
Kampfgruppe 17.. ID
Kampfgruppe 306. ID
258. ID
302. ID
Masse 294. ID
Masse Kgr. 9. PzD
97. Jäg Div.
3. Geb Div.
16. PGD
Teile 24. PzD
15. ID
Kampfgruppe 23. PzD
Kampfgruppe 46. ID
Kampfgruppe 123. ID
 Teile Kampfgruppe 9. PzD
Kampfgruppe 62. ID
Teile 294. ID
257. ID
76. ID
284. ID
Sperrverband Oberst Nagl.
```

The following units belonged to *Heeresgruppe Süd-Ukraine* 2 May 1944:

```
Rum. Infanterieverband 110
Kgr. LwFDiv
Sicherungseinheiten
4./24. Rum. ID
Alarmeinheiten 21. Rum. ID
15. Rum. ID
Kampfgruppe 335. ID
153. FAD
304. ID
Kampfgruppe 76. ID
Masse Kampfgruppe 258. ID
9. ID
Masse 3. Geb Div.
306. ID
15. ID
Teile Kampfgruppe 258. ID
257. ID
Teile 3. Geb Div.
302. ID
Teile Korpsabt. A
Teile Kampfgruppe 294. ID
Masse Korpsabt. A
14. PzD
Kampfgruppe 320. ID
13. PzD
Masse 4. Geb Div.
Masse Kampfgruppe 294. ID
Teile 4. Geb Div.
Kampfgruppe 2. FeldJDiv.
Kampfgruppe 17. ID
Korpsabt. F
Kampfgruppe 282. ID
10. PGD
11. PzD
14. Rum. ID
106. ID
370. ID
in Reserve 3. PzD
376. ID
Teile 79. ID
23. PzD, Masse 79. ID
18. Rum. Geb Div.
5. Kav Div.
in Reserve 102. Rum. Geb Brig.
Rum. Brigade Cojucaru
18. Rum. Geb. Div.
3. Rum. ID
in Reserve 101. Rum. Geb. Brig.
46. ID
24. PzD
PzD "GD"
Waffen-SS-PZD "T"
```

```
Masse 1. Rum. Garde
6. Rum. ID
Masse 1. Rum. PzD
20. Rum. ID
in Reserve 1. Rum. Brig.
103. Rum. Geb. Brig.
104. Rum. Geb Brig.
Grenadier-Ako 7
Rum. Gren.Rgt. 1030
Rum. Gren.Rgt. 3
Rum. Gren.Rgt. 1029 mit zwei deutschen Bataillonen
```

Korps-Abteilung A

(eingesetzt am 02.11.1943; umbenannt in 161.InfDiv am 27.04.1944)
Unterstellungen: ab Dez.1943 LVII.AK/1.PzArmee; ab Feb.1944 LII.AK

```
                              Stab KorpsAbt A
                              (Stab 161.InfDiv)
                                     |
   ┌─────────────────────────────────┼─────────────────────────────────┐
Divisionsgruppe 161          Divisionsgruppe 293              Divisionsgruppe 355
(Stab GrenRgt 371)           (Stab GrenRgt 512)                (Stab GrenRgt 866)
        |                            |                                 |
  Regimentsgruppen             Regimentsgruppen                  Regimentsgruppen
   ┌────┴────┐                  ┌────┴────┐                       ┌────┴────┐
  336       371                511       512                     510       866

(II./GR 336) (II./GR 371)  (II./GR 511) (II./GR 512)    (I./GR 510,293.ID) (I.GR 866)
                                                        umbenannt:II./GR 866
```

Artillerie-Regiment 241
(161.InfDiv)

I./ArtRgt 241	II./ArtRgt 241	III./ArtRgt 241	IV./ArtRgt 241 (s)
(I./ArtRgt 355)		(III./ArtRgt 293)	

NaAbt 241	DivFüsBtl 241	PzJgAbt 241	PiBtl 241	FeldErsBtl 241
(161.InfDiv)	(I./GR 364,161.InfDiv)	(161.ID,ergänzt aus 293.u.355.ID)	(161.ID,ergänzt aus 293.u.355.ID)	(161.InfDiv)

Nachschubtruppen 241 u.Dinafü 241*
(161.InfDiv)

(* Dinafü=Divisionsnachschubführer)

ORDERS OF BATTLE

```
                        K o r p s - - A b t e i l u n g   B
                              (eingesetzt am 02.11.1943)
         Nach Ausbruch aus Kessel Korssun:Reste zur Auffüllung 57.ID u.88.ID

                                    Stab KorpsAbt B
                                    (Stab 112.InfDiv)
                                           |
        ┌──────────────────────────┬───────────────────────────┐
Divisionsgruppe 112         Divisionsgruppe 255        Divisionsgruppe 332
(Stab GrenRgt 258)          (Stab GrenRgt 465)         (Stab GrenRgt 475/255.ID)
    Regimentsgruppen            Regimentsgruppen            Regimentsgruppen
      ┬─────┬                     ┬─────┬                     ┬─────┬
     110   258                   465                         677   678
(III./GR 110) (II./GR 258)  (I./GR 465) (III./GR 465)  (I./GR 475,255.ID) (II./GR 475,255.ID)

                                  Artillerie-Regiment 86*
                             (mit eingegliederter III./ArtRgt 332)

     I./ArtRgt 86        II./ArtRgt 86        III./ArtRgt 86        IV./ArtRgt 86 (s)

  NaAbt 112      DivFüsBtl 112        PzJgAbt 112        PiBtl 112        FeldErsBtl 112
              (AA 112+Tle 255.u.332.ID)  (+Rest PzJgAbt 255)              (+ Tle 255.u.332.ID)

                                Nachschubtruppen 112
                           (ergänzt mit Teilen 255.ID u.332.ID)

                                                        (* ArtRgt 86,112.InfDiv)
```

Korps-Abteilung C
(eingesetzt am 02./03.11.1943, LIX.AK)
Aufgelöst am 12.August 1944

Stab KorpsAbt C
(Stab 183.InfDiv)

Divisionsgruppe 183
(Stab GrenRgt 330)
Regimentsgruppen
330   351
(I./GR 330) (II./GR 351)

Divisionsgruppe 217
(Stab GrenRgt 346)
Regimentsgruppen
311   389
(I./GR 311) (II./GR 389)

Divisionsgruppe 339
(Stab GrenRgt 693)
Regimentsgruppen
691*   692
(I./GR 691) (I./GR 692)

Artillerie-Regiment 219
(183.InfDiv)

I./ArtRgt 219
(I./ArtRgt 217)

II./ArtRgt 219

III./ArtRgt 219
unterstellt: sHArtAbt 101

IV./ArtRgt 219 (s)

DivFüsBtl 217

PzJgAbt 219
(ergänzt aus
217.u.339.ID)

PiBtl 219

FeldErsBtl 217
(+DivKampfschule 217)

NaAbt 219
(183.InfDiv)

Nachschubtruppen 219
(ergänzt mit Teilen aus 217.u.339.ID)

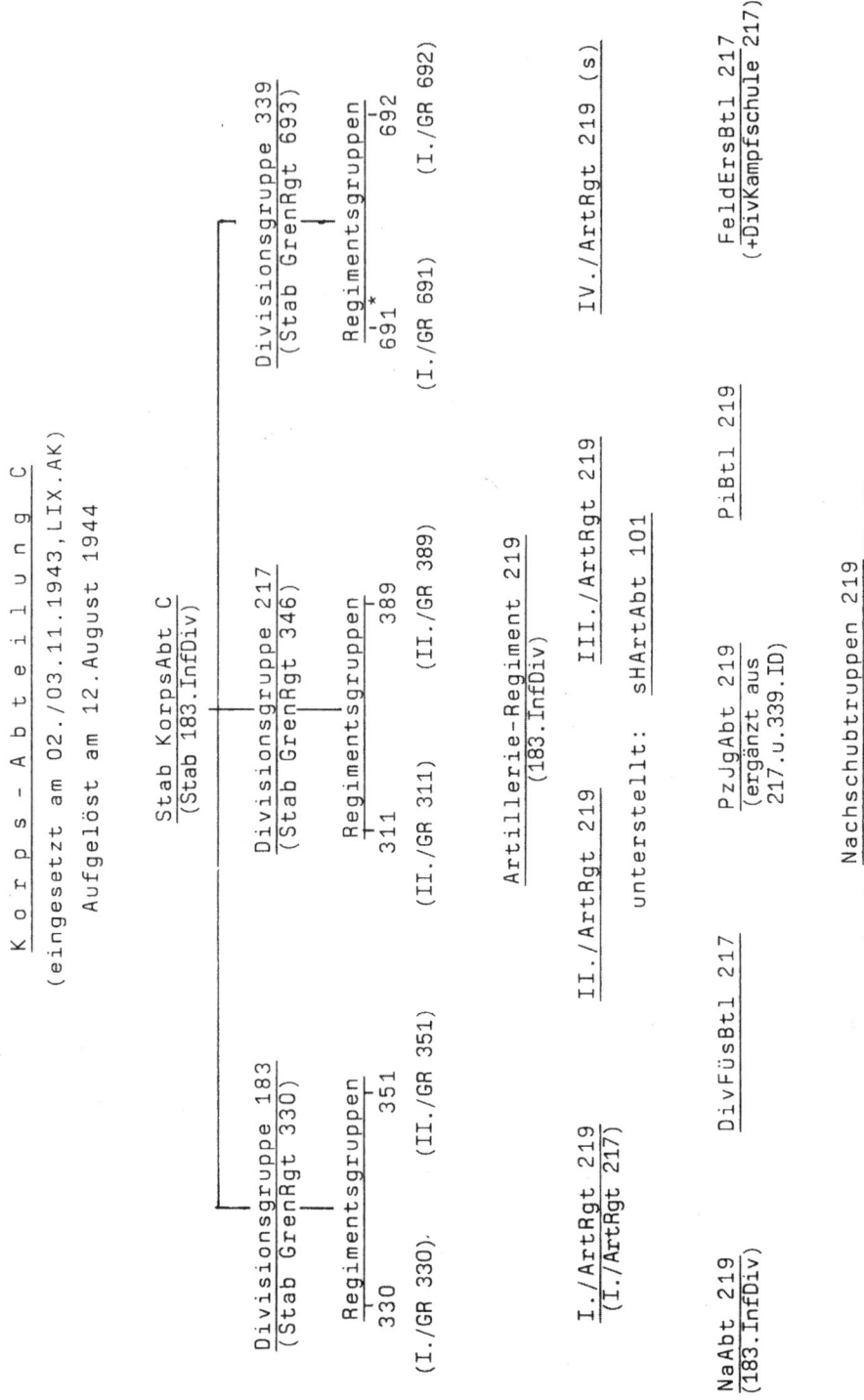

ORDERS OF BATTLE 487

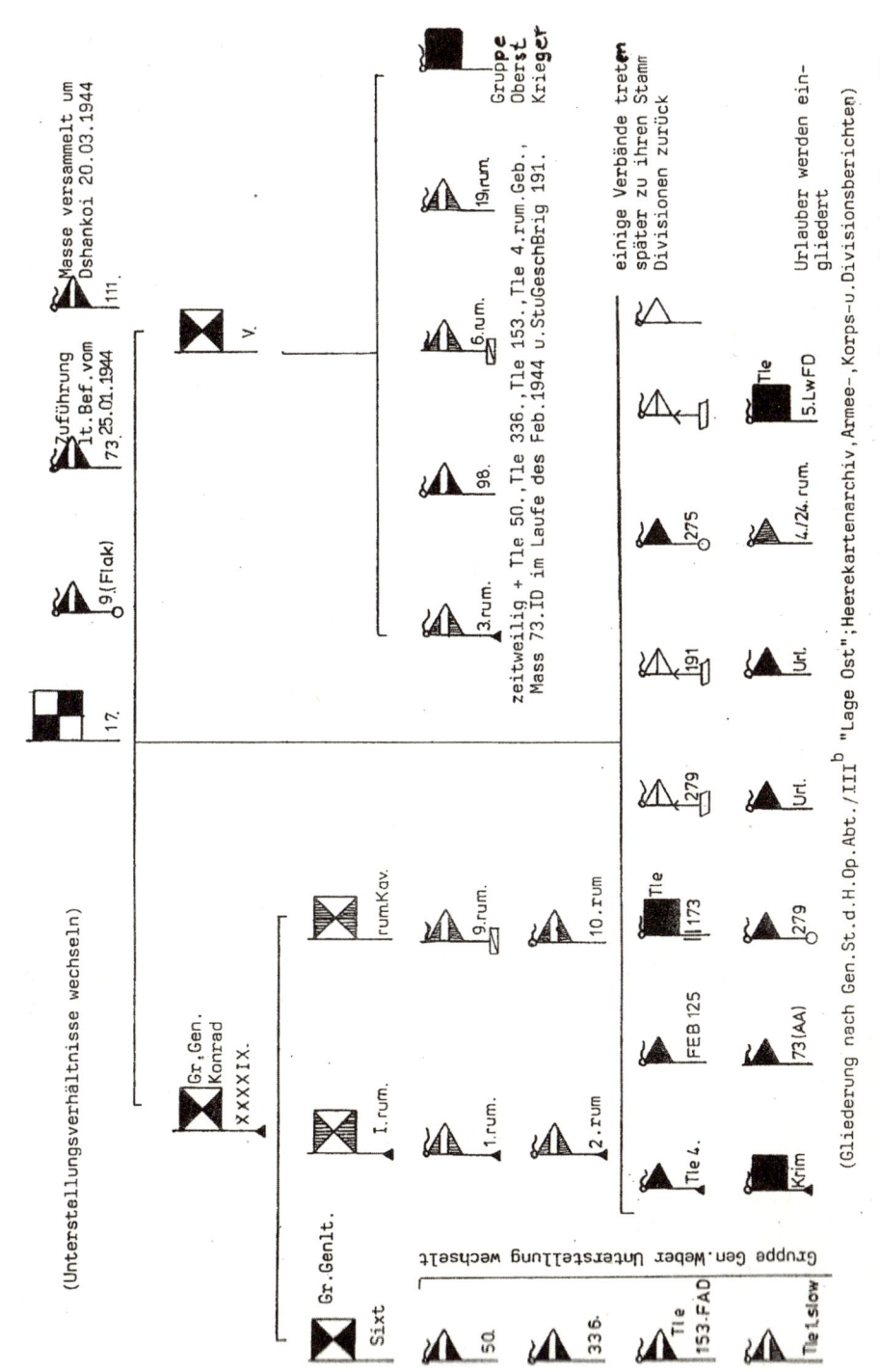

17. Armee Stand Oktober / November 1943

(Unterstellungsverhältnisse wechseln)

Gr.Gen. Konrad XXXXIX.

Gr.Genlt. Sixt

Gruppe Gen. Weber Unterstellung wechselt

I.rum.

rumKav.

1.rum.
2.rum
9.rum.
10.rum

50.
336.
Tle 153.FAD
Tle 1.slow

Tle 4.
FEB 125
Tle 173
279

Krim
73(AA)
279
Url.

9.(Flak)
Zuführung lt.Bef. vom 73 25.01.1944
Masse versammelt um Dshankoi 20.03.1944
111.

V.

3.rum.
98.
6.rum.
19.rum.

zeitweilig + Tle 50., Tle 336., Tle 153., Tle 4.rum.Geb.,
Mass 73.ID im Laufe des Feb.1944 u.StuGeschBrig 191.

191
275
4./24.rum.
Url.
5.LwFD

Gruppe Oberst Krieger

einige Verbände treten später zu ihren Stamm Divisionen zurück

Urlauber werden eingliedert

(Stand ab Oktober/November 194

(Gliederung nach Gen.St.d.H.Op.Abt./III[b] "Lage Ost";Heerekartenarchiv,Armee-, Korps-u.Divisionsberichten)

488 CRUCIBLE OF COMBAT

454. Sicherungs-Division

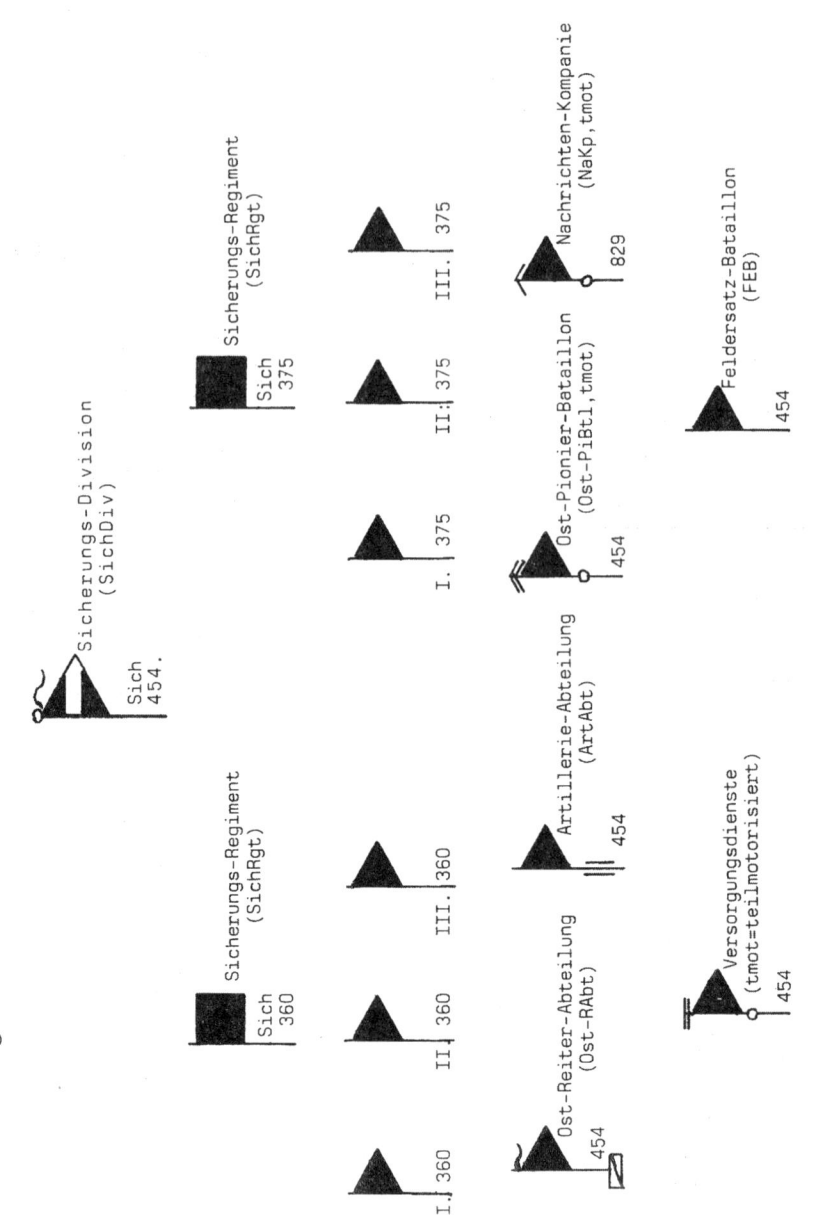

- Sicherungs-Division (SichDiv) — Sich 454.
  - Sicherungs-Regiment (SichRgt) — Sich 360
    - I. 360
    - II. 360
    - III. 360
  - Sicherungs-Regiment (SichRgt) — Sich 375
    - I. 375
    - II. 375
    - III. 375
  - Ost-Reiter-Abteilung (Ost-RAbt) — 454
  - Artillerie-Abteilung (ArtAbt) — 454
  - Ost-Pionier-Bataillon (Ost-PiBtl, tmot) — 454
  - Nachrichten-Kompanie (NaKp, tmot) — 829
  - Versorgungsdienste (tmot=teilmotorisiert) — 454
  - Feldersatz-Bataillon (FEB) — 454

ORDERS OF BATTLE 489

Organisation of the garrison of "Feste Platz"
Tarnopol on the day of its encirclement
(23 March 1944)

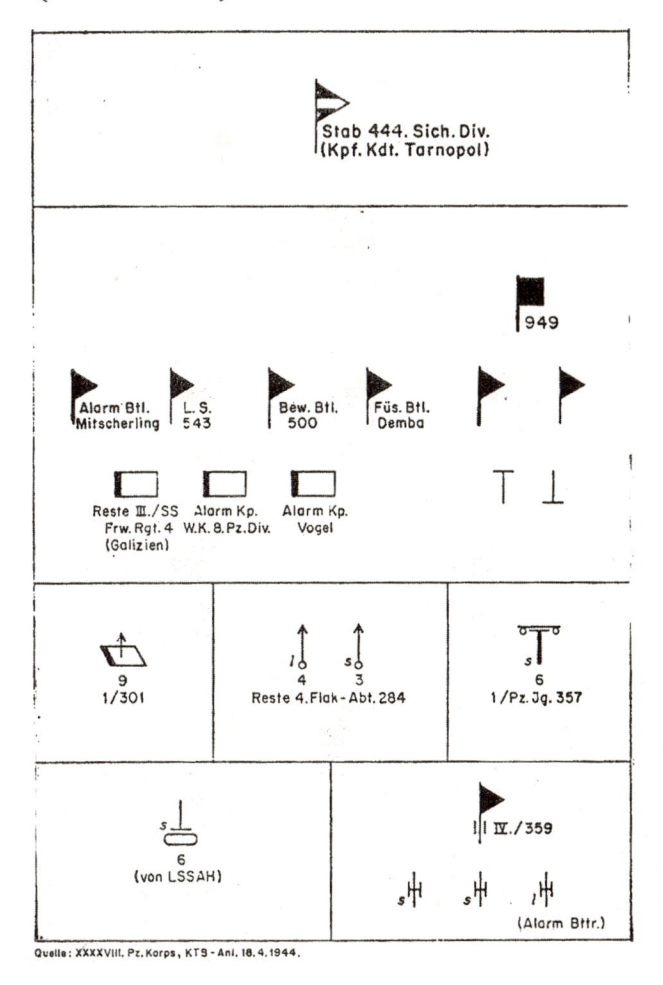

⚑ Stab 444. Sich. Div.
(Kpf. Kdt. Tarnopol)

⚑ 949

| Alarm Btl. Mitscherling | L.S. 543 | Bew. Btl. 500 | Füs. Btl. Demba | | |

Reste III./SS Alarm Kp. Alarm Kp.
Frw. Rgt. 4   W.K.8.Pz.Div. Vogel
(Galizien)

9 1/301 | 1 4 / s 3 Reste 4.Flak-Abt. 284 | s 6 1/Pz.Jg. 357

s 6 (von LSSAH) | ⚑ IV./359 (Alarm Bttr.)

Quelle: XXXXVIII. Pz.Korps, KTB-Anl. 18.4.1944.

Gliederung der Korps-Abteilung C

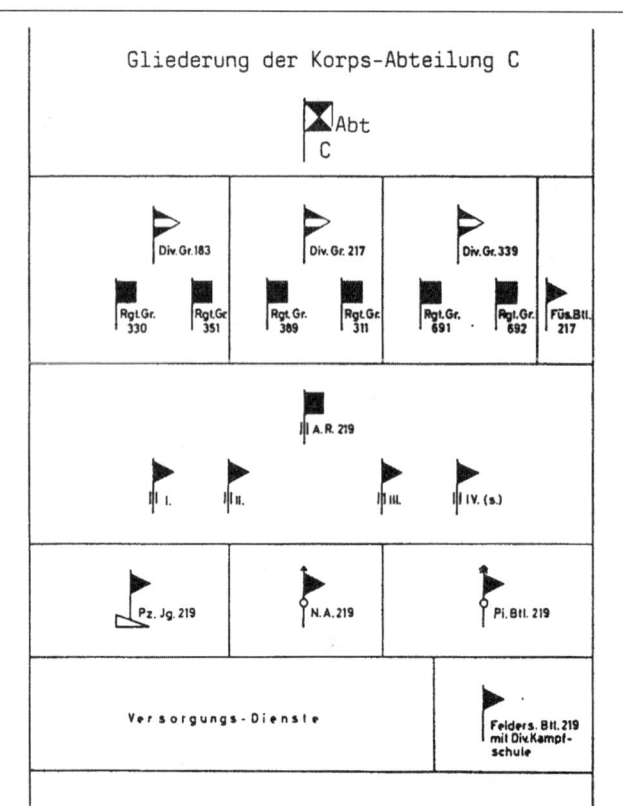

- Abt C
  - Div. Gr. 183
    - Rgt.Gr. 330
    - Rgt.Gr. 351
  - Div. Gr. 217
    - Rgt.Gr. 389
    - Rgt.Gr. 311
  - Div. Gr. 339
    - Rgt.Gr. 691
    - Rgt.Gr. 692
    - Füs.Btl. 217
- A.R. 219
  - I.
  - II.
  - III.
  - IV. (s.)
- Pz. Jg. 219
- N.A. 219
- Pi. Btl. 219
- Versorgungs-Dienste
- Felders. Btl. 219 mit Div.Kampfschule

Korpsabteilung C war aus 3 abgekämpften Inf.Diven. gebildet und entsprach einer Inf.Div. normaler Gliederung. Die Inf. Rgter. führten die Bezeichnung „Div. Gr.", die Inf. Btle. „Rgts. Gr." unter Beibehalt ihrer alten Div.-bzw. Rgts-Nummern.

Die Korps-Abteilung C wurde am 04.11.1943 gebildet und am 12.08.1944 aufgelöst.

Glossary

Abteilung   Battalion (cavalry, reconnaissance or artillery), tactical detachment or unit, administrative department or section.
Aufklärungs-   Reconnaissance.
Flak   Anti-aircraft artillery
Feld Ersatz Bataillon   Field replacement battalion. A division's replacements were first sent to its *Feldersatzbataillon* where they received additional training to make them ready for combat in the field. From it they were dispatched , as needed, to the parent division. In emergencies the *Feldersatzbataillon* might be committed directly to action.
Felgendarmerie   Military police.
Fliegerkorps   Air force corps – subordinate operational command of a *Luftflotte*.
Führerbefehl   *Führer* order, direct from Hitler.
Gebirgs-   Mountain-
Haft-Hohlladung,   3 kg magnetic anti-tank demolition charge. The shaped charge of 1.47 kg of explosive had a steel casing with three powerful horseshoe magnets attached to the plywood or plastic base to hold it to and the right distance from the armour. A penetration of 110 mm of armour was reported. There were two models with time delays of four seconds and seven seconds from the time the friction igniter was pulled.[1]
Heeresgruppe   Army Group (*Süd* = South, *Nord* = North, *Mitte* = Center)
Hiwi, Hilfswilliger   Russian 'volunteer', a prisoner-of-war who chose to work for the German army in a non-combatant support role as an alternative to prison camp.
Hornisse   Formerly called the *'Nashorn',* (rhinoceros), the *'Hornisse'* (hornet), *SdKfz* 164, was a self-propelled antitank gun with an 8.8 cm *Pak* 43/1 L/71 on the *PzKfz* III/IV chassis.
'Hummel'   15 cm *Panzerhaubitze* 18 (M) on *PzKpfw* III/IV chassis, *'Hummel'* (Sd. Kfz. 165.) 15 cm self-propelled gun.
Infanterie Geschütz   Infantry gun. In addition to the division's *Artillerie Regiment* with its three *Abteilungen* (battalions) of artillery, each German infantry regiment included, as its 13th *Kompanie*, an *Infanteriegeschützkompanie* with thee light infantry gun platoons (*leichte Infanteriegeschützzüge*) with two 7.5 cm light infantry guns and one heavy infantry gun platoon (*schweren Infanteriegeschützzug*) with two heavy 15 cm infantry guns. These infantry guns were lighter than those of the regular artillery and they could not use as heavy propelling charges as the regular artillery of the same caliber. They were accurate and effective and were to provide immediate support at the battalion level. Toward the end of the war they were in part replaced by medium and heavy mortars.
Jäger   (lit. 'hunter') light infantry, either in a *Jäger* (light infantry) division or a *Gebirgs* (mountain) division.

---

1   Chamberlain, Doyle & Gander, *Deutsche Panzerabwehr*, 1998.

Kampfgruppe   Combat command, often referring to a combat group formed of remnants of a division that had been reduced to a level that could no longer be referred to as a division. Also used, as in English usage, for a more-or-less balanced team of combat specialties assembled or employed for a particular combat task.

Kampfkommandant   There is no English equivalent term. The *Kampfkommandant* was appointed to command the battle in his designated location. Any and all troops or units entering the bounds of his area fell under his command. On occasion, that led units to circumvent such an area so as not to be dragooned into the local defense.

Kodina   *Kommandeur der Divisions Nachschubtruppen*, formerly *Dinafü*, *Divisionsnachschub Führer*, commander of the division's logistical elements.

KoPiFü   *Korps Pionier Führer*, Commander of the *Korps* pioneer units.

Kommandant der Rückwärtiges Armee Gebiet   Commandant of the Army Rear Area

Kettenkrad   Tracked motorcycle.

Muli, or *Maultier*   The *Muli*, Sd. Kfz 3, or *Maultier*, (Mule) was a half-tracked supply lorry made by replacing the rear axle of a standard lorry such as the three-ton Opel or Ford, with a tracked rear drive unit. The load capacity was reduced from three to two tons due to the weight of the new drive unit. A heavier Mercedes-Benz 4½ ton *Maultier* was introduced later.

Nachrichten   Communications

Nachschub   Supply, logistical support

Nebelwerfer   See *Werfer*.

Oberkommando des Heeres, OKH   Army High Command

Offenrohr   'Stovepipe', also called the *'Panzerschreck'*, Tank Terror, the German version of the American 'Bazooka' fired a heavier, 88mm, 3.25 kg projectile capable of penetrating 160 mm of armor at 60°.[2]

Ostheer   The German Eastern Army

Pak   Anti-tank gun

Pak-Front   A carefully organized, mutually supporting array of anti-tank guns with infantry support.

Panjewagon   Universal Russian two-wheeled sturdy peasant cart.

Schlucht   Ravine

Schwadron   Troop (cavalry or reconnaissance)

Schwerpunkt   Point of main effort, center of gravity

Siebel – Fähre   Originally constructed for the intended invasion of England, the *Siebel Fähre* (ferry) consisted of two pioneer pontoons with an additional engine compartment at the rear, the gap between them bridged over with a deck. Siebel ferries came in various models for special functions. Some were heavily armed and proved tough opponents for allied gunboats in the Mediterranean.

Stellung   Position

Sturmgeschütz   Assault gun.

Unternehmen   Operation

Wehrmacht   Armed Forces

---

2   See Ian Hogg, *The Encyclopedia of Infantry Weapons of World War II* and P. Chamberlain, H. Doyle & T. Gander, *Deutsche Panzerabwehr,1916-1918 & 1930-1945*.

GLOSSARY 493

Werfer, Nebelwerfer   *Nebelwerfer* were rocket launchers, not guns or mortars. Although laying smoke screens and delivering chemicals were among their original capabilities, the abstention from the use of poison gas in WWII led to the rapid development of high explosive projectiles, and the primary mission of the *Nebelwerfer* batteries became delivering massive volumes of high explosive rounds with powerful blast effect or incendiary-oil projectiles and also laying smoke screens.

Holes around the rim of the *Turbine* plate at the base of the solid-fuel rocket motor drilled at an angle to the axis of the rocket caused it to rotate rapidly, stabilizing it in flight. Because the spin-stabilized rocket projectiles for the *15 cm NbWf 41* had the rocket motor in front, the high-explosive payload in the rear, and detonated when the nose struck the ground, the bursting point was elevated above the ground surface, giving a devastatingly effective fragmentation and blast effect. Salvos from an entire battery of multiple-tube *Nebelwerfer* bursting over an area in rapid sequence gave waves of high and low pressure that, in the early Russian campaigns, resulted in discovery of many enemy dead with no visible signs of external injuries, their lungs apparently burst by the extreme pressure differential.

A 15 cm *Werfer-Abteilung* (battalion), with its three batteries of 6 launchers each, could deliver a salvo of 108 rounds from its 18 launchers in 10 seconds, followed by successive salvoes on the same target at 80-90 second intervals, giving 5 salvoes in 5 minutes. The 15 cm rockets came in both high-explosive and smoke rounds. Larger rockets had the rocket-motor in the rear, the bursting charge in the front. The 21 cm *Werfer-Abteilung* could deliver 90 rounds (18 launchers at 5 tubes each) in 10 seconds, with one salvo every 2.5 minutes, giving 3 salvos in 5 minutes. The 30 cm *Werfer 42 Abteilung* could deliver 108 rounds in 10 seconds, with 3 minutes between salvos, giving 3 salvoes in six minutes. The *28/32 cm Werfer 41 Abteilung* could deliver 108 rounds in 10 seconds, with five minutes between salvos.

Because, even after the switch from black-powder to smokeless propellent reduced the massive smoke-trails of the rockets, the clouds of dust raised by the exhausts of the rockets in the launching area made it easy for the enemy to rapidly identify the location of launching sites, standard practice was to launch a few rapid salvos, laying down a sudden, massive application of high explosive saturating an area, then immediately change positions to avoid retaliation.

Thanks to the relatively light weight of the launchers, they could move over terrain that would not support conventional artillery and could be shifted around by manpower or almost any powered vehicle.

21 cm rockets were only made in high-explosive. 28 cm rounds were high-explosive, 32 cm were *Flammöl* (incendiary). 30 cm rockets were high-explosive only. Because of the sound of the rockets in flight, American troops in Normandy dubbed them 'Screeming Meemies', the British, 'Moaning Minnies'.

The name *Nebelwerfer* was taken over from the 10 cm *Nebelwerfer 35*, which was a true 'trench mortar' employed by the *Nebeltruppen* for laying smoke screens. After 1940 the *Nebel-Abteilungen* gradually converted from mortars (*Werfer*) to rocket launchers, such as the six-tube electrically ignited breech-loading rocket launcher, the 15 cm *Nebelwerfer 41*, which retained the 'smoke mortar' designation for reasons of deception. There were *Nebelwerfer Brigaden* consisting of two *Nebelwerfer* regiments and separate *Nebelwerfer* regiments. Regiments included three *Abteilungen* (battalions) of three batteries each. There were also independent *Abteilungen*. There were *Abteilungen* of the 15 cm six-tube *Nebelwerfer 15 cm-41*, five-tube *21 cm Nebelwerfer 42* and of the 28/32 cm *Nebelwerfer 41*, which was a carriage mounting frames for six rockets, either the 32 cm *Flammöl*, incendiary, rockets or, with inserts, the 28 cm high-explosive rockets. The heavy 28 and 32 cm *Wurfkörper* could be launched from their wood or metal packing boxes either separately or arranged on simple frames or racks.

From the very start, all *Nebeltruppen* were motorized. The final organization of the *Nebeltruppe* in World War II was as independent *Nebelwerferabteilungen (mot.)*, *Werferregimenter (mot.)* and *schwere* [heavy] *Werferregimenter (mot.)*. The independent *Nebelwerferabteilungen* were capable of employing smoke rounds, gas rounds or (for limited missions) high explosive rounds. Their *forte* was, aside from firing gas rounds, in the ability to provide smoke coverage rapidly and for extended periods (several hours) and over extensive areas. Effective in the spring of 1943, a *Werferregiment (mot.)* consisted of two *Abteilungen* of 15 cm *Nebelwerfer* and one *Abteilung* of either 30 or 21 cm *Nebelwerfer*.. A *schwere Werferregiment (mot.)* consisted of two *Abteilungen* 30 cm *Nebelwerfer* and one *Abteilung* of either 15 or 21 cm *Nebelwerfer*.

Panzer-Pioniere , the combat engineer companies of *Panzer* divisions, had half-tracks with six individual launching racks, three on each side, for launching the heavy rockets.

The *Panzer-Werfer 42* (15 cm) consisted of ten tubes in two superimposed rows of five mounted on a very lightly armoured *Maultier* half-track, the armour merely providing splinter protection and protection against the exhaust of the rockets. Between the armour (8 mm on body, 10mm on cab) and the rocket-launcher, the vehicle was overloaded, resulting in breakdowns. However, the half-track mount permitted rapid position changes.

The SS developed an 8 cm multiple-track launcher with 24 double-rails firing fiin-stabilized 8 cm rockets. Although a successful design, production factors prevented general introduction.

The 30 cm *R-Werfer 56* , introduced in the closing months of the war, no longer carried the deception-designation, *Nebelwerfer*, but the word *Raketen* was still not written out. With inserted rails, it could also fire the 15 cm and 21 cm rockets.

The range of the rockets was only half or less than that of artillery and the rockets were ineffective against point-targets, concrete or armoured emplacements or structures. The mission of the rocket troops was strictly defined as application of sudden, massive concentrations of fire on area targets, whereas the missions of artillery was to deliver fire against point targets, deliver harrassing fire and final protective fire (blocking barrages), as well as rolling barrages in front of attacks. *Nebelwerfer* were not effective in any of these roles. Dispersion of the rockets prevented employment against point targets or in close proximity to friendly troops, thus excluding final protective fire close to friendly positions. Because of the dispersion of rockets, the launchers were to be used in *Abteilung* (battalion) or larger groupings, in which case the areas targeted would be saturated with impacts. The launchers were not intended, nor were they effective, for use as individual weapons. Availability of the precious ammunition was always limited, so employment was always limited, concentrated in both time and area.

Nebelwerfer were never to be employed for missions that could be accomplished by division artillery.

Artillery shells have to withstand the high pressures of the propellant gasses in the gun-barrel and the sudden acceleration, which determine minimum wall thicknesses, limiting the space available for the bursting charge. Rockets are accelerated over a longer period of time by their own motors, allowing far thinner walls and a far greater bursting charge in relation to projectile weight. Since the launchers consisted of open tubes or racks that merely aimed the rockets, and did not have to absorb recoil, the projectors were inexpensive to produce and the tubes did not wear out as rapidly as rifled artillery tubes. Optimum range for the 15 cm rockets was between 4000 and 6500 meters, for the 21 cm rockets between 5500 and 7850 meters. The large rockets had extremely short ranges, the 28 cm between 750 and 1925 meters, the 32 cm between 875 and 2200 meters. The 30 cm *Nebelwerfer 42* was a six-rocket rack on a wheeled carriage, similar to the 28/32 cm *Nebelwerfer 41*. Its rocket was developed to improve on the extremely short range of the earlier heavy rockets and had an effective range between 800 and 4550 meters, with a minimum possible range of about 500 meters.

Wespe(n)   Self-propelled 10.5 cm light field howitzer on *Panzer* II chassis.

Wurfkörper   Special projectiles for signal pistols. The German *Wurfkörper* 361 was a pistol-grenade formed by attaching the *Eierhandgranate* [egg hand grenade] to a plastic tube and fired from a flare-pistol.[3]

Zerstörer   Destroyer

Zug   Platoon

---

[3] Terry Gander & Peter Chamberlain, *Weapons of the Third Reich*, Doubleday and Company, Inc., Garden City NY, 1979.

Bibliography

Anon.	*Die 50. ID 1939 – 1945*
	Augsburg 1965
Anon.	*Die 291. Infanterie-Division (Elchdivision) von 1940-1945 im 2. Weltkrieg*
	Wuppertal 1983
Anon.	*Nie außer Dienst, zum 80. Geburtstag des GFM von Manstein*
	Köln 1967
Anon.	*Der Kessel von Tscherkassy. 5. SS-Panzer-Division "Wiking"; die Flut verschlang sich selbst, nicht uns*
	Osnabrück 1969
Benary	*Die Berliner Bären-Division, Geschichte der 257. ID 1939-1945*
	Bad Nauheim 1955
von Bentheim	*Der Weg der 46. Infanterie-Division*
	Bayreuth 1952
Blankenhagen	*Im Zeichen des Schwertes (131. ID)*
	Osterode 1982
Brehm	*Mein Kriegstagebuch 1939-1945, 7. Panzerdivision*
	Kassel 1953
Braun	*Enzian und Edelweiß, die 4. Gebirgs-Div. 1944-45*
	Bad Nauheim 1955
Buchner	*Ostfront 1944*
	Friedberg/Hessen 1988
Carell	*Der Rußland-Krieg*
	Berlin-Frankfurt/Main-Wien 1967
Conze	*Die Geschichte der 291. Infanterie-Division*
	Bad Nauheim 1953
Dahms	*Psyche des 2. Weltkriegs*
	Tübingen 1965
Degrelle	*28. SS-PGD . "Wallonien", die verlorene Legion*
	Preußisch-Oldendorf 1972
Drews	*Der Weg der 11. Panzerdivision 1939-1945*
	Bad Wörishofen 1982
Fredmann	*Sie kamen übers Meer: die größte Rettungsaktion der Geschichte*
	Köln 1971
Fricke	*Fester Platz Tarnopol 1944*
	Freiburg 1969
Froben	*Aufklärende Artillerie: Geschichte der Beobachtungsabteilungen u. selbständigen Beobachtungsbatterien bis 1945*
	München 1972

Gareis	*Kampf und Ende der fränkisch-sudetendeutschen 98. Infanteriedivision* Freiburg 1956
Grams	*Die 14. Panzer-Division 1940-1945* Bad Nauheim 1957
Gruber	*Das Infanterie-Regiment 213, 1939-45* Nürnberg 1963
Haupt	*Die Schlachten der Heeresgruppe Süd* Friedberg 1985
Held	*Verbände und Truppen der deutschen Wehrmacht und Waffen-SS 1939-1945: Bibliographie, Band II* Osnabrück 1983
Hake	*Das waren wir! Das erlebten wir! Der Schicksalsweg der 13. Panzer-Division* Wunstorf 1971
Hillgruber	*Hitler, König Carol und Marschall Antunescu. Die deutsch-rumänischen Beziehungen 1938-44* Wiesbaden 1954
Jacobsen & Dollinger	*Der Weltkrieg 1939-1945* München, Wien/Basel, 1962
Klatt	*Die 3. Gebirgs-Division 1939 – 1945* Bad Nauheim 1958
Kreidler	*Die Eisenbahnen im Machtbereich der Achsenmachte während des 2. Weltkriegs* Göttingen 1975
Kurowski	*Fränkische Infanterie* Bochum-Langendreer 1970
Lang	*Geschichte der 384. Infanterie-Division 1942-44* Rodenkirchen b. Köln 1965
Lange	*Korpsabteilung C – Vom Dniepr bis nach Polen* Neckargemünd 1961
Lehmann	*Die Leibstandarte, Band III* Osnabrück 1982
Lehmann & Tiemann	*Die Leibstandarte, Band IV/I* Osnabrück
Löser	*Bittere Pflicht, Kampf und Untergang der 76. Berlin-Brandenburgischen Infanterie-Division* Osnabrück 1986
von Lucke	*Die Geschichte des Panzer-Regiments 2* Gut Wöhrden/Stade 1953
von Manteuffel	*Die 7. Panzerdivision im 2. Weltkrieg* Friedberg 1986
Mazulenko	*Die Zerschlagung der Heeresgruppe Süd-Ukraine August bis September 1944* Berlin 1959

von Mellenthin	*Panzerschlachten*
	Neckargemünd 1963
Midelldorf	*Taktik im Rußland-Feldzug*
	Darmstadt 1956
Morzik	*Die deutschen Transportflieger im 2. Weltkrieg. Die Geschichte des "Fußvolks der Luft"*
	Frankfurt/Main 1966
Musculus	*Geschichte der 111.Infanterie-Division 1940–44*
	Hamburg 1980
Ostry	*Rollbahn in die Hölle, der wandernde Kessel von Tscherkassy-Korsun*
	Rastatt 1967
Ott	*Jäger am Feind, Geschichte und Opfer der 97. Jag.Div. 1940 – 1945*
	München 1966
Paul	*Brennpunkte, 6. Panzer-Division 1937–1945*
	Osnabrück 1993
Paul	*Geschichte der 18. Panzerdivision 1940-1943; mit Geschichte der 18. Artillerie-Division 1943–44; Anhang Heeresartillerie-Brigade 88, 1944–1945*
	Preußisch-Oldendorf 1989
Peckert	*Vom Küban-Brückenkopf bis Sewastopol*
	Heidelberg 1955
Pfister	*Abriß der Geschichte der 88. ID*
	Amberg 1956
von Plato	*Die Geschichte der 5. Panzer-Division von 1938 bis 1945*
	Regensburg 1978
Ploetz	*Geschichte der Weltkriege*
	Freiburg-Würzburg 1981
Pohlmann	*Geschichte der 96. Infanterie-Division 1939 – 45*
	Bad Nauheim 1959
Pottgießer	*Die Reichsbahn im Ostfeldzug*
	Neckargemünd 1960
Rebentisch	*Zum Kaukasus und zu den Tauern, die Geschichte der 23. Panzerdivision 1941-1945*
	Esslingen 1963
Redelis	*Partisanenkrieg*
	Heidelberg 1958
Rehm	*Jassy, Schicksal einer Division oder einer Armee*
	Neckargemünd 1959
Richter	*Die 1. (ostpreußische) Infanterie-Division*
	München 1975
Rieker	*Ein Mann verliert einen Weltkrieg*
	Frankfurt/Main 1969
Scheibert	*Die Gespenster-Division (7. PzD)*
	Bad Nauheim 1981

Schmidt	*Geschichte der 10. Division, 10. Infanterie-Division (mot), 10. Panzer-Grenadier-Division 1933 – 1945* Bad Nauheim 1963
Schmitz	*Die 16. Panzerdivision 1938 – 1945* Friedberg 1977
Schrodek	*Ihr Glaube gehört dem Vaterland, die Geschichte des Panzer-Regiments 15 (11. PzD)* München 1976
Selz	*Das grüne Regiment, der Weg der 256. ID aus der Sicht des Regiments 481* Freiburg/Breisgau 1970
von Senger und Etterlin	*Der Gegenschlag: Kampfbeispiele und Führungsgrundsätze der beweglichen Abwehr* Neckargemünd 1959
von Senger und Etterlin	*Die 24. Panzerdivision, vormals 1. Kav.Div. 1939 bis 1945* Neckargemünd 1962
Shilin	*Die wichtigsten Operationen des großen vaterländischen Krieges* Berlin 1958
Spaeter	*Die Geschichte des Panzerkorps Großdeutschland, Band II* Bielefeld 1958
Spaeter	*Die Einsätze der Panzergrenadier-Division "Großdeutschland"* Friedberg 1986
Spaeter	*Panzerkorps Großdeutschland* Friedberg 1988
Steiner	*Die Freiwilligen* Göttingen 1958
Stoves	*1. Panzer-Division 1935-1945, Chronik einer der drei Stamm-Divisionen der deutschen Panzerwaffe* Bad Nauheim 1961
Tessin	*Verbände und Truppen der deutschen Wehrmacht und der Waffen-SS im 2. Weltkrieg, Band II und Band III* Osnabrück, 1970-1971
von Tettau	*Geschichte der 24. ID 1935-45* Stollberg 1956
Telpuchowsky	*Die sowjetische Geschichte des großen vaterländischen Krieges 1941–1945* 1961
Tieke	*Kampf um die Krim 1941–1944* Gummersbach 1975
Tippelskirch, von	*Geschichte des 2.Weltkrieges* Bonn 1956
Tschuikow	*Gardisten auf dem Weg nach Berlin* Berlin 1976
Tschuikow	*Das Ende des 3. Reiches* München 1966
Voigt	*Der verlorene Haufen (unpublished)*

Wagener	*Die Heeresgruppe Süd*
	Bad Nauheim 1981
Walther	*Divisionen der Waffen-SS im Einsatz*
	Friedberg 1985
Weidinger	*Division Das Reich, Band IV 1943*
	Osnabrück 1979
Weidinger	*Division Das Reich, Band V*
	Osnabrück 1982
Weidinger	*Division "Das Reich", der Weg der 2. Waff-SSPGD*
	"Das Reich", Geschichte der Stammdivision der Waffen-SS 1941-43
	Osnabrück 1973
Weinmann	*Die 101. Jag. Div.*
	Offenburg 1965
Werthen	*Geschichte der 16. Panzerdivision 1939-45*
	Bad Nauheim 1958
Willemer	*Die 15. Infanterie-Division im 2. Weltkrieg*
	Wiesbaden 1968

Supplementary bibliography[1]

Anon. *Der Kessel von Tscherkassy, 5. SS-Panzer-Division "Wiking", die Flut Verschlang sich selbst, nicht uns*, Munin Verlag GmbH, Osnabrück, 1969.

Bender, Roger James & Hugh Page Taylor, *Uniforms, Organization and History of the Waffen-SS*, R. James Bender Publishing, San Jose, California, 1969–1982, 5 volumes

Buchner, Alex, *Das Handbuch der Deutschen Infanterie, 1939 – 1945*, Podzun Pallas Verlag, Friedberg, 1987. Although there is an English translation of this, the English translation is flawed by serious and substantial errors in translation.

Chamberlain, P,. H. Doyle & T. Gander, *Deutsche Panzerabwehr 1916-1918 & 1930–1945. German Anti-Tank Weapons*, Cannon Publications, Retford, 1998.

Fricke, Gert, *Fester Platz Tarnopol 1944. Einzelschriften zur militärishen Geschichte des Zweiten Weltkrieges*, Verlag Rombach, Freiburg, 1986.

Fürbringer, Herbert, *SS-Panzer-Division Hohenstaufen, 1944: Normandie – Tarnopol – Arnhem*, Editions Heimdal, Bayeux, 1984.

Haupt, W., *Die 8. Panzer-Division im 2. Weltkrieg*, Podzun-Pallas, Friedberg, 1987.

Jentz, Thomas, *Germany's Panther Tanks*, Schiffer, Atglen, Pennsylvania, 1995.

Kaltenegger, Roland, *Gebirgsoldaten unter dem Zeichen des "Enzian", Schicksalsweg und Kampf der 4. Gebirgs-Division 1940–1945*, Leopold Stocker Verlag, Graz – Stuttgart, 1983.

---

[1] This supplementary bibliography details the sources utilised by this book's editor and translator, Frederick P. Steinhardt.

Klatt, Paul, *Die 3. Gebirgs-Division 1939–1945,* Verlag Hans-Henning Podzun, Bad Nauheim, 1958.

Koch, Fred, *Kettenschlepper der Wehrmacht, 1935–1945,* Podzun–Pallas, Wölfersheim-Berstadt, 1996

Lange, Wolfgang, *Korps-Abteilung C, vom Dnjepr bis nach Polen (November 1943 bis Juli 1944). Die Wehrmacht im Kampf Band 28,* Scharnhorst Buchkameradschaft, Neckargemünd, 1961.

Lehmann, Rudolf & Ralf Tiemann, *Die Leibstandarte, Band IV/1,* Munin Verlag GmbH, Osnabrück 1986. (Also available in English translation from J. J. Fedorowicz, Winnipeg Canada)

Lochmann, Dr Franz Wilhelm, Richard Freiherr von Rosen & Alfred Rubbel (eds.), *Erinnerungen schwere Panzer Abteilung 503, 1942–1945,* manuscript dated 1992 which was translated by Dr. F.P. Steinhardt and published by J.J. Fedorowicz as, Rubbel, Alfred, *The Combat History of schwere Panzer–Abteilung 503. In Action in the East and West with the Tiger I and II*

Nash, Douglas E., *Hell's Gate: The Battle of the Cherkassy Pocket January–February 1944,* RZM Imports, Inc., Stamford CT, 2005

Paul, Wolfgang, *Brennpunkte. Die Geschichte der 6. Panzerdivision (1. Leichte) 1937-1945,* Biblio Verlag, Osnabrück, 1993.

Pohlmann, H., *Geschichte der 96. Infanterie-Division 1939–1945,* Verlag Hans-Henning Podzun, Bad Nauheim, 1959.

Ruef, Karl, *Odysee einer Gebirgs-Division, die 3. Geb. Div. im Einsatz,* Leopold Stocker Verlag, Graz – Stuttgart, 1976.

von Senger und Etterlin, F.M., *Die deutschen Geschütze, 1939 – 1945,* Bernard & Graefe Verlag, Bonn, 1998.

von Senger und Etterlin, F.M., *Die deutschen Panzer, 1926 – 1945,* Bernard & Graefe Verlag, Bonn, 2000.

Spaeter, Helmuth, *Die Geschichte des Panzerkorps Großdeutschland",* Selbstverlag Hilfswerk ehem. Soldaten für Kriegsopfer und Hinterbliebene e.V., Duisburg–Ruhrort, der Traditionsgemeinschaft Panzerkorps Grossdeutschland, 1958, 3 volumes. Also available in English translation as *The History of Panzerkorps Grossdeutschland* in three volumes from J. J. Fedorowicz.

Stoves, Rolf, *1. Panzer Division, 1935 – 1945, Chronik einer der drei Stamm-Divisionen der deutschen Panzerwaffe,* Verlag Hans-Henning Podzun, Bad Nauheim, 1961.

Strassner, Peter, *Europäische Freiwillige, die 5. SS-Panzerdivision "Wiking",* Munin Verlag GmbH, Osnabrück, 3rd rev. ed. 1977. Available in English translation as *European Volunteers, the 5 SS-Panzer-Division WIKING* from J. J. Fedorowicz.

Tessin, Georg, *Verbände und Truppen der deutschen Wehrmacht und Waffen-SS, 1939 – 1945,* Biblio Verlag, Osnabrück, 1979-, 16 volumes.

Tieke, Wilhelm, *Im Feuersturm letzter Kriegsjahre, II. SS-Panzerkorps mit 9. und 10. SS-Divisionen "Hohenstaufen" und "Fründsberg"*, Munin Verlag GmbH, Osnabrück, 1975. Available in English translation by Dr. F. P. Steinhardt as *In the Firestorm of the Last Year of the War* from J. J. Fedorowicz.

Vopersal, Wolfgang, *Soldaten Kämpfer Kameraden, Marsch und Kämpfe der SS-Totenkopfdivision, Band III*. Im Selbstverlag der Truppenkameradschaft der 3. SS-Panzer-Division e. V. Auslieferung durch Biblio Verlag, Osnabrück 1987.

Vopersal, Wolfgang, *Soldaten Kämpfer Kameraden, Marsch und Kämpfe der SS-Totenkopfdivision, Band IVa*. Im Selbstverlag der Truppenkameradschaft der 3. SS-Panzer-Division e. V. Auslieferung durch Biblio Verlag, Osnabrück 1988.

Vopersal, Wolfgang, *Soldaten Kämpfer Kameraden, Marsch und Kämpfe der SS-Totenkopfdivision, Band IVb*. Im Selbstverlag der Truppenkameradschaft der 3. SS-Panzer-Division e. V. Auslieferung durch Biblio Verlag, Osnabrück 1988.

Weidinger, Otto, *Division Das Reich, der Weg der 2. SS-Panzer – Division "Das Reich", die Geschichte der Stammdivision der Waffen-SS, Band IV, 1943*, Munin Verlag GmbH, Osnabrück 1979. English translation by Dr. F.P. Steinhardt available from J.J. Fedorowicz.

Weidinger, Otto, *Division Das Reich, der Weg der 2. SS-Panzer – Division "Das Reich", die Geschichte der Stammdivision der Waffen-SS, Band V, 1943 – 1945*, Munin Verlag GmbH, Osnabrück 1982. English translation by Dr. F.P. Steinhardt and Robert Edwards soon to be released by J.J. Fedorowicz.

Werthen, Wolfgang, *Weg und Schicksal der 16. Infanterie Division and 16. Panzer-Division*, herausgeben vom Kameradschaftsbund 16. Panzer – und Infanterie-Division Kameradenhilfswerk e. V., Podzun-Pallas Verlag GmbH, Friedberg, 1958.

Ziemke, Earl F., *Stalingrad to Berlin, The German Defeat in the East*, Army Historical Series, Center of Military History, United States Army, Washington D.C., 1968.

Related titles published by Helion & Company

After Stalingrad. The Red Army's Winter Offensive 1942-1943
David M. Glantz
536pp, photos, maps
Hardback
ISBN 978-1-906033-26-2

Battle in the Baltics 1944-45
Ian Baxter
112pp, photos
Hardback
ISBN 978-1-906033-33-0

A selection of forthcoming titles:

Steel Bulwark. The Last Years of the German Panzerwaffe on the Eastern Front 1943-45, a Photographic History
Ian Baxter
ISBN 978-1906033-40-8

Barbarossa Derailed. The Battles for Smolensk, July-August 1941
David M. Glantz
ISBN 978-1906033-72-9

Entrapment. Soviet Operations to Capture Budapest, December 1944
Kamen Nevenkin
ISBN 978-1906033-73-6

HELION & COMPANY
26 Willow Road, Solihull, West Midlands B91 1UE, England
Telephone 0121 705 3393   Fax 0121 711 4075
Website: http://www.helion.co.uk